Lecture Notes in Computer Scie

Edited by G. Goos, J. Hartmanis and J. van

T0238120

Springer

Berlin
Heidelberg
New York
Barcelona
Hong Kong
London
Milan
Paris
Singapore
Tokyo

Jan Van den Bussche   Victor Vianu (Eds.)

Database Theory – ICDT 2001

8th International Conference
London, UK, January 4-6, 2001
Proceedings

 Springer

Series Editors

Gerhard Goos, Karlsruhe University, Germany
Juris Hartmanis, Cornell University, NY, USA
Jan van Leeuwen, Utrecht University, The Netherlands

Volume Editors

Jan Van den Bussche
Limburg University (LUC)
3590 Diepenbeek, Belgium
E-mail: jan.vandenbussche@luc.ac.be

Victor Vianu
University of California, Department of Computer Science and Engineering
La Jolla, CA 92093-0114, USA
E-mail: vianu@cs.ucsd.edu

Cataloging-in-Publication Data applied for

Die Deutsche Bibliothek - CIP-Einheitsaufnahme

Database theory : 8th international conference ; proceedings / ICDT
2001, London, UK, January 4 - 6, 2001. Jan VandenBussche ; Victor
Vianu (ed.). - Berlin ; Heidelberg ; New York ; Barcelona ; Hong Kong ;
London ; Milan ; Paris ; Singapore ; Tokyo : Springer, 2000
  (Lecture notes in computer science ; Vol. 1973)
  ISBN 3-540-41456-8

CR Subject Classification (1998): H.2, F.1.3, F.4.1, I.2.1, H.4, F.2, H.3

ISSN 0302-9743
ISBN 3-540-41456-8 Springer-Verlag Berlin Heidelberg New York

Springer-Verlag Berlin Heidelberg New York
a member of BertelsmannSpringer Science+Business Media GmbH
© Springer-Verlag Berlin Heidelberg 2001
Printed in Germany

Typesetting: Camera-ready by author, data conversion by PTP-Berlin, Stefan Sossna
Printed on acid-free paper   SPIN: 10781153   06/3142   5 4 3 2 1 0

Preface

The papers contained in this volume were presented at ICDT 2001, the 8th International Conference on Database Theory, held from 4 to 6 January 2001 in the Senate House of Birckbeck College, University of London, UK.

The series of ICDT conferences provides a biennial, international forum for the communication of research advances on the principles of database systems. ICDT is traditionally held in beautiful European locations: Rome in 1986, Bruges in 1988, Paris in 1990, Berlin in 1992, Prague in 1995, Delphi in 1997, and Jerusalem in 1999. Since 1992, ICDT has merged with the Symposium on Mathematical Fundamentals of Database Systems (MFDBS), initiated in Dresden in 1987, and continued in Visegrad in 1989 and Rostock in 1991.

This volume contains 26 papers describing original research on fundamental aspects of database systems, selected from 75 submissions. The paper by Chung Keung Poon was awarded as Best Newcomer to the field of database theory. In addition, this volume contains two invited papers by Leonid Libkin and Philip Wadler. A third invited talk was given by Andrei Broder.

We wish to thank all the authors who submitted papers, the members of the program committee, the external referees, the organizing committee, and the sponsors for their efforts and support.

Jan Van den Bussche
Victor Vianu

Organization

ICDT 2001 was organized by the Department of Computer Science, Birkbeck College, University of London, in cooperation with ACM SIGACT and SIGMOD.

Organizing Committee

George Loizou (chair)
James Bailey
Mark Levene
Alex Poulovassilis
Betty Walters

Sponsors

European Union
European Research Consortium for Informatics and Mathematics

Program Committee

Michael Benedikt (Bell Labs)
Nicole Bidoit (U Bordeaux)
Surajit Chaudhuri (Microsoft Research)
Thomas Eiter (TU Vienna)
Martin Grohe (UI Chicago)
Maurizio Lenzerini (U Rome La Sapienza)
Mark Levene (UC London)
Tova Milo (Tel Aviv U)
Ken Ross (Columbia U)
Thomas Schwentick (U Mainz)
Luc Segoufin (INRIA)
Timos Sellis (NTU Athens)
Dan Suciu (U Washington)
Val Tannen (U Pennsylvania)
Jerzy Tyszkiewicz (U Warsaw)
Jan Van den Bussche, co-chair (Limburg U)
Dirk Van Gucht (Indiana U)
Moshe Vardi (Rice U)
Victor Vianu, co-chair (UC San Diego)
Gottfried Vossen (U Muenster)
Peter Widmayer (ETH Zurich)
Limsoon Wong (Kent Ridge Digital Labs)

External Referees

Catriel Beeri

Yuri Breitbart

Francois Bry

Gautam Das

Anat Eyal

Chris Giannella

Carmem Hara

Georg Lausen

Jens Lechtenboerger

Jorge Lobo

Sofian Maabout

Holger Meuss

Martin Otto

Lucian Popa

Torsten Schlieder

Wang-Chiew Tan

Dimitri Theodoratos

Panos Vassiliadis

Mathias Weske

Andreas Behrend

Nicolas Bruno

Diego Calvanese

Alin Deutsch

Joerg Flum

Georg Gottlob

Hans-Joachim Klein

Clemens Lautemann

Leonid Libkin

Thomas Lukasiewicz

Alberto Mendelzon

Mohamed Mosbah

HweeHwa Pang

Arnaud Sahuguet

Nicole Schweikardt

Avi Telyas

Denis Therien

Michalis Vazirgiannis

Graham Wills

Table of Contents

Expressive Power of SQL

Leonid Libkin[1]

University of Toronto and Bell Laboratories
Email: libkin@cs.toronto.edu

Abstract. It is a folk result in database theory that SQL cannot express recursive queries such as reachability; in fact, a new construct was added to SQL3 to overcome this limitation. However, the evidence for this claim is usually given in the form of a reference to a proof that relational algebra cannot express such queries. SQL, on the other hand, in all its implementations has three features that fundamentally distinguish it from relational algebra: namely, grouping, arithmetic operations, and aggregation.

In the past few years, most questions about the additional power provided by these features have been answered. This paper surveys those results, and presents new simple and self-contained proofs of the main results on the expressive power of SQL. Somewhat surprisingly, tiny differences in the language definition affect the results in a dramatic way: under some very natural assumptions, it can be proved that SQL cannot define recursive queries, no matter what aggregate functions and arithmetic operations are allowed. But relaxing these assumptions just a tiny bit makes the problem of proving expressivity bounds for SQL as hard as some long-standing open problems in complexity theory.

1 Introduction

What queries can one express in SQL? Perhaps more importantly, one would like to know what queries cannot be expressed in SQL – after all, it is the inability to express certain properties that motivates language designers to add new features (at least one hopes that this is the case).

This seems to be a rather basic question that database theoreticians should have produced an answer to by the beginning of the 3rd millennium. After all, we've been studying the expressive power of query languages for some 20 years now (and in fact more than that, if you count earlier papers by logicians on the expressiveness of first-order logic), and SQL is the de-facto standard of the commercial database world – so there surely must be an answer somewhere in the literature.

When one thinks of the limitations of SQL, its inability to express reachability queries comes to mind, as it is well documented in the literature (in fact, in many database books written for very different audiences, e.g. [1,5,7,25]). Let us consider a simple example: suppose that R(Src,Dest) is a relation with flight information: Src stands for source, and Dest for destination. To find pairs of

J. Van den Bussche and V. Vianu (Eds.): ICDT 2001, LNCS 1973, pp. 1–21, 2001.

cities (A, B) such that it is possible to fly from A to B with one stop, one would use a self-join:

```
SELECT R1.Src, R2.Dest
FROM   R AS R1, R AS R2
WHERE  R1.Dest=R2.Src
```

What if we want pairs of cities such that one makes two stops on the way? Then we do a more complicated self-join:

```
SELECT R1.Src, R3.Dest
FROM   R AS R1, R AS R2, R AS R3
WHERE  R1.Dest=R2.Src AND R2.Dest=R3.Src
```

Taking the union of these two and the relation R itself we would get the pairs of cities such that one can fly from A to B with *at most* two stops. But often one needs a general reachability query in which no a priori bound on the number of stops is known; that is, whether it possible to get to B from A.

Graph-theoretically, this means computing the transitive closure of R. It is well known that the transitive closure of a graph is *not* expressible in relational algebra or calculus; in particular, expressions similar to those above (which happen to be unions of conjunctive queries) cannot possibly express it. This appears to be a folk result in the database community; while many papers do refer to [2] or some other source on the expressive power of first-order logic, many texts just state that relational algebra, calculus and SQL cannot express recursive queries such as reachability.

With this limitation in mind, the SQL3 standard introduced recursion explicitly into the language [7,12]. One would write the reachability query as

```
WITH RECURSIVE TrCl(Src,Dest) AS
      R
   UNION
      SELECT TrCl.Src, R.Dest
      FROM   TrCl, R
      WHERE  TrCl.Dest = R.Src
SELECT * FROM TrCl
```

This simply models the usual datalog rules for transitive closure:

$$trcl(x, y) :\text{-} r(x, y)$$
$$trcl(x, y) :\text{-} trcl(x, z), r(z, y)$$

When a new construct is added to a language, a good reason must exist for it, especially if the language is a declarative query language, with a small number of constructs, and with programmers relying heavily on its optimizer. The reason for introducing recursion in the next SQL standard is precisely this folk result stating that it cannot be expressed in the language. But when one looks at what evidence is provided to support this claim, one notices that all the references point to papers in which it is proved that *relational algebra and calculus* cannot express recursive queries. Why is this not sufficient? Consider the following query

```
SELECT R1.A
FROM   R1, R2
WHERE (SELECT COUNT(*) FROM R1) >
         (SELECT COUNT(*) FROM R2)
```

This query tests if $|\text{R1}| > |\text{R2}|$: in that case, it returns the A attribute of R1, otherwise it returns the empty set. However, logicians proved it long time ago that first-order logic, and thus relational calculus, cannot compare cardinalities of relations, and yet we have a very simple SQL query doing precisely that.

The conclusion, of course, is that SQL has more power than relational algebra, and the main source of this additional power is its *aggregation* and *grouping* constructs, together with *arithmetic* operations on numerical attributes. But then one cannot say that the transitive closure query is not expressible in SQL simply because it is inexpressible in relational algebra. Thus, it might appear that the folk theorem about recursion and SQL is an unproven statement.

Fortunately, this is not the case: the statement was (partially) proved in the past few years; in fact, a series of papers proved progressively stronger results, finally establishing good bounds on the expressiveness of SQL.

My main goal here is twofold:

(a) I give an overview of these recent results on the expressiveness of SQL. We shall see that some tiny differences in the language definition affect the results in a dramatic way: under some assumptions, it can be shown that reachability and many other recursive queries aren't expressible in SQL. However, under a slightly different set of assumptions, the problem of proving expressivity bounds for SQL is as hard as separating some complexity classes.

(b) Due to a variety of reasons, even the simplest proofs of expressivity results for SQL are not easy to follow; partly this is due to the fact that most papers used the setting of their predecessors that had unnecessary complications in the form of nested relations, somewhat unusual (for mainstream database people) languages and infinitary logics. Here I try to get rid of those complications, and present a simple and self-contained proof of expressivity bounds for SQL.

Organization. In the next section, we discuss the main features that distinguish SQL from relational algebra, in particular, aggregate functions. We then give a brief overview of the literature on the expressive power of SQL.

Starting with Section 3, we present those results in more detail. We introduce relational algebra with grouping and aggregates, ALG_{aggr}, that essentially captures basic SQL statements. Section 4 states the main result on the expressive power of SQL, namely that queries it can express are *local*. If one thinks of queries on graphs, it means that the decision whether a tuple $\vec{t}$ belongs to the output is determined by a small neighborhood of $\vec{t}$ in the input graph; the reachability query does not have this property.

Section 5 defines an *aggregate logic* $\mathcal{L}_{aggr}$ and shows a simple translation of the algebra with aggregates ALG_{aggr} into this logic. Then, in Section 6, we present a self-contained proof of locality of $\mathcal{L}_{aggr}$ (and thus of ALG_{aggr}).

In Section 7, we consider an extension $ALG_{aggr}^{<}$ of ALG_{aggr} in which non-numerical order comparisons are allowed, and show that it is more powerful than the unordered version. Furthermore, no nontrivial bounds on the expressiveness of this language can be proved without answering some deep open problems in complexity theory.

Section 8 gives a summary and concluding remarks.

2   SQL vs. Relational Algebra

What exactly is SQL? There is, of course, a very long standard, that lists numerous features, most of which have very little to do with the expressiveness of queries. As far as expressiveness is concerned, the main features that distinguish SQL from relational algebra, are the following:

- Aggregate functions: one can compute, for example, the average value in a column. The standard aggregates in SQL are COUNT, TOTAL, AVG, MIN, MAX.
- Grouping: not only can one compute aggregates, one can also group them by values of different attributes. For example, it is possible to compute the average salary for each department.
- Arithmetic: SQL allows one to apply arithmetic operations to numerical values.

For example, for relations S1(Empl,Dept) and S2(Empl,Salary), the following query (assuming that Empl is a key for both relations) computes the average salary for each department which pays total salary at least 100,000:

```
        SELECT  S1.Dept, AVG(S2.Salary)
        FROM    S1, S2
(*)     WHERE   S1.Empl=S2.Empl
        GROUPBY S1.Dept
        HAVING  TOTAL(S2.Salary) > 100000
```

Next, we address the following question: what is an aggregate function? The first paper to look into this was probably [20]: it defined aggregate functions as $f : \mathcal{R} \to \mathsf{Num}$, where $\mathcal{R}$ is the set of all relations, and Num is a numerical domain. A problem with this approach is that it requires a different aggregate function for each relation and each numerical attribute in it; that is, we do not have just one aggregate AVG, but infinitely many of those. This complication arises from dealing with duplicates in a correct manner. However, duplicates can be incorporated in a much more elegant way, as suggested in [14], which we shall follow here. According to [14], an aggregate function $\mathcal{F}$ is a collection

$$\mathcal{F} = \{f_0, f_1, f_2, \ldots, f_\omega\}$$

where f_k is a function that takes a k-element multiset (bag) of elements of Num and produces an element of Num. For technical reasons, we also add a constant

$f_\omega \in$ Num whose intended meaning is the value of $\mathcal{F}$ on infinite multisets. For example, if Num is $\mathbb{N}$, or $\mathbb{Q}$, or $\mathbb{R}$, we define the aggregate $\sum = \{s_0, s_1, \ldots\}$ by $s_k(\{|x_1, \ldots, x_k|\}) = \sum_{i=1}^{k} x_i$; furthermore, $s_0 = s_\omega = 0$ (we use the $\{| \ |\}$ brackets for multisets). This corresponds to SQL's TOTAL. For COUNT, one defines $\mathcal{C} = \{c_0, c_1, \ldots\}$ with c_k returning k (we may again assume $c_\omega = 0$). The aggregate AVG is defined as $\mathcal{A} = \{a_0, a_1, \ldots\}$ with $a_k(X) = \frac{s_k(X)}{c_k(X)}$, $a_0 = a_\omega = 0$.

Languages That Model SQL and Their Expressive Power

It is very hard to prove formal statements about a language like SQL: to put it mildly, its syntax is not very easy to reason about. The research community has come up with several proposals of languages that capture the expressiveness of SQL. The earliest one is perhaps Klug's extension of relational algebra by grouping and aggregation [20]: if e is an expression producing a relation with m attributes, $\vec{A}$ is a set of attributes, and f is an aggregate function, then $e\langle \vec{A}, f \rangle$ is a new expression that produces a relation with $m + 1$ attributes. Assuming f applies to attribute A', and $\vec{B}$ is the list of all attributes of the output of e, the semantics is best explained by SQL:

> SELECT $\vec{B}, f(A')$
> FROM e
> GROUPBY $\vec{A}$

Klug's paper did not analyze the expressive power of this algebra, nor did it show how to incorporate arithmetic operations. The main contribution of [20] is an equivalence result between the algebra and an extension of relational calculus. However, the main focus of that extension is its safety, and the resulting logic is extremely hard to deal with, due to many syntactic restrictions.

To the best of my knowledge, the first paper that directly addressed the problem of the expressive power of SQL, was the paper by Consens and Mendelzon in ICDT'90 [6]. They have a datalog-like language, whose nonrecursive fragment is exactly as expressive as Klug's algebra. Then they show that this language cannot express the transitive closure query under the assumption that DLOGSPACE is properly included in NLOGSPACE. The reason is simple: Klug's algebra (with some simple aggregates) can be evaluated in DLOGSPACE, while transitive closure is complete for NLOGSPACE.

That result can be viewed as a strong evidence that SQL is indeed incapable of expressing reachability queries. However, it is not completely satisfactory for three reasons. First, nobody knows how to separate complexity classes. Second, what if one adds more complex aggregates that increase the complexity of query evaluation? And third, what if the input graph has a very simple structure (for example, no node has outdegree more than 1)? In this case reachability is in DLOGSPACE, and the argument of [6] does not work.

In early 90s, many people were looking into languages for collection types. Functional statically typechecked query languages became quite fashionable, and they were produced in all kinds of flavors, depending on particular collection types they had to support. It turned out that a set language capturing essentially the expressive power of a language for bags, could also model all the essential features of SQL [23]. The problem was that the language dealt with nested relations, or complex objects. But then [23] proved a *conservativity* result, stating that nested relations aren't really needed if the input and output don't have them. That made it possible to use a non-nested fragment of languages inspired by structural recursion [4] and comprehensions [28] as a "theoretical reconstruction of SQL."

Several papers dealt with this language, and proved a number of expressivity bounds. The first one, appearing in PODS'94 [23], showed that the language could not express reachability queries. The proof, however, was very far from ideal. It only proved inexpressibility of transitive closure in a way that was very unlikely to extend to other queries. It relied on a complicated syntactic rewriting that wouldn't work even for a slightly different language. And the proof wouldn't work if one added more aggregate functions.

The first limitation was addressed in [8] where a certain general property of queries expressible in SQL was established. However, the other two problems not only remained, but were exacerbated: the rewriting of queries became particularly unpleasant. In an attempt to remedy this, [21] gave an indirect encoding of a fragment of SQL into first-order logic with counting, FO(C) (it will be formally defined later). The restriction was to natural numbers, thus excluding aggregates such as AVG. The encoding is bound to be indirect, since SQL is capable of expressing queries that FO(C) cannot express. The encoding showed that for any query Q in SQL, there exists a FO(C) query Q' that shares some nice properties with Q. Then [21] established some properties of FO(C) queries and transferred them to that fragment of SQL. The proof was much cleaner than the proofs of [23,8], at the expense of a less expressive language.

After that, [24] showed that the coding technique can be extended to SQL with rational numbers and the usual arithmetic operations. The price to pay was the readability of the proof – the encoding part became very unpleasant.

That was a good time to pause and see what must be done differently. How do we prove expressivity bounds for relational algebra? We do it by proving bounds on the expressiveness of first-order logic (FO) over finite structures, since relational algebra has the same power as FO. So perhaps if we could put aggregates and arithmetic directly into logic, we would be able to prove expressivity bounds in a nice and simple way?

That program was carried out in [18], and I'll survey the results below. One problem with [18] is that it inherited too much unnecessary machinery from its predecessors [23,8,24,21,22]: one had to deal with languages for complex objects and apply conservativity results to get down to SQL; logics were infinitary to start with, although infinitary connectives were not necessary to translate SQL; and expressivity proofs went via a special kind of games invented elsewhere [16].

Here we show that all these complications are completely unnecessary: there is indeed a very simple proof that reachability is not expressible in SQL, and this proof will be presented below. Our language is a slight extension of Klug's algebra (no nesting!). We translate it into an aggregate logic (with no infinitary connectives!) and prove that it has nice locality properties (without using games!)

3   Relational Algebra with Aggregates

To deal with aggregation, we must distinguish numerical columns (to which aggregates can be applied) from non-numerical ones. We do it by typing: a type of a relation is simply a list of types of its attributes.

We assume that there are two base types: a non-numerical type b with domain Dom, and a numerical type n, whose domain is denoted by Num (it could be $\mathbb{N}, \mathbb{Z}, \mathbb{Q}, \mathbb{R}$, for example).

A type of a relation is a string over the alphabet $\{b, n\}$. A relation R of type $a_1 \ldots a_m$ has m columns, the ith one containing entries of type a_i. In other words, such a relation is a finite subset of

$$\prod_{i=1}^{m} \mathrm{dom}(a_i)$$

where $\mathrm{dom}(b) = \mathsf{Dom}$ and $\mathrm{dom}(n) = \mathsf{Num}$. For example, the type of S2(Empl, Salary) is bn. For a type t, $t.i$ denotes the ith position in the string. The length of t is denoted by $|t|$.

A *database schema* SC is a collection of relation names R_i and their types t_i; we write $R_i : t_i$ if the type of R_i is t_i.

Next we define expressions of relational algebra with aggregates, parameterized by a collection Ω of functions and predicates on Num, and a collection Θ of aggregates, over a given schema SC. Expressions are divided into three groups: the standard relational algebra, arithmetic, and aggregation/grouping. In what follows, m stands for $|t|$, and $\{i_1, \ldots, i_k\}$ for a sequence $1 \leq i_1 < \ldots < i_k \leq m$.

Relational Algebra

SCHEMA RELATION If $R : t$ is in SC, then R is an expression of type t.

PERMUTATION If e is an expression of type t and θ is a permutation of $\{1, \ldots, m\}$, then $\rho_\theta(e)$ is an expression of type $\theta(t)$.

BOOLEAN OPERATIONS If e_1, e_2 are expressions of type t, then so are $e_1 \cup e_2, e_1 \cap e_2, e_1 - e_2$.

CARTESIAN PRODUCT For $e_1 : t_1$, $e_2 : t_2$, $e_1 \times e_2$ is an expression of type $t_1 \cdot t_2$.

PROJECTION If e is of type t, then $\pi_{i_1, \ldots, i_k}(e)$ is an expression of type t' where t' is the string composed of $t.i_j$s, in their order.

SELECTION If e is an expression of type t, $i, j \leq m$, and $t.i = t.j$, then $\sigma_{i=j}(e)$ is an expression of type t.

Arithmetic

NUMERICAL SELECTION If $P \subseteq \mathsf{Num}^k$ is a k-ary numerical predicate from Ω, and $i_1, \ldots, i_k$ are such that $t.i_j = n$, then $\sigma[P]_{i_1, \ldots, i_k}(e)$ is an expression of type t for any expression e of type t.

FUNCTION APPLICATION If $f : \mathsf{Num}^k \to \mathsf{Num}$ is a function from Ω, $i_1, \ldots, i_k$ are such that $t.i_j = \mathsf{n}$, and e is an expression of type t, then $\mathrm{Apply}[f]_{i_1,\ldots,i_k}(e)$ is an expression of type $t \cdot \mathsf{n}$. If $k = 0$ (i.e. f is a constant), then $\mathrm{Apply}[f]_\epsilon(e)$ is an expression of type $t \cdot \mathsf{n}$.

Aggregation and Grouping

AGGREGATION Let $\mathcal{F}$ be an aggregate from Θ. For any expression e of type t and i such that $t.i = \mathsf{n}$, $\mathrm{Aggr}[i : \mathcal{F}](e)$ is an expression of type $t \cdot \mathsf{n}$.

GROUPING Assume $e : u$ is an expression over $SC \cup \{S : s\}$. Let e' be an expression of type $t \cdot s$ over SC, where $|t| = l$. Then $\mathrm{Group}_l[\lambda S.e](e')$ is an expression of type $t \cdot u$.

Semantics. For the relational algebra operations, this is standard. The operation ρ_θ is permutation: each tuple $(a_1, \ldots, a_m)$ is replaced by $(a_{\theta(1)}, \ldots, a_{\theta(m)})$. The condition $i = j$ in the selection predicate means equality of the ith and the jth attribute: $(a_1, \ldots, a_m)$ is selected if $a_i = a_j$. Note that using Boolean operations we can model arbitrary combinations of equalities and disequalities among attributes.

For numerical selection, $\sigma[P]_{i_1,\ldots,i_k}$ selects $(a_1, \ldots, a_m)$ iff $P(a_{i_1}, \ldots, a_{i_k})$ holds. Function application replaces each $(a_1, \ldots, a_m)$ with $(a_1, \ldots, a_m, f(a_{i_1}, \ldots, a_{i_k}))$.

The aggregate operation is SQL SELECT $\vec{A}, \mathcal{F}(A_i)$ FROM e, where $\vec{A} = (A_1, \ldots, A_m)$ is the list of attributes. More precisely, if e evaluates to $\vec{a}_1, \ldots, \vec{a}_p$ where $\vec{a}_j = (a_j^1, \ldots, a_j^m)$, then $\mathrm{Aggr}[i : \mathcal{F}](e)$ replaces each $\vec{a}_j$ with $(a_j^1, \ldots, a_j^m, f)$ where $f = \mathcal{F}(\{a_1^i, \ldots, a_p^i\})$.

Finally, $\mathrm{Group}_l[\lambda S.e](e')$ groups the tuples by the values of their first l attributes and applies e to the sets formed by this grouping. For example:

assuming that e returns $\{d_1, d_2\}$ when $S = \{b_1, b_2\}$, and e returns $\{g_1\}$ for $S = \{c_1, c_2\}$.

Formally, let e' evaluate to $\{\vec{a}_1, \ldots, \vec{a}_p\}$. We split each tuple $\vec{a}_j = (a_j^1, \ldots, a_j^m)$ into $\vec{a}_j' = (a_j^1, \ldots, a_j^l)$ that contains the first l attributes, and $\vec{a}_j'' = (a_j^{l+1}, \ldots, a_j^m)$ that contains the remaining ones. This defines, for each $\vec{a}_j$, a set $S_j = \{\vec{a}_r'' \mid \vec{a}_r' = \vec{a}_j'\}$. Let $T_j = \{\vec{b}_j^1, \ldots, \vec{b}_j^{m_j}\}$ be the result of applying e with S interpreted as S_j. Then $\mathrm{Group}_l[\lambda S.e](e')$ returns the set of tuples of the form $(\vec{a}_j', \vec{b}_j^i)$, $1 \le j \le p$, $1 \le i \le m_j$.

Klug's algebra. It combines grouping and aggregation in the same operation as follows:

GROUPING & AGGREGATION Let t be of length m. Let $l < i_1 < \ldots < i_k$ with $t.i_j = n$, and let $\mathcal{F}_1, \ldots, \mathcal{F}_k$ be aggregates from Θ. Then, for e an expression of type t, $\mathrm{Aggr}_l[i_1 : \mathcal{F}_1, \ldots, i_k : \mathcal{F}_k]$ is an expression of type $t \cdot n \ldots n$ (t with k ns added at the end).

The semantics is best explained by SQL:

SELECT $\#1, \ldots, \#m, \mathcal{F}_1(\#i_1), \ldots, \mathcal{F}_k(\#i_k)$
FROM   E
GROUPBY $\#1, \ldots, \#l$

where E is the result of the expression e. (As presented in [20], the algebra does not have arithmetic operations, and the aggregates are limited to the standard five.)

Note that there are no higher-order operators in Klug's algebra, and that it is expressible in our algebra with aggregates, as $\mathrm{Aggr}_l[i_1 : \mathcal{F}_1, \ldots, i_k : \mathcal{F}_k](e')$ is equivalent to $\mathrm{Group}_l[\lambda S.e](e')$, where e is

$$\mathrm{Aggr}[i_k - l : \mathcal{F}_k](\mathrm{Aggr}[i_{k-1} - l : \mathcal{F}_{k-1}](\cdots (\mathrm{Aggr}[i_1 - l : \mathcal{F}_1](S)) \cdots))$$

Example. The query (∗) from Section 2 is defined by the following expression (which uses the operator combining grouping with aggregation):

$$\pi_{1,4}(\sigma[> 100000]_5((\mathrm{Aggr}_1[3 : \mathcal{A}, 3 : \Sigma](\pi_{2,3,4}(\sigma_{1=3}(S_1 \times S_2)))))))$$

where $\mathcal{A}$ is the aggregate AVG, Σ is TOTAL, and > 100000 is a unary predicate on $\mathbb{N}$ which holds of numbers $n > 100000$.

Example. The only aggregate that can be applied to non-numerical attributes in SQL is COUNT that returns the cardinality of a column. It can be easily expressed in $\mathrm{ALG}_{\mathrm{aggr}}$ as long as the summation aggregate Σ and constant 1 are present. We show how to define $\mathrm{Count}_m(e)$:

SELECT $\#1, \ldots, \#m - 1, \mathrm{COUNT}(\#m)$
FROM   E
GROUPBY $\#1, \ldots, \#m$

First, we add a new column, whose elements are all 1s: $e_1 = \mathrm{Apply}[1]_\epsilon(e)$. Then define an expression $e' = \mathrm{Aggr}[2 : \Sigma](S)$, and use it to produce

$$e_2 = \mathrm{Group}_{m-1}[\lambda S.e'](e_1).$$

This is almost the answer: there are extra 2 attributes, the mth attribute of e, and those extra 1s. So finally we have

$$\mathrm{Count}_m(e) = \pi_{1,\ldots,m-1,m+2}(\mathrm{Group}_{m-1}[\lambda S.\mathrm{Aggr}[2 : \Sigma](S)](\mathrm{Apply}[1]_\epsilon(e)))$$

Remark In previous papers on the expressive power of SQL [23,24,21,18], we used languages of a rather different flavor, based on structural recursion [4] and comprehensions [28]. One can show, however, that those language and $\mathrm{ALG}_{\mathrm{aggr}}$ have the same expressiveness, provided they are supplied with the same set of aggregates and arithmetic functions. The proof of this will be given in the full version.

4   Locality of SQL Queries

What kind of general statement can one provide that would give us strong evidence that SQL cannot express recursive queries? For that purpose, we shall use the *locality* of queries. Locality was the basis of a number of tools for proving expressivity bounds of first-order logic [15,13,11], and it was recently studied on its own and applied to more expressive logics [17,22].

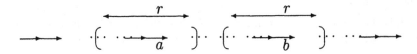

Fig. 1. A local formula cannot distinguish (a, b) from (b, a).

The general idea of this notion is that a query can only look at a small portion of its input. If the input is a graph, "small" means a neighborhood of a fixed radius. For example, Fig. 1 shows that reachability is not local: just take a graph like the one shown in the picture so that there would be two points whose distance from the endpoints and each other is more than $2r$, where r is the fixed radius. Then locality of query says that (a, b) and (b, a) are indistinguishable, as the query can only look at the r-neighborhoods of a and b. Transitive closure, on the other hand, does distinguish between (a, b) and (b, a), since b is reachable from a but not vice versa.

We now define locality formally. We say that a schema SC is *purely relational* if there are no occurrences of the numerical type n in it. Let us first restrict our attention to graph queries. Suppose we have a purely relational schema $R : bb$; that is, the relation R contains edges of a directed graph. Suppose e is an expression of the same type bb; that is, it returns a directed graph. Given a pair of nodes a, b in R, and a number $r > 0$, the *r-neighborhood of a, b in R*, $N_r^R(a, b)$, is the subgraph on the set of nodes in R whose distance from either a or b is at most r. The distance is measured in the undirected graph corresponding to R, that is, $R \cup R^{-1}$.

We write $(a, b) \approx_r^R (c, d)$ when the two neighborhoods, $N_r^R(a, b)$ and $N_r^R(c, d)$, are isomorphic; that is, when there exists a (graph) isomorphism h between them such that $h(a) = c, h(b) = d$. Finally, we say that e is *local* if there is a number r, depending on e only, such that

$$(a, b) \approx_r^R (c, d) \quad \Rightarrow \quad (a, b) \in e(R) \text{ iff } (c, d) \in e(R).$$

We have seen that reachability is not local. Another example of a non-local query is a typical example of recursive query called *same-generation*:

$$sg(x, x) :\text{-}$$
$$sg(x, y) :\text{- } R(x', x), R(y', y), sg(x', y')$$

This query is not local either: consider, for example, a graph consisting of two chains: $(a, b_1), (b_1, b_2), \ldots, (b_{m_1}, b_m)$ and $(a, c_1), (c_1, c_2), \ldots, (c_{m_1}, c_m)$. Assume that *same-generation* is local, and $r > 0$ witnesses that. Take $m > 2r + 3$, and note that the r-neighborhoods of (b_{r+1}, c_{r+1}) and (b_{r+1}, c_{r+2}) are isomorphic. By locality, this would imply that these pairs agree on the same-generation query, but in fact we have $(b_{r+1}, c_{r+1}) \in sg(R)$ and $(b_{r+1}, c_{r+2}) \notin sg(R)$.

We now state our main result on locality of queries, that applies to the language in which no limit is placed on the available arithmetic and aggregate functions – all are available. We denote this language by $\text{ALG}_{\text{aggr}}(\text{All}, \text{All})$.

Theorem 1 (Locality of SQL). *Let e be a pure relational graph query in* $\text{ALG}_{\text{aggr}}(\text{All}, \text{All})$, *that is, an expression of type bb over the scheme of one symbol* $R : \text{bb}$. *Then e is local.* □

That is, neither reachability, nor same-generation, is expressible in SQL over the base type b, no matter what aggregate functions and arithmetic operations are available. Inexpressibility of many other queries can be derived from this, for example, tests for graph connectivity and acyclicity.

Our next goal is to give an elementary, self-contained proof of this result. The restriction to graph queries used in the theorem is not necessary; the result can be stated in greater generality, but the restriction to graphs makes the definition of locality very easy to understand. The proof will consist of three steps:

1. It is easier to prove expressivity bounds for a logic than for an algebra. We introduce an *aggregate logic* $\mathcal{L}_{\text{aggr}}$, as an extension of first-order logic, and show how ALG_{aggr} queries are translated into it.
2. The logic $\mathcal{L}_{\text{aggr}}$ is still a bit hard to deal with it, because of the aggregate terms. We show that we can replace aggregate terms by *counting quantifiers*, thereby translating $\mathcal{L}_{\text{aggr}}$ into a simpler logic $\mathcal{L}_{\text{C}}$. The price to pay is that $\mathcal{L}_{\text{C}}$ has infinitary connectives.
3. We note that any use of an infinitary connective resulting from translation of $\mathcal{L}_{\text{aggr}}$ into $\mathcal{L}_{\text{C}}$ applies to a rather uniform family of formulae, and use this fact to give a simple inductive proof of locality of $\mathcal{L}_{\text{C}}$ formulae.

5   Aggregate Logic and Relational Algebra

Our goal here is to introduce a logic $\mathcal{L}_{\text{aggr}}$ into which we translate ALG_{aggr} expressions. The structures for this logic are precisely relational databases over two base types with domains Dom and Num; that is, vocabularies are just schemas. This makes the logic *two-sorted*; we shall also refer to Dom as *first-sort* and to Num as *second-sort*.

We now define formulae and terms of $\mathcal{L}_{\text{aggr}}(\Omega, \Theta)$; as before, Ω is a set of predicates and functions on Num, and Θ is a set of aggregates. The logic is just a slight extension of the two-sorted first-order logic.

A SC-structure D is a tuple $\langle A, R_1^D, \ldots, R_k^D \rangle$, where A is a finite subset of Dom, and R_i^D is a finite subset of

$$\prod_{j=1}^{|t.|} \mathrm{dom}_j(D)$$

where $\mathrm{dom}_j(D) = A$ for $t_i.j = \mathsf{b}$, and $\mathrm{dom}_j(D) = \mathsf{Num}$ for $t_i.j = \mathsf{n}$.

- A variable of sort i is a term of sort i, $i = 1, 2$.
- If $R : t$ is in SC, and $\vec{u}$ is a tuple of terms of type t, then $R(\vec{u})$ is a formula.
- Formulae are closed under the Boolean connectives $\vee, \wedge, \neg$ and quantification (respecting sorts). If x is a first-sort variable, $\exists x$ is interpreted as $\exists x \in A$; if k is a second-sort variable, then $\exists k$ is interpreted as $\exists k \in \mathsf{Num}$.
- If P is an n-ary predicate in Ω and $\tau_1, \ldots, \tau_n$ are second-sort terms, then $P(\tau_1, \ldots, \tau_n)$ is a formula.
- If f is an n-ary function in Ω and $\tau_1, \ldots, \tau_n$ are second-sort terms, then $f(\tau_1, \ldots, \tau_n)$ is a second-sort term.
- If $\mathcal{F}$ is an aggregate in Θ, $\varphi(\vec{x}, \vec{y})$ is a formula and $\tau(\vec{x}, \vec{y})$ a second-sort term, then $\tau'(\vec{x}) = \mathrm{Aggr}_{\mathcal{F}}\vec{y}. \, (\varphi(\vec{x}, \vec{y}), \tau(\vec{x}, \vec{y}))$ is a second-sort term with free variables $\vec{x}$.

The interpretation of all the constructs except the last one is completely standard. The interpretation of the aggregate term-former is as follows: fix an interpretation $\vec{a}$ for $\vec{x}$, and let $B = \{\vec{b} \mid D \models \varphi(\vec{a}, \vec{b})\}$. If B is infinite, then $\tau'(\vec{a})$ is f_ω. If B is finite, say $\{\vec{b}_1, \ldots, \vec{b}_l\}$, then $\tau'(\vec{a})$ is the result of applying f_l to the multiset whose elements are $\tau(\vec{a}, \vec{b}_i)$, $i = 1, \ldots, l$.

It is now possible to translate $\mathrm{ALG}_{\mathrm{aggr}}$ into $\mathcal{L}_{\mathrm{aggr}}$:

Theorem 2. *Let $e : t$ be an expression of $\mathrm{ALG}_{\mathrm{aggr}}(\Omega, \Theta)$. Then there is a formula $\varphi_e(\vec{x})$ of $\mathcal{L}_{\mathrm{aggr}}(\Omega, \Theta)$, with $\vec{x}$ of type t, such that for any SC-database D,*

$$e(D) \;=\; \{\vec{a} \mid D \models \varphi_e(\vec{a})\}$$

Proof. For the usual relational algebra operators, this is the same as the standard textbook translation of algebra expressions into calculus expression. So we only show how to translate arithmetic operations, aggregation, and grouping.

- Numerical selection: Let $e' = \sigma[P]_{i_1, \ldots, i_k}(e)$, where P is a k-ary predicate in Ω. Then $\varphi_{e'}(\vec{x})$ is defined as $\varphi_e(\vec{x}) \wedge P(x_{i_1}, \ldots, x_{i_k})$.
- Function application: Let $e' = \mathrm{Apply}[f]_{i_1, \ldots, i_k}(e)$, where $f : \mathsf{Num}^k \to \mathsf{Num}$ is in Ω. Then $\varphi_{e'}(\vec{x}, q) \equiv \varphi_e(\vec{x}) \wedge (q = f(x_{i_1}, \ldots, x_{i_k}))$.
- Aggregation: Let $e' = \mathrm{Aggr}[i : \mathcal{F}](e)$. Then $\varphi_{e'}(\vec{x}, q) \equiv \varphi_e(\vec{x}) \wedge (q = \mathrm{Aggr}_{\mathcal{F}}\vec{y}. \, (\varphi_e(\vec{y}), y_i))$.
- Grouping: Let $e' = \mathrm{Group}_m[\lambda S.e_1](e_2)$, where $e_1 : u$ is an expression over $SC \cup \{S\}$, and e_2 over SC is of type $t \cdot s$. Let $\vec{x}, \vec{y}, \vec{z}$ be of types t, s, u, respectively. Then

$$\varphi_{e'}(\vec{x}, \vec{z}) \;\equiv\; \exists \vec{y} \, \varphi_{e_2}(\vec{x}, \vec{y}) \,\wedge\, \varphi_{e_1}(\vec{z})[\varphi_{e_2}(\vec{x}, \vec{v})/S(\vec{v})]$$

where the second conjunct is $\varphi_{e_1}(\vec{z})$ in which every occurrence of $S(\vec{v})$ is replaced by $\varphi_{e_1}(\vec{x}, \vec{v})$.

The converse does not hold: formulae of $\mathcal{L}_{\mathrm{aggr}}$ need not define safe queries, while all $\mathrm{ALG}_{\mathrm{aggr}}$ queries are safe. It is possible, however, to prove a partial converse result; see [18] for more details.

6   SQL Is Local: The Proof

We start by stating our main result in greater generality, without restriction to graph queries.

Let SC be pure relational (no occurrences of type n), and D an instance of SC. The *active domain* of D, $adom(D)$, is the set of all elements of Dom that occur in relations of D. The *Gaifman graph* of D is the undirected graph $G(D)$ on $adom(D)$ with $(a, b) \in G(D)$ iff a, b belong to the same tuple of some relation in D. The *r-sphere* of $a \in adom(D)$, $S_r^D(a)$, is the set of all b such that $d(a, b) \leq r$, where the distance $d(\cdot, \cdot)$ is taken in $G(D)$. The *r-sphere* of $\vec{a} = (a_1, \ldots, a_k)$ is $S_r^D(\vec{a}) = \bigcup_{i \leq k} S_r^D(a_i)$. The *r-neighborhood* of $\vec{a}$, $N_r^D(\vec{a})$, is a new database, whose active domain is $S_r^D(\vec{a})$, and whose SC-relations are simply restrictions of those relations in D. We write $\vec{a} \approx_r^D \vec{b}$ when there is an isomorphism of relational structures $h : N_r^D(\vec{a}) \to N_r^D(\vec{b})$ such that in addition $h(\vec{a}) = \vec{b}$. Finally, we say that a query e of type b...b is *local* if there exists a number $r > 0$ such that, for any database D, $\vec{a} \approx_r^D \vec{b}$ implies that $\vec{a} \in e(D)$ iff $\vec{b} \in e(D)$. The minimum such r is called the locality rank of e and denoted by $\mathsf{lr}(e)$.

Theorem 3. *Let e be a pure relational query in* $\mathrm{ALG}_{\mathrm{aggr}}(\mathsf{All}, \mathsf{All})$*, that is, an expression of type b...b over a pure relational schema. Then e is local.*   □

Since $\mathrm{ALG}_{\mathrm{aggr}}(\mathsf{All}, \mathsf{All})$ can be translated into $\mathcal{L}_{\mathrm{aggr}}(\mathsf{All}, \mathsf{All})$, we must prove that the latter is local. The proof of this is in two steps: we first introduce a simpler counting logic, $\mathcal{L}_{\mathbf{C}}$, and show how to translate $\mathcal{L}_{\mathrm{aggr}}$ into it. We then give a simple proof of locality of $\mathcal{L}_{\mathbf{C}}$.

The logic $\mathcal{L}_{\mathbf{C}}$ is simpler than $\mathcal{L}_{\mathrm{aggr}}$ in that it does not have aggregate terms. There is a price to pay for this – $\mathcal{L}_{\mathbf{C}}$ has infinitary conjunctions and disjunctions. However, the translation ensures that for each infinite conjunction or disjunction, there is a uniform bound on the *rank* of formulae in it (to be defined a bit later), and this property suffices to establish locality.

Logic $\mathcal{L}_{\mathbf{C}}$. The structures for $\mathcal{L}_{\mathbf{C}}$ are the same as the structures for $\mathcal{L}_{\mathrm{aggr}}$. The only terms are variables (of either sort); in addition, every constant $c \in \mathsf{Num}$ is a term of the second sort.

Atomic formulae are $R(\vec{x})$, where $R \in SC$, and $\vec{x}$ is a tuple of terms (that is, variables and perhaps constants from Num) of the appropriate sort, and $x = y$, where x, y are terms of the same sort.

Formulae are closed under the Boolean connectives, and *infinitary connectives*: if φ_i, $i \in I$, is a collection of formulae, then $\bigvee_{i \in I} \varphi_i$ and $\bigwedge_{i \in I} \varphi_i$ are $\mathcal{L}_{\mathbf{C}}$

formulae. Furthermore, they are closed under both first and second-sort quantification.

Finally, for every $i \in \mathbb{N}$, there is a quantifier $\exists i$ that binds one first-sort variable: that is, if $\varphi(x, \vec{y})$ is a formula, then $\exists i x\ \varphi(x, \vec{y})$ is a formula whose free variables are $\vec{y}$. The semantics is as follows: $D \models \exists i x \varphi(x, \vec{a})$ if there are i distinct elements $b_1, \ldots, b_i \in A$ such that $D \models \varphi(b_j, \vec{a})$, $1 \leq j \leq i$. That is, the existential quantifier is witnessed by at least i elements. Note that the first-sort quantification is superfluous as $\exists x \varphi$ is equivalent $\exists 1 x\ \varphi$.

We now introduce the notion of a *rank* of a formula, $\mathrm{rk}(\varphi)$, for both $\mathcal{L}_{\mathbf{C}}$ and $\mathcal{L}_{\mathrm{aggr}}$. For $\mathcal{L}_{\mathbf{C}}$, this is the quantifier rank, but the second-sort quantification does not count:

- For each atomic φ, $\mathrm{rk}(\varphi) = 0$.
- For $\varphi = \bigvee_i \varphi$, $\mathrm{rk}(\varphi) = \sup_i \mathrm{rk}(\varphi)$, and likewise for $\bigwedge$.
- $\mathrm{rk}(\neg\varphi) = \mathrm{rk}(\varphi)$.
- $\mathrm{rk}(\exists i x\ \varphi) = \mathrm{rk}(\varphi) + 1$ for x first-sort; $\mathrm{rk}(\exists k \varphi) = \mathrm{rk}(\varphi)$ for k second-sort.

For $\mathcal{L}_{\mathrm{aggr}}$, the definition differs slightly.

- For a variable or a constant term, the rank is 0.
- The rank of an atomic formula is the maximum rank of a term in it.
- $\mathrm{rk}(\varphi_1 * \varphi_2) = \max(\mathrm{rk}(\varphi_1), \mathrm{rk}(\varphi_2))$, for $* \in \{\vee, \wedge\}$; $\mathrm{rk}(\neg\varphi) = \mathrm{rk}(\varphi)$.
- $\mathrm{rk}(f(\tau_1, \ldots, \tau_n)) = \max_{1 \leq i \leq n} \mathrm{rk}(\tau_i)$.
- $\mathrm{rk}(\exists x \varphi) = \mathrm{rk}(\varphi) + 1$ if x is first-sort; $\mathrm{rk}(\exists k \varphi) = \mathrm{rk}(\varphi)$ if k is second-sort.
- $\mathrm{rk}(\mathrm{Aggr}_{\mathcal{F}} \vec{y}.\ (\varphi, \tau)) = \max(\mathrm{rk}(\varphi), \mathrm{rk}(\tau)) + m$, where m is the number of first-sort variables in $\vec{y}$.

Translating $\mathcal{L}_{\mathrm{aggr}}$ into $\mathcal{L}_{\mathbf{C}}$. This is the longest step in the proof, but although it is somewhat tedious, conceptually it is quite straightforward.

Proposition 1. *For every formula $\varphi(\vec{x})$ of $\mathcal{L}_{\mathrm{aggr}}(\mathsf{All}, \mathsf{All})$, there exists an equivalent formula $\varphi^\circ(\vec{x})$ of $\mathcal{L}_{\mathbf{C}}$ such that $\mathrm{rk}(\varphi^\circ) \leq \mathrm{rk}(\varphi)$.*

Proof. We start by showing that one can define a formula $\exists i \vec{x} \varphi$ in $\mathcal{L}_{\mathbf{C}}$, whose meaning is that there exist at least i tuples $\vec{x}$ such that φ holds. Moreover, its rank equals $\mathrm{rk}(\varphi)$ plus the number of first-sort variables in $\vec{x}$. The proof is by induction on the length of $\vec{x}$. If $\vec{x}$ is a single first-sort variable, then the counting quantifier is already in $\mathcal{L}_{\mathbf{C}}$. If k is a second-sort variable, then $\exists i k \varphi(k, \cdot)$ is equivalent to $\bigvee_C \bigwedge_{c \in C} \varphi(c, \cdot)$, where C ranges over i-element subsets of Num – this does not increase the rank. Suppose we can define it for $\vec{x}$ being of length n. We now show how to define $\exists i(y, \vec{x}) \varphi$ for y of the first sort, and $\exists i(k, \vec{x}) \varphi$ for k of the second sort.

1. Let $\psi(\vec{z}) \equiv \exists i(y, \vec{x}) \varphi(y, \vec{x}, \vec{z})$ It is the case that there are i tuples $(b_j, \vec{a}_j)$ satisfying $\varphi(y, \vec{x}, \cdot)$ iff one can find an l-tuple of pairs $((n_1, m_1), \ldots, (n_l, m_l))$ with all m_js distinct, such that
   - there are at least n_j tuples $\vec{a}$ for which the number of elements b satisfying $\varphi(b, \vec{a}, \cdot)$ is precisely m_j, and

$- \sum_{j=1}^{l} n_j \cdot m_j \geq i.$

Thus, $\psi(\vec{z})$ is equivalent to

$$\bigvee \bigwedge_{j=1}^{l} \exists n_j \vec{x} \; (\exists! m_j y \; \varphi(y, \vec{x}, \vec{z}))$$

where the disjunction is taken over all the tuples satisfying $n_j, m_j > 0$, m_js distinct, and $\sum_{j=1}^{l} n_j \cdot m_j \geq i$ (it is easy to see that a finite disjunction would suffice), and $\exists! nu\varphi$ abbreviates $\exists nu\varphi \wedge \neg\exists(n+1)u\varphi$.

The rank of this formula equals $\mathrm{rk}(\exists! m_j y\varphi) = \mathrm{rk}(\varphi) + 1$, plus the number of first-sort variables in $\vec{x}$ (by the induction hypothesis) – that is, $\mathrm{rk}(\varphi)$ plus the number of first-sort variables in $(y, \vec{x})$.

2. Let $\psi(\vec{z}) \equiv \exists i(k, \vec{x})\varphi(k, \vec{x}, \vec{z})$. The proof is identical to the proof above up to the point of writing down the quantifier $\exists! m_j k\varphi(k, \cdot)$ – it is replaced by the formula $\bigvee_C (\bigwedge_{c \in C} \varphi(c, \cdot) \wedge \bigwedge_{c \notin C} \neg\varphi(c, \cdot))$ where C ranges over m_j-element subsets of Num. As the rank of this equals $\mathrm{rk}(\varphi)$, we conclude that the rank of the formula equivalent to $\psi(\vec{z})$ equals $\mathrm{rk}(\varphi)$ plus the number of first-sort variables in $\vec{x}$.

This concludes the proof that counting over tuples is definable in $\mathcal{L}_C$. With this, we prove the proposition by induction on the formulae and terms. We also produce, for each second-sort term $\tau(\vec{x})$ of $\mathcal{L}_{\mathrm{aggr}}$, a formula $\psi_\tau(\vec{x}, z)$ of $\mathcal{L}_C$, with z of the second sort, such that $D \models \psi_\tau(\vec{a}, q)$ iff the value of $\tau(\vec{a})$ on D is q.

We may assume, without loss of generality, that parameters of atomic $\mathcal{L}_{\mathrm{aggr}}$ formulae $R(\cdot)$ and $P(\cdot)$ are tuples of variables: indeed, if a second-sort term occurs in $R(\cdot \tau_i \cdot)$, it can be replaced by $\exists k \; (k = \tau_i) \wedge R(\cdot k \cdot)$ without increasing the rank. We now define the translation as follows:

- For a second-sort term t which is a variable q, $\psi_t(q, z) \equiv (z = q)$. If t is a constant c, then $\psi_t(z) \equiv (z = c)$.
- For an atomic φ of the form $x = y$, where x, y are first-sort, $\varphi^\circ = \varphi$.
- For an atomic φ of the form $P(\tau_1(\vec{x}), \ldots, \tau_n(\vec{x}))$, $\varphi^\circ(\vec{x})$ is $\bigvee_{(c_1, \ldots, c_n) \in P} \bigwedge_{i=1}^{n} \psi_{\tau_i}(\vec{x}, c_i)$. Note that $\mathrm{rk}(\varphi^\circ) = \max_i \mathrm{rk}(\psi_{\tau_i}) \leq \max_i \mathrm{rk}(\tau_i) = \mathrm{rk}(\varphi)$.
- $(\varphi_1 \vee \varphi_2)^\circ = \varphi_1^\circ \vee \varphi_2^\circ$, $(\varphi_1 \wedge \varphi_2)^\circ = \varphi_1^\circ \wedge \varphi_2^\circ$, $(\neg\varphi)^\circ = \neg\varphi^\circ$, $(\exists x \varphi)^\circ = \exists x \varphi^\circ$ for x of either sort. Clearly, this does not increase the rank.
- For a term $\tau(\vec{x}) = f(\tau_1(\vec{x}), \ldots, \tau_n(\vec{x}))$, we have

$$\psi_\tau(\vec{x}, z) = \bigvee_{(c, c_1, \ldots, c_n) : c = f(\vec{c})} (z = c) \wedge \bigwedge_{j=1}^{n} \psi_{\tau_j}(\vec{x}, c_j)$$

Again it is easy to see that $\mathrm{rk}(\psi_\tau) \leq \mathrm{rk}(\tau)$.
- For a term $\tau'(\vec{x}) = \mathrm{Aggr}_{\mathcal{F}}\vec{y}. (\varphi(\vec{x}, \vec{y}), \tau(\vec{x}, \vec{y}))$, $\psi_{\tau'}(\vec{x}, z)$ is defined as

$$[\varphi_\infty^\circ(\vec{x}) \wedge (z = f_\infty)] \vee [\neg\varphi_\infty^\circ(\vec{x}) \wedge \psi'(\vec{x}, z)]$$

where $\varphi_\infty^\circ(\vec{x})$ tests if the number of $\vec{y}$ satisfying $\varphi(\vec{x}, \vec{y})$ is infinite, and ψ' produces the value of the term in the case the number of such $\vec{y}$ is finite.

The formula $\varphi_\infty^\circ(\vec{x})$ can be defined as

$$\bigvee_{i:y_i \text{ of 2nd sort}} \quad \bigvee_{C \subseteq \text{Num}, |C| = \infty} \quad \bigwedge_{c \in C} \varphi_i^\circ(\vec{x}, c)$$

where $\varphi_i^\circ(\vec{x}, y_i) \equiv \exists(y_1, \ldots, y_{i-1}, y_{i+1}, \ldots, y_m)\varphi^\circ(\vec{x}, \vec{y})$.
The formula $\psi'(\vec{x}, z)$ is defined as the disjunction of $\neg\exists\vec{y}\varphi^\circ(\vec{x}, \vec{y}) \wedge z = f_0$
and

$$\bigvee_{c,(c_1,n_1),\ldots,(c_l,n_l)} \left(\begin{array}{l} z = c \\ \wedge \exists! n_1 \vec{y} \, (\varphi^\circ(\vec{x}, \vec{y}) \wedge \psi_\tau(\vec{x}, \vec{y}, c_1)) \\ \wedge \cdots \\ \wedge \exists! n_l \vec{y} \, (\varphi^\circ(\vec{x}, \vec{y}) \wedge \psi_\tau(\vec{x}, \vec{y}, c_l)) \\ \wedge \forall \vec{y} \bigwedge_{a \in \text{Num}} (\varphi^\circ(\vec{x}, \vec{y}) \wedge \psi_\tau(\vec{x}, \vec{y}, a) \rightarrow \bigvee_{i=1}^l (a = c_i)) \end{array} \right)$$

where the disjunction is taken over all tuples $(c_1, n_1), \ldots, (c_l, n_l)$, $l > 0$, $n_i > 0$ and values $c \in \text{Num}$ such that

$$\mathcal{F}(\{\underbrace{c_1, \ldots, c_1}_{n_1 \text{ times}}, \ldots, \underbrace{c_l, \ldots, c_l}_{n_l \text{ times}}\}) \;\; = \;\; c$$

Indeed, this formula asserts that either $\varphi(\vec{x}, \cdot)$ does not hold and then $z = f_0$, or that $c_1, \ldots, c_l$ are exactly the values of the term $\tau(\vec{x}, \vec{y})$ when $\varphi(\vec{x}, \vec{y})$ holds, and that n_is are the multiplicities of the c_is.
A straightforward analysis of the produced formulae shows that $\text{rk}(\psi_{\tau'}) \leq \max(\text{rk}(\varphi^\circ), \text{rk}(\psi_\tau))$ plus the number of first-sort variables in $\vec{y}$; that is, $\text{rk}(\psi_{\tau'}) \leq \text{rk}(\tau')$. This completes the proof of the proposition.

$\mathcal{L}_C$ is local. Formulae of $\mathcal{L}_{\text{aggr}}$ have finite rank; hence they are translated into $\mathcal{L}_C$ formulae of finite rank. We now show by a simple induction argument that those formulae are local. More precisely, we show that for every finite-rank $\mathcal{L}_C$ formula $\varphi(\vec{x}, \vec{\imath})$ ($\vec{x}$ of first-sort, $\vec{\imath}$ of second-sort) over pure relational SC, there exists a number $r \geq 0$ such that $\vec{a} \approx_r^D \vec{b}$ implies $D \models \varphi(\vec{a}, \vec{\imath}_0) \leftrightarrow \varphi(\vec{b}, \vec{\imath}_0)$ for any $\vec{\imath}_0$. The smallest such r will be denoted by $\text{lr}(\varphi)$. The proof is based on:

Lemma 1 (Permutation Lemma). Let D be first-sort, with $A = \text{adom}(D)$, and $r > 0$. If $\vec{a} \approx_{3r+1}^D b$, then there exists a permutation $\rho : A \rightarrow A$ such that $\vec{a}c \approx_r^D \vec{b}\rho(c)$ for every $c \in A$.

Proof. Fix an isomorphism $h : N_{3r+1}^D(\vec{a}) \rightarrow N_{3r+1}(\vec{b})$ with $h(\vec{a}) = \vec{b}$. For any $c \in S_{2r+1}^D(\vec{a})$, $h(c) \in S_{2r+1}^D(\vec{b})$ has the same isomorphism type of its r-neighborhood. Thus, for any isomorphism type T of an r-neighborhood of a single element, there are equally many elements in $A - S_{2r+1}^D(\vec{a})$ and in $A - S_{2r+1}^D(\vec{b})$ that realize T. Thus, we have a bijection $g : A - S_{2r+1}^D(\vec{a}) \rightarrow A - S_{2r+1}^D(\vec{b})$ such that $c \approx_r^D g(c)$. Then ρ can be defined as h on $S_{2r+1}^D(\vec{a})$, and as g on $A - S_{2r+1}^D(\vec{a})$. $\qquad\square$

Based on the lemma, we show that every $\mathcal{L}_C$ formula φ of finite rank is local, with $\mathsf{lr}(\varphi) \leq (3^{\mathsf{rk}(\varphi)} - 1)/2$. Note that for the sequence $r_0 = 0, \ldots, r_{i+1} = 3r_i + 1, \ldots$, we have $r_k = (3^k - 1)/2$; we show $\mathsf{lr}(\varphi) \leq r_{\mathsf{rk}(\varphi)}$.

The proof of this is by induction on the formulae, and it is absolutely straightforward for all cases except counting quantifiers. For example, if $\varphi(\vec{x}, \vec{\imath}) = \bigvee_j \varphi_j$ $(\vec{x}, \vec{\imath})$, and $m = \mathsf{rk}(\varphi)$, then by the hypothesis, $\mathsf{lr}(\varphi_j) \leq r_m$, as $\mathsf{rk}(\varphi_j) \leq \mathsf{rk}(\varphi)$. So fix $\vec{\imath}_0$, and let $\vec{a} \approx_{r_m}^D \vec{b}$. Then $D \models \varphi_j(\vec{a}, \vec{\imath}_0) \leftrightarrow \varphi_j(\vec{b}, \vec{\imath}_0)$ for all j by the induction hypothesis, and thus $D \models \varphi(\vec{a}, \vec{\imath}_0) \leftrightarrow \varphi(\vec{b}, \vec{\imath}_0)$.

Now consider the case of the counting quantifier $\psi(\vec{x}, \vec{\imath}) \equiv \exists i z \varphi(\vec{x}, z, \vec{\imath})$. Let $\mathsf{rk}(\varphi) = m$, then $\mathsf{rk}(\psi) = m + 1$ and $r_{m+1} = 3r_m + 1$. Fix $\vec{\imath}_0$, and let $\vec{a} \approx_{r_{m+1}}^D \vec{b}$. By the Permutation Lemma, we get a permutation $\rho : A \to A$ such that $\vec{a}c \approx_{r_m}^D \vec{b}\rho(c)$. By the hypothesis, $\mathsf{lr}(\varphi) \leq r_m$, and thus $D \models \varphi(\vec{a}, c, \vec{\imath}_0) \leftrightarrow \varphi(\vec{b}, \rho(c), \vec{\imath}_0)$. Hence, the number of elements of A satisfying $\varphi(\vec{a}, \cdot, \vec{\imath}_0)$ is exactly the same as the number of elements satisfying $\varphi(\vec{b}, \cdot, \vec{\imath}_0)$, which implies $D \models \psi(\vec{a}, \vec{\imath}_0) \leftrightarrow \psi(\vec{b}, \vec{\imath}_0)$. This concludes the proof of locality of $\mathcal{L}_C$.

Putting everything together, let e be a pure relational expression of $\mathrm{ALG}_{\mathrm{aggr}}$ (All, All). By Theorem 2, it is expressible in $\mathcal{L}_{\mathrm{aggr}}$(All, All), and by Proposition 1, by a $\mathcal{L}_C$ formula of finite rank. Hence, it is local.

7   SQL over Ordered Domains

So far the only nonnumerical selection was of the form $\sigma_{i=j}$, testing equality of two attributes. We now extend the language to $\mathrm{ALG}_{\mathrm{aggr}}^<$ by allowing selections of the form $\sigma_{i<j}(e)$, where both i and j are of the type b, and $<$ is some fixed linear ordering on the domain Dom.

This small addition changes the situation dramatically, and furthermore in this case we can't make blanket statements like "queries are local" – a lot will depend on the numerical domain Dom and available arithmetic operations.

7.1   Natural Numbers

Let $\mathrm{Num} = \mathbb{N}$. We consider a version of $\mathrm{ALG}_{\mathrm{aggr}}$ that has the most usual set of arithmetic and aggregate operators: namely, $+, \cdot, <$ and constants for arithmetic, and the aggregate $\sum$. This suffices to express aggregates MIN, MAX, COUNT, TOTAL, but certainly not AVG, which produces rational numbers.

We shall use the notations:

- $\mathrm{SQL}_\mathbb{N}$ for $\mathrm{ALG}_{\mathrm{aggr}}(\{+, \cdot, <, 0, 1\}, \{\sum\})$, and
- $\mathrm{SQL}_\mathbb{N}^<$ for $\mathrm{ALG}_{\mathrm{aggr}}^<(\{+, \cdot, <, 0, 1\}, \{\sum\})$.

It is sufficient to have constants just for 0 and 1, as all other numbers are definable with $+$.

We show how a well-known counting logic FO(C) [3] can be embedded into $\mathrm{SQL}_\mathbb{N}^<$. The importance of this lies in the fact that FO(C) over ordered structures captures a complexity class, called TC^0 [3,26], for which no nontrivial general lower bounds are known. In fact, although TC^0 is contained in DLOGSPACE, the containment is not known to be proper, and to this day we don't even know if $TC^0 \neq NP$. Moreover, there are indications that proving such a separation result, at least by traditional methods, is either impossible, or would have some very unexpected cryptographic consequences [27].

Definition of FO(C). (see [3,10,19]) It is a two-sorted logic, with second sort being the sort of natural numbers. That is, a structure D is of the form

$$\langle \{a_1, \ldots, a_n\}, \{1, \ldots, n\}, <, +, \cdot, \underline{1}, \underline{n}, R_1, \ldots, R_l \rangle,$$

where the relations R_i are defined on the domain $\{a_1, \ldots, a_n\}$, while on the numerical domain $\{1, \ldots, n\}$ one has $\underline{1}, \underline{n}, <$ and $+, \cdot$ interpreted as ternary predicates (e.g., $+(x, y, z)$ holds iff $x + y = z$). This logic extends first-order by counting quantifiers $\exists i x\ \varphi(x)$, meaning that at least i elements satisfy φ; here i refers to the numerical domain $\{1, \ldots, n\}$ and x to the domain $\{a_1, \ldots, a_n\}$. These quantifiers bind x but not i.

Theorem 4. *Over ordered structures, FO(C) $\subseteq$ SQL$_{\mathbb{N}}^{\leq}$. In particular,*

$$\text{uniform } TC^0 \ \subseteq \ \text{SQL}_{\mathbb{N}}^{\leq}.$$

Proof sketch. With order and aggregate TOTAL, one can define the set $\{1, \ldots, m\}$ where $m = |\ adom(D)\ |$ (by counting the number of elements not greater than each element in the active domain). On this set, one defines $+, \cdot, <$, and then uses the standard translation of calculus into algebra, except for using the aggregate $\sum$ to translate counting quantifiers. $\square$

Corollary 1. *Assume that reachability is not expressible in SQL$_{\mathbb{N}}^{\leq}$. Then uniform TC^0 is properly contained in NLOGSPACE.*

As separation of complexity classes is currently beyond reach, so is proving expressivity bounds for SQL$_{\mathbb{N}}^{\leq}$.

One can also show a closely-related upper bound on the class of decision problems expressible in SQL$_{\mathbb{N}}^{\leq}$:

Proposition 2. *Every Boolean query in SQL$_{\mathbb{N}}^{\leq}$ is contained in P-uniform TC^0.*

Notice that the reachability query, even over ordered domains of nodes, is *order-independent*; that is, the result does not depend on a particular ordering on the nodes, just on the graph structure. Could it be that order-independent queries in SQL$_{\mathbb{N}}$ and SQL$_{\mathbb{N}}^{\leq}$ are the same? Of course, such a result would imply that TC^0 is properly contained in DLOGSPACE, and several papers suggested this approach towards separating complexity classes. Unfortunately, it does not work, as shown in [17]:

Proposition 3. *There exist order-independent non-local queries expressible in* $\text{SQL}_\mathbb{N}^<$. *Thus, there are order-independent* $\text{SQL}_\mathbb{N}^<$ *queries not expressible in* $\text{SQL}_\mathbb{N}$.

Proof sketch. On the graph of an n-element successor relation with an extra predicate P interpreted as the first $\lfloor \log_2 n \rfloor$ elements, one can define the reachability query restricted to the elements of P. □

Counting abilities of $\text{SQL}_\mathbb{N}$ are essential for this result, as its analog for relational calculus does not hold [9].

7.2   Rational Numbers

The language $\text{SQL}_\mathbb{N}^<$ falls short of the class of queries real SQL can define, as it only uses natural numbers. To deal with rational arithmetic (and thus to permit aggregates such as AVG), we extend the numerical domain Num to that of rational numbers $\mathbb{Q}$, and introduce the language

$$\text{SQL}_\mathbb{Q}^< \text{ as } \text{ALG}_{\text{aggr}}^<(\{+, -, \cdot, \div, <, 0, 1\}, \{\Sigma\}).$$

This is a stronger language than $\text{SQL}_\mathbb{N}^<$ (and thus than $\text{FO}(\mathbf{C})$) – to see this, note that it can define rational numbers, and if one represents those by pairs of natural numbers, in some queries these numbers may grow exponentially with the size of the database: something that cannot happen in the context of $\text{SQL}_\mathbb{N}^<$.

The most interesting feature of $\text{SQL}_\mathbb{Q}^<$ is perhaps that it is capable of coding inputs with numbers:

Theorem 5. *Let SC be a pure relational schema. Then there is an* $\text{SQL}_\mathbb{Q}^<$ *expression* e_{SC} *of type* n *such that for every SC-database D,* $e_{SC}(D)$ *is a single rational number, and*

$$D_1 \neq D_2 \quad \Rightarrow \quad e_{SC}(D_1) \neq e_{SC}(D_2)$$

Proof sketch. The proof is based on the following: if P_1 and P_2 are two distinct nonempty sets of prime numbers, then $\sum_{p \in P_1} \frac{1}{p} \neq \sum_{p \in P_2} \frac{1}{p}$. We then code tuples with prime numbers (at most polynomial in the size of the input) and add up inverses of those codes. □

Thus, with the addition of some arithmetic operations, $\text{SQL}_\mathbb{Q}^<$ can express many queries; in particular, $\text{SQL}_\mathbb{Q}^<$ extended with all computable numerical functions expresses all computable queries over pure relational schemas! In fact, to express all computable Boolean queries over such schemas, it suffices to add all computable functions from $\mathbb{Q}$ to $\{0, 1\}$. In contrast, one can show that adding all computable functions from $\mathbb{N}$ to $\{0, 1\}$ to $\text{SQL}_\mathbb{N}^<$ does not give us the same power, as the resulting queries can be coded by non-uniform TC^0 circuits. Still, the coding is just of theoretical interest; even for graphs with 20 nodes it can produces codes of the form $\frac{p}{q}$ with p, q relatively prime, and $q > 10^{1000}$; for $q > 10^{10000}$ one needs only 60 nodes.

8 Conclusion

Did SQL3 designers really have to introduce recursion, or is it expressible with what's already there? Our results show that they clearly had a good reason for adding a new construct, because:

1. Over unordered types, reachability queries cannot be expressed by the basic SQL SELECT-FROM-WHERE-GROUPBY-HAVING statements; in fact, all queries expressible by such statements are local.
2. Over ordered domains, with limited arithmetic, reachability queries are most likely inexpressible, but proving this is hard as separating some complexity classes (and perhaps as hard as refuting some cryptographic assumptions). Adding more arithmetic operations might help, but only at the expense of encodings which are several thousand digits long – so the new construct is clearly justified.

Being a theoretician, I like to see proofs of theorems (even folk theorems!), hence writing all those papers [23,21,24,18] on the expressiveness of SQL. Having finished [18] just over a year ago, I felt that the whole story can be presented in a nice and clean fashion, without asking the reader to spend days studying the prerequisites. I've attempted to give such a presentation here. I hope I convinced you that next-generation database theory texts shouldn't just state that certain queries are inexpressible in SQL, they should also include simple proofs of these results.

Acknowledgements. Although the presentation here is new, it is based entirely on previous results obtained jointly with other people. Special thanks to Limsoon Wong, with whom many of those papers were coauthored, and who in fact suggested back in '93 that we look at the expressiveness of aggregation. The aggregate logic was developed jointly with Limsoon, Lauri Hella, and Juha Nurmonen, who also collaborated with me on various aspects of locality of logics. Simple proofs of locality of logics were discovered in an attempt to answer some questions posed by Moshe Vardi. For their comments on the paper I thank Limsoon, Lauri, Juha, Martin Grohe, Thomas Schwentick, and Luc Segoufin. Part of this work was done while I was visiting the Verso group at INRIA-Rocquencourt.

References

1. S. Abiteboul, R. Hull and V. Vianu. *Foundations of Databases*, Addison Wesley, 1995.
2. A. V. Aho and J. D. Ullman. Universality of data retrieval languages. In *POPL'79*, pages 110–120.
3. D.M. Barrington, N. Immerman, H. Straubing. On uniformity within NC^1. *JCSS*, 41:274–306, 1990.
4. P. Buneman, S. Naqvi, V. Tannen, L. Wong. Principles of programming with complex objects and collection types. *TCS*, 149 (1995), 3–48.

5. J. Celko. *SQL for Smarties: Advanced SQL Programming*. Morgan Kaufmann, 2000.
6. M. Consens and A. Mendelzon. Low complexity aggregation in GraphLog and Datalog, *TCS* 116 (1993), 95–116. Extended abstract in *ICDT'90*.
7. C. J. Date and H. Darwen. *A Guide to the SQL Standard*. Addison Wesley, 1997.
8. G. Dong, L. Libkin and L. Wong. Local properties of query languages. *TCS* 239 (2000), 277–308. Extended abstract in *ICDT'97*.
9. M. Grohe and T. Schwentick. Locality of order-invariant first-order formulas. *ACM TOCL*, 1 (2000), 112–130.
10. K. Etessami. Counting quantifiers, successor relations, and logarithmic space, *JCSS*, 54 (1997), 400–411.
11. R. Fagin, L. Stockmeyer and M. Vardi, On monadic NP vs monadic co-NP, *Information and Computation*, 120 (1995), 78–92.
12. S. Finkelstein, N. Mattos, I.S. Mumick, and H. Pirahesh. Expressing recursive queries in SQL. ANSI Document X3H2-96-075r1, 1996.
13. H. Gaifman. On local and non-local properties, *Proceedings of the Herbrand Symposium, Logic Colloquium '81*, North Holland, 1982.
14. E. Grädel and Y. Gurevich. Metafinite model theory. *Information and Computation* 140 (1998), 26–81.
15. W. Hanf. Model-theoretic methods in the study of elementary logic. In J.W. Addison et al, eds, *The Theory of Models*, North Holland, 1965, pages 132–145.
16. L. Hella. Logical hierarchies in PTIME. *Information and Computation*, 129 (1996), 1–19.
17. L. Hella, L. Libkin and J. Nurmonen. Notions of locality and their logical characterizations over finite models. *J. Symb. Logic*, 64 (1999), 1751-1773.
18. L. Hella, L. Libkin, J. Nurmonen and L. Wong. Logics with aggregate operators. In *LICS'99*, pages 35–44.
19. N. Immerman. *Descriptive Complexity*. Springer Verlag, 1998.
20. A. Klug. Equivalence of relational algebra and relational calculus query languages having aggregate functions. *J. ACM* 29 (1982), 699–717.
21. L. Libkin. On the forms of locality over finite models. In *LICS'97*, pages 204–215.
22. L. Libkin. Logics with counting and local properties. *ACM TOCL*, 1 (2000), 33–59. Extended abstract in *LICS'98*.
23. L. Libkin, L. Wong. Query languages for bags and aggregate functions. *JCSS* 55 (1997), 241–272. Extended abstract in *PODS'94*.
24. L. Libkin and L. Wong. On the power of aggregation in relational query languages. In *DBPL'97*, pages 260–280.
25. P. O'Neil. *Database: Principles, Programming, Performance*. Morgan Kaufmann, 1994.
26. I. Parberry and G. Schnitger. Parallel computation and threshold functions. *JCSS* 36 (1988), 278–302.
27. A. Razborov and S. Rudich. Natural proofs. *JCSS* 55 (1997), 24–35.
28. P. Wadler. Comprehending monads. *Mathematical Structures in Computer Science* 2 (1992), 461–493.

Query Evaluation via Tree-Decompositions
Extended Abstract

Jörg Flum[1], Markus Frick[1], and Martin Grohe[2]

[1] Institut für Mathematische Logik, Albert-Ludwigs-Universität Freiburg,
Eckerstr. 1, 79104 Freiburg, Germany.
Email: `flum@uni-freiburg.de`, `frick@logik.mathematik.uni-freiburg.de`
[2] Department of Mathematics, Statistics, and Computer Science, UIC,
851 S. Morgan St. (M/C 249), Chicago, IL 60607-7045, USA.
Email: `grohe@math.uic.edu`

Abstract. A number of efficient methods for evaluating first-order and monadic-second order queries on finite relational structures are based on tree-decompositions of structures or queries. We systematically study these methods. In the first-part of the paper we consider tree-like structures. We generalize a theorem of Courcelle [7] by showing that on such structures a monadic second-order formula (with free first-order and second-order variables) can be evaluated in time linear in the structure size plus the size of the output. In the second part we study tree-like formulas. We generalize the notions of acyclicity and bounded tree-width from conjunctive queries to arbitrary first-order formulas in a straightforward way and analyze the complexity of evaluating formulas of these fragments. Moreover, we show that the acyclic and bounded tree-width fragments have the same expressive power as the well-known guarded fragment and the finite-variable fragments of first-order logic, respectively.

1 Introduction

Evaluating first-order, or relational calculus, queries against a finite relational database is well-known to be PSPACE-complete [17]. The complexity we refer to here is called the *combined complexity* of the query language [22], i.e. the complexity of the evaluation problem measured both in terms of the length of the query and the size of the database. Many research efforts went into handling this high worst case complexity. In practice, various query optimization heuristics are used; they are based both on the structure of the queries and the (expected) structure of the databases.

One of the important theoretical notions is that of *acyclic conjunctive queries* (cf. [1]). Yannakakis [24] proved that acyclic conjunctive queries can be recognized and evaluated efficiently. In the last few years, there has been renewed interest in acyclic conjunctive queries and related notions based on the graph theoretic concept of *tree-width* [6,15,12, 13]. Whereas these approaches concentrate on conjunctive queries, there have also been attempts to isolate larger fragments of first-order logic whose combined complexity is in PTIME. In particular, Vardi [23] observed that this is the case for the *finite variable fragments* of first-order logic. A fragment of first-order logic that has recently received a lot of attention is the *guarded fragment* [3]. Gottlob, Grädel, and Veith [11] proved

J. Van den Bussche and V. Vianu (Eds.): ICDT 2001, LNCS 1973, pp. 22–38, 2001.

that its combined complexity is both linear in the length of the formula and the size of the database.

There is a different way of using tree-width to evaluate queries that originated in the area of graph algorithms. Here we do not restrict the class of queries, but the class of input structures, or databases. This approach does not only work for first-order logic, but even for the much stronger monadic second-order logic. Courcelle [7] proved that Boolean monadic second-order queries on structures of bounded tree-width can be evaluated in time linear in the size of the input structure, or more precisely in time $f(l) \cdot n$, where l is the length of the query, n is the size of the structure, and $f : \mathbb{N} \to \mathbb{N}$ is some (fast-growing) function.[1] Arnborg, Lagergren, and Seese [4] extended Courcelle's result by showing that on structures of bounded tree-width the number of satisfying assignments of a monadic second-order formula with free variables can be computed in time linear in the size of the input structure.

In the first part of this paper we shall further extend this approach by proving that on structures of bounded tree-width the set of all satisfying assignments of a monadic second-order formula (with free first and second-order variables) can be computed in time linear in the size of the input structure and the size of the output. For example, *all* cliques of a graph $\mathcal{G}$ of bounded tree-width can be computed in time $O(|G| + \sum_{C \text{ clique in } \mathcal{G}} |C|)$. Similarly, all Hamiltonian cycles of a graph of bounded tree-width can be computed in time linear in the size of the graph and the output.

In the second part of the paper we study fragments of first-order logic whose formulas have a tree-like structure. We start by reviewing Yannakakis's [24] algorithm for evaluating acyclic conjunctive queries. Practically the same algorithm can be used to evaluate conjunctive queries of bounded tree-width [6,15], bounded query-width [6], or bounded hypertree-width [13]. We extend the notions of acyclicity and tree-width from conjunctive queries to full first-order logic. Our approach is based on the well-known correspondence between first-order formulas and non-recursive stratified datalog programs (cf. [1]). We generalize acyclicity and tree-width in a straightforward way to such programs. Yannakakis's algorithm immediately gives us algorithms for evaluating queries defined by acyclic or bounded-tree-width programs.

Then we show that the tree-like fragments of first-order logic obtained by this approach are closely related to the two fragments mentioned earlier: Acyclic programs correspond to guarded first-order formulas and bounded tree-width programs correspond to finite-variable first-order formulas. The latter extends an observation Kolaitis and Vardi [15] made on the level of conjunctive queries. In particular the result on the guarded fragment, though not difficult to prove, is quite remarkable, since the motivation for introducing the guarded fragment was completely different. Nevertheless, it turns out that this new fragment can be described in terms of the well-known concept of acyclicity. The second part of our paper thus shows that Yannakakis's method of evaluating tree-like queries is very far reaching and comprises all the methods used to evaluate queries in the other fragments of first-order logic mentioned here.

---

[1] Another way to phrase Courcelle's result is to say that the *data complexity* [22] of monadic second-order logic on graphs of bounded tree-width is in linear time. However, in this paper we consequently maintain the view of combined complexity.

In the last section we discuss the connections between the two parts of the paper. The algorithms in both parts are very similar, and we give an explanation of why that is using tree-automata.

It is one of our main objectives to analyze the running times of the algorithms as precisely as possible, instead of just saying that we have polynomial time algorithms. Occasionally, this requires considerable additional efforts. Furthermore, we are always interested in evaluating formulas with free-variables and not just sentences. Let us also emphasize that we are not fixing a vocabulary for our formulas and structures in advance, but let the vocabulary vary with the inputs.

Due to space limitations, we can at most sketch the proofs of our results in this extended abstract. For details and additional background information, we refer the reader to the full version of this paper [10].

2 Preliminaries

Structures and Queries. A *vocabulary* τ is a finite set of relation symbols. The arity of a vocabulary is the maximum of the arities of the relation symbols it contains. A τ-*structure* $\mathcal{A}$ consists of a non-empty set A, called the *universe* of $\mathcal{A}$, and a relation $R^{\mathcal{A}} \subseteq A^r$ for each r-ary relation symbol $R \in \tau$. If $\mathcal{A}$ is a structure and $B \subseteq A$ non-empty, then $\langle B \rangle^{\mathcal{A}}$ denotes the substructure induced by $\mathcal{A}$ on B. We only consider finite structures. It is convenient to assume that elements of a structure are natural numbers. In other words, *the universe of every structure considered here is a finite subset of* $\mathbb{N}$.

STR denotes the class of all structures. If C is a class of structures, $C[\tau]$ denotes the subclass of all τ-structures in C. We consider graphs as $\{E\}$-structures $\mathcal{G} = (G, E^{\mathcal{G}})$, where $E^{\mathcal{G}}$ is an anti-reflexive and symmetric binary relation. A *colored graph* is a structure $\mathcal{B} = (B, E^{\mathcal{B}}, P_1^{\mathcal{B}}, \ldots, P_n^{\mathcal{B}})$, where $(B, E^{\mathcal{B}})$ is a graph and the unary relations $P_1^{\mathcal{B}}, \ldots, P_n^{\mathcal{B}}$ form a partition of the universe B.

A k-*ary query* of vocabulary τ is a mapping χ that associates with each structure $\mathcal{A} \in \text{STR}[\tau]$ a k-ary relation $\chi(\mathcal{A}) \subseteq A^k$ such that for every isomorphism $f : \mathcal{A} \to \mathcal{B}$ between structures $\mathcal{A}, \mathcal{B} \in \text{STR}[\tau]$ we have $\chi(\mathcal{B}) = f(\chi(\mathcal{A}))$. We admit $k = 0$ and let A^0 consist of one element (the empty tuple) for every A. We identify A^0 with TRUE and $\emptyset$ with FALSE. 0-ary queries are usually called Boolean queries.

Logics. FO and MSO denote the classes of formulas of first-order logic and of monadic second-order logic, respectively. If L is a class of formulas, then $L[\tau]$ denotes the class of all formulas of vocabulary τ in L. For a structure $\mathcal{A} \in \text{STR}$ and a formula $\varphi(X_1, \ldots, X_l, x_1, \ldots, x_m)$ with free monadic second-order variables $X_1, \ldots, X_l$ and free first-order variables $x_1, \ldots, x_m$ we let

$$\varphi(\mathcal{A}) := \{(A_1, \ldots, A_l, a_1, \ldots, a_m) \mid \mathcal{A} \models \varphi(A_1, \ldots, A_l, a_1, \ldots, a_m)\}.$$

For sentences we have $\varphi(\mathcal{A}) =$ TRUE if, and only if, $\mathcal{A}$ satisfies φ. If φ has no free second-order variables, then we call the mapping $\mathcal{A} \mapsto \varphi(\mathcal{A})$ the query *defined* by φ.

In this paper, for various logics L and classes C of structures we will study the following *evaluation problem for* L *on* C:

> *Input:* Structure $\mathcal{A} \in C$, formula $\varphi \in$ L.
> *Problem:* Compute $\varphi(\mathcal{A})$.

For the class C of all structures we call this problem the *evaluation problem for* L.

We often denote tuples $(a_1, \ldots, a_k)$ of elements of a set A by $\bar{a}$, and we write $\bar{a} \in A$ instead of $\bar{a} \in A^k$. Similar notations are used for tuples of subsets, tuples of variables, etc.

Coding Issues. Our underlying model of computation is the standard RAM-model with addition and subtraction as arithmetic operations (cf. [2,21]). We use the uniform cost measure. We will carefully distinguish between the *size* $||o||$ of an object o, which is the length of a natural encoding of o, and, if o is a set, its *cardinality*, denoted by $|o|$. For example, if R is an r-ary relation on a set A, then for a reasonable encoding of R we have $||R|| = O(r \cdot |R| + 1)$. The size $||\mathcal{A}||$ of a τ-structure $\mathcal{A}$ is $O(|A| + \sum_{R \in \tau} ||R^{\mathcal{A}}||)$.

Tree-Decompositions. A *tree* is a connected acyclic graph $\mathcal{T}$. We always fix an (arbitrary) *root* $r^{\mathcal{T}} \in T$ in a tree $\mathcal{T}$. Then we have a natural partial order $\leq^{\mathcal{T}}$ on T, which is defined by: $(t \leq^{\mathcal{T}} u \iff t$ appears on the path from $r^{\mathcal{T}}$ to u). We say that u is a *child* of t or t is the *parent* of u if $(t, u) \in E^{\mathcal{T}}$ and $t \leq^{\mathcal{T}} u$. For every $t \in T$ we let $\mathcal{T}_t := \langle \{u \mid t \leq^{\mathcal{T}} u\}\rangle^{\mathcal{T}}$ be the subtree rooted at t. A tree $\mathcal{T}$ is *binary* if every node has either 0 or 2 children.

It will be convenient to work with hypergraphs (as an abstraction of relational structures). A *hypergraph* $\mathcal{H}$ is a pair $(H, E^{\mathcal{H}})$ consisting of a non-empty set H of *vertices* and a set $E^{\mathcal{H}}$ of non-empty subsets of H called *hyperedges*.

A *tree-decomposition* of a hypergraph $\mathcal{H}$ is a pair $(\mathcal{T}, (H_t)_{t \in T})$, where $\mathcal{T}$ is a tree and $(H_t)_{t \in T}$ a family of subsets of H (called the *blocks* of the decomposition) such that

(1) For every $v \in H$, the set $\{t \in T \mid v \in H_t\}$ is non-empty and connected (i.e. a subtree).
(2) For every $e \in E^{\mathcal{H}}$ there is a $t \in T$ such that $e \subseteq H_t$.

The *width* of a tree-decomposition $(\mathcal{T}, (H_t)_{t \in T})$ is $\max\{|H_t| \mid t \in T\} - 1$. The *tree-width* $\mathrm{tw}(\mathcal{H})$ of $\mathcal{H}$ is the minimum width over all possible tree-decompositions of $\mathcal{H}$.

A *tree-decomposition of a τ-structure* $\mathcal{A}$ is a tree-decomposition of the hypergraph

$$\Big(A, \{\{a_1, \ldots, a_r\} \mid \exists R \in \tau, \ R \ r\text{-ary}, (a_1, \ldots, a_r) \in R^{\mathcal{A}}\}\Big);$$

the *tree-width* of $\mathcal{A}$ is defined accordingly.

A tree-decomposition $(\mathcal{T}, (H_t)_{t \in T})$ of a hypergraph $\mathcal{H}$ is *reduced* if for all $t, u \in T, t \neq u$, we have $H_t \not\subseteq H_u$. For a reduced tree-decomposition $(\mathcal{T}, (H_t)_{t \in T})$ of $\mathcal{H}$ we have $|T| \leq |H|$.

Theorem 2.1 (Bodlaender [5]). *There are a polynomial $p(X)$ and an algorithm that, given a hypergraph $\mathcal{H}$, computes a reduced tree-decomposition of $\mathcal{H}$ of width $w :=$ $\mathrm{tw}(\mathcal{H})$ in time $2^{p(w)} \cdot |H|$.*

3 Tree-Like Structures

In this section we present algorithms for evaluating monadic-second order formulas. We first deal with trees and then show how to extend the results to arbitrary structures parameterized by tree-width. Our automata theoretic approach is based on ideas of Arnborg, Lagergren, and Seese [4].

For a finite alphabet Γ we let τ_Γ be the vocabulary consisting of a binary relation symbol E and a unary relation symbol P_γ for all $\gamma \in \Gamma$. A Γ-*tree* is a colored graph of vocabulary τ_Γ whose underlying graph is a binary tree, and a *colored tree* is a Γ-tree for some Γ.

We say that a vertex t of a colored tree $\mathcal{T}$ has *color* γ (and write $\gamma(t) := \gamma$), if $t \in P_\gamma^{\mathcal{T}}$.

A (bottom-up) Γ-*tree automaton* is a tuple $\mathfrak{A} = (Q, \delta, \Delta, F)$, where Q is a finite set, the set of *states*, $\Delta : \Gamma \to Q$ is the *starting function*, $F \subseteq Q$ is the set of *accepting states* and $\delta : [Q]^{\leq 2} \times \Gamma \to Q$ is the *transition function* (hence we only consider deterministic automata). Here, $[Q]^{\leq 2} := \{\{q, q'\} \mid q, q' \in Q\}$ is the set of singletons and pairs of elements of Q. The *run* $\rho : T \to Q$ of $\mathfrak{A}$ on Γ-tree $\mathcal{T}$ is defined in a bottom-up manner (i.e., from leaves to the root): If t is a leaf, then $\rho(t) := \Delta(\gamma(t))$; if t has children s_1, s_2, then $\rho(t) := \delta(\{\rho(s_1), \rho(s_2)\}, \gamma(t))$. The automaton $\mathfrak{A}$ *accepts* $\mathcal{T}$ if $\rho(r^{\mathcal{T}}) \in F$. A class of colored trees is *recognizable*, if it is the class of colored trees accepted by some tree automaton.

Theorem 3.1 (Thatcher and Wright [19]). *Let Γ be a finite alphabet. A class of Γ-trees is recognizable if, and only if, it is definable by an* MSO$[\tau_\Gamma]$-*sentence. Furthermore, there is an algorithm that computes the tree automaton corresponding to a given MSO-sentence.*

Theorem 3.2. *There exist a function $f : \mathbb{N} \to \mathbb{N}$ and an algorithm that solves the evaluation problem for MSO-formulas on colored trees in time $f(\|\varphi\|) \cdot (|T| + \|\varphi(\mathcal{T})\|)$.*

Proof: We can restrict our attention to MSO-formulas without free first-order variables.

Let Γ be an alphabet and $\varphi(X_1, \ldots, X_k) \in$ MSO$[\tau_\Gamma]$. Theorem 3.1 only applies to sentences. Therefore, we replace the variables $X_1, \ldots, X_k$ by new unary relation symbols appropriately. We set $\Gamma' := \Gamma \times \{0, 1\}^k$. A Γ-tree $\mathcal{T}$ together with $B_1, \ldots, B_k \subseteq T$ leads to a Γ'-tree $\mathcal{T}' := (\mathcal{T}; B_1, \ldots, B_k)$ in a natural way: Denoting the color of $t \in T$ in $\mathcal{T}'$ by $\gamma'(t)$, we let

$$\gamma'(t) = (\gamma, \bar{\epsilon}) \iff \gamma(t) = \gamma \text{ and } (t \in B_i \leftrightarrow \epsilon_i = 1) \text{ for } i = 1, \ldots, k.$$

We call $\bar{\epsilon}$ the *additional color* of t.

The class of Γ'-trees $\{(\mathcal{T}; \bar{B}) \mid \mathcal{T} \text{ colored } \tau\text{-tree}, \bar{B} \subseteq T, \bar{B} \in \varphi(\mathcal{T})\}$ is definable in MSO; hence, there is a Γ'-automaton $\mathfrak{A} = (Q, \Delta, \delta, F)$ recognizing it. Let $\mathcal{T}$ be a Γ-tree. We describe how to compute the set $\varphi(\mathcal{T}) = \{\bar{B} \subseteq T \mid \mathfrak{A} \text{ accepts } (\mathcal{T}; \bar{B})\}$. To do so, we pass through the tree $\mathcal{T}$ three times:

(1) Bottom-up. By induction from the leaves to the root, we first compute, for every $t \in T$, a set P_t of "potential states" at t: If t is a leaf, then $P_t := \{\Delta((\gamma(t), \bar{\epsilon})) \mid \bar{\epsilon} \in \{0, 1\}^k\}$. For an inner vertex t with children s_1 and s_2, we set

$$P_t := \{\delta(\{q_1, q_2\}, (\gamma(t), \bar{\epsilon})) \mid q_1 \in P_{s_1}, q_2 \in P_{s_2}, \bar{\epsilon} \in \{0, 1\}^k\}.$$

Then for all $t \in T$ and $q \in Q$ we have: $q \in P_t$ if, and only if, there are sets $B_1, \ldots, B_k \subseteq T$ such that for the run ρ of $\mathfrak{A}$ on $(\mathcal{T}; \bar{B})$ we have $\rho(t) = q$. If $P_r \cap F = \emptyset$ we have $\varphi(\mathcal{T}) = \emptyset$, and no further action is required.

(2) *Top-down.* Starting at the root $r := r^{\mathcal{T}}$ we compute, for every $t \in T$, the subset S_t of P_t of "success states" at t: We let $S_r := F \cap P_r$. If t has parent s and sibling t', then

$$S_t := \{q \in P_t \mid \text{there are } q' \in P_{t'}, \bar{\epsilon} \in \{0,1\}^k \text{ such that } \delta(\{q, q'\}, (\gamma(s), \bar{\epsilon})) \in S_s\}.$$

Then for all $t \in T$ and $q \in Q$ we have: $q \in S_t$ if, and only if, there are sets $B_1, \ldots, B_k \subseteq T$ such that $\mathfrak{A}$ accepts $(\mathcal{T}; \bar{B})$ and $\rho(t) = q$ for the run ρ of $\mathfrak{A}$ on $(\mathcal{T}; \bar{B})$.

(3) *Bottom-up again.* Recall that for $t \in T$, by $\mathcal{T}_t$ we denote the subtree of $\mathcal{T}$ rooted in t. For $t \in T$ and $q \in S_t$ we let

$$\mathrm{Sat}_{t,q} := \{\bar{B} \subseteq \mathcal{T}_t \mid \text{for } 1 \le i \le k \text{ there is } B_i' \subseteq T \text{ such that } B_i' \cap T_t = B_i,$$
$$\mathfrak{A} \text{ accepts } (\mathcal{T}; \bar{B}'), \text{ and for the run } \rho \text{ of } \mathfrak{A} \text{ on } (\mathcal{T}; \bar{B}'): \rho(t) = q\}.$$

We compute the sets $\mathrm{Sat}_{t,q}$ inductively from the leaves to the root. Let $t \in T$ and $q \in S_t$. Set $B_1^t := \{t\}$ and $B_0^t = \emptyset$. If t is a leaf, then $\mathrm{Sat}_{t,q} = \{(B_{\epsilon_1}^t, \ldots, B_{\epsilon_k}^t) \mid \Delta((\gamma(t), \bar{\epsilon})) = q\}$. If t has children s and s', then

$$\mathrm{Sat}_{t,q} = \Big\{(B_1 \cup B_1' \cup B_{\epsilon_1}^t, \ldots, B_k \cup B_k' \cup B_{\epsilon_k}^t) \mid \bar{\epsilon} \in \{0,1\}^k, \text{ there exist}$$
$$q' \in S_s, q'' \in S_{s'} \text{ such that } \bar{B} \in \mathrm{Sat}_{s,q'}, \bar{B}' \in \mathrm{Sat}_{s',q''}, \delta(\{q', q''\}, (\gamma(t), \bar{\epsilon})) = q\Big\}.$$

Note that $\varphi(\mathcal{T}) = \bigcup_{q \in S_r} \mathrm{Sat}_{r,q}$. Now we describe an algorithm evaluating a formula on a tree:

Input: Colored tree $\mathcal{T}$, MSO-formula $\varphi(X_1, \ldots, X_k)$.
1. Check if there is an alphabet Γ such that $\mathcal{T}$ is a colored Γ-tree and φ is an MSO$[\tau_\Gamma]$-formula; if this is not the case then return $\emptyset$.
2. Compute the Γ'-tree automaton $\mathfrak{A}$ corresponding to φ.
3. For all $t \in T$, compute P_t.
4. For all $t \in T$, compute S_t.
5. For all $t \in T$ and $q \in S_t$, compute $\mathrm{Sat}_{t,q}$.
6. Return $\bigcup_{q \in S_r} \mathrm{Sat}_{r,q}$.

This algorithm can be implemented to work within the desired time bounds. The most difficult step is 5; it is also the only step where we need the automaton to be deterministic.
□

The following corollary easily follows from the proof of Theorem 3.2:

Corollary 3.3. *There exist a function* $f : \mathbb{N} \to \mathbb{N}$ *and an algorithm that, given a colored tree* $\mathcal{T}$ *and an MSO-formula* $\varphi(X_1, \ldots, X_l, x_1, \ldots, x_m)$, *decides in time* $f(\|\varphi\|) \cdot |T|$ *if there are sets* $B_1, \ldots, B_l \subseteq T$ *and elements* $a_1, \ldots, a_m \in T$ *such that* $\mathcal{T} \models \varphi(B_1, \ldots, B_l, a_1, \ldots, a_m)$, *and, if this is the case, computes such sets and elements.*

For a given structure $\mathcal{A}$, by using a tree-decomposition $(\mathcal{T}, (H_t)_{t \in T})$ of $\mathcal{A}$ with underlying binary tree $\mathcal{T}$ and by encoding the isomorphism type of $\mathcal{A}$ in a coloring of $\mathcal{T}$ appropriately, we obtain from Theorem 3.2:

Theorem 3.4. *There exist a function $f : \mathbb{N} \times \mathbb{N} \to \mathbb{N}$ and an algorithm that solves the evaluation problem for MSO-formulas in time $f(\|\varphi\|, \mathrm{tw}(\mathcal{A})) \cdot (|A| + \|\varphi(\mathcal{A})\|)$.*

Remark 3.5. Courcelle and Mosbah [8] get an algorithm for evaluating MSO-formulas on graphs of bounded tree-width out of a more algebraic framework. However, they did not analyze the complexity of their algorithm, and it does not seem to be linear in the size of the output (as ours is).

Corollary 3.6. *There exist a function $f : \mathbb{N} \times \mathbb{N} \to \mathbb{N}$ and an algorithm that, given a structure $\mathcal{A}$ and an MSO-formula $\varphi(X_1, \dots, X_l, x_1, \dots, x_m)$, decides in time $f(\|\varphi\|, \mathrm{tw}(\mathcal{A})) \cdot |A|$, if there are sets $B_1, \dots, B_l \subseteq T$ and elements $a_1, \dots, a_m \in T$ such that $\mathcal{T} \models \varphi(B_1, \dots, B_l, a_1, \dots, a_m)$, and, if this is the case, computes such sets and elements.*

Remark 3.7. There is a trick that can sometimes improve the running time of our algorithms considerably, in particular if the arity of the vocabulary, say τ, is high:

We let τ_b be the vocabulary that contains a unary relation symbol P_R for $R \in \tau$ and binary relation symbols $E_1, \dots, E_s$, where s is the arity of τ. Then with every τ-structure $\mathcal{A}$ we associate a τ_b-structure $\mathcal{A}_b$, the *bipartite structure* associated with $\mathcal{A}$. The universe consists of A together with a new vertex $b_{R\bar{a}}$ for all $R \in \tau$ and $\bar{a} \in R^A$. The relation E_i holds for all pairs $(a_i, b_{Ra_1 \dots a_r})$, and $P_R^{\mathcal{A}_b} := \{b_{R\bar{a}} \mid \bar{a} \in R^A\}$. $\mathcal{A}_b$ can be computed from $\mathcal{A}$ in linear time, and we have $|A_b| = O(\|A\|)$. Moreover, $\mathrm{tw}(\mathcal{A}_b) \leq \mathrm{tw}(\mathcal{A}) + 1$. If the arity of τ is at most $\mathrm{tw}(\mathcal{A})$, this can be improved to $\mathrm{tw}(\mathcal{A}_b) \leq \mathrm{tw}(\mathcal{A})$. The tree-width of $\mathcal{A}_b$ can be considerably smaller than that of $\mathcal{A}$. For example, if R is a 1000-ary relation, then the tree width of $\mathcal{A} = (\{1, \dots, 1000\}, \{(1, \dots, 1000)\})$ is 999, whereas the tree-width of $\mathcal{A}_b$ is 1. For graphs $\mathcal{G}$ we have $\mathrm{tw}(\mathcal{G}) = \mathrm{tw}(\mathcal{G}_b)$.

It is easy to see that there is a linear-time algorithm that associates with every MSO-formula φ an MSO-formula φ_b such that for all structures $\mathcal{A}$ we have $\varphi(\mathcal{A}) = \varphi_b(\mathcal{A}_b)$. Thus to evaluate MSO-formulas we can also proceed as follows: Given a formula φ and a structure $\mathcal{A}$, we first compute φ_b and $\mathcal{A}_b$. Then we compute $\varphi_b(\mathcal{A}_b)$ using our algorithms. By Theorem 3.4, this requires time $O(f(\|\varphi_b\|, \mathrm{tw}(\mathcal{A}_b)) \cdot (\|A\| + \|\varphi(\mathcal{A})\|))$, which can be much better than $f(\|\varphi\|, \mathrm{tw}(\mathcal{A})) \cdot (|A| + \|\varphi(\mathcal{A})\|)$.

There is another advantage in working with the structure $\mathcal{A}_b$ instead of $\mathcal{A}$: MSO becomes more expressive. Intuitively, the reason is that in $\mathcal{A}_b$ we can talk about sets of "edges". For example, it is easy to see that there is an MSO-formula $\varphi(X)$ such that for every graph $\mathcal{G}$, $\varphi(\mathcal{G}_b)$ consists of all sets $\{b_{Eab} \mid ab \in H\}$, where H ranges over the edge sets of all Hamiltonian cycles of $\mathcal{G}$. Thus in a sense φ defines the set of all Hamiltonian cycles of a graph. This is not possible by an MSO-formula in the original $\mathcal{G}$. As a matter of fact, there is not even an MSO-sentence that holds in a graph $\mathcal{G}$ if, and only if, $\mathcal{G}$ is Hamiltonian [16].

4 Tree-Like Formulas

In this section, we restrict our attention to first-order formulas. Recall that *atomic formulas*, or *atoms*, are formulas of the form $x = y$ or $Rx_1 \ldots x_r$ for an r-ary relation symbol R. The set of all atoms occurring in a formula φ is denoted by $at(\varphi)$. *Literals* are atomic or negated atomic formulas. The set of all variables occurring in a formula φ is denoted by $var(\varphi)$, the set of free variables of φ by $free(\varphi)$. With every formula φ we associate a hypergraph $\mathcal{H}_\varphi := \big(var(\varphi), \{var(\alpha) \mid \alpha \in at(\varphi)\}\big)$. A *tree-decomposition* of a formula φ is a tree-decomposition of $\mathcal{H}_\varphi$. A tree-decomposition $(\mathcal{T}, (X_t)_{t \in T})$ of a formula φ is *strict* if there exists a $t \in T$ such that $free(\varphi) \subseteq X_t$. Tree-decompositions turn out to be quite useful when it comes to evaluating formulas of a very simple form, which are known as *conjunctive queries*.

Acyclic Conjunctive Queries. A *conjunctive query* is a first-order formula of the form $\exists y_1 \ldots \exists y_m \bigwedge_{i=1}^{n} \alpha_i$ with atomic formulas $\alpha_1, \ldots, \alpha_n$. In this subsection we explain an algorithm due to Yannakakis for evaluating *acyclic* conjunctive queries.

We have to recall some basic notions of relational database theory. An X-relation $\mathcal{R}$, for a finite set X, is a finite set of mappings with domain X. We let $range(\mathcal{R}) := \bigcup_{\gamma \in \mathcal{R}} \gamma(X)$. We think of an X-relation as an $|X|$-ary relation on $range(\mathcal{R})$ in which we have associated a name (an element of X) with every place of the relation. Usually, X is a set of variables and $range(\mathcal{R})$ is contained in the universe of some structure. For $Y \subseteq X$, the Y-projection of an X-relation $\mathcal{R}$ is the set $\pi_Y(\mathcal{R}) := \{\gamma|_Y \mid \gamma \in \mathcal{R}\}$. For sets X, Y of variables, the *join* of an X-relation $\mathcal{R}$ and a Y-relation $\mathcal{S}$ is the $X \cup Y$-relation $\mathcal{R} \bowtie \mathcal{S} := \{\gamma : X \cup Y \to A \mid \gamma|_X \in \mathcal{R}, \gamma|_Y \in \mathcal{S}\}$. For every formula $\varphi(x_1, \ldots, x_l)$ and structure $\mathcal{A}$ the set $\varphi(\mathcal{A})$ is an $\{x_1, \ldots, x_l\}$-relation over A. On the logical level, projections correspond to existential quantifications and joins correspond to conjunctions. In particular, for a conjunctive query $\varphi(x_1, \ldots, x_l) = \exists y_1 \ldots \exists y_m \bigwedge_{i=1}^{n} \alpha_i$ we have $\varphi(\mathcal{A}) = \pi_{\{x_1, \ldots, x_l\}}\big(\alpha_1(\mathcal{A}) \bowtie \cdots \bowtie \alpha_n(\mathcal{A})\big)$. The following two lemmas describe Yannakakis's basic algorithm. The idea behind these lemmas is the following: We want to evaluate a conjunctive query φ in a structure $\mathcal{A}$. Suppose we can efficiently compute a tree-decomposition $(\mathcal{T}, (X_t)_{t \in T})$ of φ and, for every $t \in T$, the X_t-relation

$$\mathcal{P}_t := \underset{\substack{\alpha \in at(\varphi) \\ var(\alpha) \subseteq X_t}}{\bowtie} \alpha(\mathcal{A}).$$

Then, noting that $\varphi(\mathcal{A}) := \pi_{free(\varphi)}\big(\bowtie_{t \in T} \mathcal{P}_t\big)$, we can use Lemma 4.2 to compute $\varphi(\mathcal{A})$. Moreover, if the tree-decomposition is strict, i.e. if $free(\varphi) \subseteq X_t$ for some $t \in T$, we can even do better using Lemma 4.1.

Lemma 4.1. *There is an algorithm solving the following problem in time* $O\big(|T| \cdot \max_{t \in T} \|\mathcal{P}_t\|\big)$:

> *Input:* Tree-decomposition $(\mathcal{T}, (X_t)_{t \in T})$, an X_t-relation $\mathcal{P}_t$ for every $t \in T$.
> *Problem:* Compute $\mathcal{R}_t := \pi_{X_t}\big(\bowtie_{t \in T} \mathcal{P}_t\big)$ for all $t \in T$.

Proof: The algorithm passes the tree twice.

(1) Bottom-up. For every $t \in T$ we let $\mathcal{Q}_t := \pi_{X_t}\left(\underset{u \geq^T t}{\bowtie} \mathcal{P}_u\right)$. Then if t is a leaf, we have $\mathcal{Q}_t = \mathcal{P}_t$, and if t is an inner node with children $t_1, \dots, t_m$, we have

$$\mathcal{Q}_t = \pi_{X_t}\left(\mathcal{P}_t \bowtie \underset{1 \leq j \leq m}{\bowtie} \mathcal{Q}_{t_j}\right) = \mathcal{P}_t \bowtie \pi_{X_t}\left(\underset{1 \leq j \leq m}{\bowtie} \mathcal{Q}_{t_j}\right) = \mathcal{P}_t \bowtie \underset{1 \leq j \leq m}{\bowtie} \pi_{X_t}(\mathcal{Q}_{t_j}).$$

(2) Top-down. Note that for the root $r := r^T$ we have $\mathcal{R}_r = \mathcal{Q}_r$. For a node $t \in T \setminus \{r\}$ with parent s we have $\mathcal{R}_t = \pi_{X_t}(\mathcal{R}_s) \bowtie \mathcal{Q}_t$.

Thus to compute $\mathcal{Q}_t$ for all $t \in T$ amounts to computing at most one projection and one join of relations of size at most $\max_{t \in T} \|\mathcal{P}_t\|$ for every tree-node. The same applies to $\mathcal{R}_t$. $\square$

Lemma 4.2. *There is an algorithm solving the following problem in time* $O\big(|T| \cdot \max_{t \in T} \|\mathcal{P}_t\| \cdot \|\mathcal{S}\|\big)$:

> *Input:* Tree-decomposition $(\mathcal{T}, (X_t)_{t \in T})$, a subset $X \subseteq \bigcup_{t \in T} X_t$, an X_t-relation $\mathcal{P}_t$ for every $t \in T$.
> *Problem:* Compute $\mathcal{S} := \pi_X\big(\underset{t \in T}{\bowtie} \mathcal{P}_t\big)$.

Proof: We first compute the family $(\mathcal{R}_t)_{t \in T}$ as in Lemma 4.1. For every $t \in T$, let $Y_t := \bigcup_{u >^T t}(X \cap X_u)$. If t has a parent s, then let $Z_t := X_t \cap X_s$, and let $Z_r := \emptyset$. Let $\mathcal{S}_t := \pi_{Y_t \cup Z_t}\big(\underset{u \geq^T t}{\bowtie} \mathcal{R}_u\big)$. Then $\mathcal{S} = \mathcal{S}_r$.

We can compute the relations $\mathcal{S}_t$ inductively in a bottom-up manner, noting that for a leaf t we have $\mathcal{S}_t = \pi_{Y_t \cup Z_t}(\mathcal{R}_t)$ and for an inner node t with children $t_1, \dots, t_m$ we have

$$\mathcal{S}_t = \pi_{Y_t \cup Z_t}\Big(\mathcal{R}_t \bowtie \mathcal{S}_{t_1} \bowtie \cdots \bowtie \mathcal{S}_{t_m}\Big).$$ $\square$

A hypergraph $\mathcal{H}$ is *acyclic* if there is a tree-decomposition $(T, (H_t)_{t \in T})$ of $\mathcal{H}$ such that for every $t \in T$ there exists a hyperedge $e \in E^H$ such that $e = X_t$. We call such a tree-decomposition a *chordal decomposition* of $\mathcal{H}$. A conjunctive query φ is *acyclic* if its hypergraph $\mathcal{H}_\varphi$ is. φ is *strictly acyclic* if $\mathcal{H}_\varphi$ has a chordal decomposition that is a strict tree-decomposition of φ.

Theorem 4.3 (Tarjan, Yannakakis [18]). *Given a hypergraph $\mathcal{H}$, it can be decided in linear time if $\mathcal{H}$ is acyclic. If this is the case, a reduced and chordal decomposition of $\mathcal{H}$ can be computed in linear time.*

Theorem 4.4 (Yannakakis [24]). *There is an algorithm that solves the evaluation problem for acyclic conjunctive queries in time $O\big(\|\varphi\| \cdot \|\mathcal{A}\| \cdot \|\varphi(\mathcal{A})\|\big)$.*

For strictly acyclic conjunctive queries, this can be improved to $O\big(\|\varphi\| \cdot \|\mathcal{A}\|\big)$.

Proof: Given $\mathcal{A}$ and φ, we first compute a reduced chordal decomposition $(\mathcal{T}, (X_t)_{t \in T})$ of φ in time $O(\|\varphi\|)$.

For every atomic formula $\alpha \in \text{at}(\varphi)$, we let $\text{node}(\alpha)$ be the smallest $t \in T$ (with respect to $\leq^T$) such that $\text{var}(\alpha) \subseteq X_t$. It can be shown that $\text{node}(\alpha)$ can be computed in time $O(||\mathcal{A}||)$. Furthermore, $\alpha(\mathcal{A})$ can be computed in time $O(||\mathcal{A}||)$. For $t \in T$ we let

$$\mathcal{P}_t := \underset{\substack{\alpha \in \text{at}(\varphi) \\ \text{node}(\alpha)=t}}{\bowtie} \alpha(\mathcal{A}).$$

Then $\varphi(\mathcal{A}) = \pi_{\text{free}(\varphi)}\left(\underset{t \in T}{\bowtie}\mathcal{P}_t\right)$. For $t \in T$ we let $\alpha_t \in \text{at}(\varphi)$ such that $\text{var}(\alpha_t) = X_t$. Then $\mathcal{P}_t \subseteq \alpha_t(\mathcal{A})$, thus $||\mathcal{P}_t|| \leq ||\alpha_t(\mathcal{A})|| \leq ||\mathcal{A}||$. We can compute the family $(\mathcal{P}_t)_{t \in T}$ in time $O(||\varphi|| \cdot ||\mathcal{A}||)$, because we only have to compute at most one join per atom of φ, and if these joins are computed in the right order, the intermediate relations obtained while computing $\mathcal{P}_t$ are all contained in $\alpha_t(\mathcal{A})$. We now apply Lemma 4.2. The stronger statement for strictly acyclic φ follows from Lemma 4.1. □

The *tree-width* tw(φ) of a formula φ is the tree-width of $\mathcal{H}_\varphi$. The *strict tree-width* stw(φ) of φ is the minimum width over all possible strict tree-decomposition of φ. By a similar proof we get:

Theorem 4.5 (Chekuri and Rajaraman [6]). *The evaluation problem for conjunctive queries can be solved in time* $O\left(2^{p(w)} \cdot ||\varphi|| + ||\varphi|| \cdot (|A|^{w+1} + ||\mathcal{A}||) \cdot ||\varphi(\mathcal{A})||\right)$, *where* $w := \text{tw}(\varphi)$, *and in time* $O\left(2^{p(s)} \cdot ||\varphi|| + ||\varphi|| \cdot (|A|^{s+1} + ||\mathcal{A}||)\right)$, *where* $s := \text{stw}(\varphi)$.

Remark 4.6. Recall Remark 3.7, where we evaluated a query by first translating the input structure $\mathcal{A}$ to a bipartite structure $\mathcal{A}_b$ and the input formula φ to a formula φ_b with $\varphi(\mathcal{A}) = \varphi_b(\mathcal{A}_b)$. A similar approach yields a variant of Theorem 4.5 which is sometimes better. Chekuri and Rajaraman [6] took this approach.

Remark 4.7. Acyclicity and bounded tree-width of a conjunctive query are incomparable — all queries $Ex_1x_2 \wedge Ex_2x_3 \wedge \ldots \wedge Ex_{n-1}x_n \wedge Ex_nx_1$, for $n \geq 3$, are of tree-width 2, but cyclic. On the other hand, the queries $R_nx_1 \ldots x_n$, for $n \geq 1$ and n-ary R_n, are acyclic, but their tree-width grows with n. The connection between acyclicity and bounded tree-width has also been discussed in the full version of [15].

Chekuri and Rajaraman [6] defined a common generalization of both acyclicity and tree-width they called *query-width*. Acyclic queries are precisely those of query-width 1, and for all queries φ we have query-width$(\varphi) \leq \text{tw}(\mathcal{B}_\varphi)$. Chekuri and Rajaraman [6] showed that conjunctive queries of bounded query-width can be evaluated in polynomial time (in the size of the input and the output). However, query-width has one big disadvantage: Queries of bounded query-width cannot be recognized in polynomial time. More precisely, for every $q \geq 4$ it is NP-complete to decide whether a given query has query-width at most q [13]. Gottlob, Leone, and Scarcello [13] therefore introduced yet another width, the *hypertree-width* of a conjunctive query. Acyclic queries are precisely the queries of hypertree-width 1, and for every query φ we have hypertree-width$(\varphi) \leq$ query-width(φ). Moreover, for every $h \geq 1$ there is a polynomial time algorithm that recognizes the queries of hypertree-width at most h.

Although we do not want to give the details here, the basic idea of query-width and hypertree-width is easy to explain: Suppose that we are given a tree-decomposition $(\mathcal{T}, (X_t)_{t \in T})$ of a query φ, and a mapping λ that associates with every $t \in T$ a set $\lambda(t)$ of atoms of φ such that $X_t \subseteq \bigcup_{\alpha \in \lambda(t)} \text{var}(\alpha)$. Suppose, moreover, that $|\lambda(t)| \leq h$ for all $t \in T$ (very roughly, the hypertree-width of φ is the smallest h such that a tree-decomposition and a mapping λ with these properties exist). Then to evaluate φ in a structure $\mathcal{A}$, we can proceed as follows: For $t \in T$ we let

$$\mathcal{P}_t := \underset{\alpha \in \lambda(t)}{\bowtie} \pi_{X_t}(\alpha(\mathcal{A})) \bowtie \underset{\substack{\alpha \in \operatorname{at}(\varphi) \\ \operatorname{node}(\alpha) = t}}{\bowtie} \alpha(\mathcal{A}).$$

Then $\varphi(\mathcal{A}) = \pi_{\operatorname{free}(\varphi)}(\underset{t \in T}{\bowtie} \mathcal{P}_t)$. Thus we can use Lemmas 4.1 and 4.2 to compute $\varphi(\mathcal{A})$.

Tree-decompositions and related notions have also extensively been studied in AI, [14] is a survey.

Let us now try to extend the results on conjunctive queries to larger classes of formulas. A *conjunctive query with negation* is a formula of the form $\exists \bar{y} \bigwedge_{i=1}^{n} \lambda_i$, where $\lambda_1, \ldots, \lambda_n$ are literals, i.e. atomic or negated atomic formulas. We let $\operatorname{at}^+(\varphi)$ $(\operatorname{at}^-(\varphi))$ denote the set of all atoms occurring positively (negatively, resp.) in φ.

The first observation we make is a disappointment: Evaluating conjunctive queries with negation whose hypergraph is acyclic is just as hard as evaluating arbitrary conjunctive queries with negation. To see this, let $\varphi = \exists \bar{y} \bigwedge_{i=1}^{n} \lambda_i$ be an arbitrary conjunctive query with negation of vocabulary τ. Let R be a new $|\operatorname{var}(\varphi)|$-ary relation symbol, $\bar{x}$ a tuple that contains all variables of φ, and $\varphi^* := \exists \bar{y}(\neg R\bar{x} \wedge \bigwedge_{i=1}^{n} \lambda_i)$. Then $\mathcal{H}_{\varphi^*}$ is acyclic, because the one node tree yields a chordal tree-decomposition of $\mathcal{H}_{\varphi^*}$. For every τ-structure $\mathcal{A}$ let $\mathcal{A}^*$ be the $\tau \cup \{R\}$-expansion of $\mathcal{A}$ with $R^{\mathcal{A}^*} := \emptyset$. Then $\|\mathcal{A}^*\| = O(\|\mathcal{A}\|)$ and $\varphi(\mathcal{A}) = \varphi^*(\mathcal{A}^*)$. Thus evaluating φ is not harder than evaluating φ^*.

However, there is a refined notion of acyclicity for conjunctive queries with negation: A conjunctive query with negation φ is *acyclic* if it has a chordal decomposition $(\mathcal{T}, (X_t)_{t \in T})$ such that for every $t \in T$ there is an atom $\alpha \in \operatorname{at}^+(\varphi)$ with $X_t = \operatorname{var}(\alpha)$. If φ has such a chordal decomposition that, in addition, is a strict tree-decomposition, then φ is *strictly acyclic*.

It is now easy to extend the previous results:

Corollary 4.8. *The evaluation problem for acyclic conjunctive queries with negation can be solved in time $O(\|\varphi\| \cdot \|\mathcal{A}\| \cdot \|\varphi(\mathcal{A})\|)$. For strictly acyclic queries, this can be improved to $O(\|\varphi\| \cdot \|\mathcal{A}\|)$.*

Corollary 4.9. *The evaluation problem for conjunctive queries with negation can be solved in time $O(2^{p(w)} \cdot \|\varphi\| + \|\varphi\| \cdot (|A|^{w+1} + \|\mathcal{A}\|) \cdot \|\varphi(\mathcal{A})\|)$, where $w := \operatorname{tw}(\varphi)$, and in time $O(2^{p(s)} \cdot \|\varphi\| + \|\varphi\| \cdot (|A|^{s+1} + \|\mathcal{A}\|))$, where $s := \operatorname{stw}(\varphi)$.*

Non-recursive Stratified Datalog. A *datalog rule (with negation)* ρ is an expression of the form $\gamma \leftarrow \lambda_1 \wedge \ldots \wedge \lambda_n$, where γ is an atom of the form $Qx_1 \ldots x_l$ with pairwise distinct variables $x_1, \ldots, x_l \in \operatorname{var}(\lambda_1 \wedge \ldots \wedge \lambda_n)$ and $\lambda_1, \ldots, \lambda_n$ are literals. γ is called the *head* and $\lambda_1 \wedge \ldots \wedge \lambda_n$ the *body* of ρ.

To define the semantics, suppose that $\gamma = Qx_1 \ldots x_l$ and let $\mathcal{A}$ be a structure whose vocabulary contains all relation symbols occurring in the body of ρ. Then we let

$$\rho(\mathcal{A}) := \pi_{\{x_1, \ldots, x_l\}}\left(\underset{1 \leq i \leq n}{\bowtie} \lambda_i(\mathcal{A})\right).$$

If $\bar{y}$ is a tuple that consists of all variables in $\bigcup_{1 \leq i \leq n} \mathrm{var}(\lambda_i) \setminus \{x_1, \ldots, x_l\}$ and $\varphi(\bar{x}) := \exists \bar{y} \bigwedge_{1 \leq i \leq n} \lambda_i$, then $\rho(\mathcal{A}) = \varphi(\mathcal{A})$. Thus datalog rules are just another way of writing conjunctive queries with negation.

A *datalog program* is a finite set Π of datalog rules. The *intensional vocabulary* $\mathrm{int}(\Pi)$ of Π is the set of all relation symbols that occur in the head of some rule of Π. The extensional vocabulary $\mathrm{ext}(\Pi)$ is the set of all relation symbols that occur in the body of some rule of Π and are not contained in $\mathrm{int}(\Pi)$. Program Π is *non-recursive*, if no relation symbol that occurs in the head of a rule also occurs in the body of a rule. *In the following we restrict our attention to non-recursive datalog programs.*

To define the semantics, let $Q \in \mathrm{int}(\Pi)$ and $\mathcal{A}$ an $\mathrm{ext}(\Pi)$-structure. Then we let

$$\Pi_Q(\mathcal{A}) := \bigcup \{ \rho(\mathcal{A}) \mid \rho \in \Pi, \ Q \text{ occurs in the head of } \rho \}.$$

The query $\mathcal{A} \mapsto \Pi_Q(\mathcal{A})$ can be defined by an existential first-order formula; conversely every query definable by an existential first-order formula can also be defined by a datalog program.

A *non-recursive stratified datalog (NRSD) program* is a sequence $\Pi := (\Pi^1, \ldots, \Pi^n)$ of non-recursive datalog programs with the property that no $Q \in \mathrm{int}(\Pi^j)$ occurs in Π_i for $1 \leq i < j \leq n$. We set $\mathrm{int}(\Pi) := \bigcup_{i=1}^{n} \mathrm{int}(\Pi_i)$, and $\mathrm{ext}(\Pi) := \bigcup_{i=1}^{n} (\mathrm{ext}(\Pi^i) \setminus \bigcup_{j=1}^{i-1} \mathrm{int}(\Pi^j))$. The programs $\Pi_1, \ldots, \Pi_n$ are called the *strata* of Π.

To define the semantics, let $\mathcal{A}$ be an $\mathrm{ext}(\Pi)$-structure. We let $\mathcal{A}_0 := \mathcal{A}$. Inductively over $i, 1 \leq i \leq n$, we define $\mathcal{A}_i$ and $\Pi_Q(\mathcal{A})$ for all $Q \in \mathrm{int}(\Pi^i)$ as follows: Suppose that $1 \leq i \leq n$ and that the $\mathrm{ext}(\Pi) \cup \bigcup_{j=1}^{i-1} \mathrm{int}(\Pi^j)$-structure $\mathcal{A}_{i-1}$ is already defined. For $Q \in \mathrm{int}(\Pi^i)$ we let $\Pi_Q(\mathcal{A}) := \Pi_Q^i(\mathcal{A}_{i-1})$. Let $\mathcal{A}_i$ be the $\mathrm{ext}(\Pi) \cup \bigcup_{j=1}^{i} \mathrm{int}(\Pi^j)$-expansion of $\mathcal{A}_{i-1}$ with $Q^{\mathcal{A}_i} := \Pi_Q(\mathcal{A})$ for $Q \in \mathrm{int}(\Pi_i)$.

In the following, we assume that every NRSD-program has a distinguished intensional relational symbol, the *goal predicate*, which we always denote by Q. Then we write $\Pi(\mathcal{A})$ instead of $\Pi_Q(\mathcal{A})$; $\mathcal{A} \mapsto \Pi_Q(\mathcal{A})$ is the *query defined by* Π. An NRSD-program Π is *Boolean*, if it defines a Boolean query, i.e. if its goal predicate is 0-ary. An NRSD-program Π is *equivalent* to a formula φ or to another program Π' if they define the same query. It is easy to prove the following (well-known) fact:

Fact 4.10. *A query is first-order definable if, and only if, it is NRSD-definable.*

The *evaluation problem* for a class P of datalog programs is the following problem:

> *Input:* Structure $\mathcal{A}$, program $\Pi \in$ P.
> *Problem:* Compute $\Pi(\mathcal{A})$.

Tree-decompositions, tree-width, acyclicity, etc. of a datalog rule ρ are defined with respect to the corresponding conjunctive query with negation. For example, a tree-decomposition of a datalog rule $\rho := \gamma \leftarrow \bigwedge_{i=1}^{n} \lambda_i$ is a tree-decomposition of the hypergraph $(\mathrm{var}(\rho), \{\mathrm{var}(\lambda_i) \mid 1 \leq i \leq n\})$, and a tree-decomposition $(\mathcal{T}, (X_t)_{t \in T})$ of ρ is *strict* if there is a $t \in T$ such that $\mathrm{var}(\gamma) \subseteq X_t$.

Definition 4.11. Let $\Pi = (\Pi_1, \ldots, \Pi_n)$ be an NRSD-program.
(1) Π is *strictly acyclic* if every rule of Π is strictly acyclic.

(2) Π is *acyclic* if $(\Pi_1, \ldots, \Pi_{n-1})$ is strictly acyclic and every rule ρ of Π_n is acyclic.

(3) The *strict tree-width* of Π is the number $\mathrm{stw}(\Pi) := \max\{\mathrm{stw}(\rho) \mid \rho \in \bigcup_{i=1}^{n} \Pi_i\}$.

(4) The *tree-width* of Π is the number $\mathrm{tw}(\Pi) := \max\{\mathrm{stw}((\Pi_1, \ldots, \Pi_{n-1}))\} \cup \{\mathrm{tw}(\rho) \mid \rho \in \Pi_n\}$.

The following example shows why it is necessary that in an acyclic program we require all strata except for the last one to be *strictly* acyclic:

Example 4.12. Let $\Pi = (\Pi_1, \ldots, \Pi_n)$ be an NRSD-program. We construct an equivalent program $\Pi' = (\Pi'_0, \Pi'_1, \ldots, \Pi'_n)$ such that all rules of Π' are acyclic. Let m be the maximal number of variables occurring in a rule of Π and $X \notin \mathrm{int}(\Pi) \cup \mathrm{ext}(\Pi)$ a new m-ary relation symbol. Let ρ_0 be the acyclic datalog rule $X x_1 \ldots x_m \leftarrow x_1 = x_1 \wedge \ldots \wedge x_m = x_m$. Π'_0 just consists of the rule ρ_0, and for $1 \leq i \leq n$ the stratum Π'_i is obtained from Π_i by adding an atom $X\bar{y}$ to the body of every rule ρ of Π_i, where $\bar{y}$ is a tuple of variables that contains all variables of ρ. Clearly, Π' is equivalent to Π, and all of its rules are acyclic.

An NRSD-program $\Pi = (\Pi_1, \ldots, \Pi_n)$ is in *normal form* if for $1 \leq i < j \leq n$ and $X \in \mathrm{int}(\Pi_i) \cap \mathrm{ext}(\Pi_j)$ the relation symbol X only occurs negatively in Π_j.

Lemma 4.13. *There is an exponential time algorithm that associates with every acyclic NRSD-program Π an equivalent acyclic NRSD-program Π' in normal form. Furthermore, if Π is strictly acyclic, then Π' is also strictly acyclic.*

The results of Section 4 on conjunctive queries yield:

Corollary 4.14. *(1) The evaluation problem for acyclic NRSD-programs in normal form can be solved in time $O(\|\Pi\| \cdot \|\mathcal{A}\| \cdot \|\Pi(\mathcal{A})\|)$. For strictly acyclic NRSD-programs in normal form, this can be improved to $O(\|\Pi\| \cdot \|\mathcal{A}\|)$.*

(2) The evaluation problem for NRSD-programs can be solved in time $O(2^{p(w)} \cdot \|\varphi\| + \|\Pi\| \cdot (|\mathcal{A}|^{w+1} + \|\mathcal{A}\|)\|\Pi(\mathcal{A})\|)$, where $w := \mathrm{tw}(\Pi)$, and in time $O(2^{p(s)} \cdot \|\varphi\| + \|\Pi\| \cdot (|\mathcal{A}|^{s+1} + \|\mathcal{A}\|))$, where $s := \mathrm{stw}(\Pi)$.

The following example shows why we need the normal form in (1) and that there is no polynomial time translation of arbitrary acyclic programs into normal form programs. A similar example occurs in [11].

Example 4.15. Let $n \geq 2$ and $X_1, \ldots, X_n$ be n-ary relation symbols. For $1 \leq i < j \leq n, 1 \leq k \leq n - 1$ let $\rho^k_{\{i,j\}}$ be the datalog rule

$$X_{k+1} x_1 \ldots x_{i-1} x_j x_{i+1} \ldots x_{j-1} x_i x_{j+1} \ldots x_n \leftarrow X_k x_1 \ldots x_n$$

and let ρ^k_{id} be the rule $X_{k+1}\bar{x} \leftarrow X_k\bar{x}$. Set $\Pi_k := \{\rho^k_{\mathrm{id}}\} \cup \{\rho^k_{\{i,j\}} \mid 1 \leq i < j \leq n - 1\}$. Then $\Pi = (\Pi_1, \ldots, \Pi_{n-1})$ is a strictly acyclic NRSD-program with $\|\Pi\| = O(n^4)$. For the $\{X_1\}$-structure $\mathcal{A} := (\{1, \ldots, n\}, \{(1, \ldots, n)\})$ we have $|\Pi_{X_n}(\mathcal{A})| = n!$, and therefore $\Pi_{X_n}(\mathcal{A})$ cannot be computed in time $O(\|\Pi\| \cdot \|\mathcal{A}\|) = O(n^5)$.

Similar results can be obtained for stratified datalog programs with recursion (by iterating the results for programs without recursion).

Tractable Fragments of First-Order Logic. The classes of strictly acyclic NRSD-programs and programs of strictly bounded tree-width correspond to well-known fragments of first-order logic.

The *guarded fragment* GF is the smallest fragment of FO containing all atoms, closed under the Boolean operations $\neg$, $\wedge$, $\vee$ and satisfying:

> If α is atomic and φ is a GF-formula with free$(\varphi) \subseteq$ var(α), then for every tuple $\bar{y}$ of variables $\exists \bar{y}(\alpha \wedge \varphi)$ is a GF-formula.

A GF-formula is *strictly guarded* if it is of the form $\exists \bar{y}(\alpha \wedge \varphi)$, where free$(\varphi) \subseteq$ var(α). Here we allow the degenerated case that $\bar{y}$ is empty, i.e. that the formula is just $\alpha \wedge \varphi$. Every GF-formula is a Boolean combination of atomic formulas and strictly guarded formulas. Furthermore, any GF-sentence φ is equivalent to the strictly guarded sentence $\exists y(y = y \wedge \varphi)$.

Theorem 4.16. *(1) There is a quadratic time algorithm that associates with every strictly guarded formula an equivalent strictly acyclic NRSD-program in normal form.*
(2) There is an algorithm that associates with every strictly acyclic NRSD-program an equivalent disjunction of strictly guarded formulas.
In particular, every GF-sentence is equivalent to an acyclic Boolean NRSD-program and vice versa.

Remark 4.17. It seems possible to improve the translation algorithm in (1) to an $O(n \cdot \log(n))$-algorithm. We do not believe that it can be made linear, although we cannot prove this. The following strictly acyclic formulas $(\varphi_n)_{n \geq 1}$ seem to require NRSD-programs of superlinear size: We let $P_1, P_2, \ldots$ be unary and, for $n \geq 1$, R_n n-ary. Then we let $\varphi_n := R_n x_1 \ldots x_n \wedge \bigvee_{i=1}^{n} P_i x_i$.

The translation from NRSD-programs to first-order formulas cannot be made polynomial; this has nothing to do with being acyclic or guarded. Intuitively, it is due to the fact that programs correspond to directed acyclic graphs, whereas formulas correspond to trees.

Remark 4.18. Gottlob, Grädel, and Veith [11] give a similar translation between sentences of the guarded fragment and so-called *Datalog LITE*-programs, which are essentially stratified datalog programs where every rule has a strict chordal decomposition whose tree only consists of one node.

The following theorem generalizes a result for conjunctive queries due to Kolaitis and Vardi:

Theorem 4.19. *Let $k \geq 1$ and let FO^k be the set of all first-order formulas with at most k variables.*
(1) There is a linear time algorithm that associates with every FO^k-formula an equivalent NRSD-program of strict tree-width at most $(k-1)$.
(2) There is an algorithm that associates with every NRSD-program of strict tree-width at most $(k-1)$ an equivalent FO^k-formula.

5 The Overall Picture

The query-evaluation algorithms of Sections 3 and 4 are very similar. First we compute a tree-decomposition, either of the structure or the formula. Then we pass the tree three times. The first (bottom-up) pass is to compute all reachable states of the automaton at some tree-node (the sets P_t in the proof of Theorem 3.2) or all reachable assignments to the variables occurring at the node (the relation $\mathcal{Q}_t$ in the proof of Lemma 4.1). In the second (top-down) pass we filter out all states that do not lead to an accepting configuration (S_t in the proof of Theorem 3.2, $\mathcal{R}_t$ in Lemma 4.1). The third (bottom-up) pass is to assemble the satisfying assignments from the pieces computed at every node ($\mathrm{Sat}_{t,q}$ in the proof of Theorem 3.2, S_t in Lemma 4.2). Note that in both cases for sentences we only need the first pass.

The connection becomes clearer if in Section 4 we view the structures as automata: We define a non-deterministic[2] tree-automaton $\mathfrak{A}_\mathcal{A} := (Q, \delta, \Delta, F)$ for every τ-structure $\mathcal{A}$. Let r be the arity of τ. The alphabet is $\Sigma_\tau := \tau \times \mathrm{Pow}(\{(i,j) \mid 1 \le i, j \le r\})$ $\times \mathrm{Pow}(\{(i,j) \mid 1 \le i, j \le r\})$. The state space consists of a state $q^=_{(a,a)}$ for every $a \in A$ and a state $q^R_{\bar a}$ for every $R \in \tau, \bar a \in R^\mathcal{A}$. In the following we just view '=' as a relation symbol in τ with $=^\mathcal{A} := \{(a, a) \mid a \in A\}$. The transition relation δ consists of all tuples $(q^R_{\bar a}, q^{R'}_{\bar a'}, (R'', e, e'), q^{R''}_{\bar a''})$ where $((i,j) \in e \implies a_i = a''_j)$ and $((i,j) \in e' \implies a'_i = a''_j)$. The starting relation Δ consists of all pairs $((R, \emptyset, \emptyset), q^R_{\bar a})$. Every state of $\mathfrak{A}_\mathcal{A}$ is accepting, i.e. we let $F := Q$.

Now let φ be an acyclic conjunctive query of vocabulary τ. Then, starting from an arbitrary chordal decomposition of φ, we can find a chordal decomposition $(\mathcal{T}, (X_t))$ of φ where $\mathcal{T}$ is a binary tree, together with an onto mapping $\lambda : T \to \mathrm{at}(\varphi)$ such that for every $t \in T$ we have $\mathrm{var}(\lambda(t)) = X_t$. We define a mapping $\sigma : T \to \Sigma_\tau$ as follows: For the leaves $t \in T$ we let $\sigma(t) = (R, \emptyset, \emptyset)$, where R is the relation symbol occurring in $\lambda(t)$. For a node t with children u_1 and u_2 we let $\sigma(t) = (R, e_1, e_2)$, where again R is the relation symbol occurring in $\lambda(t)$, and e_i is defined as follows (for $i = 1, 2$): If $\lambda(t) = Rx_1 \ldots x_m$ and $\lambda(u_i) = R'y_1 \ldots y_n$ (note that $1 \le m, n \le r$), then $e_i := \{(k, l) \mid y_k = x_l\}$.

Suppose now that φ is a sentence. Then the automaton $\mathfrak{A}_\mathcal{A}$ accepts the colored tree $(\mathcal{T}, \gamma)$ if, and only if, $\mathcal{A} \models \varphi$. The fact that our automaton is not deterministic does not play a role as long as we just want to decide acceptance; in the algorithm of Theorem 3.2 we used the fact that there we had a deterministic automaton only in the third pass in order to compute the output efficiently.

The correspondence breaks down for formulas with free variables. If we want to evaluate an MSO-formula on a structure of bounded tree-width then in the third pass of the automaton we have to collect additional colorings of the tree that lead to accepting runs. If we want to evaluate an acyclic conjunctive query in a structure $\mathcal{A}$ using the automaton $\mathfrak{A}_\mathcal{A}$, then in the third pass we have to collect projections of accepting runs of the automaton.

---

[2] In Section 3 we only defined deterministic tree-automata. In a non-deterministic automaton (Q, δ, Δ, F) of alphabet Σ, instead of functions we have a *transition relation* $\delta \subseteq Q \times Q \times \Sigma \times Q$ and a *starting relation* $\Delta \subseteq \Sigma \times Q$.

If we restrict our attention to monadic second-order sentences of a very special form, there is an abstract explanation for the connection between evaluation of the MSO-sentences and Boolean conjunctive queries due to Feder and Vardi [9]: Both problems amount to deciding whether there is a homomorphism between two relational structures. And in both cases we use the fact that it is decidable in polynomial time if an arbitrary structure $\mathcal{A}$ contains a homomorphic image of a structure $\mathcal{B}$ of bounded tree-width.

References

1. S. Abiteboul, R. Hull, and V. Vianu. *Foundations of Databases*. Addison-Wesley, 1995.
2. A.V. Aho, J.E. Hopcroft, and J.D. Ullman. *The Design and Analysis of Computer Algorithms*. Addison-Wesley, 1974.
3. H. Andréka, J. van Benthem, and I. Németi. Modal languages and bounded fragments of first-order logic, 1996. ILLC Research Report ML-96-03, University of Amsterdam.
4. S. Arnborg, J. Lagergren, and D. Seese. Easy problems for tree-decomposable graphs. *Journal of Algorithms*, 12:308–340, 1991.
5. H.L. Bodlaender. A linear-time algorithm for finding tree-decompositions of small treewidth. *SIAM Journal on Computing*, 25:1305–1317, 1996.
6. Ch. Chekuri and A. Rajaraman. Conjunctive query containment revisited. In Ph. Kolaitis and F. Afrati, editors, *Proceedings of the 5th International Conference on Database Theory*, volume 1186 of *Lecture Notes in Computer Science*, pages 56–70. Springer-Verlag, 1997.
7. B. Courcelle. Graph rewriting: An algebraic and logic approach. In J. van Leeuwen, editor, *Handbook of Theoretical Computer Science*, volume 2, pages 194–242. Elsevier Science Publishers, 1990.
8. B. Courcelle and M. Mosbah. Monadic second-order evaluations on tree-decomposable graphs. *Theoretical Computer Science*, 103:49–82, 1993.
9. T. Feder and M.Y. Vardi. Monotone monadic SNP and constraint satisfaction. In *Proceedings of the 25th ACM Symposium on Theory of Computing*, pages 612–622, 1993.
10. J. Flum and M. Frick and M. Grohe. Query evaluation via tree-decompositions. Full version of this paper, available at http://www.math.uic.edu/~grohe/pub.html.
11. G. Gottlob, E. Grädel, and H. Veith. Datalog lite: Temporal versus deductive reasoning in verification. Technical Report DBAI-TR-98-22, Technische Universität Wien, 1998.
12. G. Gottlob, N. Leone, and F. Scarcello. The complexity of acyclic conjunctive queries. In *Proceedings of the 39th Annual IEEE Symposium on Foundations of Computer Science*, pages 706–715, 1998.
13. G. Gottlob, N. Leone, and F. Scarcello. Hypertree decompositions and tractable queries. In *Proceedings of the 18th ACM Symposium on Principles of Database Systems*, pages 21–32, 1999.
14. G. Gottlob, N. Leone, and F. Scarcello. A Comparison of Structural CSP Decomposition Methods. In *Proceedings of the Sixteenth International Joint Conference on Artificial Intelligence*, pages 394–399, 1999.
15. Ph.G. Kolaitis and M.Y. Vardi. Conjunctive-query containment and constraint satisfaction. In *Proceedings of the 17th ACM Symposium on Principles of Database Systems*, pages 205–213, 1998.
16. J. Makowsky. Model theory in computer science: An appetizer. In S. Abramsky, D.M. Gabbay, and T.S.E. Maibaum, editors, *Handbook of Logic in Computer Science*, volume 1, chapter 6. Oxford University Press, 1992.
17. L.J. Stockmeyer. *The Complexity of Decision Problems in Automata Theory*. PhD thesis, Department of Electrical Engineering, MIT, 1974.

18. R.E. Tarjan and M. Yannakakis. Simple linear-time algorithms to test chordality of graphs, test acyclicity of hypergraphs, and selectively reduce acyclic hypergraphs. *SIAM Journal on Computing*, 13:566–579, 1984.
19. J.W. Thatcher and J.B. Wright. Generalized finite automata with an application to a decision problem of second order logic. *Math. Syst. Theory*, 2:57–82, 1968.
20. C. Thomassen. Embeddings and minors. In R. Graham, M. Grötschel, and L. Lovász, editors, *Handbook of Combinatorics*, volume 1, chapter 5, pages 301–349. Elsevier, 1995.
21. P. van Emde Boas. Machine models and simulations. In J. van Leeuwen, editor, *Handbook of Theoretical Computer Science*, volume 1, pages 1–66. Elsevier Science Publishers, 1990.
22. M.Y. Vardi. The complexity of relational query languages. In *Proceedings of the 14th ACM Symposium on Theory of Computing*, pages 137–146, 1982.
23. M.Y. Vardi. On the complexity of bounded-variable queries. In *Proceedings of the 14th ACM Symposium on Principles of Database Systems*, pages 266–276, 1995.
24. M. Yannakakis. Algorithms for acyclic database schemes. In *7th International Conference on Very Large Data Bases*, pages 82–94, 1981.

Scalar Aggregation in FD-Inconsistent Databases

Marcelo Arenas[1], Leopoldo Bertossi[2], and Jan Chomicki[3]

[1] University of Toronto, Department of Computer Science, marenas@cs.toronto.edu
[2] Pontificia Universidad Catolica de Chile, Escuela de Ingeniería, Departamento de Ciencia de Computacion, bertossi@ing.puc.cl
[3] University at Buffalo, Department of Computer Science and Engineering, chomicki@cse.buffalo.edu

Abstract. We consider here scalar aggregation queries in databases that may violate a given set of functional dependencies. We show how to compute consistent answers (answers true in every minimal repair of the database) to such queries. We provide a complete characterization of the computational complexity of this problem. We also show how tractability can be obtained in several special cases (one involves a novel application of the perfect graph theory) and present a practical hybrid query evaluation method.

1 Introduction

While integrity constraints capture important semantic properties of data, they are often unenforceable if data comes from different, autonomous sources (thus the integrated database may be inconsistent with the constraints). The notion of a *consistent query answer* [2] attempts to reduce this tension by using constraints to qualify query answers. A consistent answer is, intuitively, true regardless of the way the database is fixed to remove constraint violations. Thus answer consistency serves as an indication of its reliability.

Consistent query answers are potentially important in a datawarehouse context, where inconsistencies are likely to occur as the effect of the integration of data sources, with duplicate information, or delayed refreshment of the warehouse. In addition, it is in datawarehousing where aggregation queries are particularly important because they are used, in combination with OLAP methodologies, to better understand, in a global way, the peculiarities of clients, market and business behavior, and to support decision making.

In [2], in addition to a formal definition of a consistent query answer, a computational mechanism for obtaining such answers was presented. However, the queries considered were just first-order queries. Here we address in the same context the issue of *aggregation queries*. We limit, however, ourselves to single relations that possibly violate a given set of functional dependencies (FDs).

In defining consistent answers to aggregation queries we distinguish between queries with *scalar* and *aggregation* functions. The former return a single value for the entire relation. The latter perform grouping on an attribute (or a set of attributes) and return a single value for each group. Both kinds of queries use

J. Van den Bussche and V. Vianu (Eds.): ICDT 2001, LNCS 1973, pp. 39–53, 2001.
© Springer-Verlag Berlin Heidelberg 2001

the same standard set of SQL-2 aggregate operators: MIN, MAX, COUNT, SUM, and AVG. In this paper, we address only aggregation queries with scalar functions.

Example 1. Assume we have the following database instance *Salary* (we are identifying the table with the database instance)

Salary	Name	Amount
	V.Smith	5000
	V.Smith	8000
	P.Jones	3000
	M.Stone	7000

and F is *Name* $\rightarrow$ *Amount*, meaning that *Name* functionally determines *Amount*, that is violated by the table *Salary*, actually by the tuples with the value *V.Smith* in attribute *Name*. If we pose the query MIN(Amount) to this database, we should get, independently of how the violation is fixed, the value 3000. Nevertheless, if we ask MAX(Amount), we have a problem, because the maximum, 8000, comes from a tuple that participates in the violation of the functional dependency.

In [2] we defined an answer to a query posed to an inconsistent database as *consistent* when that same answer is obtained from every possible repair of the given database instance. Here, a repair is a new database instance that satisfies the given integrity constraints (ICs) and departs in a minimal way from the original database (see Section 2.1). In our case, the possible repairs are

Salary$_1$	Name	Amount
	V.Smith	5000
	P.Jones	3000
	M.Stone	7000

Salary$_2$	Name	Amount
	V.Smith	8000
	P.Jones	3000
	M.Stone	7000

In each repair MIN(Amount) returns the same value: 3000. On the other hand, MAX(Amount) returns a different value in each repair: 7000 or 8000. Thus, in the second case, there is no single consistent answer in the sense we had defined it. Nevertheless, an answer given by the initial database in the form of the interval [6000, 9000], meaning that in every repair the maximum lies between 6000 and 9000, could be considered a consistent answer. In particular, we might be interested in getting, as a more accurate consistent answer, the smallest possible interval (the optimal lower and upper bounds), in this case the interval [7000, 8000].

Example 2. Consider the *FD*: *StNumber* $\rightarrow$ *Name* and the inconsistent database instance

Jobs	StNumber	Name	Activity
	980134	D.Singh	TeachAsst
	980134	F.Chen	ResAsst
	980134	D.Singh	Programmer

This instance has two possible repairs

$Jobs_1$	StNumber	Name	Activity
	980134	D.Singh	TeachAsst
	980134	D.Singh	Programmer

$Jobs_2$	StNumber	Name	Activity
	980134	F.Chen	ResAsst

If we pose the query COUNT(Jobs) to these repairs, we obtain two different answers, 2 and 1, respectively. Thus, the optimal consistent answer is the interval [1,2]. □

Therefore, for aggregation queries we have to weaken a bit the notion of consistent query answer to allow answers that are not single values, but intervals.

In Section 2, we provide a general definition of consistent answer to an aggregation query with scalar functions. We also define a graph-theoretical representation of the database repairs, which is specifically geared towards FDs. In Section 3, we study the data complexity of the problem of computing consistent answers to aggregation queries in inconsistent databases. In Section 4, we show how to reduce the computational cost of computing such answers by decomposing the computation into two parts: one that involves standard relational query evaluation and one that computes the consistent answers in a smaller instance. In Section 5, we show that the complexity of computing consistent answers can be reduced by exploiting special properties of the given set of FDs or the given instances. In Section 6 we discuss related and further work.

2 Basic Notions

In this paper we assume that we have a fixed database schema containing only one relation schema R with the set of attributes U. We will denote elements of U by $A, B, \ldots$, subsets of U by $X, Y, \ldots$, and the union of X and Y by XY. We also have two fixed, disjoint infinite database domains: D (uninterpreted constants) and N (numbers). We assume that elements of the domains with different names are different. The database instances can be seen as first order structures that share the domains D and N. Every attribute in U is typed, thus all the instances of R can contain only elements either of D or N in a single attribute. Since each instance is finite, it has a finite active domain which is a subset of $D \cup N$. As usual, we allow built-in predicates over N that have infinite extensions, identical for all database instances. There is also a set of functional dependencies F over R that captures the semantics of the database. E.g., it may express the property that an employee has only a single salary. The instances of the database do not have to satisfy F (because the database may contain integrated data from multiple sources). A database that violates a given set of FDs is called *FD-inconsistent*.

2.1 Repairs

Given a database instance r, we denote by $\Sigma(r)$ the set of formulas $\{P(\bar{a}) \mid r \models P(\bar{a})\}$, where P is a relation name and $\bar{a}$ a ground tuple.

Definition 1. *The* distance $\Delta(r, r')$ *between data-base instances* r *and* r' *is the symmetric difference:* $\Delta(r, r') = (\Sigma(r) - \Sigma(r')) \cup (\Sigma(r') - \Sigma(r))$.

Definition 2. *For the instances* r, r', r'' , $r' \leq_r r''$ *if* $\Delta(r, r') \subseteq \Delta(r, r'')$, *i.e., if the distance between* r *and* r' *is less than or equal to the distance between* r *and* r''.

Definition 3. *Given a set of FDs* F *and database instances* r *and* r', *we say that* r' *is a* repair *of* r *w.r.t.* F *if* $r' \models F$ *and* r' *is* $\leq_r$*-minimal in the class of database instances that satisfy the set of FDs* F. □

We denote by $Repairs_F(r)$ the set of repairs of r w.r.t. F. Examples 1 and 2 illustrate the notion of repair. For a set of FDs, F, repairs are always obtained by deleting tuples from the table. For every instance r, the union of all repairs of r w.r.t. F is equal to r. These properties are not necessarily shared by other classes of ICs.

Definition 4. *The* core *of* r *is defined as* $Core_F(r) = \bigcap_{r' \in Repairs_F(r)} r'$. □

The *core* is a new database instance. If r consists of a single relation, then the core is the intersection of all the repairs of r. The core of r itself is not necessarily a repair of r. In example 1, the core is the table containing the tuples $(P.Jones, 3000)$ and $(M.Stone, 7000)$ only. In example 2, the core is empty.

2.2   Consistent Query Answers

First Order Queries. Query answers for first order queries are defined in the standard way.

Definition 5. *Given a set of integrity constraints* F, *we say that a (ground) tuple* $\bar{t}$ *is a* consistent answer *to a query* $Q(\bar{x})$ *in a database instance* r, *and we write* $r \models_F Q(\bar{t})$ *(or* $r \models_F Q(\bar{x})[\bar{t}]$*), if for every* $r' \in Repairs_F(r)$, $r' \models Q(\bar{t})$. *If* Q *is a sentence, then* true *(*false*) is a consistent answer to* Q *in* r, *and we write* $r \models_F Q$ *(*$r \models_F \neg Q$*), if for every* $r' \in Repairs_F(r)$, $r' \models Q$ *(*$r' \not\models Q$*).*

Aggregation Queries. The aggregation queries we consider are queries of the form: SELECT f(...) FROM R, where f is one of the aggregate operators MIN, MAX, COUNT, SUM, and AVG, applied to an attribute or the entire relation (as with the COUNT(*)). These queries return single numerical values by applying the corresponding *scalar function*, i.e., minimum for MIN, etc. In general, f will denote an aggregation query (or a scalar function itself). We write $r \models f = a$ to express that the aggregation query f returns the value a in the instance r.

Definition 6. *Given a set of integrity constraints* F, *we say that a numerical interval* $[a, b]$, *with* $-\infty < a \leq b < \infty$, *is a* consistent answer *to an aggregation query* f *in a database instance* r, *and we write* $r \models_F f \in [a, b]$ *(or* $r \models_F a \leq$

$f \leq b$) *if for every* $r' \in Repairs_F(r)$, r' *returns to the query* f *a value* v *such that* $a \leq v \leq b$. *If* $[a, b]$ *is a consistent answer, then* a *is called a lower-bound-answer and* b *an* upper-bound-answer. *An interval is an* optimal consistent answer *if no subinterval is a consistent answer. If* $[a, b]$ *is an optimal consistent answer, then* a *is called the greatest-lower-bound-answer* (glb-answer) *and denoted* $glb_F(f, r)$, *and* b *the least-upper-bound-answer* (lub-answer) *and denoted* $lub_F(f, r)$.   □

We will be particularly interested in obtaining optimal consistent answers by querying the possibly inconsistent database, without computing and checking all possible repairs.

Note: Our notion of consistent query answer for aggregation queries with scalar functions has some shortcomings. For instance, while we guarantee that the value of the scalar function in every repair falls within the returned interval, clearly not every value in this interval will correspond to the value of the function obtained in some repair. Perhaps it is more natural for such queries to return a *set of values*, each corresponding to the value of the function in some repair. Along the same lines, one could represent such a set as an OR-object [12] or a C-table [11]. However, the interval-based representation is exponentially more compact than any explicit set-based representation.

Example 3. Consider the functional dependency $A \rightarrow B$ and the following database instance r_0 (columns represent tuples):

r_0							
A	1	1	2	2	$\cdots$	n	n
B	0	1	0	2	$\cdots$	0	2^{n-1}

The scalar function involving summing on the B attribute will assume each value between 0 and $2^n - 1$ in some repair of r_0. Therefore, any set-based representation of set of all of those values will be of exponential size. On the other hand, the interval-based representation $[0, 2^n - 1]$ has polynomial size.   □

In addition to consistent answers, we will also consider other auxiliary notions of query answers in inconsistent databases.

Definition 7. *A value* v *is a* core answer *w.r.t.* F *to* f *in* r *if*

$$v = f(\bigcap_{r' \in Repairs_F(r)} r').$$

A value v *is a* union answer *w.r.t.* F *to* f *in* r *if*

$$v = f(\bigcup_{r' \in Repairs_F(r)} r').$$

Union answers are trivial for FDs, as the union of all the repairs of r is r itself, so the union answer reduces to $f(r)$.

2.3   Graph Representation

Given a set of FDs F and an instance r, all the repairs of r w.r.t. F can be succinctly represented as a graph.

Definition 8. *The* conflict graph $G_{F,r}$ *is an undirected graph whose set of vertices is the set of tuples in r and whose set of edges consists of all the edges (t_1, t_2) such that there is a dependency $X \to Y \in F$ for which $t_1[X] = t_2[X]$ and $t_1[Y] \neq t_2[Y]$. The* complement conflict graph $\bar{G}_{F,r}$ *is the complement of the conflict graph.*

Example 4. Consider a schema $R(AB)$, the set F of two functional dependencies $A \to B$ and $B \to A$, and an instance $r = \{(a_1, b_1), (a_1, b_2), (a_2, b_2), (a_2, b_1)\}$ over this schema. The conflict graph $G_{F,r}$ looks as follows:

$$
\begin{array}{cc}
(a_1, b_1) \!-\!\!-\!\!-\! (a_1, b_2) \\
\mid \qquad\qquad \mid \\
(a_2, b_1) \!-\!\!-\!\!-\! (a_2, b_2)
\end{array}
$$

Proposition 1. *Each repair in $Repairs_F(r)$ corresponds to a maximal independent set in $G_{F,r}$ (or a maximal clique in $\bar{G}_{F,r}$) and vice versa.*   □

The above graphs are geared specifically towards FDs. The repairs of other classes of constraints do not necessarily have similar representations.

2.4   Computational Complexity

Data Complexity. The data complexity assumption [7,15] makes it possible to study the complexity of query processing as a function of the size of the database instance.

Definition 9. *Given a class of databases $\mathcal{D}$, a class of queries $\mathcal{L}$ and a class of integrity constraints, the* data complexity *of computing consistent query answers is defined to be the complexity of (deciding the membership of) the sets $D_{F,\phi} = \{(D, \bar{t}) : D \models_F \phi[\bar{t}]\}$ for a fixed $\phi \in \mathcal{L}$ and a fixed finite set F of integrity constraints. This problem is C-data-hard for a complexity class C if there is a query $\phi \in \mathcal{L}$ and a finite set of integrity constraints F such that $D_{F,\phi}$ is C-hard.*

Upper and Lower Complexity Bounds. We view computing glb- and lub-answers as an *optimization* problem. It is easy to see that for all SQL scalar aggregation queries the data complexity of this problem is in NPO - the class of optimization problems whose associated decision problems are in NP [4]. In several cases, we will show that computing glb- and lub-answers is in PO (polynomial-time computable optimization problems). To show intractability of computing a glb- (or lub)-answer to $f(r)$ for an aggregation query f, we will demonstrate that the decision problem $glb_F(\mathbf{f}, r)$ (or $lub_F(\mathbf{f}, r)$) θk (where $\theta \in \{\leq, \geq\}$) is NP-hard. If the latter is the case, then clearly computing the appropriate consistent answer is not in PO, unless P=NP.

3   Scalar Aggregation

Computing consistent answers by producing all the repairs of a database instance and then computing the aggregation queries for each of them may have a high complexity. The following instance r_1 with $2n$ tuples (columns represent tuples):

r_1							
A	1	1	2	2	$\cdots$	n	n
B	0	1	0	1	$\cdots$	0	1

has 2^n possible repairs for the single FD $A \rightarrow B$. So, in general, computing all repairs and then evaluating a query in each repair is not feasible. We have identified two ways of computing consistent answers by querying the given, inconsistent database instance, without having to compute all the repairs. Query transformation modifies the original query, Q, into a new query, $T(Q)$, that returns only consistent answers. We have applied this approach in [2] to restricted first order queries and universal integrity constraints. Except in some simple cases, this approach does not seem applicable to aggregation queries. For example, even when MAX(A) and MIN(A) queries can be written as first order queries, their resulting syntax does not allow to apply the methodology developed in [2] to them. Here, we use instead the fact that for FDs, the set of all repairs of an instance can be compactly represented as the conflict graph or its complement. We develop techniques and algorithms geared specifically towards this representation.

3.1   Core Answers

We start by considering *core answers*. For some aggregation operators, e.g., COUNT and SUM of nonnegative values, a core answer is a lower-bound-answer, but not necessarily a glb-answer. As we will see in Section 4, computing core answers to aggregation queries can be useful for computing consistent answers.

Theorem 1. *The data complexity of computing core answers for any scalar function is in PTIME.*

Proof: The core consists of all the isolated vertices in the conflict graph.   □

In general, computing glb-answers and lub-answers is considerably more involved than computing core answers. We consider each aggregation operator in turn. In the following, r denotes an instance of a schema R.

3.2   MIN and MAX

Consider MAX(A) (MIN(A) is symmetric). In this case computing the lub-answer in r w.r.t. an arbitrary set of FDs F consists of evaluating MAX(A) in r. However, it is not obvious how to compute the glb-answer, namely the minimum of the set of maximums obtained by posing the query MAX(A) in every repair. Computing MAX(A) in $Core_F(r)$ gives us only a lower-bound-answer which does not have to be the glb-answer. We first provide a definition and prove a lemma which will also be useful later. Recall that U is the set of all attributes of the schema R.

Definition 10. *An FD $X \to Y$ is a* partition dependency *over R if $X \cup Y = U$ and $X \cap Y = \emptyset$.*

Lemma 1. *For any instance r of R and any partition dependency $d = X \to Y$ over R, the conflict graph $G_{d,r}$ is a union of disjoint cliques.*

Proof: Assume (t_1, t_2) and (t_2, t_3) are two edges in $G_{d,r}$ such that $t_1 \neq t_3$. Then $t_1[X] = t_2[X]$, $t_1[Y] \neq t_2[Y]$, $t_2[X] = t_3[X]$, and $t_2[Y] \neq t_3[Y]$. Therefore $t_1[X] = t_3[X]$. Also, $t_1[Y] \neq t_3[Y]$ because otherwise t_1 and t_3 would be the same tuple. So (t_1, t_3) is an edge in $G_{d,r}$. □

Theorem 2. *The data complexity of computing $glb_F(\text{MAX}(A), r)$ in r for a set of FDs F consisting of a single FD $X \to Y$ is in PTIME.*

Proof: Consider first the case where the FD is a partition dependency. Then by Lemma 1 the conflict graph $G_{F,r}$ is a union of disjoint cliques $C_1, \dots, C_k$. Every repair picks exactly one tuple from each clique. Consider a tuple t in a clique C_j, $1 \leq j \leq k$. The value $t[A]$ is a maximum in a repair iff for every clique C_i, $1 \leq i \leq k$, there is a tuple t' in C_i such that $t'[A] \leq t[A]$. This condition can be tested in PTIME because the cliques are in our case just the connected components. Denote the set of all maximum values determined in this way as S. Then the glb-answer to $\text{MAX}(A)$ is the minimum value in S.

A slight complication arises if the FD is not a partition dependency. The schema may contain some attributes other than those in XY. Let's call two tuples t and t' XY-*overlapping* if $t[XY] = t'[XY]$. There may be two different XY-overlapping tuples which are not in conflict although they are both in conflict with some other tuple. Thus, the conflict graph is not necessarily a union of disjoint cliques. However, it is easy to see that XY-overlapping tuples are always together in a repair. Therefore only the tuples with the maximum value of A among all XY-overlapping tuples can have a maximum value in a repair. All the remaining tuples can be removed without affecting the set of maximum values in repairs. If there is more than one tuple with the maximum value, an arbitrary one is selected. Denote the instance obtained in this way as r'. The conflict graph $G_{F,r'}$ is a union of disjoint cliques and the procedure described in the previous paragraph can be applied. □

Theorem 3. *There is a set of 2 FDs F_0 for which deciding whether $glb_{F_0}(\text{MAX}$ (A), r) \leq k$ in r is NP-data-hard.*

Proof: We reduce SAT to our problem. Consider a propositional formula φ : $C_1 \wedge \cdots \wedge C_n$ in CNF. Let $p_1, \dots p_m$ be the propositional variables in φ. Construct a relation r with the list of attributes A, B, C, D and containing exactly the following tuples:
1. $(p_i, 1, C_j, 1)$ if making p_i true makes C_j true,
2. $(p_i, 0, C_j, 1)$ if making p_i false makes C_j true,
3. $(w, w, C_j, 2)$, $1 \leq j \leq n$, where w is a new symbol.

Consider also the FDs $A \to B$ (each propositional variable cannot have more than one truth value) and $C \to D$. The crucial observation is that the $glb_{F_0}(\text{MAX}$ (D), r) = 1$ iff φ is satisfiable. □

3.3   COUNT(*) and SUM

We consider only COUNT(*): SUM is very similar.

Theorem 4. *If the set of FDs F is equivalent to a single dependency $X \rightarrow Y$, $X \cap Y = \emptyset$, the data complexity of computing $glb_F(\text{COUNT}(*), r)$ (or lub_F (COUNT(*), r)) in r is in PTIME.*

Proof: The glb-answer can be computed using the following set of SQL views (the lub-answer is obtained in a similar way):

```
CREATE VIEW S(X,Y,C) AS
  SELECT X,Y,COUNT(*) FROM R
  GROUP BY X,Y;
CREATE VIEW T(X,C) AS
  SELECT X, MIN(C) FROM S
  GROUP BY X;

SELECT SUM(C) FROM T;                                            □
```

To characterize the remaining cases, we prove two lemmas about maximum cliques in conflict graphs.

Lemma 2. *There is a set of 2 FDs F_1 for which the problem of determining the existence of a repair of r of size $\geq k$ is NP-data-hard.*

Proof: Reduction from 3-COLORABILITY. Given a graph $G = (N, E)$, with $N = \{1, 2, \ldots, n\}$, and given the colors w (white), b (blue) and r (red), we define the relation $P(A, B, C, D)$ by means of the following rules:

1. for every $1 \leq i \leq n$, $(i, w, i, w) \in P$, $(i, b, i, b) \in P$ and $(i, r, i, r) \in P$.
2. for every $(i, j) \in E$, $(i, w, j, b) \in P$, $(i, w, j, r) \in P$, $(i, b, j, w) \in P$, $(i, b, j, r) \in P$, $(i, r, j, w) \in P$ and $(i, r, j, b) \in P$.

We consider the set of functional dependencies $A \rightarrow B$ and $C \rightarrow D$. The crucial property is that G is 3-colorable iff there is a repair P' of P with exactly $n+2\cdot|E|$ tuples (the maximum possible number of tuples in a repair).   □

Lemma 3. *There is a set of 2 FDs F_2 for which the problem of determining the existence of a repair of r of size $\leq k$ is NP-data-hard.*

Proof: Modification of the lower bound proof of Theorem 3. We build the instance by using the same tuples of the kind (1) and (2), as well as sufficiently many tuples of the kind (3), each with a different new symbol w. It is enough to have $3n(n + 1)$ such tuples, where n is the number of clauses. The formula is satisfiable iff there is a repair of size $\leq 3n$.   □

The lemmas 2 and 3 imply the following theorems.

Theorem 5. *There is a set of two FDs F_1 for which determining whether $lub_{F_1}(\text{COUNT}(*), r) \geq k$ in r is NP-data-hard.*

Theorem 6. *There is a set of two FDs F_2 for which determining whether $glb_{F_2}(\texttt{COUNT}(*), r) \leq k$ in r is NP-data-hard.*   □

The above results establish the intractability of determining lub-answers and glb-answers to `COUNT(*)` in a general setting. Similar results hold for `SUM`. We will see that the boundary between the tractable and the intractable can be pushed farther in several special cases.

3.4   COUNT(A)

We assume here that distinct values of A are counted (`COUNT (DISTINCT A)`).

Theorem 7. *There is a single FD $d_0 = B \to A$ for which determining whether $glb_{d_0}(\texttt{COUNT}(A), r) \leq k$ in r is NP-data-hard.*

Proof: To see that the lower bound holds, we will encode an instance of the HITTING SET problem in r. For every set S_i in the given collection C and every element $x \in S_i$ we put the tuple (i, x) in r. There is in C a hitting set of size less than or equal to k iff there is a repair of r with at most k different values of the first attribute A.   □

Theorem 8. *There is a single FD $d_1 = B \to A$ for which determining whether $lub_{d_1}(\texttt{COUNT}(A), r) \geq k$ in r is NP-data-hard.*

Proof: We reduce SAT to this problem. Let the instance r be the conjunction of clauses $\varphi : C_1 \wedge \ldots \wedge C_n$. Consider the functional dependency $X \to Y$ and the database instance $r(X, Y, A)$ with the following tuples:
1. $(p_i, 1, C_j)$ if making p_i true makes C_j true.
2. $(p_i, 0, C_j)$ if making p_i false makes C_j true.
Then, φ is satisfiable iff $lub_{d_1}(\texttt{COUNT}(A), r) \geq n$.   □

3.5   AVG

Theorem 9. *If a set of FDs F is equivalent to a single dependency $X \to Y$, with $X \cap Y = \emptyset$, then the data complexity of the problem of computing $glb_F(\texttt{AVG}(A), r)$ (or $lub_F(\texttt{AVG}(A), r)$) in r is in PTIME.*

Proof:[1] First, the problems of finding the glb and lub answers for `AVG` with one functional dependency can be reduced in polynomial time to the following problem:
P1:   There are m bins. Each bin contains objects of different colors. No two bins have objects of the same color. All objects of the same color have the same weight. One has to choose exactly one color for each bin in such a way that the sum of the weights of all objects of the chosen colors divided by the total number of such objects (i.e., the average weight AVG of objects of the chosen colors) is maximized.

---

[1] The proof of this theorem is due to Vijay Raghavan and Jeremy Spinrad.

To solve **P1**, consider the well-known "*2-OPT*" strategy of starting with an arbitrary selection $\langle c_1, c_2, ..., c_m \rangle$ of one color each from each of the m bins. The *2-OPT* strategy is simply to replace a color from one bin with a different color from the same bin if so doing increases the value of the average weight of objects of the colors in the selection.

This *2-OPT* strategy can be shown to converge to the optimum. In addition, it can be designed in such a way the it runs in polynomial time.   □

Theorem 10. *There is a set of two FDs F_3 for which determining whether $glb_{F_3}(\mathtt{AVG(A)}, r) \le k$ in r is NP-data-hard.*

Proof: We can use the same reduction as in theorem 3. There is a satisfying assignment iff there is a repair for which $\mathtt{AVG(D)} = 1$ (otherwise the glb-answer is bigger than 1) iff $glb_{F_3}(\mathtt{AVG(D)}, r) \le 1$.   □

Theorem 11. *There is a set of two FDs F_4 for which determining whether $lub_{F_4}(\mathtt{AVG(A)}, r) \ge k$ in r is NP-data-hard.*

Proof: We reduce SAT to our problem. Change the tuples of the instance in the proof of theorem 3 as follows:
3'. $(w, w, C_j, -2)$, $1 \le j \le n$, where w is a new symbol.
There is a satisfying assignment iff $glb_{F_4}(\mathtt{AVG(D)}, r) \ge 1$.   □

3.6   Summary of Complexity Results

It is easy to show that each of the problems considered before belong to the class NP.

	glb-answer		lub-answer	
	$|F| = 1$	$|F| \ge 2$	$|F| = 1$	$|F| \ge 2$
MIN(A)	PTIME	PTIME	PTIME	NP-complete
MAX(A)	PTIME	NP-complete	PTIME	PTIME
COUNT(*)	PTIME	NP-complete	PTIME	NP-complete
COUNT(A)	NP-complete	NP-complete	NP-complete	NP-complete
SUM(A)	PTIME	NP-complete	PTIME	NP-complete
AVG(A)	PTIME	NP-complete	PTIME	NP-complete

4   Hybrid Computation

As we have seen, determining glb-answers and lub-answers is often computationally hard. However, it seems that hard instances of those problems are unlikely to occur in practice. We expect that in a typical instance a large majority of tuples are not involved in any conflicts. If this is the case, it is advantageous to break up the computation of an lub-answer to f in r into three parts: (1) the computation of f in the core of r, (2) the computation of an lub-answer to f in the complement of the core of r (which should be small), and (3) the combination of the results of (1) and (2). The step (1) can be done using a DBMS because the core of r can be computed using a first-order query (Theorem 1).

Definition 11. *The scalar function f admits a g-decomposition of its lub-answers (resp. glb-answers) w.r.t. a set of FDs F if for every instance r of R, the lub-answer (resp. glb-answer) v to f satisfies the condition $v = g(f(Core_F(r)), v')$, where $v' = lub_F(f, r - Core_F(r))$ (resp. $v' = glb_F(f, r - Core_F(r))$).*

Theorem 12. *The following pairs describe g-decompositions admitted by scalar functions f:*
1. *$f = $ MIN(A), $g = $ min;*
2. *$f = $ MAX(A), $g = $ max;*
3. *$f = $ COUNT(*), $g = +$;*
4. *$f = $ SUM(A), $g = +$.*

5   Special Cases

We consider here various cases when the conflict graph (or its complement) has some special form that could be used to reduce the complexity of computing answers to aggregation queries.

5.1   BCNF

We show here that if the set of FDs F has two dependencies and the schema R is in BCNF, computing lub-answers can be done in PTIME. This should be contrasted with Theorem 5 which showed that two dependencies without the BCNF assumption are sufficient for NP-hardness.

Lemma 4. *If R is in BCNF and F is equivalent to a set of FDs with 2 dependencies, then F is equivalent to a set of FDs with 2 partition dependencies $X_1 \rightarrow Y_1$ and $X_2 \rightarrow Y_2$.*   □

Therefore, WLOG we can assume that $|F| = 2$ and $F = \{d_1, d_2\}$ where d_1 and d_2 are different partition dependencies. (The case of $|F| = 1$ has already been shown to be in PTIME, even without the BCNF assumption.)

Definition 12. *A chord in a cycle is an edge connecting two nonconsecutive vertices of the cycle.*

Lemma 5. *Every cycle of length k where k is odd and $k > 3$ in $G_{\{d_1, d_2\}, r}$ has a chord.*

Proof: Such a cycle has two consecutive edges (t_1, t_2) and (t_2, t_3) that belong both to $G_{d_1, r}$ or both to $G_{d_2, r}$. Therefore, by Lemma 1 the edge (t_1, t_3), which is a chord, also belongs to one of those graphs, and consequently to $G_{\{d_1, d_2\}, r}$.
□

Note: For the above property to hold, it is essential for the cycle in the conflict graph to be odd. Example 4 shows an even cycle of length 4 that does not have a chord. That implies that conflict graphs in the case of two FDs are not necessarily *chordal* [5] and thus efficient algorithms for the computation of maximum independent set in such graphs [9] are not applicable.

Lemma 6. *Every cycle of length k where k is odd and $k > 3$ in the complement conflict graph $\bar{G}_{\{d_1,d_2\},r}$ has a chord.*

Proof: To give the idea of the proof, we consider the case of $R(A, B)$ and $d_1 = A \rightarrow B$ and $d_2 = B \rightarrow A$.

Assume $(t_1, t_2, \ldots, t_k, t_1)$ is a cycle in $\bar{G}_{\{d_1,d_2\},r}$. Let $t_i = (a_i, b_i)$, $1 \leq i \leq k$, where the a_i's and b_i's are distinct variables. We write down the formula ϕ that expresses the property that the consecutive vertices in the cycle are in $\bar{G}_{\{d_1,d_2\},r}$:
$\phi \equiv \bigwedge a_i \neq a_{i+1} \wedge \bigwedge b_i \neq b_{i+1}$, where the indexes are interpreted cyclically, i.e., $k + 1 = 1$. Now we write down the formula ψ that expresses the property that there are no chords in the cycle. This formula is a conjunction of the formulas $\psi_{i,j}$ (for every pair (i, j) of nonconsecutive vertices in the cycle) that express the property that there is a conflict between t_i and t_j: $\psi_{i,j} \equiv (a_i = a_j \wedge b_i \neq b_j \vee b_i = b_j \wedge a_i \neq a_j) \equiv (a_i = a_j \vee b_i = b_j) \wedge (a_i \neq a_j \vee b_i \neq b_j)$. Therefore $\psi_{i,j}$ postulates at least one equality: $a_i = a_j$ or $b_i = b_j$.

Now the counting argument. Assume $\phi \wedge \psi$ is satisfiable. The formula ϕ postulates n inequalities between the a_i's and n inequalities between the b_i's. The formula ψ postulates $\frac{n(n-3)}{2}$ inequalities and the same number of equalities that involve either a_i's or b_i's. WLOG we assume that at least half of them, i.e., $\lceil \frac{n(n-3)}{4} \rceil$ involve a_i's. Therefore, for $n \geq 5$, the equalities imply together yet another equality. (The assumption that all the equalities holding have disjoint variables leads to contradiction.) Thus the total number of equalities is $\frac{n(n-3)}{2} + 1$. Now

$$2n + \frac{n(n-3)}{2} + \frac{n(n-3)}{2} + 1 = n(n-1) + 1$$

and is greater than the number of 2-element sets consisting only of a_i's or b_i's. Therefore for some i and j, we have both $a_i = a_j$ and $a_i \neq a_j$ (or $b_i = b_j$ and $b_i \neq b_j$), which contradicts the satisfiability of $\phi \wedge \psi$. Thus an odd cycle of length ≥ 5 has to have a chord.   □

Definition 13. *A graph is* perfect *if its chromatic number is equal to the size of its maximum clique.*

Strong Perfect Graph Conjecture: A graph G is perfect iff every odd cycle in G or $\bar{G}$ has a chord.

This conjecture has been shown to hold for many classes of graphs, including claw-free graphs [5].

Definition 14. *A graph is* claw-free *if it does not contain an induced subgraph* (V_0, E_0) *where* $V_0 = \{t_1, t_2, t_3, t_4\}$ *and* $E_0 = \{(t_2, t_1), (t_3, t_1), (t_4, t_1)\}$.

Lemma 7. *If R is in BCNF over $F = \{d_1, d_2\}$, then for every instance r of R, the conflict graph $G_{\{d_1,d_2\},r}$ is claw-free and perfect.*

Proof: Assume that the conflict graph contains a claw (V_0, E_0) where $V_0 = \{t_1, t_2, t_3, t_4\}$ and $E_0 = \{(t_2, t_1), (t_3, t_1), (t_4, t_1)\}$. Then two of the edges in E_0, say (t_2, t_1) and (t_3, t_1) come from one of $G_{d_1,r}$ or $G_{d_2,r}$. But the by Lemma 1, the edge (t_3, t_2) also belongs to that graph, and consequently to $G_{\{d_1, d_2\}, r}$. Thus the subgraph induced by V_0 is not a claw.

As the conflict graph is claw-free, the Strong Perfect Graph Conjecture holds for it and Lemmas 5 and 6 yield together the fact that it is perfect.   □

Theorem 13. *If R is in BCNF and the given set of FDs F is equivalent to one with at most two dependencies, computing $lub_F(\text{COUNT}(*), r)$ in any instance r of R can be done in PTIME.*

Proof: The theorem follows from Lemma 7 and the fact that in perfect claw-free graphs computing a maximum independent set can be done in $O(n^{5.5})$ [10].   □

What about $|F| > 2$? In this case the conflict graph does not have to be claw-free, so it is not clear whether the Strong Perfect Graph Conjecture holds for it. The conflict graph does not even have to be perfect. Take a conflict graph consisting of a cycle of length 5 where the edges corresponding to the dependencies d_1, d_2 and d_3 alternate. The chromatic number of this graph is 3, while the size of the maximum clique is 2.

5.2   Disjoint Union

Theorem 14. *If the instance r is the disjoint union of two instances that separately satisfy F, computing $lub_F(\text{COUNT}(*), r)$ can be done in PTIME.*

Proof: In this case, the only conflicts are between the parts of r that come from different databases. Thus the conflict graph is a bipartite graph. For bipartite graphs determining the maximum independent set can be done in PTIME.   □

Note that the assumption in Theorem 14 is satisfied when the instance r is obtained by merging together two consistent databases in the context of database integration.

6   Related and Further Work

We can only briefly survey the related work here. A more comprehensive discussion can be found in [2]. The need to accommodate violations of functional dependencies is one of the main motivations for considering disjunctive databases [12,14] and has led to various proposals in the context of data integration [1, 3,8,13]. A purely proof-theoretic notion of consistent query answer comes from Bry [6]. None of the above approaches considers aggregation queries.

Many further questions suggest themselves. First, is it possible to identify more tractable cases and to reduce the degree of the polynomial in those already identified? Second, is it possible to use approximation in the intractable cases? The INDEPENDENT SET problem is notoriously hard to approximate, but perhaps the special structure of the conflict graph may be helpful. Finally, it would be very interesting to see if our approach can be generalized to broader classes of queries and integrity constraints.

Finally, alternative definitions of repairs and consistent query answers that include, for example, preferences are left for future work. Also, one can apply further aggregation to the results of aggregation queries in different repairs, e.g., the average of all MAX(A) answers.

Acknowledgments.   Work supported in part by FONDECYT Grant 1000593 and NSF grant INT-9901877/CONICYT Grant 1998-02-083. The comments of the anonymous referees are gratefully acknowledged.

References

1. S. Agarwal, A.M. Keller, G. Wiederhold, and K. Saraswat. Flexible Relation: An Approach for Integrating Data from Multiple, Possibly Inconsistent Databases. In *IEEE International Conference on Data Engineering*, 1995.
2. M. Arenas, L. Bertossi, and J. Chomicki. Consistent Query Answers in Inconsistent Databases. In *Proc. ACM Symposium on Principles of Database Systems (ACM PODS'99, Philadelphia)*, pages 68–79, 1999.
3. C. Baral, S. Kraus, J. Minker, and V.S. Subrahmanian. Combining Knowledge Bases Consisting of First-Order Theories. *Computational Intelligence*, 8:45–71, 1992.
4. D. P. Bovet and P. Crescenzi. *Introduction to the Theory of Complexity*. Prentice Hall, 1994.
5. A. Brandstädt, V. B. Le, and J. P. Spinrad. *Graph Classes: A Survey*. SIAM, 1999.
6. F. Bry. Query Answering in Information Systems with Integrity Constraints. In *IFIP WG 11.5 Working Conference on Integrity and Control in Information Systems*. Chapman &Hall, 1997.
7. A. K. Chandra and D. Harel. Computable Queries for Relational Databases. *Journal of Computer and System Sciences*, 21:156–178, 1980.
8. Phan Minh Dung. Integrating Data from Possibly Inconsistent Databases. In *International Conference on Cooperative Information Systems*, Brussels, Belgium, 1996.
9. Fanica Gavril. Algorithms for Minimum Coloring, Maximum Clique, Minimum Covering by Cliques, and Maximum Independent Set of a Chordal Graph. *SIAM Journal on Computing*, 1(2):180–187, 1972.
10. W-L. Hsu and G.L. Nemhauser. Algorithms for Minimum Covering by Cliques and Maximum Clique in Claw-free Perfect Graphs. *Discrete Mathematics*, 37:181–191, 1981.
11. T. Imieliński and W. Lipski. Incomplete Information in Relational Databases. *Journal of the ACM*, 31(4):761–791, 1984.
12. T. Imieliński, S. Naqvi, and K. Vadaparty. Incomplete Objects - A Data Model for Design and Planning Applications. In *ACM SIGMOD International Conference on Management of Data*, pages 288–297, Denver, Colorado, May 1991.
13. J. Lin and A. O. Mendelzon. Merging Databases under Constraints. *International Journal of Cooperative Information Systems*, 7(1):55–76, 1996.
14. R. van der Meyden. Logical Approaches to Incomplete Information: A Survey. In J. Chomicki and G. Saake, editors, *Logics for Databases and Information Systems*, chapter 10. Kluwer Academic Publishers, Boston, 1998.
15. M. Y. Vardi. The Complexity of Relational Query Languages. In *ACM Symposium on Theory of Computing*, pages 137–146, 1982.

On Decidability and Complexity of Description Logics with Uniqueness Constraints*

Vitaliy L. Khizder, David Toman, and Grant Weddell

Department of Computer Science
University of Waterloo, Canada

Abstract. We establish the equivalence of: (1) the logical implication problem for a description logic dialect called DLClass that includes a concept constructor for expressing uniqueness constraints, (2) the logical implication problem for path functional dependencies (PFDs), and (3) the problem of answering queries in deductive databases with limited use of successor functions. As a consequence, we settle an open problem concerning lower bounds for the PFD logical implication problem and show that a regularity condition for DLClass that ensures low order polynomial time decidability for its logical implication problem is tight.

1   Introduction

Description Logics (DLs) have many applications in information systems [2]. They can facilitate data access to heterogenous data sources because of their ability to capture integrity constraints manifest in object relational database schema, in ER diagrams or UML class diagrams and that arise in practical XML applications, including the constraints that underly XML *document type definitions* (DTDs) [10]. They are particularly valuable for solving problems in information integration and that arise in query optimization [4,8,16,17]. However, in many of these applications, it becomes essential for a particular DL dialect to capture knowledge that relates to various kinds of *uniqueness constraints* that are satisfied by the possible data sources.

For example, consider a hypothetical integrated patient management system depicted in Figure 1. It can be crucial to know for this system

1. that *a hospital has a unique name*,
2. that *a patient is uniquely identified by hospital and patient number*, and
3. that *a person admitted to a hospital has a valid unique social security number*.

DL dialects that enable capturing keys in the standard database sense and simple forms of functional dependencies have been proposed in [4,7]. Such a facility was a nagging missing ingredient for prior DL dialects that had efficient subsumption checking algorithms. This was achieved by adding a new kind of *concept constructor* (fd). Also, Calvanese et al. have recently demonstrated how a variety of keys with set-valued components can be added to a very general DL dialect without increasing the complexity of reasoning [9].

---

* An earlier version of this paper has appeared in the informal proceedings of the International Workshop on Description Logics DL2000.

J. Van den Bussche and V. Vianu (Eds.): ICDT 2001, LNCS 1973, pp. 54–67, 2001.
© Springer-Verlag Berlin Heidelberg 2001

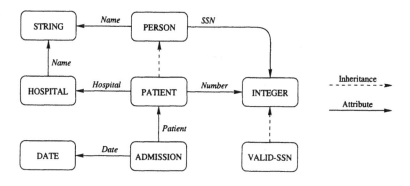

Fig. 1. Patient Data Integration.

In this paper, we consider a more general version of fd in which component attribute descriptions may now correspond to *attribute* or *feature paths* [15,16, 17,20]. To focus on the essential idea, we define a very simple DL dialect called DLFD that consists of a single concept constructor corresponding to this more general version of fd. The logical implication problem for DLFD is therefore a special case of the logical implication problem for *path functional dependencies* (PFDs), a variety of uniqueness constraints for data models supporting complex objects that was first proposed in [20] and studied more fully in a subsequent series of papers [15,19,21].

Although DLFD is extremely simple, it can be used to simulate logical implication problems in a more general *object relational* dialect via a linear translation. DLClass, as we shall call it, includes additional concept constructors that directly capture class inheritance and attribute typing, a capability that is essential to the convenient capture of meta-data relating to possible data sources in information systems.

For example, consider again the hospital schema in Figure 1 for the above-mentioned patient management system. The schema captures many of the constraints that underly an information source that contains XML data with the structure illustrated in Figure 2. The schema, perhaps given more directly by an associated DTD for the data, can be captured in DLClass as a *terminology* that consists of the following *subsumption constraints* (cf. Definition 1).

> ADMISSION < (and (all *Date* DATE) (all *Patient* PATIENT))
> PATIENT < (all *Hospital* HOSPITAL)
> PATIENT < (and PERSON (all *Number* INTEGER))
> PERSON < (and (all *Name* STRING) (all *SSN* INTEGER))
> HOSPITAL < (all *Name* STRING)
> VALID-SSN < INTEGER

Furthermore, DLClass can be used to capture the three uniqueness constraints for the patient management system listed at the beginning of this section by adding the following additional subsumption constraints to the terminology.

```
<ADMISSION>
    <PATIENT Number=123>
        <PERSON SSN=45678>
            <NAME>Fred</NAME>
        </PERSON>
        <HOSPITAL>
            <NAME>Sunny Brook</NAME>
        </HOSPITAL>
    </PATIENT>
    <DATE>20-January-2000</DATE>
</ADMISSION>
```

Fig. 2. Patient Data in XML.

$$\text{HOSPITAL} < (\text{fd HOSPITAL} : Name \rightarrow Id)$$
$$\text{PATIENT} < (\text{fd PATIENT} : Hospital, Number \rightarrow Id)$$
$$\text{ADMISSION} < (\text{all } Patient \text{ (and (all } SSN \text{ VALID-SSN)}$$
$$(\text{fd PERSON} : SSN \rightarrow Id)))$$

Again, we show that DLFD is sufficiently powerful to simulate all inferences in DLClass by exhibiting a linear answer preserving translation of DLClass to DLFD. However, this translation is indirect: it relates the logical implication problems in DLFD and DLClass to query answering in Datalog_{nS}, a deductive query language with limited use of successor functions [11,12]. This relationship leads to the main contribution of the paper; an open issue relating to the complexity of reasoning about PFDs is resolved. By proving an equivalence to query answering in Datalog_{nS}, the logical implication problems for DLFD and DLClass are DEXPTIME-complete, and therefore the exponential time decision procedure [15] becomes tight.

The example constraints in DLClass given above have a restricted form that satisfies a syntactic *regularity* condition (cf. Section 5), which leads to incremental polynomial time algorithms for a restricted class of logical implication problems in DLClass [16]. Using the tight translation between DLClass and Datalog_{nS} we show that a similar condition can be applied to Datalog_{nS} programs. This leads to a PTIME query evaluation procedure for a syntactically restricted class of Datalog_{nS} programs. In addition, the condition turns out to be as general as one can hope for while ensuring the existence of such efficient algorithms.

The remainder of the paper is organized as follows. Section 2 defines the syntax and semantics for DLClass and Datalog_{nS}. Section 3 reduces the problem of answering queries in Datalog_{nS} to the logical implication problem for DLFD and subsequently to logical implication problems in DLClass. Section 4 completes the picture by reducing the logical implication problem for DLClass to Datalog_{nS}. Section 5 discusses special cases in which PTIME reasoning is possible. We conclude with a summary in Section 6.

2 Definitions

The syntax and semantics of DLClass and Datalog$_{nS}$ are given by the following.

Definition 1 (Description Logic DLClass) *Let F be a set of attribute names. We define a* path *expression by the grammar "Pf ::= f.Pf | Id" for $f \in F$.*

Let C be primitive concept description(s). We define derived *concept descriptions using the following grammar:*

$$
\begin{aligned}
D ::=\ & C \\
| &\ (\text{all } f\ D) \\
| &\ (\text{fd } C : \text{Pf}_1, \dots, \text{Pf}_k \to \text{Pf}), k > 0 \\
| &\ (\text{and } D\ D)
\end{aligned}
$$

A subsumption constraint *is an expression of the form $C < D$.*

The semantics *of expressions is given with respect to a structure $(\Delta, .^I)$, where Δ is a domain of "objects" and $.^I$ an interpretation function, that fixes the interpretations of primitive concepts to be subsets of the domain, $C^I \subseteq \Delta$, and primitive attributes to be total functions on the domain, $f^I : \Delta \to \Delta$. This interpretation is extended to path expressions, $Id^I = \lambda x.x$ and $f.\text{Pf}^I = \text{Pf}^I \circ f^I$, and to derived descriptions*

$$
\begin{aligned}
(\text{all } f\ D)^I &= \{o \in \Delta : f^I(o) \in D^I\} \\
(\text{fd } C : \text{Pf}_1, \dots, \text{Pf}_k \to \text{Pf})^I &= \{o \in \Delta : \forall o' \in C^I. \\
&\quad \textstyle\bigwedge_{i=1}^{k} \text{Pf}_i^I(o) = \text{Pf}_i^I(o') \Rightarrow \text{Pf}^I(o) = \text{Pf}^I(o')\} \\
(\text{and } D_1\ D_2)^I &= D_1^I \cap D_2^I
\end{aligned}
$$

An interpretation *satisfies a subsumption constraint $C < D$ if $C^I \subseteq D^I$.*

For a given set of subsumption constraints $\Sigma = \{C_i < D_i : 0 < i \leq n\}$ (a terminology*) and a subsumption constraint $C < D$ (a* posed question*), the* logical implication problem *asks if $\Sigma \models C < D$ holds, i.e, if all interpretations that satisfy Σ must also satisfy $C < D$.*

Limiting the left-hand-side of subsumption constraints in terminologies to be primitive concepts is a common assumption to avoid reasoning about equality between general concept descriptions. In contrast, requiring the left-hand-side of the posed question to be a primitive concept is not a real limitation since a more general logical implication problem of the form $\Sigma \models D_1 < D_2$ can always be rephrased as $\Sigma \cup \{C < D_1\} \models C < D_2$, where C is a primitive concept not occurring in $\Sigma \cup \{D_1 < D_2\}$.

In the rest of the paper we simplify the notation for path expressions by omitting the trailing Id. We also allow a syntactic composition $\text{Pf}_1 . \text{Pf}_2$ of path expressions that stands for their concatenation.

Definition 2 (Datalog$_{nS}$ [12]) *Let p_i be predicate symbols, f_i function symbols such that $p_i \neq f_i$, and $X, Y, \ldots$ variables. A logic program P is a finite set of Horn clauses of the form*

$$p_0(t^0, s_1^0, \ldots, s_k^0) \leftarrow p_1(t^1, s_1^1 \ldots, s_{l_1}^1), \ldots, p_k(t^k, s_1^k, \ldots, s_{l_k}^k)$$

for $k \geq 0$, where the terms t^i and s_j^i are constructed from constants, function symbols and variables. We say that P is a Datalog$_{nS}$ program if

1. *t^i is a functional term: a variable, a distinguished constant 0, or a term of the form $f(t, s_1, \ldots s_l)$ where f is a function symbol, t is a functional term, and $s_1, \ldots, s_l$ are data terms,*
2. *s_j^i are data terms: variables or constants different from 0, and*
3. *no variable appears both in a functional and a data term.*

We say that a Datalog$_{nS}$ program is in normal form *if the only predicate and functions symbols used are unary, and whenever a variable appears in any predicate p_i of a clause then the same variable appears in all the predicates of the same clause.*

A recognition problem *for a Datalog$_{nS}$ program P and a ground (variable-free) atom $q(t, s_1, \ldots, s_k)$ is the question does $P \models q(t, s_1, \ldots, s_k)$ hold, i.e., $q(t, s_1, \ldots, s_k)$ is true in all models of P?*

It is known that every Datalog$_{nS}$ program can be encoded as a normal Datalog$_{nS}$ program [11,12]. Moreover, every normal Datalog$_{nS}$ program can be divided into a set of clauses with non-empty bodies and a set of ground *facts* (clauses with empty bodies). Proofs of theorems in the paper rely on the following two observations about logic programs [18]:

1. The recognition problem $P \models q$ for a ground q is equivalent to checking $q \in M_P$ where M_P is the unique *least Herbrand model* of P.
2. M_P can be constructed by iterating an *immediate consequence operator* T_P associated with P until reaching fixpoint; $M_P = T_P^\omega(\emptyset)$.

To establish the complexity bounds we use the following result about Datalog$_{nS}$ programs:

Proposition 3 ([12,14]) *The recognition problem for Datalog$_{nS}$ programs (under the data-complexity[1] measure) is DEXPTIME-complete. The lower bound holds even for programs in normal form.*

3   Lower Bounds

In this section we show that the recognition problem for Datalog$_{nS}$ can be reduced to the (infinite) implication problem for path-functional dependencies. We

---

[1] Complexity of the problem for a fixed set of symbols.

study this problem in a DL dialect DLFD in which all subsumption constraints are of the form

$$\mathsf{THING} < (\mathsf{fd}\ \mathsf{THING} : \mathsf{Pf}_1, \ldots, \mathsf{Pf}_k \to \mathsf{Pf}).$$

THING is a primitive concept interpreted as the domain Δ. In the rest of this section we use the shorthand $\mathsf{Pf}_1, \ldots, \mathsf{Pf}_k \to \mathsf{Pf}$ for the above constraint.

It is easy to see that DLFD problems can be trivially embedded into DLClass. We simply consider THING to be a single primitive concept description such that THING $<$ (all f THING) for every primitive attribute f. Therefore, lower bounds for DLFD also apply to DLClass.

Notation: we associate two Datalog$_{nS}$ functional terms $\overline{\mathsf{Pf}}(0) = f_k(\cdots f_1(0) \cdots)$ and $\overline{\mathsf{Pf}}(X) = f_k(\cdots f_1(X) \cdots)$ with every path expression $\mathsf{Pf} = f_1 \cdots \cdot f_k . \mathit{Id}$, where 0 is a distinguished constant and X is a variable. Similarly, for every Datalog$_{nS}$ term $t = f_1(\cdots f_k(X) \cdots)$ there is a path expression $\mathsf{Pf} = f_k \cdots \cdot f_1$. Id such that $t = \overline{\mathsf{Pf}}(X)$. In the rest of the paper we overload the symbols p_i and f_i to stand both for unary predicate and function symbols in Datalog$_{nS}$ and for primitive attribute names in the appropriate description logic, and use $\overline{\mathsf{Pf}}(X)$ and $\overline{\mathsf{Pf}}(0)$ to stand for Datalog$_{nS}$ terms.

Theorem 4 Let P be an arbitrary normal Datalog$_{nS}$ program and $G = p(\overline{\mathsf{Pf}}(0))$ a ground atom. We define

- $\Sigma_P = \{\mathsf{Pf}'_1 . p'_1, \ldots, \mathsf{Pf}'_k . p'_k \to \mathsf{Pf}' . p' :$
  $$p'(\overline{\mathsf{Pf}}'(X)) \leftarrow p'_1(\overline{\mathsf{Pf}}'_1(X)), \ldots, p'_k(\overline{\mathsf{Pf}}'_k(X)) \in P\}, \text{ and}$$
- $\varphi_{P,G} = \mathsf{Pf}_1 . p_1, \ldots, \mathsf{Pf}_k . p_k \to \mathsf{Pf} . p$
  where $p_1(\overline{\mathsf{Pf}}_1(0)), \ldots, p_k(\overline{\mathsf{Pf}}_k(0))$ are all facts in P.

Then $P \models G \iff \Sigma_P \models \varphi_{P,G}$.

Proof: $\Rightarrow$: We show that $p(\overline{\mathsf{Pf}}(0)) \in T_P^\omega(\emptyset)$ implies $\Sigma_P \models \varphi_{P,G}$.

If $p(\overline{\mathsf{Pf}}(0)) \in T_P^\omega(\emptyset)$ then there must be $m > 0$ such that $p(\overline{\mathsf{Pf}}(0)) \in T_P^m(\emptyset)$. Then, by induction on m, we have:

$m = 1$: immediate as it must be the case that $p(\overline{\mathsf{Pf}}(0))$ must be one of the facts in P, e.g., $p_i(\overline{\mathsf{Pf}}_i(0))$ and therefore also $\mathsf{Pf} . p = \mathsf{Pf}_i . p_i$. Consequently, $\Sigma_P \models \varphi_{P,G}$ as $\varphi_{P,G}$ is a trivial path-functional dependency.

$m > 1$: if $p(\overline{\mathsf{Pf}}(0)) \in T_P^m(\emptyset)$ then there is a term $t(0)$ (to be substituted for X) and A clause $p(\overline{\mathsf{Pf}}'(X)) \leftarrow p_1(\overline{\mathsf{Pf}}'_1(X)), \ldots, p_l(\overline{\mathsf{Pf}}'_l(X))$ in P such that $\overline{\mathsf{Pf}}(0) = \overline{\mathsf{Pf}}'(t(0))$ and $p_i(\overline{\mathsf{Pf}}'_i(t(0))) \in T_P^{m-1}(\emptyset)$. By the IH we have $\Sigma_P \models \varphi_{P,p_i(\overline{\mathsf{Pf}}'_i(t(0)))}$ and therefore, by composition with the path-functional dependency $\mathsf{Pf}'_1 . p_1, \ldots, \mathsf{Pf}'_l . p_l \to \mathsf{Pf} . p \in \Sigma_P$ we have $\Sigma_P \models \varphi_{P,G}$.

$\Leftarrow$: Assume $p(\overline{\mathsf{Pf}}(0)) \notin T_P^\omega(\emptyset)$. We construct an counterexample interpretation as follows: let $o_1, o_2 \in \Delta$ be two distinct objects and T_1, T_2 two complete infinite trees rooted by these two objects with edges labeled by primitive attributes, in this case f_i and p_i. Moreover, if $p'(\overline{\mathsf{Pf}'}(0)) \in T_P^\omega(\emptyset)$ we merge the two subtrees identified by the path $\mathsf{Pf}'.p'$ starting from the respective roots of the trees. The resulting graph provides an interpretation for DLFD (the nodes of the trees represent elements of Δ, the edges give interpretation to primitive attributes) such that:

(i) $(\mathsf{Pf}_i.p_i)^I(o_1) = (\mathsf{Pf}_i.p_i)^I(o_2)$ for all $p_i(\overline{\mathsf{Pf}}_i(0)) \in P$, and

(ii) every constraint in Σ_P is satisfied by the constructed interpretation: Assume the interpretation violated a constraint $\mathsf{Pf}'_1.p'_1, \ldots, \mathsf{Pf}'_l.p'_l \rightarrow \mathsf{Pf}'.p' \in \Sigma_P$. Then there must be two distinct elements x_1, x_2 such that $(\mathsf{Pf}'_i.p'_i)^I(x_1) = (\mathsf{Pf}'_i.p'_i)^I(x_2)$. From the construction of the interpretation and the fact that the sets of predicate and function symbols are disjoint we know that $p'_i(\overline{\mathsf{Pf}'}_i(t(0))) \in T_P^\omega(\emptyset)$ where t is a term corresponding to the paths from o_1 and o_2 to x_1 and x_2, respectively (note that all the paths that end in a particular common node in the constructed interpretation are symmetric). However, then $p'(\overline{\mathsf{Pf}'}(t(0))) \in T_P^\omega(\emptyset)$ using the clause in P associated with the violated constraint in Σ_P, and thus $(\mathsf{Pf}'.p')^I(x_1) = (\mathsf{Pf}'.p')^I(x_2)$, a contradiction.

On the other hand, $(\mathsf{Pf}.p)^I(o_1) \neq (\mathsf{Pf}.p)^I(o_2)$ as $p(\overline{\mathsf{Pf}}(0)) \notin T_P^\omega(\emptyset)$, a contradiction. □

For the constructed DLFD problem we have $|\Sigma_P| + |\varphi_{P,G}| \in \mathcal{O}(|P| + |G|)$. Thus:

Corollary 5 *The logical implication problem for DLFD is DEXPTIME-hard.*

Since DLFD problems can be embedded into DLClass, we have:

Corollary 6 *The logical implication problem for DLClass is DEXPTIME-hard.*

4   Upper Bound and Decision Procedure for DLClass

To complete the picture we exhibit a DEXPTIME decision procedure for DL-Class by reducing an arbitrary logical implication problem to the recognition problem for Datalog$_{nS}$ [12]. We start with two lemmas that are used to simplify complex DLClass constraints.

Lemma 7 *Let C_1 be a primitive concept not in $\Sigma \cup \{C' < D'\}$. Then*

$$\Sigma \cup \{C < (\mathsf{and}\ D_1\ D_2)\} \models C' < D' \iff \Sigma \cup \{C < D_1, C < D_2\} \models C' < D',$$

$$\Sigma \cup \{C < (\mathsf{all}\ f\ D)\} \models C' < D' \iff \Sigma \cup \{C < (\mathsf{all}\ f\ C_1), C_1 < D\} \models C' < D'.$$

We say that a terminology Σ is *simple* if it does not contain descriptions of the form (and D_1 D_2) and whenever (all f D) appears in Σ then D is a primitive concept description. Lemma 7 shows that every terminology can be converted to an equivalent simple terminology.

Lemma 8 *Let Σ be a simple terminology and C_1 a primitive concept not present in $\Sigma \cup \{C < D, C' < D'\}$. Then*

$$\Sigma \models C < (\text{and } D_1 \ D_2) \iff \Sigma \models C < D_1 \text{ and } \Sigma \models C < D_2,$$

$$\Sigma \models C < (\text{all } f \ D) \iff \Sigma \cup \{C < (\text{all } f \ C_1)\}$$
$$\cup \{C_1 < C_2 : \Sigma \models C < (\text{all } f \ C_2)\} \models C_1 < D.$$

We say that a subsumption constraint $C < D$ is *simple* if it is of the form $C < C'$, $C < (\text{all } f \ C')$, and $C < (\text{fd } C' : \text{Pf}_1, \ldots, \text{Pf}_k \to \text{Pf})$; Lemmas 7 and 8 allow us to convert general logical implication problems to (sets of) problems where all subsumption constraints are simple. For each such problem $\Sigma \models \varphi$ we define a Datalog$_{nS}$ recognition problem $P_\Sigma \cup P_\varphi \models G_\varphi$ as follows:

$$
\begin{aligned}
P_\Sigma = \{ \ & \text{cl}(X, c_j, Y) \leftarrow \text{cl}(X, c_i, Y) && \text{for all } C_i < C_j \in \Sigma && (1)\\
& \text{cl}(f(X), c_j, Y) \leftarrow \text{cl}(X, c_i, Y) && \text{for all } C_i < (\text{all } f \ C_j) \in \Sigma && (2)\\
& \text{cl}(X, Y, 1) \leftarrow \text{eq}(X), \text{cl}(X, Y, 2) &&&& (3)\\
& \text{cl}(X, Y, 2) \leftarrow \text{eq}(X), \text{cl}(X, Y, 1) &&&& (4)\\
& \text{eq}(f(X)) \leftarrow \text{eq}(X) && \text{for all primitive attributes } f && (5)\\
& \text{eq}(\overline{\text{Pf}}(X)) \leftarrow \text{cl}(X, c_i, 1), \text{cl}(X, c_j, 2), \text{eq}(\overline{\text{Pf}}_1(X)), \ldots, \text{eq}(\overline{\text{Pf}}_k(X)) && (6)\\
& \text{eq}(\overline{\text{Pf}}(X)) \leftarrow \text{cl}(X, c_i, 2), \text{cl}(X, c_j, 1), \text{eq}(\overline{\text{Pf}}_1(X)), \ldots, \text{eq}(\overline{\text{Pf}}_k(X)) && (7)\\
& \qquad \text{for all } C_i < (\text{fd } C_j : \text{Pf}_1, \ldots, \text{Pf}_k \to \text{Pf}) \in \Sigma \ \}
\end{aligned}
$$

The clauses stand for the inferences of inheritance (1), direct typing (2), typing inferred from equalities (3-4), propagation of equality by primitive attributes (5), and path FD inference (6-7), respectively. In addition we use a set of facts to represent the left-hand-side of the posed question[2]:

$$
P_\varphi = \begin{cases}
\{\text{cl}(0, c_i, 1)\} & \text{for } C_i < C_j\\
\{\text{cl}(0, c_i, 1)\} & \text{for } C_i < (\text{all } f \ C_j)\\
\{\text{cl}(0, c_i, 1), \text{cl}(0, c_j, 2), \text{eq}(\overline{\text{Pf}}_1(0)), \ldots, \text{eq}(\overline{\text{Pf}}_k(0))\} & \\
& \text{for } C_i < (\text{fd } C_j : \text{Pf}_1, \ldots, \text{Pf}_k \to \text{Pf})
\end{cases}
$$

and a ground atom to represent the right-hand-side of the posed question:

$$
G_\varphi = \begin{cases}
\text{cl}(0, c_j, 1) & \text{for } C_i < C_j\\
\text{cl}(f(0), c_j, 1) & \text{for } C_i < (\text{all } f \ C_j)\\
\text{eq}(\overline{\text{Pf}}(0)) & \text{for } C_i < (\text{fd } C_j : \text{Pf}_1, \ldots, \text{Pf}_k \to \text{Pf})
\end{cases}
$$

Intuitively, the ground facts $\text{cl}(\overline{\text{Pf}}(0), c_j, i)$ and $\text{eq}(\overline{\text{Pf}}(0))$ derived from P_φ using P_Σ stand for properties of two distinguished nodes o_1 and o_2 and their descendents, in particular for $\text{Pf}^I(o_i) \in C_j$ and $\text{Pf}^I(o_1) = \text{Pf}^I(o_2)$, respectively. In addition $|P_\Sigma| + |P_\varphi| \in \mathcal{O}(|\Sigma| + |\varphi|)$ and $|G_\varphi| \in \mathcal{O}(|\varphi|)$.

---

[2] Essentially an application of the Deduction theorem.

Theorem 9 *Let Σ be an arbitrary simple DLClass terminology and φ a simple DLClass subsumption constraint. Then $\Sigma \models \varphi \iff P_\Sigma \cup P_\varphi \models G_\varphi$.*

<u>Proof:</u>   (sketch)

$\Leftarrow$: By induction on stages of $T_{P_\Sigma \cup P_\varphi}$ showing that every clause in $P_\Sigma \cup P_\varphi$ represents a valid inference (essentially the same as the "only-if" part of the proof of Theorem 4).

$\Rightarrow$: By contradiction we assume that $G_\varphi \notin T^\omega_{P_\Sigma \cup P_\varphi}$. We again construct an interpretation for DLClass starting with two complete infinite trees with edges labeled by primitive attribute names. We merge the two nodes accessible from the two distinct roots by the path Pf whenever $\mathrm{eq}(\overline{\mathrm{Pf}}(0)) \in T_{P_\Sigma \cup P_\varphi}$ (all children of such nodes are merged as well due to the clause $\mathrm{eq}(f(X)) \leftarrow \mathrm{eq}(X) \in P_\Sigma$). In addition we label each node n in the resulting graph by a set of class (identifier) labels c_i if $n = o_j.\mathrm{Pf}$ and $\mathrm{cl}(\overline{\mathrm{Pf}}(0), c_i, j) \in T_{P_\Sigma \cup P_\varphi}$ $(j = 1, 2)$.

Nodes of the resulting graph then provide the domain Δ of the interpretation; primitive concept C_i is interpreted as the set of nodes labeled c_i and the interpretation of primitive attributes is given by the edges of the graph.

The resulting interpretation satisfies Σ (by case analysis for the individual constraints in Σ using the corresponding clauses in P_Σ) and the "left-hand" side of φ (follows from the definition of P_φ), but falsifies the "right-hand" side of φ. $\Box$

This result completes the circle of reductions

$$\text{(normal) Datalog}_{nS} \longrightarrow \text{DLFD} \longrightarrow \text{DLClass} \longrightarrow \text{Datalog}_{nS}$$

Corollary 10 *Logical implication problems in DLFD and DLClass are DEXP-TIME-complete.*

In particular, this also means that every DLClass problem can be reformulated as a DLFD problem, and consequently that *typing* and *inheritance* constraints do not truly enhance the expressive power of DLClass.

5   Polynomial Cases

Previous sections have established DEXPTIME-completeness for DLClass. However, there is an interesting syntactic restriction on uniqueness constraints in DLClass that (a) allows for a low-order polynomial time decision procedure that solves the logical implication problem, and (b) has a number of practical applications in the database area [16,17]. In particular, the restriction requires all fd descriptions in a terminology Σ to be regular; in other words, to have one of the forms

1. $(\mathrm{fd}\ C : \mathrm{Pf}_1, \ldots, \mathrm{Pf} . \mathrm{Pf}', \ldots, \mathrm{Pf}_k \to \mathrm{Pf})$ or
2. $(\mathrm{fd}\ C : \mathrm{Pf}_1, \ldots, \mathrm{Pf} . \mathrm{Pf}', \ldots, \mathrm{Pf}_k \to \mathrm{Pf} . f)$.

Given the connection between DLFD and Datalog$_{nS}$ established by Theorem 4, a natural question is whether there is a syntactic restriction of Datalog$_{nS}$ programs that leads to an efficient decision procedure. We identify such a restriction in the following definition.

Definition 11 (Regular Datalog$_{nS}$) *Let P be a normal Datalog$_{nS}$ program. We say that P is* regular *if every clause with a non-empty body has the form*

$$p(t(X)) \leftarrow p_1(t_1(X)), \ldots, q(t'(t(X))), \ldots, p_k(t_k(X))$$

for some terms $t, t', t_1, \ldots, t_k$ (note that any of the terms may be just the variable X itself).

Theorem 12 *The recognition problem $P \models G$ for regular Datalog$_{nS}$ programs has a low-order polynomial time decision procedure.*

Proof: Consider the conversion of P to Σ_P presented in Theorem 4. It is not hard to see that such a conversion of any clause with non-empty body in P to a constraint in DLFD would obtain a regular fd description. The statement of the theorem then follows since the conversion of the recognition problem takes $\mathcal{O}(|P| + |G|)$ time, $|\Sigma_P| + |\varphi_{P,G}| \in \mathcal{O}(|P| + |G|)$, and the obtained (equivalent) logical implication problem can be solved using a $\mathcal{O}(|\Sigma_P| \cdot |\varphi_{P,G}|)$ procedure for regular DLClass problems [16].   □

In addition, a slight generalization of the regularity condition in DLClass leads to intractability [16]. The same turns out to be true for regular Datalog$_{nS}$.

Definition 13 (Nearly-regular Datalog$_{nS}$) *We define P as a* nearly regular *Datalog$_{nS}$ program if every clause with non-empty body has one of the forms*

1. $p(f(t(X))) \leftarrow p_1(t_1(X)), \ldots, q(t'(t(X))), \ldots, p_k(t_k(X))$ *or*
2. $p(t(f(X))) \leftarrow p_1(t_1(X)), \ldots, q(t'(t(X))), \ldots, p_k(t_k(X))$.

Essentially, near-regularity allows an additional function symbol f to appear in the head of a clause.

Theorem 14 *For an arbitrary normal Datalog$_{nS}$ program P there is an equivalent nearly regular Datalog$_{nS}$ program P'.*

Proof: Consider P' that contains the same facts as P, and for every clause

$$p(f_1(\ldots f_k(X) \ldots)) \leftarrow p_1(t_1(X)), \ldots, p_l(t_l(X)) \in P$$

with non-empty body, contains a set of clauses

$$q_1(f_k(X)) \leftarrow p_1(t_1(X)), \ldots, p_l(t_l(X)),$$
$$q_2(f_{k-1}(f_k(X))) \leftarrow q_1(f_k(X)),$$
$$\vdots$$
$$q_k(f_1(\ldots f_k(X)\ldots)) \leftarrow q_{k-1}(f_2(\ldots f_k(X)\ldots)),$$
$$p(f_1(\ldots f_k(X)\ldots)) \leftarrow q_k(f_1(\ldots f_k(X)\ldots))$$

for some predicate symbols $q_1, \ldots, q_k$ not occurring in P. Each of the generated clauses is nearly regular (by satisfying the first form in Definition 13). Similarly, we could have generated P' where all clauses have satisfied the second form in Definition 13.

In both cases, the statement of the theorem is easy to establish from the construction of P'. □

Corollary 15 *The recognition problem for nearly regular Datalog$_{nS}$ programs is DEXPTIME-complete.*

6   Summary and Discussion

We have presented a description logic dialect called DLClass that is capable of capturing many important object relational database constraints including inheritance, typing, primary keys, foreign keys, and object identity. Although DLClass and its applications in information systems has been explored in earlier work [4,16,17], this paper establishes a strong connection with Datalog$_{nS}$. We have explored this connection and obtained the following results:

- An open problem relating to the complexity of DLFD (and therefore to the complexity of DLClass) that was originally considered in [15,20] has been resolved. In particular, the result implies that the regularity condition for DLClass [16] is a boundary between tractable and intractable problems in DLClass.
- A consequence of our relatively straightforward linear reduction of DLClass to DLFD implies that inheritance and typing constraints do not appreciatively add to the utility of DLFD for capturing object relational schema. Such constraints are straightforwardly expressed in DLFD.
- We have identified a subset of the Datalog$_{nS}$ recognition problems that can be solved in PTIME. Moreover, we have shown that the regularity condition for Datalog$_{nS}$ programs is a boundary between polynomial and exponential time problems in Datalog$_{nS}$.

In general, a DL dialect is obtained by a selection of concept constructors that will in turn determine the tradeoff between the utility of the dialect for capturing schema structure and the complexity of the associated implication problem. For example, CLASSIC [3] opts for a less expressive selection that excludes negation and disjunction constructors in order to ensure an efficient polynomial time algorithm for its implication problem. Similarly, DLClass may be viewed as a minimal core of CLASSIC extended with uniqueness constraints. Conversely, other dialects opt for a more expressive selection that includes such constructors with the expectation that *model building* implication checking procedures work well on typical real world schema structure [10].

Note that DLCLass excludes any consideration for so-called *roles* which are essentially set-valued attributes. Allowing roles to be used in formulating uniqueness constraints is an interesting avenue for future work, although allowing them to be used only at the end of path expressions is a straightforward generalization of our results that would accommodate the notion of key in [9]. Also note that DLClass interprets attributes as total functions. However, partial functions can be straightforwardly simulated by employing a simple notational convention.

It is worth mentioning other work on various forms of path constraints for graph based data models relating to semi-structure data and object relational schema [5,6,13] that have similar objectives to research in the area of DLs. Indeed, many of the results in this work appear to have close analogies to corresponding work on DLs, although a more thorough exploration of this relationship is an interesting avenue for further research.

Another direction for future research relates to a property that DLFD shares with many DL dialects: its arbitrary and finite logical implication problems do not coincide. In particular,

$$\{\mathsf{THING} < (\mathsf{fd}\ \mathsf{THING} : A.B \to Id)\} \models \mathsf{THING} < (\mathsf{fd}\ \mathsf{THING} : B \to Id)$$

holds if and only if one requires the domain for any interpretation to be finite [15]. Furthermore, there is some evidence that existing techniques for finite model reasoning are not suited to more general information integration problems that involve access to large finite information sources such as the WEB [1].

Acknowledgements. The authors gratefully acknowledge the Natural Sciences and Engineering Research Council of Canada and the Communications and Information Technology of Ontario for their support of this research. We also wish to thank the many helpful suggestions and comments by the anonymous referees.

References

1. Serge Abiteboul and Victor Vianu. Queries and computation on the web. In *6th International Conference on Database Theory ICDT'97*, volume 1186 of *Lecture Notes in Computer Science*, pages 262–275. Springer, 1997.
2. Alexander Borgida. Description logics in data management. *IEEE Transactions on Knowledge and Data Engineering*, 7(5):671–682, 1995.
3. Alexander Borgida, Ronald J. Brachman, Deborah L. McGuinness, and Lori Alperin Resnick. Classic: A structural data model for objects. In James Clifford, Bruce G. Lindsay, and David Maier, editors, *Proceedings of the 1989 ACM SIGMOD International Conference on Management of Data*, pages 58–67. ACM Press, 1989.

4. Alexander Borgida and Grant Weddell. Adding uniqueness constraints to description logics (preliminary report). In *International Conference on Deductive and Object-Oriented Databases*, pages 85–102, 1997.

5. Peter Buneman, Wenfei Fan, and Scott Weinstein. Path constraints in semistructured and structured databases. In *Proceedings of the Seventeenth ACM SIGACT-SIGMOD-SIGART Symposium on Principles of Database Systems*, pages 129–138, 1998.

6. Peter Buneman, Wenfei Fan, and Scott Weinstein. Interaction between path and type constraints. In *Proceedings of the Eighteenth ACM SIGACT-SIGMOD-SIGART Symposium on Principles of Database Systems*, pages 56–67, 1999.

7. Diego Calvanese, Giuseppe De Giacomo, and Maurizio Lenzerini. Structured Objects: modeling and reasonning. In *International Conference on Deductive and Object-Oriented Databases*, pages 229–246, 1995.

8. Diego Calvanese, Giuseppe De Giacomo, and Maurizio Lenzerini. Answering Queries Using Views in Description Logics. In *6th International Workshop on Knowledge Representation meets Databases (KRDB'99)*, pages 6–10, 1999.

9. Diego Calvanese, Giuseppe De Giacomo, and Maurizio Lenzerini. Keys for free in description logics. In *International Workshop on Description Logics DL2000*, pages 79–88, 2000.

10. Diego Calvanese, Maurizio Lenzerini, and Daniele Nardi. Description logics for conceptual data modelling. In Jan Chomicki and Gunter Saake, editors, *Logics for Databases and Information Systems*, chapter 8. Kluwer, 1998.

11. Jan Chomicki. *Functional Deductive Databases: Query Processing in the Presence of Limited Function Symbols*. PhD thesis, Rutgers University, New Brunswick, New Jersey, January 1990. Also Laboratory for Computer Science Research Technical Report LCSR-TR-142.

12. Jan Chomicki and Tomasz Imieliński. Finite Representation of Infinite Query Answers. *ACM Transactions on Database Systems*, 18(2):181–223, June 1993.

13. Wenfei Fan and Jérôme Siméon. Integrity constraints for xml. In *Proceedings of the Nineteenth ACM SIGMOD-SIGACT-SIGART Symposium on Principles of Database Systems*, pages 23–34, 2000.

14. Martin Fürer. Alternation and the Ackermann Case of the Decision Problem. *L'Enseignement Math.*, 27:137–162, 1981.

15. Minoru Ito and Grant Weddell. Implication Problems for Functional Constraints on Databases Supporting Complex Objects. *Journal of Computer and System Sciences*, 49(3):726–768, 1994.

16. Vitaliy L. Khizder. *Uniqueness Constraints in Object-Relational Databases and Description Logics*. PhD thesis, University of Waterloo, 1999.

17. Vitaliy L. Khizder, David Toman, and Grant Weddell. Reasoning about Duplicate Elimination with Description Logic. Technical report, Dept. of Computer Science, University of Waterloo, 2000. (accepted to DOOD 2000).

18. John W. Lloyd. *Foundations of Logic Programming*. Springer-Verlag, 2nd edition, 1987.

19. Martin F. van Bommel and Grant Weddell. Reasoning About Equations and Functional Dependencies on Complex Objects. *IEEE Transactions on Knowledge and Data Engineering*, 6(3):455–469, 1994.

20. Grant Weddell. A Theory of Functional Dependencies for Object Oriented Data Models. In *International Conference on Deductive and Object-Oriented Databases*, pages 165–184, 1989.
21. Grant Weddell. Reasoning about Functional Dependencies Generalized for Semantic Data Models. *ACM Transactions on Database Systems*, 17(1):32–64, 1992.

Expressiveness Issues and Decision Problems for Active Database Event Queries

James Bailey and Szabolcs Mikulás*

Department of Computer Science, Birkbeck College, Univ. of London
Malet Street, London WC1E 7HX, UK. {james,szabolcs}@dcs.bbk.ac.uk

Abstract. A key facility of active database management systems is their ability to detect and react to the occurrence of events. Such events can be either atomic in nature, or specified using an event algebra to form complex events. An important role of an event algebra is to define the semantics of when events become invalid (event consumption). In this paper, we examine a simple event algebra and provide a logical framework for specification of various consumption policies. We then study the problems of equivalence and implication, identifying a powerful class of complex events for which equivalence is decidable. We then demonstrate how extensions of this class lead to undecidability.

1 Introduction

First we briefly introduce the context of our work, list our contributions and survey related works.

1.1 Events in Active Databases

Active databases provide the functionality of traditional databases and additionally are capable of reacting automatically to state changes without user intervention. This is achieved by means of Event-Condition-Action (ECA) rules of the form *on* event *if* condition *do* action. The event part of an ECA rule specifies the points in time when the rule should become triggered and is the focus of this paper. Events are of two kinds: primitive events correspond to atomic, detectable occurrences, while complex events are combinations of simple events specified using an *event algebra*. Detecting the occurrence of a complex event corresponds to the problem of evaluating an *event query* (specified using the event algebra) over a history of all previously occurring primitive events.[1] A notable characteristic of active database prototypes has been the rich and expressive event algebras developed [11]. An interesting feature of such algebras is the notion of *event consumption policies*. These are used to specify when certain instances of an event should no longer be considered in the detection of other

---

* Supported by EPSRC No. GR/L26872.

[1] In this paper, we will use the terms complex event detection and (complex) event query evaluation over a history synonymously.

J. Van den Bussche and V. Vianu (Eds.): ICDT 2001, LNCS 1973, pp. 68–82, 2001.

events depending on it. Previous work has predominantly dealt with the definition of policies for a range of applications, without focusing on their formal foundations. Indeed, there is not even widespread agreement on which policies should be standard features of an event algebra. In contrast, one of the purposes of our work is to give a framework for specifying event consumption policies and investigate what consequences their inclusion has for the expressiveness of the event query language as a whole.

In addition to expressiveness, another important question is to consider what kinds of analysis are possible for different classes of event queries. For example, the histories over which event queries may be evaluated can be very large and it is important to avoid redundant evaluation. In fact, efficient event detection has been identified as being a major challenge in improving active DBMS system performance ([6]). One possible optimisation involves being able to reason about event query equivalence and implication. Given event queries q_1 and q_2, if $q_1 \Leftrightarrow q_2$, then only one of $\{q_1, q_2\}$ needs be evaluated over the event history (whichever is less expensive, according to some cost model). Alternatively, if $q_1 \Rightarrow q_2$, then one need not evaluate q_2 whenever q_1 is true. Being able to decide these questions is therefore a useful property for an event query language to possess and the second half of this paper provides (un)decidability results for a core event language and a selection of consumption policies.

1.2 Contributions

We make two main contributions in this paper. The first is a formal procedure for the specification of event consumption which is then useful for comparison of consumption policies. The second contribution is the presentation of decidability and undecidability results for implication and equivalence of event queries. We define a powerful query class for which equivalence is decidable, yet implication is undecidable. Our results also highlight the important role that event consumption has in determining whether an effective analysis is possible. To our knowledge, this is the first paper to consider decision questions for event queries making use of different consumption policies.

1.3 Related Work

A number of active database prototypes have been built providing sophisticated event algebras (e.g. SNOOP, REACH, NAOS, CHIMERA [11]), but there are not associated results on the expressiveness of these algebras which could be used as the basis for (global) reasoning about implication and equivalence of event queries. The event language of the system ODE [5], however, has been shown to have the power of regular expressions, but event consumption policies are not an explicit feature of the language. [10] proposes the use of Datalog$_{1S}$ for expressing complex event queries. The advantage being that it has a well-defined formal semantics. Such a language is rather more powerful than the algebras we consider in this paper, however, and indeed equivalence of Datalog$_{1S}$ expressions can easily be shown to be undecidable. Similar considerations apply to work on modelling complex events using the Kowalski–Sergot event calculus [3] or coloured Petri nets [4] as used in SAMOS.

An early work which recognised the importance of event consumption is [1], where a variety of so-called parameter contexts were proposed for matching and consuming events. Work in [15] provides a meta-model for classifying a number of properties of complex event formalisms.

Equivalence and implication are of course important problems elsewhere in database theory, e.g., for conjunctive queries. It is not obvious how to use these results for reasoning about event queries, since the queries considered usually lack one of the following features: an ordering on the underlying domain, negation, or the ability to mimic event consumption. Work on temporal logics, however, is directly relevant for event reasoning, and we discuss and make use of these results in the following section.

Other work on temporal aspects of active databases includes [2] and [13], where the focus is on evaluation and expressiveness of temporal conditions. A characteristic that distinguishes conditions from events, however, is that they do not have associated consumption policies. Event languages are also used in other database areas, such as multimedia, where they are used in specifying interaction with documents [9].

2   Semantics for Complex Events

We assume the following about events in the spirit of [15]: a) The time domain is the set of natural numbers. b) Primitive events are detected by the system at points in time — that is, we can treat primitive events as primitive symbols interpreted in time. c) Event types are independent and they can be freely used as components to generate complex events — i.e., we can treat them as propositional variables that we can use for building compound formulas. d) The occurrence time of the terminator of a complex event is the occurrence time of the complex event, i.e., an event occurs when the last component of the event has occurred. e) Events can occur simultaneously.

Note that we model complex events as boolean queries over the history of all previously occurring primitive events. An event query is true over a history iff it is true at the last point in the history (of course it may well be true for prefixes of the history also).

Remark 1. We give two preliminary observations concerning our approach.

a) In practice, primitive or complex events could have other information associated with them (e.g., parameters or variables describing why they occurred)[2]. We ignore such a refinement in this paper, instead concentrating on the problem of recognising whether an event has occurred, as opposed to explaining why it occurred.

---

[2] If the domain of such parameters is finite, then we could of course model them by defining extra primitive events.

b) We are considering the definition of event queries and not techniques for their evaluation. In practice, incremental methods may be appropriate, but such evaluation methods are an orthogonal issue to the problems of expressiveness and analysis that we address.

2.1 Operations on Events

Next we review the most often used operations on events. We also propose a concise and formal way to express events occurring in time by using temporal logic over natural numbers.

We will model events occurring in active databases in time. Let $\mathfrak{N} = (\mathbb{N}, <, I)$ be a structure such that $\mathbb{N} = \{0, 1, \ldots\}$ is the set of natural numbers, $<$ is their usual ordering according to magnitude, and I is an interpretation function associating a subset $I(p)$ of $\mathbb{N}$ to every primitive event p (i.e., when it occurred).

Basic operations. For given events e and e', we first consider the following basic operations:

- *sequence operation* $e \,;\, e'$: events e and e' should occur in this order;
- *simultaneous operation* $e \parallel e'$: the events occur simultaneously;
- *conjunction operation* $e \sqcap e'$: both occur but it can happen in any order;
- *disjunction operation* $e \sqcup e'$: at least one of them occurs;
- *negation operation* $\sim e$: e does not occur (at a given time point).

Using the semantics above, it is straightforward to define when an event e occurs at a time-point $t \in \mathbb{N}$ — notation: $\mathfrak{N}, t \models e$. Note that $e \sqcap e'$ can be defined in terms of $\sqcup$, $\parallel$ and $;$: $(e \parallel e') \sqcup (e \,;\, e') \sqcup (e' \,;\, e)$.

We will see shortly how to express the above events using temporal logic, and we will also extend this translation to more complex event definitions as well.

2.2 Temporal Logic

Next we briefly recall the basics of temporal logic.[3] The language of our propositional temporal logic contains the usual propositional connectives *conjunction* $\land$ and *negation* $\neg$ and the binary temporal connectives *until* $\mathcal{U}$ and *since* $\mathcal{S}$. We also assume that a countable set P of propositional variables is at hand.

Other propositional connectives (disjunction $\lor$, implication $\to$, true $\top$, false $\bot$) are defined in the usual way. We define the unary temporal connectives *future* $\mathcal{F}$ and *past* $\mathcal{P}$:

$$\mathcal{F}\varphi \stackrel{\text{def}}{=} \mathcal{U}(\varphi, \top) \quad \text{and} \quad \mathcal{P}\varphi \stackrel{\text{def}}{=} \mathcal{S}(\varphi, \top).$$

As usual, $\mathcal{G}\varphi$ denotes $\neg\mathcal{F}\neg\varphi$ and $\mathcal{H}\varphi$ stands for $\neg\mathcal{P}\neg\varphi$, while $\Diamond\varphi$ is a shorthand for $\mathcal{P}\varphi \lor \mathcal{F}\varphi \lor \varphi$, and $\Box\varphi \stackrel{\text{def}}{=} \neg\Diamond\neg\varphi$. We will use the following definitions as well:

---

[3] We will use only past operators for modelling events in this paper, but we present a general framework that will enable us to include, e.g., rules as well.

$\triangleright\varphi \overset{\text{def}}{=} \mathcal{U}(\varphi, \bot)$ for *next*, $\triangleleft\varphi \overset{\text{def}}{=} \mathcal{S}(\varphi, \bot)$ for *previous*, and $\odot\varphi \overset{\text{def}}{=} \Diamond(\varphi \wedge \neg\mathcal{P}\top)$ for *beginning*.

In some applications, e.g., for expressing periodic events, it will be useful to consider a temporal language with an additional fixed point operation $\mu p.\varphi$. It is defined in the usual way: roughly speaking, if the free occurrences of the propositional symbol p are in the scope of past temporal operators in φ, then we can form the formula $\mu p.\varphi$. Since at any time point the past is finite (we have natural numbers flow of time), this guarantees the existence of a fixed point; see [7] for more details.

We are going to interpret temporal formulas over flows of time on the natural numbers. In more detail, let $\mathbb{N} = 0, 1, \ldots, n, \ldots$ be the set of natural numbers and $<$ their usual ordering (according to magnitude). Let v be an evaluation of the propositional variables in P, i.e., $v : P \to \mathcal{P}(\mathbb{N})$. Then truth of formulas in the model $\mathfrak{N} = (\mathbb{N}, <, v)$ is defined in the usual way; the case of the temporal connectives is as follows: for every $n \in \mathbb{N}$,

$$\mathfrak{N}, n \Vdash \mathcal{U}(\varphi, \psi) \iff \text{for some } m > n, \mathfrak{N}, m \Vdash \varphi$$
$$\text{and for all } l \text{ with } n < l < m, \mathfrak{N}, l \Vdash \psi$$
$$\mathfrak{N}, n \Vdash \mathcal{S}(\varphi, \psi) \iff \text{for some } m < n, \mathfrak{N}, m \Vdash \varphi$$
$$\text{and for all } l \text{ with } m < l < n, \mathfrak{N}, l \Vdash \psi.$$

Finally, the interpretation of fixed point formulas is as follows.

$$(\mathbb{N}, <, v), n \Vdash \mu p.\varphi \quad \text{iff} \quad n \in w(p)$$

for that unique evaluation w of the propositional variables that satisfies

- for every atom q distinct from p, $w(q) = v(q)$,
- $n \in w(p)$ iff $(\mathbb{N}, <, w), n \Vdash \varphi$.

Theorem 1. *The complexity of the decision problem for temporal logic of $\mathcal{U}$ and $\mathcal{S}$ over natural numbers flow of time is* PSPACE, *[12]. This remains true even if we include the fixed point operator, [7].*

2.3   Complex Event Definitions

First we give the translations of the basic operations on events into temporal logic:

- $e_{tr} \equiv e$ for primitive event e;
- $(e \,;\, e')_{tr} \equiv e'_{tr} \wedge \mathcal{P}e_{tr}$;
- $(e \parallel e')_{tr} \equiv e_{tr} \wedge e'_{tr}$;
- $(e \sqcap e')_{tr} \equiv (e_{tr} \wedge e'_{tr}) \vee (e_{tr} \wedge \mathcal{P}e'_{tr}) \vee (e'_{tr} \wedge \mathcal{P}e_{tr})$;
- $(e \sqcup e')_{tr} \equiv e_{tr} \vee e'_{tr}$;
- $(\sim e)_{tr} \equiv \neg e_{tr}$.

3   Consumption Policies

Event consumption policies are used to specify when certain instances of an event should no longer be considered in the detection of other events that depend on it. There are many ways in which event instances might be consumed (or not) when composite events are detected. In this section, we recall some representative policies for consuming events, similar to those of [1]. We propose a formal logic-based definition for consumption policies that will enable us to look at the problem of the complexity of deciding if two events together with consumption policies are equivalent.

Several consumption policies have been considered for the sequence operation on events. First we give a general definition, then look at particular policies and express them in the general framework. In the next section, we will consider the complexity of deciding equivalence and implication between event queries using consumption policies.

Definition 1. *Let $\mathfrak{N} = (\mathbb{N}, <, I)$ be a model with natural numbers universe $\mathbb{N}$ together with the usual ordering $<$ and an interpretation function I that associates a subset $I(p)$ of $\mathbb{N}$ to every primitive event p. Let e and e' be events and $R \subseteq \mathbb{N} \times \mathbb{N}$ be a binary relation that may depend on e and e'. Then we define the sequence operation $;_R$ as follows:*

$$\mathfrak{N}, t \models (e \, ;_R e') \iff \mathfrak{N}, t \models e' \text{ and } \mathfrak{N}, t' \models e \text{ for some } t' < t \text{ such that } R(t', t).$$

That is, $e \, ;_R e'$ holds at a time-point t iff $e \, ; e'$ occurs at t and the witness t' for e is related to t by R.

Note that by this definition we have a recursive way of defining more complex events under consumption policies. For instance, given two relations R and S, the definition of the event $(p \, ;_R q) \, ;_S r$ is as follows. Given a model $\mathfrak{N}$, first apply the definition of $;_R$ to determine for each $t \in \mathbb{N}$ if $p \, ;_R q$ occurs at t; then apply the definition of $;_S$ to $e \, ;_S r$ where e is the event $p \, ;_R q$. In other words, we compute a composite event by first computing the participating events and then, treating them as atomic events, the composite event. We also note that the above definition is in the style of modal logic, where the extra-boolean operations are evaluated according to accessibility relations. More generally, our definition of event consumption is compositional in the sense that the meaning (or truth) of a formula is determined by the meaning of its subformulas (plus the structure of the model).

Particular consumption policies are defined by imposing certain conditions on the relation R. For instance, the sequence operation $;$ can be treated as an operation with the most permissive consumption policy. In this case, we can take R as the universal binary relation, i.e., there is no further restriction on the p-witness t' for $\mathfrak{N}, t \models p \, ; q$ other than $t' < t$. Furthermore, as we will see below for the most-recent and cumulative consumption policies, there are cases when R is essentially a unary predicate. This suggests a definition of a subclass CP_1 of consumption policies when R can be substituted by a first-order formula using only unary predicates and the ordering $<$ in Definition 1. We already mentioned that the temporal logic of $\mathcal{U}$ and $\mathcal{S}$ is expressively complete w.r.t. first-order logic over natural numbers. Then for every operation $;_R \in CP_1$, there is an equivalent temporal logic formula φ_R with parameters:

$$\mathfrak{N}, t \models p \;;_R q \iff \mathfrak{N}, t \Vdash \varphi_R(p, q). \tag{1}$$

We can further strengthen this result by allowing definitions of R using monadic second-order logic $S1S$. Let CP_{S1S} be the resulting class of consumption policies. Again we have the equivalence result that the temporal logic of $\mathcal{U}$, $\mathcal{S}$ and fixed point is expressively complete w.r.t. $S1S$ over natural numbers, [7]. Thus the above equivalence 1 holds for CP_{S1S} and fixed point temporal logic.

We will demonstrate the idea of consumption policies on the example of the composite event e which is the sequential composition of the (primitive) events p and q. We will use the following example, see Figure 1. Let us assume that we are at time point 11 and the events p and q happened as follows;

$$I(p) = \{0, 1, 2, 5, 9, 10\}$$
$$I(q) = \{3, 4, 6, 7, 8, 11\}.$$

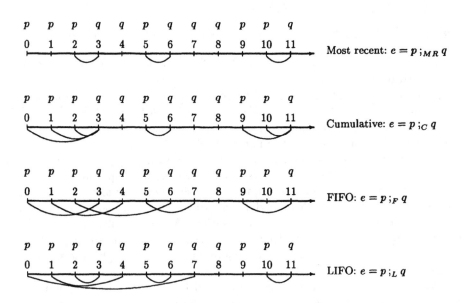

Fig. 1. Consumption policies

Most recent. In this context, only the most recent occurrence of the initiator (the first component of the event e) p is used. After detecting e, that occurrence of p which initiated e is "consumed", i.e., it cannot initiate other occurrence of *e*. Also the terminator (the final component of the event *e*) is consumed, i.e., it cannot be the terminator of another occurrence of *e*. Such a policy is useful for situations where events occur rapidly and successive occurrences only refine the previous value (e.g., sensor applications).

In the example above, *e* is first detected at 3 when *e* is initiated by the occurrence of *p* at 2 and terminated by the occurrence of *q* at 3; we will denote this by $(e, 3) = (p, 2; q, 3)$. Then other occurrences of *e* are as follows: $(e, 6) = (p, 5; q, 6)$ and $(e, 11) = (p, 10; q, 11)$.

This consumption policy can be defined by the following relation R in the above definition:

$$R(t, t') \iff \mathfrak{N}, t \models q, \; \mathfrak{N}, t' \models p, \; t' < t,$$
$$\text{and for each } t'', \text{ if } t' < t'' < t \text{ then } \mathfrak{N}, t'' \not\models p \text{ and } \mathfrak{N}, t'' \not\models q.$$

That is, R is the partial function that associates consecutive *p*- and *q*-points. Note that in the above definition of R, there was no binary relation apart from $<$. Thus there is a temporal formula expressing this consumption policy:

$$\mathfrak{N}, t \Vdash q \wedge S(p, \neg p \wedge \neg q) \iff \mathfrak{N}, t \models p \, ;_R q.$$

We will use the notation $e;_{MR} e'$ for denoting the event $e; e'$ using the most-recent consumption policy.[4]

Cumulative. In this version, all occurrences of the initiator are accumulated until the composite event is detected, and all these occurrences are consumed when the composite event is detected. Such a policy is useful where multiple occurrences of an event need to be grouped together (e.g. multiple deposits preceding a withdrawal). Using the above notation, we have $(e, 3) = (p, 0, 1, 2; q, 3)$, $(e, 6) = (p, 5; q, 6)$ and $(e, 11) = (p, 9, 10; q, 11)$. The definition of R is as follows:

$$R(t, t') \iff \mathfrak{N}, t \models q, \; \mathfrak{N}, t' \models p, \; t' < t,$$
$$\text{and for each } t'', \text{ if } t' < t'' < t \text{ then } \mathfrak{N}, t'' \not\models q.$$

Again, we can express this by a temporal formula $q \wedge S(p, \neg q)$. We will use the notation $e \, ;_C e'$ for denoting the event $e \, ; e'$ using the cumulative consumption policy.

Using the above definition of 'most recent' and 'cumulative' (or the corresponding temporal logic formulas), one easily shows the following.

Claim. The most-recent and cumulative consumption policies are equivalent. That is, for any given model $\mathfrak{N}$ and $t \in \mathbb{N}$, we have

$$\mathfrak{N}, t \models e \, ;_{MR} e' \iff \mathfrak{N}, t \models e \, ;_C e'.$$

---

[4] From now on, the subscript X in $;_X$ will stand for a particular consumption policy instead of the underlying binary relation.

FIFO. [5] The event e is detected whenever q occurs and there is an "unconsumed" earlier occurrence of p, further the *earliest* such occurrence of p is the initiator of the event. An example use of this policy could be if p represented the availability of a service instance and q represented a request for such a service. We have $(e, 3) = (p, 0; q, 3)$, $(e, 4) = (p, 1; q, 4)$, $(e, 6) = (p, 2; q, 6)$, $(e, 7) = (p, 5; q, 7)$ and $(e, 11) = (p, 9; q, 11)$.

The underlying relation R is defined in a recursive way in this case. For every $n \in \mathbb{N}$, let $\mathfrak{N}_n$ be the initial segment of $\mathfrak{N}$ defined by n: $\mathfrak{N}_n$ is the model $\mathfrak{N}$ relativized to $\mathbb{N}_n = \{t \in \mathbb{N} : t \leq n\}$, i.e., we restrict the universe and the interpretation of events to $\{t \in \mathbb{N} : t \leq n\}$. We define R_0 be the empty relation. Now let us assume that $R_n \subseteq \mathbb{N}_n \times \mathbb{N}_n$ has been already defined. R_{n+1} is defined as follows. If $\mathfrak{N}, n + 1 \not\models q$, then $R_{n+1} = R_n$. If $\mathfrak{N}, n + 1 \models q$, then we define $R_{n+1} = R_n \cup \{(m, n + 1)\}$, where $m \leq n$ satisfies

$\mathfrak{N}, m \models p$, for each $t \leq n$, $(m, t) \notin R_n$,
and for each $t < m$, if $\mathfrak{N}, t \models p$ then $R_n(t, t')$ for some $t' \leq n$,

provided such m exists; otherwise we define $R_{n+1} = R_n$. We let R be the union of the chain $(R_i : i \in \mathbb{N})$. Thus R is a partial injective function that associates every q-point x to the earliest p-point y such that $y < x$ and there is no $z < x$ with $R(y, z)$. Then $;_R$ defines the sequence operation under the FIFO consumption policy. We will use the notation $e ;_F e'$ for denoting the event $e ; e'$ using the FIFO consumption policy.

LIFO. [6] This is a similar policy to the previous one, but the event e is initiated by the *last* "unconsumed" previous occurrence of p. In our example, we have the following occurrences: $(e, 3) = (p, 2; q, 3)$, $(e, 4) = (p, 1; q, 4)$, $(e, 6) = (p, 5; q, 6)$, $(e, 7) = (p, 0; q, 7)$ and $(e, 11) = (p, 10; q, 11)$.

Again the corresponding relation R is defined recursively. We define R_0 be the empty relation. Now let us assume that $R_n \subseteq \mathbb{N}_n \times \mathbb{N}_n$ has been already defined. First assume that $\mathfrak{N}, n + 1 \not\models q$ and in this case define $R_{n+1} = R_n$. If $\mathfrak{N}, n + 1 \models q$, then $R_{n+1} = R_N \cup \{(m, n + 1)\}$ where $m \leq n$ satisfies

$\mathfrak{N}, m \models p$, for each $t \leq n$, $(m, t) \notin R_n$,
for each t, if $m < t < n + 1$ and $\mathfrak{N}, t \models p$ then $R_n(t, t')$ for some t',

provided such m exists; otherwise $R_{n+1} = R_n$. We let R be the union of the chain $(R_i : i \in \mathbb{N})$. Then $;_R$ defines the sequence operation under the FIFO consumption policy. We will use the notation $e ;_L e'$ for denoting the event $e ; e'$ using the LIFO consumption policy. Again, R satisfies the following condition: it is a partial function that maps every p-point x to the first q-point y such that $x < y$ and there is no $z < y$ with $R(x, z)$. Then it is not surprising that satisfiability of FIFO and LIFO events coincide.

Claim. The FIFO and LIFO consumption policies are equivalent.

---

[5] First in first out.
[6] Last in first out.

Remark 2. Although we have only looked at four examples, there are obviously (infinitely many) other consumption policies in the classes CP_1 and CP_{S1S}. The purpose of defining these two classes is as a classification mechanism and, as we shall see, CP_1 and CP_{S1S} represent classes of policies for which analysis is "easy".

Remark 3. The results of the next section imply that $;_L$ and $;_F$ are not definable in terms of CP_1 or CP_{S1S} operations. Intuitively, this is because their definition requires the relation R to be a "true" binary relation (one that can't be simulated by operations on unary relations).

4   Decidability of Events

In this section we look at the problem of deciding equivalence between events using consumption policies. We will consider several *event algebras* determined by various choices of operations. Let $\mathcal{E}_1$ be the event algebra in which events are generated by the following operations: sequence ; with any consumption policy from $CP_1 \cup CP_{S1S}$, $\parallel$, $\sqcap$, $\sqcup$, $\sim$. In the definition of $\mathcal{E}_2$, we allow any basic operation $\parallel$, $\sqcap$, $\sqcup$, $\sim$, plus the sequence operation under the most-recent, cumulative, FIFO and LIFO policies $;_I$ where $I \in \{MR, C, F, L\}$.[7] So, $\mathcal{E}_1$ is an event algebra that includes the basic operations plus the ability to define "well behaved" consumption policies. $\mathcal{E}_2$ is an event algebra including the same basic operations, but allowing the use of the more expressive policies $;_L$ and $;_F$.

Our aim is to find out the complexity of implication and equivalence. The *implication problem* is defined by:

given two events e and e', whether for every $\mathfrak{N}$ and $t \in \mathbb{N}$, $\mathfrak{N}, t \models e$ implies
$$\mathfrak{N}, t \models e'.$$

We will write $e \Rightarrow e'$ if e' is implied by e. *Equivalence* of events, in symbols $e \Leftrightarrow e'$, is defined by mutual implication.

Theorem 2. *Let e and e' be two event queries written in the event algebra $\mathcal{E}_1$. The complexity of deciding implication and equivalence between e and e' is in* PSPACE.

Next we look at the problem of equivalence between queries that can use either the $;_F$ and $;_L$ operator (but not both). An additional restriction is that the chosen operator from $\{;_L, ;_F\}$ can be used no more than once. Such a restriction would seem realistic in practice, given the likely difficulty in understanding/writing event queries using $\{;_L, ;_F\}$ multiple times.

Theorem 3. *Let q_1 and q_2 be event queries of the event algebra $\mathcal{E}_2$ such that each uses one instance of either $;_F$ or $;_L$. Then the problem of whether $q_1 \Leftrightarrow q_2$ is decidable.*

---

[7] As future work, we plan to extend the definition of $\mathcal{E}_2$ to also allow any policy in $CP_1 \cup CP_{S1S}$.

Proof. We show how to translate each q_i ($i \in \{1,2\}$) into a deterministic one counter machine. Since equivalences of such machines is decidable (in exponential time of the size of the machines [14]), it follows that equivalence of q_1 and q_2 is decidable. The difficulty of the translation arises from ensuring that the constructed machine is deterministic.

A deterministic one counter machine (docm) is a deterministic pushdown automaton having a stack alphabet of only one symbol. In more detail,

$$M = (\Sigma, Acc, St, A, \delta)$$

where Σ is a finite set of states, $Acc \subseteq \Sigma$ is the set of accepting states, $St \in \Sigma$ is the starting state, A is an alphabet and $\delta : A \times \Sigma \times \mathbb{N} \to \Sigma \times \mathbb{N}$ is a deterministic transition function such that if $\delta(a, S, n) = (S', m)$, then $m \in \{n, n+1, n-1\} \cap \mathbb{N}$.

Recall that an event q is satisfiable if there is an initial segment $\mathfrak{N}_n$ of $\mathfrak{N}$ such that $\mathfrak{N}, n \models q$. The *event history of* q, $H(q)$, is the set of models for q in the above sense. For any q using at one instance of the LIFO/FIFO operator, we show how to construct a docm M_q such that $L(M) = H(q)$ (where $L(M)$ is the set of input histories accepted by the machine and $H(q)$ is the set of event histories for which q is true).

We show how to build docm for recognizing events in our algebra. We wish the docm to enter an accepting state every time the query q is true in the history.

Let us fix a language L of primitive events consisting of those events which occur in q_1 or q_2. The alphabet will consist of subsets of L (this is needed to model histories when events can occur simultaneously; otherwise single events as letters would do). We will construct the machines equivalent to q_1 and q_2 by recursion.

e where e is a primitive event. We define $M = (\Sigma, Acc, St, L, \delta)$ as follows. The machine has 3 states, a start state $S_1 = St$, an intermediate state S_2 and an accepting state $S_3 \in Acc$. The transition function δ is defined regardless of the counter which will remain empty during the transitions (and will be omitted below):

$$\delta(E, S_1) = S_3, \delta(F, S_1) = S_2, \delta(F, S_2) = S_2,$$
$$\delta(E, S_2) = S_3, \delta(E, S_3) = S_3, \delta(F, S_3) = S_2$$

where F and E are any subsets of L such that $e \in E$ and $e \notin F$.

$e_1 \parallel e_2$. Recursively build a docm $M_1 = (\Sigma_1, Acc_1, St_1, L, \delta_1)$ for recognizing e_1 and a docm $M_2 = (\Sigma_2, Acc_2, St_2, L, \delta_2)$ for recognizing e_2. We now build a docm $M = (\Sigma, Acc, St, L, \delta)$ which is the "product" of M_1 and M_2. Each state in M corresponds to a pair of states from M_1 and M_2: $\Sigma = \Sigma_1 \times \Sigma_2$. The start state of M corresponds to the start states of M_1 and M_2: $St = (St_1, St_2)$. The pairing of states and transitions then obey the following conditions $\delta(E, (S_i, T_j)) = (S_m, T_n)$ where $\delta_1(E, S_i) = S_m$ and $\delta_2(E, T_j) = T_n$. (S_i, T_j) is accepting for M iff S_i is accepting for M_1 and T_j is accepting for M_2: $Acc = Acc_1 \times Acc_2$.

$\sim e_1$. Build a docm for recognizing e_1. Change all accepting states into non-accepting states and vice versa (except for the start state which remains the same).

$e_1 \sqcup e_2$. Similar to $e_1 \parallel e_2$, but now (S_i, T_j) is accepting for M iff S_i is accepting for M_1 or T_j is accepting for M_2.

$e_1 ; e_2$. Build a docm M_1 for recognizing e_1. Construct a new accept state for M_1 called S_a and $\delta(E, S_a) = S_a$ (for any set E of primitive events). For each accepting state $S_i \neq S_a$ in M_1, make it non accepting and alter the transitions such that $\delta(E, S_i) = S_a$ for any set E of primitive events. Call the new machine M_1'. Construct a docm M_2 for recognizing M_2. Now apply the "product" construction (used above for recognizing $e_1 \parallel e_2$) on M_1' and M_2. Intuitively, the state S_a has a "delaying" effect, the machine M will reach an accepting state if M_2 is in an accepting state (i.e., e_2 occurs now), and M_1 was in an accepting state before (i.e., e_1 occurred in the past).

$e_1 ;_L e_2$. Build docm $M_1 = (\Sigma_1, Acc_1, St_1, L, \delta_1)$ and $M_2 = (\Sigma_2, Acc_2, St_2, L, \delta_2)$ for recognizing e_1 and e_2, respectively. Let Σ_1^+ be a set of the same cardinality as Σ_1 such that the two sets are disjoint. We denote the bijection from Σ to Σ^+ by $^+$. This is the only stage of the construction where we need the counter c. The definition of the new machine $M = (\Sigma, Acc, St, L, \delta)$ is a modification of the "product" construction. We define $\Sigma = (\Sigma_1 \cup \Sigma_1^+) \times \Sigma_2$, $St = (St_1, St_2)$ and $Acc = \{(S^+, T) : T \in Acc_2\}$. Initially, we let the counter c be 0. The definition of the transition function δ is as follows. In all cases below we assume that $\delta_1(S_i) = S_m$ and $\delta_2(T_j) = T_n$. We have

$$\delta(E, (S_i, T_j), c) = \begin{cases} ((S_m^+, T_n), c+1) & \text{if } S_m \in Acc_1 \text{ and } T_n \notin Acc_2 \\ ((S_m, T_n), c+1) & \text{if } S_m \in Acc_1, T_n \in Acc_2 \text{ and } c = 0 \\ ((S_m^+, T_n), c) & \text{if } S_m \in Acc_1, T_n \in Acc_2 \text{ and } c > 1 \\ ((S_m, T_n), c) & \text{if } S_m \notin Acc_1, T_n \in Acc_2 \text{ and } c = 0 \\ ((S_m^+, T_n), c-1) & \text{if } S_m \notin Acc_1, T_n \in Acc_2 \text{ and } c > 0 \\ ((S_m, T_n), c) & \text{if } S_m \notin Acc_1, T_n \notin Acc_2 \text{ and } c = 0 \\ ((S_m^+, T_n), c) & \text{if } S_m \notin Acc_1, T_n \notin Acc_2 \text{ and } c > 0; \end{cases}$$

and

$$\delta(E, (S_i^+, T_j), c) = \begin{cases} ((S_m^+, T_n), c+1) & \text{if } S_m \in Acc_1 \text{ and } T_n \notin Acc_2 \\ ((S_m^+, T_n), c) & \text{if } S_m \in Acc_1, T_n \in Acc_2 \text{ and } c > 0 \\ ((S_m, T_n), c+1) & \text{if } S_m \in Acc_1, T_n \in Acc_2 \text{ and } c = 0 \\ ((S_m, T_n), c) & \text{if } S_m \notin Acc_1 \text{ and } c = 0 \\ ((S_m^+, T_n), c) & \text{if } S_m \notin Acc_1, T_n \notin Acc_2 \text{ and } c > 0 \\ ((S_m^+, T_n), c-1) & \text{if } S_m \notin Acc_1, T_n \in Acc_2 \text{ and } c > 0. \end{cases}$$

$e_1 ;_{MR} e_2$ and $e_1 ;_C e_2$. These are similar to $e_1 ; e_2$. Also, the proof would be virtually identical if $;_F$ had been chosen instead of $;_L$.

Now it is routine to check that the machine M we built for the event q has the required property: an n-long string of sets of primitive events is accepted iff the corresponding initial segment $\mathfrak{N}_n$ under the obvious evaluation of primitive events satisfies q. Further, the size of M is double exponential in terms of the size of q. Thus the above decision procedure works in triple exponential time. □

Corollary 1. *Let q be an event query in the algebra $\mathcal{E}_2$, such that it uses one instance of either $;_F$ or $;_L$. Then satisfiability of q is decidable.*

We now examine the problem of implication for event queries of the above type. The problem now becomes undecidable. Intuitively, this is because the individual queries can use their $;_L$ or $;_F$ operation in a co-operative fashion to simulate a machine with two counters.

Theorem 4. *Let q_1 and q_2 be event queries in the algebra $\mathcal{E}_2$ where each uses one instance of either $;_F$ or $;_L$. Then the problem of whether $q_1 \Rightarrow q_2$ is undecidable.*

Proof. We present a proof for the LIFO consumption semantics, it is virtually identical for FIFO. Given a Minsky machine [8] (abbreviated MM and defined below), we define a set of primitive and complex events used by an event query q, which checks whether the event history is a faithful representation of the computation of the MM. q is satisfiable iff the MM terminates. It also has the property that it can be rewritten in the form $q = q_1 \|\sim q_2$ and is thus satisfiable iff $\neg(q_1 \Rightarrow q_2)$. Thus, we are able to define two queries q_1 and q_2 (each using one instance of LIFO), which depend on the MM specification, and $q_1 \Rightarrow q_2$ iff the Minsky machine terminates — a problem which is undecidable.

An MM [8] is a sequence of n instructions $S_0 : com_0; S_1 : com_1; \ldots ; S_n : com_n$ where each instruction com_i has one of the following forms

$$S_i : c_1 = c_1 + 1; goto\ S_j$$
$$S_i : c_2 = c_2 + 1; goto\ S_j$$
$$S_i : if\ c_1 = 0\ goto\ S_j\ else\ c_1 = c_1 - 1; goto\ S_k$$
$$S_i : if\ c_2 = 0\ goto\ S_j\ else\ c_2 = c_2 - 1; goto\ S_k$$

where c_1 and c_2 are both counters. Execution begins at instruction S_0, with c_1 and c_2 initialised to zero. Thereafter, the machine executes the given instruction, appropriately changes the value of the given counter and jumps to the directed instruction. The machine halts iff it reaches instruction S_n. So, the computation of the machine can be understood as a (possibly infinite sequence) $S_{i_1}, S_{i_2}, \ldots$. We now define a number of events to ensure that the event history is a faithful representation of this sequence (if it is finite).

- For each machine instruction S_i, let e_{S_i} be an event.
- $e_c^1 = e_{push}^1 ;_L e_{pop}^1$ — used for maintaining the value of the 1st counter. Intuitively, e_{push}^1 increases it by one and e_{pop}^1 decreases it by one.
- $e_c^2 = e_{push}^2 ;_L e_{pop}^2$ — used for maintaining the value of the second counter.
- $e_{bad1}, e_{bad2}, e_{BAD1}, e_{BAD2}$ — events that occur if the history somehow deviates from the MM computation. Each uses multiple definitions and so they should in fact be interpreted as the disjunction of their individual definitions.
- e_{any} — this event is true at any point in the history. It can be written as the disjunction of all defined primitive events.
- $e_{first} = e_{any} \|\sim (e_{any}; e_{any})$ — the first event in the history.

We also rely on the following fact to guarantee correctness of the counters.

The event $e_c^1 = e_{push}^1 ;_L e_{pop}^1$ occurs iff the number of unconsumed instances of e_{push}^1 was > 0 when e_{pop}^1 occurred. Similarly for $e_c^2 = e_{push}^2 ;_L e_{pop}^2$.

Each point of the history corresponds to the machine being in a certain state.

$$e_{bad1} = e_{any} \|\sim (e_{S_1} \sqcup e_{S_2} \sqcup \ldots \sqcup e_{S_n})$$
$$e_{bad1} = e_{S_i} \| e_{S_j} \quad (\forall i, j \in \{1, \ldots, n\}, i \neq j)$$

Let N be the set of all instruction numbers, I_1 (I_2) be the set of all instruction numbers where counter one (two) is increased. Then for each $i \in I_1, j \in (N \setminus I_1)$, $a \in I_2, b \in (N \setminus I_2)$, we define

$$e_{bad1} = (e_{S_i} \|\sim e_{push}^1) \sqcup (e_{S_j} \| e_{push}^1)$$
$$e_{bad2} = (e_{S_a} \|\sim e_{push}^2) \sqcup (e_{S_b} \| e_{push}^2).$$

Let D_1 be the set of all instruction numbers where counter one is tested by an *if*-statement and D_2 be the set of all instruction numbers where counter 2 is tested by an *if*-statement. Each such test is simulated by an e_{pop}^1 or e_{pop}^2 event occurring. So, for each $i \in D_1, j \in (N \setminus D_1), a \in D_2, b \in (N \setminus D_2)$ we define

$$e_{bad1} = (e_{S_i} \|\sim e_{pop}^1) \sqcup (e_{S_j} \| e_{pop}^1)$$
$$e_{bad2} = (e_{S_a} \|\sim e_{pop}^2) \sqcup (e_{S_b} \| e_{pop}^2).$$

We need to check that the correct 'gotos' of the machine are followed. Firstly:

$$e_{bad1} = e_{first} \|\sim e_{S_0}.$$

We will use the abbreviation $succ(e_a)$ as shorthand for the next event immediately following the occurrence of e_a: $succ(e_a) \equiv e_a ;_{MR} e_{any}$. For an instruction of the form $S_i : c_i = c_i + 1; goto\ S_j$ we define

$$e_{bad1} = succ(e_{S_i}) \|\sim e_{S_j}$$

For an instruction of the form $S_i : if\ c_1 = 0\ goto\ S_j\ else\ c_1 = c_1 - 1; goto\ S_k$

$$e_{bad1} = succ(e_{S_i} \|\sim e_c^1) \|\sim e_{S_j}$$
$$e_{bad1} = succ(e_{S_i} \| e_c^1) \|\sim e_{S_k}.$$

Lastly, we ensure that if an e_{bad1} or e_{bad2} occurs at some point in the history, then it will also occur if and when the halt instruction is reached.

$$e_{BAD1} = e_{bad1} ; e_{S_n}$$
$$e_{BAD2} = e_{bad2} ; e_{S_n}$$

We can now define the query q by

$$q = (e_{S_n} \|\sim e_{BAD1} \|\sim e_{BAD2}) = (q_1 \|\sim q_2)$$

where $q_1 = e_{S_n} \|\sim e_{BAD1}$ and $q_2 = e_{BAD2}$. Observe that q_1 doesn't depend on the event e_c^2 and q_2 doesn't depend on the event e_c^1. Thus, they each use exactly one instance of the LIFO operator. □

Corollary 2. *Let q_1 be an event query in the event algebra $\mathcal{E}_2$ using two instances of either $;_F$ or $;_L$. Let q_2 be an event query written in $\mathcal{E}_1$. Then satisfiability of q_1 is undecidable and the problem of whether $q_1 \Leftrightarrow q_2$ is undecidable.*

5   Summary and Future Work

We have defined a simple core event language and defined a formal mechanism for specifying event consumption policies. We identified a class of policies for which equivalence and implication is in PSPACE. For more elaborate policies, we presented a class of event queries for which equivalence was decidable, provided each query used the policy only once. We then showed how this then became undecidable when testing for implication. In our future work, we plan to investigate a) the use of our results for understanding theories of natural numbers in fragments of first-order logic with order (e.g., the guarded fragment); b) the use of temporal logics such as CTL for expressing properties of interest in event languages and for active databases generally.

References

1. S. Chakravarthy, V. Krishnaprasad, E. Anwar, and S.-K. Kim. Composite events for active databases: semantics, contexts and detection. In *20th International Conference on Very Large Data Bases*, pages 606–617, 1994.
2. J. Chomicki and D. Toman. Implementing temporal integrity constraints using an active dbms. *IEEE TKDE*, 7(4):566–581, 1995.
3. O. Diaz, N.W. Paton, and J. Iturrioz. Formalizing and validating behavioral models through the event calculus. *Information Systems*, 23(3–4):179–196, 1998.
4. S. Gatziu and K. Dittrich. Detecting composite events in active database systems using Petri nets. In *Proceedings of the 4th International Workshop on Research Issues in Data Engineering*, pages 2–9, Houston, Texas, 1994.
5. N. Gehani, H. V. Jagadish, and O. Shmueli. Composite event specification in active databases: Model and implementation. In *VLDB'92*, pages 327–338, 1992.
6. A. Geppert and K. Dittrich. Performance assessment. In N. Paton, editor, *Active Rules in Database Systems*, pages 103–123. Springer–Verlag, 1999.
7. I. Hodkinson. On Gabbay's temporal fixed point operator. *Journal of Theoretical Computer Science*, 139:1–25, 1995.
8. M. Minsky. *Computation: Finite and Infinite Machines*. Prentice Hall, 1967.
9. I. Mirbel, B. Pernici, T. Sellis, S. Tserkezoglou, and M. Vazirgiannis. Checking temporal integrity of interactive multimedia documents. *The VLDB Journal*, 9(2):111–130, 2000.
10. I. Motakis and C. Zaniolo. Formal semantics for composite temporal events in active database rules. *Journal of Systems Integration*, 7(3–4):291–325, 1997.
11. N. Paton, editor. *Active Rules in Database Systems*. Springer-Verlag, 1999.
12. A. Sistla and E. Clark. Complexity of propositional linear temporal logics. *Journal of the ACM*, 32:733–749, 1985.
13. A. P. Sistla and O. Wolfson. Temporal triggers in active databases. *IEEE Transaction on KNowledge and Data Engineering*, 7(3):471–486, 1995.
14. L. G. Valiant and Paterson M. S. Deterministic one-counter automata. *Journal of Computer and System Sciences*, 10(3):340–250, 1975.
15. D. Zimmer and R. Unland. On the semantics of complex events in active database management systems. In *ICDE'99*, pages 392–399, 1999.

A Theory of Transactions on Recoverable Search Trees

Seppo Sippu[1] and Eljas Soisalon-Soininen[2]

[1] Department of Computer Science, University of Helsinki,
P. O. Box 26 (Teollisuuskatu 23), FIN–00014 University of Helsinki, Finland
sippu@cs.helsinki.fi
[2] Department of Computer Science and Engineering, Helsinki University of
Technology, Konemiehentie 2, FIN–02015 HUT, Finland
ess@cs.hut.fi

Abstract. We consider transactions running on a database that consists of records with unique totally-ordered keys and is organized as a sparse primary search tree such as a B-tree index on disk storage. We extend the classical read-write model of transactions by considering inserts, deletes and key-range scans and by distinguishing between four types of transaction states: forward-rolling, committed, backward-rolling, and rolled-back transactions. A search-tree transaction is modelled as a two-level transaction containing structure modifications as open nested subtransactions that can commit even though the parent transaction aborts. Isolation conditions are defined for search-tree transactions with nested structure modifications that guarantee the structural consistency of the search tree, a required isolation level (including phantom prevention) for database operations, and recoverability for structure modifications and database operations.

1 Introduction

The classical theory of concurrency control and recovery [4] defines transactions as strings of abstract read and write operations. This model is inadequate for describing transactions on index structures in which data items are identified with ordered keys and in which inserts, deletes, and key-range scans are important operations. Most importantly, the interplay of the logical database operations and the physical, page-level actions is not discussed in the theoretical database literature in such a detail that would allow for a rigorous analysis of practical database algorithms. This is in contrast to the fact that key-range locking, page latching and physiological logging of record-level operations on pages are a standard in industrial-strength database systems [5,6,12,13,14,15].

Also the actions done by an aborted transaction in its backward-rolling phase, or the actions needed at restart recovery when both forward-rolling and backward-rolling transactions are present, are not adequately treated in the formal transaction models. In [1,17,19] general recoverability results are derived for extended transaction models by treating an aborted transaction as a string

J. Van den Bussche and V. Vianu (Eds.): ICDT 2001, LNCS 1973, pp. 83–98, 2001.
© Springer-Verlag Berlin Heidelberg 2001

$\alpha\alpha^{-1}$, where the prefix α consists of reads and writes (forming the forward-rolling phase), and the suffix α^{-1} is the reversed string of undos of the writes in α (forming the backward-rolling phase), thus capturing the idea of logical undos of database operations. In this paper we present a transaction model that makes explicit the notions of forward-rolling, committed, backward-rolling, and rolled-back transactions. Our model allows for recovery aspects to be presented in a unified manner, covering aborts of single transactions during normal processing, as well as the actions needed at restart recovery after a system failure for a transaction in any of the above four states.

In our model, the logical database is assumed to consist of records with unique keys taken from a totally ordered domain. The database operations include update operations of the forms "insert a record with key x" and "delete the record with key x", and retrieval operations of the form "retrieve the record with the least key $x \geq a$ (or $x > a$)", which allow a key range to be scanned in ascending key order, simulating an SQL cursor. A database transaction can contain any number of these operations. Isolation aspects are discussed following the approach of [3], where different isolation anomalies are defined and analyzed. The definitions of dirty writes, dirty reads, unrepeatable (or fuzzy) reads, and phantoms are adapted to the model. Isolation anomalies are prevented by key-range locking [5] (also called key-value locking in [12,13]).

We assume that our database is organized physically as a primary search-tree structure such as a B-tree [2] or a B-link-tree [7,16] whose nodes are disk pages. The non-leaf pages (or index pages) store router information (index terms), while the leaf pages (or data pages) store database items (data terms). Algorithms on search trees can achieve more concurrency than would be possible if strict conflict serializability were required for accesses of index terms as well as for accesses of data terms. This is because an internal database algorithm can exploit the fact that many valid search-tree states represent one database state [2,7,16,18]. Accordingly, all index-management algorithms in industrial-strength database management systems allow nonserializable histories as regards read and write accesses on index pages. A shared latch held on an index page when searching for a key is released as soon as the next page in the search path has been latched, and exclusive latches held on pages involved in a structure modification such as a page split or merge are released as soon as the structure modification is complete [5,9,10,11,12,13,14,15].

Following [9], we model a search-tree transaction as a two-level transaction that in its higher or database level contains database operations, that is, data-term retrievals, inserts and deletes on leaf pages of the tree, together with index-term retrievals needed to locate the leaf pages. In its lower or structure-modification level, all update operations that change the structure of the tree are grouped into one or more lower-level or structure-modification transactions. When the process that is generating a higher-level transaction finds that a change (such as a page split) in the structure of the tree is needed, it starts executing a lower-level transaction to do the structure modification, and when that is done (committed), the execution of the higher-level transaction is continued. It is the responsibility of the designer of the search-tree algorithms to determine the boundaries of the lower-level transactions and to guarantee that each such transaction, when run alone in the absence of failures on a structurally consistent search tree, always produces a structurally consistent search tree as a result. The commit of a structure-modification subtransaction is independent of the outcome of the parent search-tree transaction, so that once a subtransaction has committed it will not be undone even if its parent aborts. On the other hand, the abort of a subtransaction will also imply the abort of the parent. Thus, the model is a variant of the "open nested" transaction model, see e.g. [5,20].

We derive isolation conditions for search-tree operations and structure modifications that guarantee that a history of search-tree transactions with nested structure-modification transactions preserves the consistency of both the logical and physical database. We also show that, given a history $\hat{H}$ of database transactions on a database D where the transactions are sufficiently isolated and $\hat{H}$ can be run on D, then for any structurally consistent search tree B that represents D there exists a history H of isolated search-tree transactions with nested structure-modification transactions on B that implements $\hat{H}$, that is, maps the logical database operations (key inserts, deletes and retrievals) into physiological operations (data-term inserts, deletes and retrievals) on leaf pages of the search tree such that the tree produced by running H on B is structurally consistent and represents the database produced by running $\hat{H}$ on D.

The isolation conditions can be enforced by standard key-range locking and page latching protocols, and they also guarantee a recoverability property that allows an ARIES-based [14] algorithm to be used for restart recovery. For structure modifications, both redo and undo recovery is physiological [5], that is, page-oriented. For database updates, redo recovery is physiological, but undo recovery can also be logical, so that the undo of a key insert involves a traversal down the tree in order to locate the page in which the key currently resides, unless the key is still found in the same page into which it was originally inserted, in which case the update can be undone physiologically [9,12,13,15].

2   Database Operations and Transactions

We assume that our database D consists of *database records* of the form (x, v), where x is the *key* of the record and v is the *value* of the record. Keys are unique, and there is a total order, $\leq$, among the keys. The least key is denoted by $-\infty$ and the greatest key is denoted by ∞. We assume that the keys $-\infty$ and ∞ do not appear in database records; they can only appear in search-tree index terms.

In normal transaction processing, a *database transaction* can be in one of the following four states: forward-rolling, committed, backward-rolling, or rolled-back. A *forward-rolling transaction* is a string of the form $b\alpha$, where b denotes the *begin* operation and α is a string of *database operations*. In this paper we consider the following set of database operations (cf. [12,13,15]):

1) $r[x, \theta z, v]$: *retrieve* the first matching record (x, v). Given a key z, find the least key x and the associated value v such that $x \ \theta \ z$ and the record (x, v) is

in the database. Here θ is one of the comparison operators ">" or ">". We also say that the operation *reads the key range* $[z, x]$ (if θ is ">") or $(z, x]$ (if θ is ">").

2) $n[x, v]$: *insert* a new record (x, v). Given a key x and a value v such that x does not appear in the database, insert the record (x, v) into the database.

3) $d[x, v]$: *delete* the record with key x. Given a key x in the database, delete the record, (x, v), with key x from the database.

A *committed transaction* is of the form $b\alpha c$, where $b\alpha$ is a forward-rolling transaction and c denotes the *commit* operation. An *aborted transaction* is one that contains the *abort* operation, a. A *backward-rolling transaction* is an aborted transaction of the form $b\alpha\beta a\beta^{-1}$, where $b\alpha\beta$ is a forward-rolling transaction and β^{-1} is the inverse of β (defined below). The string $\alpha\beta$ is called the *forward-rolling phase*, and the string β^{-1} the *backward-rolling phase*, of the transaction.

The *inverse* β^{-1} of an operation string β is defined inductively as follows. For the empty operation string, ϵ, the inverse ϵ^{-1} is defined as ϵ. The inverse $(\beta o)^{-1}$ of a non-empty operation string βo, where o is a single operation, is defined as $o^{-1}\beta^{-1}$, where o^{-1} denotes the *inverse* of operation o. The inverses for our set of database operations are defined by (cf. [1,17,19]): (1) $r^{-1}[x, \theta z, v] = \epsilon$; (2) $n^{-1}[x, v] = d[x, v]$; (3) $d^{-1}[x, v] = n[x, v]$.

A backward-rolling transaction $b\alpha\beta a\beta^{-1}$ thus denotes an aborted transaction that has *undone* a suffix, β, of its forward-rolling phase, while the prefix, α, is still not undone. An aborted transaction of the form $b\alpha a\alpha^{-1}c$ is a *rolled-back transaction* or an aborted transaction that has *completed its rollback*. Thus we use the operation name c to denote the completion of the rollback of an aborted transaction as well as the commit of a committed transaction. A forward-rolling or a backward-rolling transaction is called an *active transaction*.

For example, $br[x, \geq z, v]d[x, v]n[x, v+t]ad[x, v+t]n[x, v]c$, where z and t are constants and x and v are free variables, is a rolled-back aborted transaction which in its forward-rolling phase retrieves the record, (x, v), with the least key $x \geq z$ (thus reading the key range $[z, x]$) and increases the value for that record by t and which in its backward-rolling phase undoes its updates.

An operation o, an operation string α, or a transaction T, is *ground*, if it contains no free variables. A ground operation string represents a specific execution of the operation string. A *history* for a set of ground transactions is a string H in the shuffle of those transactions. H is a *complete history* if all its transactions are committed or rolled-back.

For a forward-rolling transaction $b\alpha$, the string $a\alpha^{-1}c$ is the *completion string*, and $b\alpha a\alpha^{-1}c$ the *completed transaction*. For the backward-rolling transaction $b\alpha\beta a\beta^{-1}$, the string $\alpha^{-1}c$ is the *completion string*, and $b\alpha\beta a\beta^{-1}\alpha^{-1}c$ the *completed transaction*. A *completion string* γ for an incomplete history H is any string in the shuffle of the completion strings of all the active transactions in H; the complete history $H\gamma$ is a *completed history* for H.

Let D be a database. We define when a ground operation or operation string *can be run on* D and what is the *database produced*. Any retrieval operation $r[x, \theta z, v]$ can always be run on D, and so can the operations b, c, and a; the database produced is D. If D does not contain a record with key x, an insert operation $n[x, v]$ can be run on D and produces $D \cup \{(x, v)\}$. If D contains (x, v), the delete operation $d[x, v]$ can be run on D and produces $D \setminus \{(x, v)\}$. The empty string ϵ can be run on D and produces D. If an operation string α can be run on D and produces D' and an operation o can be run on D' and produces D'', then the string αo can be run on D and produces D''.

3 Isolation of Database Transactions

In this section we give simple isolation conditions that can be enforced by standard key-range locking and that guarantee both execution correctness (serializability) and recoverability of transaction histories. In [3], the SQL isolation levels are analyzed and different *isolation anomalies*, such as dirty writes, dirty reads, unrepeatable (or fuzzy) reads, and phantoms, are defined for a non-serial history of transactions. For our model, we redefine dirty writes, dirty reads and unrepeatable reads so as to encompass also different types of phantoms.

Let $H = \alpha\beta$ be a history and T a transaction of H such that the begin-transaction operation b of T is contained in α. Let T' be the prefix of T contained in α. We say that T is *forward-rolling, committed, backward-rolling, rolled-back*, or *active, in α*, if T' is forward-rolling, committed, backward-rolling, rolled-back, or active, respectively.

A key x inserted or deleted in α has an *uncommitted update* by T in α if one of the following three statements holds: (1) T is forward-rolling in α and the last update (i.e., insert or delete) on x in α is by T; (2) T is backward-rolling in α and the last update on x in α is by the forward-rolling phase of T (which update thus has not yet been undone); (3) T is backward-rolling in α and the last update on x in α is an inverse operation $o^{-1}[x]$ by T where the corresponding forward operation $o[x]$ by T is not the first update on x by T (so that there remain updates on x by T that have not yet been undone). Once the first update on x in the forward-rolling phase of T has been undone, we regard x as committed, because in our transaction model the inverse operations done in the backward-rolling phase are never undone [12,13,14].

Let o_i be a database operation, α, β and γ operation strings, and $H = \alpha o_i \beta \gamma$ a history containing any number of forward-rolling, committed, backward-rolling, and rolled-back transactions. Further let T_i and T_j be two distinct transactions of H.

1) o_i is a *dirty write* on key x by T_i in H if o_i is an update by T_i on x, where x has an uncommitted update by T_j in α.

2) o_i is a *dirty read* by T_i in H if o_i is a retrieval operation that reads a key range containing some key x that has an uncommitted update by T_j in α.

3) o_i is an *unrepeatable read* by T_i in H if o_i is a retrieval operation that reads a key range containing some key x, T_i is forward-rolling in $\alpha o_i \beta$, and the first operation in γ is an update on x by T_j. Note that o_i is not considered unrepeatable in the case that T_i is backward-rolling in $\alpha o_i \beta$, because T_i will

eventually undo all its updates, including those possibly based on the retrieved record.

When given an incomplete history H describing the state of transaction processing at the moment of a system crash, we should be able to roll back all the forward-rolling transactions and complete the rollback of all the backward-rolling transactions in H. In other words, we should find a completed history $H\gamma$ that can be run on every database on which H can be run. Such a history does not necessarily exist at all if H is non-strict [4], that is, contains dirty writes by committed transactions. On the other hand, if H contains no dirty writes at all, then for any completion string γ of H, the completed history $H\gamma$ contains no dirty writes and can be run on every database on which H can be run. Thus, each active transaction in H can be rolled back independently of other active transactions. It is also easy to see that if H contains no dirty writes, dirty reads or unrepeatable reads, then any completed history $H\gamma$ is also free of those anomalies and is conflict-equivalent to some serial history of the transactions of $H\gamma$ and equivalent to (i.e., produces the same database as) some serial history of the committed transactions of H. Such a history H is also prefix-reducible, forward-safe and backward-safe [1,17,19].

Using the standard *key-range locking protocol* [5,12,13], all of the above anomalies can be avoided. In this protocol, transactions acquire in their forward-rolling phase commit-duration X-locks on inserted keys and on the next keys of deleted keys, short-duration X-locks on deleted keys and on the next keys of inserted keys, and commit-duration S-locks on retrieved keys. Short-duration locks are held only for the time the operation is being performed. Commit-duration X-locks are released after the transaction has committed or completed its rollback. Commit-duration S-locks can be released after the transaction has committed or aborted. No additional locks are acquired for operations done in the backward-rolling phase of aborted transactions: an inverse operation $o^{-1}[x]$ is performed under the protection of the commit-duration X-lock acquired for the corresponding forward operation $o[x]$. Thus we have:

Lemma 1. If a history H can be run on a database D under the key-range locking protocol, then for any completion string γ for H, the completed history $H\gamma$ can be run on D under the key-range locking protocol. □

4   Search-Tree Operations and Transactions

We assume that our search trees are similar to B-trees [2] or B-link-trees [7,16]. In a B-tree, each child node is directly accessible from its parent node, while in a B-link-tree some children (except the eldest) may only be accessed via a side link from the next elder sibling. In a B-tree, only the leaf nodes are sideways linked from left to right (to allow efficient key-range scans, cf. [12,13,15]), while in a B-link-tree there is a left-to-right side-link chain on every level of the tree. We assume the tree is used as a sparse index to the database, so that the database records are directly stored in the leaf nodes.

Formally, a *search tree* is an array $B[0, \ldots, N]$ of *disk pages* $B[p]$ indexed by unique *page numbers* $p = 0, \ldots, N$. The page $B[p]$ with number p is called page p, for short. Each page (other than page 0) is labelled either *allocated*, in which case it is part of the tree structure, or *deallocated* otherwise. Page 0 is assumed to contain a *storage map* (a bit vector) that indicates which pages are allocated and which are deallocated. Page 1, the *root*, is always allocated. The allocated pages form a tree rooted at 1.

Each page p *covers* a half-open range of keys x, low-key$(p) \leq x <$ high-key(p). For each level of the tree, the sequence $p_1, \ldots, p_n$ of pages on that level must form a partition of the key space $(-\infty, \infty)$. Accordingly, on each level, the low key of the first (or leftmost) page is $-\infty$, the high key of the last (or rightmost) page is ∞, and high-key$(p_i) =$ low-key(p_{i+1}), for $i = 1, \ldots, n-1$.

An allocated page is an index page or a data page. An *index page* p is a non-leaf page and it contains *index terms* of the form (x, q), where x is a key, q is a page number, low-key$(p) \leq x \leq$ high-key(p), and (if $x < \infty$) $x =$ low-key(q). Index terms (x, q) with $x <$ high-key(p) are *child terms*, and the term (x, q) with $x =$ high-key(p) (if present) is the *high-key term*. The high-key term is present in a B-link-tree. The page number q in the high-key term is that of next(p), the page next to p on the same level (when $x < \infty$). A *data page* p is a leaf page and always contains the high-key term and a set of *data terms* (x, v) with low-key(p) $\leq x <$ high-key(p). The set of data terms in the data pages of a search tree B is called the *database represented by* B and denoted by db(B).

A search tree is *structurally consistent* if it satisfies the above definition and any additional conditions required by the specific tree type in question, such as B-tree balance conditions (minimum fill factor for pages, etc).

A search-tree transaction can contain the following *search-tree operations*.

1) $r[p, x, \theta z, v]$: given a data page p and a key $z \geq$ low-key(p), retrieve from p the term (x, v) with the least key $x \, \theta \, z$ (if $z <$ high-key(p)) or the high-key term (x, v) (if $z \geq$ high-key(p)). When the least key $x \, \theta \, z$ is not greater than the key of the last data term in p, the operation corresponds to database transaction operation $r[x, \theta z, v]$; the difference is that the search-tree operation requires a page p onto which the operation is applied. The operation is then called a *data-term retrieval* on page p. Otherwise, the operation retrieves the high-key term of p, and the operation is then called an *index-term retrieval* on p.

2) $r[p, x, \theta z, q]$: given an index page p and a key $z \geq$ low-key(p), retrieve from p the index term (x, q) with the least key $x \, \theta \, z$ (if $z <$ high-key(p)) or the high-key term (x, q) (if $z \geq$ high-key(p)). The operation is used to traverse from one page to another in the search tree. The operation is called an *index-term retrieval on p*.

3) $n[p, x, v]$: given a data page p, a key x and a value v such that low-key(p) $\leq x <$ high-key(p) and p does not contain a data term with key x and p can accommodate (x, v), insert the data term (x, v) into p. The operation corresponds to database transaction operation $n[x, v]$.

4) $d[p, x, v]$: given a data page p and a key x such that p contains a data term, (x, v), with key x, and p will not underflow if (x, v) is deleted from p, delete (x, v)

from p. The operation corresponds to database transaction operation $d[x, v]$. — We say that $n[p, x, v]$ and $d[p, x, v]$ are *data-term updates on p*.

Operations 1 to 4 above do not change the structure of the tree. The structure can be changed by operations 5 to 9 below, which are called *structure modifications* (or *sm's*, for short).

5) $n[p, t]$: allocate a new page p of type $t = i$ (for index page) or $t = d$ (for data page).

6) $d[p, t]$: deallocate an empty page p. Operations 5 and 6 also update the storage map page 0.

7) $n[p, x, q]$: insert a new index term (x, q) into an index page p that can accommodate (x, q).

8) $d[p, x, q]$: delete an index term (x, q) from an index page p. Operations 7 and 8 are called *index-term updates on p*.

9) $m[p, x, v, p']$: move an index or data term (x, v) from page p to a non-full page p'. — We say that $n[p, t]$ and $d[p, t]$ are *sm's on* pages 0 and p and that $n[p, x, q]$ and $d[p, x, q]$ are *sm's on* p and that $m[p, x, v, p']$ is an *sm on* p and p'.

For example, a page split in a B-link-tree could be implemented by sm's as follows. Assume that page p is found to be full. First, $n[p', t]$ is used to allocate a new page p'. Then $m[p, x, v, p']$ is used to move the upper half of the terms (including the high-key term) from page p to page p', moving one term (x, v) at a time. Finally a new high-key term (x', p') is inserted into p by the operation $n[p, x', p']$, where x' is the least key in p'.

In a natural way we can define when a ground index-term retrieval, a data-term retrieval, data-term update, an sm, or any string of such operations *can be run on* a given search tree B and what is the search tree thus produced. For an operation to be runnable, all the stated preconditions for that operation must be satisfied. For example, a ground operation $d[p, t]$ can be run on B if and only if page p is allocated, empty, and of type t. The search tree produced is obtained from B by marking p as deallocated in the storage-map page 0. Similarly, a ground operation $n[p, x, v]$ can be run on B only if p is a data page with $y \leq x <$ high-key(p) and some index page of B contains the index term (y, p) (indicating that $y = $ low-key(p)). Then if p has room for (x, v) and does not yet contain a term with key x, (x, v) can be inserted into p.

All data-term retrievals and data-term updates have *projections* onto their corresponding database operations: $\pi(r[p, x, \theta z, v]) = r[x, \theta z, v]$; $\pi(n[p, x, v]) = n[x, v]$; $\pi(d[p, x, v]) = d[x, v]$. For index-term retrievals and for all sm's o we set $\pi(o) = \epsilon$. The projection operation π is extended in the natural way to operation strings α: $\pi(\epsilon) = \epsilon$; $\pi(\alpha o) = \pi(\alpha)\pi(o)$.

Lemma 2. Let B be a structurally consistent search tree. If $o[p, \bar{x}]$ is a ground data-term retrieval or update on data page p of B that can be run on B, then $\pi(o[p, \bar{x}]) = o[\bar{x}]$ can be run on db(B). $\square$

For the data-term updates and sm's, *physiological inverses* are defined: $n^{-1}[p, x, v] = d[p, x, v]$; $d^{-1}[p, x, v] = n[p, x, v]$; $n^{-1}[p, t] = d[p, t]$; $d^{-1}[p, t] = n[p', t]$; $n^{-1}[p, x, q] = d[p, x, q]$; $d^{-1}[p, x, q] = n[p, x, q]$; $m^{-1}[p, x, v, p'] = m[p', x, v, p]$. A physiological operation [5] is always applied to a given page, whose number is given as an input argument of the operation. All sm's are always undone physiologically, while a data-term update may be undone either physiologically or logically.

The sm's can only appear in a *structure-modification transaction*, or an *sm transaction*, for short, which is an open transaction nested in a search-tree transaction. An open transaction can commit independently from the outcome (commit or abort) of the parent transaction [5]. This property is essential in allowing sufficient concurrency between search-tree transactions that contain multiple data-term retrievals and updates. Once an sm transaction nested in a search-tree transaction T has been successfully completed, the X-latches on the modified pages can be released so that the pages can be accessed by other transactions while T is still active (and thus may later abort). However, if an sm transaction aborts, then the parent transaction will also be aborted once the sm transaction has been rolled back.

An sm transaction may take one of the forms $b\alpha$, $b\alpha c$, $b\alpha\beta a\beta^{-1}$, or $b\alpha a\alpha^{-1}c$, that is, *forward-rolling, committed, backward-rolling,* or *rolled-back.* Here the forward-rolling operation strings α and β consist of sm's, and α^{-1} and β^{-1} consist of their physiological inverses. A committed sm transaction T is *correct* if, for any structurally consistent search tree on which T can be run, T produces a structurally consistent tree as a result. We assume that a correct sm transaction exists for handling any overflow or underflow situation that might appear.

For example, a page split in a B-tree must be embedded in an sm transaction. When a page split propagates up the tree, due to parent pages in the search path that are full and therefore cannot accommodate the child terms for the new pages created by the splits, then, in a conventional B-tree, the entire series of page splits must be embedded into one sm transaction (a "nested top action" in [12,13,15]). This is necessary because a B-tree is not in a structurally consistent state in the middle of two splits in the series. On the contrary, a B-link-tree is kept consistent between any two splits done on neighboring levels of the tree, thus making possible the design of shorter sm transactions [9,10,11].

Every sm transaction is nested in some higher-level transaction, called a *search-tree transaction*, which is the *parent* of the sm transaction. Let φ be any string over index-term retrievals, data-term retrievals, data-term updates, and committed sm transactions. A search-tree transaction T is *forward-rolling* if it is a string of the form $b\varphi$ or $b\varphi S$, where S is a forward-rolling sm transaction, and *committed* if it is of the form $b\varphi c$. T is *aborted during a structure modification* if it is of the form $b\varphi S$, where S is a backward-rolling sm transaction. T is *backward-rolling* if it is of the form $b\varphi(\epsilon|S_1)a\delta(\epsilon|S_2)$, where S_1 is a rolled-back sm transaction, δ is a string over index-term retrievals, data-term updates, and committed and rolled-back sm transactions and S_2 is a backward-rolling sm transaction such that $\pi(\delta) = \pi(\varphi')^{-1}$, for some suffix φ' of φ. (Here $(\alpha_1|\alpha_2)$ denotes α_1 or α_2.) T is *rolled-back* if it is of the form $b\varphi(\epsilon|S)a\delta c$, where S is a rolled-back sm transaction and δ is a string over index-term retrievals, data-term updates, and committed and rolled-back sm transactions such that $\pi(\delta) = \pi(\varphi)^{-1}$. Note that a logical undo may cause sm transactions to be invoked, and those sm transactions may have to be rolled back should a failure occur during the rollback.

Completion strings and *completed transactions* are defined in analogy with database transactions. For an active sm transaction, the completion string is uniquely defined and consists of the physiological inverses of the sm's, while for an active search-tree transaction we only require that the projection of a completion string on the database operations must give the inverse of the projection of the not-yet-undone portion of the forward-rolling phase.

Let D be a database and $o[\bar{x}]$ (with parameter list $\bar{x}$) a ground retrieval or update on some key x that can be run on D. Let B be a structurally consistent search tree with $\mathrm{db}(B) = D$ and let p be a data page of B. We define that the search-tree operation $o[p, \bar{x}]$ on B is a *physiological implementation* of $o[\bar{x}]$ on B if the list of parameters $p, \bar{x}$ satisfies the preconditions stated above for a data-term retrieval or update o and if $o[p, \bar{x}]$ can be run on B. Thus a data-term retrieval $r[p, x, \theta z, v]$ is a physiological implementation of $r[x, \theta z, v]$ if low-key$(p) \leq z$, $x <$ high-key(p), and (x, v) is the data term in p with the least key $x \theta z$. A data-term insert $n[p, x, v]$ is a physiological implementation of $n[x, v]$ if low-key$(p) \leq x <$ high-key(p), p contains no data term with key x, and p has room for (x, v).

Physiological implementations of operations can be used, if possible, when previous operations of the search-tree transaction provide good guesses of the data page p on which the next operation will go. For example, in implementing a string of retrievals $r[x_1, \geq x_0, v_1]$, $r[x_2, > x_1, v_2]$, the two data terms to be retrieved most probably reside in the same page p, so that when p has been located by a root-to-leaf traversal in search for the key x_0 and (x_1, v_1) has been retrieved from p and p has been unlatched, the page number of p is remembered and a physical implementation of the latter retrieval is tried by relatching p and (if this succeeds) by examining the contents of p in order to find out if p indeed is the page on which the retrieval should be run.

Clearly, a physiological implementation does not always exist. A data page p may be too full to accommodate an insert or too underfull to allow a delete. In the case of a retrieval $r[x, \theta z, v]$ the data page p that covers the key z may not be the one that holds (x, v), so that the side link to the next page p' must be followed, and the search-tree operation used to retrieve (x, v) will take the form $r[p', x, \geq z', v]$, for $z' = $ low-key$(p') > z$.

The definition of a structurally consistent search tree B with $\mathrm{db}(B) = D$ implies that for any retrieval $r[x, \theta z, v]$ that can be run on D there is a search-tree operation string of the form

$$\gamma = r[p_1, x_1, \theta_1 z_1, p_2] r[p_2, x_2, \theta_2 z_2, p_3] \ldots r[p_n, x_n, \theta_n z_n, p_{n+1}] r[p_{n+1}, x, \theta' z', v]$$

that can be run on B. Here p_1 is the root of the tree, $r[p_i, x_i, \theta_i z_i, p_{i+1}]$ is an index-term retrieval, $i = 1, \ldots, n$ ($n \geq 0$), and $r[p_{n+1}, x, \theta' z', v]$ is a data-term retrieval. Also, if $z = z'$ then $\theta = \theta'$; else $z < z'$, θ' is "$\geq$" and $\mathrm{db}(B)$ contains no key y with $z < y < z'$. We call γ a *logical implementation* of $r[x, \theta z, v]$ on B.

For an update $o[x, v]$, $o \in \{n, d\}$, that can be run on $D = \mathrm{db}(B)$, there exists a *logical implementation on B* of the form $\alpha o[p, x, v]\beta$ that can be run on B. Here p is a data page of B, and α and β consist of index-term retrievals and correct committed sm transactions. Note that this general form captures strategies in which page splits or merges are performed bottom-up, as well as strategies in which they are performed top-down.

For a data-term update $o[p, x, v]$, $o \in \{n, d\}$, a *logical inverse* is any logical implementation $\alpha o^{-1}[p', x, v]\beta$ of $o^{-1}[x, v]$ $(= \pi(o[p, x, v])^{-1})$. Note that a record (x, v) inserted into page p may have moved to page p' by the time the insert is undone. Similarly, the page that covers key x at the time a delete of (x, v) is undone may be different from the page the record was deleted from.

5   Isolation of Search-Tree Transactions

Let T_i and T_j be two search-tree or sm transactions that potentially can run concurrently in a history H, that is, neither is the parent of the other and they are not both sm transactions of the same parent. In the case that both T_i and T_j are search-tree transactions we define *dirty writes*, *dirty reads* and *unrepeatable reads* in the same way as for database transactions taking into account only retrievals and updates of data terms, so that there is an anomaly between T_i and T_j in H if and only if the same anomaly exists between $\pi(T_i)$ and $\pi(T_j)$ in $\pi(H)$. Since search-tree transactions cannot update index pages, no anomalies are defined between operations on index pages by two search-tree transactions.

In the case that one or both of T_i and T_j are sm transactions we have to consider anomalies arising from conflicting accesses to index or data pages. Let H be of the form $\alpha\beta$ and let T be an sm transaction of H. A page p has an *uncommitted structure modification* by T in α if one of the following three statements holds: (1) T is forward-rolling in α and the last sm on p in α is by T; (2) T is backward-rolling in α and the last sm on p in α is by the forward-rolling phase of T; (3) T is backward-rolling in α and the last sm on p in α is the inverse of an sm o on p by T where o (in the forward-rolling phase of T) is not the first sm on p by T. Cf. the definition of an uncommitted update in Section 3.

Now consider the case in which T_i and T_j are both sm transactions of $H = \alpha o_i \beta$, where o_i is an sm on page p by T_i. We define that o_i is a *dirty write* on p by T_i if p has an uncommitted sm by T_j in α. Thus, for example, an insert operation $o_i = n_i[p, x, q]$ on an index page p is a dirty write in H if T_j is forward-rolling in α and the last sm in α on p is $d_j[p, x', q']$, even if $x' \neq x$. Updates on page p by T_i that consume space released by T_j must be prevented, so that p would not overflow when T_i commits but T_j is rolled back [12,13,15]. Note that an sm transaction can only do physiological undo. Also updates by T_i that release space consumed by T_j must be prevented, so that the page would not underflow unexpectedly when T_i commits but T_j is rolled back.

Then consider the case in which T_j is a search-tree transaction and T_i is an sm transaction. T_j can retrieve index and data terms and insert and delete data terms, while T_i can insert and delete index terms, allocate and deallocate empty index and data pages, and move index and data terms. No dirty writes are defined in this case. In particular note that it is not a dirty write if T_i moves a data term inserted by an active T_j. Nor is it a dirty write if T_i deallocates a data page p from which an active T_j has deleted the last data term. No dirty reads are defined, because sm transactions do no reads. Unrepeatable reads appear in the case that T_j retrieves a key range of index terms while traversing down the tree, and then T_i inserts or deletes terms in that range. However, in order that such an anomaly could violate database integrity, T_j should use the retrieved information for updating. Since T_j can only update data terms, and it is reasonable to assume that those updates in no way depend on the particular search path followed, we do not define any anomaly in this case either.

Finally consider the case in which T_j is an sm transaction and T_i is a search-tree transaction of $H = \alpha o_i \beta$, where o_i is an operation by T_i on a page p that has an uncommitted sm by T_j in α. We define that o_i is a *dirty write* on p by T_i if o_i is a data-term update on p. The justification for this anomaly is as for the dirty writes between two sm transactions. We define that o_i is a *dirty read* on p by T_i if o_i is an index-term or data-term retrieval on p. No unrepeatable read can appear since T_j does no reads.

Theorem 3. Let H be a history of search-tree transactions with nested sm transactions such that every sm transaction is either committed or rolled-back, all the committed sm transactions are correct, and H contains no dirty writes defined above for pairs of transactions of which at least one is an sm transaction. Assume that H can be run on a structurally consistent search tree B and produces a search tree B'. Then B' is structurally consistent, and $\mathrm{db}(B')$ is the database produced by running $\pi(H)$ on $\mathrm{db}(B)$. □

Latching [5,14] is used to guarantee the physical consistency of pages under updates. The process that generates a search-tree transaction and its nested sm transactions must acquire a shared latch (S-latch) on any page retrieved for reading and an exclusive latch (X-latch) on any page retrieved for updating. The action of acquiring a latch is sometimes combined with the buffer manager operation that is used to fix a page into the buffer. The unlatching of a page is similarly combined with the unfixing of the page. *Latch-coupling* [2,5,12] is a common way to guarantee the validity of traversed search-tree paths. The latching protocol used is assumed to be deadlock-free. This is guaranteed if an S-latch is never upgraded to an X-latch and if a parent or elder sibling page is never latched when holding a latch on a child or a younger sibling. We assume that any logical or physiological implementation on a search tree B of a database operation on $\mathrm{db}(B)$ can be run on B under the latching protocol, starting with an empty set of latched pages and ending with an empty set of latched pages (see e.g. [9,11,12]). Full isolation for sm transactions is obtained if each page p accessed by an sm transaction S is kept X-latched until S commits or, if S is aborted, until all updates by S on p have been undone.

Lemma 4. Let $\hat{H}$ be a history of transactions on database D. Construct from $\hat{H}$ a history $\hat{H}'$ by replacing some retrievals $r[x, \theta z, v]$ by $r[x, \geq z', v]$ where $x \geq z' \theta z$. Then $\hat{H}$ can be run on D under the key-range locking protocol if and only if $\hat{H}'$ can be run on D under the key-range locking protocol. □

Let $\hat{H}$ be a history of database transactions that can be run on a database D and let B be a structurally consistent search tree with $\mathrm{db}(B) = D$. A history H

of search-tree transactions with nested sm transactions is an *implementation of* $\hat{H}$ *on* B if H can be run on B, every sm transaction in H is either committed and correct or rolled-back, and $\pi(H) = \hat{H}'$ where $\hat{H}'$ can be constructed from $\hat{H}$ as in Lemma 4. Here $\hat{H}'$ is a history of transactions $\pi(T)$, where T is a search-tree transaction in H.

Theorem 5. Let $\hat{H}$ be a history of database transactions that can be run on a database D under the key-range locking protocol. Then for any structurally consistent search tree B with $db(B) = D$, there exists an implementation H of $\hat{H}$ such that all the sm transactions in H are committed and correct, and H can be run on B under the latching and locking protocols. □

Theorem 6. Let H be a history of search-tree transactions with nested sm transactions such that all the committed sm transactions are correct and H contains no isolation anomalies and can be run on a structurally consistent search tree B. Then $\pi(H)$ is conflict-equivalent to a serial history $\hat{H}_1$ of the transactions in $\pi(H)$ and there exists an implementation H_1 of $\hat{H}_1$ on B that is a serial history of some search-tree transactions with nested committed and correct sm transactions. □

The result of Theorem 6 can be characterized by saying that H is "data-equivalent" [16] to a serial history H_1. Note however that the transactions in H_1 are usually not the same as those in H. Nor is the search tree produced by running H_1 on B necessarily the same as that produced by H on B, although it is true that they represent the same database.

6   Recoverability

Following ARIES [14], we assume that each data-term update $o[p, x, v]$, $o \in \{n, d\}$, performed by a search-tree transaction T in its forward-rolling phase is logged by writing the physiological log record $\langle T, o, p, x, v, n \rangle$, where n is the log sequence number (LSN) of the log record for the previous data-term update of T, and that the inverse $o^{-1}[p', x, v]$ of such an update performed by an aborted search-tree transaction T in its backward-rolling phase is logged by writing the compensation log record $\langle T, o^{-1}, p', x, v, n \rangle$. Similarly, we assume that any sm (i.e., page allocation, page deallocation, index-term update or term move) performed by an sm transaction S in its forward-rolling phase is logged by writing a physiological log record that contains the transaction identifier S, the name and arguments of the sm operation, and the previous LSN n of S, and that the (physiological) inverse of such an sm is logged by writing the corresponding compensation log record. The LSN of the log record is stamped in the PageLSN field of every page involved in the update. The write-ahead logging protocol [5, 14] is applied, so that a data or index page with PageLSN n may be flushed onto disk only after flushing first all log records with LSNs less than or equal to n.

Let H be an incomplete history representing the state of transaction processing after a system crash when the redo pass of restart recovery [14] has been completed and the undo pass is about to begin. In the standard ARIES algorithm, the undo pass is performed by a single backward sweep of the log, rolling back all the active transactions. As noted in [9,12,13,15], this may not be possible when active sm transactions are present, because the logical inverse of a data-term update logged after an sm performed by an active sm transaction may see a structurally inconsistent tree. The following theorem states that it is possible to recover by rolling back all the active sm transactions first (cf. [9]).

Theorem 7. Let H be a history of search-tree transactions with nested sm transactions such that all the committed sm transactions are correct and H can be run on a structurally consistent search tree B under the latching protocol (with full isolation for sm transactions) and under the key-range locking protocol. Further let γ be any string in the shuffle of the completion strings for the active sm transactions in H. We have:

(1) $H\gamma$ can be run on B under the latching and locking protocols and produces a structurally consistent search tree B'.

Now let $\hat{\psi}$ be any string in the shuffle of the completion strings for the active database transactions in $\pi(H)$. Then there exists a search-tree operation string ψ such that the following statements hold.

(2) $\pi(\psi) = \hat{\psi}$ and $\gamma\psi$ is a completion string for H.

(3) All the sm transactions in ψ are committed and correct.

(4) ψ can be run on B' under the latching and locking protocols and produces a structurally consistent search tree B_1. □

Theorem 7 covers the general case in which sm transactions may be of arbitrary length, as is the case with the conventional B-tree in which a series of page splits or merges propagating from a leaf page up to the root page must all be enclosed within a single sm transaction. In the event of a crash, such an sm transaction may have some of its effects reflected on disk and on the log while some effects are not, so that the sm transaction must first be rolled back before the (logical) undoing of the database updates can begin. If a new crash occurs while the undo pass is still in progress there may be new sm transactions active, caused by the logical inverses, which then must be rolled back before completing the rollback of the parent search-tree transaction. It is easy to see that there is no upper limit on the number of sm's that repeated crashes can cause.

In the case of a B-link-tree, on the other hand, sm transactions can be made short: an sm transaction may consist of a single index-term insert, a single index-term delete, a single page split, or a single page merge (cf. [9,10,11]). Each of these operations retains the structural consistency of a B-link-tree, when our balance conditions allow a page to have several sibling pages that are not directly child-linked to their parent page but are only accessible via the side links. Moreover, each of the four operations only involves a small fixed number of pages that need to be fixed and latched in the buffer during the operation, and the operation can be logged by a set of log records that fit into a single page. For example, an sm transaction for the split of a page p includes a page allocation $n[p', t]$, a number of term moves $m[p, x, v, p']$ that are used to move about a half of the terms in page p into page p', and an index-term insert $n[p, y, p']$ that inserts into p the high-key term (y, p') where y is the least key in p'.

The log records describing the split, together with the begin and commit log records of the sm transaction, can be packed into a single log record that occupies only about a half of a page. That log record is written and the pages p and p' are unlatched and unfixed only after the completion of the split operation, so that in the event of a crash, either the log on disk contains no trace of the split (in which case there is no trace of it in the database pages on disk either), or the entire log record is found on disk. In the latter case the log record may have to be replayed in the redo pass of recovery. In neither case is there anything to be done for rolling back sm transactions. Then in Theorem 7 we may restrict ourselves to the case in which $\gamma = \epsilon$ and all the sm transactions in H are committed. This means that the undo pass of ARIES can readily be started to run the (logical) inverses of the data-term updates of active search-tree transactions.

7 Conclusion

Industrial-strength database systems use index-management algorithms that are based on a sophisticated interplay of the logical record-level operations and the physical page-level operations so that maximal concurrency is achieved while not sacrificing recoverability [12,13,15]. A key solution is to regard a series of structure modifications (sm's) on the physical database as an open nested transaction that can commit even if the parent transaction aborts. A light-weight implementation of such sm transactions can be provided by ARIES nested top actions [14].

We have presented a transaction model that serves as a theoretical framework for analysing index-management algorithms in the context of B-trees and B-link-trees. Transactions on the logical database can contain an arbitrary number of record inserts, record deletes, and key-range scans. Transactions on the physical database are modelled as two-level search-tree transactions that on the higher level do index-term retrievals and data-term inserts, deletes and retrievals and that on the lower level consist of sm transactions as open nested subtransactions. The semantics of the search tree is used to derive isolation conditions that guarantee the structural consistency of the search tree, isolation of logical database operations, and recoverability of both the search-tree structure and the database operations. The isolation conditions can be enforced by standard key-range locking and page-latching protocols.

General correctness and recoverability results are derived for search-tree transaction histories that contain any number of forward-rolling, committed, backward-rolling, and rolled-back transactions. In the case of specific B-tree structures and algorithms the general results serve as a basis for establishing more stringent results on the efficiency of transaction processing in the presence of failures. In this extended abstract, proofs of the results are omitted.

References

1. G. Alonso, R. Vingralek, D. Agrawal, Y. Breitbart, A. El Abbadi, H.-J. Schek, and G. Weikum. Unifying concurrency control and recovery of transactions. *Information Systems* **19** (1994), 101–115.
2. R. Bayer and M. Schkolnick. Concurrency of operations on B-trees. *Acta Informatica* **9** (1977), 1–21.
3. H. Berenson, P. Bernstein, J. Gray, J. Melton, E. O'Neil, and P. O'Neil. A critique of ANSI SQL isolation levels. In: *Proc. of the 1995 ACM SIGMOD Internat. Conf. on Management of Data*, 1–10.
4. P. H. Bernstein, V. Hadzilacos, and N. Goodman. *Concurrency Control and Recovery in Database Systems*, Addison-Wesley, 1987.
5. J. Gray and A. Reuter. *Transaction Processing: Concepts and Techniques*, Morgan Kaufmann, 1993.
6. D. Lomet. Key range locking strategies for improved concurrency. In: *Proc. of the 19th VLDB Conference*, 1993, 655–664.
7. P. L. Lehman and S. B. Yao. Efficient locking for concurrent operations on B-trees. *ACM Trans. Database Systems* **6** (1981), 650–670.
8. D. Lomet. MLR: a recovery method for multi-level systems. In: *Proc. of the 1992 ACM SIGMOD Internat. Conf. on Management of Data*, 185–194.
9. D. Lomet. Advanced recovery techniques in practice. In: *Recovery Mechanisms in Database Systems* (V. Kumar and M. Hsu, eds), Prentice Hall, 1998, 697–710.
10. D. Lomet and B. Salzberg. Access method concurrency with recovery. In: *Proc. of the 1992 ACM SIGMOD Internat. Conf. on Management of Data*, 351–360.
11. D. Lomet and B. Salzberg. Concurrency and recovery for index trees. *The VLDB Journal* **6** (1997), 224–240.
12. C. Mohan. Concurrency control and recovery methods for B^+-tree indexes: ARIES/KVL and ARIES/IM. In: *Performance of Concurrency Control Mechanisms in Centralized Database Systems* (V. Kumar, ed), Prentice Hall, 1996, 248–306.
13. C. Mohan. ARIES/KVL: a key-value locking method for concurrency control of multiaction transactions operating on B-tree indexes. In: *Proc. of the 16th VLDB Conference*, 1990, 392–405.
14. C. Mohan, D. Haderle, B. Lindsay, H. Pirahesh, and P. Schwartz. ARIES: a transaction recovery method supporting fine-granularity locking and partial rollbacks using write-ahead logging. *ACM Trans. Database Systems* **17** (1992), 94–162.
15. C. Mohan and F. Levine. ARIES/IM: an efficient and high concurrency index management method using write-ahead logging. In: *Proc. of the 1992 ACM SIGMOD Internat. Conf. on Management of Data*, 371–380.
16. Y. Sagiv. Concurrent operations on B*-trees with overtaking. *J. Computer and System Sciences* **33** (1986), 275–296.
17. H-J. Schek, G. Weikum and H. Ye. Towards a unified theory of concurrency control and recovery. In: *Proc. of the 12th ACM SIGACT-SIGMOD-SIGART Symp. on Principles of Database Systems*, 1993, 300–311.
18. D. Shasha and N. Goodman. Concurrent search structure algorithms. *ACM Trans. Database Systems* **13** (1988), 53–90.
19. R. Vingralek, H. Hasse-Ye, Y. Breitbart and H.-J. Schek. Unifying concurrency control and recovery of transactions with semantically rich operations. *Theoretical Computer Science* **190** (1998), 363–396.
20. G. Weikum. Principles and realization strategies of multi-level transaction management. *ACM Trans. Database Systems* **16** (1991), 132–180.

Minimizing View Sets without Losing Query-Answering Power

Chen Li, Mayank Bawa, and Jeffrey D. Ullman

Computer Science Department, Stanford University, CA 94305, USA
{chenli,bawa,ullman}@db.stanford.edu

Abstract. The problem of answering queries using views has been studied extensively due to its relevance in a wide variety of data-management applications. In these applications, we often need to select a subset of views to maintain due to limited resources. In this paper, we show that traditional query containment is *not* a good basis for deciding whether or not a view should be selected. Instead, we should minimize the view set without losing its *query-answering power*. To formalize this notion, we first introduce the concept of "p-containment." That is, a view set $\mathcal{V}$ is *p-contained* in another view set $\mathcal{W}$, if $\mathcal{W}$ can answer all the queries that can be answered by $\mathcal{V}$. We show that p-containment and the traditional query containment are *not* related. We then discuss how to minimize a view set while retaining its query-answering power. We develop the idea further by considering p-containment of two view sets with respect to a given set of queries, and consider their relationship in terms of maximally-contained rewritings of queries using the views.

1 Introduction

The problem of answering queries using views [2,3,9,13,17,22] has been studied extensively, because of its relevance to a wide variety of data management problems, such as information integration, data warehousing, and query optimization. The problem can be stated as follows: given a query on a database schema and a set of views over the same schema, can we answer the query using only the answers to the views? Recently, Levy compiled a good survey [16] about the different approaches to this problem.

In the context of query optimization, computing a query using previously materialized views can speed up query processing, because part of the computation necessary for the query may have been done while computing the views. In a data warehouse, views can preclude costly access to the base relations and help answer queries quickly. In web-site designs, precomputed views can be used to improve the performance of web-sites [11]. Before choosing an optimal design, we must assure that the chosen views can be used to answer the expected queries at the web-site. A system that caches answers locally at the client can avoid accesses to base relations at the server. Cached result of a query can be thought of as a materialized view, with the query as its view definition. The client could use the cached answers from previous queries to answer future queries.

J. Van den Bussche and V. Vianu (Eds.): ICDT 2001, LNCS 1973, pp. 99–113, 2001.

However, the benefits presented by views are not without costs. Materialized views often compete for limited resources. Thus, it is critical to select views carefully. For instance, in an information-integration system [24], a view may represent a set of web pages at an autonomous source. The mediator [26] in these systems often needs to crawl these web pages periodically to refresh the cached data in its local repository [8]. In such a scenario, the cost manifests itself as the bandwidth needed for such crawls and the efforts in maintaining the cache up-to-date. Correspondingly, in a query-optimization and database-design scenario, the materialized views may have part of the computation necessary for the query. When a user poses a query, we need to decide how to answer the query using the materialized views. By selecting an optimal subset of views to materialize, we can reduce the computation needed to decide how to answer typical queries. In a client-server architecture with client-side caching, storing all answers to past queries may need a large storage space and will add to the maintenance costs. Since the client needs to deal with an evolving set of queries, any of these can be used to answer future queries. Thus, redundant views need not be cached.

The following example shows that views can have redundancy to make such a minimization possible, and that traditional query containment is *not* a good basis for deciding whether a view should be selected or not. Instead, we should consider the *query-answering* power of the views.

Example 1. Suppose we have a client-server system with client-side caching for improving performance, since server data accesses are expensive. The server has the following base relation about books:

$$book(Title, Author, Pub, Price)$$

For example, the tuple ⟨databases, smith, prenhall, $60⟩ in the relation means that a book titled databases has an author smith, is published by Prentice Hall (prenhall), and has a current price of $60. Assume that the client has seen the following three queries, the answers of which have been cached locally. The cached data (or views), denoted by the view set $\mathcal{V} = \{V_1, V_2, V_3\}$, are:

$V_1: v_1(T, A, P) :\text{-} book(T, A, B, P)$
$V_2: v_2(T, A, P) :\text{-} book(T, A, prenhall, P)$
$V_3: v_3(A_1, A_2) :\text{-} book(T, A_1, prenhall, P_1), book(T, A_2, prenhall, P_2)$

The view V_1 has title-author-price information about all books in the relation, while the view V_2 includes this information only about books published by Prentice Hall. The view V_3 has coauthor pairs for books published by Prentice Hall. Since the view set has redundancy, we might want to eliminate a view to save costs of its maintenance and storage. At the same time, we want to be assured that such an elimination does not cause increased server accesses in response to future queries.

Clearly, view V_2 is contained in V_1, i.e., V_1 includes all the tuples in V_2, so we might be tempted to select $\{V_1, V_3\}$, and eliminate V_2 as a redundant view.

However, with this selection, we cannot answer the query:

$$Q_1 : q_1(T, P) \text{ :- } book(T, smith, prenhall, P)$$

which asks for titles and prices of books written by smith and published by prenhall. The reason is that even though V_1 includes title-author-price information about all books in the base relation, the publisher attribute is projected out in the view's head. Thus, using V_1 only, we cannot tell which books are published by prenhall. On the other hand, the query Q_1 can be answered trivially using V_2:

$$P_1 : q_1(T, P) \text{ :- } v_2(T, smith, P)$$

In other words, by dropping V_2 we have lost some *power* to answer queries. In addition, note that even though view V_3 is not contained in V_1 and V_2, it can be eliminated from $\mathcal{V}$ without changing the query-answering power of $\mathcal{V}$. The reason is that V_3 can be computed from V_2 as follows:

$$v_3(A_1, A_2) \text{ :- } v_2(T, A_1, P_1), v_2(T, A_2, P_2)$$

To summarize, we should not select $\{V_1, V_3\}$ but $\{V_1, V_2\}$, even though the former includes all the tuples in $\mathcal{V}$, while the latter does not. The rationale is that the latter is as "powerful" as $\mathcal{V}$ while the former is not. *Caution:* One might hypothesize from this example that only projections in view definitions cause such a mismatch, since we do not lose any "data" in the body of the view. We show in Section 3 that this hypothesis is wrong.

In this paper we discuss how to minimize a view set without losing its query-answering power. We first introduce the concept of *p-containment* between two view sets, where "p" stands for query-answering *power* (Sections 2 and 3). A view set $\mathcal{V}$ is *p-contained* in another view set $\mathcal{W}$, or $\mathcal{W}$ is *at least as powerful* as $\mathcal{V}$, if $\mathcal{W}$ can answer all the queries that can be answered using $\mathcal{V}$. Two view sets are called *equipotent* if they have the same power to answer queries. As shown in Example 1, two view sets may have the same tuples, yet have different query-answering power. That is, traditional view containment [6,23] does not imply p-containment. The example further shows that the reverse direction is also *not* implied. In Section 3.2 we show that given a view set $\mathcal{V}$ on base relations, how to find a minimal subset of $\mathcal{V}$ that is equipotent to $\mathcal{V}$. As one might suspect, a view set can have multiple equipotent minimal subsets.

In some scenarios, users are restricted in the queries they can ask. In such cases, equipotence may be determined *relative* to the expected (possibly infinite) set of queries. In Section 4, we investigate the above questions of equipotence testing given this extra constraint. In particular, we consider infinite query sets defined by finite parameterized queries, and develop algorithms for testing this relative p-containment.

In information-integration systems, we often need to consider not only equivalent rewritings of a query using views, but also maximally-contained rewritings (MCR's). Analogous to p-containment, which requires equivalent rewritings, we introduce the concept of *MCR-containment* that is defined using maximally-contained rewritings (Section 5). Surprisingly, we show that p-containment implies MCR-containment, and vice-versa.

The containments between two finite sets of conjunctive views discussed in this paper are summarized in Table 1. In the full version of the paper [19] we discuss how to generalize the results to other languages, such as conjunctive queries with arithmetic comparisons, unions of conjunctive queries, and datalog.

Table 1. Containments between two finite sets of conjunctive views: $\mathcal{V}$ and $\mathcal{W}$.

Containment	Definition	How to test
v-containment $\mathcal{V} \sqsubseteq_v \mathcal{W}$	For any database, a tuple in a view in $\mathcal{V}$ is in a view in $\mathcal{W}$.	Check if each view in $\mathcal{V}$ is contained in some view in $\mathcal{W}$.
p-containment $\mathcal{V} \preceq_p \mathcal{W}$	If a query is answerable by $\mathcal{V}$, then it is answerable by $\mathcal{W}$.	Check if each view in $\mathcal{V}$ is answerable by $\mathcal{W}$.
relative p-containment $\mathcal{V} \preceq_{\mathcal{Q}} \mathcal{W}$	For each query Q in a given set of queries $\mathcal{Q}$, if Q is answerable by $\mathcal{V}$, then Q is answerable by $\mathcal{W}$.	Test by the definition if $\mathcal{Q}$ is finite. See Section 4.2 for infinite queries defined by parameterized queries.
MCR-containment $\mathcal{V} \preceq_{MCR} \mathcal{W}$	For each query Q, for any maximally-contained rewriting $MCR(Q,\mathcal{V})$ (resp. $MCR(Q,\mathcal{W})$) of Q using $\mathcal{V}$ (resp. $\mathcal{W}$), $MCR(Q,\mathcal{V}) \sqsubseteq MCR(Q,\mathcal{W})$.	Same as testing if $\mathcal{V} \preceq_p \mathcal{W}$, since $\mathcal{V} \preceq_p \mathcal{W} \Leftrightarrow \mathcal{V} \preceq_{MCR} \mathcal{W}$.

2   Background

In this section, we review some concepts about answering queries using views [17]. Let $r_1, \ldots, r_m$ be m *base relations* in a database. We first consider queries on the database in the following conjunctive form:

$$h(\bar{X}) :\text{-} g_1(\bar{X}_1), \ldots, g_k(\bar{X}_k)$$

In each subgoal $g_i(\bar{X}_i)$, predicate g_i is a base relation, and every argument in the subgoal is either a variable or a constant. We consider views defined on the base relations by safe conjunctive queries, i.e., every variable in a query's head appears in the body. Note that we take the closed-world assumption [1], since the views are computed from existing database relations. We shall use names beginning with lower-case letters for constants and relations, and names beginning with upper-case letters for variables.

Definition 1. *(query containment and equivalence) A query Q_1 is contained in a query Q_2, denoted by $Q_1 \sqsubseteq Q_2$, if for any database D of the base relations, $Q_1(D) \subseteq Q_2(D)$. The two queries are equivalent if $Q_1 \sqsubseteq Q_2$ and $Q_2 \sqsubseteq Q_1$.*

Definition 2. *(expansion of a query using views) The expansion of a query P on a set of views $\mathcal{V}$, denoted by P^{exp}, is obtained from P by replacing all the views in P with their corresponding base relations. Existentially quantified variables in a view are replaced by fresh variables in P^{exp}.*

Definition 3. *(rewritings and equivalent rewritings) Given a query Q and a view set $\mathcal{V}$, a query P is a rewriting of query Q using $\mathcal{V}$ if P uses only the views in $\mathcal{V}$, and $P^{exp} \sqsubseteq Q$. P is an equivalent rewriting of Q using $\mathcal{V}$ if P^{exp} and Q are equivalent. We say a query Q is answerable by $\mathcal{V}$ if there exists an equivalent rewriting of Q using $\mathcal{V}$.*

In Example 1, P_1 is an equivalent rewriting of the query Q_1 using view V_2, because the expansion of P_1:

$$P_1^{exp} : q_1(T, P) \text{ :- } book(T, smith, prenhall, P)$$

is equivalent to Q_1. Thus, query Q_1 is answerable by V_2, but it is not answerable by $\{V_1, V_3\}$.

In this paper we consider *finite* view sets. Several algorithms have been developed for answering queries using views, such as the bucket algorithm [18,12], the inverse-rule algorithm [22,10], and the algorithms in [20,21]. See [1,17] for a study of the complexity of answering queries using views. In particular, it has been shown that the problem of rewriting a query using views is $\mathcal{NP}$-complete.

3   Comparing Query-Answering Power of View Sets

In this section we first introduce the concept of *p-containment*, and compare it with traditional query containment. Then we discuss how to minimize a view set without losing its query-answering power with respect to all possible queries.

Definition 4. *(p-containment and equipotence) A view set $\mathcal{V}$ is p-contained in another view set $\mathcal{W}$, or "$\mathcal{W}$ is at least as powerful as $\mathcal{V}$," denoted by $\mathcal{V} \preceq_p \mathcal{W}$, if any query answerable by $\mathcal{V}$ is also answerable by $\mathcal{W}$. Two view sets are equipotent, denoted by $\mathcal{V} \asymp_p \mathcal{W}$, if $\mathcal{V} \preceq_p \mathcal{W}$, and $\mathcal{W} \preceq_p \mathcal{V}$.*

In Example 1, the two view sets $\{V_1, V_2\}$ and $\{V_1, V_2, V_3\}$ are equipotent, since the latter can answer all the queries that can be answered by the former, and vice-versa. (We will give a formal proof shortly.) However, the two view sets, $\{V_1, V_3\}$ and $\{V_1, V_2, V_3\}$, are not equipotent, since the latter can answer the query Q_1, which cannot be answered by the former. The following lemma suggests an algorithm for testing p-containment.

Lemma 1. *Let $\mathcal{V}$ and $\mathcal{W}$ be two view sets. $\mathcal{V} \preceq_p \mathcal{W}$ iff for every view $V \in \mathcal{V}$, if treated as a query, V is answerable by $\mathcal{W}$.*[1]

---

[1] Due to space limitations, we do not provide all the proofs of the lemmas and theorems. Some proofs are given in the full version of the paper [19].

The importance of this lemma is that we can test $V \preceq_p W$ simply by checking if every view in V is answerable by W. That is, we can just consider a *finite* set of queries, even though $V \preceq_p W$ means that W can answer *all* the infinite number of queries that can be answered by V. We can use the algorithms in [10,12,18, 22] to do the checking. It is easy to see that the relationship "$\preceq_p$" is reflexive, antisymmetric, and transitive. Using the results of [17] for the complexity of testing whether a query is answerable by a set of views, we have:

Theorem 1. *The problem of whether a view set is p-contained in another view set is $\mathcal{NP}$-hard.*

Example 2. As we saw in Example 1, view V_3 is answerable by view V_2. By Lemma 1, we have $\{V_1, V_2, V_3\} \preceq_p \{V_1, V_2\}$. Clearly the other direction is also true, so $\{V_1, V_2\} \asymp_p \{V_1, V_2, V_3\}$. On the other hand, V_2 cannot be answered using $\{V_1, V_3\}$, which means $\{V_1, V_2, V_3\} \npreceq_p \{V_1, V_3\}$.

3.1   Comparing P-Containment and Traditional Query Containment

We are interested in the relationship between p-containment and the traditional concept of query containment (as in Definition 1). Before making the comparisons, we first generalize the latter to a concept called *v-containment* to cover the cases where the views in a set have different schemas.

Definition 5. *(v-containment and v-equivalence) A view set V is v-contained in another view set W, denoted by $V \sqsubseteq_v W$, if the following holds. For any database D of the base relations, if tuple t is in $V(D)$ for a view $V \in V$, then there is a view $W \in W$, such that $t \in W(D)$. The two sets are v-equivalent, if $V \sqsubseteq_v W$, and $W \sqsubseteq_v V$.*

In Example 1, the two view sets $\{V_1, V_2, V_3\}$ and $\{V_1, V_3\}$ are v-equivalent, while their views have different schemas. The example shows that v-containment does not imply p-containment, and vice-versa. One might guess that if we do not allow projections in the view definitions (i.e., all the variables in the body of a view appear in the head), then v-containment could imply p-containment. However, the following example shows that this guess is incorrect.

Example 3. Let $e(X_1, X_2)$ be a base relation, where a tuple $e(x, y)$ means that there is an edge from vertex x to vertex y in a graph. Consider two view sets:

$$V = \{V_1\}, \quad V_1: \ v_1(A, B, C) :\text{-} \ e(A, B), e(B, C), e(A, C)$$
$$W = \{W_1\}, \quad W_1: \ w_1(A, B, C) :\text{-} \ e(A, B), e(B, C)$$

As illustrated by Figure 1, view V_1 stores all the subgraphs shown in Figure 1(a), while view W_1 stores all the subgraphs shown in Figure 1(b). The two views do not have projections in their definitions, and $V \sqsubseteq_v W$. However, $V \npreceq_p W$, since V_1 cannot be answered using W_1.

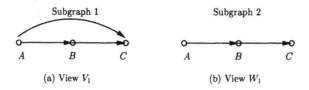

(a) View V_1 (b) View W_1

Fig. 1. Diagram for the two views in Example 3

The following example shows that p-containment does not imply v-containment, even if the views in the sets have the same schemas.

Example 4. Let $r(X_1, X_2)$ and $s(Y_1, Y_2)$ be two base relations on which two view sets are defined:

$$\begin{aligned}
\mathcal{V} &= \{V_1\}, & V_1: v_1(A, C) &:\text{-} r(A, B), s(B, C) \\
\mathcal{W} &= \{W_1, W_2\}, & W_1: w_1(A, B) &:\text{-} r(A, B) \\
& & W_2: w_2(B, C) &:\text{-} s(B, C)
\end{aligned}$$

Clearly $\mathcal{V} \not\sqsubseteq_v \mathcal{W}$, but $\mathcal{V} \preceq_p \mathcal{W}$, since there is a rewriting of V_1 using $\mathcal{W}$: $v_1(A, C) :\text{-} w_1(A, B), w_2(B, C)$.

3.2   Finding an Equipotent Minimal Subset

In many applications, each view is associated with a cost, such as its storage space or the number of web pages that need to be crawled for the view [8]. We often need to find a subset of views that has the same query-answering power.

Definition 6. *(equipotent minimal subsets) A subset M of a view set $\mathcal{V}$ is an equipotent minimal subset (EMS for short) of $\mathcal{V}$ if $M \asymp_p \mathcal{V}$, and for any $V \in M : M - \{V\} \not\succeq_p \mathcal{V}$.*

Informally, an equipotent minimal subset of a view set $\mathcal{V}$ is a minimal subset that is as powerful as $\mathcal{V}$. For instance, in Example 1, the view set $\{V_1, V_2\}$ is an EMS of $\{V_1, V_2, V_3\}$. We can compute an EMS of a view set $\mathcal{V}$ using the following Shrinking algorithm.

Algorithm Shrinking initially sets $M = \mathcal{V}$. For each view $V \in M$, it checks if V is answerable by the views $M - \{V\}$. If so, it removes V from M. It repeats this process until no more views can be removed from M, and returns the resulting M as an EMS of $\mathcal{V}$.

Example 5. This example shows that, as suspected, a view set may have multiple EMS's. Suppose $r(A, B)$ is a base relation, on which the following three views are defined:

$$\begin{aligned}
V_1&: v_1(A) & &:\text{-} r(A, B) \\
V_2&: v_2(B) & &:\text{-} r(A, B) \\
V_3&: v_3(A, B) & &:\text{-} r(A, X), r(Y, B)
\end{aligned}$$

Let $\mathcal{V} = \{V_1, V_2, V_3\}$. Then $\mathcal{V}$ has two EMS's: $\{V_1, V_2\}$, and $\{V_3\}$, as shown by the following rewritings:

$$\begin{array}{lll}
\text{rewrite } V_1 \text{ using } V_3: & v_1(A) & :\text{-} v_3(A, B) \\
\text{rewrite } V_2 \text{ using } V_3: & v_2(B) & :\text{-} v_3(A, B) \\
\text{rewrite } V_3 \text{ using } \{V_1, V_2\}: & v_3(A, B) :\text{-} v_1(A), v_2(B)
\end{array}$$

We often want to find an EMS such that the total cost of selected views is minimum. We believe that the problem of finding an optimal EMS efficiently deserves more investigations.

4   Testing P-Containment Relative to a Query Set

Till now, we have considered p-containment between two view sets with respect to a "universal" set of queries, i.e., users can ask *any* query on the base relations. However, in some scenarios, users are restricted in the queries they can ask. In this section, we consider the relationship between two view sets with respect to a given set of queries. In particular, we consider infinite query sets defined by finite parameterized queries.

Definition 7. *(relative p-containment) Given a (possibly infinite) set of queries $\mathcal{Q}$, a view set $\mathcal{V}$ is p-contained in a view set $\mathcal{W}$ w.r.t. $\mathcal{Q}$, denoted by $\mathcal{V} \preceq_{\mathcal{Q}} \mathcal{W}$, iff for any query $Q \in \mathcal{Q}$ that is answerable by $\mathcal{V}$, Q is also answerable by $\mathcal{W}$. The two view sets are equipotent w.r.t. $\mathcal{Q}$, denoted by $\mathcal{V} \asymp_{\mathcal{Q}} \mathcal{W}$, if $\mathcal{V} \preceq_{\mathcal{Q}} \mathcal{W}$ and $\mathcal{W} \preceq_{\mathcal{Q}} \mathcal{V}$.*

Example 6. Assume we have relations $car(Make, Dealer)$ and $loc(Dealer, City)$ that store information about cars, their dealers, and the cities where the dealers are located. Consider the following two queries and three views:

$$\begin{array}{lll}
\text{Queries: } Q_1: & q_1(D, C) & :\text{-} car(toyota, D), loc(D, C) \\
Q_2: & q_2(D, C) & :\text{-} car(honda, D), loc(D, C) \\
\text{Views: } W_1: & w_1(D, C) & :\text{-} car(toyota, D), loc(D, C) \\
W_2: & w_2(D, C) & :\text{-} car(honda, D), loc(D, C) \\
W_3: & w_3(M, D, C) :\text{-} car(M, D), loc(D, C)
\end{array}$$

Let $\mathcal{Q} = \{Q_1, Q_2\}$, $\mathcal{V} = \{W_1, W_2\}$, and $\mathcal{W} = \{W_3\}$. Then $\mathcal{V}$ and $\mathcal{W}$ are equipotent w.r.t. $\mathcal{Q}$, since Q_1 and Q_2 can be answered by $\mathcal{V}$ as well as $\mathcal{W}$. Note that $\mathcal{V}$ and $\mathcal{W}$ are not equipotent in general.

Given a view set $\mathcal{V}$ and a query set $\mathcal{Q}$, we define an *equipotent minimal subset* (EMS) of $\mathcal{V}$ w.r.t. $\mathcal{Q}$ in the same manner as Definition 6. We can compute an EMS of $\mathcal{V}$ w.r.t. $\mathcal{Q}$ in the same way as in Section 3.2, if we have a method to test relative p-containment. This testing is straightforward when $\mathcal{Q}$ is finite; i.e., by definition, we can check for each query $Q_i \in \mathcal{Q}$ that is answerable by $\mathcal{V}$, whether Q_i is also answerable by $\mathcal{W}$. However, if $\mathcal{Q}$ is infinite, testing relative p-containment becomes more challenging, since we cannot use this enumerate-and-test paradigm for all the queries in $\mathcal{Q}$. In the rest of this section we consider ways to test relative p-containment w.r.t. infinite query sets defined by finite parameterized queries.

4.1 Parameterized Queries

A *parameterized query* is a conjunctive query that contains *placeholders* in the argument positions of its body, in addition to constants and variables. A placeholder is denoted by an argument name beginning with a "$" sign.

Example 7. Consider the following parameterized query Q on the two relations in Example 6:

$$Q : q(D) \text{ :- } car(\$M, D), loc(D, \$C)$$

This query represents all the following queries: a user gives a car make m for the placeholder $\$M$, and a city c for the placeholder $\$C$, and asks for the dealers of the make m in the city c. For example, the following are two instances of Q:

$$I_1: q(D) \text{ :- } car(toyota, D), loc(D, sf)$$
$$I_2: q(D) \text{ :- } car(honda, D), loc(D, sf)$$

which respectively ask for dealers of Toyota and Honda in San Francisco (sf).

In general, each *instance* of a parameterized query Q is obtained by assigning a constant from the corresponding domain to each placeholder. If a placeholder appears in different argument positions, then the same constant must be used in these positions. Let $IS(Q)$ (resp. $IS(\mathcal{Q})$) denote the set of all instances of the query Q (resp. a query set $\mathcal{Q}$). We assume that the domains of placeholders are infinite (independent of an instance of the base relations), causing $IS(Q)$ to be infinite. Thus we can represent an infinite set of queries using a finite set of parameterized queries.

Example 8. Consider the following three views:

$$V_1: v_1(M, D, C) \text{ :- } car(M, D), loc(D, C)$$
$$V_2: v_2(M, D) \quad \text{ :- } car(M, D), loc(D, sf)$$
$$V_3: v_3(M) \quad\quad \text{ :- } car(M, D), loc(D, sf)$$

Clearly, view V_1 can answer all instances of Q in Example 7, since it includes information for cars and dealers in all cities. View V_2 cannot answer all instances, since it has only the information about dealers in San Francisco. But it can answer instances of the following more restrictive parameterized query, which replaces the placeholder $\$C$ by sf:

$$Q' : q(D) \text{ :- } car(\$M, D), loc(D, sf)$$

That is, the user can only ask for information about dealers in San Francisco. Finally, view V_3 cannot answer any instance of Q, since it does not have the *Dealer* attribute in its head.

Given a finite set of parameterized queries $\mathcal{Q}$ and two view sets $\mathcal{V}$ and $\mathcal{W}$, the example above suggests the following strategy of testing $\mathcal{V} \preceq_{IS(\mathcal{Q})} \mathcal{W}$:

1. Deduce *all* instances of $\mathcal{Q}$ that can be answered by $\mathcal{V}$.
2. Test if $\mathcal{W}$ can answer *all* such instances.

In the next two subsections we show how to perform each of these steps. We show that all answerable instances of a parameterized query for a given view set can be represented by a *finite* set of parameterized queries. We give an algorithm for deducing this set, and an algorithm for the second step. Although our discussion is based on one parameterized query, the results can be easily generalized to a finite set of parameterized queries.

4.2   Complete Answerability of a Parameterized Query

We first consider the problem of testing whether all instances of a parameterized query Q can be answered by a view set $\mathcal{V}$. If so, we say that Q is *completely answerable* by $\mathcal{V}$.

Definition 8. *(canonical instance) A* canonical instance *of a parameterized query Q (given a view set $\mathcal{V}$) is an instance of Q, in which each placeholder is replaced by a new distinct constant that does not appear in Q and $\mathcal{V}$.*

Lemma 2. *A parameterized query Q is completely answerable by a view set $\mathcal{V}$ if and only if $\mathcal{V}$ can answer a canonical instance of Q (given $\mathcal{V}$).*

The lemma suggests an algorithm TestComp for testing whether all instances of a parameterized query Q can be answered by a view set $\mathcal{V}$.

Algorithm TestComp first constructs a canonical instance Q_c of Q (given $\mathcal{V}$). Then it tests if Q_c can be answered using $\mathcal{V}$ by calling an algorithm of answering queries using views, such as those in [10,12,18,22]. It outputs "yes" if $\mathcal{V}$ can answer Q_c; otherwise, it outputs "no."

Example 9. Consider the parameterized query Q in Example 8. To test whether view V_1 can answer all instances of Q, we use two new distinct constants m_0 and c_0 to replace the two placeholders $\$M$ and $\$C$, and obtain the following canonical instance:

$$Q_c : q(D) :\text{-} car(m_0, D), loc(D, c_0)$$

Clearly Q_c can be answered by view V_1, because of the following equivalent rewriting of Q_c:

$$P_c : q(D) :\text{-} v_1(m_0, D, c_0)$$

By Lemma 2, view V_1 can answer all instances of Q. In addition, since V_2 cannot answer Q_c (which is also a canonical instance of Q given V_2), it cannot answer *some* instances of Q. The same argument holds for V_3.

4.3   Partial Answerability of a Parameterized Query

As shown by view V_2 and query Q in Example 8, even if a view set cannot answer all instances of a parameterized query, it can still answer some instances. In general, we want to know what instances can be answered by the view set, and whether these instances can also be represented as a set of more "restrictive" parameterized queries. A parameterized query Q_1 is more *restrictive* than a parameterized query Q if every instance of Q_1 is also an instance of Q. For example, query $q(D)$:- $car(\$M, D), loc(D, sf)$ is more restrictive than query $q(D)$:- $car(\$M, D), loc(D, \$C)$, since the former requires the second argument of the loc subgoal to be sf, while the latter allows any constant for placeholder $\$C$. For another example, query $q(M, C)$:- $car(M, \$D_1), loc(\$D_1, C)$ is more restrictive than query $q(M, C)$:- $car(M, \$D_1), loc(\$D_2, C)$, since the former has one placeholder in two argument positions, while the latter allows two different constants to be assigned to its two placeholders.

All the parameterized queries that are more restrictive than Q can be generated by adding the following two types of restrictions:

1. Type I: Some placeholders must be assigned the same constant. Formally, let $\{\$A_1, \ldots, \$A_k\}$ be *some* placeholders in Q. We can put a restriction $\$A_1 = \cdots = \$A_k$ on the query Q. That is, we can replace all these k placeholders with any of them.

2. Type II: For a placeholder $\$A_i$ in Q and a constant c in Q or V, we put a restriction $\$A_i = c$ on Q. That is, the user can only assign constant c to this placeholder in an instance.

Consider all the possible (finite) combinations of these two types of restrictions. For example, suppose Q has two placeholders, $\{\$A_1, \$A_2\}$, and Q and V have one constant c. Then we consider the following restriction combinations: $\{\}, \{\$A_1 = \$A_2\}, \{\$A_1 = c\}, \{\$A_2 = c\}$, and $\{\$A_1 = \$A_2 = c\}$. Note that we allow a combination to have restrictions of only one type. In addition, each restriction combination is consistent, in the sense that it does not have a restriction $\$A_1 = \$A_2$ and two restrictions $\$A_1 = c_1$ and $\$A_2 = c_2$, while c_1 and c_2 are two different constants in Q and V. For each restriction combination RC_i, let $Q(RC_i)$ be the parameterized query that is derived by adding the restrictions in RC_i to Q. Clearly $Q(RC_i)$ is a parameterized query that is more restrictive than Q. Let $\Phi(Q, V)$ denote all these more restrictive parameterized queries.

Suppose I is an instance of Q that can be answered by V. We can show that there exists a parameterized query $Q_i \in \Phi(Q, V)$, such that I is a canonical instance of Q_i. By Lemma 2, Q_i is completely answerable by V. Therefore, we have proved the following theorem:

Theorem 2. *All instances of a parameterized query Q that are answerable by a view set V can be generated by a finite set of parameterized queries that are more restrictive than Q, such that all these parameterized queries are completely answerable by V.*

We propose the following algorithm GenPartial. Given a parameterized query Q and a view set V, the algorithm generates all the parameterized queries that are more restrictive than Q, such that they are completely answerable by V, and they define *all* the instances of Q that are answerable by V.

Algorithm GenPartial first generates all the restriction combinations, and creates a parameterized query for each combination. Then it calls the algorithm TestComp to check if this parameterized query is completely answerable by V. It outputs all the parameterized queries that are completely answerable by V.

4.4   Testing P-Containment Relative to Finite Parameterized Queries

Now we give an algorithm for testing p-containment relative to parameterized queries. Let Q be a query set with only one parameterized query Q. Let V and W be two view sets. The algorithm tests $V \preceq_{IS(Q)} W$ as follows. First call the algorithm GenPartial to find all the more restrictive parameterized queries of Q that are completely answerable by V. For each of them, call the algorithm TestComp to check if it is also completely answerable by W. By Theorem 2, $V \preceq_{IS(Q)} W$ iff all these parameterized queries that are completely answerable by V are also completely answerable by W. The algorithm can be easily generalized to the case where Q is a finite set of parameterized queries.

5   MCR-Containment

So far we have considered query-answering power of views with respect to equivalent rewritings of queries. In information-integration systems, we often need to consider maximally-contained rewritings. In this section, we introduce the concept of *MCR-containment*, which describes the relative power of two view sets in terms of their maximally-contained rewritings of queries. Surprisingly, MCR-containment is essentially the same as p-containment.

Definition 9. *(maximally-contained rewritings) A maximally-contained rewriting P of a query Q using a view set V satisfies the following conditions: (1) P is a finite union of conjunctive queries using only the views in V; (2) For any database, the answer computed by P is a subset of the answer to Q; and (3) No other unions of conjunctive queries that satisfy the two conditions above can properly contain P.*

Intuitively, a maximally-contained rewriting (henceforth "MCR" for short) is a plan that uses only views in V and computes the maximal answer to query Q. If Q has two MCR's, by definition, they must be equivalent as queries. If Q is answerable by V, then an equivalent rewriting of Q using V is also an MCR of Q.

Example 10. Consider the following query Q and view V on the two relations in Example 6:

$$Q: q(M, D, C) :\text{-} car(M, D), loc(D, C)$$
$$V: v(M, D, sf) :\text{-} car(M, D), loc(D, sf)$$

Suppose we have the access to view V only. Then $q(M, D, sf) :\text{-} v(M, D, sf)$ is an MCR of the query Q using the view V. That is, we can give the user only the information about car dealers in San Francisco as an answer to the query, but not anything more.

Definition 10. *(MCR-containment) A view set V is MCR-contained in another view set W, denoted by $V \preceq_{MCR} W$, if for any query Q, we have $MCR(Q, V) \sqsubseteq MCR(Q, W)$, where $MCR(Q, V)$ and $MCR(Q, W)$ are MCR's of Q using V and W, respectively.*[2] *The two sets are MCR-equipotent, denoted by $V \asymp_{MCR} W$, if $V \preceq_{MCR} W$, and $W \preceq_{MCR} V$.*

Surprisingly, MCR-containment is essentially the same as p-containment.

Theorem 3. *For two view sets V and W, $V \preceq_p W$ if and only if $V \preceq_{MCR} W$.*

Proof. "If": Suppose $V \preceq_{MCR} W$. Consider each view $V \in V$. Clearly V itself is an MCR of the query V using V, since it is an equivalent rewriting of V. Let $MCR(V, W)$ be an MCR of V using W. Since $V \preceq_{MCR} W$, we have $V \sqsubseteq MCR(V, W)$. On the other hand, by the definition of MCR's, $MCR(V, W) \sqsubseteq V$. Thus $MCR(V, W)$ and V are equivalent, and $MCR(V, W)$ is an equivalent rewriting of V using W. By Lemma 1, $V \preceq_p W$.

"Only if": Suppose $V \preceq_p W$. By Lemma 1, every view has an equivalent rewriting using W. For any query Q, let $MCR(Q, V)$ and $MCR(Q, W)$ be MCR's of Q using V and W, respectively. We replace each view in $MCR(Q, V)$ with its corresponding rewriting using W, and obtain a new rewriting MCR' of query Q using W, which is equivalent to $MCR(Q, V)$. By the definition of MCR's, we have $MCR' \sqsubseteq MCR(Q, W)$. Thus $MCR(Q, V) \sqsubseteq MCR(Q, W)$, and $V \preceq_{MCR} W$.

6 Related Work

There has been a lot of work on the problem of selection of views to materialize in a data warehouse. In [5,14,15,25], a data warehouse is modeled as a repository of integrated information available for querying and analysis. A subset of queries are materialized to improve responsiveness, and base relations are accessed for the rest of the queries. Base relations can change over time, and the query results can be huge, resulting in costs for maintenance and space. The study in this setting has, therefore, emphasized on modeling the view-selection problem as cost-benefit analysis. For a given set of queries, various sets of sub-queries are

---

[2] We extend the query-containment notation "$\sqsubseteq$" in Definition 1 to unions of conjunctive queries in the obvious way.

considered for materialization. Redundant views in a set that increase costs are deduced using query containment, and an optimal subset is chosen.

Such a model is feasible when all queries can be answered in the worst case by accessing base relations, and not by views alone. This assumption is incorporated in the model by replicating base relations at the warehouse. Thus, the base relations themselves are considered to be normalized, independent, and minimal. However, when real-time access to base relations is prohibitive, such an approach can lead to wrong conclusions, as was seen in Example 1. In such a scenario, it is essential to ensure the *computability* of queries using *only* maintained views.

Our work is directed towards scenarios where the following assumptions hold. (1) Real-time access to base relations is prohibitive, or possibly denied, and (2) cached views are expensive to maintain over time, because of the high costs of propagating changes from base relations to views. Therefore, while minimizing a view set, it is important to retain its *query-answering* power. We believe the power of answering queries and the benefit/costs of a view set are orthogonal issues, and their interplay would make an interesting work in its own right.

The term "query-answering" has been used in [4] to mean deducing tuples that satisfy a query, given the view definitions and their extensions. In our framework, this term stands for the ability of a set to answer queries. Another related work is [13] that studies information content of views. It develops a concept *subsumption* between two sets of queries, which is used to characterize their capabilities of distinguishing two instances of a database.

Recently, [7] has proposed solutions to the following problem: given a set of queries on base relations, which views do we need to materialize in order to decrease the query answering time? The authors show that even for conjunctive queries and views only, there can be an infinite number of views that can answer the same query. At the same time, the authors show that the problem is decidable: for conjunctive queries and views, it is enough to consider a finite space of views where all views are superior, in terms of storage space and query answering time, to any other views that could answer the given queries. The problem specification in that paper is different from ours: they start with a set of given queries and no views. In our framework, we assume that a set of views are given, and queries can be arbitrary. We would like to deduce a minimal subset of views that can answer *all* queries answerable by the original set.

Currently we are working on some open problems in our framework, including ways to find an optimal EMS of a view set efficiently, to find a v-equivalent minimal subset of a view set efficiently, and to find cases where v-containment can imply p-containment, and vice-versa.

Acknowledgments. We thank Arvind Arasu for his valuable comments.

References

1. S. Abiteboul and O. M. Duschka. Complexity of answering queries using materialized views. In *PODS*, pages 254–263, 1998.

2. F. N. Afrati, M. Gergatsoulis, and T. G. Kavalieros. Answering queries using materialized views with disjunctions. In *ICDT*, pages 435–452, 1999.
3. D. Calvanese, G. D. Giacomo, M. Lenzerini, and M. Y. Vardi. Query answering using views for data integration over the Web. *WebDB*, pages 73–78, 1999.
4. D. Calvanese, G. D. Giacomo, M. Lenzerini, and M. Y. Vardi. What is view-based query rewriting. In *KRDB*, 2000.
5. S. Ceri and J. Widom. Deriving production rules for incremental view maintenance. In *Proc. of VLDB*, 1991.
6. A. K. Chandra and P. M. Merlin. Optimal implementation of conjunctive queries in relational data bases. *STOC*, pages 77–90, 1977.
7. R. Chirkova and M. R. Genesereth. Linearly bounded reformulations of conjunctive databases. *DOOD*, 2000.
8. J. Cho and H. Garcia-Molina. Synchronizing a database to improve freshness. *SIGMOD*, 2000.
9. O. M. Duschka. Query planning and optimization in information integration. *Ph.D. Thesis, Computer Science Dept., Stanford Univ.*, 1997.
10. O. M. Duschka and M. R. Genesereth. Answering recursive queries using views. In *PODS*, pages 109–116, 1997.
11. D. Florescu, A. Y. Levy, D. Suciu, and K. Yagoub. Optimization of run-time management of data intensive web-sites. In *Proc. of VLDB*, pages 627–638, 1999.
12. G. Grahne and A. O. Mendelzon. Tableau techniques for querying information sources through global schemas. In *ICDT*, pages 332–347, 1999.
13. S. Grumbach and L. Tininini. On the content of materialized aggregate views. In *PODS*, pages 47–57, 2000.
14. J. Hammer, H. Garcia-Molina, J. Widom, W. Labio, and Y. Zhuge. The Stanford Data Warehousing Project. In *IEEE Data Eng. Bulletin, Special Issue on Materialized Views and Data Warehousing*, 1995.
15. W. H. Inmon and C. Kelley. *Rdb/VMS: Developing the Data Warehouse*. QED Publishing Group, Boston, Massachussetts, 1993.
16. A. Levy. Answering queries using views: A survey. *Technical report, Computer Science Dept., Washington Univ.*, 2000.
17. A. Y. Levy, A. O. Mendelzon, Y. Sagiv, and D. Srivastava. Answering queries using views. In *PODS*, pages 95–104, 1995.
18. A. Y. Levy, A. Rajaraman, and J. J. Ordille. Querying heterogeneous information sources using source descriptions. In *Proc. of VLDB*, pages 251–262, 1996.
19. C. Li, M. Bawa, and J. D. Ullman. Minimizing view sets without losing query-answering power (extended version). *Technical report, Computer Science Dept., Stanford Univ.*, http://dbpubs.stanford.edu:8090/pub/2001-1, 2000.
20. P. Mitra. An algorithm for answering queries efficiently using views. In *Technical Report, Stanford University*, 1999.
21. R. Pottinger and A. Levy. A scalable algorithm for answering queries using views. In *Proc. of VLDB*, 2000.
22. X. Qian. Query folding. In *ICDE*, pages 48–55, 1996.
23. Y. Sagiv and M. Yannakakis. Equivalences among relational expressions with the union and difference operators. *Journal of the ACM*, 27(4):633–655, 1980.
24. J. D. Ullman. Information integration using logical views. In *ICDT*, pages 19–40, 1997.
25. J. Widom. Research problems in data warehousing. In *Proc. of the Intl. Conf. on Information and Knowledge Management*, 1995.
26. G. Wiederhold. Mediators in the architecture of future information systems. *IEEE Computer*, 25(3):38–49, 1992.

Cost Based Data Dissemination in Broadcast Networks[*]

Bo Xu[1], Ouri Wolfson[1], and Sam Chamberlain[2]

[1] University of Illinois at Chicago
{bxu,wolfson}@eecs.uic.edu
[2] Army Research Laboratories
wildman@arl.mil

Abstract. We consider the problem of data dissemination in a broadcast network. In contrast to previously studied models, broadcasting is among peers, rather than client server. Such a model represents, for example, satellite communication among widely distributed nodes, sensor networks, and mobile ad-hoc networks. We introduce a cost model for data dissemination in peer to peer broadcast networks. The model quantifies the tradeoff between the inconsistency of the data, and its transmission cost; the transmission cost may be given in terms of dollars, energy, or bandwidth. Using the model we first determine the parameters for which eager (i.e. consistent) replication has a lower cost than lazy (i.e. inconsistent) replication. Then we introduce a lazy broadcast policy and compare it with several naive or traditional approaches to solving the problem.

1 Introduction

A mobile computing problem that has generated a significant amount of interest in the database community is data broadcasting (see for example [19]). The problem is how to organize the pages in a broadcast from a server to a large client population in the dissemination of public information (e.g. electronic news services, stock-price information, etc.). A strongly related problem is how to replicate (or cache) the broadcast data in the Mobile Units that receive the broadcast.

In this paper we study the problems of broadcasting and replication in a peer to peer rather than client server architecture. More precisely, we study the problem of dissemination, i.e. full replication at all the nodes in the system. This architecture is motivated by new types of emerging wireless broadcast networks such as Mobile Ad-hoc Networks (see [6])[1], sensor and "smart dust" networks ([12]), and satellite networks. These networks enable novel applications in which

[*] This research was supported in part by Army Research Labs grant DAAL01-96-2-0003, DARPA grant N66001-97-2-8901, NSF grants CCR-9816633, CCR-9803974, IRI-9712967, EIA-0000516, and INT-9812325.

[1] A Mobile Ad-hoc Network (MANET) is a system of mobile computers (or nodes) equipped with wireless broadcast transmitters and receivers which are used for com-

the nodes of a network collaborate to assemble a complete database. For instance, in the case of sensors that are parachuted or sprayed from an airplane, the database renders a global picture of an unknown terrain from local images collected by individual sensors. Or, the database consists of the current location of each member in a military unit (in a MANET case), or another meaningful database constructed from a set of widely distributed fragments.

We model such applications using a "master" replication environment (see [10]), in which each node i "owns" the master copy of a data item D_i, i.e. it generates all the updates to D_i. For example, D_i may be the latest in a sequence of images taken periodically by the node i of its local surroundings. Each new image updates D_i. Or, D_i may be the location of the node which is moving; D_i is updated when the Global Positioning System (GPS) on board the node i indicates a current location that deviates from D_i by more than a prespecified threshold. The database of interest is $D = \{D_1,...,D_n\}$, where n is the number of nodes and also the number of items in the database.[2]

It is required that D is accessible from each node in the network,[3] thus each node stores a (possibly inconsistent) copy of D. [4] Our paper deals with various policies of broadcasting updates of the data items. In each broadcast a data item is associated with its version number, and a node that receives a broadcasted data item updates its local database if and only if the local version is older than the newly arrived version. In the broadcast policies there is a tradeoff between data consistency and communication cost. In satellite networks the communication cost is in terms of actual dollars the customer is charged by the network provider; in sensor networks, due to the small size of the battery, the communication cost is in terms of energy consumption for message transmission; and in MANET's the critical cost component is bandwidth (see [6]). Bandwidth for (secure) communication is an important and scarce resource, particularly in military applications (see [17]).

Now let us discuss the broadcast policies. One obvious policy is the following: for each node i, when D_i is updated, node i broadcasts the new version of D_i to the other nodes in the network. We call this the Single-item Broadcast

---

municating within the system. Such networks provide an attractive and inexpensive alternative to the cellular infrastructures when this infrastructure is unavailable (e.g. in remote and disaster areas), or inefficient, or too expensive to use. Mobile Ad-hoc Networks are used to communicate among the nodes of a military unit, in rescue and disaster relief operations, in collaborative mobile data exchange (e.g the set of attendees at a conference), and other "micronetworking" technologies ([14]).

[2] In case D_i is the location of i, the database D is of interest in what are called Moving Objects Database (MOD) applications (see [13]). If D_i is the location of object i in a battlefield situation, then a typical query may be: retrieve the friendly helicopters that are in a given region. Other MOD applications involve emergency (fire, police) vehicles and local transportation systems (e.g. city bus system).

[3] For example, the location of the members of a platoon should be viewable by any member at any time.

[4] By inconsistency of D we mean that some data items may not contain the most recent version.

Dissemination (SBD) policy. In the networks and applications we discuss in this paper, nodes may be disconnected, turned off or out of battery. Thus the broadcast of D_i may not be received by all the nodes in the system. A natural way to deal with this problem is to rebroadcast an update to D_i until it is acknowledged by all the nodes, i.e. Reliable Broadcast Dissemination (RBD). Clearly, if the new version is not much different than the previous one and if the probability of reception is low (thus necessitating multiple broadcasts), then this increase in communication cost is not justified. An alternative option, which we adopt in SBD, is to broadcast each update once, and let copies diverge. Thus the delivery of updates is unreliable, and consequently the dissemination of D_i is "lazy" in the sense that the copy of D_i stored at a node may be inconsistent.

How can we quantify the tradeoff between the increase in consistency afforded by a reliable broadcast and its increase in communication cost? In order to answer this question we introduce the concept of *inconsistency-cost* of a data item. This concept, in turn, is quantified via the notion of the cost difference between two versions of a data item D_i. In other words, the inconsistency cost of using an older version v rather than the latest version w is the distance between the two versions. For example, if D_i represents a location, then the cost difference between two versions of D_i can be taken to be the distance between the two locations. If D_i is an image, an existing algorithm that quantifies the difference between two images can be used (see for example [5]). If D_i is the quantity-on-hand of a widget, then the difference between the two versions is the difference between the quantities. Now, in order to quantify the tradeoff between inconsistency and communication one has to answer the question: what amount of bandwidth/energy/dollars am I willing to spend in order to reduce the inconsistency cost on a data item by one unit? Using this model we establish the cost formulas for RBD and SBD, i.e reliable and unreliable broadcasting, and based on them formulas for selecting one of the two policies for a given set of system parameters.

For the cases when unreliable broadcast, particularly SBD, is more appropriate, consistency of the local databases can be enhanced by a policy that we call Full Broadcast Dissemination (FBD). In FBD, whenever D_i is updated, i broadcasts its local copy of the whole database D, called $D(i)$. In other words, i broadcasts D_i, as well as its local version of each one of the other data items in the database. When a node j receives this broadcast, j updates its version of D_i, and j also updates its local copy of each other item D_k, for which the version number in $D(i)$ is more recent. Thus these indirect broadcasts of D_k (to j via i) are "gossip" messages that increase the consistency of each local database. However, again, this comes at the price of an increase in communication cost due to the fact that each broadcast message is n times longer.

The SBD and FBD policies represent in some sense two extreme solutions on a consistency-communication spectrum of lazy dissemination policies. SBD has minimum communication cost and minimum local database consistency, whereas FBD has maximum communication cost and maximum (under the imperfect circumstances) local database consistency.

In this paper we introduce and analyze the Adaptive Broadcast Dissemination (ABD) policy that optimizes the tradeoff between consistency and communication using a cost based approach. In the ABD policy, when node i receives an update to D_i it first determines whether the expected reduction in inconsistency justifies broadcasting a message. If so, then i "pads" the broadcast message that contains D_i with a set S of data items (that i does not own) from its local database, such as to optimize the total cost. One problem that we solve in this paper is how to determine the set S, i.e. how node i should select for each broadcast message which data items from the local database to piggyback on D_i. In order to do so, i estimates for each j and k the expected benefit (in terms of inconsistency reduction) to node k of including in the broadcast message its local version of D_j.

Let us now put this paper in the context of existing work on consistency in distributed systems. Our approach is new as far as we know. Although gossiping has been studied extensively in distributed systems and databases (see for exampe [3,8]), none of the existing works uses an inconsistency-communication tradeoff cost function in order to determine what gossip messages to send. Furthermore, in the emerging resource constrained environments (e.g. sensor networks, satellite communication, and MANET's) this tradeoff is crucial. Also our notion of consistency is appropriate for the types of novel applications discussed in this paper, and is different than the traditional notion of consistency in distributed systems discussed in the literature (e.g., [3]). Specifically, in contrast to the traditional approaches, our notion of consistency does not mean consistency of different copies of a data item at different nodes, and it does not mean mutual consistency of different data items at a node. In this paper a copy of a data item at a node is consistent if it has the latest version of the data item. Otherwise it is inconsistent, and the inconsistency cost is the distance between the local copy and the latest version of the data item. Inconsistency of a local database is simply the sum of the inconsistencies of all data items. We employ gossiping to reduce inconsistency, not to ensure consistency as in using vector clocks ([3]).

In this paper we provide a comparative analysis of dissemination policies. The analysis is probabilistic and experimental, and it achieves the following objectives. First, it gives a formula for the expected total cost of SBD and RBD, and a complete characterization of the parameters for which each policy has a cost lower than the other. Second, for ABD we prove cost optimality for the set of data items broadcast by a node i, for i's level of knowledge of the system state. Third, the analysis compares the three unreliable policies discussed above, namely SBD, FBD, and ABD, and a fourth traditional one called flooding (FLD)[5] [18]. ABD proved to consistently outperform the other two policies, often having a total cost (that includes the cost of inconsistency and the cost of communication) that is several times lower than that of the other policies. Due to space limitations, the comparison of the policies is omitted from this paper.

In summary, the key contributions of this paper are as follows.

---

[5] In flooding a node i broadcasts each new data item it receives either as a results of a local update of D_i, or from a broadcast message.

- Introduction of a cost model to quantify the tradeoff between consistency and communication.
- Analyzing the performance of eager and lazy dissemination via reliable and unreliable broadcasts respectively, obtaining cost formulas for each case and determining the data and communication parameters for which eager is superior to lazy, and vice versa.
- Developing and analyzing the Adaptive Broadcast Dissemination policy, and comparing it to the other lazy dissemination policies.

The rest of the paper is organized as follows. In section 2 we introduce the operational model and the cost model. In section 3 we analyze and compare reliable and unreliable broadcasting. In section 4 we describe the ABD policy, and in section 5 we analyze it. In section 6 we discuss relevant work.

2   The Model

In subsection 2.1 we precisely define the overall operational model, and in subsection 2.2 we define the cost model.

2.1   Operational Model

The system consists of a set of n nodes that communicate by message broadcasting. Each node i $(1 < i < n)$ has a data item D_i associated with it. Node i is called D_i's owner. This data item may contain a single numeric value, or a complex data structure such as a motion plan, or an image of the local environment. Only i, and no other nodes, has the authorization to modify the state of D_i. A data item is updated at discrete time points. Each update creates a new version of the data item. In other words, the *kth version of* D_i, denoted $D_i(k)$, is generated by the kth update. We denote the latest version of D_i by $\overline{D_i}$. Furthermore, we use $v(D_i)$ to represent the version number of D_i, i.e. $v(D_i(k)) = k$. For two versions $D_i(k)$ and $D_i(k')$, we say that $D_i(k)$ is *newer than* $D_i(k')$ if $k > k'$, and $D_i(k)$ is *older than* $D_i(k')$ if $k < k'$.

An owner i periodically broadcasts its data item D_i to the rest of the system. Each such broadcast includes the version number of D_i. Since nodes may be disconnected, some broadcasts may be missed by some nodes, thus each node j has a version of each D_i which may be older than $\overline{D_i}$. The *local database* of node i at any given time is the set $< D_1^i, D_2^i, ..., D_n^i >$, where each D_j^i (for $1 \leq j \leq n$) is a version of D_j. Observe that since all the updates of D_i originate at i, then $D_i^i = \overline{D_i}$. Node i updates D_j^i $(j \neq i)$ in its local database when it receives a broadcast from j.

Nodes may be disconnected (e.g. shut down) and thus miss messages. Let p_i be the percentage of time a node i is connected. Then p_i is also the probability that i receives a message from any other node j. For example, if i is connected 60% of the time (i.e. $p_i = 0.6$), then a message from j is received by i with probability 0.6. We call p_i the *connection probability* of i.

2.2   Cost Model

In this subsection we introduce a cost function that quantifies the tradeoff between consistency and communication. The function has two purposes. First, to enable determining the items that will be included in each broadcast of the ABD policy, and second, to enable comparing the various policies.

Inconsistency cost. Assume that the distance between any two versions of a data item can be quantified. For example, in moving objects database (MOD) applications, the distance between two data item versions may be taken to be the Euclidean distance between the two locations. If D_i is an image, one of the many existing distance functions between images (e.g. the cross-correlation distance ([5])) can be used.

Formally, the *distance* between two versions $D_i(k)$ and $D_i(j)$, denoted $DIST(D_i(k), D_i(j))$, is a function whose domain is the nonnegative reals, and it has the property that the distance between two identical versions is 0. If the data item owned by each node consists of two or more types of logical objects, each with its own distance function, then the distance between the items should be taken to be the weighted averages of the pairwise distances.

We take the $DIST$ function to represent the cost, or the penalty, of using the older version rather than the newer one. More precisely, consider two consecutive updates on D_i, namely the kth update and the $(k + 1)$st update. Assume that the kth update happened at time t_k and the $(k + 1)$st update at time t_{k+1}. Intuitively, at time t_{k+1} each node j that did not receive the kth version $D_i(k)$ during the interval $[t_k, t_{k+1})$, pays a price which is equal to the distance between the latest version of D_i that j knows and $D_i(k)$. In other words, this price is the penalty that j pays for using an older version during the time in which j should have used $D_i(k)$. If j receives $D_i(k)$ sometime during the interval $[t_k, t_{k+1})$, then the price that j pays on D_i is zero. Formally, assume that at time t_{k+1} the latest version of D_i that j knows is v ($v \leq k$). Then j's *inconsistency cost on version k of D_i* is $COST\_INCO_j(D_i(k)) = DIST(D_i(v), D_i(k))$.

The *inconsistency cost of the system on $D_i(k)$* is $COST\_INCO(D_i(k)) = \sum_{1 \leq j \leq n} COST\_INCO_j(D_i(k))$.

The *total inconsistency cost of the system on D_i up to* the mth update of D_i, denoted $COST\_INCO(i, m)$, is $\sum_{1 \leq k < m} COST\_INCO(D_i(k))$.

The *total inconsistency cost for the system up to time t* is $COST\_INCO(t) = \sum_{1 \leq i \leq n} COST\_INCO(i, m_i)$, where m_i is the highest version number of D_i at time t.

Communication cost. The cost of a message depends on the length of the message. In particular, if there are m data items in a message, the cost of the message is $C_1 + m \cdot C_2$. C_1 is called the *message initiation cost* and C_2 is called the *message unit cost*. C_1 represents the cost of energy consumed by the CPU to prepare and send the message. C_2 represents the incremental cost of adding a data item to a message. The values of C_1 and C_2 are given in inconsistency cost units. They are determined based on the amount of resource that one is willing to spend in order to reduce the inconsistency cost on a version by one unit. For example, if $C_1 = C_2$ and one is willing to spend one message of one data item in order to reduce the inconsistency by at least 50, then $C_1 = C_2 = 1/100$.

The *total communication cost up to time* t is the sum of the costs of all the messages that have been broadcast from the beginning (time 0) until t.

System cost. The *system cost up to time* t, denoted $COST\_SYS(t)$, is the sum of the total inconsistency for the system up to t, and the total communication cost up to t. The system cost is the objective function optimized by the ABD policy.

3   Reliable Versus Unreliable Broadcasting

In this section we completely characterize the cases in which lazy dissemination by unreliable broadcasting outperforms eager dissemination by reliable broadcasting, and vice versa. Lazy dissemination is executed by the Single-item Broadcast Dissemination policy, in which each node i unreliably broadcasts each update it receives, when i receives it. Eager dissemination is executed by the Reliable Broadcast Dissemination (RBD) policy, in which each node i reliably broadcasts each update it receives, when i receives it; by reliable broadcast we mean that i retransmits the message until it is acknowledged by all the other nodes. Performance of the two policies is measured in terms of the system cost, as defined at the end of the previous section. We first derive the closed formulas for the system costs of SBD and RBD. Then, based on these formulas, we compare SBD and RBD.

In the following discussion, we assume that for each node i, the updates at i are generated by a Poisson process with intensity λ_i. Let $\lambda = \sum_{1 \leq i \leq n} \lambda_i$. The number of nodes in the system is n, the connection probability p_i for each node i, message initiation cost C_1, and the message unit cost C_2.

The following theorem gives the system cost of SBD up to a given point in time.

Theorem 1 The system cost of SBD up to time t (i.e. $COST\_SYS_{SBD}(t)$) is a random variable whose expected value is

$$E[COST\_SYS_{SBD}(t)] = \lambda \cdot t \cdot (C_1 + C_2) + \sum_{1 \leq i \leq n} \sum_{m=1}^{\infty} \left(\frac{e^{-\lambda_i \cdot t} \cdot (\lambda_i \cdot t)^m}{m!} \cdot \right.$$

$$\sum_{q=1}^{m-1} \sum_{1 \leq j \leq n}^{j \neq i} ((1 - p_j)^q \cdot DIST(D_i(0), D_i(q))$$

$$\left. + \sum_{k=1}^{q-1} p_j \cdot (1 - p_j)^{q-k} \cdot DIST(D_i(k), D_i(q)))) \right)$$

□

Now we analyze the system cost of the reliable broadcast dissemination (RBD) policy. First let us introduce a lemma which gives the expected number of times that a message is transmitted from node i (remember that in RBD a message is retransmitted until it is acknowledged by all the other nodes).

Lemma 1 Let R_i be the number of times that a message is transmitted. Then R_i is a random variable whose expected value is:

$$E[R_i] = \sum_{k=1}^{\infty}(k \cdot (\prod_{\substack{1 \leq j \leq n \\ j \neq i}} (1 - (1 - p_j)^k) - \prod_{\substack{1 \leq j \leq n \\ j \neq i}} (1 - (1 - p_j)^{k-1})))$$

$\square$

Theorem 2 The system cost of RBD up to time t (i.e. $COST\_SYS_{RBD}(t)$) is a random variable whose expected value is:

$$E[COST\_SYS_{RBD}(t)] = (C_1 + C_2) \cdot t \cdot \sum_{i=1}^{n}(\lambda_i \cdot E[R_i]) + (n - 1) \cdot C_1 \cdot \lambda \cdot t$$

(the value of $E[R_i]$ was derived in Lemma 1) $\square$

Based on Theorems 1 and 2, we identify the situations in which SBD outperforms RBD, and vice versa. But due to space limitations, this result is omitted.

4   The Adaptive Broadcast Dissemination Policy

In this section we describe the Adaptive Broadcast Dissemination policy. Intuitively, a node i executing the policy behaves as follows. When it receives an update to D_i, node i constructs a broadcast message by evaluating the benefit of including in the message each one of the data items in its local database. Specifically, the ABD policy executed by i consists of the following two steps.

(1) Benefit estimation: For each data item in the local database, estimate how much the inconsistency of the system could be reduced if that data item is included in the message.

(2) Message construction: Construct the message which is a subset of the local database so that the total estimated net benefit of the message is maximized (The net benefit is the difference between the inconsistency reduced by the message and the cost of the message). Observe that the set of data items to be broadcast may be empty. In other words, when D_i is updated, node i may estimate that the net benefit of broadcasting any data item is negative.

Each one of the above steps is executed by an algorithm which is described in one of the next two subsections.

4.1   Benefit Estimation

Intuitively, the benefit to the system of including a data item D_j in a message that node i broadcasts is in terms of inconsistency reduction. This reduction depends on the nodes that receive the broadcast, and on the latest version of D_j at each one of these nodes. Node i maintains data structures that enable it to estimate the latest version of D_j at each node. Then the benefit of including a data item D_j in a message that i broadcasts is simply the sum of the expected inconsistency reductions at all the nodes.

In computing the inconsistency reduction for a node k we attempt to be as accurate as possible, and we do so as follows. Node i maintains a "knowledge matrix" which stores in entry (k, j) the last version number of D_j that node i received from node k (this version is called $v(D_j^k)$), and the time when it was received. Additionally, i saves in the "real history" for each D_j all the versions of D_j that i has "heard" from other nodes, the times at which it has done so, and from which node they were received[6]. The reason for maintaining all this information is that now, in estimating which version of D_j node k has, node i can take into consideration two factors: (1) the last version of D_j that i received from k at time, say t, and (2) the fact that since time t node k may have received updates of D_j by "third party" messages that were transmitted after time t, and "heard" by both, k and i. Node i also saves with each version v of D_j that it "heard", the distance (i.e. the inconsistency caused by the version difference) between v and the last version of D_j that i knows; this difference is the parameter necessary in order to compute the inconsistency cost reduction that is obtained if node i broadcasts its latest version of D_j.

In subsection 4.1.1 we describe the data structures that are used by a node i in benefit estimation. In subsection 4.1.2 we present i's benefit estimation method.

4.1.1 Data Structures

(1) The Knowledge matrix: For each data item D_j ($j \neq i$), denote by $v(D_j^k)$ the latest version number of D_j that i received from k, and denote by $t(D_j^k)$ the last time when D_j^k was received at i. The *knowledge matrix* at node i is:

$$M_i = \begin{pmatrix} (t(D_1^1), v(D_1^1)) & (t(D_2^1), v(D_2^1)) & \cdots & (t(D_n^1), v(D_n^1)) \\ (t(D_1^2), v(D_1^2)) & (t(D_2^2), v(D_2^2)) & \cdots & (t(D_n^2), v(D_n^2)) \\ \vdots & \vdots & \ddots & \vdots \\ (t(D_1^n), v(D_1^n)) & (t(D_2^n), v(D_2^n)) & \cdots & (t(D_n^n), v(D_n^n)) \end{pmatrix}$$

Node i updates the matrix whenever it receives a message. Specifically, when i receives a message from k that includes D_j, i updates the entry (k,j) of the matrix. In addition, if the version of D_j received is newer than the version in i's local database, then the newer version updates D_j in the local database.

(2) Version sequence: A version sequence records all the version numbers that i has ever known about a data item. Due to unreliability, it is possible that i has not received all the versions of a data item. In particular, the *version sequence* of D_j is $VS_j = < v_1, v_2, ..., v_h >$ where $v_1 < v_2 < ... < v_h$ are all the version numbers that i has ever known about D_j. For each $v \in VS_j$, i saves in the distance between $D_j(v)$ and $D_j(v_h)$.

(3) Dissemination history: For each version number v in each VS_j, i maintains a *dissemination history* $DH_j(v)$. This history records every time point at which

---

[6] There is a potential storage problem here, which we address, but we postpone the discussion for now.

i received $D_j(v)$ from a node. $DH_j(v)$ also contains every time point at which i broadcast $D_j(v)$.

Now we discuss how we limit the amount of storage used. Observe that the lengths of each version sequence VS_j and dissemination history $DH_j(v)$ increases unboundedly as i receives more broadcasts. This presents a storage problem. A straight-forward solution to this problem is to limit the length of each version sequence to α and the length of each dissemination history to β. We call this variant of the ABD policy $\text{ABD}(\alpha, \beta)$. The drawback of $\text{ABD}(\alpha, \beta)$ is that when the length of a dissemination history $DH_j(v)$ is smaller than β, since each dissemination history is limited to β, other dissemination histories can not make use of the free storage of $DH_j(v)$. A better solution, which we adopt in this paper, is to limit the sum of the lengths of each dissemination history in each version sequence. In particular, we use ABD-s to denote the ABD policy in which $\sum_{1 \le j \le n} \sum_{v \in VS_j} |DH_j(v)|$ is limited to s [7]. s must be at least n.

4.1.2 The Benefit Estimation Method

When an update on D_i occurs, node i estimates the benefit of including its latest version of D_j in the broadcast message, for each D_j in the local database. Intuitively, i does so using the following procedure. For each node k compute the set of versions of D_j that k can have, i.e. the set of versions that were received at i after D_j^k was received. Assume that there are m such versions. Then, compute the set of broadcasts from which k could have learned each one of these versions. Based on this set compute the probabilities $q_1, q_2, ..., q_m$ that k has each one of the possible versions $v_1, v_2, ..., v_m$. Finally, compute the expected benefit to k as the sum $q_1 \cdot DIST(v(D_j), v_1) + q_2 \cdot DIST(v(D_j), v_2) + ... + q_m \cdot DIST(v(D_j), v_m)$.

Formally, node i performs the benefit estimation in five steps:

(1) Construct an *effective version sequence* (EVS) of D_j^k which is a subsequence of VS_j:

$$EVS_j^k = \{ v | v \in VS_j \text{ and } v \ge v(D_j^k) \text{ and there exists } t \in DH_j(v) \text{ such that } t \ge t(D_j^k) \}$$

Intuitively, EVS_j^k is the set of versions of D_j that k can have, as far as i knows. In other words, EVS_j^k contains each version v that satisfies the following two properties: (i) v is higher than or equal to the latest version of D_j that i has received from k (i.e. $v(D_j^k)$), and (ii) i has received at least one broadcast which includes $D_j(v)$, and that broadcast arrived later than D_j^k.

(2) For each v in EVS_j^k that is higher than $v(D_j^k)$, count the *effective dissemination number* which is the size of the set $\{t | t \in DH_j(v) \text{ and } t > t(D_j^k)\}$, and denote this number $EDN_j^k(v)$. Intuitively, $EDN_j^k(v)$ is the number of broadcasts from which k could have learned $D_j(v)$, based on i's knowledge.

(3) For each v in EVS_j^k, compute η_v which, as we will prove, is the probability that the version number of D_j in k's local database is v. If $v = v(D_j^k)$, $\eta_v = \prod_{v' \in EVS_j^k}^{v' > v} (1 - p_k)^{EDN_j^k(v')}$. Otherwise, $\eta_v = (1 - (1 - p_k)^{EDN_j^k(v)}) \prod_{v' \in EVS_j^k}^{v' > v} (1 - p_k)^{EDN_j^k(v')}$

---

[7] $|A|$ denotes the size of the set A.

(4) If the version number of D_j in k's local database is v, then the estimated benefit to k of including D_j^i in the broadcast message is taken to be the distance between $D_j(v)$ and D_j^i (i.e. $DIST(D_j(v), D_j^i)$). Denote this benefit $B(D_j^i, k, v)$.

(5) The estimated benefit to k of including D_j^k in the broadcast message is taken to be $p_k \cdot \sum_{v \in EVS_j^k} (\eta_v \cdot B(D_j^i, k, v))$. Denote this benefit by $B(D_j^i, k)$. Then the estimated benefit $B(D_j^i)$ of including D_j^i in the broadcast message is:

$$B(D_j^i) = \sum_{\substack{1 \le k \le n \\ k \ne i,j}} B(D_j^i, k) \qquad (1)$$

4.2   Message Construction Step

The objective of this step is for node i to select a subset S of data items from the local database for inclusion in the broadcast message. The set S is chosen such that the expected net benefit of the message (i.e. the total expected inconsistency-reduction benefit minus the cost of the message) is maximized.

First, node i sorts the estimated benefits of the data items in descending order. Thus we have the benefit sequence $B(D_{k_1}^i) \ge B(D_{k_2}^i) \ge \dots \ge B(D_{k_n}^i)$. Then i constructs the message as follows. If there is no number t between 1 and n such that the sum of the first t members in the sequence is bigger than $(C_1 + t \cdot C_2)$, then i will not broadcast a message. Else, i finds the shortest prefix of the benefit sequence such that the sum of all the members in the prefix is greater than $(C_1 + m \cdot C_2)$, where m is the length of the prefix. i places the data items corresponding to the prefix in the broadcast message. Then i considers each member j that succeeds the prefix. If $B(D_j^i)$ is greater than or equal to C_2, then i puts D_j^i in the message.

In section 5 we show that the procedure in this step broadcasts the subset S of data items whose net benefit is higher than that of any other subset.

This concludes the description of the ABD-s policy, which consists of the benefit estimation and message construction steps. It is easy to see that the time complexity of the policy is $O(n \cdot s)$.

5   Analysis of the ABD Algorithm

In this section we prove cost optimality of ABD based on the level of knowledge that node i has about the other nodes in the system. The following definitions are used in the analysis.

Definition 1 If at time t there is a broadcast from i which includes D_j, we say that a *dissemination of D_j* occurs at time t, and denote it $r_j(i, v, t)$ where v is the version number of D_j included in that broadcast. □

Definition 2 A *dissemination sequence of D_j at time t* is the sequence of all the disseminations of D_j that occurred from the beginning until time t:

$$RS_j(t) = < r_j(n_1, v_1, t_1), r_j(n_2, v_2, t_2), \dots r_j(n_m, v_m, t_m) >$$

where $t_1 < t_2 < \dots < t_m \le t$. □

Definition 3 Suppose k receives a message from i which includes D_j^i. Denote $\overline{D_j^k}$ the version of D_j in k's local database immediately before the broadcast. If the version of D_j^i is higher than the version of $\overline{D_j^k}$, then the *actual benefit to k of receiving* D_j^i, denoted $\overline{B}(D_j^i)$, is: $\overline{B}(D_j^i, k) = DIST(\overline{D_j^k}, \overline{D_j}) - DIST(D_j^i, \overline{D_j})$. Otherwise the actual benefit is 0. □

In other words, the actual benefit to k of receiving D_j^i is the reduction in the distance of D_j^k from $\overline{D_j}$. Observe that the actual benefit can be negative. For example, consider the case where D_j is a numeric value and $DIST(D(k), D(k')) = |D(k) - D(k')|$. If $\overline{D_j} = 300$, $D_j^i = 100$ and $\overline{D_j^k} = 200$, then $\overline{B}(D_j^i, k) = -100$.

Definition 4 The *actual benefit of dissemination* $r_j(i, v, t)$, denoted $\overline{B}(D_j^i)$, is the sum of the actual benefits to each node k that receives the message from i at t which included D_j^i. The *actual benefit of a broadcast message* is the sum of the actual benefits of each data item included in the message. □

Now we discuss two levels of knowledge of i about the other nodes in the system.

Definition 5 Node i is *absolutely reliable on D_j for node k by time t* if i has received all the broadcast messages which included D_j and were sent between $t(D_j^k)$ and t. i is *absolutely reliable on D_j by time t* if i is absolutely reliable on D_j for each node k by t. i is *absolutely reliable by time t* if i is absolutely reliable on each D_j by t. □

Definition 6 Node i is *strictly synchronized with D_j at time t* if at t D_j in i's local database is the latest version of D_j at t. i is *strictly synchronized at time t* if i is strictly synchronized with each D_j at t. □

Obviously, if i is strictly synchronized at time t, then i's local database is identical to the system state at t.

Observe that if each node j broadcasts D_j whenever an update on D_j occurs, then a node i which is absolutely reliable on D_j by time t is strictly synchronized with D_j at time t. However, in the ABD policy a node j may decide not to broadcast the new version of D_j, and thus i is not necessarily strictly synchronized with D_j even if i is absolutely reliable on D_j. On the other hand, i can be strictly synchronized even if it is not absolutely reliable. In other words, "absolutely reliable" and "strictly synchronized" are two independent properties.

Theorem 3 Let $RS_j(t)$ be a dissemination sequence of D_j in which the last dissemination is $r_j(i, v, t)$. The actual benefit of $r_j(i, v, t)$ (i.e. $\overline{B}(D_j^i)$) is a random variable. If i is absolutely reliable on D_j by t and strictly synchronized with D_j at t, then $B(D_j^i)$ given by the ABD policy(see Equality 1) is the expected value of $\overline{B}(D_j^i)$.□

Now we devise a function which allows us to measure the cost efficiency of a broadcast.

Definition 7 The *actual net benefit* of a broadcast message is the difference between the actual benefit of the message and the cost of the message. Denote $\overline{NB}(M)$ the actual net benefit of broadcasting a set of data items M. □

Definition 8 A *broadcast sequence at time t* is the sequence of all the broadcasts in the system from the beginning (time 0) until time t:

$$BS(t) =< M(n_1, t_1), M(n_2, t_2), ..., M(n_m, t_m) > \qquad (2)$$

where $M(n_l, t_l)$ is a message that is broadcast from n_l at time t_l, and $t_1 < t_2 < ... < t_m \leq t$. □

For a node which is both absolutely reliable by t and strictly synchronized at t, we have the following theorem concerning the optimality of the ABD policy.

Theorem 4 Let $BS(t)$ be a broadcast sequence in which the last broadcast is $M(i, t)$. The actual net benefit of broadcast $M(i, t)$ (i.e. $\overline{NB}(M(i, t))$) is a random variable. In particular, let $M = \{D_{k_1}^i, D_{k_2}^i, ..., D_{k_m}^i\}$ be the set of data items broadcast by the ABD policy at time t. If i is absolutely reliable by t and strictly synchronized at t, then:

(1) $E[\overline{NB}(M)] \geq 0$

(2) For any M' which is a subset of k's local database, $E[\overline{NB}(M')] \leq E[\overline{NB}(M)]$. □

Theorem 4 shows that the message broadcast by the ABD policy is optimized because the expected net benefit of broadcasting any subset of i's local database is not higher than that of broadcasting this message. Granted, this theorem holds under the assumption of strict synchronization and absolute reliability, but i can base its decision only on the information it knows.

In some cases, Theorems 3 and 4 hold for a node which is not strictly synchronized.

Consider a data item D_i which is a single numeric value that monotonously increases as the version number of D_i increases. We call this a *monotonous data item*. Assume that the distance function is: $DIST(D_i(k), D_i(k')) = |D_i(k) - D_i(k')|$. We call this the *absolute distance function*.

For monotonous data items and absolute distance functions, Theorems 3 and 4 are true when i is absolutely reliable but not necessarily strictly synchronized at t. Thus we have the following two theorems.

Theorem 5 Let $RS_j(t)$ be a dissemination sequence where the last dissemination is $r_j(i, v, t)$. The actual benefit of $r_j(i, v, t)$ (i.e. $\overline{B}(D_j^i)$) is a random variable. For monotonous data items and absolute distance functions, if i is absolutely reliable on D_j by t, then $B(D_j^i)$ given by the ABD policy (see Equality 1) is the expected value of $\overline{B}(D_j^i)$. □

Theorem 6 Let $BS(t)$ be a broadcast sequence, where the last broadcast is $M(i, t)$. The actual net benefit of broadcast $M(i, t)$ (i.e. $\overline{NB}(M(i, t))$) is a random variable. In particular, let $M = \{D_{k_1}^i, D_{k_2}^i, ..., D_{k_m}^i\}$ be the message broadcast by the ABD policy at time t. For monotonous data items and absolute distance functions, if i is absolutely reliable by t, then:

(1) $E[\overline{NB}(M)] > 0$

(2) For any M' which is a subset of k's local database, $E[\overline{NB}(M')] \leq E[\overline{NB}(M)]$. □

6 Relevant Work

The problem of data dissemination in peer to peer broadcast networks has not been analyzed previously as far as we know. The data broadcasting problem studied in [11,20] is how to organize the broadcast and the cache in order to reduce the response time. The above works assume a centralized system with a single server and multiple clients communicating over a reliable network with large bandwidth. In contrast, in our environment these assumptions about the network do not always hold, and the environment is totally distributed and each node is both a client and a server.

Pagani et al. ([9]) proposed a reliable broadcast protocol which provides an exactly once message delivery semantics and tolerates host mobility and communication failures. Birman et al. ([4]) proposed three multicast protocols for transmitting a message reliably from a sender process to some set of destination processes. Unlike these works, we consider a "best effort" reliability model and allow copies to diverge.

Lazy replication by gossiping has been extensively investigated in the past (see for example [2]). Epidemic algorithms ([16]) such as the one used in Grapevine ([15]) also propagate updates by gossiping. However, there are two major differences between our work and the existing works. First, none of these works considered the cost of communication; this cost is important in the types of novel applications considered in this paper. Second, we consider the tradeoff between communication and inconsistency, whereas the existing works do not. Alonso, Barbara, and Garcia-Molina ([1]) studied the tradeoff between the gains in query response time obtained from quasi-caching, and the cost of checking coherency conditions. However, they assumed point to point communication and a centralized (rather than a distributed) environment.

A recent work similar to ours is TRAPP (see [7]). The similarity is in the objective of quantifying the tradeoff between consistency and performance. However, the main differences are in the basic assumptions. First, the TRAPP system deals with numeric data in traditional relational databases. Second, it quantifies the tradeoff for aggregation queries. Actually, probably the most fundamental difference is that it deals with the problem of answering a particular instantaneous query, whereas we deal with database consistency. Specifically, we want the consistency of the whole database to be maximized for as long as possible. In other words, we maximize consistency in response to continuous queries that retrieve the whole database.

References

1. R. Alonso, D. Barbara, and H. Garcia-Molina, *Data Caching Issues in an Information Retrieval System*, ACM Transactions on Database Systems, Vol. 15, No. 3, Sept. 1990.
2. R. Ladin, B. Liskov, S. Ghemawat, *Providing High Availability Using Lazy Replication*, ACM Transactions on Computer Systems, Vol. 10, No. 4, November 1992.

3. K. Birman, A. Schiper, P. Stephenson, *Lightweight Causal and Atomic Group Multicast*, ACM Transactions on Computer Systems, Vol. 9, No. 3, August 1991.
4. K. Birman, T. A. Joseph, *Reliable Communication in the Presence of Failures*, ACM Transactions on Computer Systems, Vol. 5, No. 1, Feb. 1987.
5. L. G. Brown, *A Survey of Image Registration Techniques*, ACM Computing Surveys, 24(4):325-376, December 1992.
6. J. P. Macker and M. S. Corson, *Mobile Ad Hoc Networking and the IETF*, Mobile Computing and Communications Review, Vol. 2, No. 1, January 1998.
7. C. Olston, J. Widom, *Offering a precision-performance tradeoff for aggregation queries over replicated data*, http://www-db.stanford.edu/pub/papers/trapp-ag.ps.
8. A. Schiper, J. Eggli, and A. Sandoz, *A new algorithm to implement causal ordering*, in the Proceedings of the 3rd International Workshop on Distributed Algorithms, Lecture Notes on Computer Science 392, Springer-Verlag, New York, 1989.
9. E. Pagani and G. P. Rossi, *Reliable Broadcast in Mobile Multihop Packet Networks*, Proc. ACM MOBICOM'97, pp. 34-42, Budapest, Hungary, 1997.
10. J. Gray, P. Helland, P. O'Neil, D. Shasha, *The dangers of replication and a solution*, Proc. ACM SIGMOD 96, pp. 173-182, Montreal, Canada, 1996.
11. S. Jiang, N. H. Vaidya, *Scheduling data broadcast to "impatient" users*, Proceedings of ACM International Workshop on Data Engineering for Wireless and Mobile Access, Seattle, Washington, August 1999.
12. J. M. Kahn, R. H. Katz and K. S. J. Pister, *Next century challenges: mobile networking for "Smart Dust"*, Proceedings of the fifth ACM/IEEE International Conference on Mobile Computing and Networking (MOBICOM99), Seattle, WA, August, 1999.
13. O. Wolfson, B. Xu, S. Chamberlain, L. Jiang, Moving Objects Databases: Issues and Solutions, Proceedings of the 10th International Conference on Scientific and Statistical Database Management (SSDBM98), Capri, Italy, July 1-3, 1998, pp. 111-122.
14. F. Bennett, D. Clarke, J. Evans, A. Hopper, A. Jones, and D. Leask, *Piconet: Embedded Mobile Networking*, IEEE Personal Communications, 4(5), October 1997.
15. M. D. Schroeder, A. D. Birrell, R. M. Needham, *Experience with Grapevine: the growth of a distributed system*, ACM Transactions on Computer Systems, vol. 2, No. 1, pp. 3-23, Feb. 1984.
16. R. Golding, *A weak-consistency architecture for distributed information services*, Computing Systems, vol. 5, No. 4, 1992. Usenix Association.
17. S. Chamberlain, *Model-Based Battle Command: A Paradigm Whose Time Has Come*, 1995 Symposium on C2 Research & Technology, NDU, June 1995
18. A. S. Tanenbaum, *Computer networks*, Prentice Hall, 1996.
19. S. Acharya, M. Franklin, S. Zdonik, *Balancing push and pull for data broadcast*, Proc. ACM SIGMOD 97, pp. 183-194, Tucson, Arizona, 1997.
20. S. Acharya, M. Franklin, and S. Zdonik, *Prefetching from a broadcast disk*, in 12th International Conference on Data Engineering, Feb. 1996.

Parallelizing the Data Cube

Frank Dehne[1], Todd Eavis[2], Susanne Hambrusch[3], and Andrew Rau-Chaplin[2]

[1] Carleton University, Ottawa, Canada
frank@dehne.net, http://www.dehne.net
[2] Dalhousie University, Halifax, Canada
eavis@cs.dal.ca, arc@cs.dal.ca, http://www.cs.dal.ca/~arc
[3] Purdue University, West Lafayette, Indiana, USA
seh@cs.purdue.edu, http://www.cs.purdue.edu/people/seh

Abstract. This paper presents a general methodology for the *efficient parallelization of existing data cube construction algorithms*. We describe two different partitioning strategies, one for top-down and one for bottom-up cube algorithms. Both partitioning strategies assign subcubes to individual processors in such a way that the loads assigned to the processors are balanced. Our methods reduce inter-processor communication overhead by partitioning the load in advance instead of computing each individual group-by in parallel as is done in previous parallel approaches. In fact, after the initial load distribution phase, each processor can compute its assigned subcube without any communication with the other processors. Our methods enable code reuse by permitting the use of existing sequential (external memory) data cube algorithms for the subcube computations on each processor. This supports the transfer of optimized sequential data cube code to a parallel setting.

The bottom-up partitioning strategy balances the number of single attribute external memory sorts made by each processor. The top-down strategy partitions a weighted tree in which weights reflect algorithm specific cost measures like estimated group-by sizes. Both partitioning approaches can be implemented on any *shared disk* type parallel machine composed of p processors connected via an interconnection fabric and with access to a shared parallel disk array. Experimental results presented show that our partitioning strategies generate a close to optimal load balance between processors.

1 Introduction

Data cube queries represent an important class of On-Line Analytical Processing (OLAP) queries in decision support systems. The precomputation of the different group-bys of a data cube (i.e., the forming of aggregates for every combination of GROUP BY attributes) is critical to improving the response time of the queries [16]. Numerous solutions for generating the data cube have been proposed. One of the main differences between the many solutions is whether they are aimed at sparse or dense relations [4,17,20,21,27]. Solutions within a

J. Van den Bussche and V. Vianu (Eds.): ICDT 2001, LNCS 1973, pp. 129–143, 2001.
© Springer-Verlag Berlin Heidelberg 2001

category can also differ considerably. For example, top-down data cube computations for dense relations based on sorting have different characteristics from those based on hashing.

To meet the need for improved performance and to effectively handle the increase in data sizes, parallel solutions for generating the data cube are needed. In this paper we present a general framework for the efficient parallelization of existing data cube construction algorithms. We present load balanced and communication efficient partitioning strategies which generate a subcube computation for every processor. Subcube computations are then carried out using existing sequential, external memory data cube algorithms.

Balancing the load assigned to different processors and minimizing the communication overhead are the core problems in achieving high performance on parallel systems. The heart of this paper are two partitioning strategies, one for top-down and one for bottom-up data cube construction algorithms. Good load balancing approaches generally make use of application specific characteristics. Our partitioning strategies assign loads to processors by using metrics known to be crucial to the performance of data cube algorithms [1,4,21]. The bottom-up partitioning strategy balances the number of single attribute external sorts made by each processor [4]. The top-down strategy partitions a weighted tree in which weights reflect algorithm specific cost measures such as estimated group-by sizes [1,21].

The advantages of our load balancing methods compared to the previously published parallel data cube construction methods [13,14] are:

- Our methods reduce inter-processor communication overhead by partitioning the load in advance instead of computing each individual group-by in parallel (as proposed in [13,14]). In fact, after our load distribution phase, each processor can compute its assigned subcube without any inter-processor communication.
- Our methods maximize code reuse from existing sequential data cube implementations by using existing sequential (external memory) data cube algorithms for the subcube computations on each processor. This supports the transfer of optimized sequential data cube code to the parallel setting.

Our partitioning approaches are designed for standard, *shared disk* type, parallel machines: p processors connected via an interconnection fabric where the processors have standard-size local memories and access to a shared disk array. We have implemented our top-down partitioning strategy in MPI and tested it on a multiprocessor cluster. We also tested our bottom-up partitioning strategy through a simulation. Our experimental results indicate that our partitioning strategies generate close to optimal load balancing. Our tests on the multiprocessor cluster showed close to optimal (linear) speedup.

The paper is organized as follows. Section 2 describes the parallel machine model underlying our partitioning approaches as well as the input and the output configuration for our algorithms. Section 3 presents our partitioning approach for parallel bottom-up data cube generation and Section 4 outlines our method for parallel top-down data cube generation. In Section 5 we indicate how our top-down cube parallelization can be easily modified to obtain an efficient parallelization of the ArrayCube method [27]. Section 6 presents the performance analysis of our partitioning approaches. Section 7 concludes the paper and discusses possible extensions of our methods.

2   Parallel Computing Model

We use the standard *shared disk* parallel machine model. That is, we assume p processors connected via an interconnection fabric where processors have standard size local memories and concurrent access to a shared disk array. For the purpose of parallel algorithm design, we use the *Coarse Grained Multicomputer* (CGM) model [5,8,15,18,23]. More precisely, we use the *EM-CGM* model [6,7,9] which is a multi-processor version of Vitter's *Parallel Disk Model* [24,25,26].

For our parallel data cube construction methods we assume that the d-dimensional input data set R of size N is stored on the shared disk array. The output, i.e. the group-bys comprising the data cube, will be written to the shared disk array. For the choice of output file format, it is important to consider the way in which the data cube will be used in subsequent applications. For example, if we assume that a visualization application will require fast access to individual group-bys then we may want to store each group-by in striped format over the entire disk array.

3   Parallel Bottom-Up Data Cube Construction

In many data cube applications, the underlying data set R is sparse; i.e., N is much smaller than the number of possible values in the given d-dimensional space. Bottom-up data cube construction methods aim at computing the data cube for such cases. Bottom-up methods like *BUC* [4] and *PartitionCube* [part of [20]] calculate the group-bys in an order which emphasizes the reuse of previously computed sort orders and in-memory sorts through data locality. If the data has previously been sorted by attribute A then, creating an AB sort order does not require a complete resorting. A local resorting of *A-blocks* (blocks of consecutive elements that have the same attribute A) can be used instead. The sorting of such A-blocks can often be performed in local memory and, hence, instead of another external memory sort, the AB order can be created in one single scan through the disk. Bottom-up methods [4,20] attempt to break the problem into a sequence of single attribute sorts which share prefixes of attributes and can be performed in local memory with a single disk scan. As outlined in [4,20], the total computation time of these methods is dominated by the number of such *single attribute sorts*.

In this section we describe a partitioning of the group-by computations into p independent subproblems. Our goal is to balance the number of single attribute sorts required to solve each subproblem and to ensure that each subproblem has overlapping sort sequences in the same way as for the sequential methods (thereby avoiding additional work).

Let A_1, ..., A_d be the attributes of the data cube such that $|A_1| \geq |A_2| \geq \cdots$ $\geq |A_d|$ where $|A_i|$ is the number of different possible values for attribute A_i. As observed in [20], the set of all groups-bys of the data cube can be partitioned into those that contain A_1 and those that do not contain A_1. In our partitioning approach, the groups-bys containing A_1 will be sorted by A_1. We indicate this by saying that they contain A_1 as a *prefix*. The group-bys not containing A_1 (i.e., A_1 is projected out) contain A_1 as a *postfix*. We then recurse with the same scheme on the remaining attributes. We shall utilize this property to partition the computation of all group-bys into independent subproblems computing group-bys. The load between subproblems will be balanced and they will have overlapping sort sequences in the same way as for the sequential methods. In the following we give the details of our partitioning method.

Let x, y, z be sequences of attributes representing sort orders and let A be an arbitrary single attribute. We introduce the following definition of sets of attribute sequences representing sort orders (and their respective group-bys):

$$B_1(x, A, z) = \{x, xA\} \tag{1}$$
$$B_i(x, Ay, z) = B_{i-1}(xA, y, z) \cup B_{i-1}(x, y, Az), 2 \leq i \leq \log p + 1 \tag{2}$$

The entire data cube construction corresponds to the set $B_d(\emptyset, A_1 \ldots A_d, \emptyset)$ of sort orders and respective group-bys, where d is the dimension of the the data cube. We refer to i as the *rank* of $B_i(\ldots)$. The set $B_d(\emptyset, A_1 \ldots A_d, \emptyset)$ is the union of two subsets of rank $d - 1$: $B_{d-1}(A_1, A_2 \ldots A_d, \emptyset)$ and $B_{d-1}(\emptyset, A_2 \ldots A_d, A_1)$. These, in turn, are the union of four subsets of rank $d - 2$. A complete example for a 4-dimensional data cube with attributes A, B, C, D is shown in Figure 1.

$B_4(\emptyset, ABCD, \emptyset)$	$B_3(\emptyset, BCD, A)$	$B_2(\emptyset, CD, BA)$	$B_1(\emptyset, D, CBA) = \{\emptyset, D\}$
			$B_1(C, D, BA) = \{C, CD\}$
		$B_2(B, CD, A)$	$B_1(B, D, CA) = \{B, BD\}$
			$B_1(BC, D, A) = \{BC, BCD\}$
	$B_3(A, BCD, \emptyset)$	$B_2(A, CD, B)$	$B_1(A, D, CB) = \{A, AD\}$
			$B_1(AC, D, B) = \{AC, ACD\}$
		$B_2(AB, CD, \emptyset)$	$B_1(AB, D, C) = \{AB, ABD\}$
			$B_1(ABC, D, \emptyset) = \{ABC, ABCD\}$

Fig. 1. Partitioning For A 4-Dimensional Data Cube With Attributes A, B, C, D.

For the sake of simplifying the discussion, we assume that p is a power of 2. Consider the $2p$ B-sets of rank $d - \log_2(p) - 1$. Let $\beta = (B^1, B^2, \ldots B^{2p})$ be these $2p$ sets in the order defined by Equation (2). Define

$$\text{Shuffle}(\beta) = < B^1 \cup B^{2p}, B^2 \cup B^{2p-1}, B^3 \cup B^{2p-2}, \ldots, B^p \cup B^{p+1} >$$
$$= < \Gamma_1, \ldots, \Gamma_p >$$

We assign set $\Gamma_i = B^i \cup B^{2p-i+1}$ to processor P_i, $1 \leq i \leq p$. Observe that from the construction of all group-bys in each Γ_i it follows that every processor performs the same number of single attribute sorts.

Algorithm 1 Parallel Bottom-Up Cube Construction.

Each processor P_i, $1 \leq i \leq p$, performs the following steps, independently and in parallel:

(1) Calculate Γ_i as described above.

(2) Compute all group-bys in Γ_i using a sequential (external-memory) bottom-up cube construction method.

— End of Algorithm —

Algorithm 1 can easily be generalized to values of p which are not powers of 2. We also note that Algorithm 1 requires $p \leq 2^{d-1}$. This is usually the case in practice. However, if a parallel algorithm is needed for larger values of p, the partitioning strategy needs to be augmented. Such an augmentation could, for example, be a partitioning strategy based on the number of data items for a particular attribute. This would be applied after partitioning based on the number of attributes has been done. Since the range $p \in \{2^0 \ldots 2^{d-1}\}$ covers current needs with respect to machine and dimension sizes, we do not further discuss such augmentations in this paper.

Algorithm 1 exhibits the following properties:

(a) *The computation of each group-by is assigned to a unique processor.*

(b) *The calculation of the group-bys in Γ_i, assigned to processor P_i, requires the same number of single attribute sorts for all $1 \leq i \leq p$.*

(c) *The sorts performed at processor P_i share prefixes of attributes in the same way as in [4,20] and can be performed with disk scans in the same manner as in [4,20].*

(d) *The algorithm requires no inter-processor communication.*

These four properties are the basis of our argument that our partitioning approach is load balanced and communication efficient. In Section 6, we will also present an experimental analysis of the performance of our method.

4   Parallel Top-Down Data Cube Construction

Top-down approaches for computing the data cube, like the sequential *PipeSort*, *Pipe Hash*, and *Overlap* methods [1,10,21], use more detailed group-bys to compute less detailed ones that contain a subset of the attributes of the former. They apply to data sets where the number of data items in a group-by can shrink considerably as the number of attributes decreases (data reduction). A group-by is called a child of some parent group-by if the child can be computed from the parent by aggregating some of its attributes. This induces a partial ordering of the group-bys, called the *lattice*. An example of a 4-dimensional lattice is shown in Figure 2, where A, B, C, and D are the four different attributes. The *PipeSort*, *PipeHash*, and *Overlap* methods select a spanning tree T of the lattice, rooted at the group-by containing all attributes. *PipeSort* considers two cases of parent-child relationships. If the ordered attributes of the child are a prefix of the ordered attributes of the parent (e.g., ABCD → ABC) then a simple

scan is sufficient to create the child from the parent. Otherwise, a sort is required to create the child. *PipeSort* seeks to minimize the total computation cost
by computing minimum cost matchings between successive layers of the lattice.
PipeHash uses hash tables instead of sorting. *Overlap* attempts to reduce sort
time by utilizing the fact that overlapping sort orders do not always require a
complete new sort. For example, the ABC group-by has A partitions that can
be sorted independently on C to produce the AC sort order. This may allow to
perform these independent sorts in memory rather than using external memory
sort.

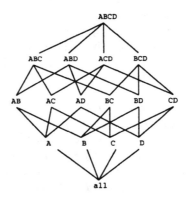

Fig. 2. A 4-Dimensional Lattice.

Next, we outline a partitioning approach which generates p independent
subproblems, each of which can be solved by one processor using an existing
external-memory top-down cube algorithm. The first step of our algorithm determines a spanning tree T of the lattice by using one of the existing approaches
like *PipeSort*, *PipeHash*, and *Overlap*, respectively. To balance the load between
the different processors we next perform a storage estimation to determine approximate sizes of the group-bys in T. This can be done, for example, by using
methods described in [11] and [22]. We now work with a weighted tree. The
most crucial part of our solution is the partitioning of the tree. The partitioning of T into subtrees induces a partitioning of the data cube problem into p
subproblems (subsets of group-bys). Determining an optimal partitioning of the
weighted tree is easily shown to be an NP-complete problem (by making, for
example, a reduction to p processor scheduling). Since the weights of the tree
represent estimates, a heuristic approach which generates p subproblems with
"some control" over the sizes of the subproblems holds the most promise. While
we want the sizes of the p subproblems balanced, we also want to minimize the
number of subtrees assigned to a processor. Every subtree may require a scan-

ning of the entire data set R and thus too many subtrees can result in poor IO performance. The solution we develop balances these two considerations.

Our heuristics makes use of a related partitioning problem on trees for which efficient algorithms exist, the *min-max tree k-partitioning problem* [3].

Definition 1. *Min-max tree k-partitioning: Given a tree T with n vertices and a positive weight assigned to each vertex, delete k edges in the tree such that the largest total weight of a resulting subtree is minimized.*

The min-max tree k-partitioning problem has been studied in [3,12,19], and an $O(n)$ time algorithm has been presented in [12]. A min-max k-partitioning does not necessarily compute a partitioning of T into subtrees of equal size and it does not address tradeoffs arising from the number of subtrees assigned to a processor. We use tree-partitioning as a preprocessing step for our partitioning. To achieve a better distribution of the load we apply an over partitioning strategy: instead of partitioning the tree T into p subtrees, we partition it into $s \times p$ subtrees, where s is an integer, $s \geq 1$. Then, we use a *"packing heuristic"* to determine which subtrees belong to which processors, assigning s subtrees to every processor. Our packing heuristic considers the weights of the subtrees and pairs subtrees by weights to control the number of subtrees. It consists of s matching phases in which the p largest subtrees (or groups of subtrees) and the p smallest subtrees (or groups of subtrees) are matched up. Details are described in Step 2b of Algorithm 2.

Algorithm 2 Sequential Tree-partition(T, s, p).
Input: A spanning tree T of the lattice with positive weights assigned to the nodes (representing the cost to build each node from it's ancestor in T). Integer parameters s (oversampling ratio) and p (number of processors).
Output: A partitioning of T into p subsets $\Sigma_1, \ldots, \Sigma_p$ of s subtrees each.
  (1) Compute a min-max tree $s \times p$ -partitioning of T into $s \times p$ subtrees $T_1, \ldots, T_{s \times p}$.
  (2) Distribute subtrees $T_1, \ldots, T_{s \times p}$ among the p subsets $\Sigma_1, \ldots, \Sigma_p$, s subtrees per subset, as follows:
      (2a) Create $s \times p$ sets of trees named Υ_i, $1 \leq i \leq sp$, where initially $\Upsilon_i = \{T_i\}$. The weight of Υ_i is defined as the total weight of the trees in Υ_i.
      (2b) For $j = 1$ to $s - 1$
          • Sort the Υ-sets by weight, in increasing order. W.l.o.g., let Υ_1, $\ldots$, $\Upsilon_{sp-(j-1)p}$ be the resulting sequence.
          • Set $\Upsilon_i := \Upsilon_i \cup \Upsilon_{sp-(j-1)p-i+1}$, $1 \leq i \leq p$.
          • Remove $\Upsilon_{sp-(j-1)p-i+1}$, $1 \leq i \leq p$.
      (2c) Set $\Sigma_i = \Upsilon_i$, $1 \leq i \leq p$.
— End of Algorithm —

The above tree partition algorithm is embedded into our parallel top-down data cube construction algorithm. Our method provides a framework for parallelizing any sequential top-down data cube algorithm. An outline of our approach is given in the following Algorithm 3.

Algorithm 3 Parallel Top-Down Cube Construction.

Each processor P_i, $1 \leq i \leq p$, performs the following steps independently and in parallel:

(1) Select a sequential top-down cube construction method (e.g., *Pipe-Sort*, *PipeHash*, or *Overlap*) and compute the spanning tree T of the lattice as used by this method.

(2) Apply the storage estimation method in [22] and [11] to determine the approximate sizes of all group-bys in T. Compute the weight of each node of T; i.e., the cost to build each node from it's ancestor in T.

(3) Execute Algorithm *Tree-partition(T, s, p)* as shown above, creating p sets Σ_1, ..., Σ_p. Each set Σ_i contains s subtrees of T.

(4) Compute all group-bys in subset Σ_i using the sequential top-down cube construction method chosen in Step 1.

— End of Algorithm —

Our performance results described in Section 6 show that an over partitioning with $s = 2$ or 3 achieves very good results with respect to balancing the loads assigned to the processors. This is an important result since a small value of s is crucial for optimizing performance.

5   Parallel Array-Based Data Cube Construction

Our method in Section 4 can be easily modified to obtain an efficient parallelization of the *ArrayCube* method presented in [27]. The *ArrayCube* method is aimed at dense data cubes and structures the raw data set in a d-dimensional array stored on disk as a sequence of "*chunks*". Chunking is a way to divide the d-dimensional array into small size d-dimensional chunks where each chunk is a portion containing a data set that fits into a disk block. When a fixed sequence of such chunks is stored on disk, the calculation of each group-by requires a certain amount of buffer space [27]. The *ArrayCube* method calculates a minimum memory spanning tree of group-bys, *MMST*, which is a spanning tree of the lattice such that the total amount of buffer space required is minimized. The total number of disk scans required for the computation of all group-bys is the total amount of buffer space required divided by the memory space available. The *ArrayCube* method can now be parallelized by simply applying Algorithm 3 with T being the *MMST*. More details will be given in the full version of this paper.

6   Experimental Performance Analysis

We have implemented and tested our parallel *top-down* data cube construction method presented in Section 4. We implemented sequential pipesort [1] in C++, and our parallel top-down data cube construction method (Section 4) in C++ with MPI [2]. As parallel hardware platform, we use a 9-node cluster. One node is used as the *root node*, to partition the lattice and distribute the work among

the other 8 machines which we refer to as *compute nodes*. The root is an IBM
Netfinity server with two 9-G scsi disks, 512 MB of Ram and a 550-MHZ Pentium
processor. The compute nodes are 133 MHZ Pentium processors, with 2G IDE
hard drives and 32 MB of RAM. The processors run LINUX and are connected
via a 100 Mbit Fast Ethernet switch with full wire speed on all ports.

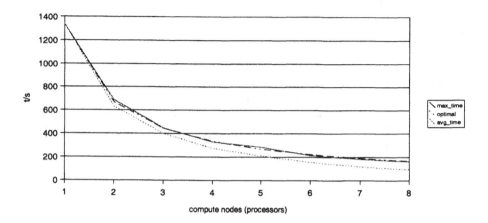

Fig. 3. Running Time (in seconds) As A Function Of The Number of Compute Nodes
(Processors)

Figure 3 shows the running time observed (in seconds) as a function of the
number of compute nodes used. For the same data set, we measured the sequential time (sequential pipesort [1]) and the parallel time obtained through our
parallel top-down data cube construction method (Section 4), using an oversampling ratio of $s = 2$. The data set consisted of 100,000 records with dimension
6. The attribute cardinalities for dimensions 1 to 6 where 5, 15, 500, 20, 1000,
and 2, respectively. Our test data values were sparse and uniformly distributed.
Figure 3 shows the running times (in seconds) of the algorithm as we increase
the number of compute nodes. There are three curves shown. *Max-time* is the
time taken by the slowest compute node (i.e. the node that received the largest
workload). *Avg-time* is the average time taken by the compute nodes. The time
taken by the *root node*, to partition the lattice and distribute the work among
the compute nodes, was insignificant. The *optimal* time shown in Figure 3 is the
sequential pipesort time divided by the number of compute nodes (processors)
used.

We observe that the *max-time* and *optimal* curves are essentially identical.
That is, for an oversampling ratio of $s = 2$, the speedup observed is very close
to optimal.

Note that, the difference between *max-time* and *avg-time* represents the load
imbalance created by our partitioning method. As expected, the difference grows
with increasing number of processors. However, we observed that a good part

of this growth can be attributed to the estimation of the cube sizes used in the tree partitioning. We are currently experimenting with improved estimators which appear to improve the result. Interestingly, the *avg-time* curve is below the *optimal* curve, while the *max-time* and *optimal* curves are essentially identical. One would have expected that the *optimal* and *avg-time* curves are similar and that the *max-time* curve is slightly above. We believe that this is caused by another effect which benefits our parallel method: improved I/O. When sequential pipesort is applied to a 10 dimensional data set, the lattice is partitioned into pipes of length up to 10. In order to process a pipe of length 10, pipesort needs to write to 10 open files at the same time. It appears that the number of open files can have a considerable impact on performance. For 100,000 records, writing them to 4 files took 8 seconds on our system. Writing them to 6 files took 23 seconds, not 12, and writing them to 8 files took 48 seconds, not 16. This benefits our parallel method, since we partition the lattice first and then apply pipesort to each part. Therefore, the pipes generated in the parallel method are considerably shorter.

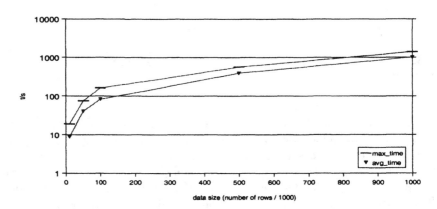

Fig. 4. Running Time (in seconds) As A Function Of The Size Of The Data Set (number of rows / 1000)

Figure 4 shows the running times (in seconds) of our top-down data cube parallelization as we increase the data size from 100,000 to 1,000,000 rows. Note that, the scale is logarithmic. The main observation is that the parallel running time (*max-time*) increases essentially linear with respect to the data size.

Figure 5 shows the running times as a function of the oversampling ratio s. We observe that the parallel running time (i.e., $max - time$) is best for $s = 3$. This is due to the following tradeoff. Clearly, the workload balance improves as s increases. However, as the total number of subtrees, $s \times p$, generated in the tree partitioning algorithm increases, we need to perform more sorts for the root nodes of these subtrees. The optimal tradeoff point for our test case is $s = 3$.

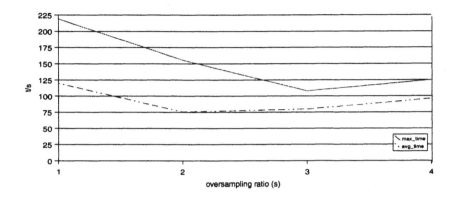

Fig. 5. Running Time (in seconds) As A Function Of The Oversampling Ratio (s)

Figure 6 shows the running times (in seconds) of our top-down data cube parallelization as we increase the dimension of the data set from 2 to 10. Note that, the number of group-bys to be computed grows exponentially with respect to the dimension of the data set. In Figure 6, we observe that the parallel running time grows essentially linear with respect to the output. We also executed our parallel algorithm for a 15-dimensional data set of 10,000 rows, and the resulting data cube was of size more than 1G.

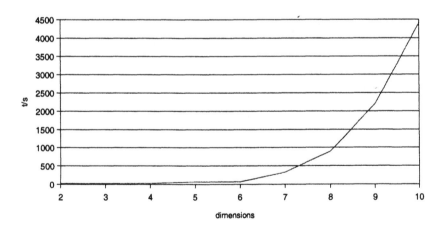

Fig. 6. Running Time (in seconds) As A Function Of The Number Of Dimensions Of The Data Set.

Simulation results for our *bottom-up* data cube parallelization in Section 3 are shown in Figure 7. For this method we have so far measured its load balancing characteristics through simulation only. As indicated in [4,20], the main indicator for the load generated by a bottom-up data cube computation is the number

of single attribute sorts. Our partitioning method in Section 3 for bottom-up
data cube parallelization does in fact *guarantee* that the subcube computations
assigned to the individual processor do all require *exactly* the same number
of single attribute sorts. There are no heuristics (like oversampling) involved.
Therefore, what we have measured in our simulation is whether the *output sizes*
of the subcube computations assigned to the processors are balanced as well. The
results are shown in Figure 7. The x-axis represents the number of processors
$p \in \{2, \ldots, 64\}$ and the y-axis represents the largest output size as a percentage
of the total data cube size. The two curves shown are the largest output size
measured for a processor and the optimal value (total data cube size / number of
processors). Five experiments were used to generate each data point. We observe
that the actual values are very close to the optimal values. The main result is
that our partitioning method in Section 3 not only balances the number of single
attribute sorts but also the sizes of the subcubes generated on each processor.

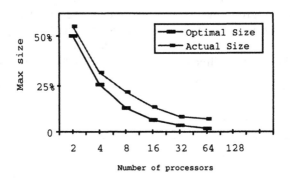

Fig. 7. Bottom-Up Cube. Maximum Output Size For One Processor As Percentage Of
Total Data Cube Size.

7   Conclusion

We presented two different, partitioning based, data cube parallelizations for
standard shared disk type parallel machines. Our partitioning strategies for
bottom-up and top-down data cube parallelization balance the loads assigned to
the individual processors, where the loads are measured as defined by the original proponents of the respective sequential methods. Subcube computations
are carried out using existing sequential data cube algorithms. Our top-down
partitioning strategy can also be easily extended to parallelize the ArrayCube
method. Experimental results indicate that our partitioning methods produce

well balanced data cube parallelizations. Compared to existing parallel data cube methods, our parallelization approach brings a significant reduction in inter-processor communication and has the important practical benefit of enabling the re-use of existing sequential data cube code.

A possible *extension* of our data cube parallelization methods is to consider a *shared nothing* parallel machine model. If it is possible to store a duplicate of the input data set R on each processor's disk, then our method can be easily adapted for such an architecture. This is clearly not always possible. It does solve most of those cases where the total output size is considerably larger than the input data set; for example *sparse* data cube computations. In fact, we applied this strategy for our implementation presented in Section 6. As reported in [20], the data cube can be several hundred times as large as R. Sufficient total disk space is necessary to store the output (as one single copy distributed over the different disks) and a p times duplication of R may be smaller than the output. Our data cube paralelization method would then partition the problem in the same way as described in Sections 3 and 4, and subcube computations would be assigned to processors in the same way as well. When computing its subcube, each processor would read R from its local disk. For the output, there are two alternatives. Since the output data sizes are well balanced, each processor could simply write the subcubes generated to its local disk. This could, however, create a bottleneck if there is, for example, a visualization application following the data cube construction which needs to read a single group-by. In such a case, each group-by should be distributed over all disks, for example in striped format. To obtain such a data distribution, all processors would not write their subcubes directly to their local disks but buffer their output. Whenever the buffers are full, they would be permuted over the network. In summary we observe that, while our approach is aimed at shared disk parallel machines, its applicability to shared nothing parallel machines depends mainly on the distribution and availability of the input data set R. We are currently considering the problem of identifying the "ideal" distribution of input R among the p processors when a fixed amount of replication of the input data is allowed (i.e., R can be copied r times, $1 \leq r < p$).

Acknowledgements. The authors would like to thank Steven Blimkie, Khoi Manh Nguyen, and Suganthan Sivagnanasundaram for their contributions towards the implementation described in Section 6. The first, second, and fourth author's research was partially supported by the Natural Sciences and Engineering Research Council of Canada. The third author's research was partially supported by the National Science Foundation under Grant 9988339-CCR.

References

1. S. Agarwal, R. Agarwal, P.M. Deshpande, A. Gupta, J.F. Naughton, R. Ramakrishnan, and S. Srawagi. On the computation of multi-dimensional aggregates. In *Proc. 22nd VLDB Conf.*, pages 506–521, 1996.

2. Argonne National Laboratory, http://www-unix.mcs.anl.gov/mpi/index.html. *The Message Passing Interface (MPI) standard.*

3. R.I. Becker, Y. Perl, and S.R. Schach. A shifting algorithm for min-max tree partitioning. *J. ACM*, (29):58–67, 1982.

4. K. Beyer and R. Ramakrishnan. Bottom-up computation of sparse and iceberg cubes. In *Proc. of 1999 ACM SIGMOD Conference on Management of data*, pages 359–370, 1999.

5. T. Cheatham, A. Fahmy, D. C. Stefanescu, and L. G. Valiant. Bulk synchronous parallel computing - A paradigm for transportable software. In *Proc. of the 28th Hawaii International Conference on System Sciences. Vol. 2: Software Technology*, pages 268–275, 1995.

6. F. Dehne, W. Dittrich, and D. Hutchinson. Efficient external memory algorithms by simulating coarse-grained parallel algorithms. In *Proc. 9th ACM Symposium on Parallel Algorithms and Architectures (SPAA'97)*, pages 106–115, 1997.

7. F. Dehne, W. Dittrich, D. Hutchinson, and A. Maheshwari. Parallel virtual memory. In *Proc. 10th Annual ACM-SIAM Symposium on Discrete Algorithms*, pages 889–890, 1999.

8. F. Dehne, A. Fabri, and A. Rau-Chaplin. Scalable parallel computational geometry for coarse grained multicomputers. In *ACM Symp. Computational Geometry*, pages 298–307, 1993.

9. F. Dehne, D. Hutchinson, and A. Maheshwari. Reducing i/o complexity by simulating coarse grained parallel algorithms. In *Proc. 13th International Parallel Processing Symposium (IPPS'99)*, pages 14–20, 1999.

10. P.M. Deshpande, S. Agarwal, J.F. Naughton, and R Ramakrishnan. Computation of multidimensional aggregates. Technical Report 1314, University of Wisconsin, Madison, 1996.

11. P. Flajolet and G.N. Martin. Probablistic counting algorithms for database applications. *Journal of Computer and System Sciences*, 31(2):182–209, 1985.

12. G.N. Frederickson. Optimal algorithms for tree partitioning. In *Proc. ACM-SIAM Symposium on Discrete Algorithms (SODA)*, pages 168–177, 1991.

13. S. Goil and A. Choudhary. High performance OLAP and data mining on parallel computers. *Journal of Data Mining and Knowledge Discovery*, 1(4), 1997.

14. S. Goil and A. Choudhary. A parallel scalable infrastructure for OLAP and data mining. In *Proc. International Data Engineering and Applications Symposium (IDEAS'99)*, Montreal, August 1999.

15. M. Goudreau, K. Lang, S. Rao, T. Suel, and T. Tsantilas. Towards efficiency and portability: Programming with the BSP model. In *Proc. 8th ACM Symposium on Parallel Algorithms and Architectures (SPAA '96)*, pages 1–12, 1996.

16. J. Gray, S. Chaudhuri, A. Bosworth, A. Layman, D. Reichart, M. Venkatrao, F. Pellow, and H. Pirahesh. Data cube: A relational aggregation operator generalizing group-by, cross-tab, and sub-totals. *J. Data Mining and Knowledge Discovery*, 1(1):29–53, April 1997.

17. V. Harinarayan, A. Rajaraman, and J.D. Ullman. Implementing data cubes efficiently. *SIGMOD Record (ACM Special Interest Group on Management of Data)*, 25(2):205–216, 1996.

18. J. Hill, B. McColl, D. Stefanescu, M. Goudreau, K. Lang, S. Rao, T. Suel, T. Tsantilas, and R. Bisseling. BSPlib: The BSP programming library. *Parallel Computing*, 24(14):1947–1980, December 1998.

19. Y. Perl and U. Vishkin. Efficient implementation of a shifting algorithm. *Disc. Appl. Math.*, (12):71–80, 1985.

20. K.A. Ross and D. Srivastava. Fast computation of sparse datacubes. In *Proc. 23rd VLDB Conference*, pages 116–125, 1997.
21. S. Sarawagi, R. Agrawal, and A. Gupta. On computing the data cube. Technical Report RJ10026, IBM Almaden Research Center, San Jose, CA, 1996.
22. A. Shukla, P. Deshpende, J.F. Naughton, and K. Ramasamy. Storage estimation for mutlidimensional aggregates in the presence of hierarchies. In *Proc. 22nd VLDB Conference*, pages 522–531, 1996.
23. J.F. Sibeyn and M. Kaufmann. BSP-like external-memory computation. In *Proc. of 3rd Italian Conf. on Algorithms and Complexity (CIAC-97)*, volume LNCS 1203, pages 229–240. Springer, 1997.
24. D.E. Vengroff and J.S. Vitter. I/o-efficient scientific computation using tpie. In *Proc. Goddard Conference on Mass Storage Systems and Technologies*, pages 553–570, 1996.
25. J.S. Vitter. External memory algorithms. In *Proc. 17th ACM Symp. on Principles of Database Systems (PODS '98)*, pages 119–128, 1998.
26. J.S. Vitter and E.A.M. Shriver. Algorithms for parallel memory. i: Two-level memories. *Algorithmica*, 12(2-3):110–147, 1994.
27. Y. Zhao, P.M. Deshpande, and J.F.Naughton. An array-based algorithm for simultaneous multidimensional aggregates. In *Proc. ACM SIGMOD Conf.*, pages 159–170, 1997.

Asymptotically Optimal Declustering Schemes for Range Queries

Rakesh K. Sinha[1], Randeep Bhatia[1], and Chung-Min Chen[2]

[1] Bell Laboratories
Murray Hill, NJ 07974
rsinha@ciena.com, randeep@research.bell-labs.com
[2] Telcordia Technologies, Inc.
Morristown, NJ 07960
chungmin@research.telcordia.com

Abstract. Declustering techniques have been widely adopted in parallel storage systems (e.g. disk arrays) to speed up bulk retrieval of multidimensional data. A declustering scheme distributes data items among multiple devices, thus enabling parallel I/O access and reducing query response time. We measure the performance of any declustering scheme as its worst case additive deviation from the ideal scheme. The goal thus is to design declustering schemes with as small an additive error as possible. We describe a number of declustering schemes with additive error $O(\log M)$ for 2-dimensional range queries, where M is the number of disks. These are the first results giving such a strong bound for any value of M. Our second result is a lower bound on the additive error. In 1997, Abdel-Ghaffar and Abbadi showed that except for a few stringent cases, additive error of any 2-dim declustering scheme is at least one. We strengthen this lower bound to $\Omega((\log M)^{\frac{d-1}{2}})$ for d-dim schemes and to $\Omega(\log M)$ for 2-dim schemes, thus proving that the 2-dim schemes described in this paper are (asymptotically) optimal. These results are obtained by establishing a connection to geometric discrepancy, a widely studied area of mathematics. We also present simulation results to evaluate the performance of these schemes in practice.

1 Introduction

The past decade has brought dramatic improvement in computer processor speed and storage capacity. In contrast, improvement in disk access time has been relatively flat. As a result, disk I/O is bound to be the bottleneck for many modern data-intensive applications. To cope with the I/O bottleneck, multi-disk systems, coupled with a declustering scheme, are usually used. The idea is to distribute data blocks across multiple disk devices, so they can be retrieved in parallel (i.e., in parallel disk seek operations). Meanwhile, emerging technologies in storage area network (e.g. Fibre Channel-Arbitrated Loop, switch-based I/O bus, and Gigabit Ethernet) have also enabled one to build a massively parallel storage system that contains hundreds or even thousands of disks [1,17]. As

J. Van den Bussche and V. Vianu (Eds.): ICDT 2001, LNCS 1973, pp. 144–158, 2001.

the number of disks increases, the efficacy of the adopted declustering scheme becomes even crucial.

Many applications that adopt declustering schemes have to deal with multidimensional data. These applications include, for example, remote-sensing databases [8,9], parallel search trees [5], and multidimensional databases [12]. In this paper, we concentrate on multi-dimensional data that is organized as a uniform grid. A good example is remote-sensing (satellite) data in raster format, which may contain dimensions such as latitude, longitude, time, and spectrum. An important class of queries against multidimensional data is **range query**. A range query requests a hyper-rectangular subset of the multidimensional data space. The **response time** of the query is measured by the access time of the disk that has the maximum number of data blocks to retrieve, and our goal is to design declustering schemes that minimize query response time.

Declustering schemes for range queries are proposed in [6,7,3,15,19,22,23, 21,12,18,11]. We measure the performance of any declustering scheme as its **worst-case additive deviation** from the ideal scheme. Based on this notion, we describe a number of 2-dim schemes with (asymptotically) optimal performance. This is done by giving an upper bound on the performance of each of these schemes as well as a lower bound on the performance of *any* declustering scheme. These are the first schemes with provably optimal behavior. Our results are obtained by establishing a connection to geometric discrepancy, a widely studied area of Combinatorics. We have been able to borrow some deep results and machinery from discrepancy theory to prove our results on declustering.

The rest of the paper is organized as follows. First, we formally define the declustering problem. Then, in Section 2, we summarize related work and present a summary of our contributions. In Section 3, we state the intuition behind our results. We briefly describe the relevant results in discrepancy theory and how we use them to prove results on declustering schemes. This is followed in Section 4 by a description of a general technique for constructing good declustering schemes from good discrepancy placements. In Section 5, we describe a number of declustering schemes, all with provably (asymptotically) optimal performance. In Section 6, we present a lower bound argument on the performance of *any* declustering scheme. Finally, in Section 7, we present brute-force simulation results on 2-dim schemes to show their exact (not asymptotic) performance. The results show that in practice, all the schemes have very good performance: their worst case deviation from the ideal scheme is within 5 for a large range of number of disks (up to 500 disks for some of the cases).

Notation: Even though our techniques can be generalized to any number of dimensions, our theoretical upper bound holds only for the case of two dimensions. For this reason, in sections 3, 4, and 5, we describe our techniques and the resulting declustering schemes for the case of two dimensions. The lower bound (presented in Section6) applies to any number of dimensions.

1.1   Problem Definition

Consider a dataset organized as a multi-dimensional grid of $N_1 \times N_2 \times N_3 \times \cdots \times N_d$ tiles. Let $(x_1, x_2, \ldots x_d)$ denote a point with coordinate x_i in dimension i. Given M disks, a declustering scheme, s, assigns tile $(x_1, x_2, \ldots x_d)$ to the disk numbered $s(x_1, x_2, \ldots x_d)$. A **range query** retrieves a hyper-rectangular set of tiles contained within the grid. We define the (nominal) **response time** of query Q under scheme s, $RT(s, Q)$, to be the maximum number of tiles from the query that get assigned to the same disk. Formally, let $tile_i(s, Q)$, $i = 0, 1, \ldots, M - 1$, represent the number of tiles in Q that get assigned to disk i under scheme s. Then $RT(s, Q) = max_{0 \le i < M} \, tile_i(s, Q)$. One may consider the unit of response time to be the average disk access time (including seek, rotational, and transfer time) to retrieve a data block. Thus, the notion of response time indicates the expected I/O delay for answering the query. The problem, therefore, is to devise a declustering scheme that would minimize the query response time.

An ideal declustering scheme would achieve, for each query Q, the **optimal response time** $ORT(Q) = \lceil |Q|/M \rceil$, where $|Q|$ is the number of tiles in Q. The **additive error** of any declustering scheme s is defined as the maximum (over all queries) difference between response time and optimal response time. Formally,

$$\text{additive error of scheme } s = \max_{all\ Q} \left(RT(Q, s) - ORT(Q) \right).$$

Note the above definition is independent of grid size. That is, query Q could be as large as possible, and the additive error is not necessarily finite.

The additive error is a measure of the performance of a declustering scheme and thus our goal is to design schemes with the smallest possible additive error. Finally, when proving our theoretical results, we will frequently omit the ceiling in the expression of the optimal response time. This will change the additive error by at most one.

2   Related Work and Our Contributions

Declustering has been a very well studied problem and a number of schemes for uniform data have been proposed [11,18,12,10,22,9,6,7,8]. However, very few of these schemes have a good worst case behavior. (e.g., the 2-dim disk modulo scheme [11] can have additive error as large as $\sqrt{M}$.) We are aware of three schemes with limited guarantee in 2-dimensions. These include two of our earlier schemes – GRS scheme [6] and Hierarchical scheme [7] – and a scheme of Atallah and Prabhakar [3]. For the GRS scheme, we also give some analytical evidence of an excellent *average* case performance. Even these 2-dim guarantees are somewhat weak. For the GRS scheme [6], we could prove a bound only when M is a Fibonacci number. Atallah and Prabhakar's scheme is defined only when M is a power of two. The hierarchical scheme [7] is constructed recursively from other base schemes and the resulting performance depends on the performance of these base schemes.

In this paper, for the first time, we prove that a number of 2-dim schemes have additive error $O(\log M)$ for *all* values of M. We also present brute-force simulation results to show that the exact (not asymptotic) additive error is within 5 for a large range of number of disks (up to 500 disks in some of the cases).

The case of higher (than two) dimensions appears intrinsically very difficult. None of the proposed schemes provide any non-trivial theoretical guarantees in higher dimensions. We believe that generalization of the techniques described in this paper will result in good higher dimensional declustering schemes in practice.

A related question is what is the smallest possible error of a declustering scheme. Abdel-Ghaffar and Abbadi [2] showed that except for a few stringent cases, additive error of any 2-dim scheme is at least one. We strengthen this lower bound to $\Omega(\log M)$ for 2-dim schemes, thus proving that the 2-dim schemes described in this paper are (asymptotically) optimal. We have also been able to generalize our lower bound to $\Omega((\log M)^{\frac{d-1}{2}})$ for d-dim schemes.

These results have been proved by relating the declustering problem to discrepancy problem – a well studied sub-discipline of Combinatorics. We have borrowed some deep results and machinery from discrepancy theory research to prove our results.

We present a general technique for constructing good declustering schemes from good discrepancy placements. Given that discrepancy theory is an active area of research, we feel that this may be our most important technical contribution. It leaves open the possibility that one may take new and improved discrepancy placements and translate them into even better declustering schemes. As an evidence of power and generality of our present technique, a straightforward corollary of our main theorem implies a significantly better bound for the GRS scheme than what we had proved in an earlier paper [6].

3 Intuition of Our Results

All our schemes are motivated by results in discrepancy theory [20]. We give a very brief description of the relevant results from discrepancy theory.

3.1 Discrepancy Theory

Given any integer M, the goal is to determine positions of M points in a 2-dimensional unit square such that these points are placed as uniformly as possible. There are several possible ways of measuring uniformity of any placement scheme. The definition most relevant to us is following:

Fix a placement P of M points and consider any rectangle R (whose sides are parallel to the sides of the unit square). If the points were placed completely uniformly in a unit square, we will expect R to contain about $area(R)*M$ points, where $area(R)$ denotes the area of R.

Measure the absolute difference between (number of points falling in R) and $area(R) * M$. This defines the "discrepancy" of placement P with respect to rectangle R. The discrepancy of placement P is defined as the highest value of discrepancy with respect to any rectangle R. The goal is to design placement schemes with smallest possible discrepancy.

It is known that any placement scheme must have discrepancy at least $\Omega(\log M)$ [20] and several placement schemes with discrepancy $O(\log M)$ are known in literature. The definition of discrepancy can be generalized to arbitrary dimensions. In d-dimensions, the known lower and upper bounds are $\Omega((\log M)^{\frac{d-1}{2}})$ and $O((\log M)^{d-1})$, respectively. These results form the basis of our upper and lower bound arguments.

3.2 Relationship with Declustering Schemes

We informally argue that a declustering scheme with small additive error can be used to construct a placement scheme with small discrepancy, and vice versa.

Consider a good declustering scheme on an $M \times M$ grid G. Because we are distributing M^2 points among M disks, a good declustering scheme will have roughly M instances of each disk. Let us focus on just one disk, say M instances of disk zero. For any query Q, its response time is defined as the maximum number of instances of any disk contained within Q. We will approximate the response time with the number of instances of disk zero contained within Q.

Then the additive error of Q is approximately equal to

$$\text{number of instances of disk zero contained within } Q - \tfrac{|Q|}{M}.$$

Now suppose we compress the grid into a unit square (so that both x and y dimensions are compressed by a factor of M) and consider the positions of disk zero. The original query Q gets compressed into a rectangle R of area $\frac{|Q|}{M^2}$. So that the discrepancy of this placement scheme with respect to R is the difference of (number of instances of disk zero contained within R) and $area(R) * M$. But the number of instances of disk zero contained within R is equal to the number of instances of disk zero contained within Q, and $area(R) * M$ is equal to $\frac{|Q|}{M}$. This implies that the discrepancy of the placement scheme is equal to the additive error of the declustering scheme.

The next section describes how to obtain a good declustering scheme from a good placement scheme.

4   From Discrepancy to Declustering

Our overall strategy can be stated in the following three steps:

1. Start with a placement scheme P_0 in the unit square with M points. By multiplying x and y dimensions by M, we obtain M points in an $M \times M$ grid. We can think of these as approximate positions of disk zero. We call this placement P.
2. The positions of disk zero in P may not correspond to grid points (i.e., their x or y-coordinates may not be integer). In this step we map these M arbitrary points to M grid points.

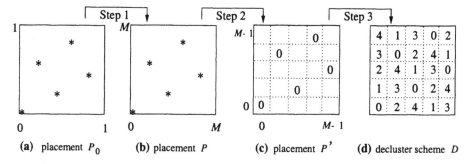

Fig. 1. Progress of Steps 1-3 for $M = 5$, starting with an initial placement scheme $P_0 = (0,0), (0.2, 0.56), (0.4, 0.22), (0.6, 0.78), (0.8, 0.44)$. $N_x = N_y = M$.

3. The M grid points in the previous step give the instances of disk zero in an $M \times M$ grid. Based on this "template", we first place all other disks in the $M \times M$ grid and then generalize it to a declustering scheme for an arbitrary $N_x \times N_y$ grid.

The goal is to be able to start with a placement scheme P_0 with small discrepancy k, and still guarantee a small additive error for the resulting declustering scheme obtained from Steps 1-3 above. Indeed, our construction guarantees that if we start with a placement scheme P_0 with discrepancy k, then the additive error of the resulting declustering scheme is at most $O\left(k + \frac{k^2}{M}\right)$. Thus, picking any placement scheme P_0 with $k = O(\log M)$ from the discrepancy theory literature (e.g. [25,13]), we can construct a declustering scheme with $O(\log M)$ additive error. In the rest of this section, we describe Steps 1-3 in detail, along with the necessary claims and their proofs.

4.1   Step-1

Start with a placement scheme P_0 on M points for a unit grid and scale up each dimension by a factor of M. Let the resulting points be $(x_0, y_o), \ldots (x_{M-1}, y_{M-1})$. We call this new placement scheme P.

Figures 1 (a) and (b) show an example for $M = 5$. The resulting placement P in Figure 1 (b) contains points $(0,0), (1.0, 2.80), (2.0, 1.10), (3.0, 3.90)$ and $(4.0, 2.20)$.

We redefine discrepancy for scheme P, which is imposed on an $M \times M$ grid rather than on an unit grid. Our definition differs in two aspects from the standard definition. First of all, we have scaled up the area of any rectangle by a factor of M^2 (a scaling of M in each dimension). Second we allow more general rectangles for measuring discrepancy: we consider rectangles whose x or y-coordinates may come from a "wrap-around" interval, i.e., an interval of the form $[j, j+1, \ldots, M-1, 0, 1, 2, k]$. We denote these as "wrap-around" rectangles. The introduction of the notion of "wrap-around" rectangles is needed when we generalize the scheme to arbitrary grids in Step-3.

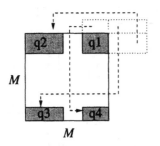
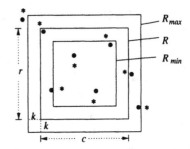

Fig. 2. An example wrap-around rectangle $q_1 \cup q_2 \cup q_3 \cup q_4$.

Fig. 3. Points of placement P are denoted by asterisks; points of P' are denoted by dots. For each point in P, its mapping in P' is the nearest dot point. In this example, $|S_{min}| = 3, |S_R| = 5$ and $|S_{max}| = 6$.

Pictorially, imagine that the left and right sides of the grid are joined and similarly the top and the bottom sides of the grid are joined. Because each "wrap-around" interval is a disjoint union of one or two (standard) intervals, a "wrap-around" rectangle is a disjoint union of one, two, or four disjoint (standard) rectangles in the grid. Pictorially, the last case will correspond to four standard rectangles in the four corners of the grid. Figure 2 shows an example.

Definition 1. *Fix a placement P of M points in an $M \times M$ grid. Then given any rectangle (which could be a 'wrap-around" rectangle) R, discrepancy of P with respect to R is defined as*

$$\left| number\ of\ points\ falling\ in\ R - \frac{area(R)}{M} \right|$$

The discrepancy of placement P is defined as the highest value of discrepancy with respect to any (including "wrap-around") rectangle R.

Lemma 1. *The discrepancy of P is at most four times the discrepancy of P_0.*

Proof. This can be easily verified by observing that (1) the scaling of P_0 to P does not affect the discrepancy value, and (2) the introduction of "wrap-around" rectangles in P may multiply the discrepancy by at most a factor of four.

4.2   Step-2:

We place the point with the smallest x-coordinate in the zeroth column, the point with the next smallest x-coordinate in the first column and so on. We do an analogous thing with y-coordinates and rows.

Formally the process is: sort $x_0, x_1, x_2, \ldots, x_{M-1}$ in increasing order (break ties arbitrarily) and let $0 \leq w_i < M$ be the rank of x_i within the sorted order.

Similarly sort $y_1, y_2, \ldots, y_M$ in increasing order (break ties arbitrarily) and let $0 \le z_i < M$ be the rank of y_i within the sorted order. Then map (x_i, y_i) to the grid point (w_i, z_i). Let us call the new placement scheme P'. Figure 1 (c) shows the resulting P' following the same example.

We will use the following claim in Steps 2 and 3.

Claim. Because w_i's are all distinct, each column contains exactly one point. Similarly z_i's are all distinct, and thus each row contains exactly one point.

Lemma 2. *If discrepancy of scheme P is k then the discrepancy of scheme P' is at most $5k + \frac{4k^2}{M}$. (In all declustering schemes we describe later in Section 5, we will start with an initial placement scheme P_0 with discrepancy $O(\log M)$, so that the $\frac{4k^2}{M}$ term will be equal to $\frac{(\log M)^2}{M}$, which is vanishingly small.)*

Proof. We will first prove that the positions of point in P do not change too much as we shift them around to obtain P'. We will prove that $|w_i - x_i| \le k$ and $|z_i - y_i| \le k$.

Consider the rectangle R whose four corners are $(0, 0), (x_i, 0), (0, M)$, and (x_i, M). The area of R is $x_i * M$ and the number of points falling in R is equal to the number of points whose x-coordinate is less than or equal to x_i, which is equal to the rank of x_i in the sorted ordering of $x_0, x_1, x_2, \ldots, x_{M-1}$, which is w_i. So by discrepancy theory, $|w_i - \frac{x_i * M}{M}| \le k$, thus $|w_i - x_i| \le k$. By a similar argument we can prove that $|z_i - y_i| \le k$.

We are ready to prove the lemma. Consider any rectangle R of dimension $c \times r$. Let S_R denote the set of points that fall inside R under scheme P'. We are interested in the cardinality of S_R.

Consider the rectangle R_{min} of dimension $(c - 2k) \times (r - 2k)$ that is obtained by pushing in each side of R by a distance of k. Also consider the rectangle R_{max} of dimension $(c + 2k) \times (r + 2k)$ that is obtained by pushing out each side of R by a distance of k. Let S_{min} (resp. S_{max}) denote the set of points that fall inside R_{min} (resp. R_{max}) under scheme P. Figure 3 shows the situation.

We already showed $|w_i - x_i| \le k$ and $|z_i - y_i| \le k$. Thus it follows that all the points in R_{min} (under scheme P) must fall in R (under scheme P') and no point outside R_{max} (under scheme P) can fall in R (under scheme P'). We conclude

$$|S_{min}| \le |S_R| \le |S_{max}|. \tag{1}$$

Because scheme P has discrepancy k,

$$|S_{min}| \ge \frac{area(R_{min})}{M} - k = \frac{(c - 2k)(r - 2k)}{M} - k, \tag{2}$$

and

$$|S_{max}| \le \frac{area(R_{max})}{M} + k = \frac{(c + 2k)(r + 2k)}{M} + k. \tag{3}$$

From Equations 1, 2, and 3, $\frac{(c-2k)(r-2k)}{M} - k \le |S_R| \le \frac{(c+2k)(r+2k)}{M} + k$.

Discrepancy of P' with respect to R is

$$\left|\|S_R\| - \frac{c \cdot r}{M}\right| \leq \max \left(\frac{cr}{M} - \frac{(c-2k)(r-2k)}{M} + k, \; \frac{(c+2k)(r+2k)}{M} + k - \frac{cr}{M} \right)$$

$$= \frac{2k(c+r) + 4k^2}{M} + k.$$

Since $c, r \leq M$, we get that discrepancy of P' is bounded by $5k + \frac{4k^2}{M}$.

4.3   Step-3

We know from Claim 4.2 that the placement scheme P' contains exactly one point in each column of the $M \times M$ grid. Let $\sigma(x)$ be the row index of the point in column x. Then, given any arbitrary $N_x \times N_y$ grid, the declustering scheme maps the point (x, y), $0 \leq x < N_x, 0 \leq y < N_y$, to disk $(y - \sigma(x \bmod M)) \bmod M$. Figure 1(d) shows the disk assignment of the left-bottom $M \times M$ subgrid. Pictorially, the decluster scheme takes this "pattern" and repeats it throughout the rest of the grid.

Theorem 1. *If we start with a placement scheme P_0 with discrepancy k then the resulting declustering scheme D' will have additive error at most $O\left(k + \frac{k^2}{M}\right)$. This implies that by starting with a placement scheme with $O(\log M)$ discrepancy, we can construct a declustering scheme with $O(\log M)$ additive error.*

We omit the proof (these can be found in www.cs.umd.edu/users/randeep/disc.ps) because of a lack of space. In Section 6, we state a converse of this theorem (Theorems 2, 3).

Higher-dimensional Extensions. There are several possible ways of extending the technique described above to obtain higher-dim declustering schemes. We can start with a higher-dimensional placement scheme with good discrepancy to obtain a higher-dimensional declustering scheme. Alternatively, we can start with a 2-dim declustering scheme (obtain using the technique outlined in the previous section) and generalize it to higher dimension, using a recursive technique as described in [6,7]

5   Description of Declustering Schemes

In this section, we present several 2-dim declustering schemes with $O(\log M)$ additive error. We describe more than one schemes in the hope that users may have other constraints (besides trying to minimize worst case response time) and some of these schemes may be better suited than the others.

5.1 Corput's Scheme

The first placement scheme we consider is given by Van der Corput[25]. The M points given by this scheme are

$$\left\{\left(\frac{i}{M}, key_i\right), 0 \le i < M\right\},$$

where key_i is computed as following: Let $a_{k-1}\dots a_1 a_0$ be the binary representation of i, where a_0 is the least significant bit. Then $key_i = \frac{a_0}{2} + \frac{a_1}{4} + \frac{a_2}{8} + \cdots + \frac{a_{k-1}}{2^k}$.

Now we apply the three steps outlined in the previous section. In Step 1, we multiply each co-ordinate by M to obtain the set $\{(i, M * key_i), 0 \le i < M\}$. In Step 2, we need to map these points to integer co-ordinates. The x-coordinate is already an integer. The y-coordinate $M * key_i$ gets mapped to the rank of $M * key_i$ in the set $\{M * key_i, 0 \le i < M\}$. We observe that this is equal to the rank of key_i in the set $\{key_i, 0 \le i < M\}$. Let RANK(i) denote the rank of this element. Then step 3 dictates that the point (x, y) should map to disk $(y - RANK(x \bmod M)) \bmod M$.

We summarize these steps below.

step-1: construct M pairs (i, key_i) for $0 \le i < M$, where key_i is computed as following: Let $a_{k-1}\dots a_1 a_0$ be the binary representation of i, where a_0 is the least significant bit. Then $key_i = \frac{a_0}{2} + \frac{a_1}{4} + \frac{a_2}{8} + \cdots + \frac{a_{k-1}}{2^k}$.

step-2: sort the first components based on key values. This will give a permutation on $0, 1, .., M - 1$. Call the resulting permutation PERM(M). Compute the inverse permutation, $RANK$ by

for $i = 0$ to $M - 1$ $\{RANK(PERM(i)) = i\}$

step-3: map point (x, y) to disk $(y - RANK(x \bmod M)) \bmod M$.

The next two schemes, GRS and Faure's scheme, are constructed in an analogous manner, except that they start with a different initial placement. Rather than describing the steps from discrepancy to declustering scheme, we present the declustering schemes directly.

5.2 GRS Scheme

The GRS scheme was first described by us in [6] and we proved that whenever M is a Fibonacci number, the response time of any query is at most three times its optimal response time. Our proof was in terms of "gaps" of any permutation and worked only when M was a Fibonacci number.

It turns out that the same scheme can be obtained from a placement scheme with discrepancy $O(\log M)$ [16][20, page 80, exercise 3] (described below). Thus Theorem 1 implies that the additive error of GRS scheme is $O(\log M)$ for any M. This is another evidence of the generality and power of Theorem 1.

step-1: construct M pairs (i, key_i) for $0 \le i < M$, where key_i is the fractional part of $\frac{2i}{(1+\sqrt{5})}$.

Step-2 and step-3 are the same as those described in Section 5.1.

5.3   Faure's Scheme

The following scheme is based on Faure's placement scheme [14]. This scheme has two parameters: a base b and a permutation σ on $\{0, 1, \ldots, b-1\}$. For suitable choice of the parameters, this is the best known construction (in terms of the constant factor in the discrepancy bound).

step-1: construct M pairs (i, key_i) for $0 \leq i < M$, where key_i is computed as following: Let $a_{k-1} \ldots a_1 a_0$ be the representation of i in base b (i.e. $i = \sum_{j=0}^{k-1} a_j b^j$), where $0 \leq a_j \leq b-1$ for all j and a_0 is the least significant digit. Then $key_i = \frac{\sigma(a_0)}{b} + \frac{\sigma(a_1)}{b^2} + \frac{\sigma(a_2)}{b^3} + \cdots + \frac{\sigma(a_{k-1})}{(b^k)}$.

Step-2 and step-3 are the same as in Section 5.1.

Please note that the CORPUT scheme is a special case with $b = 2$ and σ being the identity permutation.

5.4   Generalized Hierarchical Scheme

The Hierarchical Scheme is presented in [7]. It is based on a technique of constructing declustering scheme for $M = m_1 \times m_2 \times \ldots \times m_k$ disks, given declustering schemes D_i for $m_i, 1 \leq i \leq k$, disks. Note that m_i may be the same as m_j for $i \neq j$. The idea is that using strictly optimal declustering schemes for all $M \leq p$ for some prime p one can construct good declustering schemes for any M that can be expressed as a product of the first p prime numbers. The hierarchical declustering scheme, for a fixed p, is therefore only defined for those M which can be expressed as a product of the first p prime numbers. Due to space limit, we refer the readers to [7] for the detailed description of hierarchical schemes.

We now extend the hierarchical scheme to any number of disks. The original hierarchical declustering scheme is a column permutation declustering scheme (CPDS). A CPDS scheme is defined by a function $F : \{0 \ldots M-1\} \to \{0 \ldots M-1\}$, such that the grid point $(x, F(x))$, $x = 0, 1, \ldots, M-1$, is assigned to disk zero and, in general, point (x, y) is assigned to disk $(y - F(x \bmod M)) \bmod M$. We have seen one such scheme earlier: the declustering scheme D in Figure 1(d) is a CPDS. Given a CPDS which is only defined for certain values of M, we extend it to all values of M as following: Given $M = n$ for which the CPDS is not defined, we find the smallest number $n' \geq n$, such that the CPDS is defined for $M = n'$. Consider a $n' \times n'$ grid G under the CPDS. Again, we will restrict our attention to disk zero in this grid. We construct a CPDS for $M = n$ as follows. Take the first n columns of G. Note that there are n instances of disk zero in these columns. We assign each of these disks a unique rank (essentially sort them, break ties in any way) between 0 and $n - 1$, based on their row positions (y-coordinates). Let the rank of disk zero in column i be r_i. Define a function $F'(i) = r_i$. The CPDS defined by function F' is the CPDS for $M = n$.

We call this the generalized hierarchical declustering scheme. We can show that the generalized hierarchical declustering scheme has a $O(\log M)$ additive error (proof omitted).

6   Lower Bound

An ideal declustering scheme is the one whose performance is strictly optimal on all range queries. An interesting question is whether any realizable declustering scheme is ideal, and if not how close can any declustering scheme get to the ideal scheme. Abdel-Ghaffar and Abbadi [2] showed that except for a few stringent cases, additive error of any 2-dim scheme is at least one. We strengthen their result to give (asymptotically) tight lower bound of $\Omega(\log M)$ in 2-dim and a lower bound of $\Omega((\log M)^{\frac{d-1}{2}})$ for any d-dim scheme, thus proving that the 2-dim schemes described in this paper are (asymptotically) optimal.

Theorem 2. *Given any 2-dim declustering scheme D for M disks and any $M \times M$ grid G, there exists a query Q in the grid G, such that for query Q, $RT(Q) - ORT(Q) = \Omega(\log M)$. In other words, for any 2-dim declustering scheme, there are queries on which the response time is at least $\Omega(\log M)$ more than the optimal response time.*

Theorem 3. *Given any d-dim declustering scheme D for M disks and any d-dim grid G with all side lengths M, there exists a query Q in the grid G, such that for query Q, $RT(Q) - ORT(Q) = \Omega((\log M)^{\frac{d-1}{2}})$. In other words, for any d-dim declustering scheme, there are queries on which the response time is at least $\Omega((\log M)^{\frac{d-1}{2}})$ more than the optimal response time. (The actual lower bound is slightly larger, based on the discrepancy lower bound of [4].)*

We will sketch a proof of Theorem 2. Proof of Theorem 3 requires several additional tricks and is omitted.

Proof. Let D be a declustering scheme and G be an $M \times M$ grid as in the statement of the theorem. Since the M^2 grid points in G are mapped to the disks $\{0 \ldots M-1\}$, there must exist a disk $i \in \{0 \ldots M-1\}$, such that there are at least $n \geq M$ instances of disk i in G. W.l.o.g. we assume $i = 0$. Let us remove all disks except disk 0 from G. Let us also remove $n - M$ instances of disk 0 from G, thus leaving exactly M points(disks) in G. We will denote by $p(Q)$ the number of points contained in a rectangular query Q. We will show that there is a query Q such that $p(Q) - ORT(Q) = \Omega(\log M)$. Because there are at least $p(Q)$ instances of disk 0 in Q under the declustering scheme D, this will imply $RT(Q) - ORT(Q) \geq p(Q) - ORT(Q) = \Omega(\log M)$.

Our proof strategy is following: We will obtain a placement scheme from the positions of the M points in G. It is known that any placement scheme has discrepancy $\Omega(\log M)$ with respect to at least one rectangle R. We want to use R to construct the query Q with large additive error. There are two problems with this simple plan. The first problem is that the boundary of R may not be aligned with the grid lines. This is fixed by taking a slightly smaller rectangle whose boundary lies on the grid lines and arguing that this new rectangle also has a high discrepancy. The second problem is more serious. Remember that discrepancy is defined as the *absolute* difference of expected and actual number

Table 1. Additive errors of various schemes. Each entry in the table indicates the maximum number of disks for which the corresponding additive error is guaranteed.

additive error =	0	1	2	3	4	5
Corput	3	8	34	130	273	470
Faure-b5	3	10	27	106	140	275
Faure-b9	3	9	45	90	414	538
Faure-b36	3	11	36	109	306	368
GRS	3	22	94	391	553	–
Hierarchical	3	11	45	95	200	–

of points. So it is possible that R may be receiving *fewer* points than expected. In this case, we can only claim that the corresponding query is receiving fewer (than OPT) instances of disk zero, not enough to prove a large additive error. The way around is to observe that the grid G as a whole has zero discrepancy. So if R receives fewer points than expected, some other rectangle must be receiving more points than expected, and we construct a query from that rectangle.

7   Simulation Results

We present simulation results that compare the actual additive errors of the various schemes described in the previous section. For Faure's scheme, we tried three variations: $b = 5, \sigma = 0, 3, 2, 1, 4$; $b = 9, \sigma = 0, 5, 2, 7, 4, 1, 6, 3, 8$; and $b = 36, \sigma = $ 0,25,17,7,31,11,20,3,27, 13,34,22,5,15,29,9,23,1,18,32,8,28,14,4,21,33,12, 26,2,19,10, 30,6,16,24,35. For the generalized hierarchical scheme, it is constructed solely based on the three optimal schemes for $M = 2, 3$ and 5.

We compute additive error of each scheme for a large range of M. Fix M, it is known [6,7] that in order to compute the additive error of any permutation declustering scheme, it is enough to consider all possible queries, including "wrap-around" queries, in an $M \times M$ grid. We vary M from two to a few hundreds. Because the simulation is time consuming [1], the results we present here are what can be obtained in reasonable times (the longest runs took a week).

We present the results in a tabular format as shown in Table 1. The numbers at the top row represent additive errors, ranging from 0 to 5. The number in each of the table cells represents the max number of disks for which the corresponding additive error is guaranteed. For example, Corput's scheme guarantees that when $M \leq 3$ the additive error is zero; when $M \leq 8$ its additive error is at most 1; when $M \leq 34$, the additive error is at most 2, etc.

The table shows that all schemes provide very good worst case performance: the deviation from the ideal scheme are at most 5 for a large range of M. The most notable is GRS, which guarantees an additive error at most 4 for $M \leq 553$.

---

[1] Given M, it takes $O(M^6)$ to compute the additive error of a scheme. For some schemes, we manage to reduce the complexity to $O(M^5)$ or $O(M^4)$ by taking advantage of a dynamic programming technique and some special properties of the schemes.

Note this does not mean that GRS is better than all other schemes for all values of M. A better strategy is to use a hybrid scheme: given M, select the scheme with the lowest additive error.

Given the small additive errors of these schemes, we feel that other performance metrics, such as average additive error and ratio to the optimal, are of less importance. An additive error within 5 translates into less than 50 milli-second difference in practice (assuming 10 ms disk seek time). Taking into account seek time variation, the response time is already optimal in a statistical sense. Nonetheless, we leave it to the users to select from these schemes the one that best fits their requirements (for example in a multiuser environment the average response time may be more important).

8 Conclusion

Declustering is a popular technique to speed up bulk retrieval of multidimensional data. This paper focuses on range queries for uniform data. Even though this is a very well-studied problem, none of the earlier proposed schemes have provable good behavior. We measure the additive error of any declustering scheme as its worst case additive deviation from the ideal scheme. In this paper, for the first time, we describe a number of 2-dimensional schemes with additive error $O(\log M)$ for *all* values of M. We also present brute-force simulation results to show that the exact (not asymptotic) additive error is quite small for a large range of number of disks. We prove that this is the best possible analytical bound by giving a matching lower bound of $\Omega(\log M)$ on the performance of any 2-dimensional declustering scheme. We generalize this lower bound to $\Omega((\log M)^{\frac{d-1}{2}})$ for d-dimensional schemes.

Our main technical contribution is a connection between declustering problem and discrepancy theory, a well studied sub-discipline of Combinatorics. We give a general technique for mapping any good discrepancy placement scheme into a good declustering scheme. Using this technique, we construct new declustering schemes built upon Van der Corput's and Faure's discrepancy placements. We note there exist many more sophisticated discrepancy schemes that are known to have good discrepancy in practice (e.g. the Net-based schemes [24, 20]). Whether they will result in better declustering schemes (than Corput's and Faure's schemes) is an interesting question that requires more experiments to answer.

References

1. NCR WorldMark/Teradata 1 TB TPC-D Executive Summary. available from http://www.tpc.org/.
2. K. Abdel-Ghaffar and A. E. Abbadi. Optimal allocation of two-dimensional data. In *Proceedings of the International Conference on Database Theory*, 1997.
3. M.J. Atallah and S. Prabhakar. (Almost) optimal parallel block access for range queries. In *ACM Symp. on Principles of Database Systems*, May 2000.

4. R. C. Baker. On irregularities of distribution, II. *Journal of London Math. Soc.* To appear.

5. S. Berchtold, C. Böhm, B. Braunmüller, D.A. Keim, and H.-P. Kriegel. Fast parallel similarity search in multimedia databases. In *Proc. of ACM Int'l Conf. on Management of Data*, 1997.

6. R. Bhatia, R. K. Sinha, and C. M. Chen. Declustering using golden ratio sequences. In *16th Int'l Conf. on Data Engineering*, Feb 2000.

7. R. Bhatia, R. K. Sinha, and C. M. Chen. Hierarchical declustering schemes for range queries. In *7th Int'l Conf. on Extending Database Technology*, Mar 2000.

8. C. Chang, B. Moon, A. Acharya, C. Shock, A. Sussman, and J. Saltz. Titan: a high-performance remote-sensing database. In *13th Int. Conf. on Data Engineering*, 1997.

9. C.M. Chen and R. Sinha. Raster-spatial data declustering revisited: an interactive navigation perspective. In *15th Int. Conf. on Data Engineering*, 1999.

10. L.T. Chen and D. Rotem. Declustering objects for visualization. In *Proc. of the 19th International Conference on Very Large Data Bases*, 1993.

11. H.C. Du and J.S. Sobolewski. Disk allocation for cartesian product files on multiple disk systems. *ACM Trans. Database Systems*, pages 82–101, 1982.

12. C. Faloutsos and P. Bhagwat. Declustering using fractals. In *Proceedings of the 2nd International Conference on Parallel and Distributed Information Systems*, 1993.

13. H. Faure. Discrepancy of sequences associated with a number system (in dimension s) (in french). *Acta Arithmetic*, 41(4):337–351, 1982.

14. H. Faure. Good permutations for extreme discrepancy. *J. Number Theory*, 42:47–56, 1992.

15. H. Ferhatosmanoglu and D. Agrawal. Concentric hyperspaces and disk allocations for fast parallel range searching. In *Proc. of 15th Int. Conf. on Data Engineering*, pages 608–615, 1999.

16. E. Hlawka. *The theory of uniform distribution*. A B Academic Publ, Berkhamasted, Herts, 1984.

17. K. Keeton, D.A. Patterson, and J.M. Hellerstein. A case for intelligent disks (idisks). *SIGMOD Record*, 27(3), 1998.

18. M.H. Kim and S. Pramanik. Optimal file distribution for partial match retrieval. In *Proceedings of the ACM International Conference on Management of Data*, 1988.

19. S. Kou, M. Winslett, Y. Cho, and J. Lee. New gdm-based declustering methods for parallel range queries. In *Int'l Database Engineering and Applications Symposium (IDEAS)*, Aug. 1999.

20. J. Matousek. *Geometric discrepancy, an illustrated guide*. Springer-Verlag, 1999.

21. B. Moon, A. Acharya, and J. Saltz. Study of scalable declustering algorithms for parallel grid files. In *Proceedings of the 10th International Parallel Processing Symposium*, 1996.

22. S. Prabhakar, K. Abdel-Ghaffar, D. Agrawal, and A. E. Abbadi. Cyclic allocation of two-dimensional data. In *14th Int. Conf. on Data Engineering*, 1998.

23. S. Prabhakar, K. Abdel-Ghaffar, D. Agrawal, and A.E. Abbadi. Efficient retrieval of multidimensional datasets through parallel I/O. In *5th Int. Conf. on High Performance Computing*, 1998.

24. I. M. Sobol. Distribution of points in a cube and approximate evaluation of integrals (in russian). *Zh. Vychisl. Mat. i Mat. Fiz.*, 7:784–802, 1967.

25. J. G. van der Corput. Verteilungsfunktionen i. In *Akad. Wetensch Amsterdam*, pages 813–821, 1935.

Flexible Data Cubes for Online Aggregation

Mirek Riedewald, Divyakant Agrawal, and Amr El Abbadi

Dept. of Computer Science, University of California, Santa Barbara CA 93106, USA*
{mirek, agrawal, amr}@cs.ucsb.edu

Abstract. Applications like Online Analytical Processing depend heavily on the ability to quickly summarize large amounts of information. Techniques were proposed recently that speed up aggregate range queries on MOLAP data cubes by storing pre-computed aggregates. These approaches try to handle data cubes of any dimensionality by dealing with all dimensions at the same time and treat the different dimensions uniformly. The algorithms are typically complex, and it is difficult to prove their correctness and to analyze their performance. We present a new technique to generate Iterative Data Cubes (IDC) that addresses these problems. The proposed approach provides a modular framework for combining one-dimensional aggregation techniques to create space-optimal high-dimensional data cubes. A large variety of cost tradeoffs for high-dimensional IDC can be generated, making it easy to find the right configuration based on the application requirements.

1 Introduction

Data cubes are used in Online Analytical Processing (OLAP) [4] to support the interactive analysis of large data sets, e.g., as stored in data warehouses. Consider a data set where each data item has d *functional attributes* and a *measure attribute*. The functional attributes constitute the dimensions of a d-dimensional hyper-rectangle, the data cube. A *cell* of the data cube is defined by a unique combination of dimension values and stores the corresponding value of the measure attribute. An example of a data cube defined for a view on the TPC-H benchmark database [19] might have the total price of an order as the measure attribute and the region of a customer and the order date as the dimensions. It provides the aggregated total orders for all combinations of regions and dates. Queries issued by an analyst who wants to examine how the customer behavior in different regions changes over time do not need to access and join the "raw" data in the different tables. Instead the information is readily available and hence can be aggregated and summarized from the data cube. Our work focuses on Multidimensional OLAP (MOLAP) systems [14] where data cubes are represented in terms of multidimensional arrays (e.g., dense data cubes).

An *aggregate range query* selects a hyper-rectangular region of the data cube and computes the aggregate of the values of the cells in this region. For interactive analysis it is mandatory to provide fast replies for these queries, no matter

---

* This work was partially supported by NSF grants EIA-9818320, IIS-98-17432, and IIS-99-70700.

J. Van den Bussche and V. Vianu (Eds.): ICDT 2001, LNCS 1973, pp. 159–173, 2001.

how large the selected region. To achieve this, aggregate values for regions of the data cube are pre-computed and stored to reduce on-the-fly aggregation costs. We will refer to a data cube that contains such pre-computed values as a *pre-aggregated* data cube. Whenever necessary, the term *original* data cube is used for a cube without such pre-computed aggregates (i.e., which is obtained directly from the data set). Note, that pre-computation increases update costs since an update to a single cell of the original data cube has to be propagated to all cells in the pre-computed data cube that depend on the updated value. Also, storing *additional* values increases the storage cost. The choice of the query-update-storage cost tradeoff depends on the application. While "what-if" scenarios and stock trading applications require fast updates, for other applications overnight batch processing of updates suffices. But even batch processing poses limits on the update cost which depend on the frequency of updates and the tolerated period of inaccessibility of the data.

In this paper space-optimal techniques for MOLAP systems are explored, i.e., Iterative Data Cubes are generated by *replacing* values of the original data cube with pre-computed aggregates. The space-optimality argument would not apply to sparse data cubes where empty cells are not stored (e.g., Relational OLAP [14]). The main contributions of Iterative Data Cubes are:

1. For each dimension a different one-dimensional technique for pre-computing aggregate values can be selected. Thus specific properties of a dimension, e.g., hierarchies and domain sizes, can be taken into account.
2. Combining the one-dimensional techniques is easy. This greatly simplifies developing, implementing and analyzing IDCs. In contrast to previous approaches, dealing with a high-dimensional IDC is as simple as dealing with the one-dimensional case.
3. IDCs offer a greater variety of cost tradeoffs between queries and updates than any previous technique and cause no space overhead.
4. They generalize some of the previous approaches, thus providing a new framework for comparing and analyzing them. For the other known techniques we show analytically that our approach at least matches their query-update performance tradeoffs.

In Sect. 2 related work is presented. The Iterative Data Cube technique is described in Sect. 3. There algorithms for querying and updating Iterative Data Cubes are discussed as well. Section 4 contains examples for one-dimensional pre-aggregation techniques and illustrates how those techniques can be used for an application. In Sect. 5 we discuss how IDC performs compared to the previous approaches. Section 6 concludes this paper.

2   Related Work

An elegant algorithm for pre-aggregation on MOLAP data cubes is presented in [11]. We refer to it as the *Prefix Sum* technique (PS). The essential idea is to store pre-computed aggregate information so that range queries are answered in constant time (i.e., independent of the selected ranges). This kind of pre-aggregation results in high update costs. In the worst case, an update to a single cell of the original data cube requires recomputing the whole PS cube. The *Relative Prefix Sum* technique (RPS) [6] reduces the high update costs of PS, while still guaranteeing a constant query cost. RPS is improved by the *Space-Efficient Relative Prefix Sum* (SRPS) [17] which guarantees the same query and update costs as RPS, but uses less space. For dynamic environments Geffner et al. proposed the *Dynamic Data Cube* (DDC) [5] which balances query and update costs such, that both are provably poly-logarithmic in the domain size of the dimensions for any data cube. DDC causes a space overhead which is removed by the *Space-Efficient Dynamic Data Cube* (SDDC) [17]. SDDC improves on DDC by reducing the storage costs, while at the same time providing less or equal costs for both queries and updates. The *Hierarchical Cubes* techniques (HC) [3] generalize the idea of RPS and SRPS by allowing different tradeoffs between update and query cost. Two different schemes are proposed – Hierarchical Rectangle Cubes (HRC) and Hierarchical Band Cubes (HBC).

The above techniques are the ones that are most related to IDC. They explore query-update cost tradeoffs at no extra storage space (except RPS and DDC, which were replaced with the space-efficient SRPS and SDDC) for MOLAP data cubes. Like IDC they are only applicable when the aggregate operator is invertible (e.g., SUM) or can be expressed with invertible operators (e.g., AVG (average)). Iterative Data Cubes generalize PS, SRPS, and SDDC. For Hierarchical Cubes we show that no better query-update cost tradeoffs than for IDC can be obtained. Note that all of the above techniques, except PS, are difficult to analyze when the data cube has more than one dimension. For instance, the cost formulas for the Hierarchical Cubes are so complex, that they have to be evaluated experimentally in order to find the "best suited" HC for an application.

In [7] a new SQL operator, CUBE or "data cube", was proposed to support online aggregation by pre-computing query results for queries that involve grouping operations (GROUP BY). Our notion of a data cube is slightly different from the terminology in [7]. More precisely, the *cuboids* generated by CUBE (i.e, the results of grouping the data by subsets of the dimensions) are data cubes as defined in this paper. The introduction of the CUBE operator generated a significant level of interest in techniques for efficient computation and support of this operator [1,2,8,9,10,12,13]. These techniques do not concentrate on efficient range queries, but rather on which cuboids to pre-compute and how to efficiently access them (e.g., using index structures). Since our technique can be applied to any cuboid which is dense enough to be stored as a multidimensional array, IDC complements research regarding the CUBE operator. For instance, by adapting the formulas for query and update costs, support for range queries can be included into the framework for selecting "optimal" cuboids to be materialized. The fact that Iterative Data Cubes are easy to analyze greatly simplifies this process.

Smith et al. [18] develop a framework for decomposing the result of the CUBE operator into view elements. Based on that framework algorithms are developed that for a given population of queries select the optimal non-redundant set of view elements that minimizes the query cost. An Iterative Data Cube has properties similar to a non-redundant set of view elements. It contains aggregates for regions of the original data cube, does not introduce space overhead, and allows the reconstruction of the values of the cells of the original data cube. However, in contrast to [18] the goal of IDC is to support *all* possible range queries in order to provide provably good worst case or average query and update costs.

Vitter et al. [20,21] propose approximating data cubes using the wavelet transform. While [20] explicitly deals with the aspect of sparseness (which is not addressed in this paper) [21], like IDC, targets MOLAP data cubes. Wavelets offer a compact representation of the data cube on multiple levels of resolution. This makes them particularly suited for returning fast approximate answers. Using wavelets to encode the original data cube, however, increases the update costs and does not result in a better worst case performance when exact results are required. While [21] proposes encoding the pre-aggregated data cube which is used for the PS technique, any pre-aggregated (or the original) data cube can be encoded using wavelets. In that sense wavelet transform and IDC are orthogonal techniques[1]. Once an appropriate Iterative Data Cube is selected, approximate answers to queries can be supported by encoding this IDC using wavelet transform.

3   The Iterative Data Cubes Technique

In this paper we focus on techniques for MOLAP data cubes that are handled similar to multidimensional arrays. The query cost is measured in terms of the number of cells that need to be accessed in order to answer the query. Similarly the update cost is measured as the number of cells of the pre-aggregated data cube whose values must be updated to reflect a single update on the data set. Since the data cubes are stored and accessed using multidimensional arrays, this cost model is realistic for both, internal (main memory) and external (disk, tape) algorithms.

In general the IDC technique can be applied to an attribute whose domain forms an Abelian group under the aggregate operator. Stated differently, it can be applied to an aggregate operator $\oplus$ if there exists an inverse operator $\ominus$, such that for all attribute values a and b it holds that $(a \oplus b) \ominus b = a$ (e.g., COUNT, but also AVG when expressed with "invertible" operators SUM and COUNT). For the sake of simplicity, the technique is described for the aggregate operator SUM and a measure attribute whose domain is the set of integers.

3.1   Notation

Let A be a data cube of dimensionality d, and let without loss of generality the domain of each dimension attribute δ_i be $\{0, 1, \ldots, n_i - 1\}$. A cell $c =$

---

[1] Note, however, that wavelet encoding typically increases the update cost.

$[c_1, \ldots, c_d]$, where each c_i is an element of the domain of the corresponding dimension, contains the measure value $A[c]$. With $e : f$ we denote a *region* of the data cube, more precisely the set of all cells c that satisfy $e_i \leq c_i \leq f_i$ for all $1 \leq i \leq d$ (i.e., $e : f$ is a hyper-rectangular region of the data cube). Cell e is the *anchor* and cell f the *endpoint* of the region. The anchor and endpoint of the entire data cube are $[0, \ldots, 0]$ and $[n_1 - 1, \ldots, n_d - 1]$, respectively. The term $op(A[e] : A[f])$ denotes the result of applying the aggregate operator op to the values in region $e : f$. Consequently, $SUM(A[e] : A[f])$ is a *range sum*. The range sum $SUM(A[0, \ldots, 0] : A[f])$ will be referred to as a *prefix sum*.

3.2   Creating Iterative Data Cubes

Iterative Data Cubes are constructed by applying one-dimensional pre-aggregation techniques along the dimensions. To illustrate this process, it is first described for one-dimensional data cubes and then generalized. Let Θ be a one-dimensional pre-aggregation technique and A be the original one-dimensional data cube with n cells. Technique Θ generates a pre-aggregated array A_Θ of size n, such that each cell of A_Θ stores a *linear combination* of the cells of A:

$$\forall 0 \leq j \leq n - 1: \quad A_\Theta[j] = \sum_{k=0}^{n-1} \alpha_{j,k} A[k] . \tag{1}$$

The variables $\alpha_{j,k}$ are real numbers that are determined by the pre-aggregation technique. Figure 1 shows an example. The array SRPS is the result of applying the SRPS technique with block size 3 to the original array A. SRPS pre-aggregates a one-dimensional array as follows. A is partitioned into blocks of equal size. The anchor of a block $a : e$ (its leftmost cell) contains the corresponding prefix sum of A, i.e., $SRPS[a] = SUM(A[0] : A[a])$. Any other cell c of the block stores the "local prefix sum" $SRPS[c] = SUM(A[a+1] : A[c])$. Consequently, the coefficients in the example are $\alpha_{0,0} = 1$, $\alpha_{1,1} = 1$, $\alpha_{2,1} = \alpha_{2,2} = 1$, $\alpha_{3,k} = 1$ for $0 \leq k \leq 3$, $\alpha_{4,4} = 1$, $\alpha_{5,4} = \alpha_{5,5} = 1$, $\alpha_{6,k} = 1$ for $0 \leq k \leq 6$, and $\alpha_{j,k} = 0$ for all other combinations of j and k.

Fig. 1. Original array A and corresponding SRPS (block size 3) and PS arrays (query range and updated cell are framed, accessed cells are shaded)

For a two-dimensional data cube A two (possibly different) one-dimensional pre-aggregation techniques Θ_1 and Θ_2 are selected. Θ_1 is first applied along dimension δ_1, i.e., each row of A is pre-aggregated as described above. Let A_1 denote the resulting pre-aggregated data cube. The columns of A_1 are then processed using technique Θ_2, returning the final pre-aggregated data cube A_2. Figure 2 shows an example. For both dimensions the SRPS technique with block size 3 was selected. Note that applying the two-dimensional SRPS technique directly would generate the same pre-aggregated data cube.

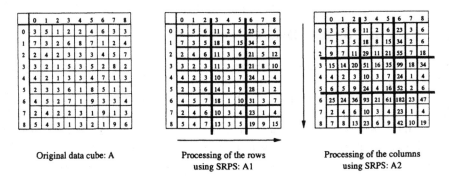

Original data cube: A   Processing of the rows using SRPS: A1   Processing of the columns using SRPS: A2

Fig. 2. Original data cube A, intermediate cube A_1, and final SRPS cube A_2 (fat lines indicate partitioning into blocks by SRPS)

Generalizing the two-dimensional IDC construction to d dimensions is straightforward. First, for each dimension δ_i, $1 \leq i \leq d$, a one-dimensional technique Θ_i is selected. Then Θ_1 is applied along dimension δ_1, i.e., to each array $[0, c_2, c_3, \ldots, c_d] : [n_1 - 1, c_2, c_3, \ldots, c_d]$ for any combination of c_j, $0 \leq c_j < n_j$ and $j \in \{2, 3, \ldots, d\}$ (intuitively only the first dimension value varies, while the others are fixed). Let the resulting pre-aggregated data cube be A_1. Each cell $c = [c_1, \ldots, c_d]$ in A_1 now contains a linear combination of the values in the original array A which are in the same "row" along δ_1. Formally,

$$A_1[c_1, c_2, \ldots, c_d] = \sum_{k_1=0}^{n_1-1} \alpha_{1,c_1,k_1} A[k_1, c_2, \ldots, c_d] \ . \tag{2}$$

Clearly A_1 does not contain more cells than A (since Θ_1 does not use additional space) and can be computed at a cost of $n_2 \cdot n_3 \cdots n_d \cdot C_1(n_1)$, where $C_i(n_i)$ denotes the cost of applying technique Θ_i to an array of size n_i. In the next step technique Θ_2 is similarly applied to dimension δ_2, but now with A_1, the result of the previous step, as the input data cube. For all cells in the resulting cube A_2 it holds that

$$A_2[c_1, c_2, \ldots, c_d] = \sum_{k_2=0}^{n_2-1} \alpha_{2,c_2,k_2} A_1[c_1, k_2, c_3, \ldots, c_d] \tag{3}$$

$$= \sum_{k_2=0}^{n_2-1} \alpha_{2,c_2,k_2} \sum_{k_1=0}^{n_1-1} \alpha_{1,c_1,k_1} A[k_1, k_2, c_3, \ldots, c_d] \qquad (4)$$

$$= \sum_{k_1=0}^{n_1-1} \sum_{k_2=0}^{n_2-1} \alpha_{1,c_1,k_1} \alpha_{2,c_2,k_2} A[k_1, k_2, c_3, \ldots, c_d] . \qquad (5)$$

This process continues until all dimensions are processed. The final result, the pre-aggregated data cube A_d, contains values which are the linear combination of the values in the original data cube. More precisely

$$A_d[c_1, c_2, \ldots, c_d] = \sum_{k_1=0}^{n_1-1} \sum_{k_2=0}^{n_2-1} \cdots \sum_{k_d=0}^{n_d-1} \alpha_{1,c_1,k_1} \alpha_{2,c_2,k_2} \cdots \alpha_{d,c_d,k_d} A[k_1, k_2, \ldots, k_d] .$$
$$(6)$$

The cost for processing dimension δ_j is $C_j(n_j) \cdot \prod_{i \neq j} n_i$. This results in a total construction cost of $\prod_{i=1}^{d} n_i \cdot (\sum_{j=1}^{d} C_j(n_j)/n_j)$ which is equal to d times the size of the data cube if a one-dimensional pre-aggregation technique processes an array of size n_j at cost n_j.

3.3 Querying an Iterative Data Cube

Aggregate range queries as issued by a user or application select ranges on the *original* data cube. This data cube, however, was replaced by an Iterative Data Cube where cells contain pre-computed aggregate values. The query therefore needs to be translated to match the different contents. We will show that the problem of querying a high-dimensional IDC can be reduced to the one-dimensional cases.

Let Θ be a one-dimensional pre-aggregation technique, and let A and A_Θ denote the original and pre-aggregated data cubes, respectively. Technique Θ has to be *complete* in the sense that it must be possible to answer each range sum query on A by using A_Θ. Formally, for each range r on A there must exist coefficients $\beta_{r,l}$, such that

$$\sum_{j \in r} A[j] = \sum_{l=0}^{n-1} \beta_{r,l} A_\Theta[l] \qquad (7)$$

where the $\beta_{r,l}$ are variables whose values depend on the pre-aggregation technique and the selected range. In the example in Fig. 1 the coefficients for SRPS (range $r = 2 : 5$) are $\beta_{r,0} = \beta_{r,1} = -1$, $\beta_{r,3} = \beta_{r,5} = 1$, and $\beta_{r,l} = 0$ for $l \in \{2, 4, 6, 7, 8\}$.

On a d-dimensional data cube A a range sum query selects a range r_i for each dimension δ_i. The answer Q to this query is computed as

$$Q = \sum_{j_d \in r_d} \sum_{j_{d-1} \in r_{d-1}} \cdots \sum_{j_1 \in r_1} A[j_1, j_2, \ldots, j_d] . \qquad (8)$$

Recall, that the pre-aggregated cube A_d for A was obtained by iteratively applying one-dimensional pre-aggregation techniques, such that data cube A_i is computed by applying technique Θ_i along dimension δ_i to A_{i-1} (let $A_0 = A$). Consequently, range sum Q can alternatively be computed as

$$Q = \sum_{j_d \in r_d} \sum_{j_{d-1} \in r_{d-1}} \cdots \sum_{j_2 \in r_2} (\sum_{l_1=0}^{n_1-1} \beta_{1,r_1,l_1} A_1[l_1, j_2, \ldots, j_d]) \tag{9}$$

$$= \sum_{l_1=0}^{n_1-1} \beta_{1,r_1,l_1} (\sum_{j_d \in r_d} \sum_{j_{d-1} \in r_{d-1}} \cdots \sum_{j_2 \in r_2} A_1[l_1, j_2, \ldots, j_d]) \tag{10}$$

$$= \sum_{l_1=0}^{n_1-1} \beta_{1,r_1,l_1} \sum_{j_d \in r_d} \sum_{j_{d-1} \in r_{d-1}} \cdots \sum_{j_3 \in r_3} (\sum_{l_2=0}^{n_2-1} \beta_{2,r_2,l_2} A_2[l_1, l_2, j_3, \ldots, j_d]) \tag{11}$$

$$\vdots$$

$$= \sum_{l_1=0}^{n_1-1} \sum_{l_2=0}^{n_2-1} \cdots \sum_{l_d=0}^{n_d-1} \beta_{1,r_1,l_1} \beta_{2,r_2,l_2} \cdots \beta_{d,r_d,l_d} A_d[l_1, l_2, \ldots, l_d] . \tag{12}$$

The β_{i,r_i,l_i} are well defined by the aggregation technique Θ_i and the selected range r_i. There are no dependencies between the different dimensions in the sense that β_{i,r_i,l_i} does not depend on the techniques Θ_j and the ranges r_j, if $j \neq i$. This enables the efficient decomposition into one-dimensional sub-problems. Note, that cell $A_d[l_1, \ldots, l_d]$ of the pre-aggregated array A_d contributes to the query result Q if and only if the value of $\beta_{1,r_1,l_1} \beta_{2,r_2,l_2} \cdots \beta_{d,r_d,l_d}$ is not zero.

The *query algorithm* follows directly from the above discussion. For each dimension δ_i and range r_i, the set of all l_i such that β_{i,r_i,l_i} is non-zero is determined independently of the other dimensions. Then, for each possible combination of non-zero $\beta_{1,r_1,l_1}, \beta_{2,r_2,l_2}, \ldots, \beta_{d,r_d,l_d}$ the cell $A_d[l_1, l_2, \ldots, l_d]$ has to be accessed and contributes its value, multiplied by $\beta_{1,r_1,l_1} \beta_{2,r_2,l_2} \cdots \beta_{d,r_d,l_d}$, to the final result Q of the range sum query.

Figure 3 shows an example for a query that computes SUM($A[2, 4] : A[5, 6]$) on a two-dimensional pre-aggregated data cube (SRPS with box size 3 applied along both dimensions). First, for range $2 : 5$ in dimension δ_1 and range $4 : 6$ in dimension δ_2 the indices with non-zero β values are obtained together with the βs. Recall, that for range $r_1 = 2 : 5$ we obtained the values $\beta_{1,r_1,0} = \beta_{1,r_1,1} = -1$, $\beta_{1,r_1,3} = \beta_{1,r_1,5} = 1$, and $\beta_{1,r_1,l_1} = 0$ for $l_1 \in \{2, 4, 6, 7, 8\}$ (see above). Similarly, we obtain $\beta_{2,r_2,3} = -1$, $\beta_{2,r_2,6} = 1$, and $\beta_{2,r_2,l_2} = 0$ for $l_2 \in \{0, 1, 2, 4, 5, 7, 8\}$ for range $r_2 = 4 : 6$ in dimension δ_2. Combining the results leads to the correct computation of SUM($A[2, 4] : A[5, 6]$) as $A_2[0, 3] - A_2[0, 6] + A_2[1, 3] - A_2[1, 6] - A_2[3, 3] + A_2[3, 6] - A_2[5, 3] + A_2[5, 6]$.

The *query cost* of IDC, i.e., the number of cells accessed in A_d, follows directly from the algorithm. It is the product of the sizes of the sets of non-empty β values obtained for each dimension. As a consequence, once the worst case or average query cost of a one-dimensional technique is known, it is easy to compute the worst/average query cost for the d-dimensional pre-aggregated data

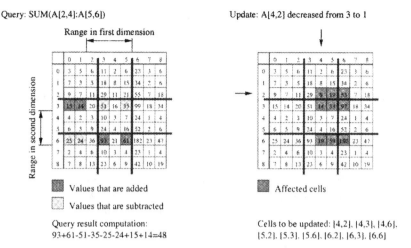

Fig. 3. Processing queries and updates on an Iterative Data Cube (SRPS technique used for both dimensions)

cube by multiplying the one-dimensional costs. In our example, one-dimensional SRPS allows each range sum to be computed from at most 4 values (computing $\texttt{SUM}(A[e] : A[f])$ with SRPS requires at most accessing the anchor of the box that contains f, cell f, and, if $e > 0$, the anchor of the box that contains $e - 1$ and cell $e - 1$). Consequently, independent of the selected ranges at most 4^d cells in the d-dimensional pre-aggregated SRPS data cube have to be accessed.

3.4   Updating an Iterative Data Cube

For the original data cube, an update to the data set only affects a single cell. Since Iterative Data Cubes store pre-computed aggregates, such an update has to be translated to updates on a set of cells in the pre-aggregated data cube. The set of affected cells in A_d follows directly from (6). Note that equations (6) and (12) are very similar, therefore the algorithms for processing queries and updates are almost identical.

Equation (1) describes the dependencies between the pre-aggregated and the original data cube for the one-dimensional case. Clearly $A_\Theta[j]$ is affected by an update to $A[k]$ if and only if $\alpha_{j,k} \neq 0$ (see Fig. 1 for an example). Based on (6) this can be generalized to d dimensions. Let $[k_1, \ldots, k_d]$ be the cell in the original data cube A which is updated by a value Δ. For each dimension δ_i, the set of all c_i such that α_{i,c_i,k_i} is non-zero is determined independently of the other dimensions. Then, for each possible combination of non-zero $\alpha_{1,c_1,k_1}, \alpha_{2,c_2,k_2}, \ldots, \alpha_{d,c_d,k_d}$ the cell $A_d[c_1, c_2, \ldots, c_d]$ has to be updated by $\Delta \cdot \alpha_{1,c_1,k_1}\alpha_{2,c_2,k_2} \cdots \alpha_{d,c_d,k_d}$.

Figure 3 shows an example for an update that decreases the value $A[4, 2]$ in the original data cube by 2. Recall, that SRPS with block size $s = 3$ was applied along both dimensions of the data cube and that the corresponding coefficients are $\alpha_{1,0,0} = 1$, $\alpha_{1,1,1} = 1$, $\alpha_{1,2,1} = \alpha_{1,2,2} = 1$, $\alpha_{1,3,k_1} = 1$ for $0 \leq k_1 \leq 3$,

$\alpha_{1,4,4} = 1$, $\alpha_{1,5,4} = \alpha_{1,5,5} = 1$, $\alpha_{1,6,k_1} = 1$ for $0 \le k_1 \le 6$, and $\alpha_{1,c_1,k_1} = 0$ for all other combinations of c_1 and k_1. In dimension δ_1 the updated cell has the index value 4, i.e., the relevant coefficients are $\alpha_{1,4,4}$, $\alpha_{1,5,4}$, and $\alpha_{1,6,4}$ which have the value 1, while all other $\alpha_{1,c_1,4}$ are zero. Similarly the non-zero coefficients $\alpha_{2,2,2} = \alpha_{2,3,2} = \alpha_{2,6,2} = 1$ are obtained. Consequently, the cells $[4,2]$, $[4,3]$, $[4,6]$, $[5,2]$, $[5,3]$, $[5,6]$, $[6,2]$, $[6,3]$, and $[6,6]$ in A_2 have to be updated by $1 \cdot (-2)$.

The *update cost* of IDC, i.e., the number of accessed cells in A_d, is the product of the sizes of the sets of non-empty α values obtained for each dimension. Thus, like for the query cost, once the worst case or average update cost of a one-dimensional technique is known, it is easy to compute the worst/average update cost for high-dimensional Iterative Data Cubes. This is done by multiplying the worst/average update costs of the one-dimensional techniques.

4   IDC for Real-World Applications

We present one-dimensional aggregation techniques and discuss how they are selected for pre-aggregating a high-dimensional data cube. The presented techniques mainly illustrate the range of possible tradeoffs between query and update cost. In the following discussion the original array is denoted with A and has n elements $A[0]$, $A[1]$,...,$A[n-1]$. The pre-aggregated array will be named like the corresponding generating technique.

4.1   One-Dimensional Pre-aggregation Techniques

The pre-aggregated array used for the PS technique [11] contains the prefix sums of the original array, i.e., $PS[j] = \sum_{k=0}^{j} A[k]$. Figure 1 shows an example for $n = 9$. Any range sum on A can be computed by accessing at most two values in PS (difference between value at endpoint and predecessor of anchor of query range). On the other hand, an update to $A[k]$ affects all $PS[j]$ where $j \ge k$. This results in worst case costs of 2 for a query and of n for an update. In Fig. 1 cells in PS which have to be accessed in order to answer $SUM(A[2] : A[5])$ and those that are affected by an update to $A[4]$ are shaded.

The SRPS technique [17] (Fig. 1) was already introduced in Sect. 3.2. Its worst case costs are 4 for queries, and $2\sqrt{n}$ (or $2\sqrt{n} - 2$ when n is a perfect square) for updates [17].

To compute the pre-aggregated array SDDC, the SDDC technique [17] first partitions the array A into two blocks of equal size. The anchor cell of each block stores the corresponding prefix sum of A. For each block, the same technique is applied recursively to the sub-arrays of non-anchor cells. The recursive partitioning defines a hierarchy, more precisely a tree of height less or equal to $\lceil \log_2 n \rceil$, on the partitions (blocks). Queries and updates conceptually descend this tree. The processing starts at the root and continues to that block that contains the endpoint of the query or the updated cell, respectively. A query $SUM(A[0] : A[c])$ is answered by adding the values of the anchors of those blocks that contain c.

Due to the construction, at most one block per level can contain c, resulting in a worst case prefix sum query cost of $\lceil \log_2 n \rceil$. Queries with ranges $[x] : [y]$ where $x > 0$ are answered as $\text{SUM}([0] : [y]) - \text{SUM}([0] : [x-1])$. Thus the cost of answering any range sum query is bounded by $2\lceil \log_2 n \rceil$. At each level an update to a cell u in a block U only propagates to those cells that have a greater or equal index than u and are an anchor of a block that has the same parent as U. Consequently, the update cost is bounded by the height of the tree ($\lceil \log_2 n \rceil$). In Fig. 4 an example of an SDDC array and how the query $\text{SUM}(A[2] : A[5])$ and an update to $A[4]$ are processed are shown. Note, that SDDC can be generalized by choosing different numbers of blocks and different block sizes when partitioning the data cube. This enables the technique to take varying attribute hierarchies into account.

Fig. 4. Original array A and corresponding SDDC and LPS ($s_1 = 3$, $s_2 = 4$, $s_3 = 3$) arrays (query range and updated cell are framed, accessed cells are shaded)

The Local Prefix Sum (LPS) technique partitions array A into t blocks of sizes $s_1, s_2, \ldots, s_t$, respectively. Any cell in the pre-aggregated array LPS contains a "local" prefix sum, i.e., the sum of its value and the values in its left neighbors until the anchor of the block it is contained in. A range query is answered by adding the values of all block endpoints that are contained in the query range, adding to it the value of the cell at the endpoint of the query range (if it is not an endpoint of a block) and subtracting the value of the cell left to the anchor of the query range (if it is not an endpoint of a block). Thus the query cost is bounded by $t + 1$. Figure 4 shows an example. Updates only affect cells with a greater or equal index than the updated cell in the same block, resulting in a worst case update cost of $\max\{s_1, \ldots, s_t\}$. For a certain t the query cost is fixed, but the worst case update cost is minimized by choosing $s_1 = s_2 = \ldots = s_t$. The corresponding family of (query cost, update cost) tradeoffs therefore becomes $(t + 1, \lceil n/t \rceil)$.

The two techniques of using A directly or using its prefix sum array PS instead, constitute the extreme cases of minimal cost of updates and minimal cost of queries for one-dimensional data. Note, that it is possible to reduce the worst case query cost to 1. This, however, requires pre-computing and storing the result for any possible range query, i.e., $\frac{n}{2}(n+1)$ values. Also, since $A[\lfloor n/2 \rfloor]$

is contained in $(\lfloor n/2 \rfloor + 1)(n - \lfloor n/2 \rfloor)$ different ranges, the update cost for this scheme is at least $n^2/4$. Since we focus on techniques that do not introduce space overhead, PS is the approach with the minimal query cost. Table 1 summarizes the query and update costs for selected one-dimensional techniques.

Table 1. Query-update cost tradeoffs for selected one-dimensional techniques

One-dimensional technique	Query cost (worst case)	Update cost (worst case)	Note
Original array	n	1	
Prefix Sum (PS)	2	n	
Space-Efficient Relative	4	$2\sqrt{n} - 2$	when n perfect square
Prefix Sum (SRPS)	4	$2\sqrt{n}$	otherwise
Space-Efficient Dynamic Data Cube (SDDC)	$2\lceil \log_2 n \rceil$	$\lceil \log_2 n \rceil$	
Local Prefix Sum (LPS)	$t + 1$	$\lceil n/t \rceil$	$2 \le t < n$

4.2   Selecting an IDC for an Application

The IDC technique provides a modular framework for choosing a suitable pre-aggregation scheme. It greatly simplifies taking advantage of a priori knowledge about an application. For instance, when it is known that a hierarchy exists for an attribute and that users typically query according to this hierarchy (e.g., it is more likely that a query aggregates monthly sales figures than sales figures for a 30-day period that starts in the middle of a month), one can set a corresponding block size for SDDC or SRPS. If a dimension has only a few values (e.g., gender), the best choice in most cases will be PS or not pre-aggregating along this dimension at all. Alternatively, if no appropriate technique is available, it is relatively easy to develop a new one and to integrate it into the framework. Recall, that all one has to do is to develop a *one*-dimensional technique and to analyze its cost tradeoffs.

The process of selecting an appropriate IDC is illustrated with a hypothetical example. Assume that the data cube has three dimensions of size n each, and a fourth dimension of size 2 (e.g., gender). Two of the three attributes with dimension size n are hierarchical and it is likely that users query according to the hierarchies. For simplicity assume further that both hierarchies are similar to a balanced binary tree. Apart from that, the query cost has to be small, but frequent updates are expected. Then the best choice for the two hierarchical attributes is the SDDC technique (depending on the actual hierarchical structure, variations of SDDC can be used). It guarantees a sublinear query and update cost and provides good expected costs for queries that aggregate according to the hierarchies. For the dimension of size 2 pre-aggregation is unnecessary.

The remaining dimension is processed with PS to enable fast queries. In total, the worst case costs are $2\log_2 n \cdot 2\log_2 n \cdot 2 \cdot 2 = 16\log_2^2 n$ for queries and $\log_2 n \cdot \log_2 n \cdot 1 \cdot n = n\log_2^2 n$ for updates. Note that all costs are *exact*, i.e., there are no hidden constants.

5   Comparing IDC to Previous Approaches

The IDC technique reduces the problem of pre-aggregating d-dimensional data cubes to the one-dimensional case. Compared to techniques that directly solve the d-dimensional problem, IDC's range of possible query-update cost tradeoffs is therefore restricted. However, as we will show below, none of the previously proposed d-dimensional pre-aggregation techniques obtains superior tradeoffs.

The PS, SRPS, and SDDC techniques constitute special cases of IDC. One can iteratively create the pre-aggregated data cubes for these techniques by applying the corresponding one-dimensional technique for each dimension of the original data cube. This results in d-dimensional Iterative Data Cubes with worst case (query, update)-cost pairs $(2^d, n^d)$, $(4^d, 2^d n^{d/2})$, and $(2^d \lceil \log_2 n \rceil^d, \lceil \log_2 n \rceil^d)$, respectively. As an interesting by-product PS, SRPS, and SDDC can be analyzed and implemented as Iterative Data Cubes. Note that for SRPS and SDDC the implementation is quite complex and the analysis difficult. For instance for a d-dimensional data cube, SDDC stores $(d-1)$-dimensional surfaces of pre-aggregated cumulative values recursively as $(d-1)$-dimensional data cubes. Thus, IDC provides a great "tool" for verifying the results of these previous approaches and for obtaining new results, like for instance average case costs.

The HC technique [3] generates a pre-aggregated data cube by hierarchically partitioning the original data cube A into smaller hyper-rectangles (blocks) of equal size. The number of recursive partitioning steps determines the height of a Hierarchical Cube. Hierarchical Rectangle Cubes (HRC) with a height of one are identical to the original data cube. In HRCs of height two each cell stores the prefix sum local to the anchor of the block it belongs to. Consequently, any HRC of height two can be constructed iteratively by applying the one-dimensional LPS technique with the corresponding block sizes along each dimension. Hierarchical Rectangle Cubes of height one and two hence are generalized by IDC. For HRCs of height greater than two, [3] does not provide analytical or experimental results. Thus we were not able to compare IDC to HRCs of height greater than two. Hierarchical Band Cubes (HBC) can not be generalized by our technique. Only HBCs of height one are identical to the PS cube, which is an IDC. For HBCs of height greater than one we prove, that no matter which hierarchical partitioning scheme is used, a d-dimensional HBC has always a worst case update cost of at least n^{d-1} (we assume without loss of generality that all dimensions have a domain of size n). The proof can be found in [15]. The range of possible update costs therefore is restricted compared to IDC. In total, the best possible HBC cube of height $h \geq 2$ has a worst case query cost of at least $2^d h = 2^{d+1}$ [3], and a worst case update cost of at least n^{d-1}. An Iterative Data Cube where the PS technique is used for $(d-2)$ dimensions and the SRPS technique is used for the remaining two dimensions, has respective worst case query and update costs of $2^{d-2}4^2 = 2^{d+2}$ and $n^{d-2}(2\sqrt{n})^2 = 4n^{d-1}$. Thus, there exists an IDC whose query and update costs are asymptotically identical to the *lower bounds* for the corresponding costs of any HBC cube.

6 Conclusion

IDC is the first pre-aggregation technique on data cubes that can take the specific properties of different dimension attributes into account. Instead of solving a d-dimensional pre-aggregation problem directly, the different dimensions are handled independently. This greatly simplifies the development, analysis, and implementation compared to earlier approaches. At the same time a greater variety of query-update cost tradeoffs can be generated. Thus Iterative Data Cubes provide a practical framework for developing pre-aggregation techniques for MOLAP data cubes.

Even though the space of possible pre-aggregation schemes is restricted by the iterative combination process, we were able to show that the query-update cost tradeoffs of previously proposed techniques are matched. It remains, however, as an open problem, to show that in general the query-update cost tradeoffs that are optimal for the IDC technique are also optimal with respect to any pre-aggregation technique on a high-dimensional data cube. We will pursue this problem, as well as the problem of sparse data sets [16] in our future research.

References

[1] E. Baralis, S. Paraboschi, and E. Teniente. Materialized view selection in a multidimensional database. In *Proc. Int. Conf. on Very Large Databases (VLDB)*, pages 156–165, 1997.

[2] K. Beyer and R. Ramakrishnan. Bottom-up computation of sparse and iceberg CUBEs. In *Proc. Int. Conf. on Management of Data (SIGMOD)*, pages 359–370, 1999.

[3] C.-Y. Chan and Y. E. Ioannidis. Hierarchical cubes for range-sum queries. In *Proc. Int. Conf. on Very Large Databases (VLDB)*, pages 675–686, 1999. Extended version published as Tech. Report, Univ. of Wisconsin, 1999.

[4] E. F. Codd. Providing OLAP (on-line analytical processing) to user-analysts: An IT mandate. Technical report, E. F. Codd and Associates, 1993.

[5] S. Geffner, D. Agrawal, and A. El Abbadi. The dynamic data cube. In *Proc. Int. Conf. on Extending Database Technology (EDBT)*, pages 237–253, 2000.

[6] S. Geffner, D. Agrawal, A. El Abbadi, and T. Smith. Relative prefix sums: An efficient approach for querying dynamic OLAP data cubes. In *Proc. Int. Conf. on Data Engineering (ICDE)*, pages 328–335, 1999.

[7] J. Gray, S. Chaudhuri, A. Bosworth, A. Layman, D. Reichart, M. Venkatrao, F. Pellow, and H. Pirahesh. Data cube: A relational aggregation operator generalizing group-by, cross-tab, and sub-totals. *Data Mining and Knowledge Discovery*, pages 29–53, 1997.

[8] H. Gupta. Selection of views to materialize in a data warehouse. In *Proc. Int. Conf. on Database Theory (ICDT)*, pages 98–112, 1997.

[9] H. Gupta, V. Harinarayan, A. Rajaraman, and J. D. Ullman. Index selection for OLAP. In *Proc. Int. Conf. on Data Engineering (ICDE)*, pages 208–219, 1997.

[10] V. Harinarayan, A. Rajaraman, and J. D. Ullman. Implementing data cubes efficiently. In *Proc. Int. Conf. on Management of Data (SIGMOD)*, pages 205–216, 1996.

[11] C. Ho, R. Agrawal, N. Megiddo, and R. Srikant. Range queries in OLAP data cubes. In *Proc. Int. Conf. on Management of Data (SIGMOD)*, pages 73–88, 1997.

[12] T. Johnson and D. Shasha. Some approaches to index design for cube forests. *IEEE Data Engineering Bulletin*, 20(1):27–35, 1997.

[13] Y. Kotidis and N. Roussopoulos. An alternative storage organization for ROLAP aggregate views based on cubetrees. In *Proc. Int. Conf. on Management of Data (SIGMOD)*, pages 249–258, 1998.

[14] N. Pendse and R. Creeth. The OLAP report. http://www.olapreport.com/Analyses.htm, 2000. Parts available online in the current edition.

[15] M. Riedewald, D. Agrawal, and A. El Abbadi. Flexible data cubes for online aggregation. Technical report, UC Santa Barbara, 2000.

[16] M. Riedewald, D. Agrawal, and A. El Abbadi. pCube: Update-efficient online aggregation with progressive feedback and error bounds. In *Proc. Int. Conf. on Scientific and Statistical Database Management (SSDBM)*, pages 95–108, 2000.

[17] M. Riedewald, D. Agrawal, A. El Abbadi, and R. Pajarola. Space-efficient data cubes for dynamic environments. In *Proc. Int. Conf. on Data Warehousing and Knowledge Discovery (DaWaK)*, pages 24–33, 2000.

[18] J. R. Smith, V. Castelli, A. Jhingran, and C.-S. Li. Dynamic assembly of views in data cubes. In *Proc. Symp. on Principles of Database Systems (PODS)*, pages 274–283, 1998.

[19] Transaction Processing Performance Council. TPC-H benchmark (1.1.0). Available at http://www.tpc.org.

[20] J. S. Vitter and M. Wang. Approximate computation of multidimensional aggregates of sparse data using wavelets. In *Proc. Int. Conf. on Management of Data (SIGMOD)*, pages 193–204, 1999.

[21] J. S. Vitter, M. Wang, and B. Iyer. Data cube approximation and histograms via wavelets. In *Proc. Intl. Conf. on Information and Knowledge Management (CIKM)*, pages 96–104, 1998.

Mining for Empty Rectangles in Large Data Sets

Jeff Edmonds[1], Jarek Gryz[1], Dongming Liang[1], and Renée J. Miller[2]

[1] York University
[2] University of Toronto

Abstract. Many data mining approaches focus on the discovery of similar (and frequent) data values in large data sets. We present an alternative, but complementary approach in which we search for empty regions in the data. We consider the problem of finding all maximal empty rectangles in large, two-dimensional data sets. We introduce a novel, scalable algorithm for finding all such rectangles. The algorithm achieves this with a single scan over a sorted data set and requires only a small bounded amount of memory. We also describe an algorithm to find all maximal empty hyper-rectangles in a multi-dimensional space. We consider the complexity of this search problem and present new bounds on the number of maximal empty hyper-rectangles. We briefly overview experimental results obtained by applying our algorithm to a synthetic data set.

1 Introduction

Much work in data mining has focused on characterizing the similarity of data values in large data sets. This work includes clustering or classification in which different techniques are used to group and characterize the data. Such techniques permit the development of more "parsimonious" versions of the data. Parsimony may be measured by the degree of compression (size reduction) between the original data and its mined characterization [3]. Parsimony may also be measured by the semantic value of the characterization in revealing hidden patterns and trends in the data [8,1].

Consider the data of Figure 1 representing information about traffic infractions (tickets), vehicle registrations, and drivers. Using association rules, one may discover that Officer Seth gave out mostly speeding tickets [1] or that drivers of BMWs usually get speeding tickets over $100 [11]. Using clustering one may discover that many expensive (over $500) speeding tickets were given out to drivers of BMW's [14]. Using fascicles, one may discover that officers Seth, Murray and Jones gave out tickets for similar amounts on similar days [8].

The data patterns discovered by these techniques are defined by some measure of similarity (data values must be identical or similar to appear together in a pattern) and some measure of degree of frequency or occurrence (a pattern is only interesting if a sufficient number of data values manifest the pattern or, in the case of outlier detection, if very few values manifest the pattern).

In this paper, we propose an alternative, but complementary approach to characterizing data. Specifically, we focus on finding and characterizing empty

J. Van den Bussche and V. Vianu (Eds.): ICDT 2001, LNCS 1973, pp. 174–188, 2001.

Registration

RegNum	Model	Owner
R43999	Saab9.5W	Owen
R44000	HondaCW	Wang
....		

Tickets

Tid	Officer	RegNum	Date	Infraction	Amt	DLNum
119	Seth	R43999	1/1/99	Speed	100	G4337
249	Murray	R00222	2/2/95	Parking	30	G7123
...						

Drivers

DLNum	Name	DOB
G16999	Smith	1970-03-22
G65000	Simon	1908-03-05
....		

Fig. 1. Schema and Data of a Traffic Infraction Database

regions in the data. In the above data set, we would like to discover if there are certain ranges of the attributes that never appear together. For example, it may be the case that no tickets were issued to BMW Z3 series cars before 1997 or that no tickets for over $1,000 were issued before 1990 or that there is no record of any tickets issued after 1990 for drivers born before 1920. Some of these empty regions may be foreseeable (perhaps BMW Z3 series cars were first produced in 1997). Others may have more complex or uncertain causes (perhaps older drivers tend to drive less and more defensively).

Clearly, knowledge of empty regions may be valuable in and of itself as it may reveal unknown correlations between data values which can be exploited in applications.[1] For example, if a DBA determines that a certain empty region is a time invariant constraint, then it may be modeled as an integrity constraint. Knowing that no tickets for over $1,000 were issued before 1990, a DBA of a relational DBMS can add a check constraint to the Tickets table. Such constraints have been exploited in semantic query optimization [5].

To maximize the use of empty space knowledge, our goal in this work is to not only find empty regions in the data, but to fully characterize that empty space. Specifically, we discover the set of all maximal empty rectangles. In Section 2, we formally introduce this problem and place our work in the context of related work from the computational geometry and artificial intelligence communities. In Section 3, we present an algorithm for finding the set of all maximal empty rectangles in a two-dimensional data set. Unlike previous work in this area, we focus on providing an algorithm that scales well to large data sets. Our algorithm requires a single scan of a sorted data set and uses a small, bounded amount of memory to compute the set of all maximal empty rectangles. In contrast, related algorithms require space that is at least on the order of the size of the data set. We describe also an algorithm that works in multiple dimensions and present complexity results along with bounds on the number of maximal hyper-rectangles. In Section 4, we present the results of experiments performed on synthetic data showing the scalability of our mining algorithm. We conclude in Section 5.

---

[1] [10] describe applications of such correlations in a medical domain.

2   Problem Definition and Related Work

Consider a data set D consisting of a set of tuples $\langle v_x, v_y \rangle$ over two totally ordered domains. Let X and Y denote the set of distinct values in the data set in each of the dimensions. We can depict the data set as an $|X| \times |Y|$ matrix M of 0's and 1's. There is a 1 in position $\langle x, y \rangle$ of the matrix if and only if $\langle v_x, v_y \rangle \in D$ where v_x is the xth smallest value in X and v_y the yth smallest in Y.

An empty rectangle is *maximal* [2] if it cannot be extended along either the X or Y axis because there is at least one 1-entry on each of the borders of the rectangle. Although it appears that there may be a huge number of overlapping maximal rectangles, [12] proves that the number is at most $\mathcal{O}(|D|^2)$, and that for a random placement of the 1-entries the expected value is $\mathcal{O}(|D| \log |D|)$ [12]. We prove that the number is at most the number of 0-entries, which is $\mathcal{O}(|X||Y|)$ (Theorem 4).

A related problem attempts to find the minimum number of rectangles (either overlapping or not) that covers all the 0's in the matrix. This problem is a special case of the problem known as Rectilinear Picture Compression and is NP-complete [7]. Hence, it is impractical for use in large data sets.

The problem of finding empty rectangles or hyper-rectangles has been studied in both the machine learning [10] and computational geometry literature [12,2,4,13]. Liu *et al* motivate the use of empty space knowledge for discovering constraints (in their terms, *impossible combinations of values*) [10]. However, the proposed algorithm is memory-based and not optimized for large datasets. As the data is scanned, a data structure is kept storing all maximal hyper-rectangles. The algorithm runs in $\mathcal{O}(|D|^{2(d-1)} d^3 (log |D|)^2)$ where d is the number of dimensions in the data set. Even in two dimensions ($d = 2$) this algorithm is impractical for large datasets. In an attempt to address both the time and space complexity, the authors propose only maintaining maximal empty hyper-rectangles that exceed an *a priori* set minimum size. This heuristic is only effective if this minimum size is set sufficiently small. Furthermore, as our experiments on real dataset will show, for a given size, there are typically many maximal empty rectangles that are largely overlapping. Hence, this heuristic may yield a set of large, but almost identical rectangles. This reduces the effectiveness of the algorithm for a large class of data mining applications where the number of discovered regions is less important that the distinctiveness of the regions. Other heuristic approaches have been proposed that use decision tree classifiers to (approximately) separate occupied from unoccupied space then post-process the discovered regions to determine maximal empty rectangles [9]. Unlike our approach, these heuristics do not guarantee that all maximal empty rectangles are found.

This problem has also been studied in the computational geometry literature [12,2,4,13] where the primary goal has been to produce run time bounds. These algorithms find all maximal empty rectangles in time $\mathcal{O}(|D| \log |D| + s)$ and space $\mathcal{O}(|D|)$, where $|D|$ is the size of the data set and s denotes the number

---

[2] Do not confuse maximal with maximum (largest).

of maximal empty rectangles. Such algorithms are particularly effective if the data set is very sparse and there happens to be only a few maximal rectangles. However, these algorithms do not scale well for large data sets because of their space requirements. The algorithms must continually access and modify a data structure that is as large as the data set itself. Because in practice this will not fit in memory, an infeasible amount of disk access is required on large data sets.

The setting of the algorithm in [13] is different because it considers points in the real plane instead of 1-entries in a matrix. The only difference that this amounts to is that they assume that points have distinct X and Y coordinates. This is potentially a problem for a database application since it would not allow any duplicate values in data (along any dimension).

Despite the extensive literature on this problem, none of the known algorithms are effective for large data sets. Even for two-dimensional data sets, the only known technique for scaling these algorithms is to provide a fixed bound on the size of the empty rectangles discovered, a technique which severally limits the application of the discovered results.

Our first contribution to this problem is an algorithm for finding all maximal empty rectangles in a two-dimensional space that can perform efficiently in a bounded amount of memory and is scalable to a large, non-memory resident data set. Unlike the algorithm of [10], our algorithm requires the data be processed in sorted order. However, sorting is a highly optimized operation within modern DBMS and by taking advantage of existing scalable sorting techniques, we have produced an algorithm with running time $\mathcal{O}(|X||Y|)$ (i.e. linear in the input size) that requires only a single scan over the sorted data. Furthermore, the memory requirements are $\Theta(|X|)$, which is an order of magnitude smaller than the size $\mathcal{O}(|X||Y|)$ of both the input and the output. (We assume without loss of generality that $|X| \leq |Y|$.) If the memory available is not sufficient, our algorithm could be modified to run on a portion of the matrix at a time at the cost of extra scans of the data set. Our second main contribution is an extension of our algorithm to find all maximal empty hyper-rectangles in multi-dimensional data. The space and time trade-off compare favorably to those of the heuristic algorithm of [10] (the time complexity of our extended algorithm is $\mathcal{O}(d|D|^{2(d-1)})$ and the space requirements are $\mathcal{O}(d^2|D|^{d-1})$), but are worse than those of incomplete classifier-based algorithms [9].

3   Algorithm for Finding All Maximal Empty Rectangles

This section presents an elegant algorithm for finding all maximal empty regions within a two dimensional data set. Although the binary matrix M representation of the data set D is never actually constructed, for simplicity we describe the algorithm completely in terms of M. In doing so, however, we must insure that only one pass is made through the data set D.

The main structure of the algorithm is to consider each 0-entry $\langle x, y \rangle$ of M one at a time row by row. Although the 0-entries are not explicitly stored, this is simulated as follows. We assume that the set X of distinct values in the (smaller) dimension is small enough to store in memory. The data set D is stored on disk sorted with respect to Y, X. Tuples from D will be read sequentially off the disk in this sorted order. When the next tuple $\langle v_x, v_y \rangle \in D$ is read from disk, we will be able to deduce the block of 0-entries in the row before this 1-entry.

When considering the 0-entry $\langle x, y \rangle$, the algorithm needs to look ahead by querying the matrix entries $\langle x+1, y \rangle$ and $\langle x, y+1 \rangle$. This is handled by having the single pass through the data set actually occur one row in advance. This extra row of the matrix is small enough to be stored in memory. Similarly, when considering the 0-entry $\langle x, y \rangle$, the algorithm will have to look back and query information about the parts of the matrix already read. To avoid re-reading the data set, all such information is retained in memory. This consists of $staircase(x-1, y)$, which is a stack of at most n tuples $\langle x_i, y_i \rangle$, a row of indexes $y_r(x', y-1)$ for $x' \in [1..n]$, and a single index $x_*(x-1, y)$.

The main data structure maintained by the algorithm is the *maximal staircase*, $staircase(x, y)$, which stores the shape of the maximal staircase shaped block of 0-entries starting at entry $\langle x, y \rangle$ and extending up and to the left as far as possible. See Figure 2. Note that the bottom-right entry separating two steps of the staircase is a 1-entry. This entry prevents the two adjoining steps from extending up or to the left and prevents another step forming between them.

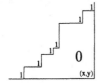

Fig. 2. The maximal staircase for $\langle x, y \rangle$.

```
loop y = 1 ... n
  loop x = 1 ... m
    (I) Construct staircase (x,y)
    (II) Output all maximal 0-rectangles with <x,y>
         as the bottom-right corner
```

Fig. 3. Algorithm Structure.

The purpose of constructing the $staircase(x, y)$ is to output all maximal rectangles that lie entirely *within* that staircase and whose bottom right corner is $\langle x, y \rangle$. The algorithm (Figure 3) traverses the matrix left-to-right and top-to-bottom creating a staircase for every entry in the matrix. We now describe the construction of the staircase and the production of maximal empty rectangles in detail.

3.1   Constructing $Staircase(x, y)$

The maximal staircase, $staircase(x, y)$, is specified by the coordinates of the top-left corner $\langle x_i, y_i \rangle$ of each of its steps. This sequence of steps $\langle \langle x_1, y_1 \rangle, \ldots, \langle x_r, y_r \rangle \rangle$ is stored in a stack, with the top step $\langle x_r, y_r \rangle$ on the top of the stack. The maximal staircase, $staircase(x, y) = \langle \langle x_1, y_1 \rangle, \ldots, \langle x_r, y_r \rangle \rangle$, is easily constructed from the staircase, $staircase(x-1, y) = \langle \langle x'_1, y'_1 \rangle, \ldots, \langle x'_{r'}, y'_{r'} \rangle \rangle$ as follows. See Figure 4.

We start by computing y_r, which will be the Y-coordinate for the highest entry in $staircase(x, y)$. This step extends up from $\langle x, y \rangle$ until it is blocked by the first 1 in column x. Searching for this 1 entry takes too much time. Instead, $y_r(x, y)$ will be computed in constant time from $y_r(x, y-1)$, which we saved from the $\langle x, y-1 \rangle$ iteration. Here, $y_r(x, y)$ is used to denote y_r to distinguish between it and the same value for different iterations. By definition $y_r(x, y)$ is the Y-coordinate of the top most 0-entry in the block of 0-entries in column x starting at entry $\langle x, y \rangle$ and extending up. $y_r(x, y-1)$ is the same except it considers the block extending up from $\langle x, y-1 \rangle$. Therefore, if entry $\langle x, y \rangle$ contains a 0, then $y_r(x, y) = y_r(x, y-1)$. On the other hand, if entry $\langle x, y \rangle$ contains a 1, then $y_r(x, y)$ is not well defined and $staircase(x, y)$ is empty.

How the rest of $staircase(x, y)$ is constructed depends on how the new height of top step y_r compares with the old one $y'_{r'}$.

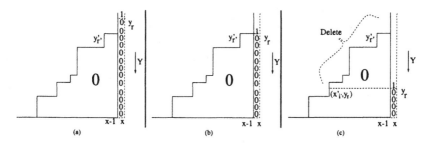

Fig. 4. The three cases in constructing maximal staircase, $staircase(x,y)$, from $staircase(x-1,y)$.

Case $y_r < y'_{r'}$: Figure 4(a). If the new top step is higher than the old top step, then the new staircase $staircase(x, y)$ is the same as the old one $staircase(x-1, y)$ except one extra high step is added on the right. This step will have width of only one column and its top-left corner will be $\langle x, y_r \rangle$. In this case, $staircase(x, y)$ is constructed from $staircase(x-1, y)$ simply by pushing this new step $\langle x, y_r \rangle$ onto the top of the stack.

Case $y_r = y'_{r'}$: Figure 4(b). If the new top step has the exact same height as the old top step, then the new staircase $staircase(x, y)$ is the same as the old one $staircase(x-1, y)$ except that this top step is extended one column to the right. Because the data structure $staircase(x, y)$ stores only the top-left corners of each step, no change to the data structure is required.

Case $y_r > y'_{r'}$: Figure 4(c). If the new top step is lower then the old top step, then all the old steps that are higher then this new highest step must be deleted. The last deleted step is replaced with the new highest step. The new highest step will have top edge at y_r and will extend to the left as far as the last step $\langle x'_{i'}, y'_{i'} \rangle$ to be deleted. Hence, top-left corner of this new top step will be at location $\langle x'_{i'}, y_r \rangle$. In this case, $staircase(x, y)$ is constructed from $staircase(x-1, y)$ simply by popping off the stack the steps $\langle x'_{r'}, y'_{r'} \rangle, \langle x'_{r'-1}, y'_{r'-1} \rangle, \ldots, \langle x'_{i'}, y'_{i'} \rangle$ as long as $y_r > y'_i$. Finally, the new top step $\langle x'_{i'}, y_r \rangle$ is pushed on top.

One key thing to note is that when constructing $staircase(x, y)$ from $staircase$ $(x-1, y)$, *at most* one new step is created.

3.2   Outputting the Maximal 0-Rectangles

The goal of the main loop is to output all maximal 0-rectangles with $\langle x, y \rangle$ as the bottom-right corner. This is done by outputting all steps of $staircase(x, y)$ that cannot be extended down or to the right.

Whether such a step can be extended depends on where the first 1-entry is located within row $y+1$ and where it is within column $x+1$. Consider the largest block of 0-entries in row $y+1$ starting at entry $\langle x, y+1 \rangle$ and extending to the left. Let $x_*(x, y)$ (or x_* for short) be the X-coordinate of this left most 0-entry (see Figure 5). Similarly, consider the largest block of 0-entries in column $x+1$ starting at entry $\langle x+1, y \rangle$ and extending up. Let $y_*(x, y)$ (or y_* for short) be the Y-coordinate of this top most 0-entry. By definition, $y_*(x, y) = y_r(x+1, y)$ and we know how to compute it. $x_*(x, y)$ is computed in constant time from $x_*(x-1, y)$ in the same way. (See Figure 6.)

The following theorem states which of the rectangles within the $staircase$ (x, y) are maximal.

Theorem 1. *Consider a step in $staircase(x, y)$ with top-left corner $\langle x_i, y_i \rangle$. The rectangle $\langle x_i, x, y_i, y \rangle$ is maximal if and only if $x_i < x_*$ and $y_i < y_*$.*

Proof. The step $\langle x_i, y_i \rangle$ of $staircase(x, y)$ forms the rectangle $\langle x_i, x, y_i, y \rangle$. If $x_i \geq x_*$, then this rectangle is sufficiently skinny to be extended down into the block of 0-entries in row $y+1$. For example, the highest step in Figure 5 satisfies this condition. On the other hand, if $x_i < x_*$, then this rectangle cannot be extended down because it is blocked by the 1-entry located at $\langle x_*-1, y+1 \rangle$. Similarly, the rectangle is sufficiently short to be extended to the right into the block of 0-entries in column $x+1$ only if $y_i \geq y_*$. See the lowest step in Figure 5. Hence, the rectangle is maximal if and only if $x_i < x_*$ and $y_i < y_*$.

To output the steps that are maximal 0-rectangles, pop the steps $\langle x_r, y_r \rangle$, $\langle x_{r-1}, y_{r-1} \rangle$, ... from the stack. The x_i values will get progressively smaller and the y_i values will get progressively larger. Hence, the steps can be divided into three intervals. At first, the steps may have the property $x_i \geq x_*$. As said, these steps are too skinny to be maximal. Eventually, the x_i of the steps will decrease until $x_i < x_*$. Then there may be an interval of steps for which $x_i < x_*$ and $y_i < y_*$. These steps are maximal. For these steps output the rectangle $\langle x_i, x, y_i, y \rangle$. However, y_i may continue to increase until $y_i \geq y_*$. The remaining steps will be too short to be maximal.

Recall that the next step after outputting the maximal steps in $staircase(x, y)$ is to construct $staircase(x+1, y)$ from $staircase(x, y)$. Conveniently, the work required for these two operations is precisely the same. This is because $y_r(x+1, y) = y_*(x, y)$. The steps from the first and second interval, i.e. $y_i < y_*(x, y) = y_r(x+1, y)$, can be thrown way as they are popped off the stack, because they are precisely the steps that are thrown away when constructing $staircase(x+1, y)$ from $staircase(x, y)$. Similarly, the staircase steps in the third interval, i.e. $y_i \geq y_*(x, y) = y_r(x+1, y)$, do not need to be popped, because they are not maximal in $staircase(x, y)$ and are required for $staircase(x+1, y)$.

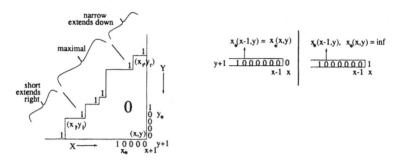

Fig. 5. Computing $staircase(x, y)$.   **Fig. 6.** Computing $x_*(x, y)$ from $x_*(x-1, y)$.

3.3   Time and Space Complexity

Theorem 2. *The time complexity of the algorithm is $\mathcal{O}(nm)$.*

Proof. Most of the algorithm is clearly constant time per $\langle x, y \rangle$ iteration of the main loop. We have already described how to compute $y_r(x, y)$, $x_*(x, y)$, and $y_*(x, y)$ in constant time. The remaining task that might take more time is popping the steps off the stack to check if they are maximal, deleting them if they are too skinny, and outputting and deleting them if they are maximal. For a particular $\langle x, y \rangle$ iteration, an arbitrary number of steps may be popped. This takes more than a constant amount of time for this iteration. However, when amortized over all iterations, at most one step is popped per iteration.

Consider the life of a particular step. During some iteration it is created and pushed onto the stack. Later it is popped off. Each $\langle x, y \rangle$ iteration creates at most one new step and then only if the $\langle x, y \rangle$ entry is 0. Hence, the total number of steps created is at most the number of 0-entries in the matrix. As well, because each of these steps is popped at most once in its life and output as a maximal 0-rectangle at most once, we can conclude that the total number of times a step is popped and the total number of maximal 0-rectangles are both at most the number of 0-entries in the matrix.

It follows that the entire computation requires only $\mathcal{O}(nm)$ time (where $n = |X|$ and $m = |Y|$).

Theorem 3. *The algorithm requires $\mathcal{O}(\min(n, m))$ space.*

Proof. If the matrix is too large to fit into main memory, the algorithm is such that one pass through the matrix is sufficient. Other than the current $\langle x, y \rangle$-entry of the matrix, only $\mathcal{O}(\min(n, m))$ additional memory is required. The stack for $staircase(x, y)$ contains neither more steps than the number of rows nor more than the number of columns. Hence, $|staircase(x, y)| = \mathcal{O}(\min(n, m))$. The previous value for x_* requires $\mathcal{O}(1)$ space. The previous row of y_* values requires $\mathcal{O}(n)$ space, but the matrix can be transposed so that there are fewer rows than columns.

3.4   Number and Distribution of Maximal 0-Rectangles

Theorem 4. *The number of maximal 0-rectangles is at most $\mathcal{O}(nm)$.*

Proof. Follows directly from the proof of Theorem 2.

We now demonstrate two very different matrices that have $\mathcal{O}(nm)$ maximal 0-rectangles. See Figure 7. The first matrix simply has $\mathcal{O}(nm)$ 0-entries each of which is surrounded on all sides by 1-entries. Each such 0-entry is in itself a maximal 0-rectangle.

For the second construction, consider the n by n matrix with two diagonals of 1-entries. One from the middle of the left side to the middle of the bottom. The other from the middle of the top to the middle of the right side. The remaining entries are 0. Choose any of the $\frac{n}{2}$ 0-entries along the bottom 1-diagonal and any of the $\frac{n}{2}$ 0-entries along the top 1-diagonal. The rectangle with these two 0-entries as corners is a maximal 0-rectangle. There are $\mathcal{O}(n^2)$ of these. Attaching $\frac{m}{n}$ of these matrices in a row will give you an n by m matrix with $\frac{m}{n}\mathcal{O}(n^2) = \mathcal{O}(nm)$ maximal 0-entries.

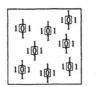

Fig. 7. Two matrices with $\mathcal{O}(nm)$ maximal 0-rectangles

Actual data generally has structure to it and hence contains large 0-rectangles. We found this to be true in all our experiments [6]. However, a randomly chosen matrix does not contain large 0-rectangles.

Theorem 5. *Let M be a $n \times n$ matrix where each entry is chosen to be 1 independently at random with probability $\alpha_1 = \frac{N_1}{n^2}$. The expected number of 1-entries is N_1. The probability of it having a 0-rectangle of size s is at most $p = (1 - \alpha_1)^s n^3$ and the expected number of disjoint 0-rectangle of size s is at least $E = (1 - \alpha_1)^s n^2 / s$.*

Proof. A fixed rectangle of size s obtains all 0's with probability $(1 - \alpha_1)^s$. There are at most n^3 different rectangles of size s in an $n \times n$ matrix. Hence, the probability that at least one of them is all 0's is at most $p = (1 - \alpha_1)^s n^3$. The number of disjoint square rectangles within a $n \times n$ matrix is n^2/s. The expected number of these that are all 0's is $E = (1 - \alpha_1)^s n^2/s$.

Example 1. If the density of 1's is only $\alpha_1 = \frac{1}{1,000}$ then the probability of having a 0-rectangle of size $s = \frac{1}{\alpha_1}[3\ln(n) + \ln(\frac{1}{p})] = 3,000\ln(n) + 7,000$ is at most $p = \frac{1}{1,000}$ and the expected number of 0-rectangle of size $s = \frac{1}{\alpha_1}[2\ln(n) - \ln\ln(n) - \ln(\frac{2E}{\alpha_1})] = 2,000\ln(n) - 1000\ln\ln(n) - 14,500$ is at least 1000.

As a second example, the probability of having a 0-rectangle of size $s = q \cdot n^2 = \frac{1}{1000}n^2$ is at most $p = \frac{1}{1000}$ when the number of 1's is at least $N_1 = \alpha_1 n^2 = \frac{1}{q}[3\ln(n) + \ln(\frac{1}{p})] = 3,000\ln(n) + 7,000$. The expected number of this size is at least $E = 100$ when the number of 1's is at most $N_1 = \alpha_1 n^2 = \frac{1}{q}\ln(\frac{1}{qE}) = 2,300$.

The expected number of rectangles can be derived as a consequence of Theorem 5 as $E(s) \leq \mathcal{O}(\min(N_1 \log N_1, N_0))$ (where N_1 is the number of 1-entries and N_0 the number of 0-entries). This value increases almost linearly with N_1 as $N_1 \log N_1$ until $N_1 \log N_1 = N_0 = n^2/2$ and then decreases linearly with $n^2 - N_1$.

3.5   Multi-dimensional Matrices

The algorithm that finds all maximal 0-rectangles in a given two dimensional matrix can be extended to find all maximal d-dimensional 0-rectangles within a given d-dimensional matrix. In the 2-dimensional case, we looped through the entries $\langle x, y \rangle$ of the matrix, maintaining the *maximal staircase*, $staircase(x, y)$ (see Figure 2). This consists of a set of *steps*. Each such step is a 0-rectangle $\langle x_i, x, y_i, y \rangle$ that cannot be extended by decreasing the x_i or the y_i coordinates. There are at most $\mathcal{O}(n)$ such "stairs", because their lower points $\langle x_i, y_i \rangle$ lie along a 1-dimensional diagonal. In the 3-dimensional case, such a maximal staircase, $staircase(x, y, z)$ looks like one quadrant of a pyramid. Assuming (for notational simplicity) that every dimension has size n, then there are at most $\mathcal{O}(n^2)$ stairs, because their lower points $\langle x_i, y_i, z_i \rangle$ lie along a 2-dimensional diagonal. In general, $staircase(x_1, x_2, \ldots x_d)$ consists of the set of at most $\mathcal{O}(n^{d-1})$ rectangles (steps) that have $\langle x_1, x_2, \ldots x_d \rangle$ as the upper corner and that cannot be extended by decreasing any coordinate.

In the 2-dimensional case, we construct $staircase(x, y)$ from $staircase(x{-}1, y)$ by imposing what amounts to a 1-dimensional staircase on to its side (see Figure 4). This 1-dimensional staircase consists of a single step rooted at $\langle x, y \rangle$ and extending in the y dimension to y_r. It was constructed from the 1-dimensional staircase rooted at $\langle x, y{-}1 \rangle$ by extending it with the 0-dimensional staircase consisting only of the single entry $\langle x, y \rangle$. The 1-dimensional staircase rooted at $\langle x, y{-}1 \rangle$ had been constructed earlier in the algorithm and had been saved in memory. The algorithm saves a line of n such 1-dimensional staircases.

In the 3-dimensional case, the algorithm saves the one 3-dimensional staircase $staircase(x-1,y,z)$, a line of n 2-dimensional staircases, and a plane of n^2 1-dimensional staircases, and has access to a cube of n^3 0-dimensional staircases consisting of the entries of the matrix. Each iteration, it constructs the 3-dimensional $staircase(x,y,z)$ from the previously saved 3-dimensional $staircase(x-1,y,z)$ by imposing a 2-dimensional staircase on to its side. This 2-dimensional staircase is rooted at $\langle x,y,z \rangle$ and extends in the y,z plain. It is constructed from the previously saved 2-dimensional staircase rooted at $\langle x,y-1,z \rangle$ by imposing a 1-dimensional staircase on to its side. This 1-dimensional staircase is rooted at $\langle x,y,z \rangle$ and extends in the z dimension. It is constructed from the previously saved 1-dimensional rooted at $\langle x,y,z-1 \rangle$ by imposing a 0-dimensional staircase. This 0-dimensional staircase consists of the single entry $\langle x,y,z \rangle$. This pattern is extended for the d-dimensional case.

The running time, $\mathcal{O}(N_0\ d\ n^{d-2})$, is dominated by the time to impose the $d-1$-dimensional staircase onto the side of the d-dimensional one. With the right data structure, this can be done in time proportional to the size of the $d-1$-dimensional staircase, which as stated is $\mathcal{O}(d\ n^{d-2})$. Doing this for every 0-entry $\langle x,y,z \rangle$ requires a total of $\mathcal{O}(N_0\ d\ n^{d-2})$ time.

When constructing $staircase(x,y,z)$ from $staircase(x-1,y,z)$ some new stairs are added and some are deleted. The deleted ones are potential maximal rectangles. Because they are steps, we know that they cannot be extended by decreasing any of the dimensions. The reason that they are being deleted is because they cannot be extended by increasing the x dimension. What remains to be determined is whether or not they can be extended by increasing either the y or the z dimension. In the 2-dimensional case, there is only one additional dimension to check and this is done easily by reading one row ahead of the current entry $\langle x,y \rangle$. In the 3-dimensional case this is harder. One possible solution is to read one y,z plane ahead. An easier solution is as follows.

The algorithm has three phases. The first phase proceeds as described above storing all large 0-rectangles that cannot be extended by decreasing any of the dimensions (or by increasing the x dimension). The second phase turns the matrix upside down and does the same. This produces all large 0-rectangles that cannot be extended by increasing any of the dimensions (or by decreasing the x dimension). The third phase finds the intersection of these two sets by sorting them and merging them together. These rectangles are maximal because they cannot be extended by decreasing or by increasing any of the dimensions. This algorithm makes only two passes through the matrix and uses only $\mathcal{O}(d\ n^{d-1})$ space.

Theorem 6. *The time complexity of the algorithm is* $\mathcal{O}(N_0\ d\ n^{d-2}) \le \mathcal{O}(d\ n^{2d-2})$ *and space complexity* $\mathcal{O}(d\ n^{d-1})$.

Theorem 7. *The number of maximal 0-hyper-rectangles in a d-dimensional matrix is* $\Theta(n^{2d-2})$.

Proof. The upper bound on the number of maximal rectangles is given by the running time of the algorithm that produces them all. The lower bound is proved by constructing a matrix that has $\Omega(n^{2d-2})$ such rectangles. The construction is very similar to that for the $d = 2$ case given in Figure 7, except that the lower and the upper diagonals each consist of a $d-1$-dimensional plain of n^{d-1} points. Taking most combinations of one point from the bottom plane and one from the top produces $\Omega(n^{d-1} \times n^{d-1}) = \Omega(n^{2d-2})$ maximal rectangles.

The number of such maximal hyper-rectangles and hence the time to produce them increases exponentially with d. For $d = 2$ dimensions, this is $\Theta(n^2)$, which is linear in the size $\Theta(n^2)$ of the input matrix. For $d = 3$ dimensions, it is already $\Theta(n^4)$, which is not likely practical in general for large data sets.

4   Performance of Mining Algorithm

In this section, we present experiments designed to verify the claims of the algorithm's scalability and usefulness on large data sets. These tests were run against synthetic data. The experiments reported here were run on an (admittedly slow) multi-user 42MHz IBM RISC System/6000 machine with 256 MB RAM.

The performance of the algorithm depends on the number of tuples $T = |D|$ (which in matrix representation is the number of 1-entries), the number n of distinct values of X, the number m of distinct values of Y, and the number of maximal empty rectangles R. We report the runtime and the number of maximal empty rectangles R (where applicable).

Effect of T, the number of tuples, on Runtime. To test the scalability of the algorithm with respect to the data set size, we held the data density (that is, the ratio of T to $n * m$) constant at one fifth. We also held n constant at 1000 since our algorithm maintains a data structure of $\mathcal{O}(n)$ size. We found these numbers to be in the middle of the ranges of the values for our real data sets. The data set is a randomly generated set of points. Initially, m is set to 500 and T to 100,000 tuples. Figure 8 plots the runtime of the algorithm with respect to the number of tuples T. The performance scales linearly as expected. The number of maximal empty rectangles also scales almost linearly with T as our analytic results of Section 3.4 predicts.

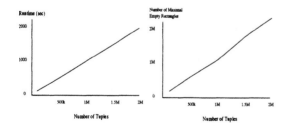
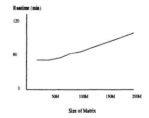
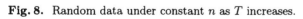

Fig. 8. Random data under constant n as T increases.

Fig. 9. Random data as the matrix size is increased (constant T).

Effect of Data Density on Runtime. Note that the algorithm requires only a single pass over the data which is why we expected this linear scale up for the previous experiment. However, the in memory processing time is $\mathcal{O}(nm)$ which may, for sparse data be significantly more than the size of the data. Hence, we verified experimentally that the algorithm's performance is dominated by the single pass over the data, not by the $\mathcal{O}(n)$ in memory computations required for each row. In this experiment, we kept both T and n constant and increased m. As we do, we increase the sparsity of the matrix. We expect the runtime performance to increase but the degree of this increase quantifies the extent to which the processing time dominates the I/O. Figure 9 plots the runtime of the algorithm with respect to the size of the matrix.

Effect of R, the number of maximal empty rectangles, on Runtime. Since the data was generated randomly in the first experiment, we could not precisely control the number of empty rectangles. In this next experiment, this number was tightly controlled. We generated a sequence of datasets shown for clarity in matrix representation in Figure 10.

Let $m = 1000$, $n = 2000$, $T = 1,000,000$. We start with a matrix that has 1000 colums filled with 1-entries separated by 1000 columns filled with 0-entries (for a total of 2000 columns). For each new test, we cluster the columns so that the number of spaces separating them decreases. We do this until there is one big square 1000x1000 filled with 1-entries, and another large square 1000x1000 filled with 0s. Thus, the number of empty rectangles decreases from 1000 to 1. We would expect that R should not affect the performance of the algorithm and this is verified by the results (Figure 10).

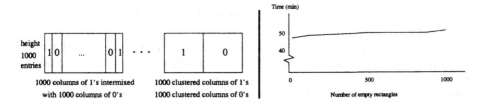

Fig. 10. Data sets and performance as the number of maximal empty rectangles R is increased.

Effect of n on the Runtime. We also tested the performance of the algorithm with respect to the number of distinct X values, n. Here, we kept T constant at 1,000,000 and R constant at 1,000 and varied both n and m. To achieve this, we constructed a sequence of data sets shown again in matrix representation in Figure 11(a).

For the first matrix, i is set to 1 so the data contains 1000 columns of 1-entries, each a single entry wide. Each column was separated by a single column of all 0's

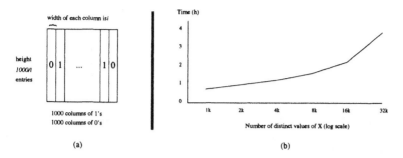

Fig. 11. Synthetic data under constant R and T. Runtime is plotted versus n.

(all columns are initially 1000 entries high). In the second matrix, the height of all columns is reduced by half (to 500 entries). The width of each column (both the columns containing 1's and the columns containing 0's) is doubled. This keeps the number of tuples constant, while increasing to 2000 the number of distinct X values. The number of columns with 0's does not change (only their width increases), hence the number of discovered empty rectangles remains constant. The process of reducing the height of the columns and multiplying their number is continued until all columns are of height 4.

The performance of the algorithm, as shown in Figure 11(b), deteriorates as expected with increasing n. Specifically, when the size of the data structures used grows beyond the size of memory, the data structures must be swapped in and out of memory. To avoid this, for data sets over two very large domains (recall that n is the minimum number of distinct values in the two attributes), the data values will need to be grouped using, for example, a standard binning or histogram technique to reduce the number of distinct values of the smallest attribute domain.

5   Conclusions

We developed an efficient and scalable algorithm that discovers all maximal empty rectangles with a single scan over a sorted two-dimensional data set. Previously proposed algorithms were not practical for large datasets since they did not scale (they required space proportional to the dataset size). We presented an extension of our algorithm to multi-dimensional data and we presented new results on the time and space complexity of these problems. Our mining algorithm can be used both to characterize the empty space within the data and to characterize any homogeneous regions in the data, including the data itself. By interchanging the roles of 0's and 1's in the algorithm, we can find the set of all maximal rectangles that are completely full (that is, they contain no empty space) and that cannot be extended without incorporating some empty space. Knowledge of empty rectangles may be valuable in and of itself as it may reveal unknown correlations or dependencies between data values and we have begun to study how it may be fully exploited in query optimization [6].

References

1. R. Agrawal, T. Imielinksi, and A. Swami. Mining Association Rules between Sets of Items in Large Databases. *ACM SIGMOD*, 22(2), June 1993.
2. M. J. Atallah and Fredrickson G. N. A note on finding a maximum empty rectangle. *Discrete Applied Mathematics*, (13):87–91, 1986.
3. D. Barbará, W. DuMouchel, C. Faloutsos, P. J. Haas, J. M. Hellerstein, Y. E. Ioannidis, H. V. Jagadish, T. Johnson, R. T. Ng, V. Poosala, K. A. Ross, and K. C. Sevcik. The New Jersey Data Reduction Report. *Data Engineering Bulletin*, 20(4):3–45, 1997.
4. Bernard Chazelle, Robert L. (Scot) Drysdale III, and D. T. Lee. Computing the largest empty rectangle. *SIAM J. Comput.*, 15(1):550–555, 1986.
5. Q. Cheng, J. Gryz, F. Koo, C. Leung, L. Liu, X. Qian, and B. Schiefer. Implementation of two semantic query optimization techniques in DB2 universal database. In *Proceedings of the 25th VLDB*, pages 687–698, Edinburgh, Scotland, 1999.
6. J. Edmonds, J. Gryz, D. Liang, and R. J. Miller. Mining for Empty Rectangles in Large Data Sets *(Extended Version)*. Technical Report CSRG-410, Department of Computer Science, University of Toronto, 2000.
7. M. R. Garey and D. S. Johnson. *Computers and Intractability*. W. H. Freeman and Co., New York, 1979.
8. H. V. Jagadish, J. Madar, and R. T. Ng. Semantic Compression and Pattern Extraction with Fascicles. In *Proc. of VLDB*, pages 186–197, 1999.
9. B. Liu, K. Wang, L.-F. Mun, and X.-Z. Qi. Using Decision Tree Induction for Discovering Holes in Data. In *5th Pacific Rim International Conference on Artificial Intelligence*, pages 182–193, 1998.
10. Bing Liu, Liang-Ping Ku, and Wynne Hsu. Discovering interesting holes in data. In *Proceedings of IJCAI*, pages 930–935, Nagoya, Japan, 1997. Morgan Kaufmann.
11. R. J. Miller and Y. Yang. Association Rules over Interval Data. *ACM SIGMOD*, 26(2):452–461, May 1997.
12. A. Namaad, W. L. Hsu, and D. T. Lee. On the maximum empty rectangle problem. *Applied Discrete Mathematics*, (8):267–277, 1984.
13. M. Orlowski. A New Algorithm for the Largest Empty Rectangle Problem. *Algorithmica*, 5(1):65–73, 1990.
14. T. Zhang, R. Ramakrishnan, and M. Livny. BIRCH: An Efficient Data Clustering Method for Very Large Databases. *ACM SIGMOD*, 25(2), June 1996.

FUN: An Efficient Algorithm for Mining Functional and Embedded Dependencies

Noël Novelli and Rosine Cicchetti

LIM, CNRS FRE-2246 - Université de la Méditerranée, Case 901
163 Avenue de Luminy, F-13288 Marseille Cedex 9 France
lastname@lim.univ-mrs.fr

Abstract. Discovering functional dependencies from existing databases is an important technique strongly required in database design and administration tools. Investigated for long years, such an issue has been recently addressed with a data mining viewpoint, in a novel and more efficient way by following from principles of level-wise algorithms. In this paper, we propose a new characterization of minimal functional dependencies which provides a formal framework simpler than previous proposals. The algorithm, defined for enforcing our approach has been implemented and experimented. It is more efficient (in whatever configuration of original data) than the best operational solution (according to our knowledge): the algorithm TANE. Moreover, our approach also performs (without additional execution time) the mining of embedded functional dependencies, i.e. dependencies holding for a subset of the attribute set initially considered (e.g. for materialized views widely used in particular for managing data warehouses).

1   Motivations

Functional Dependencies (FDs) capture usual semantic constraints within data. An FD between two sets of attributes (X, Y) holds in a relation if values of the latter set are fully determined by values of the former [11]. It is denoted by $X \rightarrow Y$. Functional dependencies are a key concept in relational theory and the foundation for data organization when designing relational databases [25,30] but also object oriented databases [39].

Discovering FDs from existing databases is an important issue, investigated for long years [20,30], and recently addressed with a data mining point of view [18, 19,26], in a novel and more efficient way.

Motivations behind addressing such an issue are originated by various application fields: database administration and design, reverse-engineering and query folding [29]. Actually extracting such a knowledge makes it possible to assess minimality of keys, control normalization and detect denormalized relations. The latter situation could be desired for optimization reasons but it could also result from design errors, or schema evolutions not controlled over time. In such cases, the database administrator is provided with a relevant knowledge for making

J. Van den Bussche and V. Vianu (Eds.): ICDT 2001, LNCS 1973, pp. 189–203, 2001.
© Springer-Verlag Berlin Heidelberg 2001

reorganization decisions. In a reverse-engineering objective, elements of the conceptual schema of data can be exhibited from the knowledge of FDs [10,32,34]. Query folding can also take benefit from the discovered knowledge by selecting the best data resource for answering a request or using specific rules satisfied by the processed instances [17,35].

Motivated by the described application fields, various approaches addressed the presented issue, known as the problem of *FD inference* [16,21]. Among them, we underline the various contributions of H. Mannila and K.J. Räihä [20,21,29,30], and an operational approach recently proposed TANE [18,19] which provides a particularly efficient algorithm when compared with previous solutions for discovering the set of minimal FDs. Due to its singleness feature, we consider this set as the *canonical cover* of FDs.

In this paper, we propose an approach for mining minimal functional dependencies. We define a new characterization of such dependencies simpler than previous proposals and based on particularly mere concepts. The associated implementation solution, the algorithm FUN, is very efficient: it is comparable to TANE or improves execution times in whatever configuration of original data. Furthermore, our approach performs the mining of embedded dependencies. Known as the *projection* of FDs [13,15,25,30], the underlying issue could be summarized as follows: being given a set of FDs holding in a relation which are those satisfied over any attribute subset of the relation? "This turns out to be a computationally difficult problem" [30].

The paper is organized as follows. In Sect. 2, we present the formal framework of our approach which is enforced through the algorithm FUN detailed in Sect. 3. Section 4 is devoted to the exhibition of embedded dependencies. Experimental and comparative results are given in Sect. 5 while Sect. 6 provides an overview of related work. As a conclusion, we discuss the advantages of our approach when compared to previous work and evoke further research work.

2   A Novel Characterization of Minimal FDs

We present, in this section, the theoretical basis of our approach. Due to lack of space, we do not recall the basic concepts of the relational theory, widely described in [25,30]. The definition of a new and mere concept along with variants of existing ones, makes it possible to provide a new characterization of minimal FDs. The introduced concept of Free Set is defined as follows.

Definition 1. *Free Set*
Let $X \subseteq R$ be a set of attributes. X is a free set in r, an instance of relation over R, if and only if: $\not\exists\ X' \subset X, |X'|_r = |X|_r$ where $|X|_r$ stands for the cardinality of the projection of r over X.

The set of all free sets in r is denoted by $\mathcal{FS}_r$. Any combination of attributes not belonging to $\mathcal{FS}_r$ is called a non free set.

Lemma 1. $\forall\ X \subseteq R,\ \forall\ X' \subset X,\ |X'|_r = |X|_r \Leftrightarrow X' \to X.$

Proof. Obvious according to the definition of FD.

Example 1. In order to illustrate this paper, our relation example (cf. Fig. 1) is supposed to be used for managing courses in a university and scheduling lectures. A lecture is characterized by the teacher giving it ($PROF$), the associated course (CSE), the day and hours (DAY, $BEGIN$, END), the room, where it takes place, and its capacity ($ROOM$, CAP).

\multicolumn{8}{c}{LECT}

IdRow	PROF	CSE	DAY	BEGIN	END	ROOM	CAP
1	NF	AL	Tuesday	09:00	11:00	A2	150
2	DM	NW	Friday	09:00	11:00	A2	150
3	ML	OS	Monday	09:00	12:00	I10	30
4	NN	PL	Monday	14:00	17:00	I10	30
5	AH	DB	Monday	09:00	12:00	I11	30
6	RC	SI	Tuesday	09:00	12:00	I10	30
7	KL	OR	Tuesday	09:00	12:00	I12	30

Fig. 1. The relation example LECT

Let us consider, in our relation example, the couple of attributes (DAY, $BEGIN$). It is particularly easy to verify that this couple is a free set since its cardinality in the relation LECT is different from the cardinalities of all its component attributes: $|DAY, BEGIN|_{LECT} = 4$; $|DAY|_{LECT} = 3$; $|BEGIN|_{LECT} = 2$. In contrast, ($ROOM$, CAP) is not a free set since $|ROOM, CAP|_{LECT} = |ROOM|_{LECT} = 4$. Thus $ROOM \to CAP$ holds in the relation $LECT$ (cf. Lemma 1). □

Lemma 2.

- *Any subset of a free set is a free set itself:* $\forall X \in \mathcal{FS}_r, \forall X' \subset X, X' \in \mathcal{FS}_r$.
- *Any superset of a non free set is non free:* $\forall X \notin \mathcal{FS}_r, \forall Y \supset X, Y \notin \mathcal{FS}_r$.

Proof. For the first point of the lemma, let us consider a free set $X \in \mathcal{FS}_r$ and assume, for the sake of a contradiction, that: $\exists X' \subset X$ such that $X' \notin \mathcal{FS}_r$. Thus, according to Definition 1, $\exists X'' \subset X'$ such that $|X''|_r = |X'|_r$. And we have $X'' \to X'$ (cf. Lemma 1). Applying the Armstrong axioms [3], we infer the following FD: $X'' \cup (X - X') \to X' \cup (X - X')$ which could be rewritten: $X - (X' - X'') \to X$. Thus $|X - (X' - X'')|_r = |X|_r$ and $X \notin \mathcal{FS}_r$ which is contradicting the initial assumption. Let us assume now that X is not a free set, thus $\exists X' \subset X$ such that $|X'|_r = |X|_r$. Since we have the FD $X' \to X$, any dependency $X' \cup Z \to X \cup Z$ is satisfied, $\forall Z \subseteq R - X$. Thus $|X' \cup Z|_r = |X \cup Z|_r$, and $X \cup Z \notin \mathcal{FS}_r$.

With the concept of free sets, we are provided with a mere characterization of sources (or left-hand sides) of minimal FDs because the source of any minimal FD is necessarily a free set (as proved by Theorem 1). In fact, a free set cannot capture any FD (cf. Definition 1 and Lemma 1) while at least an FD holds between attributes of a non free set. The following definitions are introduced for characterizing targets (or right-hand sides) of such dependencies.

Definition 2. *Attribute set closure in a relation*
Let X be a set of attributes, $X \subseteq R$. Its closure in r is defined as follows:
$X_r^+ = X \cup \{A \in R - X \ / \ |X|_r = |X \cup A|_r\}.$

Definition 3. *Attribute set quasi-closure in a relation*
The quasi-closure of an attribute set X in r, denoted by $X_r^\diamond$, is:
$X_r^\diamond = X \cup \bigcup_{A \in X}(X - A)_r^+.$

The closure of an attribute set X in the relation r encompasses any attribute A of the relation schema R, determined by X. Definition 2 guarantees that $X \rightarrow A$ holds by comparing cardinalities of X and $X \cup A$ (cf. Lemma 1). The quasi-closure of X groups the closure of all its maximal subsets and X itself. Thus any attribute $A \in X_r^\diamond - X$ is determined by a maximal subset X' of X. Since $r \models X' \rightarrow A$ (the FD holds in r), we have $r \models X \rightarrow A$, but the latter FD is not minimal because its source encompasses an extraneous attribute [5]. According to the monotonicity and extensibility properties of the closure [7,16], we have: $X \subseteq X_r^\diamond \subseteq X_r^+$. Thus Definition 2 can be rewritten (for operational reasons): $X_r^+ = X_r^\diamond \cup \{A \in R - X_r^\diamond \ / \ |X|_r = |X \cup A|_r\}.$
Through the following theorem, we state that the set of FDs characterized by using the introduced concepts is the canonical cover of FDs for the relation r, denoted by $MinDep(r)$.

Theorem 1. $MinDep(r) = \{X \rightarrow A \ / \ X \in \mathcal{FS}_r \text{ and } A \in X_r^+ - X_r^\diamond\}$

Proof. ($\supseteq$) Since $A \in X_r^+$, A is determined by X, thus $X \rightarrow A$ holds. It is minimal because $A \notin X_r^\diamond$. Thus no maximal subset of X could determine A (and a fortiori whatever subset of X).
($\subseteq$) Since $X \rightarrow A \in MinDep(r)$, we have: $\forall X' \subset X, |X'|_r \neq |X|_r$ (cf. Lemma 1). Thus $X \in \mathcal{FS}_r$ (cf. Definition 1). It is obvious that $A \in X_r^+$ since the FD holds. Moreover, no subset of X (a fortiori the maximal subsets) could determine A since the FD is minimal: $A \notin X_r^\diamond$. Thus $A \in X_r^+ - X_r^\diamond$.

Example 2. Let us consider, in our relation example (cf. Fig. 1), the following combination $X = (ROOM, DAY, BEGIN)$, which is a free set. Computing cardinality of X and cardinality of its maximal subsets results in the following quasi-closure and closure:
$X_{LECT}^\diamond = \{ROOM, DAY, BEGIN, END, CAP\}$
$X_{LECT}^+ = \{ROOM, DAY, BEGIN, END, CAP, CSE, PROF\}$
Thus both $ROOM, DAY, BEGIN \rightarrow CSE$ and $ROOM, DAY, BEGIN \rightarrow PROF$ are minimal FDs, according to Theorem 1. $\square$

For mining the canonical cover of FDs in a relation, the closure and quasi-closure of attribute sets have to be computed (cf. Theorem 1). Thus counting operations must be performed for yielding cardinality of the considered sets and all their maximal subsets (cf. Definitions 2 and 3). When introducing the following lemma, our concern is providing an efficient computation of cardinalities. Lemma 3 states that for any non free set X whose subsets are free sets, the cardinality of X is equal to the maximal cardinality of its subsets.

Lemma 3. $\forall\, X \notin \mathcal{FS}_r$ such that all its subsets X' are free sets in r:
$|X|_r = Max(\, |X'|_r \,/\, X' \subset X \text{ and } X' \in \mathcal{FS}_r \,)$.

Proof. $\forall\, X \subseteq R$ and $\forall\, X' \subseteq X$, it is obvious that $|X|_r \geq |X'|_r$ (according to the FD definition). Since we assume that $X \notin \mathcal{FS}_r$ and that its subsets are free sets, we know that it does exist, at least, a maximal subset X' determining an attribute A (according to Definition 1, Lemmas 1, and 2): $\exists\, X' \subset X$, $\exists\, A = X - X'$ such that $X' \rightarrow A$. Thus $|X|_r = |X' \cup A|_r = |X'|_r$.

With Theorem 1, we are provided with a nice characterization of minimal FDs, using particularly simple concepts. Lemma 2 gives rules specially interesting when implementing the approach using a level-wise algorithm. Lemma 3 complements this result by defining a novel way to compute FD targets *using counting inference*. This computation, proved to be correct, is moreover operational. We show in the following sections (3 and 5) that implementation based on our formal approach results in a very efficient solution.

3   The Algorithm FUN

Like various other proposals addressing data mining issues (from Apriori [2] to TANE [18,19] cf. Sect. 6), our algorithm, called FUN, is a level-wise algorithm exploring, level after level, the attribute set lattice of the input relation. We describe in more depth the general principles of FUN, detail the algorithms, and give a running example.

3.1   General Principles

FUN handles, step by step, attribute sets of increased length and, at each new level, takes benefits from the knowledge acquired at the previous iteration.
Let us assume that each level k is provided with a set of possible free sets of length k, called candidates. For controlling that a candidate is actually a free set, its cardinality must be compared to the cardinality of all its maximal subsets. If it is proved to be a free set, it is a possible source of FDs and it must be preserved. If not, the candidate encompasses at least a maximal subset with a similar cardinality and it captures at least an FD. When the latter situation occurs, we know (according to Lemma 2) that all the supersets of the candidate are non free and the candidate cannot be source of a minimal FD (according to Theorem 1). Thus it is discarded for further exploration. The kth level completes by yielding the set of all free sets encompassing k attributes, and all minimal FDs captured by the initial candidates of length k are exhibited. The set of all free sets is used for providing the next level with a new set of candidates. Such an operation is performed in a way similar to the procedure of candidate generation defined in Apriori [2] and adapted in TANE [18]. Free sets of length k are expanded for giving new candidates of length $(k+1)$, by combining two free sets whose subsets are all free sets. The algorithm completes when, at a level, no further candidates are generated.

3.2   Detailed and Commented Algorithms

The described general principles are enforced through the algorithm FUN. At each level k, the managed set of candidates is called L_k. Any element of this set is described as a quadruple: (*candidate, count, quasiclosure, closure*) in which the elements stand for the list of attributes of the candidate, its cardinality, quasi-closure and closure.

The first candidate set L_0 is initialized to a single quadruple in which *count* is assigned to 0, and the other components are empty sets (line 1 of FUN). For building L_1, all the attributes in R are considered by the algorithm (line 2). Their cardinality is computed (using the function Count). Their quasi-closure, and closure are initialized to the candidate. The set R' is built. It includes any attribute of the relation schema R excepting single attributes which are keys. Then each iteration of the loop (lines 4-9) deals with a level by computing the closure of free sets discovered at the previous level (i.e. elements of L_{k-1}) and, from this result, by computing the quasi-closure of candidates at the current level. At this point FDs, if any, having a source of $(k-1)$ attributes are extracted and displayed. Then the stages of pruning and candidate generation apply. When iterations complete, FDs captured in the last examined candidates are yielded (line 10).

Algorithm FUN
```
1    L₀ := < ∅, 0, ∅, ∅ >
2    L₁ := { < A, Count( A ), A, A > | A ∈ R }
3    R' := R − {A | A is a key }
4    for ( k := 1; Lₖ ≠ ∅; k := k + 1 ) do
5        ComputeClosure( Lₖ₋₁, Lₖ )
6        ComputeQuasiClosure( Lₖ, Lₖ₋₁ )
7        DisplayFD( Lₖ₋₁ )
8        PurePrune( Lₖ, Lₖ₋₁ )
9        Lₖ₊₁ := GenerateCandidate( Lₖ )
10   DisplayFD( Lₖ₋₁ )
end FUN
```

Apart from the procedure DisplayFD which simply yields the minimal FDs discovered at each level, functions and procedures used in FUN are described and their pseudo-code is given.

From the set of free sets in L_k, GenerateCandidate yields a new set of candidates encompassing $k+1$ attributes, supersets of keys excluded (line 1) by following from the principles of *apriori-gen* [2] (recalled in Sect. 3.1).

Function GenerateCandidate(in L_k)
```
1    Lₖ₊₁ := { l | ∀ l' ⊂ l, |l| = |l'| + 1, l' ∈ Lₖ, and |l'|ᵣ ≠ |r| }
2    for each l ∈ Lₖ₊₁ do
3        l.count := Count( l.candidate )
4    return Lₖ₊₁
end GenerateCandidate
```

ComputeClosure applies to the set of free sets achieved at the previous level and builds the closure of each free set l in the following way. Initially set to the quasi-closure of l (line 3), the closure is complemented by adding attributes determined by l. The procedure assesses whether $l \rightarrow A$ holds by comparing cardinalities of l and $l \cup \{A\}$ (line 5). Such a comparison makes use of the function FastCount (described further).

Procedure ComputeClosure(inout L_{k-1}, in L_k)
```
1    for each l ∈ L_{k-1} do
2        if l is not a key then
3            l.closure := l.quasiclosure
4            for each A ∈ R' − l.quasiclosure do
5                if FastCount( L_{k-1}, L_k, l.candidate ∪ {A} ) = l.count
6                then l.closure := l.closure ∪ {A}
end ComputeClosure
```

The procedure ComputeQuasiClosure builds the quasi-closure of each combination in the current set of candidates. Initialized to the candidate (line 2), the quasi-closure of any candidate l is achieved (line 4) by computing the union of its maximal subset closures (according to Definition 3). If the candidate under consideration is a key, its closure is also computed.

Procedure ComputeQuasiClosure(inout L_k, in L_{k-1})
```
1    for each l ∈ L_k do
2        l.quasiclosure := l.candidate
3        for each s ⊂ l.candidate and s ∈ L_{k-1} do
4            l.quasiclosure := l.quasiclosure ∪ s.closure
5        if l is a key then l.closure := R
end ComputeQuasiClosure
```

The procedure PurePrune is intended for eliminating non free sets from L_k. Making the decision of discarding a candidate is simply based on the comparison of cardinalities of the candidate and its maximal subsets which are free sets (line 3).

Procedure PurePrune(inout L_k, in L_{k-1})
```
1    for each l ∈ L_k do
2        for each s ⊂ l.candidate and s ∈ L_{k-1} do
3            if l.count = s.count then Delete l from L_k
end PurePrune
```

The function FastCount efficiently yields the cardinality of a candidate l by whether accessing its counting value or returning the maximal counting value of its subsets (cf. Lemma 3).

Function FastCount(in L_{k-1}, in L_k, in $l.candidate$)
```
1    if l.candidate ∈ L_k then return l.count
2    return Max( l'.count | l'.candidate ⊂ l.candidate, l'.candidate ∈ L_{k-1} )
end FastCount
```

Like in all other level-wise algorithms in data mining, the pruning rules are enforced in FUN for minimizing the number of candidates to be verified (without calling PurePrune, FUN would yield the very same cover). Another optimization technique used when implementing FUN is dealing with stripped partitions (thus a single pass over initial data is necessary) [12,18]. Stripped partitions provide an optimized representation of the original relation only requiring to preserve tuple identifiers, thus handled data is incomparably less voluminous.

3.3   Running Example

For exemplifying FUN running, we illustrate how the algorithm unfolds by using our relation example. In Fig. 2, attributes are denoted by their initial, excepting CAP symbolized by Ca. For the various levels, candidates (column X), their counting value ($count$), their quasi-closure (X°) and closure (X^+) are given.

Level 1				Level 2				Level 3			
X	$count$	X°	X^+	X	$count$	X°	X^+	X	$count$	X°	X^+
P	7	P	PCDBERCa	DB	4	DB	DB	DBR	7	DBERCa	PCDBERCa
C	7	C	PCDBERCa	DE	5	DBECa	DBECa	DBCa	5	DBECa	
D	3	D	D	DR	6	DRCa	DRCa	DER	7	DBERCa	PCDBERCa
B	2	B	B	DCa	4	DCa	DCa				
E	3	E	BECa	~~BE~~	3	BECa					
R	4	R	RCa	BR	5	BRCa	BERCa				
Ca	2	Ca	Ca	BCa	3	BCa	BECa				
				ER	5	BERCa	BERCa				
				~~ECa~~	3	BECa					
				~~RCa~~	4	RCa					

Fig. 2. Running example for the relation LECT

At level 1, all the attributes are considered, and their cardinality is computed. Two keys are discovered ($|P| = 7$; $|C| = 7$) and thus discarded for further search. The quasi-closure of the handled attributes is reduced to single attributes. Then the candidate generation is performed and all possible couples of remaining attributes are built. Provided with these new candidates, level 2 begins by computing the closure of free sets in the previous level, and then computes the quasi-closure of current candidates. Combinations capturing FDs are deleted (simply struck out in the figure), and of course they are not used for generating candidates for level 3. Among the latter, two keys (DBR, DER) are discovered and since it remains a single combination, no new candidate can be generated thus the algorithm completes. The extracted minimal FDs are given by using the union of their targets: $P \rightarrow CDBERCa$; $C \rightarrow PDBERCa$; $E \rightarrow BCa$; $R \rightarrow Ca$; $BR \rightarrow E$; $BCa \rightarrow E$; $DBR \rightarrow PC$; $DER \rightarrow PC$.

4   Discovering Embedded Dependencies

When being provided with a set of FDs holding in the relation r, embedded dependencies are FDs valid in the projection of r over a subset of its attributes. Embedded dependencies capture an interesting knowledge for the database administrator, particularly relevant when the number of attributes is large in a relation. In such a situation, or when the number of extracted FDs is great, the administrator can focus on particular attribute subsets, and the results of FD discovery can best be understood and more easily elucidated. Moreover, when handling materialized views, embedded dependencies exactly capture the FDs valid in the views.

Being given a set $\mathcal{F}$ of valid FDs in the relation r, embedded dependencies (also called projection of FDs [13,15]) are the FDs holding for an attribute subset X of R. In [15,30], the set of embedded FDs is defined as follows:

$\mathcal{F}[X] = \{Y \rightarrow Z \ / \ \mathcal{F} \models Y \rightarrow Z \wedge YZ \subseteq X\}$.

Computing $\mathcal{F}[X]$ cannot be solved by simply discarding from $\mathcal{F}$ dependencies having a source or a target not included in X because, due to FD properties [3], new dependencies could be introduced in $\mathcal{F}[X]$ as illustrated in the following example. In fact the problem is computationally hard [30] and computing FD projection can be exponential [13].

Example 3. Let us consider the relation schema $R(A_1, \ldots, A_n, B, C)$ and suppose that $\mathcal{F}$ encompasses the following FDs:
$\mathcal{F} = \{A_1 \rightarrow B, A_2 \rightarrow B, \ldots, A_n \rightarrow B, B \rightarrow C, C \rightarrow A_1, \ldots, C \rightarrow A_n\}$.
Then $\mathcal{F}[A_1, \ldots, A_n, C] = \{A_1 \rightarrow C, \ldots, A_n \rightarrow C, C \rightarrow A_1, \ldots, C \rightarrow A_n\}$. □

Complementing formal definitions provided in Sect. 2, minimal embedded FDs can be characterized by using the simple definition of Embedded Free Sets.

Definition 4. *Embedded Free Sets*
Let $X \subset R$ be an attribute set. The set of all free sets included in X is denoted by $\mathcal{FS}_X$ and defined by: $\mathcal{FS}_X = \{X' \ / \ X' \in \mathcal{FS}_r, X' \subset X\}$.

Lemma 4. *The set of embedded minimal FDs in X is:*
$\mathcal{F}_m[X] = \{X' \rightarrow A \ / \ X' \in \mathcal{FS}_X, A \in (X_r'^+ - X_r'^\diamond) \cap X\}$.

Proof. It is obvious that $X' \rightarrow A$ is a minimal FD (cf. Theorem 1) captured in X (because X embodies both X' and A). Since $\mathcal{FS}_X$ encompasses any free set included in X, it cannot exist a minimal embedded FD not included in $\mathcal{F}_m[X]$.

In the current implementation of FUN, free sets of whatever size, their closure and quasi-closure are preserved in main memory because allocated memory is small[1]. In such conditions, computing $\mathcal{F}_m[X]$ is straightforward. Once a free set belonging to $\mathcal{FS}_X$ is discovered, it is simply necessary to verify whether attributes in $X_r'^+ - X_r'^\diamond$ are included in X.

5   Experimental Results

In order to assess performances of FUN, the algorithm was implemented using the language C++. An executable file can be generated with Visual C++ 5.0 or

---

[1] Experiments performed for a relation encompassing 100,000 tuples and 50 attributes (with a correlation rate of 70 %) show that only 24.9 MB are required for both partitions and FUN intermediate results.

GNU g++ compilers. Experiments were performed on an AMD K6-2/400 MHz with 256 MB, running Windows NT 4.0. For a sake of an accurate comparison, a new version of TANE was implemented under the very same conditions. Both programs are available at [14]. The benchmark relations used for experiments are synthetic data sets automatically generated, using the following parameters: $|r|$ is the cardinality of the relation, $|R|$ stands for its number of attributes and c is the rate of data correlation. The more it increases, the more chances there are to have FDs captured within data.

Figure 3 details, for various values of the two latter parameters, execution times (in seconds) for FUN and TANE, setting the tuple number to 100,000. Empty cells in the table means that execution exceeded three hours and was interrupted[2]. As expected, FUN outstrips TANE in any case. More precisely, when relations have few attributes and data is weakly correlated, results are almost comparable. However, the gap between execution times of FUN and TANE regularly increases when the relation attribute set is enlarged and/or the correlation rate grows, until a threshold beyond which performances of TANE are strongly debased while FUN remains efficient. For data weakly and strongly related, curves in Figs. 4 and 5 illustrate execution times of the two algorithms when increasing the number of attributes for various values of c. These curves highlight the evoked threshold related of the number of attributes. When c is set to 30 %, TANE performance clearly debases beyond 50 attributes (cf. Fig. 4 A). When increasing the correlation rate the threshold decreases: until 40 or 30 attributes for $c = 50\%$ or 70% (cf. Figs. 4 B and 5 A). Curves in Fig. 5 B give execution times of TANE and FUN when varying the correlation rate for a relation with 100,000 tuples and 40 attributes. The gap between execution times of the two algorithms is strongly enlarged when data is highly correlated. Being given a number of attributes and a correlation rate, execution times of FUN and TANE only increase linearly in the number of tuples.

There is a twofold reason under the best performance of FUN when compared with TANE: the fast computation of FD targets and a more efficient pruning (as briefly explained in Sect. 7).

$c \backslash |R|$		10	20	30	40	50	60
30 %	FUN	2.563	11.035	25.606	46.156	77.960	131.599
	TANE	2.603	11.316	27.900	67.547	178.616	505.486
50 %	FUN	4.736	20.739	50.903	60.050	246.594	584.961
	TANE	4.816	23.964	132.921	802.544	3654.332	
70 %	FUN	6.879	30.553	73.966	205.357	404.701	1038.773
	TANE	7.080	42.050	269.737	2069.781		

Fig. 3. Execution times in seconds for correlated data ($|r| = 100,000$)

---

[2] Other experiment results are available at the URL given in [14].

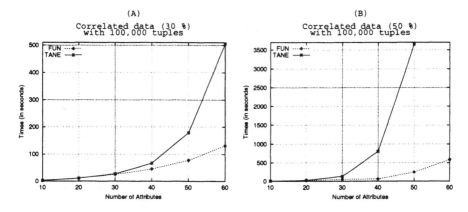

Fig. 4. Execution times in seconds for correlated data

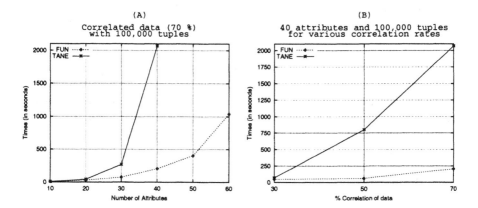

Fig. 5. Execution times in seconds for correlated data and for various correlation rates

6   Related Work

As suggested in Sect. 1 and in [31], the problem of discovering FDs is close
to other data mining issues, in particular the discovery of association rules or
sequential patterns [1,2,33]. Nevertheless, tangible differences appear[3]. In this
section, we only focus on related work addressing FD discovery.

---

[3] Algorithms mining association rules deal with itemsets. For a sake of comparison,
they could be seen as managing values of **binary** attributes [33], but when adopting
this vision, the number of attributes is extremely important, and optimized data
representation based on partition could not apply. The efficiency problem is much
more critical when considering the original data to be mined. For rules, the most
interesting raw material is historical data preserved in data warehouses, whereas
FD discovery applies to operational databases. Moreover the former approaches are
interested in extracting all (maximal) frequent itemsets whereas FD discovery approaches aim mining minimal FDs. Finally, counting operations are, in the former

The FD inference issue has received a great deal of attention and is still investigated. Let us quote, among numerous approaches, the following proposals [8,18, 26,28,29,36]. A critical concern when discovering FDs is to propose algorithms still efficient when handling large amounts of data. Earlier proposals based on repeated sorting of tuples or comparison between tuples could not meet such a requirement. The various contributions of H. Mannila, K.J. Räihä et al. must be underlined because they define the theoretical framework of the tackled problem, study its complexity, and propose algorithms for solving it [28,29] while addressing very close issues such as building Armstrong relations [27], investigating approximate inference in order to discover an approximate cover of dependencies [21], or studying FD projection [30]. However they do not provide and experiment with operational solutions. Computing the FD projection is studied in [13], and G. Gottlob proposes an algorithm called "Reduction By Resolution" (RBR) [15]. Its correctness is shown in [15,30], and its complexity is polynomial for certain classes of FDs. Various related problems such as construction of Armstrong relations, testing key minimality or normal form, study of other dependencies, are addressed [4,5,6,12,16,37], included in the context of incomplete relations [23,24,22].

According to our knowledge, the most efficient algorithm proposed until now is TANE [18,19]. TANE is based on the concept of partition [12,38] which is used as a formal basis for a new characterization of FDs and as a powerful mechanism for optimizing size of managed data. By using partitions and embodied equivalence classes, TANE characterizes sources of FDs. The associated targets are computed by using, for each examined source, a set of possible determined attributes. Initialized to R, this set is progressively reduced by discarding targets once they are discovered. The approach adopts principles of level-wise algorithms for exploring the search space, and pruning rules are enforced. Experimental results show the efficiency of the proposed algorithm and its good performance when compared to FDEP [36] chosen for its availability and efficiency.

In [26], an alternative approach Dep-Miner is proposed. Inspired from [27,29], it is based on the concepts of *agree set* [6] and *maximal set* also called meet irreducible set [16,25]. For any tuple couple, the agree set is the set of all attributes sharing the very same value. The maximal set of any attribute A is the attribute set of greatest size not determining A. The approach fits in a rigorous framework complementing proposals of [20,27,29], and introduces a characterization of minimal FD sources, based on minimal transversals of a simple hypergraph. The defined algorithm adopts the optimized representation of partitions, used in TANE, for minimizing size of handled data. New fast algorithms are proposed for computing agree sets and minimal transversals of an hypergraph. Experiments, run on various benchmark databases, show the efficiency of Dep-Miner[4]. Dep-Miner also computes small Armstrong relations.

---

case, performed level by level, requiring at each level a pass over data. When dealing with FDs, counting operates attribute by attribute.

[4] The comparison between FUN and the original version of Dep-Miner show an important gap, benefiting to FUN, between execution times. A new version of Dep-Miner

TANE and Dep-Miner particularly well illustrate what data mining contributions have brought to a problem addressed for long years and still topical and important, in particular for database administration tools.

7 Discussion and Further Work

The approach presented in this paper provides both a novel characterization of minimal FDs which can be embedded or not, and an operational algorithm FUN particularly efficient for mining the canonical cover of FDs in a relation. Experiments run on very large relations show the efficiency of our proposal compared with the best current algorithm TANE. For discovering minimal embedded dependencies, our solution is straightforward from FUN results whereas the algorithm RBR [15] can be exponential.

In order to complement experimental results given in Sect. 5, we briefly compare TANE and our approach. With the concept of partition, TANE provides a simple characterization of minimal FD sources. Nevertheless, specifying targets of such dependencies requires numerous lemmas which take into account different pruning cases. This results in the definition of the possible target set for a source (called $C+$) difficult to comprehend and relatively costly to compute. The gap observed between execution times of TANE and FUN is originated on one hand by the $C+$ computation and on the other hand by the exploration of the search space, more reduced in FUN than in TANE [14]. In fact, pruning operations in TANE are intended for discarding irrelevant candidates, among which certain capture non minimal FDs, whereas, in FUN, all examined candidates only capture (by construction) possible minimal FDs. Any candidate provided with a set $C+$ different from R is a non free set. It is deleted by FUN whereas TANE eliminates a candidate only if its associated $C+$ is empty. Thus the search space explored by FUN is smaller than the one of TANE.

The new characterization that we propose is simpler and sound. It is based on three mere concepts. Characterization proved to be correct and implementation successfully experimented are, in our approach, clear cut.

Following from the ideas introduced in [9] which aim to identify a "common data centric step" for a broad class of data mining algorithms, we would like to do likewise for database analysis. Actually, based on the discovery of free sets with FUN, various related problems, such as generation of Armstrong relations, minimal key inference, 3NF and BCNF tests, could be solved in a nice and efficient way (i.e. without significant additional time).

Acknowledgment. We would like to thank Lotfi Lakhal for his constructive comments on the paper.

---

is currently developed in order to perform valid and accurate comparisons with FUN. The first results confirm the best efficiency of FUN.

References

1. R. Agrawal, H. Mannila, R. Srikant, H. Toivonen, and A.I. Verkamo. Fast Discovery of Association Rules. *Advances in Knowledge Discovery and Data Mining*, pages 307–328, 1996.
2. R. Agrawal and R. Srikant. Fast Algorithms for Mining Association Rules. In *Proc. VLDB'94*, pages 487–499, Santiago, Chile, September 1994.
3. W.W. Armstrong. Dependency Structures of Database Relationships. In *Proc. IFIP Conf.*, pages 580–583, Amsterdam, The Netherlands, 1974. North-Holland.
4. W.W. Armstrong and C. Delobel. Decompositions and Functional Dependencies in Relations. *ACM TODS*, 5(4):404–430, Dec 1980.
5. C. Beeri and P.A. Bernstein. Computational Problems Related to the Design of Normal Form Relational Schemas. *ACM TODS*, 4(1):30–59, 1979.
6. C. Beeri, M. Dowd, R. Fagin, and R. Statman. On the Structure of Armstrong Relations for Functional Dependencies. *Journal of the ACM*, 31(1):30–46, 1984.
7. G. Birkhoff. *Lattices Theory*. Coll. Pub. XXV, vol. 25, 3rd edition, 1967.
8. D. Bitton, J. Millman, and S. Torgersen. A Feasability and Performance Study of Dependency Inference. In *Proc. ICDE'89*, pages 635–641, 1989.
9. S. Chaudhuri. Data Mining and Database Systems: Where is the Intersection? *Data Engineering Bulletin*, 21(1):4–8, 1998.
10. R.H.L. Chiang, T.M. Barron, and V.C. Storey. Reverse Engineering of Relational Databases: Extraction of an EER Model from a Relational Database. *DKE*, 10(12):107–142, 1994.
11. E.F. Codd. Further Normalization of the Data Base Model. Technical Report 909, IBM, 1971.
12. S.S. Cosmadakis, P.C. Kanellakis, and N. Spyratos. Partition Semantics for Relations. *Journal of Computer and System Sciences*, 33(2):203–233, 1986.
13. P.C. Fisher, J.H. Hou, and D.M. Tsou. Succinctness in Dependency Systems. *TCS*, 24:323–329, 1983.
14. FUN. URL. http://www.lim.univ-mrs.fr/~novelli/datamining/fun, 2000.
15. G. Gottlob. Computing Covers for Embedded Functional Dependencies. In *Proc. ACM-SIGACT-SIGMOD-SIGART'87*, pages 58–69, San Diego, US, 1987.
16. G. Gottlob and L. Libkin. Investigations on Armstrong Relations, Dependency Inference, and Excluded Functional Dependencies. *Acta Cybernetica*, 9(4):385–402, 1990.
17. J. Gryz. Query Folding with Inclusion Dependencies. In *Proc. ICDE'98*, pages 126–133, Orlando, US, Feb 1998.
18. Y. Huhtala, J. Karkkainen, P. Porkka, and H. Toivonen. Efficient Discovery of Functional and Appproximate Dependencies. In *Proc. ICDE'98*, pages 392–401, Orlando, US, Feb 1998.
19. Y. Huhtala, J. Karkkainen, P. Porkka, and H. Toivonen. TANE: An Efficient Algorithm for Discovering Functional and Approximate Dependencies. *The Computer Journal*, 42(2):100–111, 1999.
20. M. Kantola, H. Mannila, K.R. Räihä, and H. Siirtola. Discovering Functional and Inclusion Dependencies in Relational Databases. *International Journal of Intelligent Systems*, 7:591–607, 1992.
21. J. Kivinen and H. Mannila. Approximate Dependency Inference from Relations. *TCS*, 149(1):129–149, 1995.
22. M. Levene. A Lattice View of Functional Dependencies in Incomplete Relations. *Acta Cyberbernetica*, 12:181–207, 1995.

23. M. Levene and G. Loizou. Axiomatisation of Functional Dependencies in Incomplete Relations. *TCS*, 206(1-2):283–300, 1998.
24. M. Levene and G. Loizou. Database Design for Incomplete Relations. *ACM TODS*, 24(1):80–125, 1999.
25. M. Levene and G. Loizou. *A Guided Tour of Relational Databases and Beyond*. Springer-Verlag, London, 1999.
26. S. Lopes, J.M. Petit, and L. Lakhal. Efficient Discovery of Functional Dependencies and Armstrong Relations. In *Proc. EDBT'00*, pages 350–364, 2000.
27. H. Mannila and K.J. Räihä. Design by Example: An Application of Armstrong Relations. *Journal of Computer and System Sciences*, 33(2):126–141, Oct 1986.
28. H. Mannila and K.J. Räihä. On the Complexity of Inferring Functional Dependencies. *Discrete Applied Mathematics*, 40:237–243, 1992.
29. H. Mannila and K.J. Räihä. Algorithms for Inferring Functional Dependencies from Relations. *DKE*, 12(1):83–99, 1994.
30. H. Mannila and K.J. Räihä. *The Design of Relational Databases*. Addison Wesley, 1994.
31. H. Mannila and H. Toivonen. Levelwise Search and Borders of Theories in Knowledge Discovery. *Data Mining and Knowledge Discovery*, 1(3):241–258, 1997.
32. V.M. Markowitz and J.A. Makowsky. Identifying Extended Entity-Relationship Object Structure in Relational Schemas. *IEEE Transactions on Software Engineering*, 16(8):777–790, August 1990.
33. N. Pasquier, Y. Bastide, R. Taouil, and L. Lakhal. Discovering Frequent Closed Itemsets for Association Rules. In *Proc. ICDT'99*, LNCS, Vol. 1540, Springer Verlag, pages 398–416, Jan 1999.
34. J.M. Petit, F. Toumani, J.F. Boulicaut, and J. Kouloumdjian. Towards the Reverse Engineering of Denormalized Relational Databases. In *Proc. ICDE'96*, pages 218–227, Feb 1996.
35. X. Qian. Query Folding. In *Proc. ICDE'96*, pages 48–55, Feb 1996.
36. I. Savnik and P.A. Flach. Bottom-up Induction of Functional Dependencies from Relations. In *Proc. AAAI'93*, pages 174–185, 1993.
37. A.M. Silva and M.A. Melkanoff. *A Method for Helping Discover the Dependencies of a Relation*, pages 115–133. Plenum. Advances in Data Base Theory, 1981.
38. N. Spyratos. The Partition Model: a Deductive Database Model. *ACM TODS*, 12(1):1–37, 1987.
39. Z. Tari, J. Stokes, and S. Spaccapietra. Object Normal Forms and Dependency Constraints for Object-Oriented Schemata. *ACM TODS*, 22(4):513–569, Dec 1997.

Axiomatization of Frequent Sets

Toon Calders* and Jan Paredaens

Universiteit Antwerpen,
Departement Wiskunde-Informatica,
Universiteitsplein 1, B-2610 Wilrijk, Belgium.
{calders,pareda}@uia.ua.ac.be

Abstract. In data mining association rules are very popular. Most of
the algorithms in the literature for finding association rules start by searching for frequent itemsets. The itemset mining algorithms typically
interleave brute force counting of frequencies with a meta-phase for pruning parts of the search space. The knowledge acquired in the counting
phases can be represented by frequent set expressions. A frequent set expression is a pair containing an itemset and a frequency indicating that
the frequency of that itemset is greater than or equal to the given frequency. A system of frequent sets is a collection of such expressions. We
give an axiomatization for these systems. This axiomatization characterizes *complete systems*. A system is complete when it explicitly contains
all information that it logically implies. Every system of frequent sets
has a unique completion. The completion of a system actually represents
the knowledge that maximally can be derived in the meta-phase.

1 Introduction

Association rules are one of the most studied topics in data mining. They have
many applications [1]. Since their introduction, many algorithms have been proposed to find association rules [1][2][8].

We start with a formal definition of the association rule mining problem as
stated in [1]: Let $\mathcal{I} = \{I_1, I_2, \ldots, I_m\}$ be a set of symbols, called items. Let $\mathcal{D}$
be a set of transactions, where each transaction T is a set of items, $T \subseteq \mathcal{I}$, and
a unique transaction ID. We say that a transaction T *contains* X, a set of some
items in $\mathcal{I}$, if $X \subseteq T$. The fraction of transactions containing X is called the
frequency of X. An *association rule* is an implication of the form $X \Rightarrow Y$, where
$X \subseteq \mathcal{I}$, $Y \subseteq \mathcal{I}$, and $X \cap Y = \phi$. The rule holds in the transaction set $\mathcal{D}$ with
confidence c if the fraction of the transactions containing X, that also contain
Y is at least c. The rule $X \Rightarrow Y$ has *support* s in the transaction set $\mathcal{D}$ if the
fraction of the transactions in $\mathcal{D}$ that contain $X \cup Y$ is at least s.

Most algorithms start with searching itemsets that are contained in at least
a fraction s of the transactions. To optimize the search for frequent itemsets, the
algorithms use the following monotonicity principle:

---

* Research Assistant of the Fund for Scientific Research - Flanders (Belgium)(F.W.O.
- Vlaanderen).

J. Van den Bussche and V. Vianu (Eds.): ICDT 2001, LNCS 1973, pp. 204–218, 2001.

if $X \subseteq Y$, then the frequency of X will never be smaller than the frequency of Y.

This information is then used to *prune* parts of the search space *a priori*. To exploit this monotonicity as much as possible, the apriori-algorithm [2] starts by counting the single itemsets. In the second step, only itemsets $\{i_1, i_2\}$ are counted where $\{i_1\}$ and $\{i_2\}$ are frequent. All other 2-itemsets are discarded. In the third step, the algorithm proceeds with the 3-itemsets that only contain frequent 2-itemsets. This iteration continues until no itemsets that can be frequent are left. The search of frequent itemsets is thus basically an interleaving of a counting phase and a meta-phase. In the counting phase, the frequencies of some predetermined itemsets, the so-called *candidates* are counted. In the meta-phase the results of the counting phase are evaluated. Based on the monotonicity principle, some itemsets are a priori excluded.

Although the monotonicity of frequency is commonly used, there is to our knowledge no previous work that discusses whether in the general case this rule is *complete*, in the sense that it tells us everything we can derive from a given set of frequencies. In this paper we consider the notion of *a system of frequent sets*. A system of frequent sets contains, possibly incomplete, information about the frequency of every itemset. For example, $A :: 0.6, B :: 0.6, AB :: 0.1, \phi :: 0.5$ is a system of frequent sets. This system of frequent sets represents partial information (e.g. obtained in counting phases.) In this system, $A :: 0.6$ expresses the knowledge that itemset A has a frequency of at least 0.6. The system can be improved. Indeed; we can conclude that $AB :: 0.2$ holds, since $A :: 0.6$ and $B :: 0.6$ and there must be an overlap of at least a 0.2-fraction between the transactions containing A and the transactions containing B. We can also improve $\phi :: 0.5$, because $\phi :: 1$ always holds. Therefore, this system is called incomplete. When a system cannot be improved, it is complete. The completion of a system represents the maximal information that can be assumed in the meta-phase.

We give three rules **F1**, **F2**, and **F3** that characterize complete systems of frequent sets; e.g. a system is complete iff it satisfies **F1**, **F2**, **F3**. We show that, after a small modification to **F3**, this axiomatization is finite and every logical implication can be inferred using these axioms a finite number of times.

As an intermediate stage in the proofs, we introduce *rare sets*. A rare set expression $K : p_K$ expresses that at most a p_K-fraction of the transactions does not contain at least one item of K.

The structure of the paper is as follows: in Section 2 related work is discussed. In Section 3 we formally define a system of frequent sets. In Section 4, an axiomatization for complete systems of frequent sets is given. Section 5 discusses inference of complete systems using the axioms. Section 6 summarizes and concludes the paper.

Many proofs in this paper are only sketched. The full proofs can be found in [3].

Acknowledgment. We would like to thank Prof. Dirk Van Gucht and Prof. Ed Robertson from Indiana University, and Prof. Jef Wijsen from UMH (Mons, Belgium) for their preliminary thoughts and reflections on the topic of this paper. We also would like to thank the reviewers of our paper for their useful comments and for pointing out the links with probabilistic logic.

2   Related Work

In artificial intelligence literature, probabilistic logic is studied intensively. The link with this paper is that the frequency of an itemset I can be seen as the probability that a randomly chosen transaction from the transaction database satisfies I; i.e. we can consider the transaction database as an underlying probability structure.

Nilsson introduced in [12] the following *probabilistic logic problem*: given a finite set of m logical sentences $S_1, \ldots, S_m$ defined on a set $X = \{x_1, \ldots, x_n\}$ of n boolean variables with the usual boolean operators $\wedge, \vee$, and $\neg$, together with probabilities $p_1, \ldots, p_m$, does there exists a probability distribution on the possible truth assignments of X, such that the probability of S_i being true, is *exactly* p_i for all $1 \leq i \leq m$. *Georgakopoulos et al.* prove in [7] that this problem, they suggest the name *probabilistic satisfiability problem* (PSAT), is NP-complete. This problem, however, does not apply to our framework. In our framework, a system of frequent sets can *always* be satisfied. Indeed, since a system only gives *lower* bounds on the frequencies, the system is always satisfied by a transaction database where each transaction contains every item.

Another, more interesting problem, also stated by *Nilsson* in [12], is that of *probabilistic entailment*. Again a set of logical sentences $S_1, \ldots, S_m$, together with probabilities $p_1, \ldots, p_m$ is given, and one extra logical sentence S_{m+1}, the target. It is asked to find best possible upper and lower bounds on the probability that S_{m+1} is true, given $S_1, \ldots, S_m$ are satisfied with respective probabilities $p_1, \ldots, p_m$. The interval defined by these lower and upper bounds forms the so-called *tight entailment* of S_{m+1}. It is well known that both PSAT and probabilistic entailment can be solved nondeterministically in polynomial time using linear programming techniques. In our framework, a complete system of frequent sets is a system that only contains tight frequent expressions; i.e. the bounds of the frequent expressions in the complete system are the best possible in view of the system, and as such, this corresponds to the notion of tight entailment.

For a comprehensive overview of probabilistic logic, entailment and various extensions, we refer to [9][10]. Nilsson's probabilistic logic and entailment are extended in various ways, including assigning intervals to logical expressions instead of exact probability values and considering conditional probabilities [6].

In [4], *Fagin et al.* study the following extension. A *basic weight formula* is an expression $a_1 w(\phi_1) + \ldots + a_k w(\phi_k) \geq c$, where $a_1, \ldots, a_k$ and c are integers and $\phi_1, \ldots, \phi_k$ are propositional formulas, meaning that the sum of all a_i times the *weight* of ϕ_i is greater than or equal to c. A *weight formula* is a boolean combination of basic weight formulas. The semantics are introduced by an underlying probability space. The weight of a formula corresponds with the probability that it is true. The main contribution (from the viewpoint of our paper) of [4] is the description of a sound and complete axiomatization for this probabilistic logic. The logical framework in our paper is in some sense embedded into the logic in [4]. Indeed, if we introduce a propositional symbol P_i for each item i, the frequent set expression $K :: p_K$ can be translated as $w(\bigwedge_{i \in K} P_i) \geq p_K$. As such, by results obtained in [4], the implication problem in our framework is guaranteed to be decidable. Satisfiability, and thus also the implication problem, are NP-complete in Fagin's framework. Our approach differs from Fagin's approach in the sense that we only consider situations where for all expressions a probability is given.

Also in [6], axioms for a probabilistic logic are introduced. However, the authors are unable to proof whether the axioms are complete. For a sub-language (Type-A problems), they proof that their set of axioms is complete. However, this sub-language is not sufficiently powerful to express frequent itemset expressions.

On the other side of the spectrum, we have related work within the context of data mining. There have been attempts to proof some completeness results for itemsets in this area. One such attempt is described shortly in [11]. In the presence of constraints on the allowable itemsets, the authors introduce the notion of *ccc-optimality*[1]. ccc-optimality can intuitively be understood as "the algorithm only generates and tests itemsets that still can be frequent, using the current knowledge." Our approach however, is more general, since we do not restrict ourselves to a particular algorithm. No attempt is known to us in the context of data mining, that studies what we can derive from an arbitrary set of frequent itemsets.

Finally, we would like to add that in our paper the emphasis is on introducing a logical framework for frequent itemsets and not on introducing a new probabilistic logic, nor on algorithms.

3 Complete System of Frequent Sets

We formally define a system of frequent sets. We also define what it means for a system to be complete.

To represent a database with transactions, we use a matrix. The columns of the matrix represent the items and the rows represent the transactions. The matrix contains a one in the (i, j)-entry if transaction i contains item j, else this entry is zero. When R is a matrix where the columns represent the items in I, we say that R is a matrix over I. In our running example we regularly refer to the items with capital letters. With this notation, we get the following definition:

Definition 1. *Let* $I = \{I_1, \ldots, I_n\}$ *be a set of items, and* R *be a matrix over* I. *The* frequency *of an itemset* $K \subseteq I$ *in* R, *denoted* $freq(K, R)$ *is the fraction of rows in* R *that have a one in every column of* K.

---

[1] ccc-optimality stands for Constraint Checking and Counting-optimality

Example 1. In Fig. 1, a matrix is given, together with some frequencies. The frequency of DEF [2] is 0.2, because 2 rows out of 10 have a one in every column of DEF. Note that, because R is a matrix, R can have identical rows.

Matrix R					
A	B	C	D	E	F
1	0	1	0	1	1
1	0	1	0	1	1
0	1	0	1	1	0
1	1	1	0	0	1
1	0	0	1	0	1
0	1	0	1	1	1
1	1	0	1	1	1
0	0	1	0	0	1
1	1	1	0	1	0
1	0	0	1	0	1

$freq(A, R) = 0.7$
$freq(B, R) = 0.5$
$freq(AB, R) = 0.3$
$freq(DEF, R) = 0.2$

R satisfies $A :: 0.5$, $AB :: 0.3$, $DEF :: 0.1$
R does not satisfy $A :: 0.8$, $ABC :: 0.4$, $DEF :: 0.3$

Fig. 1. A matrix together with some frequent set expressions

We now introduce logical implication and completeness of a system of frequent sets.

Definition 2. *Let* $I = \{I_1, \ldots, I_n\}$ *be a set of items.*

- *A* frequent set expression *over* I *is an expression* $K :: p_K$ *with* $K \subseteq I$ *and* p_K *rational with* $0 \le p_K \le 1$.
- *A matrix* R *over* I satisfies $K :: p_K$ *iff* $freq(K, R) \ge p_K$. *Hence itemset* K *has frequency at least* p_K.
- *A* system of frequent sets *over* I *is a collection*

$$\{_{K \subseteq I} \; K :: p_K$$

of frequent set expressions, with exactly one expression for each $K \subseteq I$.
- *A matrix* R *over* I satisfies the system $\{_{K \subseteq I} \; K :: p_K$ *iff* R *satisfies all* $K :: p_K$.

Example 2. In Fig. 1, the matrix R satisfies $A :: 0.6$, because the frequency of A in R is bigger than 0.6. The matrix does not satisfy $B :: 0.7$, because the frequency of B is lower than 0.7.

Definition 3. *Let* $I = \{I_1, \ldots, I_n\}$ *be a set of items, and* $K \subseteq I$.

- *A system of frequent sets* S *over* I logically implies $K :: p_K$, *denoted* $S \models K :: p_K$, *iff every matrix that satisfies* S, *also satisfies* $K :: p_K$. *System* S_1 logically implies *system* S_2, *denoted* $S_1 \models S_2$, *iff every* $K :: p$ *in* S_2 *is logically implied by* S_1.

---

[2] DEF denotes the set $\{D, E, F\}$

B, C, BC, ABC		
A	B	C
1	1	0
1	1	1
1	0	1
1	1	1
0	1	1

A, AB, AC		
A	B	C
1	1	0
1	1	1
1	1	1
0	1	1
0	1	1

$$ABC :: 0.4$$

$$AB :: 0.6 \quad AC :: 0.4 \quad BC :: 0.6$$

$$A :: 0.6 \quad B :: 0.8 \quad C :: 0.8$$

$$\phi :: 1$$

Fig. 2. Proof-matrices for a system of frequent sets

- A system of frequent sets $S = \{_{K \subseteq I}\, K :: p_K$ is complete *iff for each* $K :: p$ *logically implied by* S, $p \leq p_K$ *holds.*

Example 3. Let $I = \{A, B, C, D, E, F\}$. Consider the following system: $S = \{_{K \subseteq I}\, K :: p_K$, where $p_A = 0.7$, $p_B = 0.5$, $p_{AB} = 0.3$, $p_{DEF} = 0.2$, and $p_K = 0$ for all other itemsets K. The matrix in Fig. 1 satisfies S. S is not complete, because in every matrix satisfying $DEF :: 0.2$, the frequency of DE must be at least 0.2, and S contains $DE :: 0$. Furthermore, S *does not* logically imply $EF :: 0.5$, since R satisfies S, and R does not satisfy $EF :: 0.5$.

Consider the following system over $I = \{A, B, C\}$:
$\{\phi :: 1, A :: 0.6, B :: 0.8, C :: 0.8, AB :: 0.6, AC :: 0.4, BC :: 0.6, ABC :: 0.4\}$.
This system is complete. We prove this by showing that for every subset K of I, there exists a matrix R_K that satisfies S, and $freq(K, R_K)$ is exactly p_K. These matrices then *prove* that for all K, we cannot further improve on K; i.e. make p_K larger. These proof-matrices are very important in the proof of the axiomatization that is given in the next section. In Fig. 2, the different proof-matrices are given.

When a system S is not complete, we can improve this system. Suppose a system $S = \{_{K \subseteq I}\, K :: p_K$ is not complete, then there is a frequent set expression $K :: p'_k$ that is logically implied by S, and $p'_K > p_K$. We can improve S by replacing $K :: p_K$ by $K :: p'_K$. The next proposition says that there exists a unique system $C(S)$, that is logically implied by S and that is complete.

Proposition 1. *Let* $I = \{I_1, \ldots, I_n\}$ *be a set of items, and* $S = \{_{K \subseteq I}\, K :: p_K$ *be a system of frequent sets. There exists a unique system* $C(S)$, *the completion of* S, *such that* $S \models C(S)$, *and* $C(S)$ *is a complete system.*

Proof. Let $M_K = \{p_K \mid S \models K :: p_K\}$. M_K always contains its supremum. This can easily be seen as follows: suppose a matrix M satisfies S. Let p be the frequency of K in M. Since M satisfies S, for all $p_K \in M_K$, $p \geq p_K$ holds, and hence $p \geq sup(M_K)$ holds. Hence, every matrix satisfying S, also satisfies $K :: sup(M_K)$, and thus $S \models K :: sup(M_K)$. It is straightforward that the system $\{_{K \subseteq I}\, K :: supp(M_K)$ is the unique completion of S.

Example 4. $I = \{A, B, C\}$. The system $\{\phi :: 1, A :: 0.6, B :: 0.8, C :: 0.8, AB ::$
$0.6, AC :: 0.4, \mathbf{BC} :: \mathbf{0.6}, ABC :: 0.4\}$ is the unique completion of the system
$\{\phi :: 0.8, A :: 0.6, B :: 0.8, C :: 0.8, AB :: 0.6, AC :: 0.4, \mathbf{BC} :: \mathbf{0.4}, ABC :: 0.4\}$.
$BC :: 0.6$ is implied by the second system, since there is an overlap of at least
0.6 between the rows having a one on B and the rows having a one on C.

Remark that when a system is complete, it is not necessary that there exists
one matrix such that for all itemsets the frequency is exactly the frequency given
in the system. Consider for example the following system: $\{\phi :: 1, A :: 0.5, B ::$
$0.5, C :: 0.1, AB :: 0, AC :: 0, BC :: 0, ABC :: 0\}$. This system is complete.
However, we will never find a matrix in which the following six conditions are
simultaneously true: $freq(A) = 0.5$, $freq(B) = 0.5$, $freq(C) = 0.1$, $freq(AB) =$
0, $freq(AC) = 0$, and $freq(BC) = 0$, because due to $freq(A) = 0.5$, $freq(B) =$
0.5, and $freq(AB) = 0$, every row has a one in A or in B. So, every row having a
one in C has also a one in A or in B, and thus violates respectively $freq(AC) = 0$,
or $freq(BC) = 0$.

4   Axiomatizations

We give an axiomatization for frequent sets. An axiomatization in this context
is a set of rules that are satisfied by the system if and only if it is complete. In
order to simplify the notation we first introduce rare sets. In Section 5 we will
show how we can build finite proofs for all logical implications using the axioms
as rules of inference.

4.1   Rare Sets

Definition 4. *Let $I = \{I_1, \ldots, I_n\}$ be a set of items, and $K \subseteq I$.*

- *Let R be a matrix over I. The* rareness *of an itemset $K \subseteq I$ in R, denoted
  $rare(K, R)$, is the fraction of rows in R that have a zero in at least one
  column of K.*
- *A* rare set expression *over I is an expression $K : p_K$ with $K \subseteq I$ and p_K
  rational with $0 \le p_K \le 1$.*
- *A matrix R over I satisfies $K : p_K$ iff $rare(K, R) \le p_K$. Hence itemset K
  has rareness at most p_K.*
- *A system of rare sets over I is a collection $\left\{_{K \subseteq I} K : p_K\right.$ of rare set expressions, with exactly one expression for each $K \subseteq I$.*
- *A matrix R over I satisfies the system $\left\{_{K \subseteq I} K : p_K\right.$ iff R satisfies all $K : p_K$.*
- *A system of rare sets S over I logically implies $K : p$, denoted $S \models K : p$ iff
  every matrix that satisfies S also satisfies $K : p$. System S_1 logically implies
  system S_2, denoted $S_1 \models S_2$, iff every $K : p$ in S_2 is logically implied by S_1.*
- *A system of rare sets $S = \left\{_{K \in I} K : p_K\right.$ is complete iff for each $K : p$ logically
  implied by S, $p_K \le p$ holds.*

Example 5. In Fig. 1, the matrix R satisfies $A : 0.4$, because the rareness of A in R is smaller than 0.4. The matrix does not satisfy $B : 0.3$, because the rareness of B is greater than 0.3. Let $I = \{A, B\}$. The system $\{AB : 0.8, A : 0.3, B : 0.4, \phi : 0.4\}$ is not complete. The unique completion of this system is $\{AB : 0.7, A : 0.3, B : 0.4, \phi : 0\}$.

The next proposition connects rare sets with frequent sets. The connection between the two is straightforward. Indeed: the set of rows that have a zero in at least one column on K is exactly the complement of the set of rows having only ones in these columns. The second part of the proposition shows that an axiomatization for rare sets automatically yields an axiomatization for frequent sets.

Proposition 2. *Let $I = \{I_1 \ldots I_n\}$ be a set of items. For every matrix R over I and every subset K of I holds that*

- $freq(K, R) + rare(K, R) = 1.$
- R *satisfies $K : p_K$ iff R satisfies $K :: 1 - p_K$.*

In the following subsection we prove an axiomatization for complete systems of rare sets. From this axiomatization, we can easily derive an axiomatization for frequent sets, using the last proposition.

4.2   Axiomatization of Rare Sets

Before we give the axiomatization, we first introduce our notation of bags.

Definition 5.

- A bag *over a set S is a total function from S into $\{0, 1, 2, \ldots\}$.*
- *Let $\mathbf{K}$ be a bag over S and $s \in S$. We say that s appears n times in $\mathbf{K}$ iff $\mathbf{K}(s) = n$.*
- *If $\mathbf{K}$ and $\mathbf{L}$ are bags over S, then we define the* bag-union *of $\mathbf{K}$ and $\mathbf{L}$, notation $\mathbf{K} \bigcup \mathbf{L}$, as follows: for all $s \in S$, $(\mathbf{K} \bigcup \mathbf{L})(s) = \mathbf{K}(s) + \mathbf{L}(s)$.*
- *Let $S = \{s_1, s_2, \ldots, s_n\}$. $\{\!\{ c_1's_1, \ldots, c_n's_n \}\!\}$ denotes the bag over S in which s_i appears c_i times for $1 \leq i \leq n$.*
- *Let S be a set, $\mathbf{K}$ a bag over S. $\sum_{s \in S} \mathbf{K}(s)$ is the* cardinality *of $\mathbf{K}$, and is denoted by $|\mathbf{K}|$.*
- *Let $\mathbf{K}$ be a bag over the subsets of a set S. Then $\bigcup \mathbf{K}$ denotes the bag $\bigcup_{K \in \mathbf{K}} K$. The* degree *of an element $s \in S$ in $\mathbf{K}$, denoted $deg(s, \mathbf{K})$ is the number of times s appears in $\bigcup \mathbf{K}$.*

Example 6. $\mathbf{K} = \{\!\{ 1'\{a, b\}, 2'\{b, c\}, 2'\{b, d\} \}\!\}$ is a bag over the subsets of $\{a, b, c, d\}$. $\bigcup \mathbf{K} = \{\!\{ 1'a, 5'b, 2'c, 2'd \}\!\}$. $deg(b, \mathbf{K}) = 5$. $|\mathbf{K}| = 5$.

The next three rules form an axiomatization for complete systems of rare sets in the sense that the complete systems are exactly the ones that satisfy these three rules. The p_K's that appear in the rules, indicate the rareness-values given in the system for the set K; i.e. $K : p_K$ is in the system.

R1 $p_\phi = 0$

R2 If $K_2 \subseteq K_1$, then $p_{K_2} \leq p_{K_1}$

R3 Let $K \subseteq I$, **M** a bag of subsets of K. Then

$$p_K \leq \frac{\sum_{M \in \mathbf{M}} p_M}{k},$$

with $k = min_{a \in K}(deg(a, \mathbf{M}))^3$

The next theorem is one of the most important results of this paper. The following lemma, proved in [3], will be used in the proof of the theorem.

Lemma 1. *Given a set of indices I and given rational numbers a_K, b_K for every non-empty $K \subseteq I$. Consider the following system of inequalities:*

$$\left\{ _{K \subseteq I} \; a_K \leq \sum_{i \in K} X_i \leq b_K \right.$$

This system has a solution $(x_1, \ldots, x_{\#I})$, x_i rational, iff for all $\mathbf{K}$ and $\mathbf{L}$, bags of subsets of I with $\bigcup \mathbf{K} = \bigcup \mathbf{L}$ holds that $\sum_{K \in \mathbf{K}} a_K \leq \sum_{L \in \mathbf{L}} b_L$.

Theorem 1. *Let $S = \{ _{K \subseteq I} K : p_K$ be a system of rare sets over I. The following two statements are equivalent:*

- *S is a complete system.*
- *S satisfies **R1**, **R2**, and **R3**.*

Proof. ($\Rightarrow$) **R1** and **R2** are trivial.

R3: Let **M** be a bag over the subsets of an itemset K, and $S = \{ _{K \subseteq I} K : p_K$ is a complete system. Let R be an arbitrary matrix that satisfies S. D_K^R is the bag that contains exactly those rows r for which there exists a k in K such that $r(k) = 0$. Then, for every L holds: $\frac{|D_L^R|}{|R|} \leq p_L$. If $r \in D_K^R$, then there exists a $a \in K$ such that $r(a) = 0$. a appears in at least $k = min_{a \in K} deg(a, \mathbf{M})$ of the sets of **M**. Thus, $k|D_K^R| \leq \sum_{M \in \mathbf{M}} |D_M^R|$. We can conclude that in every matrix satisfying S, $rare(K, R) = \frac{|D_K^R|}{|R|} \leq \frac{\sum_{M \in \mathbf{M}} p_M}{k}$.

($\Leftarrow$) We show that if $S = \{ _{K \subseteq I} K : p_K$ satisfies **R1**, **R2**, and **R3**, we can for each itemset K find a proof-matrix $\widehat{R_K}$, such that $\widehat{R_K}$ satisfies S, and $rare(K, \widehat{R_K}) = p_K$ [4]. We specify $\widehat{R_K}$ by giving the frequency of every possible row r. β_Z denotes the fraction of rows that have a zero in every column of Z, and a one elsewhere. We will show that there exists such a matrix $\widehat{R_K}$ with only rows with at most one zero, and this zero, if present, must be in a column of K; i.e. whenever $|Z| > 1$ or $Z \not\subseteq K$, $\beta_Z = 0$.

---

[3] If $k = 0$, **R3** should be interpreted as "$p_K \leq 1$"

[4] Remark the similarities with the traditional Armstrong-relations in functional dependency theory [5]

This can be expressed by the following system of inequalities:

$$\begin{cases} \forall a \in K : 0 \leq \beta_a \leq 1 & \text{(1) all fractions are between 0 and 1} \\ 0 \leq \beta_0 \leq 1 & \text{(2) idem} \\ (\sum_{a \in K} \beta_a) + \beta_0 = 1 & \text{(3) the frequencies add up to one} \\ p_K = \sum_{a \in K} \beta_a & \text{(4) the rareness of } K \text{ is exactly } p_K \\ \forall L \subset K : p_L \geq \sum_{a \in L} \beta_a & \text{(5) for other sets } L, \ p_L \geq rare(L, \widehat{R_K}) \end{cases}$$

Every solution of this system describes a matrix that satisfies S. Only (5) needs a little more explanation. For an arbitrary itemset L, $rare(L, \widehat{R_K}) = rare(L \cap K, \widehat{R_K})$ due to the construction. Because S satisfies **R2**, $p_L \geq p_{K \cap L}$. Therefore, it suffices to demand that $rare(L, \widehat{R_K}) \leq p_L$, for all $L \subset K$.

The system has a solution if the following (simpler) system has a solution:

$$\{ \forall L \subseteq K : p_K - p_L \leq \sum_{a \in K} \beta_a - \sum_{a \in L} \beta_a \leq p_K \ (1') $$

1 is ok: choose $L = K - \{a\}$, then $0 \leq^{(\mathbf{R2})} p_K - p_{K-\{a\}} \leq \beta_a \leq p_K \leq 1$

2+3 are ok: let $\beta_0 = 1 - \sum_{a \in K} \beta_a = 1 - p_K$

4 is ok: choose $L = \phi$, $p_L = 0$ (**R1**), and thus $p_K \leq \sum_{a \in K} \beta_K \leq p_K$

5 is ok: $p_L - p_K \geq \sum_{a \in L} \beta_a - \sum_{a \in K} \beta_a + 4$.

According to Lemma 1, this last system has a rational solution iff for all bags **M** and **N** over the subsets of K, such that $\bigcup \mathbf{M} = \bigcup \mathbf{N}$, $\sum_{M \in \mathbf{M}}(p_K - p_{K-M}) \leq \sum_{N \in \mathbf{N}} p_N$ holds.

Let $\mathbf{L} = \mathbf{N} \bigcup \{\!\{ K - M \mid M \in \mathbf{M} \}\!\}$. Then, by **R3** we have that $\frac{\sum_{L \in \mathbf{L}} p_L}{k} \geq p_K$, with $k = min_{a \in K} \#(\{\!\{ N \mid a \in N \wedge N \in \mathbf{N} \}\!\} \bigcup \{\!\{ M \mid M \in \mathbf{M} \wedge a \notin M \}\!\})$. Because $\#\{\!\{ M \mid M \in \mathbf{M} \wedge a \in M \}\!\} = \#\{\!\{ N \mid N \in \mathbf{N} \wedge a \in n \}\!\}$, $k = \#\mathbf{M}$.

We have: $\sum_{L \in \mathbf{L}} p_L \geq \#\mathbf{M} p_K$. Since $\sum_{L \in \mathbf{L}} p_L = \sum_{N \in \mathbf{N}} p_N + \sum_{M \in \mathbf{M}} p_{K-M}$ and $\#\mathbf{M} p_K = \sum_{M \in \mathbf{M}} p_K$, $\sum_{M \in \mathbf{M}}(p_K - p_{K-M}) \leq \sum_{N \in \mathbf{N}} p_N$ holds.

Example 7. The system $\{\phi : 0.5, A : 0.5, B : 0.25, C : 0.5, AB : 0, AC : 1, BC : 0, ABC : 1\}$ is not complete, since $\phi : 0.5$ violates **R1**.

The system $\{\phi : 0, A : 0.5, B : 0.25, C : 0.5, AB : 0, AC : 1, BC : 0, ABC : 1\}$ is not complete, since for example $AB : 0$ and $A : 0.5$ together violate **R2**.

The system $\{\phi : 0, A : 0, B : 0, C : 0, AB : 0, AC : 1, BC : 0, ABC : 1\}$ is not complete, since $A : 0$, $C : 0$, and $AC : 1$ together violate **R3**.

The system $\{\phi : 0, A : 0, B : 0, C : 0, AB : 0, AC : 0, BC : 0, ABC : 0\}$ is complete, since it satisfies **R1**, **R2**, and **R3**. This system is the unique completion of all systems in this example.

4.3 Axiomatization of Frequent Sets

From Proposition 2, we can now easily derive the following axiomatization for frequent sets.

F1 $p_\phi = 1$

F2 If $K_2 \subseteq K_1$, then $p_{K_2} \geq p_{K_1}$

F3 Let $K \subseteq I$, **M** a bag of subsets of K. Then

$$p_K \geq 1 - \frac{\#\mathbf{M} - \sum_{M \in \mathbf{M}} p_M}{k},$$

with $k = min_{a \in K}(deg(a, \mathbf{M}))$[5]

---
[5] If $k = 0$, **R3** should be interpreted as "$p_K \geq 0$"

Theorem 2. *Let* $S = \left\{ {}_{K \subseteq I} \; K :: p_K \right.$ *be a system of frequent sets over* I. *The following two statements are equivalent:*

- S *is a complete system.*
- S *satisfies* **F1**, **F2**, *and* **F3**.

5   Inference

In the rest of the text we continue working with rare sets. The results obtained for rare sets can, just like the axiomatization, be carried over to frequent sets.

  In the previous section we introduced and proved an axiomatization for complete systems of rare and frequent sets. There is however still one problem with this axiomatization. **R3** states a property that has to be checked for all bags over the subsets of K. This number of bags is infinite. In this section we show that it suffices to check only a finite number of bags: the minimal multi-covers. We show that the number of minimal multi-covers over a set is finite, and that they can be computed.

  We also look at the following problem: when an incomplete system is given, can we compute its completion using the axioms? We show that this is indeed possible. We use **R1**, **R2**, and **R3** as inference rules to adjust rareness values in the system; whenever we detect an inconsistency with one of the rules, we improve the system. When the rules are applied in a systematic way, this method leads to a complete system within a finite number of steps.

  Actually, the completion of a system of frequent sets can be computed in an obvious way by using linear programming. Indeed, when we look at the proof of theorem 1, we can compute the completion of the system of inequalities by applying linear programming. For all sets K, we can minimize p_K with respect to a system of inequalities expressing that the frequencies obey the system of rare sets. Since the system of inequalities has polynomial size in the number of frequent itemsets, this algorithm is even polynomial in the size of the system. However, in association rule mining, it is very common that the number of itemsets becomes very large and thus the system of inequalities will in practical situations certainly become prohibitive large. Therefore, solving the linear programming problem is a theoretical solution, but not a practical one. Also, as mentioned in [6], an axiomatization has as an advantage that it provides human-readable proofs, and that, when the inference is stopped before termination, still a partial solution is provided.

5.1   Minimal Multi-covers

Definition 6.

- *A k-cover of a set S is a bag* **K** *over the subsets of S such that for all $s \in S$, $deg(s, \mathbf{K}) = k$.*
- *A bag* **K** *over the subsets of a set S is a* multi-cover *of S if there exists an integer k such that* **K** *is a k-cover of S.*

− *A k-cover* $\mathbf{K}$ *of S is* minimal *if it cannot be decomposed as* $\mathbf{K} = \mathbf{K}_1 \bigcup \mathbf{K}_2$, *with* $\mathbf{K}_1$ *and* $\mathbf{K}_2$ *respectively* k_1- *and* k_2-*covers of S,* $k_1 > 0$ *and* $k_2 > 0$.

Example 8. Let $K = \{A, B, C, D\}$. $\{\!\{\ 1'AB, 1'BC, 1'CD, 1'AD, 1'ABCD\ \}\!\}$ is a 3-cover of K. It is not minimal, because it can be decomposed into the following two minimal multi-covers of K: $\{\!\{\ 1'AB, 1'BC, 1'CD, 1'AD\ \}\!\}$ and $\{\!\{\ 1'ABCD\ \}\!\}$.

The new rule that replaces **R3** states that it is not necessary to check all bags; we only need to check the minimal multi-covers. This gives the following **R3'**:

R3' Let $K \subseteq I$, $\mathbf{M}$ a minimal k-cover of K. Then

$$p_K \leq \frac{\sum_{M \in \mathbf{M}} p_M}{k}\ .$$

Theorem 3. *Let S be a system of rare sets over I. The following statements are equivalent:*

1. *S satisfies* **R1**, **R2**, *and* **R3**.
2. *S satisfies* **R1**, **R2**, *and* **R3'**.

SKETCH OF THE PROOF. (1) The direction **R1**, **R2**, **R3** implies **R1**, **R2**, **R3'** is trivial, since every k-cover of K is also a bag over the subsets of K, where the minimal degree is k.

(2) Suppose the system S satisfies **R1** and **R2**, but violates **R3**. There exists a set K and a bag $\mathbf{K}$ over the subsets of K, such that $p_K > \frac{\sum_{L \in \mathbf{K}} p_L}{k}$, with $k = min_{a \in K} deg(a, \mathbf{K})$. Starting from this bag, one can construct a minimal multi-cover of K, that violates **R3'**. We show this construction with an example. Suppose $\mathbf{K} = \{\!\{\ AB, BC, ABC\ \}\!\}$. Every element appears at least 2 times in $\mathbf{K}$. We first construct a multi-cover from $\mathbf{K}$, by removing elements that appear more than others. In this example, B appears 3 times, and all other elements appear only 2 times. We remove B from one of the sets in $\mathbf{K}$, resulting in $\{\!\{\ A, BC, ABC\ \}\!\}$. The sum over $\mathbf{K}$ became smaller by this operation, since S satisfies **R2**. This multi-cover can be split into two different minimal multi-covers: $\mathbf{K}_1 = \{\!\{\ A, BC\ \}\!\}$, and $\mathbf{K}_2 = \{\!\{\ ABC\ \}\!\}$. Because now $\frac{\sum_{L \in \mathbf{K}} p_L}{2} = \frac{\sum_{L \in \mathbf{K}_1} p_L + \sum_{L \in \mathbf{K}_2} p_L}{1+1}$, for at least one i, $\frac{\sum_{L \in \mathbf{K}_i} p_L}{1}$ is smaller than $\frac{\sum_{L \in \mathbf{K}} p_L}{2}$.

Proposition 3. *Let K be a finite set. The number of minimal multi-covers of K is finite and computable.*

The proof can be found in [3].

5.2   Computing the Completion of a System with Inference Rules

We prove that by applying **R1**, **R2**, and **R3**' as rules, we can compute the completion of any given system of rare sets. Applying for example rule **R2** means that whenever we see a situation $K_1 \subseteq K_2$, and the system states $K_1 : p_{K_1}$ and $K_2 : p_{K_2}$, and $p_{K_2} < p_{K_1}$, we improve the system by replacing $K_1 : p_{K_1}$ by $K_1 : p_{K_2}$. It is clear that **R1** can only be applied once; **R2** and **R3** never create situations in which **R1** can be applied again.

R2 is a *top-down operation*, in the sense that the rareness values of smaller sets is adjusted using values of bigger sets. So, for a given system S we can easily reach a fixpoint for rule **R2**, by going top-down; we first try to improve the frequencies of the biggest itemsets, before continuing with the smaller ones.

R3 is a *bottom-up operation*; values of smaller sets are used to adjust the values of bigger sets. So, again, for a given system S, we can reach a fixpoint for rule **R3**, by applying the rule bottom-up.

A trivial algorithm to compute the completion of a system is the following: apply **R1**, and then keep applying **R2** and **R3** until a fixpoint is reached. Clearly, the *limit* of this approach yields a complete system, but it is not clear that a fixpoint will be reached within a finite number of steps. Moreover, there are examples of situations in which infinite loops are possible. In Fig. 3, such an example is given. The completion of the first system, is clearly all rareness values equal to zero, because for every matrix satisfying the system, none of the rows have a zero in AB, and none have a zero in BC, so there are no zeros at all in the matrix. When we keep applying the rules as in Fig. 3, we never reach this fixpoint, since in step $2n$, the value for ABC is $\left(\frac{1}{2}\right)^n$. This is however not a problem; we show that when we apply the rules **R2** and **R3** in a systematic way, we always reach a fixpoint within a finite number of steps. This systematic approach is illustrated in Fig. 4. We first apply **R2** top-down until we reach a fixpoint for **R2**, and then we apply **R3** bottom-up until we reach a fixpoint for **R3**. The general systematic approach is written down in Fig. 5. We prove that for every system these two meta-steps are all there is needed to reach the completion.

Definition 7. *Let I be a set of items, $J \subseteq I$, and $S = \left\{_{K \subseteq I} K : p_K \right.$ a system of rare sets over I. The projection of S on J, denoted $proj(S, J)$, is the system $S' = \left\{_{K \subseteq J} K : p_K \right..$*

Lemma 2. *Let I be a set of items, $J \subseteq I$, and $S = \left\{_{K \subseteq I} K : p_K \right.$ a system of rare sets over I. If S satisfies **R2**, then $proj(C(S), J) = C(proj(S, J))$.*

Theorem 4. *The algorithm in Fig. 5 computes the completion of the system of rare sets S.*

SKETCH OF THE PROOF. Let $I = \{A, B, C\}$, and S be a system of rare sets over I. After the top-down step, the resulting system satisfies **R2**. First we apply **R3** to adjust the value of A. Because S satisfies **R2**, and after application of **R3** on A, the system $\{\phi : 0, A : p_A\}$ is complete, we cannot further improve on A; $proj(C(S), \{A\}) = C(S, proj(S, \{A\}))$. We can use the same argument

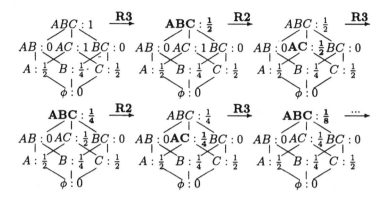

Fig. 3. "Random" application of the rules can lead to infinite loops

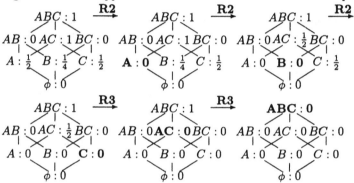

Fig. 4. Systematic application of the rules avoids infinite computations

for B and C. Then we apply **R3** to adjust the value of AC. After this step, $\{\phi : 0, A : p_A, B : p_B, AC : p_{AC}\}$ satisfies **R3**. This system also satisfies **R2**, because otherwise we could improve on A or on B, and we just showed that we cannot further improve on A or B. Thus, the system $proj(S, \{A, C\})$ is closed, and thus we cannot further improve on AC. This way, we iteratively go up, and finally we can conclude that S must be complete after the full bottom-up step.

6   Summary and Further Work

We presented an axiomatization for complete systems of frequent sets. As an intermediate stage in the proofs, we introduced the notion of a system of rare sets. The axiomatization for rare sets contained three rules **R1**, **R2**, and **R3**. From these rules we could easily derive the axiomatization, **F1**, **F2**, and **F3** for frequent sets. Because rule **R3** yields a condition that needs to be checked for an infinite number of bags, we replaced **R3** by **R3'**. We showed that the completion can be computed by applying **R1**, **R2**, and **R3'** as inference rules. If these rules are applied first top-down, and then bottom-up, the completion is reached within

Close(S)
$p_\phi = 0$
TopDown(S)
BottomUp(S)

TopDown(S)
for $i = n$ **downto** 1 **do**
   for all itemsets K of cardinality i **do**
      make $p_K = min_{K \subseteq L}(p_L)$

BottomUp(S)
for $i = 1$ **to** n **do**
   for all itemsets K of cardinality i **do**
      make $p_K = min_{K, \text{ minimal } k\text{-cover of } K} \left(\frac{\sum_{K' \in K} p_{K'}}{k} \right)$

Fig. 5. Algorithm Close for finding the completion of the system $S = \left\{ _{K \subseteq I} \ K : p_K \right\}$ over $I = \{I_1, \ldots, I_n\}$

a finite number of steps. In the future we want to study an axiomatization for systems in which not for every set a frequency is given. For some preliminary results on these *sparse systems*, we refer to [3]. Another interesting topic is expanding the axiomatization to include association rules and confidences.

References

1. R. Agrawal, T. Imilienski, and A. Swami. Mining association rules between sets of items in large databases. In *Proc. ACM SIGMOD*, 1993
2. R. Agrawal, R. Srikant. Fast Algorithms for Mining Association Rules. In *Proc. VLDB*, 1994
3. T. Calders, and J. Paredaens. A Theoretical Framework for Reasoning about Frequent Itemsets. Technical Report 006, Universiteit Antwerpen, Belgium, http://win-www.uia.ac.be/u/calders/download/axiom.ps, June 2000.
4. R. Fagin, J. Halpern, and N. Megiddo. A Logic for Reasoning about Probabilities. In *Information and Computation* 87(1,2): 78-128, 1990.
5. R. Fagin, M. Y. Vardi. Armstrong Databases for Functional and Inclusion Dependencies. In *IPL 16(1): 13-19*, 1983.
6. A. M. Frisch, P. Haddawy. Anytime Deduction for Probabilistic Logic. In *Artificial Intelligence* 69(1-2): 93-122, 1994.
7. G. Georgakopoulos, D. Kavvadias, and C. H. Papadimitriou. Probabilistic Satisfiability. In *Journal of Complexity* 4:1-11, 1988.
8. J. Han, J.Pei, and Y. Yin. Mining frequent patterns without candidate generation. In *Proc. ACM SIGMOD*, 2000
9. P. Hansen, B. Jaumard, G.-B. D. Nguetsé, M. P. de Aragão. Models and Algorithms for Probabilistic and Bayesian Logic. In *Proc. IJCAI*, 1995
10. P. Hansen, B. Jaumard. Probabilistic Satisfiability. *Les Cahiers du GERAD* G-96-31, 1996
11. L. V.S. Laksmanan, R.T. Ng, J. Han, and A. Pang. Optimization of Constrained Frequent Set Queries with 2-variable Constraints. *Proc. ACM SIGMOD*, 1999
12. N. Nilsson. Probabilistic Logic. In *Artificial Intelligence* 28: 71-87, 1986

On Answering Queries in the Presence of Limited Access Patterns

Chen Li[1] and Edward Chang[2]

[1] Computer Science Department, Stanford University, CA 94305, USA
chenli@cs.stanford.edu
[2] ECE Department, University of California, Santa Barbara, CA 93106, USA
echang@ece.ucsb.edu

Abstract. In information-integration systems, source relations often have limitations on access patterns to their data; i.e., when one must provide values for certain attributes of a relation in order to retrieve its tuples. In this paper we consider the following fundamental problem: can we compute the complete answer to a query by accessing the relations with legal patterns? The *complete* answer to a query is the answer that we could compute if we could retrieve all the tuples from the relations. We give algorithms for solving the problem for various classes of queries, including conjunctive queries, unions of conjunctive queries, and conjunctive queries with arithmetic comparisons. We prove the problem is undecidable for datalog queries. If the complete answer to a query cannot be computed, we often need to compute its maximal answer. The second problem we study is, given two conjunctive queries on relations with limited access patterns, how to test whether the maximal answer to the first query is contained in the maximal answer to the second one? We show this problem is decidable using the results of monadic programs.

1 Introduction

The goal of information-integration systems (e.g., [3,20,25]) is to support seamless access to heterogeneous data sources. In these systems, a user poses a query on a mediator [26], which computes the answer by accessing the data at the underlying source relations. One of the challenges for these systems is to deal with the diverse capabilities of sources in answering queries. For instance, a source relation *r(Star,Movie)* might not allow us to retrieve all its data "for free." Instead, the only way of retrieving its tuples is by providing a star name, and then retrieving the movies of this star. In general, relations in these systems may have limitations on access patterns to their data; i.e., one must provide values for certain attributes of a relation to retrieve its tuples. There are many reasons for these limitations, such as restrictive web search forms and concerns of security and performance.

In this paper we first study the following fundamental problem: *Given a query on relations with limited access patterns, can we compute the complete answer to the query by accessing the relations with legal patterns?* The *complete* answer to

J. Van den Bussche and V. Vianu (Eds.): ICDT 2001, LNCS 1973, pp. 219–233, 2001.
© Springer-Verlag Berlin Heidelberg 2001

the query is the answer that we could compute if we could retrieve all the tuples from the relations. Often users make decisions based on whether the answers to certain queries are complete or not. Thus the solution to this problem is important for the decision support and analysis by users. The following example shows that in some cases we can compute the complete answer to a query, even though we cannot retrieve all the tuples from relations.

Example 1. Suppose we have two relations $r(Star, Movie)$ and $s(Movie, Award)$ that store information about movies and their stars, and information about movies and the awards they won, respectively. The access limitation of relation r is that each query to this relation must specify a star name. Similarly, the access limitation of s is that each query to s must specify a movie name. Consider the following query that asks for the awards of the movies in which Fonda starred:

$$Q_1 : ans(A) :\!- r(fonda, M), s(M, A)$$

To answer Q_1, we first access relation r to retrieve the movies in which Fonda starred. For each returned movie, we access relation s to obtain its awards. Finally we return all these awards as the answer to the query. Although we did not retrieve all the tuples in the two relations, we can still claim that the computed answer *is* the complete answer to Q_1. The reason is that all the tuples of relation r that satisfy the first subgoal were retrieved in the first step. In addition, all the tuples of s that satisfy the second subgoal and join with the results of the first step were retrieved in the second step.

However, if the access limitation of the relation r is that each query to r must specify a movie title (not a star name), then we cannot compute the complete answer to query Q_1. The reason is that there can be a movie that Fonda starred, but we cannot retrieve the tuple without knowing the movie.

In general, if the complete answer to a query can be computed for any database of the relations in the query, we say that the query is *stable*. For instance, the query Q_1 in Example 1 is a stable query. As illustrated by the example, we might think that we can test the stability of a query by checking the existence of a *feasible* order of all its subgoals, as in [9,28]. An order of subgoals is feasible if for each subgoal in the order, the variables bound by the previous subgoals provide enough bound arguments that the relation for the subgoal can be accessed using a legal pattern. However, the following example shows that a query can be stable even if such a feasible order does not exist.

Example 2. We modify query Q_1 slightly by adding a subgoal $r(S, M)$, and have the following query:

$$Q_2 : ans(A) :\!- r(fonda, M), s(M, A), r(S, M)$$

This query does not have a feasible order of all its subgoals, since we cannot bind the variable S in the added subgoal. However, this subgoal is actually redundant, and we can show that Q_2 is equivalent to query Q_1. That is, there is a containment mapping [4] from Q_2 to Q_1, and vice versa. Therefore, for any database of the two relations, we can still compute the complete answer to Q_2 by answering Q_1.

Example 2 suggests that testing stability of a conjunctive query is not just checking the existence of a feasible order of all its subgoals. In this paper we study how to test stability of a variety of queries. The following are the results:

1. We show that a conjunctive query is stable iff its minimal equivalent query has a feasible order of all its subgoals. We propose two algorithms for testing stability of conjunctive queries, and prove this problem is $\mathcal{NP}$-complete (Section 3).
2. We study stability of finite unions of conjunctive queries, and give similar results as conjunctive queries. We propose two algorithms for testing stability of unions of conjunctive queries, and prove that stability of datalog queries is undecidable (Section 3).
3. We propose an algorithm for testing stability of conjunctive queries with arithmetic comparisons (Section 4).
4. We show that the complete answer to a nonstable conjunctive query can be computed for certain databases. We develop a decision tree (Figure 1) to guide the planning process to compute the complete answer to a conjunctive query (Section 5).

In the cases where we cannot compute the complete answer to a query, we often want to compute its maximal answer. The second problem we study is, *given two queries on relations with limited access patterns, how to test whether the maximal answer to the first query is contained in the maximal answer to the second one?* Clearly the solution to this problem can be used to answer queries efficiently.

Given a conjunctive query on relations with limited access patterns, [8,17] show how to construct a recursive datalog program [24] to compute the maximal answer to the query. That is, we can retrieve tuples from relations by retrieving as many bindings from the relations and the query as possible, then use the obtained tuples to answer the query. For instance, consider the relation $s(Movie, Award)$ in Example 1. Suppose we have another relation $dm(Movie)$ that provides movies made by Disney. We can use these movies to access relation s to retrieve tuples, and use these tuples to answer a query on these relations.

To test whether the maximal answer to a conjunctive query is contained in the maximal answer to another conjunctive query, we need to test whether the datalog program for the first one is contained in that for the second one. Since containment of datalog programs is undecidable [23], our problem of query containment seems undecidable. However, in Section 6 we prove this containment problem is decidable using the results of monadic programs [6]. Our results extend the recent results by Millstein, Levy, and Friedman [19], since we loosen the assumption in that paper. We also discuss how to test the containment efficiently when the program for a query in the test is inherently not recursive.

2   Preliminaries

Limited access patterns of relations can be modeled using *binding patterns* [24]. A binding pattern of a relation specifies the attributes that must be given values ("bound") to access the relation. In each binding pattern, an attribute is adorned as "*b*" (a value must be specified for this attribute) or "*f*" (the attribute can be free). For example, a relation $r(A, B, C)$ with the binding patterns $\{bff, ffb\}$ requires that every query to the relation must either supply a value for the first argument, or supply a value for the third argument.

Given a database D of relations with binding patterns and a query Q on these relations, the *complete* answer to Q, denoted by $ANS(Q, D)$, is the query's answer that could be computed if we could retrieve *all* tuples from the relations. However, we may not be able to retrieve all these tuples due to the binding patterns. The following observation serves as a starting point of our work.

> If a relation does not have an all-free binding pattern, then after some finite source queries are sent to the relation, there can always be some tuples in the relation that have not been retrieved, because we did not obtain the necessary bindings.

Definition 1. *(stable query) A query on relations with binding patterns is* stable *if for any database of the relations, we can compute the complete answer to the query by accessing the relations with legal patterns.*

We assume that if a relation requires a value to be given for a particular argument, the domain of the argument is infinite, or we do not know all the possible values for this argument. For example, the relation $r(Star, Movie)$ in Example 1 requires a star name, and we assume that we do not know all the possible star names. As a result, we do not allow the "strategy" of trying all the (infinite) possible strings as the argument to test the relation, since this approach does not terminate. Instead, we assume that each binding we use to access a relation is either from a query, or from the tuples retrieved by another access to a relation, while the value is from the appropriate domain.

Now the fundamental problem we study can be stated formally as follows: *how to test the stability of a query on relations with binding patterns?* As we will see in Section 3, in order to prove a query is stable, we need to show a legal plan that can compute the complete answer to the query for any database of the relations. On the other hand, in order to prove that a query Q is not stable, we need to give two databases D_1 and D_2, such that they have the same observable tuples. That is, by using only the bindings from the query and the relations, for both databases we can retrieve the same tuples from the relations. However, the two databases yield different answers to query Q, i.e., $ANS(Q, D_1) \neq ANS(Q, D_2)$. Therefore, based on the retrievable tuples from the relations, we cannot tell whether the answer computed using these tuples is the complete answer or not.

3 Stability of Conjunctive Queries, Unions of Conjunctive Queries, and Datalog Queries

In this section we develop two algorithms for testing stability of a conjunctive query, and prove this problem is $\mathcal{NP}$-complete. We also propose two algorithms for testing stability of a finite union of conjunctive queries. We prove that stability of datalog queries is undecidable.

3.1 Stability of Conjunctive Queries

A conjunctive query (CQ for short) is denoted by:

$$h(\bar{X}) :\text{-} g_1(\bar{X}_1), \ldots, g_n(\bar{X}_n)$$

In each subgoal $g_i(\bar{X}_i)$, predicate g_i is a relation, and every argument in $\bar{X}_i$ is either a variable or a constant. The variables $\bar{X}$ in the head are called *distinguished* variables. We use names beginning with lower-case letters for constants and relation names, and names beginning with upper-case letters for variables.

Definition 2. *(feasible order of subgoals) Some subgoals $g_1(\bar{X}_1), \ldots, g_k(\bar{X}_k)$ in a CQ form a* feasible order *if each subgoal $g_i(\bar{X}_i)$ in the order is executable; that is, there is a binding pattern p of the relation g_i, such that for each argument A in $g_i(\bar{X}_i)$ that is adorned as b in p, either A is a constant, or A appears in a previous subgoal. A CQ is* feasible *if it has a feasible order of all its subgoals.*

The query Q_1 in Example 1 is feasible, since $\big(r(fonda, M), s(M, A)\big)$ is a feasible order of all its subgoals. The query Q_2 is not feasible, since it does not have such a feasible order. A subgoal in a CQ is *answerable* if it is in a feasible order of *some* subgoals in the query. The answerable subgoals of a CQ can be computed by a greedy algorithm, called the Inflationary algorithm. That is, initialize a set Φ_a of subgoals to be empty. With the variables bound by the subgoals in Φ_a, whenever a subgoal becomes executable by accessing its relation, add this subgoal to Φ_a. Repeat this process until no more subgoals can be added to Φ_a, and Φ_a will include all the answerable subgoals of the query. Clearly a query is feasible if and only if all its subgoals are answerable. The following lemma shows that feasibility of a CQ is a sufficient condition for its stability.

Lemma 1. *A feasible CQ is stable. That is, if a CQ has a feasible order of all its subgoals, for any database of the relations, we can compute the complete answer to the query.*[1]

Corollary 1. *A CQ is stable if it has an equivalent query that is feasible.*

---

[1] We do not provide all the proofs of the lemmas and theorems in this paper due to space limitations. Refer [15,16] for details.

The query Q_2 in Example 2 is the *minimal equivalent query* of Q_1. A CQ is *minimal* if it has no redundant subgoals, i.e., removing any of its subgoals will yield a nonequivalent query. It is known that each CQ has a unique minimal equivalent up to renaming of variables and reordering of subgoals, which can be obtained by deleting its redundant subgoals [4]. Now we give two theorems that suggest two algorithms for testing the stability of a CQ.

Theorem 1. *A CQ is stable iff its minimal equivalent is feasible.*

By Theorem 1, we give an algorithm CQstable for testing the stability of a CQ Q. The algorithm first computes the minimal equivalent Q_m of Q by deleting the redundant subgoals in Q. Then it uses the Inflationary algorithm to test the feasibility of Q_m. If Q_m is feasible, then Q is stable; otherwise, Q is not stable. The complexity of the algorithm CQstable is exponential, since we need to minimize the CQ first, which is known to be $\mathcal{NP}$-complete [4]. There is a more efficient algorithm that is based on the following theorem.

Theorem 2. *Let Q be a CQ on relations with binding patterns and Q_a be the query with the head of Q and the answerable subgoals of Q. Then Q is stable iff Q and Q_a are equivalent as queries, i.e., $Q = Q_a$.*

Theorem 2 gives another algorithm CQstable* for testing the stability of a CQ Q as follows. The algorithm first computes all the answerable subgoals of Q. If all the subgoals are answerable, then Q is stable, and we do not need to test any query containment. Otherwise, the algorithm constructs the query Q_a with these answerable subgoals and the head of Q. It tests whether Q_a is contained in Q (denoted $Q_a \sqsubseteq Q$) by checking if there is a containment mapping from Q to Q_a. If so, since $Q \sqsubseteq Q_a$ is obvious, we have $Q = Q_a$, and Q is stable; otherwise, Q is not stable. The algorithm CQstable* has two advantages: (1) If all the subgoals of Q are answerable, then we do not need to test whether $Q_a \sqsubseteq Q$, thus its time complexity is polynomial in this case. (2) As we will see in Section 4, this algorithm can be generalized to test stability of conjunctive queries with arithmetic comparisons.

Theorem 3. *The problem of testing stability of a CQ is $\mathcal{NP}$-complete.*

Proof. (sketch) Algorithm CQstable shows that the problem is in $\mathcal{NP}$. It is known that given a CQ Q and a CQ Q' that has a subset of the subgoals in Q, the problem of deciding whether $Q' \sqsubseteq Q$ is $\mathcal{NP}$-complete [4]. It can be shown that this problem can be reduced to our stability problem in polynomial time [15].

3.2 Stability of Unions of Conjunctive Queries

Let $\mathcal{Q} = Q_1 \cup \cdots \cup Q_n$ be a finite union of CQ's (UCQ for short), and all its CQ's have a common head predicate. It is known that there is a unique minimal subset of $\mathcal{Q}$ that is its minimal equivalent [22].

Example 3. Suppose we have three relations r, s, and p, and each relation has only one binding pattern bf. Consider the following three CQ's:

$$Q_1: \quad ans(X) :\text{-} r(a, X)$$
$$Q_2: \quad ans(X) :\text{-} r(a, X), p(Y, Z)$$
$$Q_3: \quad ans(X) :\text{-} r(a, X), s(X, Y), p(Y, Z)$$

Clearly $Q_3 \sqsubseteq Q_2 \sqsubseteq Q_1$. Queries Q_1 and Q_3 are both stable (since they are both feasible), while query Q_2 is not. Consider the following two UCQ's: $\mathcal{Q}_1 = Q_1 \cup Q_2 \cup Q_3$ and $\mathcal{Q}_2 = Q_2 \cup Q_3$. $\mathcal{Q}_1$ has a minimal equivalent Q_1, and $\mathcal{Q}_2$ has a minimal equivalent Q_2. Therefore, query $\mathcal{Q}_1$ is stable, and $\mathcal{Q}_2$ is not.

In analogy with the results for CQ's, we have the following two theorems:

Theorem 4. *Let $\mathcal{Q}$ be a UCQ on relations with binding patterns. $\mathcal{Q}$ is stable iff each query in the minimal equivalent of $\mathcal{Q}$ is stable.*

Theorem 5. *Let $\mathcal{Q}$ be a UCQ on relations with binding patterns. Let $\mathcal{Q}_s$ be the union of all the stable queries in $\mathcal{Q}$. Then $\mathcal{Q}$ is stable iff $\mathcal{Q}$ and $\mathcal{Q}_s$ are equivalent as queries, i.e., $\mathcal{Q} = \mathcal{Q}_s$.*

Theorem 4 gives an algorithm UCQstable for testing stability of a UCQ $\mathcal{Q}$ as follows. Compute the minimal equivalent $\mathcal{Q}_m$ of $\mathcal{Q}$, and test the stability of each CQ in $\mathcal{Q}_m$ using the algorithm CQstable or CQstable*. If all the queries in $\mathcal{Q}_m$ are stable, query $\mathcal{Q}$ is stable; otherwise, $\mathcal{Q}$ is not stable. Theorem 5 gives another algorithm UCQstable* for testing stability of a UCQ $\mathcal{Q}$ as follows. Test the stability of each query in $\mathcal{Q}$ by calling the algorithms CQstable or CQstable*. If all the queries are stable, then $\mathcal{Q}$ is stable. Otherwise, let $\mathcal{Q}_s$ be the union of these stable queries. Test whether $\mathcal{Q} \sqsubseteq \mathcal{Q}_s$, i.e., $\mathcal{Q}$ is contained in $\mathcal{Q}_s$ as queries. If so, $\mathcal{Q}$ is stable; otherwise, $\mathcal{Q}$ is not stable. The advantage of this algorithm is that we do not need to test whether $\mathcal{Q} \sqsubseteq \mathcal{Q}_s$ if all the queries in $\mathcal{Q}$ are stable.

3.3 Stability of Datalog Queries

We want to know that given a datalog query on EDB predicates [24] with binding patterns, can we compute the complete answer to the query by accessing the EDB relations with legal patterns? Not surprisingly, this problem is not decidable.

Theorem 6. *Stability of datalog queries is undecidable.*

Proof. (Sketch) Let P_1 and P_2 be two arbitrary datalog queries. We show that a decision procedure for the stability of datalog queries would allow us to decide whether $P_1 \sqsubseteq P_2$. Since containment of datalog queries is undecidable, we prove the theorem.[2] Let all the EDB relations in the two queries have an all-free binding pattern; i.e., there is no restriction of retrieving tuples from these relations. Without loss of generality, we can assume that the goal predicates in P_1 and P_2, named p_1 and p_2 respectively, have arity m. Let Q be the datalog query consisting of all the rules in P_1 and P_2, and of the rules:

---

[2] The idea of the proof is borrowed from [7], Chapter 2.3.

$$r_1: ans(X_1, \ldots, X_m) :- p_1(X_1, \ldots, X_m), e(Z)$$
$$r_2: ans(X_1, \ldots, X_m) :- p_2(X_1, \ldots, X_m)$$

where e is a new 1-ary relation with the binding pattern b. Variable Z is a new variable that does not appear in P_1 and P_2. We can show that $P_1 \sqsubseteq P_2$ if and only if query Q is stable.

In [15] we give a sufficient condition for stability of datalog queries. We show that if a set of rules on EDB relations with binding patterns has a feasible rule/goal graph [24] w.r.t. a query goal, then the query is stable.

4 Stability of Conjunctive Queries with Arithmetic Comparisons

In this section we develop an algorithm for testing the stability of a conjunctive query with arithmetic comparisons (CQAC for short). This problem is more challenging than conjunctive queries, because equalities may help bind more variables, and then make more subgoals answerable. In addition, a CQAC may not have a minimal equivalent formed from a subset of its own subgoals, as shown by Example 14.8 in [24]. Therefore, we cannot generalize the algorithm CQstable to solve this problem.

Assume Q is CQAC. Let $O(Q)$ be the set of ordinary (uninterpreted) subgoals of Q that do not have comparisons. Let $C(Q)$ be the set of subgoals of Q that are arithmetic comparisons. We consider the following arithmetic comparisons: $<$, $\leq$, $=$, $>$, $\geq$, and $\neq$. In addition, we make the following assumptions about the comparisons: (1) Values for the variables in the comparisons are chosen from an infinite, totally ordered set, such as the rationals or reals. (2) The comparisons are not contradictory, i.e., there exists an instantiation of the variables such that all the comparisons are true. In addition, all the comparisons are safe, i.e., each variable in the comparisons appears in some ordinary subgoal.

Definition 3. *(answerable subquery of a CQAC) The answerable subquery of a CQAC Q on relations with binding patterns, denoted by Q_a, is the query including the head of Q, the answerable subgoals Φ_a of Q, and all the comparisons of the bound variables in Φ_a that can be derived from $C(Q)$.*

The answerable subquery Q_a of a CQAC Q can be computed as follows. We first compute all the answerable ordinary subgoals Φ_a of query Q using the Inflationary algorithm. Note that if Q contains equalities such as $X = Y$, or equalities that can be derived from inequalities (e.g., if we can derive $X \leq Y$ and $X \geq Y$, then $X = Y$), we need to substitute variable X by Y before using the Inflationary algorithm to find all the answerable subgoals. Derive all the inequalities among the variables in Φ_a from $C(Q)$. Then Q_a includes *all* the constraints of the variables in Φ_a, because $C(Q)$ may derive more constraints that these variables should satisfy. For instance, assume variable X is bound in Φ_a, and variable Y is not. If Q has comparisons $X < Y$ and $Y < 5$, then variable X in Q_a still needs to satisfy the constraint $X < 5$.

We might be tempted to generalize the algorithm CQstable* as follows. Given a CQAC Q, we compute its answerable subquery Q_a. We test the stability of Q by testing whether $Q_a \sqsubseteq Q$, which can be tested using the algorithm in [11,29] ("the GZO algorithm" for short). However, the following example shows that this "algorithm" does not always work.

Example 4. Consider query

$$P : ans(Y) \text{:-} p(X), r(X,Y), r(A,B), A < B, X \leq A, A \leq Y$$

where relation p has a binding pattern f, and relation r has a binding pattern bf. Its answerable subquery is

$$P_a : ans(Y) \text{:-} p(X), r(X,Y), X \leq Y$$

Using the GZO algorithm we know $P_a \not\sqsubseteq P$. Therefore, we may claim that query P is not stable. However, actually query P *is* stable. As we will see shortly, P is equivalent to the union of the following two queries.

$$T_1 : ans(Y) \text{:-} p(X), r(X,Y), X < Y$$
$$T_2 : ans(Y) \text{:-} p(Y), r(Y,Y), r(Y,B), Y < B$$

Note both T_1 and T_2 are stable, since all their ordinary subgoals are answerable.

The above "algorithm" fails because the only case where $P_a \not\sqsubseteq P$ is when $X = Y$. However, $X \leq A$ and $A \leq Y$ will then force $A = X = Y$, and the subgoal $r(A,B)$ becomes answerable! This example suggests that we need to consider *all* the total orders of the query variables, similar to the idea in [12].[3]

Theorem 7. *Let Q be a CQAC, and $\Omega(Q)$ be the set of all the total orders of the variables in Q that satisfy the comparisons of Q. For each $\lambda \in \Omega(Q)$, let Q^λ be the corresponding query that includes the ordinary subgoals of Q and all the inequalities and equalities of this total order λ. Query Q is stable if and only if for all $\lambda \in \Omega(Q)$, $Q_a^\lambda \sqsubseteq Q$, where Q_a^λ is the answerable subquery of Q^λ.*

The theorem suggests an algorithm CQACstable for testing the stability of a CQAC Q as follows:

1. Compute all the total orders $\Omega(Q)$ of the variables in Q that satisfy the comparisons in Q.
2. For each $\lambda \in \Omega(Q)$:
   a) Compute the answerable subquery Q_a^λ of query Q^λ;
   b) Test $Q_a^\lambda \sqsubseteq Q$ by calling the GZO algorithm;
   c) If $Q_a^\lambda \not\sqsubseteq Q$, claim that query Q is not stable and return.
3. Claim that query Q is stable.

---

[3] Formally, a total order of the variables in the query is an order with some equalities, i.e., all the variables are partitioned to sets $S_1, \ldots, S_k$, such that each S_i is a set of equal variables, and for any two variables $X_i \in S_i$ and $X_j \in S_j$, if $i < j$, then $X_i < X_j$.

For a CQAC Q on a database D, if by calling algorithm CQACstable we know Q is stable, we can compute $ANS(Q, D)$ by computing $ANS(Q_a^\lambda, D)$ for each total order λ in $\Omega(Q)$, and taking the union of these answers.

Example 5. The query P in Example 4 has the following 8 total orders:

$$\lambda_1:\ X < A = Y < B; \quad \lambda_2:\ X < A < Y < B; \quad \lambda_3:\ X < A < Y = B;$$
$$\lambda_4:\ X < A < B < Y; \quad \lambda_5:\ X = A = Y < B; \quad \lambda_6:\ X = A < Y < B;$$
$$\lambda_7:\ X = A < Y = B; \quad \lambda_8:\ X = A < B < Y.$$

For each total order λ_i, we write its corresponding query P^{λ_i}. For instance:

$$P^{\lambda_1} : ans(Y) :\text{-} p(X), r(X, Y), r(Y, B), X < Y, Y < B$$

We then compute the answerable subquery $P_a^{\lambda_i}$. All the 8 answerable subqueries are contained in P. By Theorem 7, query P is stable. Actually, the union of all the answerable subqueries except $P_a^{\lambda_5}$ is:

$$ans(Y) :\text{-} p(X), r(X, Y), r(A, B), X < Y, A < B, X \leq A, A \leq Y$$

whose answerable subquery is the query T_1 in Example 4. In addition, $P_a^{\lambda_5}$ is equivalent to the query T_2. Since P is equivalent to the union of the 8 answerable subqueries, we have proved $P = T_1 \cup T_2$.

5   Nonstable Conjunctive Queries with Computable Complete Answers

So far we have considered whether the complete answer to a query can be computed for *any* database. In this section we show that for *some* databases, even if a CQ is not stable, we may still be able to compute its complete answer. However, the computability of its complete answer is data dependent, i.e., we do not know the computability until some plan is executed. The following is an example.

Example 6. Consider the following queries on relations with binding patterns:

Relations	Binding patterns	Queries
$r(A, B, C)$	bff	$Q_1 : ans(B) \quad :\text{-} r(a, B, C), s(C, D)$
$s(C, D)$	fb	$Q_2 : ans(D) \quad :\text{-} r(a, B, C), s(C, D)$
$p(D)$	f	

The two queries have the same subgoals but different heads, and both are not stable. However, we can still try to answer query Q_1 as follows: send a query $r(a, X, Y)$ to relation r. Assume we obtain three tuples: $\langle a, b_1, c_1 \rangle$, $\langle a, b_2, c_2 \rangle$, and $\langle a, b_2, c_3 \rangle$. Thus, by retrieving these tuples, we know that the complete answer is a subset of $\{\langle b_1 \rangle, \langle b_2 \rangle\}$. Assume attributes A, B, C, and D have different domains. If relation p provides the tuples that allow us to retrieve some tuples $\langle c_1, d_1 \rangle$ and $\langle c_2, d_2 \rangle$ from s, we can know that $\{\langle b_1 \rangle, \langle b_2 \rangle\}$ *is* the complete answer. On the other hand, if relation p does not provide tuples that allow us to compute the answer $\{\langle b_1 \rangle, \langle b_2 \rangle\}$, we do not know whether we have computed the complete answer to Q_1.

We can try to answer query Q_2 in the similar way. After the first subgoal is processed, we also obtain the same three tuples from r. However, no matter what tuples are retrieved from relation s, we can never know the complete answer to Q_2, since there can always be a tuple $\langle c_1, d' \rangle$ in relation s that has not been retrieved, and d' is in the answer to Q_2. For both Q_1 and Q_2, if after processing the first subgoal we obtain no tuples from r that satisfy this subgoal, then we know that their complete answers are empty.

An important observation on these two queries is that Q_1's distinguished variable B can be bound by the answerable subgoal $r(a, B, C)$, while Q_2's distinguished variable D cannot be bound. Based on this observation, we develop a decision tree (Figure 1) that guides the planning process to compute the complete answer to a CQ. The shaded nodes in the figure are where we can conclude about whether we can compute the complete answer.

Now we explain the decision tree in details. Given a CQ Q and a database D, we first minimize a CQ Q by deleting its redundant subgoals, and compute its minimal equivalent Q_m (arc 1 in Figure 1). Then we test the feasibility of the query Q_m by calling the Inflationary algorithm; that is, we test whether Q_m has a feasible order of all its subgoals. If so (arc 2 in Figure 1), Q_m (thus Q) is stable, and its answer can be computed following a feasible order of all the subgoals in Q_m.

If Q_m is not feasible (arc 3), we compute all its answerable subgoals Φ_a, and check if all the *distinguished* variables are bound by the subgoals Φ_a. There are two cases:

1. If all the distinguished variables are bound by the subgoals Φ_a (arc 4), then the complete answer may be computed even if the supplementary relation [2, 24] (denoted I_a) of subgoals Φ_a is not empty. We compute the supplementary relation I_a of these subgoals following a feasible order of Φ_a.
   a) If I_a is empty (arc 5), then we know that the complete answer is empty.
   b) If I_a is not empty (arc 6), let I_a^P be the projection of I_a onto the distinguished variables. We use all the bindings from the query and the relations to retrieve as many tuples as possible. (See [8,17] for the details.) Let Φ_{na} denote all the nonanswerable subgoals.
      i. If for every tuple $t^P \in I_a^P$, there is a tuple $t_a \in I_a$, such that the projection of t_a onto the distinguished variables is t^P, and t_a can join with some tuples for all the subgoals Φ_{na} (tuple t^P is called *satisfiable*), then we know that I_a^P is the complete answer to the query (arc 7).
      ii. Otherwise, the complete answer is not computable (arc 8).
2. If some distinguished variables are not bound by the subgoals Φ_a (arc 9), then the complete answer is not computable, unless the supplementary relation I_a is empty. Similarly to the case of arc 4, we compute I_a by following a feasible order of Φ_a. If I_a is empty (arc 10), then the complete answer is empty. Otherwise (arc 11), the complete answer is not computable.

While traversing the decision tree from the root to a leaf node, we may reach a node where we do not know whether the complete answer is computable until we traverse one level down the tree. Two planning strategies can be adopted at this kind of nodes: a pessimistic strategy and an optimistic strategy. A *pessimistic* strategy gives up traversing the tree once the complete answer is unlikely to be computable. On the contrary, an *optimistic* strategy is optimistic about the possibility of computing the complete answer, and it traverses one more level by taking the corresponding operations.

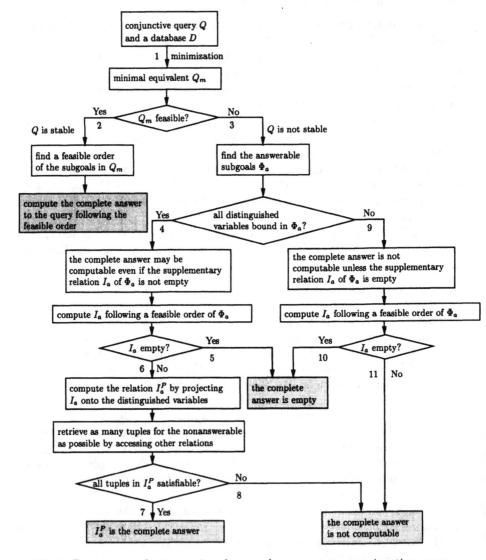

Fig. 1. Decision tree for computing the complete answer to a conjunctive query

6   Query Containment in the Presence of Binding Patterns

In the cases we cannot compute the complete answer to a query, we often want to compute the maximal answer to the query. In this section we study the following problem: *given two conjunctive queries on relations with limited access patterns, how to test whether the maximal answer to the first query is contained in the maximal answer to the second one?* We show this problem is decidable, and discuss how to test the query containment efficiently.

For a CQ Q on relations $\mathcal{R}$ with binding patterns, let $\Pi(Q, \mathcal{R})$ denote the program that computes the maximal answer to the query by using *only* the bindings from query Q and relations $\mathcal{R}$. It is shown in [8,17] how the program $\Pi(Q, \mathcal{R})$ is constructed. $\Pi(Q, \mathcal{R})$ can be a recursive datalog program, even if the query Q itself is not recursive. That is, we might access the relations repeatedly to retrieve tuples, and use the new bindings in these tuples to retrieve more tuples from the relations. Formally, our containment problem is: *Given two conjunctive queries Q_1 and Q_2 on relations $\mathcal{R}$ with limited access patterns, how to test whether $\Pi(Q_1, \mathcal{R}) \sqsubseteq \Pi(Q_2, \mathcal{R})$?* The following theorem shows that this problem is decidable, even though containment of datalog programs is undecidable [23].

Theorem 8. *For two conjunctive queries Q_1 and Q_2 on relations $\mathcal{R}$ with binding patterns, whether $\Pi(Q_1, \mathcal{R}) \sqsubseteq \Pi(Q_2, \mathcal{R})$ is decidable.*

Proof. (Sketch) We can show that $\Pi(Q_1, \mathcal{R})$ and $\Pi(Q_2, \mathcal{R})$ are monadic datalog programs. A datalog program is *monadic* if all its recursive predicates [24] are monadic (i.e., with arity one); its nonrecursive IDB predicates can have arbitrary arity. Cosmadakis et al. [6] show that containment of monadic programs is decidable. Thus our containment problem is decidable.

This containment problem is recently studied in [19]. They prove the same decidability result using a different technique. There are some differences between our approach to the decidability result and their approach. The decidability proof in that paper is based on the assumption that the set of initial bindings for the contained query is a subset of the initial bindings for the containing query. We loosen this assumption because the decidability result holds even if the two queries have different initial bindings. Another difference between the two approaches is that we assume that the contained query is a conjunctive query, while in [19] the contained query can be a recursive datalog query. Finally, [19] uses the source-centric approach to information integration [25], which is different from the query-centric approach [25] that is taken in our framework. However, we can easily extend our technique [16] to the source-centric approach.

[6] involves a complex algorithm that uses tree-automata theory to test containment of monadic programs. If one of the two programs in the test is *bounded* (i.e., it is equivalent to a finite union of conjunctive query), then the containment can be tested more efficiently using the algorithms in [4,5,22]. Therefore, we are

interested in how to test the boundedness of the program $\Pi(Q, \mathcal{R})$ for a query Q on relations $\mathcal{R}$ with binding patterns.

It is shown in [6] that boundedness is also decidable for monadic datalog programs, although it is not decidable in general [10]. However, testing boundedness of monadic programs also involves a complex algorithm [6]. In [16] we study this problem for the class of connection queries [17]. Informally, a connection query is a conjunctive query on relations whose schemas are subsets of some global attributes, and some values are given for certain attributes in the query. In [16] we give a polynomial-time algorithm for testing the boundedness of the datalog program for a connection query.

7   Related Work

Several works consider binding patterns in the context of answering queries using views [8,14,1]. Rajaraman, Sagiv, and Ullman [21] propose algorithms for answering queries using views with binding patterns. In that paper all solutions to a query compute the complete answer to the query; thus only stable queries are handled. Duschka and Levy [8] solve the same problem by translating source restrictions into recursive datalog rules to obtain the maximally-contained rewriting of a query, but the rewriting does not necessarily compute the query's complete answer. Li et al. [18] study the problem of generating an executable plan based on source restrictions. [9,28] study query optimization in the presence of binding patterns. Yerneni et al. [27] consider how to compute mediator restrictions given source restrictions. These four studies do not minimize a conjunctive query before checking its feasibility. Thus, they regard the query Q_2 in Example 2 as an unsolvable query. In [17] we study how to compute the maximal answer to a conjunctive query with binding patterns by borrowing bindings from relations not in the query, but the computed answer may not be the complete answer. As we saw in Section 5, we can sometimes use the approach in that paper to compute the complete answer to a nonstable conjunctive query. Levy [13] considers the problem of obtaining complete answers from incomplete databases, and the author does not consider relations with binding restrictions.

Acknowledgments. We thank Foto Afrati, Mayank Bawa, Rada Chirkova, and Jeff Ullman for their valuable comments on this material.

References

1. F. N. Afrati, M. Gergatsoulis, and T. G. Kavalieros. Answering queries using materialized views with disjunctions. In *ICDT*, pages 435–452, 1999.
2. C. Beeri and R. Ramakrishnan. On the power of magic. In *PODS*, pages 269–283, 1987.
3. D. Calvanese, G. D. Giacomo, M. Lenzerini, and M. Y. Vardi. Query answering using views for data integration over the Web. *WebDB*, pages 73–78, 1999.
4. A. K. Chandra and P. M. Merlin. Optimal implementation of conjunctive queries in relational data bases. *STOC*, pages 77–90, 1977.
5. S. Chaudhuri and M. Y. Vardi. On the equivalence of recursive and nonrecursive datalog programs. In *PODS*, pages 55–66, 1992.

6. S. S. Cosmadakis, H. Gaifman, P. C. Kanellakis, and M. Y. Vardi. Decidable optimization problems for database logic programs. *STOC*, pages 477–490, 1988.
7. O. M. Duschka. Query planning and optimization in information integration. *Ph.D. Thesis, Computer Science Dept., Stanford Univ.*, 1997.
8. O. M. Duschka and A. Y. Levy. Recursive plans for information gathering. In *IJCAI*, 1997.
9. D. Florescu, A. Levy, I. Manolescu, and D. Suciu. Query optimization in the presence of limited access patterns. In *SIGMOD*, pages 311–322, 1999.
10. H. Gaifman, H. G. Mairson, Y. Sagiv, and M. Y. Vardi. Undecidable optimization problems for database logic programs. *Journal of the ACM*, pages 683–713, 1993.
11. A. Gupta, Y. Sagiv, J. D. Ullman, and J. Widom. Constraint checking with partial information. In *PODS*, pages 45–55, 1994.
12. A. Klug. On conjunctive queries containing inequalities. *Journal of the ACM*, 35(1):146–160, January 1988.
13. A. Y. Levy. Obtaining complete answers from incomplete databases. In *Proc. of VLDB*, pages 402–412, 1996.
14. A. Y. Levy, A. O. Mendelzon, Y. Sagiv, and D. Srivastava. Answering queries using views. In *PODS*, pages 95–104, 1995.
15. C. Li. Computing complete answers to queries in the presence of limited access patterns (extended version). *Technical report, Computer Science Dept., Stanford Univ.*, http://dbpubs.stanford.edu:8090/pub/1999-11, 1999.
16. C. Li and E. Chang. Testing query containment in the presence of limited access patterns. *Technical report, Computer Science Dept., Stanford Univ.*, http://dbpubs.stanford.edu:8090/pub/1999-12, 1999.
17. C. Li and E. Chang. Query planning with limited source capabilities. In *ICDE*, pages 401–412, 2000.
18. C. Li, R. Yerneni, V. Vassalos, H. Garcia-Molina, Y. Papakonstantinou, J. D. Ullman, and M. Valiveti. Capability based mediation in TSIMMIS. In *SIGMOD*, pages 564–566, 1998.
19. T. Millstein, A. Levy, and M. Friedman. Query containment for data integration systems. In *PODS*, 2000.
20. T. Milo and S. Zohar. Using schema matching to simplify heterogeneous data translation. In *Proc. of VLDB*, pages 122–133, 1998.
21. A. Rajaraman, Y. Sagiv, and J. D. Ullman. Answering queries using templates with binding patterns. In *PODS*, pages 105–112, 1995.
22. Y. Sagiv and M. Yannakakis. Equivalences among relational expressions with the union and difference operators. *Journal of the ACM*, 27(4):633–655, 1980.
23. O. Shmueli. Equivalence of datalog queries is undecidable. *Journal of Logic Programming*, 15(3):231–241, 1993.
24. J. D. Ullman. *Principles of Database and Knowledge-base Systems, Volumes II: The New Technologies*. Computer Science Press, New York, 1989.
25. J. D. Ullman. Information integration using logical views. In *ICDT*, pages 19–40, 1997.
26. G. Wiederhold. Mediators in the architecture of future information systems. *IEEE Computer*, 25(3):38–49, 1992.
27. R. Yerneni, C. Li, H. Garcia-Molina, and J. D. Ullman. Computing capabilities of mediators. In *SIGMOD*, pages 443–454, 1999.
28. R. Yerneni, C. Li, J. D. Ullman, and H. Garcia-Molina. Optimizing large join queries in mediation systems. In *ICDT*, pages 348–364, 1999.
29. X. Zhang and M. Ozsoyoglu. On efficient reasoning with implication constraints. In *DOOD*, pages 236–252, 1993.

The Dynamic Complexity of Transitive Closure Is in DynTC^0

William Hesse

Department of Computer Science
University of Massachusetts
Amherst, MA 01002
whesse@cs.umass.edu

Abstract. This paper presents a fully dynamic algorithm for maintaining the transitive closure of a directed graph. All updates and queries can be computed by constant depth threshold circuits of polynomial size (TC^0 circuits). This places transitive closure in the dynamic complexity class DynTC^0, and implies that transitive closure can be maintained in databases using updates written in a first order query language plus counting operators, while keeping the size of the database polynomial in the size of the graph.

1 Introduction

Many restricted versions of transitive closure are known to be dynamically maintainable using first-order updates. In this paper we show that the transitive closure of a relation can be dynamically maintained using a polynomial-size data structure, with updates computable by constant depth threshold circuits. We show that updating the data structure upon adding or deleting an edge is in the circuit complexity class TC^0, described in Sect. 4. This means there is a first-order uniform family of constant depth threshold circuits, with size polynomial in the size of the graph, computing the new values of all the bits in the data structure[1].

Queries computed by TC^0 circuits are exactly those queries defined by first-order logic plus counting quantifiers, a class which contains those SQL queries in which no new domain elements are created [6]. Thus, our results show that the transitive closure of a relation can be maintained by ordinary SQL queries which use only polynomially sized auxiliary relations. The contents of these auxiliary relations are uniquely determined by the input relation, making this a memoryless algorithm; the state of the data structure does not depend on the order of the updates to the input relation.

This paper is organized as follows. In Sect. 3 dynamic complexity classes and the dynamic complexity of transitive closure are defined. In Sect. 4 circuit complexity classes including TC^0 are described. Sect. 5 presents the dynamic

---

[1] All complexity classes are assumed to be FO-uniform unless otherwise stated. This is discussed in Sect. 4

J. Van den Bussche and V. Vianu (Eds.): ICDT 2001, LNCS 1973, pp. 234–247, 2001.
© Springer-Verlag Berlin Heidelberg 2001

algorithm for transitive closure. Sects. 6 and 7 show that all operations in the dynamic algorithm are in the complexity class TC^0 and can be written as SQL update queries. Sects. 8 and 9 extend the algorithm to allow the addition of new elements to the relation's domain, and extend the algorithm to one dynamically maintaining the powers of an integer matrix. The final section offers some conclusions and directions for further work.

2 Previous Related Work

Patnaik and Immerman [9] introduced the complexity class DynFO (dynamic first-order) consisting of those dynamic problems such that each operation (insert, delete, change, or query) can be implemented as a first-order update to a relational data structure over a finite domain. This is similar to the definition of a first-order incremental evaluation system (FOIES) by Dong and Su [4]. Patnaik and Immerman showed that problems including undirected reachability and minimum spanning trees, whose static versions are not first-order, are nonetheless in DynFO. Dong and Su showed that acyclic reachability is in DynFO [4]. The question of whether transitive closure is in DynFO remains open; this paper proves that transitive closure is in the larger dynamic complexity class DynTC^0 (dynamic TC^0).

Libkin and Wong have previously shown that the transitive closure of a relation could be maintained using ordinary SQL updates while keeping a possibly exponential amount of auxiliary information[8][2]. Our dynamic complexity class DynTC^0 is less powerful than the class SQLIES (SQL incremental evaluation systems), that contains this algorithm. SQLIES captures all queries maintainable using SQL updates, which allow the creation of large numbers of new domain elements. DynTC^0 lacks the capability to introduce new constants, allowing as base type only a single finite domain, usually considered as the ordered integers from 1 to n, including arithmetic operations on that domain. Since dynamic computations in DynTC^0 use a constant number of relations of constant arity, they use an amount of auxiliary data polynomially bounded by the size of this domain. General SQL computations, by introducing new tuples with large integer constants as keys, can potentially square the size of the auxiliary databases at each iteration, leading to exponential or doubly exponential growth of the amount of auxiliary data kept.

A lower bound by Dong, Libkin, and Wong [3] shows that the transitive closure of a relation is not dynamically maintainable using first-order updates without auxiliary data. Our new upper bound is not strict; we still do not know if first-order updates using auxiliary data are sufficient to maintain transitive closure.

---

[2] Their algorithm creates a domain element for each path in the directed graph induced by the relation. This could be restricted to the set of simple paths, or paths of length less than the number of vertices, but it is still exponential for most graphs.

3   Problem Formulation

A binary relation induces a directed graph, by considering the domain of the relation as the vertices of a graph and the pair (s, t) as a directed edge from s to t in that graph. A tuple (s, t) is in the transitive closure of a binary relation if and only if there is a path from s to t in the corresponding graph. In the remainder of this paper, we think of a binary relation and its transitive closure in this context, allowing us to use the conventional graph-theoretic language of vertices, edges, paths, and reachability.

Computing the transitive closure of a relation is then equivalent to answering, for each pair of elements s and t, the decision problem REACH, which asks whether there is a path in the induced directed graph G from vertex s to vertex t. A dynamic algorithm maintaining the transitive closure of a relation consists of a set of auxiliary data structures and a set of update algorithms. These update the input relation, the auxiliary data structures, and the transitive closure of the input relation when a tuple is inserted into or deleted from the input relation. The complexity of this algorithm is the maximum complexity of any of these update algorithms.

We give an dynamic algorithm for the equivalent problem REACH. We define an auxiliary data structure, counting the number of paths between s and t of each length k less than a given bound, and give algorithms for updating and querying this data structure. The operations on this data structure are to add a directed edge between two vertices and to delete a directed edge between two vertices. We also specify an algorithm for querying the data structure, asking whether there is a directed path between two vertices. The update algorithms are given as circuits computing the new values for the data structure's bits, or computing the result of a query. The complexity of our algorithm is the circuit complexity class these circuits fall into. We will show that we can create a polynomial-size data structure with updates and queries computable by TC^0 circuits.

This places the problem REACH in the dynamic complexity class $DynTC^0$. In [9], the complexity class $Dyn\text{-}C$ is defined for any static complexity class C. A summary of this definition is that a query on a input structure is in $Dyn\text{-}C$ if there is some set of auxiliary data, of size polynomial in the size of the input structure, so that we can update the input structure and the auxiliary data with update queries in the complexity class C upon changes to the input structure. This additional data must allow us to answer the original query on the current state of the input structure with a query in complexity class C as well.

Remark 1. In specifying the operations for the dynamic version of REACH, we did not include operations to add or delete vertices. As this approach derives from finite model theory, we conceive of dynamic REACH as being a family of problems, parameterized by the number of graph vertices, n. We show in Sect. 8 that this algorithm can be modified to yield a SQLIES which allows addition and deletion of vertices (new domain elements) while keeping the size of the auxiliary relations polynomial in the size of the input relation. This modified problem can no longer be categorized as being in $DynTC^0$, however; it is no longer a dynamic problem of the type categorized by the dynamic complexity classes $Dyn\text{-}C$.

4 The Parallel Complexity Class TC^0

In static complexity theory, many natural low-level complexity classes have been parallel complexity classes, containing those problems which can be solved by idealized massively parallel computers in polylogarithmic or constant time. One model for these computations is as circuits made up of Boolean gates taking the values 1 and 0. A circuit is an acyclic directed graph whose vertices are the gates of the circuit and whose edges are the connections between gates. There is an input gate for each bit of the input, and a single output gate. Some of the most important parallel complexity classes are those defined by circuits with polynomial size and constant or logarithmic depth. The relations between these complexity classes are currently known to include the following inclusions:

$$AC^0 \subset ThC^0 \subseteq NC^1 \subseteq L \subseteq NL \subseteq AC^1 \subseteq ThC^1 \qquad (1)$$

The classes NC^1, AC^1, and ThC^1 are classes of logarithmic depth, polynomial-size circuits. All these circuits contain AND, OR, and NOT gates, but the class NC^1 contains only AND and OR gates with 2 inputs, while the class AC^1 contains AND and OR gates with arbitrarily many inputs, bounded only by the total number of gates in the circuit. The class ThC^1 contains threshold gates as well as AND and OR gates. The classes AC^0, and ThC^0 are the corresponding classes of constant depth circuits.

The circuit complexity class TC^0 contains all decision problems computed by a family of constant depth circuits containing AND, OR, and threshold gates, all with unbounded fan-in, as well as NOT gates. There is one circuit for each value of the input size, n, and there is a single constant and a single polynomial in n such that these circuits have a size (number of gates) bounded by that polynomial and depth bounded by that constant. The addition of threshold gates distinguishes these circuits from the circuit class AC^0, which contain only AND, OR, and NOT gates. A threshold gate accepts if more than a certain number of its inputs are true; it may have up to polynomially many inputs, and its threshold may be any number. Thus the majority function which is 1 iff more than half of its inputs are 1 is computed by a threshold gate with n inputs and threshold $\lfloor \frac{n}{2} \rfloor + 1$. Conversely, by adding enough dummy inputs, set to the constants 0 or 1, a majority gate can simulate a threshold gate with any threshold.

The importance of the classes AC^0 and ThC^0 to this paper is that first-order queries can be decided by AC^0 circuits, and that ThC^0 is the smallest important complexity class containing AC^0. It has been shown to strictly contain AC^0 because important problems including parity, majority, and integer multiplication have been shown to be computable by ThC^0 circuits but not by AC^0 circuits.

The classes L and NL denote deterministic and nondeterministic logspace computability by Turing machines. The class NL is relevant because the static version of REACH is a complete problem for this complexity class. This shows that the dynamic complexity of REACH is potentially significantly smaller than its static complexity. Finally, the class ThC^1 is important because the ThC^0

circuits we construct will be so complex that we will need to prove that they can be constructed by ThC^1 circuits, in order to eventually show that our algorithm can be implemented by SQL queries.

The complexity of constructing a circuit is called the uniformity of that circuit, and circuits whose pattern of connections can be specified by a first-order formula will be called FO-uniform. By this, we mean that, if our gates are numbered from 0 to $n - 1$, there a first-order formula $\phi(i, j)$ giving the edge relation which states whether the output of gate i is connected to an input of gate j. This formula must quantify only over variables taking values from 0 to $n-1$, and may use addition and multiplication operations and equality relations. Similar formulas must specify the type of each gate and which gates are inputs and the output from the circuit.

Repeated integer multiplication, which we require in our algorithm, is the most notorious example of a problem for which ThC^0 circuits are known, but no FO-uniform ThC^0 circuits are known. For the remainder of this paper, we will assume that all circuits are FO-uniform unless we state otherwise explicitly. For example, will say that a circuit is in ThC^1-uniform ThC^0, meaning that the circuit's description can be computed by a (FO-uniform) ThC^1 circuit.

The inclusions in (1) hold for the corresponding classes of FO-uniform circuits as well, and we have the additional property that FO-uniform $TC^0 = FO$, the class of decision problems definable with first-order formulas. If a family of TC^0 circuits is FO-uniform, the computation they perform can also be expressed by a first order formula with the addition of majority quantifiers, (Mx), specifying that for at least half of the distinct values for the variable bound by the quantifier, the following subformula is true [1]. We will show in Sect. 6, first that we can construct TC^1-uniform TC^0 circuits to implement our updates, then that they can be replaced by FO-uniform TC^0 circuits.

5   A Dynamic Algorithm for REACH

We describe our algorithm by specifying the data structures it maintains, then describing the updates necessary to maintain those data structures in a consistent state.

5.1   Data Structures

Our input structure is a directed graph on n vertices, identified with the numbers 0 to $n - 1$. It is represented by its adjacency matrix, an n by n array of bits $e_{i,j}$, where $e_{i,j}$ is 1 if there is a directed edge from i to j, 0 otherwise. The auxiliary information we will keep is the set of n^3 numbers $p_{i,j}(k)$, where $p_{i,j}(k)$ is the number of paths of length k from i to j in the graph. Note that $p_{i,i}(0) = 1$, $p_{i,j}(1) = e_{i,j}$, and that our paths are not necessarily simple paths; they may include cycles. Since the number of paths of length k from i to j is bounded by n^k, $p_{i,j}(k)$ is a number with at most $k \log n$ bits. We will only consider paths of length $n - 1$ or less. This is sufficient to decide our queries, since if two vertices are connected, they are connected by a path of length $n-1$ or less. Therefore, for $k < n$, $p_{i,j}(k) < n^n$. We will pack the values $p_{i,j}(k)$ for a fixed i and j and all k in $\{0, \ldots, n-1\}$ into an n^3 bit integer $a_{i,j}$:

$$a_{i,j} = \sum_{k=0}^{n-1} p_{i,j}(k) r^k, \tag{2}$$

where $r = 2^{n^2}$ is large enough so that in the binary representation of $a_{i,j}$, the bits of $p_{i,j}(k)$ and $p_{i,j}(k+1)$ are well separated by zeroes. Note that there is no computation involved in creating the $a_{i,j}$ from the values $p_{i,j}(k)$, $0 \le k < n$. We can regard the same array of bits as n numbers of n^2 bits or as one number with n^3 bits, depending on whether we want to reference the $p_{i,j}(k)$'s or $a_{i,j}$. We will also regard the integer $a_{i,j}$ as if it were a polynomial in r, in order to explain the proofs of the update computations more clearly. As the coefficients of this polynomial in r are small compared to r, there are no carries from one power of r to another, and thus the coefficients add and multiply as if we were multiplying polynomials. Since the coefficient of r^k in $a_{s,t}$ counts the number of paths with length k, it can be seen as a generating function counting the paths from s to t according to their weight. Since this polynomial is truncated after the nth term, it is a truncated generating function.

5.2 Adding an Edge

We now show how to calculate the updated value for $a_{s,t}$, upon adding an edge (i,j). We will see that the new value for $a_{s,t}$, which we denote $a'_{s,t}$, can be expressed as a polynomial in the previous values of $a_{s,t}, a_{s,i}, a_{j,i}$, and $a_{j,t}$.

Lemma 1. *We can calculate the new values of all $a_{s,t}$ after insertion of an edge (i,j) into our graph as follows:*

$$a'_{s,t} = a_{s,t} + \sum_{k=0}^{n-2} a_{s,i} r (r a_{j,i})^k a_{j,t} \mod r^n \tag{3}$$

Proof. We show that the sum over k in the above expression counts the paths going through the added edge, (i,j), one or more times, by showing that each term counts the number of paths using that edge exactly k times. For all $m < n$, the coefficient of r^m in $a_{s,i} r (r a_{j,i})^k a_{j,t}$ (regarded as a polynomial in r) is the number of paths of length m from s to t passing through edge (i,j) exactly $k+1$ times. Once we have shown this, then the expression $\sum_{k=0}^{n-2} a_{s,i} r (r a_{j,i})^k a_{j,t}$ can be seen to count all paths of length less than n passing through (i,j) any number of times. These counts appear as the coefficients of $r^0, \ldots r^{n-1}$, as in all our quantities $a_{s,t}$. This sum is thus the correct additive update to our counts $a_{s,t}$ upon adding the edge (i,j).

Each term counts the paths going through (i,j) k times by the standard combinatorial technique of multiplying generating functions. If polynomial P counts the elements of set A, with the coefficient of r^k counting the number of elements with weight k, and Q similarly counts the elements of set B, then the coefficient of r^k in PQ counts the numbers of pairs of one element from A with one element from B, with total weight k. Therefore, the term $a_{s,i}r(ra_{j,i})^k a_{j,t}$, as a product of $a_{s,i}$, r^{k+1}, $a_{j,i}^k$, and $a_{j,t}$, counts the number of ways of choosing a path from s to i, k paths from j to i, and a path from j to t, weighted by their total weight plus an additional weight of $k+1$. But these choices of a set of paths are in one-to-one correspondence with the unique decompositions of paths from s to t passing through edge (i,j) $k+1$ times into their $k+2$ subpaths separated by uses of the edge (i,j), as shown in Fig. 1. The total length of each path is the sum of the lengths of the subpaths, plus the additional $k+1$ uses of the edge (i,j). This one-to-one correspondence is only with the paths made up of subpaths of length less than n, but all paths of length less than n of course only contain subpaths of smaller lengths. Thus the coefficient of r^m in that term correctly counts the number of paths from s to t using edge (i,j) $k+1$ times.

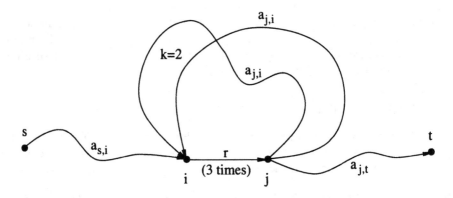

Fig. 1. the decomposition of a path passing through (i,j) $k+1$ times into $k+2$ subpaths

□

5.3 Deleting an Edge

We now show a corresponding formula which will calculate the number of paths which are removed when we delete an edge from the graph. We are given the values $a_{s,t}$ which count the number of paths from s to t, including those paths using edge (i,j) one or more times. We need to calculate the number of paths from s to t not using edge (i,j).

Lemma 2. *We can maintain the values of all $a_{s,t}$ upon deletion of an edge (i,j) by the formula*

$$a'_{s,t} = a_{s,t} - \sum_{k=0}^{n-2} a_{s,i}r(-1)^k(ra_{j,i})^k a_{j,t} \quad \mod r^n \qquad (4)$$

The values $a_{s,t}$ on the right hand side include in their counts paths using the edge (i,j) zero or more times.

Proof. We prove this by calculating the number of times a path from s to t which uses the edge (i,j) l times is counted by the term $a_{s,i}r(ra_{j,i})^k a_{j,t}$. It will turn out that a path using the edge $0 < l < n$ times will be counted $\binom{l}{k+1}$ times by the kth term.

The proof uses the same one-to-one correspondence between items counted by the above product of truncated generating functions and decompositions of paths using edge (i,j) into subpaths of length less than n. However, since the subpaths from s to i counted by $a_{s,i}$ may include uses of the edge (i,j), we no longer have a unique decomposition into subpaths.

A path which uses the edge (i,j) l times can be decomposed into $k+2$ subpaths separated by uses of the edge (i,j) in $\binom{l}{k+1}$ ways; just choose $k+1$ of the l uses. The remaining $l-k-1$ uses of the edge (i,j) are among the internal edges of the subpaths. Since these decompositions are in one-to-one correspondence with the items counted by the product $a_{s,i}r(ra_{j,i})^k a_{j,t}$, each such path is counted $\binom{l}{k+1}$ times.

The number of times each such path is counted in the sum

$$\sum_{k=0}^{n-2} a_{s,i}r(-1)^k(ra_{j,i})^k a_{j,t}$$

is

$$\sum_{k=0}^{n-2}(-1)^k\binom{l}{k+1} = 1 - 1 + \sum_{k=1}^{n-1}-(-1)^k\binom{l}{k} = 1 - \sum_{k=0}^{n-1}(-1)^k\binom{l}{k}$$

Since the alternating binomial sum $\sum_{k=0}^{n-1}(-1)^k\binom{l}{k}$ is always 0 for $0 < l < n$, we see that the sum shown above is equal to 1 for $0 < l < n$. By inspection, we see that paths not passing through (i,j) at all contribute nothing to this sum.

Since this implies that the coefficient of r^k in $\sum_{k=0}^{n-2} a_{s,i}r(-1)^k(ra_{j,i})^k a_{j,t}$ mod r^n is exactly the number of paths of length k from s to t using edge (i,j) at least once, this is exactly the correct quantity to subtract from $a_{s,t}$ to get the new value $a'_{s,t}$ counting only the paths from s to t that do not use (i,j). □

Remark 2. The formulas for updating $a_{s,t}$ upon deletion and addition of an edge can be verified by seeing that these updates are functional inverses of each other. By composing the polynomial updates for an insertion and a deletion, we verify that $a_{s,t}$ remains unchanged mod r^n when we insert and delete an edge.

The final operation we need to be able to do is to query whether s and t are connected by a directed path in our graph. But there is a path from s to t if and only if the value $a_{s,t}$ is non-zero. This can easily be checked by an FO formula, and thus by a TC^0 circuit.

6   Computing the Updates in TC^0

In this section, we first show that the updates can be computed in TC^1-uniform TC^0. Then we show how our dynamic algorithm can be modified to use only FO-uniform TC^0 circuits.

6.1   Computing the Updates Using a TC^1-Uniform TC^0 Circuit

The formula for updating the $a_{s,t}$ upon inserting an edge is

$$a'_{s,t} = a_{s,t} + \sum_{k=0}^{n-2} a_{s,i} r(r a_{j,i})^k a_{j,t} \quad \mod r^n. \tag{5}$$

The computational power of constant depth threshold circuits was investigated by Reif and Tate in [10]. They found that polynomials with size and degree bounded by $n^{O(1)}$ and with coefficients and variables bounded by $2^{n^{O(1)}}$ could be computed by polynomial-size constant depth threshold circuits (Corollary 3.4 in that paper). We cannot use the result of Reif and Tate about the evaluation of polynomials directly because they only state that there exist polynomial-time-uniform TC^0 circuits to evaluate them. We show here that this can be done by TC^1-uniform TC^0 circuits.

Evaluating this polynomial requires us to raise numbers of $O(n^3)$ bits to powers up to $n-2$, multiply the results by other numbers, add $n-1$ of the results together, and find the remainder mod r^n. Multiplying pairs of numbers and adding n numbers together can be done with TC^0 circuits [6]. If we have a number in binary, it is easy to find its remainder mod r^n by dropping all but the low order n^3 bits. To raise the number $r a_{j,i}$ to the kth power, we will need the following lemma:

Lemma 3. *Finding the $n^{O(1)}$th power of a number with $n^{O(1)}$ bits is in TC^1-uniform TC^0*

Proof. A corollary to the result of Beame, Cook, and Hoover[3] [2] shows that we can multiply n numbers with n bits each with a TC^0 circuit that is constructible in logspace from the product of the first n^2 primes [7]. The product of the first n^2 primes can be computed by a TC^1 circuit (a depth $O(\log n)$ binary tree of TC^0 circuits performing pairwise multiplications). The primes, all less than n^3, can be found by an FO formula. Since logspace is contained in TC^1, all of the operations required by our algorithm can be performed by a TC^1-uniform TC^0 circuit. Extension from the case of numbers with n bits raised to the nth power to numbers with $n^{O(1)}$ bits raised to the $n^{O(1)}$ power is trivial because the classes TC^1 and TC^0 are closed under polynomial expansion of the input.   □

---

[3] Beame, Cook, and Hoover show that n numbers can be multiplied by multiplying their remainders modulo all of the small primes with $O(\log n)$ bits. Then, knowing the remainder of the desired product modulo each of these small primes, the Chinese remainder theorem is used to find the desired product modulo the product of all the small primes

6.2 Computing a TC^1-Uniform TC^0 Circuit by an FO-Uniform TC^0 Circuit in the Dynamic Setting

Because a TC^1 circuit can be evaluated by $\log n$ rounds of a TC^0 circuit, we can compute this additional numerical data during the first $\log n$ rounds of our dynamic transitive closure algorithm. We simply add the circuit computing and storing this additional data to our existing TC^0 circuit for maintaining transitive closure. We need to add a third component to ensure that our algorithm computes transitive closure correctly during the first $\log n$ rounds, while the table of numerical data has not yet been computed. If we consider that $\log n$ rounds of updates can only add $\log n$ tuples to an initially empty relation, we see that this can be a first-order formula that finds the transitive closure of our $\log n$ size relation by brute force. We maintain a correspondence between those vertices with non-zero degree in our graph and the numbers between 1 and $2 \log n$. Then, to find out if two vertices are connected, we try (in parallel) all n^2 possible subsets of $\{1, \ldots, 2 \log n\}$ to see if they correspond to the vertices forming a path between the two vertices. It is easy to verify that a set of vertices forms a path between two given vertices, possibly with additional disconnected cycles. We simply check that all vertices have degree 2 in the induced subgraph except for the two ends of the path.

Thus we can add this first-order algorithm to our TC^0 circuit to create a circuit that correctly maintains the transitive closure of an initially empty relation, while computing the numerical data necessary for our full algorithm. The counts that our algorithm maintains of the number of paths between vertices have not yet been computed, however. To compute these, use the following $\log n$ rounds of computation to simulate 2 updates per round, catching up to the correct values of our counts after these $\log n$ rounds. Our first-order algorithm can easily be extended to work on graphs with up to $2 \log n$ edges.

Remark 3. This complex sequence of bootstrapping, computing some necessary numerical data during the first $\log n$ rounds of computation, threatens the memoryless nature of our algorithm. To ensure that all of our auxiliary data is completely determined by the state of the input relation, we must perform these rounds of bootstrapping under the control not of the clock, during the first $\log n$ rounds of computation, but under the control of the number of edges in our graph. When an update adds an edge to our graph, we compute another round in our emulation of the TC^1 circuit computing our numerical data, remembering the results of all previous rounds. When an update deletes an edge from our graph, we delete the results of the last round of numerical computation. Similarly, we emulate the second $\log n$ rounds, where 2 updates are performed on every round, during all updates where the graph has between $\log n$ and $2 \log n$ edges, performing updates so that the numerically first $2i - 2 \log n$ out of i edges are correctly represented in the counts. Thus, even the uniform TC^0 circuit maintaining the transitive closure of a relation can be made memoryless.

Because we have shown that there are uniform TC^0 circuits maintaining the transitive closure of a relation, starting with an empty relation and no precomputed data, we have our main result:

Theorem 1. *Transitive Closure* $\in DynTC^0$

7   DynTC^0 in SQL

The fact that a DynTC^0 algorithm can be implemented as a incremental database algorithm with update queries expressed in SQL, using polynomial space, follows as a corollary from the fact that safe TC^0 queries can be written as SQL expressions. Theorem 5.27 in [6] states, in part,

$$TC^0 = FO(COUNT),$$

and Theorem 14.9 states that the queries computable in SQL are exactly the safe queries in Q(FO(COUNT)).

Unfortunately, our TC^0 circuits do not correspond to safe queries. Our circuits include negation, which can only be implemented in general in SQL if we have a full relation to subtract from, leaving a tuple in the result if and only if it is not in the input. But asserting the existence of a unary relation containing the numbers from 1 to n is a negligible amount of precomputation to expect. If we extend our algorithm to allow a dynamically varying number of vertices, we can certainly add the number n to this base relation at the same time as we add the nth vertex to our set of vertices.

8   Adding and Deleting Vertices

The fact that we have a polynomial bound on the amount of auxiliary data is closely bound to our having a fixed bound n on the number of vertices of the graph. If we do not have a fixed bound n, we can still use our algorithm as a polynomial space SQLIES algorithm. We can run an instance of the algorithm using some initial bound n until the number of vertices approaches within $2 \log n$ of this bound. Then we initialize a new instance of the algorithm with bound $2n$, and are ready to start using it by the time we add the $n + 1$st vertex. After computing the auxiliary data used by this larger instance, we can copy the counts $p_{i,j}(k)$ encoded in the integers $a_{i,j}$ into the new larger copies of the integers $a_{i,j}$. Since these are stored in binary, we just copy the counts to the right positions in the new integers, leaving larger gaps. We must then also calculate the values $p_{i,j}(k)$ for values of k between n and $2n$. These are the counts of paths with lengths between n and $2n$. But as each path of length i, $n \leq i < 2n - 1$, has a unique decomposition into a path of length $n - 1$ and a path of length $i - n + 1$, we can find these values from the sum

$$\sum_{h=0}^{n-1} p_{i,h}(n-1)a_{h,j}.$$

The count of paths of length $2n - 1$ can be found by repeating this process. These are all TC^0 computations, so they can be done in a single step.

A final note is that the algorithm as stated does not allow us to delete a vertex with all of its associated edges in one step. However, an update polynomial even simpler than the update for deleting a single edge can be found, and is as follows:

$$a'_{s,t} = a_{s,t} - \sum_{k=0}^{n-2} a_{s,i}(-1)^k (a_{i,i})^k a_{i,t} \mod r^n \tag{6}$$

9   Integer Matrix Powering

The problem of directed reachability in a graph may be reduced to the problem of finding the entries of the nth power of the adjacency matrix of the graph. Our algorithm is based on this reduction, and the core algorithm can be modified to maintain dynamically the first $n^{O(1)}$ powers of an n by n integer matrix with entries of size $n^{O(1)}$. Our algorithm can be seen upon inspection to handle correctly the addition of self-loops and multiple edges to our graph, so it correctly handles adjacency matrices with non-zero diagonal and entries other than 1. In our algorithm, we picked our constant $r = 2^{n^2}$ sufficient to separate the values which would be the entries of the kth power of the adjacency matrix. For arbitrary matrices, we need to pick a larger r with polynomially many bits, sufficient to keep the entries separated. This dynamic algorithm will then compute arbitrary changes of a single matrix entry, and queries on the value of any entry of any of the computed powers of the matrix.

Note that the dynamic complexity of the multiplication of n different n by n matrices is seen to be in DynTC^0 without this result, since only one entry of one of the matrices can be changed at a time, causing a linear update of the product. The dynamic complexity of the power of an integer matrix is greater than or equal to that of iterated multiplication, and it is this complexity which we have shown to be in DynTC^0.

10   Conclusions

A major consequence of Theorem 1, Transitive Closure $\in$ DynTC^0, is that transitive closure can be maintained using SQL update queries while keeping the size of the auxiliary relations polynomial in the size of the input relation. As transitive closure has been used as the prime example of a database query not expressible in query languages without recursion, non-recursive algorithms for maintaining transitive closure are of significant interest. Our result reduces the space required by a non-recursive algorithm from exponential in the size of the input relation to polynomial in the size of the input relation.

This new algorithm does not, however, lessen the importance of finding efficient sequential algorithms for maintaining transitive closure in databases. The dynamic algorithm given here is unlikely to be usefully implemented in practice, because its work complexity is greater than the best sequential dynamic algorithms. For example, the transitive closure of a symmetric relation (i.e. undirected graph reachability) can be maintained by sequential algorithms with polylogarithmic time amortized time per operation [5].

Though this algorithm may not be practically useful in contexts where total work is the crucial constraint, it is an important upper bound for the following reason. Parallel complexity classes, using constant or logarithmic time, and polynomial work, have been seen to be the natural complexity classes smaller than P in the study of static complexity. They are robust under changes in encoding, and have natural connections to descriptive complexity classes. If dynamic complexity classes are similar to static complexity classes, then discovering what dynamic problems are in DynFO, DynTC^0, and other similar classes may be important. Since the dynamic complexity of problems is often less than the static complexity, the lower complexity classes may be even more important than in static complexity. This new upper bound for the dynamic complexity of directed reachability helps us to understand the landscape of dynamic complexity better. We now know that all special cases of reachability can be placed in dynamic complexity classes below or equal to DynTC^0.

There are open questions related to this paper in many directions. It is, of course, still an open question whether REACH is in DynFO. Many other restricted subclasses of graph reachability have not yet been investigated. We suspect that directed grid graph reachability and plane graph (planar graphs with a fixed embedding) reachability are in DynFO. There may be problems that are complete for these dynamic complexity classes, and logics that express exactly the class of queries with dynamic algorithms in some dynamic complexity class. The largest unknown, however, remains whether dynamic complexity classes exist that are as robust as the familiar static complexity classes, and whether they are orthogonal to or comparable to these static complexity classes.

References

1. Barrington, Immerman, and Straubing. On uniformity within NC^1. In *SCT: Annual Conference on Structure in Complexity Theory*, 1988.
2. Paul W. Beame, Stephen A. Cook, and H. James Hoover. Log depth circuits for division and related problems. *SIAM Journal on Computing*, 15(4):994–1003, 1986.
3. G. Dong, L. Libkin, and L. Wong. On impossibility of decremental recomputation of recursive queries in relational calculus and SQL. In *International Workshop on Database Programming Languages*, 1995.
4. Guozhu Dong and Jianwen Su. Incremental and decremental evaluation of transitive closure by first-order queries. *Information and Computation*, 120(1):101–106, July 1995.
5. Jacob Holm, Kristian de Lichtenberg, and Mikkel Thorup. Poly-logarithmic deterministic fully-dynamic algorithms for connectivity, minimum spanning tree, 2-edge and biconnectivity. In *Proceedings of the 30th Annual ACM Symposium on Theory of Computing (STOC-98)*, pages 79–89, New York, May 23–26 1998. ACM Press.
6. Neil Immerman. *Descriptive Complexity*. Springer-Verlag, New York, 1999.
7. Neil Immerman and Susan Landau. The complexity of iterated multiplication. *Information and Computation*, 116(1):103–116, January 1995.

8. Leonid Libkin and Limsoon Wong. Incremental recomputation of recursive queries with nested sets and aggregate functions. In *Proc. of Database Programming Languages (DBPL'97)*, pages 222–238, Estes Park, CO, 1998. Springer-Verlag, Lecture Notes in Computer Science 1369.
9. Sushant Patnaik and Neil Immerman. Dyn-FO: A parallel, dynamic complexity class. *Journal of Computer and System Sciences*, 55(2):199–209, October 1997.
10. John H. Reif and Stephen R. Tate. On threshold circuits and polynomial computation. *SIAM Journal on Computing*, 21(5):896–908, October 1992.

Query Languages for Constraint Databases: First-Order Logic, Fixed-Points, and Convex Hulls

Stephan Kreutzer

Lehrgebiet Mathematische Grundlagen der Informatik,
RWTH Aachen, D-52056 Aachen,
kreutzer@informatik.rwth-aachen.de

Abstract. We define various extensions of first-order logic on linear as well as polynomial constraint databases. First, we extend first-order logic by a convex closure operator and show this logic, *FO(conv)*, to be closed and to have PTIME data-complexity. We also show that a weak form of multiplication is definable in this language and prove the equivalence between this language and the multiplication part of PFOL. We then extend *FO(conv)* by fixed-point operators to get a query languages expressive enough to capture PTIME. In the last part of the paper we lift the results to polynomial constraint databases.

1 Introduction

In recent years new application areas have reached the limits of the standard relational database model. Especially, geographical information systems, which are of growing importance, exceed the power of the relational model with their need to store geometrical figures, naturally viewed as infinite sets of points. Therefore, new database models have been proposed to handle these needs. One such data model is the framework of constraint databases introduced by Kanellakis, Kuper, and Revesz in 1990 [KKR90]. Essentially, constraint databases are relational databases capable of storing arbitrary elementary sets. These sets are not stored tuple-wise but by an elementary formula defining them. We give a precise definition of the constraint database model in Section 2. See [KLP00] for a detailed study of constraint databases.

When applied to spatial databases, one usually considers either databases storing semi-algebraic sets, called *polynomial constraint databases*, or semi-linear sets, known as *linear constraint databases*. Polynomial constraint databases allow the storage of spatial information in a natural way. The interest in the linear model results from the rather high (practical) complexity of query evaluation on polynomial databases. Essentially, the evaluation of first-order queries in the polynomial model consists of quantifier-elimination in the theory of ordered real fields, for which a non-deterministic exponential-time lower bound has been proven. On the other hand, query evaluation on linear constraint databases can be

J. Van den Bussche and V. Vianu (Eds.): ICDT 2001, LNCS 1973, pp. 248–262, 2001.

done efficiently. But first-order logic on these databases yields a query language with rather poor expressive power.

It is known that first-order logic lacks the power to define queries relying on recursion. A prominent example is connectivity which is not expressible in FO on almost all interesting classes of structures. This lack of expressive power shows up on polynomial as well as linear constraint databases. In finite model theory, a standard method to solve this problem is to consider least fixed-point logic, an extension of FO by a least fixed-point operator (see [EF95].) Although this logic has successfully been used in the context of dense-order constraint databases (see [KKR90,GS97,GK99]), it is not suitable for the linear database model, as it is neither closed nor decidable on this class of databases (see [KPSV96].) Logics extending FO by fixed-point constructs can be found in [GK97] and [GK00]. Decidability and closure of these languages was achieved by including some kind of stop condition for the fixed-point induction. In [Kre00], this problem has also been attacked resulting in a language extending FO by fixed-points over a finite set of regions in the input database.

Besides queries based on recursion there are also other important queries that are not first-order definable. In the context of linear databases a very important example of a query not expressible in FO is the convex closure query. We address this problem in Section 3. Unfortunately, any extension of FO by operators capable of defining convex hulls for arbitrary sets leads to a non-closed language. Therefore, we can only hope to extend FO consistently by a restricted convex hull operator. In this paper we add an operator to compute convex hulls of finite sets only. We show that this can be done in a consistent way, resulting in a language that is closed and has PTIME data-complexity. It is also shown that this language and PFOL, an extension of FO by restricted multiplication defined by Vandeurzen, Gyssens, and Van Gucht [VGG98], have the same expressive power.

As mentioned above, a language extending FO by recursion mechanisms has been defined in [Kre00]. Although this language turns out to be rather expressive for boolean queries, it lacks the power to define broad classes of non-boolean queries. In Section 4 we present two alternative approaches to define fixed-point logics on linear constraint databases. The first approach extends the logic defined in [Kre00] by the convex closure operator mentioned above, whereas the second approach combines convex closure with fixed-point induction over finite sets. It is shown that both approaches lead to query languages capturing PTIME on linear constraint databases.

In Section 5 we address the problem whether these results extend to the class of polynomial constraint databases. Clearly, extending first-order logic by a convex closure operator does not make sense, since convex closure is already definable in FO+POLY, that is, first-order logic on polynomial constraint databases. But it will be shown that the extension by fixed-point constructs can be suitably adapted to the polynomial setting, resulting in a language strictly more expressive than FO+POLY.

2   Preliminaries

Constraint databases. We first give a precise definition of the constraint database model. See [KLP00] for a detailed introduction. The basic idea in the definition of constraint databases is to allow infinite relations which have a finite presentation by a quantifier-free formula. Let $\mathfrak{A}$ be a τ-structure, called the *context structure*, and $\varphi(x_1, \ldots, x_n)$ be a quantifier-free formula of vocabulary τ. We say that a n-ary relation $R \subseteq A^n$ is *represented by* $\varphi(x_1, \ldots, x_n)$ *over* $\mathfrak{A}$ iff R equals $\{\bar{a} \in A^n : \mathfrak{A} \models \varphi[\bar{a}]\}$. Let $\sigma := \{R_1, \ldots, R_k\}$ be a relational signature. A σ-constraint database over the context structure $\mathfrak{A}$ is a σ-expansion $\mathfrak{B} := (\mathfrak{A}, R_1, \ldots, R_k)$ of $\mathfrak{A}$ where all R_i are finitely represented by formulae φ_{R_i} over $\mathfrak{A}$. The set $\Phi := \{\varphi_{R_1}, \ldots, \varphi_{R_k}\}$ is called a *finite representation* of $\mathfrak{B}$.

To measure the complexity of algorithms taking constraint databases as inputs we have to define the size of a constraint database. Unlike finite databases, the size of constraint databases cannot be given in terms of the number of elements stored in them but has to be based on a representation of the database. Note that equivalent representations of a database need not be of the same size. Thus, the size of a constraint database depends on a particular representation. In the following, whenever we speak of a constraint database $\mathfrak{B}$, we have a particular representation Φ of $\mathfrak{B}$ in mind. The size $|\mathfrak{B}|$ of $\mathfrak{B}$ is then defined as the sum of the length of the formulae in Φ. This corresponds to the standard encoding of constraint databases by the formulae of their representation.

Constraint queries. Fix a context structure $\mathfrak{A}$. A constraint query is a mapping Q from constraint databases over $\mathfrak{A}$ to finitely representable relations over $\mathfrak{A}$. Note that queries are abstract, i.e., they depend only on the database not on their representation. That is, any algorithm that computes Q, taking a representation Φ of a database $\mathfrak{B}$ as input and producing a representation of $Q(\mathfrak{B})$ as output, has to compute on two equivalent representations Φ and Φ' output formulae that are not necessarily the same, but represent the same relation on $\mathfrak{A}$.

In the sequel we are particularly interested in queries defined by formulae of a given logic $\mathcal{L}$. Let $\varphi \in \mathcal{L}$ be a formula with k free variables. Then φ defines the query Q_φ mapping a constraint database $\mathfrak{B}$ over $\mathfrak{A}$ to the set $\varphi^{\mathfrak{B}} := \{(a_1, \ldots, a_k) : \mathfrak{B} \models \varphi[\bar{a}]\}$. In order for Q_φ to be well defined, this set must be representable by a quantifier-free formula. If φ is first-order, this means that $\mathfrak{A}$ admits quantifier elimination. For more powerful logics than first-order logic the additional operators must be eliminated as well. A logic $\mathcal{L}$ is *closed* for a class $\mathcal{C}$ of constraint databases over $\mathfrak{A}$, if for every $\varphi \in \mathcal{L}$ and every $\mathfrak{B} \in \mathcal{C}$ the set $\varphi^{\mathfrak{B}}$ can be defined by a quantifier-free first-order formula over $\mathfrak{A}$.

Typical questions that arise when dealing with constraint query languages are the complexity of query evaluation for a certain constraint query language and the definability of a query in a given language. For a fixed query formula $\varphi \in \mathcal{L}$, the *data-complexity* of the query Q_φ is defined as the amount of resources (e.g. time, space, or number of processors) needed to evaluate the function that takes a representation Φ of a database $\mathfrak{B}$ to a representation of the answer relation $Q_\varphi(\mathfrak{B})$.

3   First-Order Logic and Convex Hulls

In this section we define an extension of first-order logic on semi-linear databases such that with each definable finite set of points also its convex hull becomes definable. Defining convex hulls is a very important concept when dealing with semi-linear databases but first-order logic itself is not powerful enough to define it. Thus, adding an operator allowing the definition of convex hulls results in a language strictly more expressive than FO. Note that allowing to define the convex closure of arbitrary point sets yields a non-closed query language, since multiplication - and thus sets which are not semi-linear - becomes definable. We therefore allow the definition of convex hulls for finite sets of points only.

Proviso. In the rest of this paper, whenever we speak about the interior of a set or a set being open, we always mean "interior" or "open" with respect to the set's affine support.

Definition 1 *Let $\bar{x}_i, \bar{x}'_i, \bar{y}$ denote sequences of l variables each and $\bar{z}$ denote a sequence of variables, such that all variables are distinct. The logic FO(conv) is defined as the extension of first-order logic by the following two rules:*

  (i) *If $\varphi \in$ FO(conv) is a formula with free variables $\{\bar{x}_1, \ldots, \bar{x}_k, \bar{z}\}$ then $\psi :=$ $[\text{conv}_{\bar{x}_1, \ldots, \bar{x}_k} \varphi](\bar{y}, \bar{z})$ is also a formula, with free variables $\{\bar{y}, \bar{z}\}$.*
  (ii) *If $\varphi \in$ FO(conv) is a formula with free variables $\{\bar{x}_1, \bar{x}'_1, \ldots, \bar{x}_k, \bar{x}'_k, \bar{z}\}$ then $\psi := [\text{uconv}_{\bar{x}_1, \bar{x}'_1, \ldots, \bar{x}_k, \bar{x}'_k} \varphi](\bar{y}, \bar{z})$ is also a formula, with free variables $\{\bar{y}, \bar{z}\}$.*

The semantics of the additional operators is defined as follows. Let $\mathfrak{B}$ be the input database and ψ and φ be as in Part (i) of the definition above. Let $\varphi^{\mathfrak{B}}$ be the result of evaluating the formula φ in $\mathfrak{B}$. If $\varphi^{\mathfrak{B}}$ is infinite, then $\psi^{\mathfrak{B}} := \varnothing$. Otherwise, $\psi^{\mathfrak{B}} := \{(\bar{a}, \bar{b}) : \bar{a} \in \bigcup \{\text{conv}\{\bar{a}_1, \ldots, \bar{a}_k\} : \mathfrak{B} \models \varphi[\bar{a}_1, \ldots, \bar{a}_k, \bar{b}]\}\}$, where $\text{conv}\{\bar{a}_1, \ldots, \bar{a}_k\}$ denotes the interior (with respect to the affine support) of the convex closure of $\{\bar{a}_1, \ldots, \bar{a}_k\}$.

The semantics of the uconv operator is defined similarly. The motivation for the uconv operator is, that every set defined by the conv operator is bounded. To overcome this restriction, the uconv operator is designed to handle "points at infinity". Let φ and ψ be as indicated in Part (ii) of the definition above and let $\mathfrak{B}$ be the input database. Again, if $\varphi^{\mathfrak{B}}$ is infinite, then $\psi^{\mathfrak{B}} := \varnothing$. Otherwise, $\varphi^{\mathfrak{B}} := \{(\bar{a}, \bar{b}) : \text{there are } \bar{a}_1, \bar{a}'_1, \ldots, \bar{a}_k, \bar{a}'_k \text{ such that } \mathfrak{B} \models \varphi[\bar{a}_1, \bar{a}'_1, \ldots, \bar{a}_k, \bar{a}'_k, \bar{b}] \text{ and } \bar{a} \in \text{conv}(\bigcup_{i=1}^{k} line(\bar{a}_i, \bar{a}'_i))\}$, where $line(\bar{a}_i, \bar{a}'_i) := \{\bar{x} : (\exists b \in \mathbb{R}^{\geq 0}) \text{ such that } \bar{x} = \bar{a}_i + b(\bar{a}'_i - \bar{a}_i)\}$ defines the half line with origin $\bar{a}_i$ going through $\bar{a}'_i$.

Intuitively, each pair $(\bar{a}_i, \bar{a}'_i)$ represents two points, the point $\bar{a}_i$ and the point "reached" when starting at $\bar{a}_i$ and going in the direction of $\bar{a}'_i$ to infinite distance. Now uconv returns the union of the open convex closure (with respect to its affine support) of the $2k$ points represented by each tuple $((\bar{a}_{i,1}, \bar{a}'_{i,1}), \ldots, (\bar{a}_{i,k}, \bar{a}'_{i,k}))$.

Note that the condition on the formula φ to define a finite set is purely semantical. Since finiteness of a semi-linear set is first-order definable - consider, for example, the formula *finite*(φ) stating that there are $\epsilon, \delta > 0$ such that the Manhattan-distance between any two points in $\varphi^{\mathfrak{B}}$ is greater than ϵ and each point in $\varphi^{\mathfrak{B}}$ is contained in a hypercube of edge length δ - this condition can also be ensured on a syntactic level, thus giving the language an effective syntax.

We now give an example of a query definable in *FO(conv)*.

Example 2 *Let $\varphi(x)$ be a formula defining a finite set. The query*

$$mult_\varphi(x, y, z) := \{(a, b, c) \ : \ a \text{ satisfies } \varphi \text{ and } a \cdot b = c\}$$

is definable in FO(conv). We give a formula for the case $x, y, z \geq 0$. Let $\bar{x}_1 = (x_{1,1}, x_{1,2})$ and $\bar{x}_2 := (x_{2,1}, x_{2,2})$ be pairs of variables and $\psi(\bar{x}_1, \bar{x}_2; x) := \bar{x}_1 = (0, 0) \wedge \bar{x}_2 = (1, x)$ be a formula defining for each x the two points $(0, 0)$ and $(1, x)$ in $\mathbb{R}^2$. Then the formula

$$\psi(x, y, z) := [\text{uconv}_{\bar{x}_1, \bar{x}_2} \varphi(x) \wedge \psi(\bar{x}_1, \bar{x}_2, x)](y, z; x)$$

defines the query $mult_\varphi$. The uconv operator defines - for the parameter x - the half line with origin $(0, 0)$ and slope x. Thus the point (y, z) is on this line iff $x \cdot y = z$.

Theorem 3 *FO(conv) is closed and has* PTIME *data-complexity.*

The closure of the conv-operator follows from the finiteness of the sets, of which the convex closure is computed. PTIME data-complexity can easily be shown by induction on the structure of the queries.

We now compare the language to other extensions of FO for linear databases. Especially, we will show that *FO(conv)* and the language PFOL as defined by Vandeurzen et. al. [VGG98] have the same expressive power. We briefly recall the definition of PFOL (see [VGG98] and [Van99] for details.)

There are two different kinds of variables in PFOL, *real variables* and so-called *product variables*. A PFOL program consists of a sequence of formulae $(\varphi_1(x), \ldots, \varphi_k(x); \varphi(\bar{x}))$. Each φ_i is required to define a finite set $D_i \subset \mathbb{R}$. The formulae are allowed to use multiplication between variables $x \cdot p$, but at least p must be a product variable. All product variables must be bound at some point by a quantifier of the following form. In φ_i the quantifiers for the product variables are of the form $\exists p \in D_j$, where $j < i$. In φ all D_i may be used. Thus, essentially, the formulae φ_i define successively a sequence of finite sets and then at least one factor of each multiplication is restricted to one of these sets. In the original definition of PFOL there were also terms $t = \sqrt{|p|}$. We don't take this term building rule into account and allow only multiplication. We believe this to be the essential and important part of the language. But note that the square root operator strictly increases the expressive power of the language. Therefore we call the language considered here *restricted PFOL*.

It is known that convex closure can be defined in restricted PFOL. In Example 2 we already saw that multiplication with one factor bounded by a finite set can be defined in *FO(conv)*. Thus, the proof of the following theorem is straightforward.

Theorem 4 *Restricted PFOL = FO(conv).*

Note 5 *As the previous theorem shows, we can express atoms of the form $x \cdot_\varphi y = z$ in FO(conv), with the semantics being that $xy = z$ and $\varphi(x)$ holds, where φ is required to define a finite set. From now on, we allow atoms of this form in FO(conv)-formulae.*

The previous theorem implies that the bounds on expressiveness proven for PFOL carry over to *FO(conv)*. Here we mention one result which will be of special importance in Section 4.2.

It has been shown in [Van99] that there is a PFOL query which returns on a semi-linear set $S \subset \mathbb{R}^n$ a finite relation $S^{\text{enc}} \subseteq \mathbb{R}^{n(n+1)}$ of $(n + 1)$-tuples of points in $\mathbb{R}^n$, such that $S = \bigcup_{(\bar{a}_1,\ldots,\bar{a}_{n+1}) \in S^{\text{enc}}} \text{conv}(\bar{a}_1, \ldots, \bar{a}_{n+1})$. Thus, PFOL can compute a canonical finite representation of the input database and recover the original input from it. This will be used below to define a fixed-point query language capturing PTIME.

4   Query Languages Combining Convex Hulls and Recursion

In this section we present two approaches to combine the query language defined above with fixed-point constructs.

4.1   The Logic *RegLFP(conv)*

Let $S \subseteq \mathbb{R}^d$ be a semi-linear set. An arrangement of S is a partition of $\mathbb{R}^d$ into finitely many disjoint regions, i.e., connected subsets of $\mathbb{R}^d$, such that for each region R either $R \cap S = \varnothing$ or $R \subseteq S$. It is known that for a fixed dimension arrangements of semi-linear sets can be computed in polynomial time. See e.g. [Ede87] or [GO97] for details.

It follows from the definition that the input relation S can be written as a finite union of regions in its arrangement. In this section we consider a query language which has access to the set of regions in such an arrangement of the input database. This gives the logic access to the representation of the database increasing, thus, its expressive power. Precisely, we consider a fixed-point logic where the fixed-point induction is defined over the finite set of regions. The semantics of the logic is defined in terms of certain two-sorted structures, called *region extensions* of linear constraint databases. Let $\mathfrak{B} := ((\mathbb{R}, <, +), S)$ be a database and let $\mathcal{A}(S)$ be the set of regions in an arrangement of S. The logic then has separate variables and quantifiers for the reals and the set of regions.

We now give the precise definitions.

Definition 6 *Let $\mathfrak{B} := ((\mathbb{R}, <, +), S)$ be a linear constraint database, where S is a d-ary relation, and let $\mathcal{A}(S)$ be the set of regions of an arrangement of S. The structure $\mathfrak{B}$ gives rise to a two-sorted structure $\mathfrak{B}^{Reg} := ((\mathbb{R}, <, +), S; Reg, adj),$*

called the region extension of $\mathfrak{B}$, *with sorts* $\mathbb{R}$ *and* $Reg := A(S)$ *and the adjacency relation* $adj \subseteq Reg \times Reg$, *where two regions are adjacent if there is a point p in one of them such that every ε-neighbourhood of p has a non-empty intersection with the other region.*

The dimension of a region is defined as the dimension of its affine support, i.e., the dimension of the smallest affine subspace it is contained in. It is known that the number of regions in the arrangement is bounded polynomially in the size of the representation of S. As arrangements can be computed in polynomial time, one can compute the region extension of a given database in polynomial time as well.

We now define the logic *RegLFP(conv)* which is *FO(conv)* extended by a least fixed-point operator on the set of regions in the region extensions. In the definition of the logic we deal with three types of variables, so-called *element-*, *region-*, and *relation variables*. Element variables will be interpreted by real numbers, region variables by regions in the region extension of the database. Each relation variable is equipped with a pair $(k, l) \in \mathbb{N}^2$ of arities. Relation variables of arity (k, l) are interpreted by subsets $M \subseteq Reg^k \times \mathbb{R}^l$, such that for each $\bar{R} \in Reg^k$ the set $\{\bar{x} \ : \ (\bar{R}, \bar{x}) \in M\}$ is finitely representable.

Definition 7 *The logic RegLFP(conv) is defined as extension of FO(conv) on region extensions by a least fixed-point operator. Precisely, the logic extends FO(conv) by the following rules.*

- *If R is a region variable and $\bar{x}$ is a sequence of element variables, then $R\bar{x}$ is a formula.*
- *If φ is a formula and R a region variable, then $\exists R\varphi$ is also a formula.*
- *If M is a relation variable of arity (k, l), $\bar{R} := R_1, \ldots, R_k$ is a sequence of region variables, and $\bar{x} := x_1, \ldots, x_l$ is a sequence of element variables, then $M\bar{R}\bar{x}$ is a formula.*
- *If $\varphi(M, \bar{R}, \bar{x})$ is a formula with free element variables $\bar{x}$, free region variables $\bar{R} := R_1, \ldots, R_k$, and a free (k, l)-ary relation variable M, such that M occurs only positively in φ, then $[\text{tLFP}_{M, \bar{R}, \bar{x}}\varphi](\bar{R}, \bar{x})$ is a formula.*
- *If $\varphi(x)$ is a formula and x, y, z are element variables, then $x \cdot_\varphi y = z$ is a formula.*

RegLFP(conv)-queries are defined by RegLFP(conv)-formulae without free region or relation variables.

The semantics of the new rules is defined as follows. An atom $R\bar{x}$ states that the point $\bar{x}$ is contained in the region R; an atom $M\bar{R}\bar{x}$ states that the tuple $(\bar{R}, \bar{x})$ is contained in M; a formula $\exists R\varphi$ states that there is a region $R \in Reg$ satisfying φ. The semantics of conv, uconv, and $\cdot_\varphi$ is defined as in the previous section.

Let M be a (k, l)-ary relation variable, $\bar{R} := R_1, \ldots, R_k$ be a sequence of region variables, $\bar{x} := x_1, \ldots, x_l$ be a sequence of element variables, and $\varphi(M, \bar{R}, \bar{x})$ be a formula positive in M. The result of the formula $\psi := [\text{tLFP}_{M, \bar{R}, \bar{x}}\varphi](\bar{R}, \bar{x})$

evaluated in a database $\mathfrak{B}$ is defined as the least fixed-point of the function f_φ defined as

$$f_\varphi : \mathrm{Pow}(Reg^k \times \mathbb{R}^l) \longrightarrow \mathrm{Pow}(Reg^k \times \mathbb{R}^l)$$
$$M \longmapsto \{(\bar{R}, \bar{a}) \in Reg^k \times \mathbb{R}^l \; : \; (\exists \bar{y}\,(\bar{R}, \bar{y}) \in M \wedge (\bar{R}, \bar{a}) \in M) \vee$$
$$(\neg \exists \bar{y}(\bar{R}, \bar{y}) \in M \wedge \mathfrak{B} \models \varphi(M, \bar{R}, \bar{a}))\}.$$

Clearly, the least fixed-point of the function exists and can be computed inductively in time polynomially in the number of regions and thus also in the size of the database.

Intuitively, we can think of the stages of the fixed-point induction as a set of tuples of regions $\overline{R}$, where to each $\bar{R}$ there is a formula $\varphi_{\bar{R}}(\bar{x})$ attached to it defining a set of points in $\mathbb{R}^l$. But once a tuple of regions is contained in some stage of the fixed-point induction, the formula attached to it cannot be changed anymore. This is ensured by the first disjunct in the definition of f_φ. An example motivating this definition of the fixed-point operator is given below.

Note that there are different decompositions of $\mathbb{R}^d$ satisfying the conditions of an arrangement as presented above. Thus, the semantics of the logic depends on a particular decomposition chosen. But the results we prove below stay true for most decompositions, as long as the input can be recovered from them. Thus, for a given application area, one should choose a decomposition which is more intuitive to use.

Having defined the logic, we now give a motivating example for it.

Example 8 *Suppose we are given a road map with cities and the highways connecting them. Typically, the maps contain information about the distance between any two adjacent cities directly connected by a section of a highway. In this setup a useful decomposition of the input into regions would be to have a region for each city, one for each section of a highway between two cities, as well as regions for the other parts of the map.*

Now suppose we want to travel from one city to another on a certain highway and we want to know the distance between these two cities. Let the constants s, t denote the regions of the source and target city and assume a formula $dist(C, C', d)$, stating that C and C' are regions of adjacent cities and d is the distance between both on the chosen highway. Then the formula

$$\varphi(x) := [\mathrm{tLFP}_{M,C_1,C_2,d} \; dist(C_1, C_2, d) \vee (\exists C \, \exists d_1 \, \exists d_2 \; M(C_1, C, d_1) \wedge$$
$$dist(C, C_2, d_2) \wedge d = d_1 + d_2) \,](s, t, x)$$

defines the distance between the two cities. Here the real variable d in the fixed-point induction is used to sum up the distances.

We now show that the logic is expressive enough to capture all PTIME-queries on linear constraint databases.

Definition 9 *A linear constraint database $\mathfrak{B}$ has the small coordinate property if the absolute values of the coordinates of all points contained in a 0-dimensional region, are bounded by $2^{O(n)}$, where n is the number of regions in the region extension of $\mathfrak{B}$.*

Theorem 10 *RegLFP(conv) captures* PTIME *on the class of linear constraint databases having the small coordinate property.*

Sketch. As an arrangement of a semi-linear set can be computed in polynomial time, the region extension of the input database can be computed in PTIME as well. Now the PTIME data-complexity of *RegLFP(conv)* can be shown by induction on the structure of the queries. To prove that each PTIME-query can be defined by a *RegLFP(conv)*-query, we show that the run of a Turing-machine M computing the query can be simulated. The crucial point is that, given the input relation $S \subseteq \mathbb{R}^d$, a finite set $R \subseteq \mathbb{R}^{d(d+1)}$ of tuples of points such that $S = \bigcup\{\mathrm{conv}(\bar{a}_1, \ldots, \bar{a}_{d+1}) : (\bar{a}_1, \ldots, \bar{a}_{d+1}) \in R\}$ can be defined in *RegLFP(conv)*. Further, given such a set $R \subseteq \mathbb{R}^{l(l+1)}$ for some $l \in \mathbb{N}$, the set $\{\bar{x} : \bar{x} \in \mathrm{conv}(\bar{a}_1, \ldots, \bar{a}_{l+1})$ for some $(\bar{a}_1, \ldots, \bar{a}_{l+1}) \in R\}$ can be defined using the conv and uconv operators. This can be used to encode the input of a Turing-machine and to decode its output. The run of the Turing-machine can be simulated as usual in finite model theory, using region variables to denote positions on the Turing-tape. The restriction to databases with small coordinates comes from the fact, that in order to simulate the Turing-machine, coordinates of points have to be encoded by (tuples of) region variables. Thus, only polynomially many bits can be used to represent a coordinate of a point, restricting it to exponential size. □

4.2   Finitary Fixed-Point Logic

The query language introduced in the previous section depends on a specific decomposition of the input database. Thus, its usability relies on the existence of a decomposition which can easily be understood by the user. Although this is the case in some application areas, it will be a problem in others. In this section we present a way to overcome this dependency on a specific, intuitive decomposition.

Below we define *finitary fixed-point logic* as the extension of *FO(conv)* by a least fixed-point operator over arbitrary definable finite sets. The idea is that, as mentioned in Section 3, the language *FO(conv)* is capable of defining a finite representation of the input database. Using this one can replace the fixed-point induction on the regions by a fixed-point induction on the finite representation.

We already mentioned that finiteness of a semi-linear set is first-order definable. Therefore we use formulae finite(φ), which, given a formula φ, evaluate to true if the set defined by φ is finite and false otherwise.

Definition 11 Finitary Fixed-Point Logic (FFP) *is defined as the extension of FO(conv) by a finitary LFP operator. Precisely, if $\bar{x} := x_1, \ldots, x_k$ and $\bar{z} := z_1, \ldots, z_l$ are sequences of first-order variables, R is a $(k + l)$-ary second-order variable, $\varphi(\bar{x})$ and $\psi(R, \bar{x}, \bar{z})$ are formulae, such that R occurs only positively in ψ and does not occur in φ, then also $[\mathrm{tLFP}_{R,\bar{x}}(\varphi, \psi)](\bar{u}, \bar{v})$ is a formula with free variables $\{\bar{u}, \bar{v}\}$, where $\bar{u}, \bar{v}$ are sequences of variables of arity k and l.*

The semantics of a formula $\chi := [\text{tLFP}_{R,\bar{x}}(\varphi, \psi)](\bar{u}, \bar{v})$ is defined as the least fixed-point of the function

$$f_\chi : Pow(\mathbb{R}^{k+l}) \longrightarrow Pow(\mathbb{R}^{k+l})$$
$$R \longmapsto \{(\bar{x}, \bar{z}) : (\exists \bar{y} \, (\bar{x}, \bar{y}) \in R \wedge (\bar{x}, \bar{z}) \in R) \vee$$
$$((\neg \exists \bar{y} \, (\bar{x}, \bar{y}) \in R) \wedge \mathfrak{B} \models \text{finite}(\varphi) \wedge \varphi(\bar{x}) \wedge \psi(R, \bar{x}, \bar{z})))\},$$

where $\mathfrak{B}$ is the input database. Intuitively, the formula φ serves as a guard, ensuring that the fixed-point induction runs over the finite set defined by φ only. As before, the variables $\bar{z}$ can be used to attach some information to a tuple $\bar{x}$ contained in a induction stage.

Regarding the expressive power of this language, one can easily show that the languages *RegLFP(conv)* and FFP are equivalent. Thus, FFP captures PTIME on the class of linear constraint databases.

Theorem 12   *(i) FFP captures* PTIME *on the class of linear constraint databases having the small coordinate property.*

   (ii) RegLFP(conv) and FFP have the same expressive power on the class of linear constraint databases.

5   Polynomial Constraint Databases

In this section we extend the approach taken in Section 4 to polynomial constraint databases. Clearly, it does not make sense to add a convex closure operator to first-order logic, as convex closure is already definable in FO on polynomial constraint databases. Thus, the logic *PolyLFP* is defined as the least fixed-point logic over region extensions, but the regions will now be defined by a cylindrical algebraic decomposition of the input space.

In Section 5.1 we give a (very brief) overview of cylindrical algebraic decompositions (CADs). See [Col75] or the monograph [CJ98] for details. We then define the region extension of polynomial constraint databases and introduce the logic *PolyLFP*.

The data-complexity and expressive power of the logic is considered thereafter. When dealing with complexity issues for constraint databases, one can base the examination on the Turing-model and restrict oneself to representing formulae with rational or real algebraic coefficients. Another approach is to ignore the complexity of the storage and manipulation of real numbers and use a computation model capable of storing arbitrary real numbers. These models have built-in functions for operations like multiplication and addition which can be executed in one time step. This approach puts more focus on the complexity of the underlying logic than on the complexity of manipulating numbers. Therefore we take this approach here and base our analysis of the complexity on the Blum-Shub-Smale (BSS) model. A brief introduction to BSS-machines can be found in Appendix A.

5.1 Cylindrical Algebraic Decomposition

Fix a dimension d. A *region* is defined as a connected subset of $\mathbb{R}^d$. The *cylinder* $Z(R)$ *over a region* R is defined as $R \times \mathbb{R}$. If R is a region and $f : R \to \mathbb{R}$ is a continuous function, then the *f-section of* $Z(R)$ is defined as the graph of f, that is, the set $\{(\bar{a}, b) \ : \ \bar{a} \in R \text{ and } b = f\bar{a}\}$.

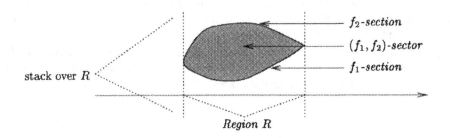

Fig. 1. Illustration of some concepts used in CADs.

Now, let $f_1, f_2 : R \to \mathbb{R}$ be continuous functions over R such that for all $\bar{a} \in R$ $f_1(\bar{a}) < f_2(\bar{a})$. The (f_1, f_2)-*sector of* $Z(R)$ is defined as the set $\{(\bar{a}, b) \ : \ \bar{a} \in R \text{ and } f_1(\bar{a}) < b < f_2(\bar{a})\}$. We allow f_1, f_2 to be the constant functions $-\infty, \infty$.

Let $X \subseteq \mathbb{R}^d$ be a set. A *decomposition* of X is a finite collection of disjoint regions whose union is X. Let R be a region and let $f_1, \ldots, f_k : R \to \mathbb{R}$ be a sequence of continuous functions from R to $\mathbb{R}$, such that $f_i(\bar{x}) < f_{i+1}(\bar{x})$ for all $\bar{x} \in R$. This sequence defines a decomposition of the cylinder $Z(R)$ into the regions defined by 1) the f_i-sections, 2) the (f_i, f_{i+1})-sectors where $i \in \{0, \ldots, k+1\}$ and $f_0(\bar{x}) = -\infty$ and $f_{k+1}(\bar{x}) = \infty$. Such a decomposition is called a *stack over* R *(determined by* $f_1, \ldots, f_k$*).* See Figure 1 for an illustration of these concepts.

A decomposition D of $\mathbb{R}^d$ is called *cylindrical* if *i)* $d = 1$ and D is a stack over $\mathbb{R}^0$, i.e. a finite number of singletons and intervals, or *ii)* $d \geq 2$ and there is a cylindrical decomposition D' of $\mathbb{R}^{d-1}$ such that for each region $R \in D'$ there is a subset $S \subseteq D$ forming a stack over R. Clearly, a cylindrical decomposition of $\mathbb{R}^d$ determines a unique cylindrical decomposition of $\mathbb{R}^{d-1}$, called the *induced* decomposition.

A decomposition of $\mathbb{R}^d$ is called *algebraic*, if every region is a semi-algebraic set. A *cylindrical algebraic decomposition (CAD) of* $\mathbb{R}^d$ is a decomposition of $\mathbb{R}^d$ which is both cylindrical and algebraic.

Let $\mathcal{A} := \{f_1, \ldots, f_m\}$ be a set of polynomials from $\mathbb{R}^d$ to $\mathbb{R}$. A decomposition D of $\mathbb{R}^d$ is called $\mathcal{A}$-*invariant*, if for each $f_i \in \mathcal{A}$ and all regions $R \in D$, either for all $\bar{x} \in R$ $f_i(\bar{x}) > 0$, $f_i(\bar{x}) = 0$, or $f_i(\bar{x}) < 0$.

Let $\mathfrak{B} := (\mathbb{R}, <, +, \cdot, S)$ be a database, where S is d-ary. A CAD D of $\mathbb{R}^d$ is *invariant for* $\mathfrak{B}$, if it is invariant for the set of polynomials occurring in the representation of S. Thus, for each region $R \in D$ either $R \cap S = \emptyset$ or $R \subseteq S$.

It is known that a CAD of $\mathbb{R}^d$ invariant for a given set $\mathcal{A}$ of polynomials can be computed in double exponential time in the dimension d and polynomial time in the size of $\mathcal{A}$. Since the dimension is fixed, the algorithm operates in polynomial time in the size of $\mathcal{A}$, resp. in the size of a database $\mathfrak{B}$, if $\mathcal{A}$ is the set of polynomials occurring in the representation of $\mathfrak{B}$.

Further, a close analysis of the algorithms shows, that if D is a CAD of $\mathbb{R}^d$ invariant for a given set of polynomials of degree at most n, then, for d fixed, the degree of the polynomials defining the regions in D is polynomially bounded in n. See [Col75] for details.

5.2   A Fixed-Point Logic for Polynomial Constraint Databases

We define a fixed-point query language for polynomial constraint databases. In analogy to Section 4 this language is based on *region extensions* of databases.

Definition 13 *Let $\mathfrak{B} := ((\mathbb{R}, <, +, \cdot), S)$ be a polynomial constraint database. The region extension $\mathfrak{B}^{Reg}$ of $\mathfrak{B}$ is defined as a two-sorted structure $\mathfrak{B}^{Reg} := ((\mathbb{R}, <, +, \cdot), S; Reg)$. The first sort consists of the reals with order, addition, and multiplication, whereas the second sort consists of the set Reg of regions decomposing $\mathbb{R}^d$ in a CAD invariant for $\mathfrak{B}$.*

We now define the language *PolyLFP* as least fixed-point logic on region extensions. As before, the fixed-point induction is defined on the (finite) set of regions only. Since every database has a unique region extension we don't distinguish between databases and their region extensions and freely speak about a database being a model of a *PolyLFP* formula instead of explicitly mentioning its region extension.

Definition 14 *The logic PolyLFP is defined as the extension of first-order logic by the following rules. As in Definition 6 there are* element, region, *and* relation *variables.*

- *If R is a region variable and $\bar{x}$ is a sequence of element variables, then $R\bar{x}$ is a formula.*
- *If φ is a formula and R a region variable, then $\exists R\varphi$ is also a formula.*
- *If M is a relation variable of arity (k, l), $\bar{R} := R_1, \ldots, R_k$ are region variables, and $\bar{x} := x_1, \ldots, x_l$ are element variables, then $M\bar{R}\bar{x}$ is a formula.*
- *If $\varphi(M, \bar{R}, \bar{x})$ is a formula with free element variables $\bar{x}$, free region variables $\bar{R} := R_1, \ldots, R_k$, and a free (k, l)-ary relation variable M, such that φ is positive in M, then $[\mathrm{tLFP}_{M, R, \bar{x}}\varphi](\bar{R}, \bar{x})$ is a formula.*

PolyLFP-queries are defined by PolyLFP-formulae without free region or relation variables.

The semantics of the logic is defined analogously to *RegLFP(conv)*, with the region variables ranging over the set of regions in the region extension of a database and relation variables being interpreted as subsets of $Reg^k \times \mathbb{R}^l$. Since the region extension of a database can be computed in polynomial time and first-order logic on polynomial constraint databases has polynomial time data-complexity, the polynomial time data-complexity of *PolyLFP* follows immediately.

We now show that $P_{\mathbb{R}}$ - the set of queries computable in polynomial time on a BSS-machine - can be captured by *PolyLFP* for a restricted class of polynomial constraint databases.

Definition 15 *A polynomial constraint database $\mathfrak{B}$ is said to be a k-degree database, if the highest degree of any variable of a polynomial in the representation of the database is at most k.*

Note that, as mentioned in Section 5.1, by bounding the degree of the polynomials in the input database, we also get a polynomial bound on the degree of the polynomials bounding the regions.

Theorem 16 *For each $k \in \mathbb{N}$, PolyLFP captures $P_{\mathbb{R}}$ on the class of k-degree databases.*

Sketch. Again, the theorem is proved by showing that the run of a BSS-machine computing a $P_{\mathbb{R}}$-query can be simulated, the crucial point being the representation of the input database. Recall from above, that the regions are either f-sectors or (f_1, f_2)-sections, for some polynomial functions f, f_1, f_2. We define a representation of the database by a disjunction of formulae defining the regions contained in it. Let region R be a f-section. Since, for some $k \in \mathbb{N}$, the input is restricted to be a k-degree database and thus the degree of f is bounded by k, the polynomial f can be defined as $f := \sum_{i \in \{0, \ldots, k\}^d} \bar{a}_i \bar{x}^i$, where, for $i := (i_0, \ldots, i_d) \in \{0, \ldots, k\}^d$, $\bar{x}^i$ denotes the product $\prod_{j=0}^d x_j^{i_j}$. The coefficients a_i in the sum can be defined by a formula $\varphi(\bar{a}) := \forall \bar{x} \exists y \left(\sum_{i \in \{0, \ldots, k\}^d} a_i \bar{x}^i = y \leftrightarrow R\bar{x}y \right)$, if the region R contains more than one point. The case where R contains only one point is trivial. The sectors can be defined similarly, since they are bounded by one or two sections. These sections are again regions and can thus be defined as described above.   □

6   Conclusion

We introduced logics extending first-order logic by recursion mechanisms on linear as well as polynomial constraint databases. For linear constraint databases we also introduced a logic extending FO by the ability to compute convex closure and showed that regarding expressive power this concept equals the logic PFOL, where multiplication with one factor bounded by a finite set is permitted.

We showed that the fixed-point logics offer query languages with rather high expressive power, while still having tractable data-complexity. For practical implementations of these query languages, arrangements or cylindrical algebraic decompositions probably offer not the most intuitive definition of the region domain. But note that the results are independent of the precise definition of the region decomposition, as long as the database can be represented by a union of regions and the region decomposition can be computed in polynomial time. Thus, in a spatial database system, where spatial information is combined with non-spatial information giving a meaning to part of the spatial image, one could use a decomposition consistent with this semantical part.

References

[BCSS98] L. Blum, F. Cucker, M. Shub, and S. Smale. *Complexity and Real Computation*. Springer, 1998.

[BSS89]   L. Blum, M. Shub, and S.Smale. On a theory of computation and complexity over the real numbers: NP-completeness, recursive functions and universal machines. *Bulletin of the American Mathmatical Society*, 21:1–46, 1989.

[CJ98]   B.F. Caviness and J.R.Johnson, editors. *Quantifier Elimination and Cylindric Algebraic Decomposition*. Springer, 1998.

[Col75]   George E. Collins. Quantifier elimination for real closed fields by cylindrical algebraic decomposition. In *Automata Theory and Formal Languages*, number 33 in LNCS, pages 134–183, Berlin, 1975. Springer-Verlag.

[Ede87]   H. Edelsbrunner. *Algorithms in Combinatorial Geometry*. EATCS Monographs on Theoretical Computer Science. Springer, 1987.

[EF95]   H.-D. Ebbinghaus and J. Flum. *Finite Model Theory*. Springer, 1995.

[GK97]   S. Grumbach and G. M. Kuper. Tractable recursion over geometric data. In *Principles and Practice of Constraint Programming*, number 1330 in LNCS, pages 450 – 462. Springer, 1997.

[GK99]   E. Grädel and S. Kreutzer. Descriptive complexity theory for constraint databases. In *Computer Science Logic*, number 1683 in LNCS, pages 67 – 82. Springer, 1999.

[GK00]   F. Geerts and B. Kuijpers. Linear approximation of planar spatial databases using transitive-closure logic. In *PODS 2000*, pages 126–135. ACM Press, 2000.

[GO97]   Jacob E. Goodman and Joseph O'Rourke, editors. *Handbook of Discrete and Computational Geometry*. CRC Press, 1997.

[GS97]   S. Grumbach and J. Su. Finitely representable databases. *Journal of Computer and System Sciences*, 55:273–298, 1997.

[KKR90]   P. C. Kanellakis, G. M. Kuper, and P. Z. Revesz. Constraint query languages. In *PODS 1990*, pages 299–313, 1990.

[KLP00]   G. Kuper, L. Libkin, and J. Paredaens, editors. *Constraint Databases*. Springer, 2000.

[KPSV96] B. Kuijpers, J. Paredaens, M. Smits, and J. Van den Bussche. Termination properties of spatial datalog programs. In *Logic in Databases*, number 1154 in LNCS, pages 101 – 116, 1996.

[Kre00]   S. Kreutzer. Fixed-point query languages for linear constraint databases. In *PODS 2000*, pages 116–125. ACM press, 2000.

[Van99]   L. Vandeurzen. *Logic-Based Query Languages for the Linear Constraint Database Model*. PhD thesis, Limburgs Universitair Centrum, 1999.

[VGG98]   L. Vandeurzen, M. Gyssens, and D. Van Gucht. An expressive language for linear spatial database queries. In *PODS 1998*, pages 109–118, 1998.

A   Blum-Shub-Smale-Machines

Blum-Shub-Smale (BSS) machines have been introduced by Blum, Shub, and Smale in 1989 [BSS89]. We give a brief review of the computation model here. For a detailed introduction see [BSS89] and the monograph on real computation [BCSS98]. Note that we use a slightly different presentation of BSS machines than the presentation given by Blum, Shub, and Smale.

Intuitively, a BSS machine is a random access machine with real registers and built-in operations for addition, subtraction, multiplication, and division. A precise definition is given below.

Definition 17 *We define $\mathbb{R}^\infty$ as the set of all infinite sequences $(a_0, a_1, \dots)$ of real numbers such that there is $k \in \mathbb{N}$ with $a_i = 0$ for all $i \geq k$.*

Definition 18 *A BSS machine consists of the input space $\mathbb{R}^\infty$, the state space $S := \mathbb{N} \times \mathbb{N} \times \mathbb{N} \times \mathbb{R}^\infty$, the output space $\mathbb{R}^\infty$ and a directed connected graph $G := (\{0, \dots, N\}, V)$ for some $N \in \mathbb{N}$. Each vertex has at most two children and one of the following five types of operations assigned to it. The graph represents the program of the machine, where vertices can be thought of as commands and successors of nodes as the possible successive commands.*

- *The node 0 is the* input node. *An input $(y_1, y_2, \dots, y_k, 0, \dots) \in \mathbb{R}^\infty$ is mapped to $(1, 1, 1, y_1, y_2, \dots) \in S$. Thus the node 0 has the successor 1.*
- *N is the* output node. *The machine stops in the position $(N, i, j, x_1, x_2, \dots)$ and outputs $(x_1, x_2, \dots)$. The node N has no successors.*
- Computation nodes: *An operation of this type transforms a state $(n, i, j, x_1, x_2, \dots) \in S$ to $(n+1, i', j', g_n(x_1, x_2, \dots)) \in S$, where $n+1$ is the successive command, $i' \in \{i+1, 1\}, j' \in \{j+1, 1\}$, and g_n is one of the following basic operations:*
    - *Two registers x_r, x_s are added, subtracted, multiplied, or divided and the result is stored in x_r.*
    - *A register x_r is set to a real constant.*
    The registers x_i with $i \notin \{r, s\}$ are not altered.
- Test nodes: *A test node n has exactly two successors $n+1$ and $\beta(n)$. On a state $(n, i, j, x_1, \dots) \in S$ the machine tests whether $x_1 \geq 0$ and continues in node $n+1$ if the answer is yes and in node $\beta(n)$ otherwise.*
- Copy nodes: *In state $(n, i, j, x_1, \dots)$, the machine sets $x_j := x_i$ and continues at node $n+1$.*

Based on BSS machines one can define complexity classes like $P_\mathbb{R}$ as the class of all problems computable on a BSS machine in polynomially many steps. See [BCSS98] for details.

A Semi-monad for Semi-structured Data
(ICDT Version)

Mary Fernandez[1], Jerome Simeon[2], and Philip Wadler[3]

[1] ATT Labs, mff@research.att.com
[2] Bell Labs, Lucent Technologies simeon@research.bell-labs.com
[3] Avaya Labs, wadler@avaya.com

Abstract. This document proposes an algebra for XML Query. The algebra has been submitted to the W3C XML Query Working Group. A novel feature of the algebra is the use of regular-expression types, similar in power to DTDs or XML Schemas, and closely related to Hasoya and Pierce's work on Xduce. The iteration construct is based on the notion of a monad, and involves novel typing rules not encountered elsewhere.

1 Introduction

This document proposes an algebra for XML Query.

This work builds on long standing traditions in the database community. In particular, we have been inspired by systems such as SQL, OQL, and nested relational algebra (NRA). We have also been inspired by systems such as Quilt, UnQL, XDuce, XML-QL, XPath, XQL, and YATL. We give citations for all these systems below.

In the database world, it is common to translate a query language into an algebra; this happens in SQL, OQL, and NRA, among others. The purpose of the algebra is twofold. First, the algebra is used to give a semantics for the query language, so the operations of the algebra should be well-defined. Second, the algebra is used to support query optimization, so the algebra should possess a rich set of laws. Our algebra is powerful enough to capture the semantics of many XML query languages, and the laws we give include analogues of most of the laws of relational algebra.

In the database world, it is common for a query language to exploit schemas or types; this happens in SQL, OQL, and NRA, among others. The purpose of types is twofold. Types can be used to detect certain kinds of errors at compile time and to support query optimization. DTDs and XML Schema can be thought of as providing something like types for XML. Our algebra uses a simple type system that captures the essence of XML Schema [42]. The type system is close to that used in XDuce. Our type system can detect common type errors and support optimization. A novel aspect of the type system (not found in Xduce) is the description of projection in terms of iteration, and the typing rules for iteration that make this viable. The algebra is based on earlier work on the use of monads to query semi-structured data, and iteration construct satisfies the three monad laws.

J. Van den Bussche and V. Vianu (Eds.): ICDT 2001, LNCS 1973, pp. 263–300, 2001.
© Springer-Verlag Berlin Heidelberg 2001

This paper describes the key features of the algebra. For simplicity, we restrict our attention to only three scalar types (strings, integers, and booleans), but we believe the system will smoothly extend to cover the continuum of scalar types found in XML Schema. Other important features that we do not tackle include attributes, namespaces, element identity, collation, and key constraints, among others. Again, we believe they can be added within the framework given here.

Two earlier versions of this paper have been distributed. The first [18] used a more ad-hoc approach to typing. The second [19] used a different notation for case analysis, and has less discussion of the relation to earlier work on monads.

The paper is organized as follows. A tutorial introduction is presented in Section 2. Section 3 explains key aspects of how the algebra treats projection and iteration. The expressions of the algebra are summarized in Section 4. The type system is reviewed in Section 5. Some laws of the algebra are presented in Section 6. Finally, the static typing rules for the algebra are described in Section 7. Section 8 discusses open issues and problems.

Cited literature includes: SQL [16], OQL [4,5,13], NRA [15,8,24,25], comprehensions [33,6], monads [33,34,35], Quilt [11], UnQL [3], XDuce [21], XML Query [40,41], XML Schema [42,43], XML-QL [17], XPath [39,36], XQL [30], and YaTL [14].

2   The Algebra by Example

This section introduces the main features of the algebra, using familiar examples based on accessing a database of books.

2.1   Data and Types

Consider the following sample data:

```
<bib>
  <book>
    <title>Data on the Web</title>
    <year>1999</year>
    <author>Abiteboul</author>
    <author>Buneman</author>
    <author>Suciu</author>
  </book>
  <book>
    <title>XML Query</title>
    <year>2001</year>
    <author>Fernandez</author>
    <author>Suciu</author>
  </book>
</bib>
```

Here is a fragment of a XML Schema for such data.

```
<xsd:group name="Bib">
  <xsd:element name="bib">
    <xsd:complexType>
      <xsd:group ref="Book"
        minOccurs="0" maxOccurs="unbounded"/>
    </xsd:complexType>
  </xsd:element>
</xsd:group>

<xsd:group name="Book">
  <xsd:element name="book">
    <xsd:complexType>
      <xsd:element name="title" type="xsd:string"/>
      <xsd:element name="year" type="xsd:integer"/>
      <xsd:element name="author" type="xsd:integer"
        minOccurs="1" maxOccurs="unbounded"/>
    </xsd:complexType>
  </xsd:element>
</xsd:group>
```

This data and schema is represented in our algebra as follows:

```
type Bib =
  bib [ Book* ]
type Book =
  book [
    title  [ String ],
    year   [ Integer ],
    author [ String ]+
  ]
let bib0 : Bib =
  bib [
    book [
      title  [ "Data on the Web" ],
      year   [ 1999 ],
      author [ "Abiteboul" ],
      author [ "Buneman" ],
      author [ "Suciu" ]
    ],
    book [
      title  [ "XML Query" ],
      year   [ 2001 ],
      author [ "Fernandez" ],
      author [ "Suciu" ]
    ]
  ]
```

The expression above defines two types, Bib and Book, and defines one global variable, bib0.

The Bib type consists of a bib element containing zero or more entries of type Book. The Book type consists of a book element containing a title element (which contains a string), a year element (which contains an integer), and one or more author elements (which contain strings).

The Bib type corresponds to a single bib element, which contains a *forest* of zero or more Book elements. We use the term forest to refer to a sequence of (zero or more) elements. Every element can be viewed as a forest of length one.

The Book type corresponds to a single book element, which contains one title element, followed by one year element, followed by one or more author elements. A title or author element contains a string value and a year element contains an integer.

The variable bib0 is bound to a literal XML value, which is the data model representation of the earlier XML document. The bib element contains two book elements.

The algebra is a strongly typed language, therefore the value of bib0 must be an instance of its declared type, or the expression is ill-typed. Here the value of bib0 is an instance of the Bib type, because it contains one bib element, which contains two book elements, each of which contain a string-valued title, an integer-valued year, and one or more string-valued author elements.

For convenience, we define a second global variable book0, also bound to a literal value, which is equivalent to the first book in bib0.

```
let book0 : Book =
  book [
    title  [ "Data on the Web" ],
    year   [ 1999 ],
    author [ "Abiteboul" ],
    author [ "Buneman" ],
    author [ "Suciu" ]
  ]
```

2.2 Projection

The simplest operation is projection. The algebra uses a notation similar in appearance and meaning to path navigation in XPath.

The following expression returns all author elements contained in book0:

```
    book0/author
==> author [ "Abiteboul" ],
    author [ "Buneman" ],
    author [ "Suciu" ]
:   author [ String ]+
```

The above example and the ones that follow have three parts. First is an expression in the algebra. Second, following the ==>, is the value of this expression.

Third, following the :, is the type of the expression, which is (of course) also a legal type for the value.

The following expression returns all `author` elements contained in `book` elements contained in `bib0`:

```
    bib0/book/author
==> author [ "Abiteboul" ],
    author [ "Buneman" ],
    author [ "Suciu" ],
    author [ "Fernandez" ],
    author [ "Suciu" ]
 :  author [ String ]*
```

Note that in the result, the document order of `author` elements is preserved and that duplicate elements are also preserved.

It may be unclear why the type of `bib0/book/author` contains *zero* or more authors, even though the type of a `book` element contains *one* or more authors. Let's look at the derivation of the result type by looking at the type of each sub-expression:

```
bib0               : Bib
bib0/book          : Book*
bib0/book/author : author [ String ]*
```

Recall that `Bib`, the type of `bib0`, may contain *zero* or more `Book` elements, therefore the expression `bib0/book` might contain zero `book` elements, in which case, `bib0/book/author` would contain no authors.

This illustrates an important feature of the type system: the type of an expression depends only on the type of its sub-expressions. It also illustrates the difference between an expression's run-time value and its compile-time type. Since the type of `bib0` is `Bib`, the best type for `bib0/book/author` is one listing zero or more authors, even though for the given value of `bib0` the expression will always contain exactly five authors.

One may access scalar data (strings, integers, or booleans) using the keyword `data()`. For instance, if we wish to select all author names in a book, rather than all author elements, we could write the following.

```
    book0/author/data()
==> "Abiteboul",
    "Buneman",
    "Suciu"
 :  String+
```

Similarly, the following returns the year the book was published.

```
    book0/year/data()
==> 1999
 :  Integer
```

This notation is similar to the use of `text()` in XPath. We chose the keyword `data()` because, as the second example shows, not all data items are strings.

2.3 Iteration

Another common operation is to iterate over elements in a document so that their content can be transformed into new content. Here is an example of how to process each book to list the authors before the title, and remove the year.

```
    for b in bib0/book do
        book [ b/author, b/title ]
==> book [
        author [ "Abiteboul" ],
        author [ "Buneman" ],
        author [ "Suciu" ],
        title  [ "Data on the Web" ]
    ],
    book [
        author [ "Fernandez" ],
        author [ "Suciu" ],
        title  [ "XML Query" ]
    ]
:   book [
        author[ String ]+,
        title[ String ]
    ]*
```

The for expression iterates over all book elements in bib0 and binds the variable b to each such element. For each element bound to b, the inner expression constructs a new book element containing the book's authors followed by its title. The transformed elements appear in the same order as they occur in bib0.

In the result type, a book element is guaranteed to contain one or more authors followed by one title. Let's look at the derivation of the result type to see why:

```
    bib0/book          : Book*
    b                  : Book
    b/author           : author [ String ]+
    b/title            : title  [ String ]
```

The type system can determine that b is always Book, therefore the type of b/author is author[String]+ and the type of b/title is title[String].

In general, the value of a for loop is a forest. If the body of the loop itself yields a forest, then all of the forests are concatenated together. For instance, the expression:

```
    for b in bib0/book do
        b/author
```

is exactly equivalent to the expression bib0/book/author.

Here we have explained the typing of for loops by example. In fact, the typing rules are rather subtle, and one of the more interesting aspects of the algebra, and will be explained further below.

2.4   Selection

Projection and for loops can serve as the basis for many interesting queries. The next three sections show how they provide the power for selection, quantification, join, and regrouping.

To select values that satisfy some predicate, we use the where expression. For example, the following expression selects all book elements in bib0 that were published before 2000.

```
    for b in bib0/book do
        where b/year/data() <= 2000 do
            b
==> book [
        title  [ "Data on the Web" ],
        year   [ 1999 ],
        author [ "Abiteboul" ],
        author [ "Buneman" ],
        author [ "Suciu" ]
    ]
:    Book*
```

An expression of the form

```
  where e₁ do e₂
```

is just syntactic sugar for

```
  if e₁ then e₂ else ()
```

where e_1 and e_2 are expressions. Here () is an expression that stands for the empty sequence, a forest that contains no elements. We also write () for the type of the empty sequence.

According to this rule, the expression above translates to

```
    for b <- bib0/book in
        if b/year/data() < 2000 then b else ()
```

and this has the same value and the same type as the preceding expression.

2.5   Quantification

The following expression selects all book elements in bib0 that have *some* author named "Buneman".

```
    for b in bib0/book do
        for a in b/author do
            where a/data() = "Buneman" do
                b
==> book [
```

```
        title  [ "Data on the Web" ],
        year   [ 1999 ],
        author [ "Abiteboul" ],
        author [ "Buneman" ],
        author [ "Suciu" ]
    ]
:   Book*
```

In contrast, we can use the empty operator to find all books that have *no* author whose name is Buneman:

```
    for b in bib0/book do
        where empty(for a in b/author do
                    where a/data() = "Buneman" do
                    a) do
            b
==> book [
        title  [ "XML Query" ],
        year   [ 2001 ],
        author [ "Fernandez" ],
        author [ "Suciu" ]
    ]
:   Book*
```

The empty expression checks that its argument is the empty sequence ().

We can also use the empty operator to find all books where all the authors are Buneman, by checking that there are no authors that are not Buneman:

```
    for b in bib0/book do
        where empty(for a in b/author do
                    where a/data() <> "Buneman" do
                    a) do
            b
==> ()
:   Book*
```

There are no such books, so the result is the empty sequence. Appropriate use of empty (possibly combined with not) can express universally or existentially quantified expressions.

Here is a good place to introduce the let expression, which binds a local variable to a value. Introducing local variables may improve readability. For example, the following expression is exactly equivalent to the previous one.

```
    for b in bib0/book do
        let nonbunemans = (for a in b/author do
                            where a/data() <> "Buneman" do
                            a) do
        where empty(nonbunemans) do
            b
```

Local variables can also be used to avoid repetition when the same subexpression appears more than once in a query.

Later we will introduce `match` expressions, and we will see how to define `empty` using `match` in Section 6.

2.6   Join

Another common operation is to *join* values from one or more documents. To illustrate joins, we give a second data source that defines book reviews:

```
type Reviews  =
  reviews [
    book [
      title  [ String ],
      review [ String ]
    ]*
  ]
let review0 : Reviews =
  reviews [
    book [
      title  [ "XML Query" ],
      review [ "A darn fine book." ]
    ],

    book [
      title  [ "Data on the Web" ],
      review [ "This is great!" ]
    ]
  ]
```

The `Reviews` type contains one `reviews` element, which contains zero or more `book` elements; each `book` contains a title and review.

We can use nested `for` loops to join the two sources `review0` and `bib0` on title values. The result combines the title, authors, and reviews for each book.

```
for b in bib0/book do
  for r in review0/book do
    where b/title/data() = r/title/data() do
      book [ b/title, b/author, r/review ]
==>
  book [
    title  [ "Data on the Web" ],
    author [ "Abiteboul" ],
    author [ "Buneman" ],
    author [ "Suciu" ]
    review [ "A darn fine book." ]
  ],
```

```
      book [
        title  [ "XML Query" ],
        author [ "Fernandez" ],
        author [ "Suciu" ]
        review [ "This is great!" ]
      ]
  :   book [
        title  [ String ],
        author [ String ]+
        review [ String ]
      ]*
```

Note that the outer-most for expression determines the order of the result. Readers familiar with optimization of relational join queries know that relational joins commute, i.e., they can be evaluated in any order. This is not true for the XML algebra: changing the order of the first two for expressions would produce different output. In Section 8, we discuss extending the algebra to support unordered forests, which would permit commutable joins.

2.7   Restructuring

Often it is useful to regroup elements in an XML document. For example, each book element in bib0 groups one title with multiple authors. This expression regroups each author with the titles of his/her publications.

```
      for a in distinct(bib0/book/author) do
        biblio [
          a,
          for b in bib0/book do
            for a2 in b/author do
              where a/data() = a2/data() do
                b/title
        ]
==> biblio [
        author [ "Abiteboul" ],
        title  [ "Data on the Web" ]
      ],
      biblio [
        author [ "Buneman" ],
        title  [ "Data on the Web" ]
      ],
      biblio [
        author [ "Suciu" ],
        title  [ "Data on the Web" ],
        title  [ "XML Query" ]
      ],
```

```
    biblio [
       author [ "Fernandez" ],
       title  [ "XML Query" ]
    ]
 :  biblio [
       author [ String ],
       title  [ String ]*
    ]*
```

Readers may recognize this expression as a self-join of books on authors. The expression distinct(bib0/book/author) produces a forest of author elements with no duplicates. The outer for expression binds a to each author element, and the inner for expression selects the title of each book that has some author equal to a.

Here distinct is an example of a built-in function. It takes a forest of elements and removes duplicates.

The type of the result expression may seem surprising: each biblio element may contain *zero* or more title elements, even though in bib0, every author co-occurs with a title. Recognizing such a constraint is outside the scope of the type system, so the resulting type is not as precise as we might like.

2.8 Aggregation

The algebra has five built-in aggregation functions: avg, count, max, min and sum. This expression selects books that have more than two authors:

```
    for b in bib0/book do
       where count(b/author) > 2 do
          b
==> book [
       title  [ "Data on the Web" ],
       year   [ 1999 ],
       author [ "Abiteboul" ],
       author [ "Buneman" ],
       author [ "Suciu" ]
    ]
 :  Book*
```

All the aggregation functions take a forest with repetition type and return an integer value; count returns the number of elements in the forest.

2.9 Functions

Functions can make queries more modular and concise. Recall that we used the following query to find all books that do not have "Buneman" as an author.

```
for b in bib0/book do
  where empty(for a in b/author do
                 where a/data() = "Buneman" do
                   a) do
       b
==> book [
    title  [ "XML Query" ],
    year   [ 2001 ],
    author [ "Fernandez" ],
    author [ "Suciu" ]
    ]
:   Book*
```

A different way to formulate this query is to first define a function that takes a string s and a book b as arguments, and returns true if book b does not have an author with name s.

```
fun notauthor (s : String; b : Book) : Boolean =
  empty(for a in b/author do
           where a/data() = s do
             a)
```

The query can then be re-expressed as follows.

```
for b in bib0/book do
  where notauthor("Buneman"; b) do
     b
==> book [
    title  [ "XML Query" ],
    year   [ 2001 ],
    author [ "Fernandez" ],
    author [ "Suciu" ]
    ]
:   Book*
```

We use semicolon rather than comma to separate function arguments, since comma is used to concatenate forests.

Note that a function declaration includes the types of all its arguments and the type of its result. This is necessary for the type system to guarantee that applications of functions are type correct.

In general, any number of functions may be declared at the top-level. The order of function declarations does not matter, and each function may refer to any other function. Among other things, this allows functions to be recursive (or mutually recursive), which supports structural recursion, the subject of the next section.

2.10   Structural Recursion

XML documents can be recursive in structure, for example, it is possible to define a **part** element that directly or indirectly contains other **part** elements. In the algebra, we use recursive types to define documents with a recursive structure, and we use recursive functions to process such documents. (We can also use mutual recursion for more complex recursive structures.)

For instance, here is a recursive type defining a part hierarchy.

```
type Part =
  Basic | Composite
type Basic =
  basic [
    cost [ Integer ]
  ]
type Composite =
  composite [
    assembly_cost [ Integer ],
    subparts [ Part+ ]
  ]
```

And here is some sample data.

```
let part0 : Part =
  composite [
    assembly_cost [ 12 ],
    subparts [
      composite [
        assembly_cost [ 22 ],
        subparts [
          basic [ cost [ 33 ] ]
        ]
      ],
      basic [ cost [ 7 ] ]
    ]
  ]
```

Here vertical bar (|) is used to indicate a choice between types: each part is either basic (no subparts), and has a cost, or is composite, and includes an assembly cost and subparts.

We might want to translate to a second form, where every part has a total cost and a list of subparts (for a basic part, the list of subparts is empty).

```
type Part2 =
  part [
    total_cost [ Integer ],
    subparts [ Part2* ]
  ]
```

Here is a recursive function that performs the desired transformation. It uses a new construct, the *match* expression.

```
fun convert(p : Part) : Part2 =
  match p
    case b : Basic do
      part[
        total_cost[ b/cost/data() ],
        subparts[]
      ]
    case c : Composite do
      let s = (for q in children(c/subparts) do convert(q)) in
      part[
        total_cost[
        c/assembly_cost/data() + sum(s/total_cost/data())
        ],
        subparts[ s ]
      ]
    else error
```

Each branch of the match expression is labeled with a type, Basic or Composite, and with a corresponding variable, b or c. The evaluator checks the type of the value of p at *run-time*, and evaluates the corresponding branch. If the first branch is taken then b is bound to the value of p, and the branch returns a new part with total cost the same as the cost of b, and with no subparts. If the second branch is taken then c is bound to the value of p. The function is recursively applied to each of the subparts of c, giving a list of new subparts s. The branch returns a new part with total cost computed by adding the assembly cost of c to the sum of the total cost of each subpart in s, and with subparts s.

One might wonder why b and c are required, since they have the same value as p. The reason why is that p, b, and c have different types.

```
p : Part
b : Basic
c : Composite
```

The types of b and c are more precise than the type of p, because which branch is taken depends upon the type of value in p.

Applying the query to the given data gives the following result.

```
    convert(part0)
==> part [
      total_cost [ 74 ],
      subparts [
        part [
          total_cost [ 55 ],
          subparts [
            part [
```

```
                total_cost [ 33 ],
                subparts []
              ]
            ]
          ],
        part [
          total_cost [ 7 ],
          subparts []
        ]
      ]
    ]
:   Part2
```

Of course, a match expression may be used in any query, not just in a recursive one.

2.11   Processing Any Well-Formed Document

Recursive types allow us to define a type that matches any well-formed XML document. This type is called UrTree:

```
type UrTree  =  UrScalar | ~[UrType]
type UrType  =  UrTree*
```

Here UrScalar is a built-in scalar type. It stands for the most general scalar type, and all other scalar types (like Integer or String) are subtypes of it. The tilde (~) is used to indicate a wild-card type. In general, ~[t] indicates the type of elements that may have any element name, but must have children of type t. So an UrTree is either an UrScalar or a wildcard element with zero or more children, each of which is itself an UrTree. In other words, any single element or scalar has type UrTree.

Types analogous to UrType and UrScalar appear in XML Schema. The use of tilde is a significant extension to XML Schema, because XML Schema has no type corresponding to ~[t], where t is some type other than UrType. It is not clear that this extension is necessary, since the more restrictive expressiveness of XML Schema wildcards may be adequate.

In particular, our earlier data also has type UrTree.

```
     book0 : UrTree
==>  book [
        title  [ "Data on the Web" ],
        year   [ 1999 ],
        author [ "Abiteboul" ],
        author [ "Buneman" ],
        author [ "Suciu" ]
     ]
:    UrTree
```

A specific type can be indicated for any expression in the query language, by writing a colon and the type after the expression.

As an example, we define a recursive function that converts any XML data into HTML. We first give a simplified definition of HTML.

```
type HTML =
  ( UrScalar
  | b [ HTML ]
  | ul [ (li [ HTML ])* ]
  )*
```

An HTML body consists of a sequence of zero or more items, each of which is either: a scalar; or a b element (boldface) with HTML content; or a ul element (unordered list), where the children are li elements (list item), each of which has HTML content.

Now, here is the function that performs the conversion.

```
fun html_of_xml( t : UrTree ) : HTML =
  match t
    case s : UrScalar do
      s
    case e : ~[UrType] do
      b [ name(e) ],
      ul [ for c in children(e) do li [ html_of_xml(c) ] ]
    else error
```

The case expression checks whether the value of t is data or an element, and evaluates the corresponding branch. If the first branch is taken, then s is bound to the value of t, which must be a scalar, and the branch returns the scalar. If the second branch is taken, then e is bound to the value of t, which must be an element. The branch returns the name of the element in boldface, followed by a list containing one item for each child of the element. The function is recursively applied to get the content of each list item.

Applying the query to the book element above gives the following result.

```
    html_of_xml(book0)
==> b [ "book" ],
    ul [
      li [ b [ "title" ],  ul [ li [ "Data on the Web" ] ] ],
      li [ b [ "year" ],   ul [ li [ 1999 ] ] ],
      li [ b [ "author" ], ul [ li [ "Abiteboul" ] ] ],
      li [ b [ "author" ], ul [ li [ "Buneman" ] ] ],
      li [ b [ "author" ], ul [ li [ "Suciu" ] ] ]
    ]
  : Html_Body
```

2.12   Top-Level Queries

A query consists of a sequence of top-level expressions, or *query items*, where each query item is either a type declaration, a function declaration, a global variable declaration, or a query expression. The order of query items is immaterial; all type, function, and global variable declarations may be mutually recursive.

A query can be evaluated by the query interpreter. Each query expression is evaluated in the environment specified by all of the declarations. (Typically, all of the declarations will precede all of the query expressions, but this is not required.) We have already seen examples of type, function, and global variable declarations. An example of a query expression is:

```
query html_of_xml(book0)
```

To transform any expression into a top-level query, we simply precede the expression by the `query` keyword.

3   Projection and Iteration

This section describes key aspects of projection and iteration.

3.1   Relating Projection to Iteration

The previous examples use the / operator liberally, but in fact we use / as a convenient abbreviation for expressions built from lower-level operators: `for` expressions, the `children` function, and `match` expressions.

For example, the expression:

```
book0/author
```

is equivalent to the expression:

```
for c in children(book0) do
  match c
    case a : author[UrType] do a
    else ()
```

Here the `children` function returns a forest consisting of the children of the element book0, namely, a title element, a year element, and three author elements (the order is preserved). The `for` expression binds the variable v successively to each of these elements. Then the `match` expression selects a branch based on the value of v. If it is an `author` element then the first branch is evaluated, otherwise the second branch. If the first branch is evaluated, the variable a is bound to the same value as x, then the branch returns the value of a. The type of a is author[String], which is the the intersection of the type of c and the type author[UrType]. If the second branch is evaluated, then then branch returns (), the empty sequence.

To compose several expressions using /, we again use `for` expressions. For example, the expression:

```
bib0/book/author
```

is equivalent to the expression:

```
for c in children(bib0) do
  match c of
    case b : book[UrType] =>
      for d in children(b) do
        match d of
          case a : author[UrType] => a
          else ()
    else ()
```

The **for** expression iterates over all **book** elements in **bib0** and binds the variable b to each such element. For each element bound to b, the inner expression returns all the **author** elements in b, and the resulting forests are concatenated together in order.

In general, an expression of the form $e\;/\;a$ is converted to the form

```
for v₁ in e do
  for v₂ in children(v₁) do
    match v₂ of
      case v₃ : a[UrType] do v₃
      else ()
```

where e is an expression, a is an element name, and v_1, v_2, and v_3 are fresh variables (ones that do not appear in the expression being converted).

According to this rule, the expression **bib0/book** translates to

```
for v1 in bib0 do
  for v2 in children(v1) do
    match v2 of
      case v3 : book[UrType] do v3
      else ()
```

In Section 3.3 we discuss laws which allow us to simplify this to the previous expression

```
for v2 in children(bib0) do
  match v2 of
    case v3 : book[UrType] do v3
    else ()
```

Similarly, the expression **bib0/book/author** translates to

```
for v4 in (for v2 in children(bib0) do
             match v2
               case v3 : book[UrType] do v3
               else ()) do
  for v5 in children(v4) do
    match v5
      case v6 : author[UrType] do v6
      else ()
```

Again, the laws will allow us to simplify this to the previous expression

```
for v2 in children(bib0) do
  match v2
    case v3 : book[UrType] do
      for v5 in children(v3) do
        match v5
          case v6 : author[UrType] do d
          else ()
    else ()
```

These examples illustrate an important feature of the algebra: high-level operators may be defined in terms of low-level operators, and the low-level operators
may be subject to algebraic laws that can be used to further simplify the expression.

3.2 Typing Iteration

The typing of for loops is rather subtle. We give an intuitive explanation here,
and cover the detailed typing rules in Section 7.

A *unit* type is either an element type $a[t]$, a wildcard type $\tilde{}[t]$, or a scalar
type s. A for loop

```
for v in e₁ do e₂
```

is typed as follows. First, one finds the type of expression e_1. Next, for each unit
type in this type one assumes the variable v has the unit type and one types
the body e_2. Note that this means we may type the body of e_2 several times,
once for each unit type in the type of e_1. Finally, the types of the body e_2 are
combined, according to how the types were combined in e_1. That is, if the type
of e_1 is formed with sequencing, then sequencing is used to combine the types
of e_2, and similarly for choice or repetition.

For example, consider the following expression, which selects all author elements from a book.

```
for c in children(book0) do
  match c
    case a : author do a
    else ()
```

The type of children(book0) is

```
title[String], year[Integer], author[String]+
```

This is composed of three unit types, and so the body is typed three times.

assuming c has type		the body has type	
title[String]			()
" year[Integer]		"	()
" author[String]		"	author[String]

The three result types are then combined in the same way the original unit types
were, using sequencing and iteration. This yields

```
(), (), author[String]+
```

as the type of the iteration, and simplifying yields

```
author[String]+
```

as the final type.

As a second example, consider the following expression, which selects all title and author elements from a book, and renames them.

```
for c in children(book0) do
  match c
    case t : title[String]  do titl [ t/data() ]
    case y : year[Integer]  do ()
    case a : author[String] do auth [ a/data() ]
    else error
```

Again, the type of children(book0) is

```
title[String], year[Integer], author[String]+
```

This is composed of three unit types, and so the body is typed three times.

```
assuming c has type title[String]  the body has type titl[String]
    "              year[Integer]        "              ()
    "              author[String]       "              auth[String]
```

The three result types are then combined in the same way the original unit types were, using sequencing and iteration. This yields

```
titl[String], (), auth[String]+
```

as the type of the iteration, and simplifying yields

```
titl[String], auth[String]+
```

as the final type. Note that the title occurs just once and the author occurs one or more times, as one would expect.

As a third example, consider the following expression, which selects all basic parts from a sequence of parts.

```
for p in children(part0/subparts) do
  match p
    case b : Basic     do b
    case c : Composite do ()
    else error
```

The type of children(part0/subparts) is

```
(Basic | Composite)+
```

This is composed of two unit types, and so the body is typed two times.

assuming p has type   `Basic`   the body has type `Basic`
"   `Composite`   "   `()`

The two result types are then combined in the same way the original unit types were, using sequencing and iteration. This yields

`(Basic | ())+`

as the type of the iteration, and simplifying yields

`Basic*`

as the final type. Note that although the original type involves repetition one or more times, the final result is a repetition zero or more times. This is what one would expect, since if all the parts are composite the final result will be an empty sequence.

In this way, we see that for loops can be combined with match expressions to select and rename elements from a sequence, and that the result is given a sensible type.

In order for this approach to typing to be sensible, it is necessary that the unit types can be uniquely identified. However, the type system given here satisfies the following law.

$$a[t_1 | t_2] = a[t_1] | a[t_2]$$

This has one unit type on the left, but two distinct unit types on the right, and so might cause trouble. Fortunately, our type system inherits an additional restriction from XML Schema: we insist that the regular expressions can be recognized by a top-down deterministic automaton. In that case, the regular expression must have the form on the left, the form on the right is outlawed because it requires a non-deterministic recognizer. With this additional restriction, there is no problem.

The method of translating projection to iteration described in the previous section combined with the typing rules given here yield optimal types for projections, in the following sense. Say that variable x has type t, and the projection $x\,/\,a$ has type t'. The type assignment is *sound* if for every value of type t, the value of $x\,/\,a$ has type t'. The type assignment is *complete* if for every value y of type t' there is a value x of type t such that $x\,/\,a = y$. In symbols, we can see that these conditions are complementary.

sound: $\forall x \in t.\,\exists y \in t'.\,x\,/\,a = y$
complete: $\forall y \in t'.\,\exists x \in t.\,x\,/\,a = y$

Any sensible type system must be sound, but it is rare for a type system to be complete. But, remarkably, the type assignment given by the above approach is both sound and complete.

3.3 Monad Laws

Investigating aspects of homological algebra in the 1950s, category theorists uncovered the concept of a *monad*, which among other things generalizes set, bag,
and list types. Investigating programming languages based on lists in the 1970s,
functional programmers adapted from set theory the notion of a *comprehension*,
which expresses iteration over set, bag, and list types. In the early 1990s, a precise connection between monads and comprehension notation was uncovered by
Wadler [33,34,35], who was inspired by Moggi's work applying monads to describe features of programming languages [27,28]. As the decade progressed this
was applied by researchers at the University of Pennsylvania to database languages for semi-structured data [6], particularly nested relational algebra (NRA)
[8,25,24] and the Kleisli system [37].

The iteration construct of the algebra corresponds to the structure of a monad. The correspondence is close, but not exact. Each monad is based on a unary
type constructor, such as $Set(t)$ or $List(t)$, representing a homogenous set or list
where all elements are of type t. In contrast, here we have more complex and
heterogenous types, such as a forest consisting of a title, a year, and a sequence
of one or more authors. Also, one important component of a monad is the unit
operator, which converts an element to a set or list. If x has type t, then $\{x\}$ is
a unit set of type $Set(t)$ or $[x]$ is a unit list of type $List(t)$. In contrast, here we
simply write, say, `author["Buneman"]`, which stands for both a tree and for the
unit forest containing that tree.

One can define comprehensions in terms of iteration:

```
[ e0 | x1 <- e1 ]           = for x1 in e1 do e0
[ e0 | x1 <- e1, x2 <- e2 ] = for x1 in e1 do for x2 in e2 do e0
                     ...
```

Conversely, one can define iterations in terms of comprehension:

$$\texttt{for } x \texttt{ in } e_1 \texttt{ do } e_2 = [\ y \ | \ x \ \texttt{<-} \ e_1, \ y \ \texttt{<-} \ e_2 \ ]$$

Here y is a fresh variable name.

Monads satisfy three laws, and three corresponding laws are satisfied by the
iteration notation given here.

First, iteration over a unit forest can be replaced by substition. This is called
the *left unit* law.

$$\texttt{for } v \texttt{ in } e_1 \texttt{ do } e_2 = e_2\{v := e_1\}$$

provided that e_1 is a unit type (e.g., is an element or a scalar constant). We
write $e_1\{v := e_2\}$ to denote the result of taking expression e_1 and replacing
occurrences of the variable v by the expression e_2. For example

$$\texttt{for v in author["Buneman"] do auth[v/data()]} = \texttt{auth["Buneman"]}$$

Second, an iteration that returns the iteration variable is equivalent to the
identity. This is called the *right unit* law.

$$\texttt{for } v \texttt{ in } e \texttt{ do } v = e$$

For example

```
for v in book0 do v = book0
```

An important feature of the type system described here is that the left side of the above equation always has the same type as the right side. (This was not true for an earlier version of the type system [18].)

Third, there are two ways of writing an iteration over an iteration, both of which are equivalent. This is called the *associative* law.

$$\text{for } v_2 \text{ in (for } v_1 \text{ in } e_1 \text{ do } e_2) \text{ do } e_3$$
$$= \text{for } v_1 \text{ in } e_1 \text{ do (for } v_2 \text{ in } e_2 \text{ do } e_3)$$

For example, a projection over a forest includes an implicit iteration, so $e \,/\, a =$ for v in e do $v \,/\, a$. Say we define a forest of bibliographies, bib1 = bib0 , bib0. Then bib1/book/author is equivalent to the first expression below, which in turn is equivalent to the second.

```
for b in (for a in bib1 do a/book) do b/author
= for a in bib1 do (for b in a/book do b/author
```

With nested relational algebra, the monad laws play a key role in optimizing queries. For instance, they are exploited extensively in the Kleisli system for biomedical data, developed by Limsoon Wong and others at the University of Pennsylvania and Kent Ridge Digital Labs, and now sold commercially [37]. Similarly, the monad laws can also be exploited for optimization in this context.

For example, if b is a book, the following find all authors of the book that are not Buneman:

```
for a in b do
  when a/data() != Buneman do
    a
```

If 1 is a list of authors, the following renames all author elements to auth elements:

```
for a' in l do
  auth[ a'/data() ]
```

Combining these, we select all authors that are not Buneman, and rename the elements:

```
for a' in (for a in b do
             when a/data() != Buneman do
               a) do
  auth[ a'/data() ]
```

Applying the associative law for a monad, we get:

```
for a in b do
  for a' in (when a/data() != Buneman do a) do
    auth[ a'/data() ]
```

Expanding the **when** clause to a conditional, we get:

```
for a in b do
  for a' in (if a/data() != Buneman then a else ()) do
    auth[ a'/data() ]
```

Applying a standard for loops over conditionals gives:

```
for a in b do
  if a/data() != Buneman then
    for a' in a do
      auth[ a'/data() ]
  else ()
```

Applying the left unit law for a monad, we get:

```
for a in b do
  if a/data() != Buneman then
    auth[ a/data() ]
  else ()
```

And replacing the conditional by a **when** clause, we get:

```
for a in b do
  when a/data() != Buneman do
    auth[ a/data() ]
```

Thus, simple manipulations, including the monad laws, fuse the two loops.

Section 3.1 ended with two examples of simplification. Returning to these, we can now see that the simplifications are achieved by application of the left unit and associative monad laws.

4   Expressions

Figure 1 contains the grammar for the algebra, i.e., the convenient concrete syntax in which a user may write a query. A few of these expressions can be rewritten as other expressions in a smaller *core* algebra; such derived expressions are labeled with "*". We define the algebra's typing rules on the smaller core algebra. In Section 6, we give the laws that relate a user expression with its equivalent expression in the core algebra. Typing rules for the core algebra are defined in Section 7.

We have seen examples of most of the expressions, so we will only point out a few details here. We include only two operators, + and =, and one aggregate function sum in the formal syntax, adding others is straightforward.

A query consists of a sequence of *query items*, where each query item is either a type declaration, a function declaration, a global variable declaration, or a query expression. The order of query items is immaterial; all type, function, and global variable declarations may be mutually recursive. Each query expression

tag	a		
function	f		
variable	v		
integer	c_{int}	$::= \cdots \mid -1 \mid 0 \mid 1 \mid \cdots$	
string	c_{str}	$::= \text{""} \mid \text{"a"} \mid \text{"b"} \mid \cdots \mid \text{"aa"} \mid \cdots$	
boolean	c_{bool}	$::= \textbf{false} \mid \textbf{true}$	
constant	c	$::= c_{\text{int}} \mid c_{\text{str}} \mid c_{\text{bool}}$	
expression	e	$::= c$	scalar constant
		$\mid v$	variable
		$\mid a[e]$	element
		$\mid \,\tilde{}e[e]$	computed element
		$\mid e , e$	sequence
		$\mid ()$	empty sequence
		$\mid \textbf{if } e \textbf{ then } e \textbf{ else } e$	conditional
		$\mid \textbf{let } v = e \textbf{ do } e$	local binding
		$\mid \textbf{for } v \textbf{ in } e \textbf{ do } e$	iteration
		$\mid \textbf{match } e_0$	match
		$\quad \textbf{case } v_1 : t_1 \textbf{ do } e_1$	
		$\quad \cdots$	
		$\quad \textbf{case } v_n : t_n \textbf{ do } e_n$	
		$\quad \textbf{else } e_{n+1}$	
		$\mid f(e;\ldots;e)$	function application
		$\mid \textbf{error}()$	error
		$\mid e + e$	plus
		$\mid e = e$	equal
		$\mid \textbf{sum}(e)$	aggregation
		$\mid \textbf{children}(e)$	children
		$\mid \textbf{name}(e)$	element name
		$\mid e \,/\, a$	element projection *
		$\mid e \,/\, \textbf{data}()$	scalar projection *
		$\mid \textbf{where } e \textbf{ then } e$	conditional *
		$\mid \textbf{empty}(e)$	empty test *
query item	q	$::= \textbf{type } x = t$	type declaration
		$\mid \textbf{fun } f(v{:}t;\ldots;v{:}t){:}t = e$	function declaration
		$\mid \textbf{let } v : t = e$	global declaration
		$\mid \textbf{query } e$	query expression
data	d	$::= c$	scalar constant
		$\mid a[d]$	element
		$\mid d , d$	sequence
		$\mid ()$	empty sequence

Fig. 1. Expressions

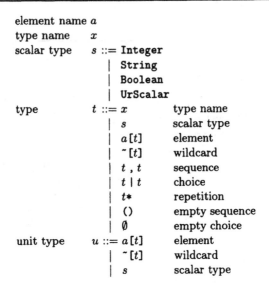

Fig. 2. Types

is evaluated in the environment specified by all of the declarations. (Typically, all of the declarations will precede all of the query expressions, but this is not required.)

We define a subset of expressions that correspond to *data values*. An expression is a data value if it consists only of scalar constant, element, sequence, and empty sequence expressions.

5   Types

Figure 2 contains the grammar for the algebra's type system. We have already seen many examples of types. Here, we point out some details.

Our algebra uses a simple type system that captures the essence of XML Schema [42]. The type system is close to that used in XDuce [21].

In the type system of Figure 2, a scalar type may be a UrScalar, Boolean, Integer, or String. In XML Schema, a scalar type is defined by one of fourteen primitive datatypes and a list of facets. A type hierarchy is induced between scalar types by containment of facets. The algebra's type system can be generalized to support these types without much increase in its complexity. We added UrScalar, because XML Schema does not support a most general scalar type.

A type is either: a type variable; a scalar type; an element type with element name a and content type t; a *wildcard* type with an unknown element name and content type t; a sequence of two types, a choice of two types; a repetition type; the empty sequence type; or the empty choice type.

The algebra's external type system, that is, the type definitions associated with input and output documents, is XML Schema. The internal types are in some ways more expressive than XML Schema, for example, XML Schema has no type corresponding to Integer* (which is required as the type of the argument to an aggregation operator like sum or min or max), or corresponding to ~[t] where t is some type other than UrTree*. In general, mapping XML Schema types into internal types will not lose information, however, mapping internal types into XML Schema may lose information.

5.1 Relating Values to Types

Recall that *data* is the subset of expressions that consists only of scalar constant, element, sequence, and empty sequence expressions. We write $\vdash d : t$ if data d has type t. The following type rules define this relation.

$$\frac{}{\vdash c_{\text{int}} : \texttt{Integer}}$$

$$\frac{}{\vdash c_{\text{str}} : \texttt{String}}$$

$$\frac{}{\vdash c_{\text{bool}} : \texttt{Boolean}}$$

$$\frac{}{\vdash c : \texttt{UrScalar}}$$

$$\frac{\vdash d : t}{\vdash a[d] : a[t]}$$

$$\frac{\vdash d : t}{\vdash a[d] : \mathord{\sim}[t]}$$

$$\frac{\vdash d_1 : t_1 \qquad \vdash d_2 : t_2}{\vdash d_1 , d_2 : t_1 , t_2}$$

$$\frac{}{\vdash () : ()}$$

$$\frac{\vdash d : t_1}{\vdash d : t_1 \mid t_2}$$

$$\frac{\vdash d : t_2}{\vdash d : (t_1 \mid t_2)}$$

$$\frac{\vdash d_1 \,:\, t \qquad \vdash d_2 \,:\, t*}{\vdash (d_1, d_2) \,:\, t*}$$

$$\frac{}{\vdash () \,:\, t*}$$

We write $t_1 <: t_2$ if for every data d such that $\vdash d \,:\, t_1$ it is also the case that $\vdash d \,:\, t_2$, that is t_1 is a subtype of t_2. It is easy to see that $<:$ is a partial order, that is it is reflexive, $t <: t$, and it is transitive, if $t_1 <: t_2$ and $t_2 <: t_3$ then $t_1 <: t_3$. Here are some of the inequations that hold.

$$
\begin{aligned}
\emptyset & <: t \\
t & <: \mathtt{UrType} \\
t_1 & <: t_1 \mid t_2 \\
t_2 & <: t_1 \mid t_2 \\
\mathtt{Integer} & <: \mathtt{UrScalar} \\
\mathtt{String} & <: \mathtt{UrScalar} \\
\mathtt{Boolean} & <: \mathtt{UrScalar} \\
a\,[t] & <: \mathtt{\tilde{}}\,[t]
\end{aligned}
$$

Further, if $t <: t'$ then

$$
\begin{aligned}
a\,[t] & <: a\,[t'] \\
t* & <: t'*
\end{aligned}
$$

And if $t_1 <: t_1'$ and $t_2 <: t_2'$ then

$$
\begin{aligned}
t_1 \,,\, t_2 & <: t_1' \,,\, t_2' \\
t_1 \mid t_2 & <: t_1' \mid t_2'
\end{aligned}
$$

We write $t_1 = t_2$ if $t_1 <: t_2$ and $t_2 <: t_1$. Here are some of the equations that hold.

$$
\begin{aligned}
\mathtt{UrScalar} & = \mathtt{Integer} \mid \mathtt{String} \mid \mathtt{Boolean} \\
(t_1 \,,\, t_2) \,,\, t_3 & = t_1 \,,\, (t_2 \,,\, t_3) \\
t \,,\, () & = t \\
() \,,\, t & = t \\
t_1 \mid t_2 & = t_2 \mid t_1 \\
(t_1 \mid t_2) \mid t_3 & = t_1 \mid (t_2 \mid t_3) \\
t \mid \emptyset & = t \\
\emptyset \mid t & = t \\
t_1 \,,\, (t_2 \mid t_3) & = (t_1 \,,\, t_2) \mid (t_1 \,,\, t_3) \\
(t_1 \mid t_2) \,,\, t_3 & = (t_1 \,,\, t_3) \mid (t_2 \,,\, t_3) \\
t \,,\, \emptyset & = \emptyset \\
\emptyset \,,\, t & = \emptyset \\
t* & = () \mid t \,,\, t*
\end{aligned}
$$

We also have that $t_1 <: t_2$ if and only iff $t_1 \mid t_2 = t_2$.

We define $t?$ and $t+$ as abbreviations, by the following equivalences.

$$
\begin{aligned}
t? & = () \mid t \\
t+ & = t \,,\, t*
\end{aligned}
$$

We define the *intersection* $t_1 \wedge t_2$ of two types t_1 and t_2 to be the largest type t that is smaller than both t_1 and t_2. That is, $t = t_1 \wedge t_2$ if $t <: t_1$ and $t <: t_2$ and if for any t' such that $t' <: t_1$ and $t' <: t_2$ we have $t <: t'$.

6 Equivalences and Optimization

6.1 Equivalences

Here are the laws that define derived expressions (those labeled with * in Figure 1) in terms of other expressions.

$$
\begin{aligned}
e \,/\, a \\
= \texttt{for } v_1 \texttt{ in } e \texttt{ do} \\
\quad \texttt{for } v_2 \texttt{ in children}(v_1) \texttt{ do} \\
\quad\quad \texttt{match } v_2 \\
\quad\quad\quad \texttt{case } v_3 \;:\; a \texttt{ do } v_3 \\
\quad\quad\quad \texttt{else ()}
\end{aligned}
\tag{1}
$$

$$
\begin{aligned}
e \,/\, \texttt{data()} \\
= \texttt{for } v_1 \texttt{ in } e \texttt{ do} \\
\quad \texttt{for } v_2 \texttt{ in children}(v_1) \texttt{ do} \\
\quad\quad \texttt{match } v_2 \\
\quad\quad\quad \texttt{case } v_3 \;:\; \texttt{UrScalar do } v_3 \\
\quad\quad\quad \texttt{else ()}
\end{aligned}
\tag{2}
$$

$$
\begin{aligned}
\texttt{where } e_1 \texttt{ then } e_2 \\
= \texttt{if } e_1 \texttt{ then } e_2 \texttt{ else ()}
\end{aligned}
\tag{3}
$$

$$
\begin{aligned}
\texttt{empty}(e) \\
= \texttt{match } e \texttt{ case } v \;:\; \texttt{() do true else false}
\end{aligned}
\tag{4}
$$

Law 1 rewrites the element projection expression $e \,/\, a$, as described previously. Law 2 rewrites the scalar projection expression $e \,/\, \texttt{data()}$, similarly. Law 3 rewrites a **where** expression as a conditional, as described previously. Law 4 rewrites an **empty** test using a **match** expression.

6.2 Optimizations

In a relational query engine, algebraic simplifications are often applied by a query optimizer before a physical execution plan is generated; algebraic simplification can often reduce the size of the intermediate results computed by a query interpreter. The purpose of our laws is similar – they eliminate unnecessary **for** or **match** expressions, or they enable other optimizations by reordering or distributing computations. The set of laws given here is suggestive, rather than complete.

Here are some simplification laws.

$$\texttt{for } v \texttt{ in () do } e = () \tag{1}$$

$$\begin{aligned}\texttt{for } v \texttt{ in } (e_1 , e_2) \texttt{ do } e_3 \\ = (\texttt{for } v \texttt{ in } e_1 \texttt{ do } e_3) , (\texttt{for } v \texttt{ in } e_2 \texttt{ do } e_3)\end{aligned} \tag{2}$$

$$\begin{aligned}\texttt{for } v \texttt{ in } e_1 \texttt{ do } e_2 \\ = e_2\{v := e_1\}, \quad \text{if } e : u\end{aligned} \tag{3}$$

$$\begin{aligned}\texttt{match } a[e_0] \texttt{ case } v : a \texttt{ do } e_1 \texttt{ else } e_2 \\ = e_1\{v := a[e_0]\}\end{aligned} \tag{4}$$

$$\begin{aligned}\texttt{match } a'[e_0] \texttt{ case } v : a \texttt{ do } e_1 \texttt{ else } e_2 \\ = e_2, \quad \text{if } a \neq a'\end{aligned} \tag{5}$$

$$\texttt{for } v \texttt{ in } e \texttt{ do } v = e \tag{6}$$

Laws 1, 2, and 3 simplify iterations. Law 1 rewrites an iteration over the empty sequence as the empty sequence. Law 2 distributes iteration through sequence: iterating over the sequence e_1 , e_2 is equivalent to the sequence of two iterations, one over e_1 and one over e_2. Law 3 is the left unit law for a monad. If e_1 is a unit type, then e_1 can be substituted for occurrences of v in e_2. Laws 4 and 5 eliminate trivial **case** expressions. Law 6 is the right unit law for a monad.

The remaining laws commute expressions. Each law actually abbreviates a number of other laws, since the *context variable* E stands for a number of different expressions. The notation $E[e]$ stands for one of the six expressions given with expression e replacing the hole $[]$ that appears in each of the alternatives.

$$\begin{aligned}E ::= \; &\texttt{if } [] \texttt{ then } e_1 \texttt{ else } e_2 \\ | \; &\texttt{let } v = [] \texttt{ do } e \\ | \; &\texttt{for } v \texttt{ in } [] \texttt{ do } e \\ | \; &\texttt{match } [] \\ &\quad \texttt{case } v_1 : t_1 \texttt{ do } e_1 \\ &\quad \cdots \\ &\quad \texttt{case } v_n : t_n \texttt{ do } e_n \\ &\quad \texttt{else } e_{n+1}\end{aligned}$$

Here are the laws for commuting expressions.

$$\begin{aligned}E[\texttt{if } e_1 \texttt{ then } e_2 \texttt{ else } e_3] \\ = \texttt{if } e_1 \texttt{ then } E[e_2] \texttt{ else } E[e_3]\end{aligned} \tag{7}$$

$$\begin{aligned}E[\texttt{let } v = e_1 \texttt{ do } e_2] \\ = \texttt{let } v = e_1 \texttt{ do } E[e_2]\end{aligned} \tag{8}$$

$$\begin{aligned}E[\texttt{for } v \texttt{ in } e_1 \texttt{ do } e_2] \\ = \texttt{for } v \texttt{ in } e_1 \texttt{ do } E[e_2]\end{aligned} \tag{9}$$

$$E[\text{match } e_0$$
$$\quad \text{case } v_1 \; : \; t_1 \; \text{do } e_1$$
$$\quad \cdots$$
$$\quad \text{case } v_n \; : \; t_n \; \text{do } e_n$$
$$\quad \text{else } e_{n+1}]$$
$$= \text{match } e_0 \qquad\qquad\qquad (10)$$
$$\quad \text{case } v_1 \; : \; t_1 \; \text{do } E[e_1]$$
$$\quad \cdots$$
$$\quad \text{case } v_n \; : \; t_n \; \text{do } E[e_n]$$
$$\quad \text{else } E[e_{n+1}]$$

Each law has the same form. Law 7 commutes conditionals, Law 8 commutes local bindings, Law 9 commutes iterations, and Law 10 commutes match expressions. For instance, one of the expansions of Law 9 is the following, when E is taken to be for v in $[]$ do e.

$$\text{for } v_2 \text{ in } (\text{for } v_1 \text{ in } e_1 \text{ do } e_2) \text{ do } e_3$$
$$= \text{for } v_1 \text{ in } e_1 \text{ do } (\text{for } v_2 \text{ in } e_2 \text{ do } e_3)$$

This will be recognized as the associative law for a monad.

7   Type Rules

We explain our type system in the form commonly used in the programming languages community. For a textbook introduction to type systems, see, for example, Mitchell [26].

7.1   Environments

The type rules make use of an environment that specifies the types of variables and functions. The type environment is denoted by Γ, and is composed of a comma-separated list of variable types, $v : t$ or function types, $f : (t_1; \ldots; t_n) \rightarrow t$. We retrieve type information from the environment by writing $(v : t) \in \Gamma$ to look up a variable, or by writing $(f : (t_1; \ldots; t_n) \rightarrow t) \in \Gamma$ to look up a function.

7.2   Type Rules

We write $\Gamma \vdash e \; : \; t$ if in environment Γ the expression e has type t. Below are all the rules except those for for and match expressions, which are discussed in the following subsections.

$$\overline{\Gamma \vdash c_{\text{int}} \; : \; \texttt{Integer}}$$

$$\overline{\Gamma \vdash c_{\text{str}} \; : \; \texttt{String}}$$

$$\overline{\Gamma \vdash c_{\text{bool}} : \text{Boolean}}$$

$$\frac{(v : t) \in \Gamma}{\Gamma \vdash v : t}$$

$$\frac{\Gamma \vdash e : t}{\Gamma \vdash a[e] : a[t]}$$

$$\frac{\Gamma \vdash e_1 : \text{String} \qquad \Gamma \vdash e_2 : t}{\Gamma \vdash \tilde{\ } e_1[e_2] : \tilde{\ }[t]}$$

$$\frac{\Gamma \vdash e_1 : t_1 \qquad \Gamma \vdash e_2 : t_2}{\Gamma \vdash e_1 , e_2 : t_1 , t_2}$$

$$\overline{\Gamma \vdash () : ()}$$

$$\frac{\Gamma \vdash e_1 : \text{Boolean} \qquad \Gamma \vdash e_2 : t_2 \qquad \Gamma \vdash e_3 : t_3}{\Gamma \vdash \text{if } e_1 \text{ then } e_2 \text{ else } e_3 : (t_2 \mid t_3)}$$

$$\frac{\Gamma \vdash e_1 : t_1 \qquad \Gamma, v : t_1 \vdash e_2 : t_2}{\Gamma \vdash \text{let } v = e_1 \text{ do } e_2 : t_2}$$

$$\frac{\begin{array}{c} (f : (t_1; \ldots; t_n) \to t) \in \Gamma \\ \Gamma \vdash e_1 : t_1' \qquad t_1' <: t_1 \\ \ldots \\ \Gamma \vdash e_n : t_n' \qquad t_n' <: t_n \end{array}}{\Gamma \vdash f(e_1; \ldots; e_n) : t}$$

$$\overline{\Gamma \vdash \text{error}() : \emptyset}$$

$$\frac{\Gamma \vdash e_1 : \text{Integer} \qquad \Gamma \vdash e_2 : \text{Integer}}{\Gamma \vdash e_1 + e_2 : \text{Integer}}$$

$$\frac{\Gamma \vdash e_1 : t_1 \qquad \Gamma \vdash e_2 : t_2}{\Gamma \vdash e_1 = e_2 : \text{Boolean}}$$

$$\frac{\Gamma \vdash e : \text{Integer*}}{\Gamma \vdash \text{sum } e : \text{Integer}}$$

7.3 Typing for Expressions

The type rule for for expressions uses the following auxiliary judgement. We write $\Gamma \vdash$ for $v : t$ do $e : t'$ if in environment Γ when the bound variable of an iteration v has type t then the body e of the iteration has type t'.

$$\frac{\Gamma, v : u \vdash e : t'}{\Gamma \vdash \text{for } v : u \text{ do } e : t'}$$

$$\overline{\Gamma \vdash \text{for } v : () \text{ do } e : ()}$$

$$\frac{\Gamma \vdash \text{for } v : t_1 \text{ do } e : t'_1 \qquad \Gamma \vdash \text{for } v : t_2 \text{ do } e : t'_2}{\Gamma \vdash \text{for } v : t_1 \, , t_2 \text{ do } e : t'_1 \, , t'_2}$$

$$\overline{\Gamma \vdash \text{for } v : \emptyset \text{ do } e : \emptyset}$$

$$\frac{\Gamma \vdash \text{for } v : t_1 \text{ do } e : t'_1 \qquad \Gamma \vdash \text{for } v : t_2 \text{ do } e : t'_2}{\Gamma \vdash \text{for } v : t_1 \mid t_2 \text{ do } e : t'_1 \mid t'_2}$$

$$\frac{\Gamma \vdash \text{for } v : t \text{ do } e : t'}{\Gamma \vdash \text{for } v : t* \text{ do } e : t'*}$$

Given the above, the type rule for for expressions is immediate.

$$\frac{\Gamma \vdash e_1 : t_1 \qquad \Gamma \vdash \text{for } v : t_1 \text{ do } e_2 : t_2}{\Gamma \vdash \text{for } v \text{ in } e_1 \text{ do } e_2 : t_2}$$

7.4 Typing Match Expressions

Due to the rule for iteration, it is possible that the body of an iteration is checked many times. Thus, when a match expression is checked, it is possible that quite a lot is known about the type of the expression being matched, and one can determine that only some of the clauses of the match apply. The definition of match uses the auxiliary judgments to check whether a given clause is applicable.

We write $\Gamma \vdash$ case $v : t$ do $e : t'$ if in environment Γ when the bound variable of the case v has type t then the body e of the case has type t'. Note the type of the body is irrelevant if $t = \emptyset$.

$$\frac{t \neq \emptyset \qquad \Gamma, v : t \vdash e : t'}{\Gamma \vdash \text{case } v : t \text{ do } e : t'}$$

$$\overline{\Gamma \vdash \text{case } v : \emptyset \text{ do } e : \emptyset}$$

We write $\Gamma \vdash t <: t'$ **else** $e : t''$ if in environment Γ when $t <: t'$ does not hold then the body e of the **else** clause has type t''. Note that the type of the body is irrelevant if $t <: t'$.

$$\frac{t <: t'}{\Gamma \vdash t <: t' \text{ else } e : \emptyset}$$

$$\frac{t \not<: t' \qquad \Gamma \vdash e : t''}{\Gamma \vdash t <: t' \text{ else } e : t''}$$

Given the above, it is straightforward to construct the typing rule for a **match** expression. Recall that we write $t \wedge t'$ for the intersection of two types.

$$\frac{\begin{array}{c} \Gamma \vdash e_0 : t_0 \\ \Gamma \vdash \text{case } v_1 : t_0 \wedge t_1 \text{ do } e_1 : t_1' \\ \cdots \\ \Gamma \vdash \text{case } v_n : t_0 \wedge t_n \text{ do } e_n : t_n' \\ \Gamma \vdash t_0 <: t_1 \mid \cdots \mid t_n \text{ else } e_{n+1} : t_{n+1}' \end{array}}{\Gamma \vdash \left(\begin{array}{l} \text{match } e_0 \\ \quad \text{case } v_1 \ : \ t_1 \ \text{do } e_1 \\ \quad \cdots \\ \quad \text{case } v_n \ : \ t_n \ \text{do } e_n \\ \quad \text{else } e_{n+1} \end{array} \right) : t_1' \mid \cdots \mid t_{n+1}'}$$

7.5   Top-Level Expressions

We write $\Gamma \vdash q$ if in environment Γ the query item q is well-typed.

$$\frac{}{\Gamma \vdash \text{type } x = t}$$

$$\frac{\Gamma, v_1 : t_1, \ldots, v_n : t_n \vdash e : t' \qquad t' <: t}{\Gamma \vdash f(v_1 : t_1; \ldots; v_n : t_n) : t = e}$$

$$\frac{\Gamma \vdash e : t' \qquad t' <: t}{\Gamma \vdash \text{let } v \ : \ t = e}$$

$$\frac{\Gamma \vdash e : t}{\Gamma \vdash \text{query } e}$$

We extract the relevant component of a type environment from a query item q with the function $environment(q)$.

$$\begin{array}{ll} environment(\text{type } x = t) & = () \\ environment(\text{fun } f(v_1 : t_1; \ldots; \ v_n : t_n) : t) & = f : (t_1; \ldots; t_n) \rightarrow t \\ environment(\text{let } v \ : \ t = e) & = v : t \end{array}$$

We write $\vdash q_1 \ldots q_n$ if the sequence of query items $q_1 \ldots q_n$ is well typed.

$$\frac{\Gamma = environment(q_1), \ldots, environment(q_n) \qquad \Gamma \vdash q_1 \quad \cdots \quad \Gamma \vdash q_n}{\vdash q_1 \ldots q_n}$$

8 Discussion

The algebra has several important characteristics: its operators are orthogonal, strongly typed, and they obey laws of equivalence and optimization.

There are many issues to resolve in the completion of the algebra. We enumerate some of these here.

Data Model. Currently, all forests in the data model are ordered. It may be useful to have unordered forests. The distinct operator, for example, produces an inherently unordered forest. Unordered forests can benefit from many optimizations for the relational algebra, such as commutable joins.

The data model and algebra do not define a global order on documents. Querying global order is often required in document-oriented queries.

Currently, the algebra does not support reference values, which are defined in the XML Query Data Model. The algebra's type system should be extended to support reference types and the data model operators ref and deref should be supported.

Type System. As discussed, the algebra's internal type system is closely related to the type system of XDuce. A potentially significant problem is that the algebra's types may lose information when converted into XML Schema types, for example, when a result is serialized into an XML document and XML Schema.

The type system is currently first order: it does not support function types nor higher-order functions. Higher-order functions are useful for specifying, for example, sorting and grouping operators, which take other functions as arguments.

The type system is currently monomorphic: it does not permit the definition of a function over generalized types. Polymorphic functions are useful for factoring equivalent functions, each of which operate on a fixed type. The lack of polymorphism is one of the principal weaknesses of the type system.

Operators. We intentionally did not define equality or relational operators on element and scalar types undefined. These operators should be defined by consensus.

It may be useful to add a fixed-point operator, which can be used in lieu of recursive functions to compute, for example, the transitive closure of a collection.

Functions. There is no explicit support for externally defined functions.

The set of builtin functions may be extended to support other important operators.

Recursion. Currently, the algebra does not guarantee termination of recursive expressions. In order to ensure termination, we might require that a recursive function take one argument that is a singleton element, and any recursive invocation should be on a descendant of that element; since any element has a finite number of descendants, this avoids infinite regress. (Ideally, we should have a simple syntactic rule that enforces this restriction, but we have not yet devised such a rule.)

References

1. S. Abiteboul, R. Hull, V. Vianu. *Foundations of Databases.* Addison Wesley, 1995.
2. Richard Bird. *Introduction to Functional Programming using Haskell.* Prentice Hall, 1998.
3. P. Buneman, M. Fernandez, D. Suciu. UnQL: A query language and algebra for semistructured data based on structural recursion. *VLDB Journal,* to appear.
4. Catriel Beeri and Yoram Kornatzky. Algebraic Optimization of Object-Oriented Query Languages. *Theoretical Computer Science* 116(1&2):59–94, August 1993.
5. Francois Bancilhon, Paris Kanellakis, Claude Delobel. *Building an Object-Oriented Database System.* Morgan Kaufmann, 1990.
6. Peter Buneman, Leonid Libkin, Dan Suciu, Van Tannen, and Limsoon Wong. Comprehension Syntax. *SIGMOD Record,* 23:87–96, 1994.
7. David Beech, Ashok Malhotra, Michael Rys. A Formal Data Model and Algebra for XML. W3C XML Query working group note, September 1999.
8. Peter Buneman, Shamim Naqvi, Val Tannen, Limsoon Wong. Principles of programming with complex object and collection types. *Theoretical Computer Science* 149(1):3–48, 1995.
9. Catriel Beeri and Yariv Tzaban, SAL: An Algebra for Semistructured Data and XML, *International Workshop on the Web and Databases (WebDB'99),* Philadelphia, Pennsylvania, June 1999.
10. R. G. Cattell. *The Object Database Standard: ODMG 2.0.* Morgan Kaufmann, 1997.
11. Don Chamberlin, Jonathan Robie, and Daniela Florescu. Quilt: An XML Query Language for Heterogeneous Data Sources. *International Workshop on the Web and Databases (WebDB'2000),* Dallas, Texas, May 2000.
12. Vassilis Christophides and Sophie Cluet and Jérôme Siméon. On Wrapping Query Languages and Efficient XML Integration. *Proceedings of ACM SIGMOD Conference on Management of Data,* Dallas, Texas, May 2000.
13. S. Cluet and G. Moerkotte. Nested queries in object bases. *Workshop on Database Programming Languages,* pages 226–242, New York, August 1993.
14. S. Cluet, S. Jacqmin and J. Siméon The New YAT$_L$: Design and Specifications. *Technical Report,* INRIA, 1999.
15. L. S. Colby. A recursive algebra for nested relations. *Information Systems* 15(5):567–582, 1990.
16. Hugh Darwen (Contributor) and Chris Date. *Guide to the SQL Standard: A User's Guide to the Standard Database Language SQL* Addison-Wesley, 1997.
17. A. Deutsch, M. Fernandez, D. Florescu, A. Levy, and D. Suciu. A query language for XML. In *International World Wide Web Conference,* 1999.
`http://www.research.att.com/-mff/files/final.html`

18. Mary Fernandez, Jerome Simeon, Philip Wadler. An Algebra for XML Query, Draft manuscript, June 2000.
19. Mary Fernandez, Jerome Simeon, Philip Wadler. An Algebra for XML Query, *Foundations of Software Technology and Theoretical Computer Science* (FSTTCS 2000), New Delhi, December 2000.
20. J. A. Goguen, J. W. Thatcher, E. G. Wagner. An initial algebra approach to the specification, correctness, and implementation of abstract data types. In *Current Trends in Programming Methodology*, pages 80–149, Prentice Hall, 1978.
21. Haruo Hosoya, Benjamin Pierce, XDuce : A Typed XML Processing Language (Preliminary Report). In *WebDB Workshop* 2000.
22. Haruo Hosoya, Benjamin Pierce, Jerome Vouillon, Regular Expression Types for XML. In *International Conference on Functional Programming (ICFP)*, September 2000.
23. M. Kifer, W. Kim, and Y. Sagiv. Querying object-oriented databases. In *Proceedings of ACM SIGMOD Conference on Management of Data*, pages 393–402, San Diego, California, June 1992.
24. Leonid Libkin and Limsoon Wong. Query languages for bags and aggregate functions. *Journal of Computer and Systems Sciences*, 55(2):241–272, October 1997.
25. Leonid Libkin, Rona Machlin, and Limsoon Wong. A query language for multi-dimensional arrays: Design, implementation, and optimization techniques. *SIGMOD 1996*.
26. John C. Mitchell *Foundations for Programming Languages*. MIT Press, 1998.
27. E. Moggi, Computational lambda-calculus and monads. In *Symposium on Logic in Computer Science*, Asilomar, California, IEEE, June 1989.
28. E. Moggi, Notions of computation and monads. *Information and Computation*, 93(1), 1991.
29. The Caml Language. `http://pauillac.inria.fr/caml/`.
30. J. Robie, editor. XQL '99 Proposal, 1999.
    `http://metalab.unc.edu/xql/xql-proposal.html`.
31. H.-J. Schek and M. H. Scholl. The relational model with relational-valued attributes. *Information Systems* 11(2):137–147, 1986.
32. S. J. Thomas and P. C. Fischer. Nested Relational Structures. In *Advances in Computing Research: The Theory of Databases*, JAI Press, London, 1986.
33. Philip Wadler. Comprehending monads. *Mathematical Structures in Computer Science*, 2:461-493, 1992.
34. P. Wadler, Monads for functional programming. In M. Broy, editor, *Program Design Calculi*, NATO ASI Series, Springer Verlag, 1993. Also in J. Jeuring and E. Meijer, editors, *Advanced Functional Programming*, LNCS 925, Springer Verlag, 1995.
35. P. Wadler, How to declare an imperative. *ACM Computing Surveys*, 29(3):240–263, September 1997.
36. Philip Wadler. A formal semantics of patterns in XSLT. Markup Technologies, Philadelphia, December 1999.
37. Limsoon Wong. An introduction to the Kleisli query system and a commentary on the influence of functional programming on its implementation. *Journal of Functional Programming*, to appear.
38. World-Wide Web Consortium XML Query Data Model, Working Draft, May 2000.
    `http://www.w3.org/TR/query-datamodel`.
39. World-Wide Web Consortium, XML Path Language (XPath): Version 1.0. November, 1999. `/www.w3.org/TR/xpath.html`
40. World-Wide Web Consortium, XML Query: Requirements, Working Draft. August 2000. `http://www.w3.org/TR/xmlquery-req`

41. World-Wide Web Consortium, XML Query: Data Model, Working Draft. May 2000. http://www.w3.org/TR/query-datamodel/
42. World-Wide Web Consortium, XML Schema Part 1: Structures, Working Draft. April 2000. http://www.w3.org/TR/xmlschema-1
43. World-Wide Web Consortium, XML Schema Part 2: Datatypes, Working Draft, April 2000. http://www.w3.org/TR/xmlschema-2.
44. World-Wide Web Consortium, XSL Transformations (XSLT), Version 1.0. W3C Recommendation, November 1999. http://www.w3.org/TR/xslt.

Algebraic Rewritings for Optimizing Regular Path Queries

Gösta Grahne and Alex Thomo

Concordia University
{grahne,thomo}@cs.concordia.ca

Abstract. Rewriting queries using views is a powerful technique that has applications in query optimization, data integration, data warehousing etc. Query rewriting in relational databases is by now rather well investigated. However, in the framework of semistructured data the problem of rewriting has received much less attention. In this paper we focus on extracting as much information as possible from algebraic rewritings for the purpose of optimizing regular path queries. The cases when we can find a complete exact rewriting of a query using a set a views are very "ideal." However, there is always information available in the views, even if this information is only partial. We introduce "lower" and "possibility" partial rewritings and provide algorithms for computing them. These rewritings are algebraic in their nature, i.e. we use only the algebraic view definitions for computing the rewritings. This fact makes them a main memory product which can be used for reducing secondary memory and remote access. We give two algorithms for utilizing the partial lower and partial possibility rewritings in the context of query optimization.

1 Introduction

Semistructured data is a self-describing collection, whose structure can naturally model irregularities that cannot be captured by relational or object-oriented data models [ABS99]. This kind of data is usually best formalized in terms of labelled graphs, where the graphs represent data found in many useful applications such web information systems, XML data repositories, digital libraries, communication networks, and so on. Almost all the query languages for semi-structured data provide the possibility for the user to query the database through regular expressions. The design of query languages using regular path expressions is based on the observation that many of the recursive queries that arise in practice amount to graph traversals. These queries are in essence graph patterns and the answers to the query are subgraphs of the database that match the given pattern [MW95,FLS98,CGLV99,CGLV2000].

For example, for answering a query containing in it the regular expression $(\_^* \cdot article) \cdot (\_^* \cdot ref \cdot \_^* \cdot (ullman + widom))$ one should find all the paths having at some point an edge labelled $article$, followed by any number of other edges then by an edge ref and finally by an edge labelled with $ullman$ or $widom$.

J. Van den Bussche and V. Vianu (Eds.): ICDT 2001, LNCS 1973, pp. 301–315, 2001.
© Springer-Verlag Berlin Heidelberg 2001

Based on practical observations, the most expensive part of answering queries on semistructured data is finding these graph patterns described by regular expressions. This is, because a regular expression can describe arbitrary long paths in the database which means in turn an arbitrary number of physical accesses. Hence it is clear that, having a good optimizer for answering regular path (sub)queries is very important. This optimizer can be used for the broader class of full fledged query languages for semistructured data.

In semistructured data, as well as in other data models such as relational and object oriented, the importance of utilizing views is well recognized [LMSS95], [CGLV99], [Lev99]. Simply stated, the problem is: Given a query Q and a set of views $\{V_1, \ldots, V_n\}$, find a representation of Q by means of the views and then answer the query on the basis of this representation. Several papers [LMSS95, Ull97,GM99,PV99] investigate this problem for the case of conjunctive queries. The methods in these papers are based on the query containment and the fact that the number of literals in the minimal rewriting is bounded from above by the number of literals in the query.

It is obvious that a method for rewriting of regular path queries requires a technique for rewriting of regular expressions, i.e. given a regular expression E and a set of regular expressions $E_1, E_2, ..., E_n$ one wants to compute a function $f(E_1, E_2, ..., E_n)$ which approximates E. As far as the authors know, there are two methods for computing such a function f which approximates E from below. The first one of Conway [Con71] is based on the derivatives of regular expressions which provide the ground for the development of an algebraic theory of factorization in the regular algebra that in turn gives the tools for computing the approximating function. The second method by Calvanese et al [CGLV99] is automata based. Both methods are equivalent in the sense that they compute the same rewriting of a query. However, these methods model –using views– only full paths of the database, i.e. paths whose labels spell a word belonging to the regular language of the query. But in practice, the cases in which we can infer from the views full paths for the query are very "ideal." The views can cover partial paths which can be satisfactory long for using them in optimization but if they are not complete paths, they are ignored by the above mentioned methods. So, it would probably be better to give a partial rewriting in order to encapture all the information provided by the views. The information provided by the views is always useful, even if it is partial and not complete. The problem of a partial rewriting is touched upon briefly in [CGLV99]. However, there this problem is considered only as an extension of the complete rewriting, enriching the set of the views with new elementary one-symbol views, and materializing them before query evaluation. The choice of the new elementary views to be materialized is done in a brute force way, using some cost criteria depending on the application.

In this paper we use a very different approach. For each word in the regular language of the query we do the best possible using views. If the word contains a sub-path that a view has traversed before, we use that view for evaluation. We present generalized query answering algorithms that access the database only when necessary. For the "been there" subpaths our algorithms use the views. Note that we do not materialize any new views, we only consult the database "on the fly," as needed.

The outline of the paper is as follows. In Section 2 we formalize the problem of query rewriting using views in the realistic framework of cached views and available database. Then we discuss the utility of algebraic rewritings. We illustrate through an example that the complete rewritings can be empty for a particular query, while the partial information provided by the views is no less than 99% of the complete "missing" information. In Section 3 we introduce and formally define a new algebraic, formal-language operator, the *exhaustive replacement*. Simply described, given two languages L_1 and L_2, the result of the exhaustive replacement of $L - 2$ in L_1 is the replacement, by a special symbol, of all the words of L_2 that occur as sub-words in the words of L_1. Then we give a theorem showing that the result of the exhaustive replacement can be represented as an intersection of a rational transduction and a regular language. The proof of the theorem is constructive and provides an algorithm for computing the exhaustive replacement operator. In Section 4 we present the partial possibility rewriting that is a generalization of the previously introduced exhaustive replacement operator. In Section 5 we define a partial lower rewriting. It is the largest subset of words in the partial possibility rewriting such that their expansions to the the database alphabet are contained in the query language. In Section 6 we review a typical query answering algorithm for regular path queries and show how two modify it into two other "lazy" algorithms for utilizing the partial lower and possibility rewritings respectively. The computational complexity is studied in Section 7. We show that, although exponential, the algorithms proposed for computing the partial possibility and partial lower rewritings are essentially optimal.

2 Background

Rewriting regular queries. Let Δ be a finite alphabet, called the *database alphabet*. Elements of Δ will be denoted $R, S, T, R', S', \ldots, R_1, S_1, \ldots$, etc. Let $\mathbf{V} = \{V_1, \ldots, V_n\}$ be a set of *view definitions*, with each V_i being a finite or infinite regular language over Δ. Associated with each view definition V_i is a view name v_i. We call the set $\Omega = \{v_1, \ldots, v_n\}$ the *outer alphabet*, or *view alphabet*. For each $v_i \in \Omega$, we set $def(v_i) = V_i$. The substitution def associates with each view name v_i in Ω alphabet the language V_i. The substitution def is applied to words, languages, and regular expressions in the usual way (see e. g. [HU79]).

A *(user) query* Q is a finite or infinite regular language over Δ. Sometimes we need to refer to regular expressions representing the languages Q and V_i. We then write $re(Q)$ and $re(V_i)$ respectively to denote these expressions.

A *maximal lower rewriting* (l-rewriting) of a user query Q using $\mathbf{V}$ is a language Q' over Ω, that includes *all* the words $v_{i_1} \ldots v_{i_k} \in \Omega$, such that

$$def(v_{i_1} \ldots v_{i_k}) \subseteq Q.$$

A *maximal possibility rewriting* (p-rewriting) of a user query Q using $\mathbf{V}$ is a language Q'' over Ω, that includes *all* the words $v_{i_1} \ldots v_{i_k} \in \Omega$, such that

$$def(v_{i_1} \ldots v_{i_k}) \cap Q \neq \emptyset.$$

For instance, if $re(Q)$ is $(RS)^*$, and we have the views V_1, V_2, V_3 and V_4 available, with $re(V_1) = R + SS$, $re(V_2) = S$, $re(V_3) = SR$ and $re(V_4) = (RS)^2$ respectively, the l-rewriting is v_4^* and the p-rewriting is $(v_4 + v_1 v_3^* v_2)^*$.

Semistructured databases. We consider a database to be an edge labeled graph. This graph model is typical in semistructured data, where the nodes of the database graph represent the objects and the edges represent the attributes of the objects, or relationships between the objects.

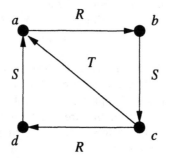

Fig. 1. An example of a graph database

Formally, we assume that we have a universe of objects D. Objects will be denoted $a, b, c, a', b', \ldots, a_1, b_2, \ldots$, and so on. A *database DB* over (D, Δ) is a pair (N, E), where $N \subseteq D$ is a set of nodes and $E \subseteq N \times \Delta \times N$ is a set of directed edges labeled with symbols from Δ. Figure 1 contains an example of a graph database.

If there is a path labeled $R_1, R_2, \ldots, R_k$ from a node a to a node b we write $a \xrightarrow{R_1 \cdot R_2 \ldots R_k} b$. Let Q be a query and $DB = (N, E)$ a database. Then the *answer to Q on DB* is defined as

$$ans(Q, DB) = \{(a, b) \in N^2 \; : \; a \xrightarrow{W} b \text{ for some } W \in Q\}.$$

For instance, if DB is the graph in Figure 1, and $Q = \{SR, T\}$, then $ans(Q, DB)$ $= \{(b, d), (d, b), (c, a)\}$

What are rewritings good for? In a scenario with a database and materialized views there are various assumptions, such as the exactness/soundness/completeness of the views, and whether the database relations are available, and if so, at what cost compared to the cost of accessing the views (see papers [AD98,GM99,Lev99]). Depending on the application (information integration, cache-based optimization, etc) different assumptions are valid. The use of rewritings in answering user queries using views have been thoroughly investigated in the case of relational databases (see e.g. the survey [Lev99]). For the case of semi-structured databases much less is currently known. Notably, Calvanese et al [CGLV99] show how to obtain l-rewritings, and the same authors, in [CGLV2000] discuss the possible use of l-rewritings in information integration applications. The present authors show in [GT2000] how p-rewritings are obtained and how they are profitable in information integration applications, where the database graph is unavailable. The paper [GT2000] shows that running an l-rewriting on the view extensions is guaranteed to produce a subset of the desired answer, while running the p-rewriting is guaranteed to produce a superset.

In particular, the l-rewriting can be empty, even if the desired answer is not. Suppose for example that query Q is $re(Q) = R_1 \ldots R_{100}$ and we have available two views V_1 and V_2, where $re(V_1) = R_1 \ldots R_{49}$ and $re(V_2) = R_{51} \ldots R_{100}$. It is easy to see that the l-rewriting is empty. However, depending on the application, a "partial rewriting" such as $v_1 R_{50} v_2$ could be useful. In the next section we develop a formal algebraic framework for the partial rewritings. This framework is flexible enough and can be easily tailored to the specific needs of the various applications. In Section 6 we demonstrate the usability of the partial rewritings in query optimization.

3   Replacement – A New Algebraic Operator

In this section we introduce and study a new algebraic operation, the exhaustive replacement in words and languages. It is similar in spirit to the deletion and insertion language operations studied in [Kari91].

Let W be a word, and M a ϵ-free language over some alphabet, and let $\dagger$ be a symbol outside that alphabet. Then we define

$$\rho_M(W) = \begin{cases} \{W_1 \dagger W_3 : \exists \ W_2 \in M \text{ such that } W = W_1 W_2 W_3\} & \text{if non-empty} \\ \{W\} & \text{otherwise.} \end{cases}$$

Furthermore, let L be a set of words over the same alphabet as M. Then define $\rho_M(L) = \bigcup_{W \in L} \rho_M(W)$. We can now define the *powers of* ρ_M as follows:

$$\rho_M^1(\{W\}) = \rho_M(W), \quad \rho_M^{i+1}(\{W\}) = \rho_M(\rho_M^i(\{W\})).$$

Let k be the smallest integer such that $\rho_M^{k+1}(\{W\}) = \rho_M^k(\{W\})$. We then set

$$\rho_M^*(W) = \rho_M^k(\{W\}).$$

(It is clear that k is at most the number of symbols in W.)

The *exhaustive replacement* of a ϵ-free language M in a language L, using a special symbol $\dagger$ not in the alphabet, can be simply defined as

$$L \triangleright M = \bigcup_{W \in L} \rho_M^*(W).$$

Intuitively, the exhaustive replacement $L \triangleright M$ replaces in every word $W \in L$ the non-overlapping occurrences of words from M with the special symbol †. Moreover, between two occurrences of words of M that have been replaced, no nonempty word from M remains as a subword.

Example 1. Let $L = \{RSRSRSR, RRSRSR, RSRRSRRSR\}$, $M = \{RSR\}$. Then

$$L \triangleright M = \{†S†, RS†SR, R†SR, RRS†, †††\},$$

being the union of the sets:

$$\rho^*_{\{RSR\}}(RSRSRSR) = \{†S†, RS†SR\},$$
$$\rho^*_{\{RSR\}}(RRSRSR) = \{R†SR, RRS†\},$$
$$\rho^*_{\{RSR\}}(RSRRSRRSR) = \{†††\}.$$

Computing the Replacement Operation. To this end, we will give first a characterization of the $\triangleright$ operator. The construction in the proof of our characterization provides the basic algorithm for computing the result of the $\triangleright$ operator on given languages. The construction is based on finite transducers.

A *finite transducer* $T = (S, I, O, \delta, s, F)$ consists of a finite set of states S, an input alphabet I, and output alphabet O, a starting state s, a set of final states F, and a transition-output function δ from finite subsets of $S \times I^*$ to finite subsets of $S \times O^*$. Intuitively, for instance $(q_1, W) \in \delta(q_0, U)$ means that if the transducer is in state q_0 and reads word U, it can go to state q_1 and emit the word W. For a given word $U \in I^*$, we say that a word $W \in O^*$ is an *output of T for U* if there exists a sequence $(q_1, W_1) \in \delta(s, U_1)$, $(q_2, W_2) \in \delta(q_1, U_2)$, ..., $(q_n, W_n) \in \delta(q_{n-1}, U_n)$ of state transitions of T, such that $q_n \in F$, $U = U_1 \ldots U_n$, and $W = W_1 \ldots W_n$. We write $W \in T(U)$, where $T(U)$ denotes the set of all outputs of T for the input word U. For a language $L \subseteq I^*$, we define $T(L) = \bigcup_{U \in L} T(U)$. It is well known that $T(L)$ is regular whenever L is.

We are now in a position to state our characterization theorem.

Theorem 1. *Let L and M be regular languages over an alphabet Δ. There exists a finite transducer T and a regular language M' such that:*

$$L \triangleright M = T(L) \cap M'.$$

Proof sketch. Let $A = (S, \Delta, \delta, s_0, F)$ be a nondeterministic finite automaton that accepts the language M. Let us consider the finite transducer:

$$T = (S \cup \{s'_0\}, \Delta, \Gamma, \delta', s'_0, \{s'_0\}),$$

where $\Gamma = \Delta \cup \{†\}$, and, written as a relation,

$$\delta' = \{(s, R, s', \epsilon) : (s, R, s') \in \delta\} \cup$$
$$\{(s_0', R, s_0', R) : R \in \Delta\} \cup$$
$$\{(s_0', R, s, \epsilon) : (s_0, R, s) \in \delta\} \cup$$
$$\{(s_0', R, s_0', \dagger) : (s_0, R, s) \in \delta \text{ and } s \in F\} \cup$$
$$\{(s, R, s_0', \dagger) : (s, R, s') \in \delta \text{ and } s' \in F\}.$$

Intuitively, transitions in the first set of δ' are the transitions of the "old" automaton modified so as to produce ϵ as output. Transitions in the second set mean that "if we like, we can leave everything unchanged," i.e. each symbol gives itself as output. Transitions in the third set are for jumping non-deterministically from the new initial state s_0' to the states of the old automaton A, that are reachable in one step from the old initial state s_0. These transitions give ϵ as output. Transitions in the fourth set are for handling special cases, when from the old initial state q_0, an old final state can be reached in one step. In these cases we can replace the one symbol words accepted by A with the special symbol $\dagger$. Finally, the transitions of the fifth set are the most significant. Their meaning is: in a state, where the old automaton has a transition by a symbol, say R, to an old final state, there will in the transducer be an additional transition $R/\dagger$ to s_0', which is also the (only) final state of T. Observe, that if the transducer T decides to leave the state s_0' while a suffix U of the input string is unscanned, and enter the old automaton A, then it can return back only if there is a prefix U' of U, such $U' \in L(A)$. In this case the trasducer replaces U', which is a subword of the input string, by the special symbol $\dagger$.

Given a word of $W \in L$ as input, the finite transducer T replaces arbitrary many occurences of words of M in W with the special symbol symbol $\dagger$.

For an example, suppose M is $R(SR)^* + RST$. Then an automaton that accepts this language is given in Figure 2 drawn with solid arrows. The corresponding finite transducer is shown in the same figure in the right. It consists of the automaton A, whose transitions now produce as output ϵ, plus the state s_0' and the additional transitions drawn with dashed arrows.

It can now be shown that

$$T(L) = L \cup \{U_1 \dagger U_2 \dagger \ldots \dagger U_k : \text{ for some } U \text{ in } L \text{ and words } W_i \text{ in } M,$$
$$U = U_1 W_1 U_2 W_2 \ldots W_{k-1} U_k\}.$$

From the transduction $T(L)$ we get all the words of L having replaced in them an arbitrary number of words from M. What we like is not an arbitrary but an exhaustive replacement of words from M. To achive this goal we will intersect the language $T(L)$ with a regular language M' which will serve as a "mask" for the words of $L \triangleright M$. We set

$$M' = (\Gamma^* M \Gamma^*)^c.$$

Now M' guarantees that no other candidate for replacing occurs inside the words of the final result. □

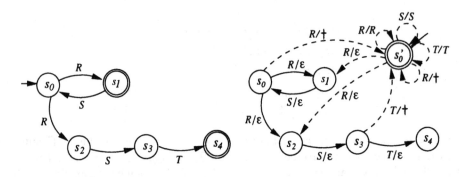

Fig. 2. An example of the construction of a replacement transducer

4   Partial P-Rewritings

We can give a natural generalization of the definition of the replacement operator for the case when we like to exhaustively replace subwords not from one language only, but from a finite set of languages (such as a finite set of view definitions). For this purpose, let W be a word and $\mathbf{M} = \{M_1, \ldots, M_n\}$ be a set of languages over some aplhabet, and let $\{\dagger_1, \ldots, \dagger_n\}$ be a set of symbols outside that alphabet. Now we define

$$\rho_{\mathbf{M}}(W) = \begin{cases} \{W_1 \dagger_i W_3 : \exists\, W_2 \in M_i \text{ such that } W = W_1 W_2 W_3\} & \text{if non-empty} \\ \{W\} & \text{otherwise.} \end{cases}$$

Then, $\rho_{\mathbf{M}}^*$ is defined similarly to ρ_M^*.

The *generalized exhaustive replacement* of $\mathbf{M} = \{M_1, \ldots, M_n\}$ in a language L, by the corresponding special symbols $\dagger_1, \ldots, \dagger_n$, is

$$L \triangleright \mathbf{M} = \bigcup_{W \in L} \rho_{\mathbf{M}}^*(W).$$

In the following we will define the notion of the *partial p-rewriting* of a database query Q using a set $\mathbf{V} = \{V_1, \ldots, V_n\}$ of view definitions.

Definition 1 The *partial p-rewriting* of a query Q over Δ using a set $\mathbf{V} = \{V_1, \ldots, V_n\}$ of view definitions over Δ is

$$Q \triangleright \mathbf{V},$$

with $\Omega = \{v_1, \ldots, v_n\}$ as the corresponding set of special symbols.

As a generalization of Theorem 1 we can give the following result about the partial p-rewriting of a query Q over Δ using a set $\mathbf{V} = \{V_1, \ldots, V_n\}$ of view definitions over Δ.

Theorem 2. *The partial p-rewriting $Q \triangleright \mathbf{V}$ can be effectively computed.*

Proof sketch. Let $A_i = (S_i, \Delta, \delta_i, s_{0i}, F_i)$, for $i \in [1, n]$ be n nondeterministic finite automata that accept the corresponding V_i languages. Let us consider the finite transducer:

$$T = (S_1 \cup \ldots \cup S_n \cup \{s'_0\}, \Delta, \Delta \cup \Omega, \delta', s'_0, \{s'_0\}),$$

where

$$
\begin{aligned}
\delta' = \ &\{(s, R, s', \epsilon) : (s, R, s') \in \delta_i, \ i \in [1, n]\} \cup \\
&\{(s'_0, R, s'_0, R) : R \in \Delta\} \cup \\
&\{(s'_0, R, s, \epsilon) : (s_{0i}, R, s) \in \delta_i, \ i \in [1, n]\} \cup \\
&\{(s'_0, R, s'_0, \dagger_i) : (s_{0i}, R, s) \in \delta_i \text{ and } s \in F_i, \ i \in [1, n]\} \cup \\
&\{(s, R, s'_0, \dagger_i) : (s, R, s') \in \delta_i \text{ and } s' \in F_i, \ i \in [1, n]\}.
\end{aligned}
$$

The transducer T performs the following task: given a word of Q as input, it replaces nondeterministically some words of $V_1 \cup \ldots \cup V_n$ from the input with the corresponding special symbols. The proof of this claim is similar as in the previous theorem.

From the tranduction $T(Q)$ we get all the words of Q having replaced in them an arbitrary number of words from $V_1 \cup \ldots \cup V_n$. But what we like is the exhaustive replacement $Q \triangleright \mathbf{V}$. For this we intersect the language $T(Q)$ with the regular language

$$\left((\Delta \cup \Omega)^* (V_1 \cup \ldots \cup V_n)(\Delta \cup \Omega)^* \right)^c,$$

which will serve as a mask for extracting the words in the exhaustive replacement.

□

We note here that the partial p-rewriting of a query is a generalization of the p-rewriting. Indeed, consider the the substitution from $\Omega \cup \Delta$ that maps each $v_i \in \Omega$ to the corresponding regular view language V_i and each database symbol $R \in \Delta$ to itself. This substitution is the extension of the *def* substitution to the Δ alphabet and we call it def'. Then the partial p-rewriting is the set of *all* the words W on $\Omega \cup \Delta$, with no subwords in any of $V_1, \ldots, V_n$, such that $def'(W)$ has a non empty intersection with Q. The conceptual similarity of the partial p-rewriting with p-rewriting can also be observed in another way; change the above mask to Ω^* and the result will be the p-rewriting, as opposed to the partial p-rewriting.

5   Partial L-Rewritings

We defined the l-rewriting of a query Q given a set of view definitions $\mathbf{V} = \{V_1, \ldots, V_n\}$ as the set of all the words W on the view alphabet Ω such that $def(W)$ is contained in the query language Q. In the same spirit we will define the partial l-rewriting. It will be the set of all "mixed" words W on the alphabet

$\Omega \cup \Delta$, with no subword in $V_1 \cup \cdots \cup V_n$, such that their substitution by the extended def' is contained in the query Q. The condition that there is no subword in $V_1 \cup \cdots \cup V_n$, says that in fact the partial l-rewriting is a subset of the partial p-rewriting.

Definition 2 The *partial l-rewriting* of a query Q on Δ is the language Q' on $\Omega \cup \Delta$ given by

$$Q' = \{W \in (Q \triangleright \mathbf{V}) : def'(W) \subseteq Q\}.$$

We now give a method for computing the partial l-rewriting, given a query Q and a set $\mathbf{V} = \{V_1, \ldots, V_n\}$ of view definitions as input.

Algorithm 1   *1. Compute the complement Q^c of the query.*
   2. Construct the transducer T used for the partial p-rewriting. Then compute the transduction $T(Q^c)$.
   3. Compute the complement $(T(Q^c))^c$ of the previous transduction.
   4. Intersect the complement $(T(Q^c))^c$ with the mask

$$M = ((\Delta \cup \Omega)^* (V_1 \cup \ldots \cup V_n)(\Delta \cup \Omega)^*)^c$$

Denote with Q' the result.   □

Theorem 3. *The mixed $\Omega \cup \Delta$ language Q' gives exactly the partial l-rewriting of Q.*

Proof. "$\subseteq$". $T(Q^c)$ is the set of all words W on $\Omega \cup \Delta$ such that $def'(W) \cap Q^c \neq \emptyset$. Hence, $(T(Q^c))^c$, being the complement of this set, will contain only $\Omega \cup \Delta$ words such that *all* the Δ-words in their substitution by def' will be contained in Q. This is the first condition for a word on $\Omega \cup \Delta$ to be in the partial l-rewriting of Q. Furthermore, intersecting with the mask M we keep in $(T(Q^c))^c$ only the $\Omega \cup \Delta$ words that do not contain Δ subwords in $V_1 \cup \cdots \cup V_n$. This is the second condition for a word on $\Omega \cup \Delta$ to be in the partial l-rewriting of Q.

"$\supseteq$". We will prove this direction by a contradiction. First observe that both the partial l-rewriting and the set Q' are subsets of the partial p-rewriting, that is, all their words "pass" the mask M. In other words their words do not have subwords in $V_1 \cup \cdots \cup V_n$. Suppose now, that the mixed $\Omega \cup \Delta$-word W is in the partial l-rewriting but not in Q'. That is $def'(W) \subseteq Q$. On the other hand, since $W \notin Q'$ it follows that $W \in Q'^c$ which means that $W \in T(Q^c) \cup M^c$. But as we mentioned before, the word W, which belongs in the partial l-rewriting, "passes" the mask M and this implies that it cannot "pass" the complement of the mask. Therefore, $W \in T(Q^c)$. Thus $def'(W) \cap Q^c \neq \emptyset$ that is, $def'(W) \not\subseteq Q$, i.e. W cannot be in the partial l-rewriting, a contradiction.   □

6 Query Optimization Using Partial Rewritings and Views

In this section we show how to utilize partial rewritings in query optimization in a scenario where we have available a set of precomputed views, as well as the database itself. The views could be materialized views in a warehouse, or locally cached results from previous queries in a client/server environment. In this scenario the views are assumed to be excact, and we are interested in answering the query by consulting the views as far as possible, and by accessing the database only when necessary.

Formally, let $\Omega = \{v_1, \ldots v_n\}$ be the view alphabet and let $\mathbf{V} = \{V_1, \ldots, V_n\}$ be a set of view definitions as before. Given a database DB, which is a graph, where the edges are labelled with database symbols from Δ, we define the *view graph* $\mathcal{V}$ over $(\mathbf{V}, \Omega)$ to be a database over (D, Ω) induced by the set

$$\bigcup_{i \in \{1, \ldots, n\}} \{(a, v_i, b) : (a, b) \in ans(V_i, DB)\}.$$

of Ω-labelled edges.

It is now straightforward to show, that if the l-rewriting Q' is exact (meaning $def(Q') = Q$), then $ans(Q, DB) = ans(Q', \mathcal{V})$ (see Calvanese et al. [CGLV2000]).

However, the cases when we are able to obtain an exact rewriting of the query using the views would be rare in practice, in the general we have in the views only part of the information needed to answer the query. So, should we ignore this partial information only beacuse it is not complete? In the previous sections we showed how this partial information can be captured algebraically by the partial rewritings. In the following, we use the partial rewritings not to avoid *completely* accesing database, but to *minimize* such access as much as possible.

However, in order to be able to utilize the partial l-rewriting Q', it should be exact, i.e. we require that $def'(Q') = Q$. We can use for testing the exactness the optimal algorithm of [CGLV99].

Given an exact partial l-rewriting, we can use it to evaluate the query on the view-graph, and accessing the database in a "lazy" fashion, only when necessary. Before describing the lazy algorithm, let us review how query answering on semistructured databases typically works [ABS99].

Algorithm 2 We are given a regular expression for Q and a database graph DB. First construct an automaton A_Q for Q. Let N be the set of nodes in the database graph, and s_0 be the initial state in A_Q. For each node $a \in N$ compute a set $Reach_a$ as follows.

1. Initialize $Reach_a$ to $\{(a, s_0)\}$.
2. Repeat 3 until $Reach_a$ no longer changes.
3. Choose a pair $(x, s) \in Reach_a$. If there is a database symbol R, such that a transition $s \xrightarrow{R} s'$ is in A_Q and an edge $a \xrightarrow{R} a'$ is in the database DB, then add the pair (x', a') to $Reach_a$.

Finally, set

$$ans(Q, DB) = \{(a, b) : a \in N, (b, s) \in Reach_a, \text{ and } s \text{ is a final state in } A_Q\}.$$

$\square$

In the following we modify this algorithm into a lazy algorithm for answering a query Q using its partial l-rewriting with respect to a set of cached exact views.

Algorithm 3 We are given an automaton $A_{Q'}$, corresponding to an exact partial l-rewriting Q' and the view graph $\mathcal{V}$. Let N be the set nodes in $\mathcal{V}$, and s_0 be the initial state in $A_{Q'}$. For each node $a \in N$ then compute a set $Reach_a$.

1. Initialize $Reach_a$ to $\{(a, s_0)\}$, and $Expanded_a$ to **false**.
2. For each database symbol R, if there is in $A_{Q'}$ a transition $s_0 \xrightarrow{R} s$ from the initial state s_0, then access the database and add to $\mathcal{V}$ the subgraph of DB induced by the R-edges.
3. Repeat 4 until $Reach_a$ no longer changes.
4. Choose a pair $(x, s) \in Reach_a$. If there is a view or database symbol R, such that a transition $s \xrightarrow{R} s'$ is in $A_{Q'}$, go to 5.
5. If there is an edge $a \xrightarrow{R} a'$ in the viewgraph, add the pair (x', a') to $Reach_a$. Otherwise, if $Expanded_a =$ **false**, set $Expanded_a =$ **true**, access the database and add to $\mathcal{V}$ the subgraph of DB induced by all edges originating from a.

Set $eval(Q', \mathcal{V}, DB) =$

$$\{(a, b) : a \in N, (b, s) \in Reach_a, \text{ and } s \text{ is a final state in } A_{Q'}\}.$$

$\square$

Theorem 4. *Given a query Q and a set of exact views, if the partial l-rewriting Q' of Q is exact, then $eval(Q', \mathcal{V}, DB) = ans(Q, DB)$.*

Next, let us discuss how to utilize the partial p-rewriting Q'' of a query Q for computing the answer set $ans(Q, DB)$. If we use the same algorithm as in the case of the partial l-rewriting we might get a proper superset of the answer. Note however that, contrary to Algorithm 3, in any case the partial p-rewriting does not need to be exact.

Theorem 5. *Given a query Q and a set $\mathcal{V}$ of exact views, if Q'' is the partial p-rewriting of Q using $\mathcal{V}$, then $ans(Q, DB) \subseteq eval(Q'', \mathcal{V}, DB)$.*

In other words, we are not sure if all the pairs are valid. To be able to discard false hits, suppose that the views are materialized using Algorithm 2. We can then associate each pair (a, b) in the view graph with their derivation. That is, for each pair (a, b) connected with an edge, say v_i, in the view graph, we associate an automaton, say A_{ab}, with start state a and final states $\{b\}$. What is this automaton? For each pair (a, b), we can consider the database graph as a non-deterministic automaton DB_{ab} with initial state a and final states $\{b\}$. It is now easy to see that

$$A_{ab} = DB_{ab} \cap A_{V_i}$$

where A_{V_i} is an automaton for the view V_i. We are now ready to formulate the algorithm for using the partial p-rewriting in query answering.

Algorithm 4

1. Compute $eval(Q'', \mathcal{V}, DB)$ using Algorithm 3. During the execution of Algorithm 3 the view graph $\mathcal{V}$ is extended with new edges and nodes as described. Call the extended view graph $\mathcal{V}'$.
2. Replace in $\mathcal{V}'$ each edge labeled with a view symbol, say v_i, between two objects a and b with the automaton A_{ab} of the derivation. Call the new graph $\mathcal{V}''$.
3. Set $verified(Q'', \mathcal{V}, DB) = eval(Q'', \mathcal{V}, DB) \cap \{(a, b) : ans(Q, \mathcal{V}''_{ab}) \neq \emptyset\}$, where $\mathcal{V}''_{ab}$ is a non-deterministic automata similar to D_{ab}.

Theorem 6. *Given a query Q and a set $\mathcal{V}$ of exact views, if Q'' is the partial p-rewriting of Q using $\mathcal{V}$, then $verified(Q'', \mathcal{V}, DB) = ans(Q, DB)$.*

7 Complexity Analysis

The following theorem establishes an upper bound for the problem of generating the exhaustive replacement $L \triangleright M$, where L and M are regular languages.

Theorem 7. *Generating the exhaustive replacement of a regular language M from another language L can be done in exponential time.*

Proof. Let us refer to the cost of the steps in the constructive proof of the Theorem 1. To construct a non-deterministic automaton for the language M and using it to construct the transducer g is polynomial. To compute the transduction of the regular language L, $g(L)$, is again polynomial. But at the end, in order to compute the subset of the words in $g(L)$, to which no more replacement can be applied, is exponential. This is because we intersect with a mask that is a language described by an extended regular language containing complementation. □

Theorem 8. *Let Γ be an alphabet and A, B be regular languages over Γ. Then the problem of deciding the emptiness of $A \cap (\Gamma^* B \Gamma^*)^c$ is PSPACE complete.*

We are now in a position to prove the following result.

Theorem 9. *There exist regular languages L and M, such that the exhaustive replacement $L \triangleright M$ cannot be computed in polynomial time, unless PTIME = PSPACE.*

Proof. Suppose that given two regular expressions A and B on alphabet Γ we like to test the emptiness of $A \cap (\Gamma^* B \Gamma^*)^c$. Without loss of generality let us assume that there exists one symbol in A that does not not appear in B. To see why even with this restriction the above problem of emptiness is still PSPACE complete, imagine that we can simply have a tape symbol which does not appear at all in the definition of the transition function of the Turing machine. Then this symbol will appear in the above set A but not in B (see Appendix). Let us denote this special symbol with †. We substitute the † symbol in A with the regular expression B. The result will be another regular expression A' which has polynomial size. Clearly, $A \cap (\Gamma^* B \Gamma^*)^c = A \cap (A' \triangleright B)$.

As a conclusion, if we had a polynomial time algorithm producing a polynomial size representation for $A' \triangleright B$, we could polynomially construct an NFA for $A \cap (A' \triangleright B)$. Then we could check in NLOGSPACE the emptiness of this NFA. This means that, the emptiness of $A \cap (\Gamma^* B \Gamma^*)^c$ could be checked in PTIME, which is a contradiction, unless PTIME=PSPACE. □

Corollary 1 *The algorithm in the proof of Theorem 2 for computing the partial p-rewriting of a query Q using a set $\mathbf{V} = \{V_1, \ldots, V_n\}$ of view definitions, is essentially optimal.*

Theorem 10. *Given a query Q and a set $\mathbf{V} = \{V_1, \ldots, V_n\}$ of view definitions, the partial l-rewriting can be computed in 2EXPTIME.*

Proof. Let us refer to the constructive proof of the Theorem 3. To compute the complement Q^c of the query is exponential. To transduce it to $T(Q^c)$ is polynomial. To complement again is exponential. So, in total we have 2EXPTIME. To compute the mask is EXPTIME and to intersect is polynomial. Finally, 2EXPTIME + EXPTIME = 2EXPTIME. □

For the partial lower rewriting we have the following.

Theorem 11. *Algorithm 1 for computing the partial l-rewriting of a query Q using a set $\mathbf{V} = \{V_1, \ldots, V_n\}$ of view definitions, is essentially optimal.*

Proof. Polynomially intersect the partial l-rewriting with Ω^* and get the l-rewriting of [CGLV99]. But, the l-rewriting is optimally computed in doubly exponential time in [CGLV99], so our algorithm is essentially optimal. □

References

[Abi97]   S. Abiteboul. Querying Semistructured Data. *Proc. of ICDT* 1997 pp. 1-18.

[ABS99]   S. Abiteboul, P. Buneman and D. Suciu. *Data on the Web : From Relations to Semistructured Data and Xml.* Morgan Kaufmann, 1999.

[AD98]   S. Abiteboul, O. M. Duschka. Complexity of Answering Queries Using Materialized Views. *Proc. of PODS* 1998 pp. 254-263

[AHV95]   S. Abiteboul, R. Hull and V. Vianu. *Foundations of Databases.* Addison-Wesley, 1995.

[AQM+97]   S. Abiteboul, D. Quass, J. McHugh, J. Widom and J. L. Wiener. The Lorel Query Language for Semistructured Data. *Int. J. on Digital Libraries* 1997 1(1) pp. 68-88.

[Bun97]   P. Buneman. Semistructured Data. *Proc. of PODS* 1997, pp. 117-121.

[BDFS97]   P. Buneman, S. B. Davidson, M. F. Fernandez and D. Suciu. Adding Structure to Unstructured Data. *Proc. of ICDT* 1997, pp. 336-350.

[CGLV99]   D. Calvanese, G. Giacomo, M. Lenzerini and M. Y. Vardi. Rewriting of Regular Expressions and Regular Path Queries. *Proc. of PODS* 1999, pp. 194-204.

[CGLV2000] D. Calvanese, G. Giacomo, M. Lenzerini and M. Y. Vardi. Answering Regular Path Queries Using Views. *Proc. of ICDE* 2000, pp. 389-398.

[CGLV2000]   D. Calvanese, G. Giacomo, M. Lenzerini and M. Y. Vardi. View-Based Query Processing for Regular Path Queries with Inverse. *Proc. of PODS* 2000, pp. 58-66.

[Con71]   J. H. Conway. *Regular Algebra and Finite Machines.* Chapman and Hall 1971.

[DFF+99]   A. Deutsch, M. F. Fernandez, D. Florescu, A. Y. Levy, D. Suciu. A Query Language for XML. *WWW8/Computer Networks 31(11-16)* 1999, pp. 1155-116.

[DG97]   O. Duschka and M. R. Genesereth. Answering Recursive Queries Using Views. *Proc. of PODS* 1997, pp. 109-116.

[FS98]   M. F. Fernadez and D. Suciu. Optimizing Regular path Expressions Using Graph Schemas *Proc. of ICDE* 1998, pp. 14-23.

[FLS98]   D. Florescu, A. Y. Levy, D. Suciu Query Containment for Conjunctive Queries with Regular Expressions *Proc. of PODS* 1998, pp. 139-148.

[GM99]   G. Grahne and A. O. Mendelzon. Tableau Techniques for Querying Information Sources through Global Schemas. *Proc. of ICDT* 1999 pp. 332-347.

[GT2000]   G. Grahne and A. Thomo. An Optimization Technique for Answering Regular Path Queries. *Proc. of WebDB* 2000.

[HU79]   J. E. Hopcroft and J. D. Ullman *Introduction to Automata Theory, Languages, and Computation.* Addison-Wesley 1979.

[HRS76]   H. B. Hunt and D. J. Rosenkrantz, and T. G. Szymanski, On the Equivalence, Containment, and Covering Problems for the Regular and Context-Free Languages. *Journal of Computing and System Sciences* 12(2) 1976, pp. 222-268

[Kari91]   L. Kari. *On Insertion and Deletion in Formal Languages.* Ph.D. Thesis, 1991, Department of Mathematics, University of Turku, Finland.

[Lev99]   A. Y. Levy. *Answering queries using views: a survey.* Submitted for publication 1999.

[LMSS95]   A. Y. Levy, A. O. Mendelzon, Y. Sagiv, D. Srivastava. Answering Queries Using Views. *Proc. of PODS* 1995, pp. 95-104.

[MW95]   A. O. Mendelzon and P. T. Wood, Finding Regular Simple Paths in Graph Databases. *SIAM J. Comp. 24:6,* (December 1995).

[MMM97]   A. O. Mendelzon, G. A. Mihaila and T. Milo. Querying the World Wide Web. *Int. J. on Digital Libraries 1(1),* 1997 pp. 54-67.

[MS99]   T. Milo and D. Suciu. Index Structures for Path Expressions. *Proc. of ICDT,* 1999, pp. 277-295.

[PV99]   Y. Papakonstantinou, V. Vassalos. Query Rewriting for Semistructured Data. proc. of SIGMOD 1999, pp. 455-466

[Ull97]   J. D. Ullman. Information Integration Using Logical Views. *Proc. of ICDT* 1997, pp. 19-40.

[Var88]   M. Y. Vardi. The universal-relation model for logical independence. *IEEE Software.*

[Yu97]   S. Yu. Reqular Languages. In: *Handbook of Formal Languages.* G. Rozenberg and A. Salomaa (Eds.). Springer Verlag 1997, pp. 41-110

Why and Where:
A Characterization of Data Provenance*

Peter Buneman, Sanjeev Khanna**, and Wang-Chiew Tan

University of Pennsylvania
Department of Computer and Information Science
200 South 33rd Street, Philadelphia, PA 19104, USA
{peter,sanjeev,wctan}@saul.cis.upenn.edu

Abstract. With the proliferation of database views and curated databases, the issue of *data provenance* – where a piece of data came from and the process by which it arrived in the database – is becoming increasingly important, especially in scientific databases where understanding provenance is crucial to the accuracy and currency of data. In this paper we describe an approach to computing provenance when the data of interest has been created by a database query. We adopt a syntactic approach and present results for a general data model that applies to relational databases as well as to hierarchical data such as XML. A novel aspect of our work is a distinction between "why" provenance (refers to the source data that had some influence on the existence of the data) and "where" provenance (refers to the location(s) in the source databases from which the data was extracted).

1 Introduction

Data provenance — sometimes called "lineage" or "pedigree" — is the description of the origins of a piece of data and the process by which it arrived in a database. The field of molecular biology, for example, supports some 500 public databases [1], but only a handful of these are "source" data in the sense that they receive experimental data. All the other databases are in some sense *views* either of the source data or of other views. In fact, some of them are views of each other, which sounds nonsensical until one understands that the individual databases are not simply computed by queries, but also have added value in the form of corrections and annotations by experts (they are "curated"). A serious problem confronting the user of one of these databases is knowing the provenance of a given piece of data. This information is essential to anyone interested in the accuracy and timeliness of the data.

Understanding provenance and the process by which one records it is a complex issue. In this paper we address an important part of the general problem. Suppose a database (a view) $V = Q(D)$ is constructed by a query Q applied to

---

* This work was partly supported by a Digital Libraries 2 grant DL-2 IIS 98-17444
** Supported in part by an Alfred P. Sloan Research Fellowship.

J. Van den Bussche and V. Vianu (Eds.): ICDT 2001, LNCS 1973, pp. 316–330, 2001.
© Springer-Verlag Berlin Heidelberg 2001

databases D and we ask for the provenance of some piece of data d in $Q(D)$: what parts of the database D contributed to d? The problem has been addressed by [7,2] for relational databases. In particular [7] considers the question : given a *tuple* in $Q(D)$ what tuples in D contributed to it. The crucial question here is what is meant by "contributed to". By examining provenance in a more general setting we draw a distinction between "where-provenance" – where does a given piece of data come from and – "why-provenance" – why is it in the database. Consider the following example:

```
SELECT name, telephone
FROM employee
WHERE salary > SELECT AVERAGE salary FROM employee
```

If one sees the tuple ("John Doe",1234) in the output one could argue that every tuple in contributed to it, for modifying any tuple in the employee relation could affect the presence of ("John Doe",1234) in the result. This is the why-provenance and it is what is studied in [7] as the set of contributing tuples. On the other hand, suppose one asks *where* the telephone number 1234 in the tuple ("John Doe",1234) comes from, the answer is apparently much simpler: from the telephone field "John Doe" tuple in the input. This statement presupposes that name is a key for the employee relation; if it is not we need some other means of identifying the tuple in the source, for SQL does *not* eliminate duplicates. (Had we used SELECT UNIQUE the answer would be a set of locations.) The point is that where-provenance requires us to identify locations in the source data. Where-provenance is important for understanding the source of errors in data (what source data should John Doe investigate if he discovers that his telephone number is incorrect in the view.) It is also important for carrying annotations through database queries. Therefore as a basis for describing where-provenance, we use the data model proposed in [6] in which there is an explicit notion of location. The model has the advantage that it allows us to study provenance in a more general context than the relational model. Existing work on provenance considers only the relational model.

Outline. In the next section we describe the *deterministic* model in [6]. We then give a *syntactic* characterization of why-provenance and show that it is invariant under query rewriting. To this end, in Section 3 we describe a natural normal form for queries and give a strong normalization result for query rewriting. The normal form is useful because it also gives us a reasonable basis for defining where-provenance which turns out to be problematic and cannot, in general be expected to be invariant under query rewriting. We discuss a possible restriction for which where-provenance has a satisfactory characterization.

Related work. Why-provenance has been studied for relations in [2,7]. To our knowledge no-one has studied where-provenance. A definition of why-provenance for relational views is given in [7], which also shows how to compute why-provenance for queries in the relational algebra. There, a semantic characterization of provenance is given which, when restricted to SPJU, has the expected properties such as invariance under query rewriting. In fact, the syntactic techniques developed in this paper, when restricted to a natural interpretation of the relational model, yield identical results to those in [7]. We do not know whether there is semantic characterization for where-provenance nor do we know whether there is a semantic characterization of why-provenance that is well behaved on anything beyond than SPJU queries.

Expressing the why-provenance for a query is loosely related to the view maintenance problem [17]. It is apparently simpler in (a) that in why-provenance we are not interested in what is not in the view (view maintenance needs to account for additions to the database) and (b) that we are not asking how to reconstruct a view under a change to the source. Conversely, there is a loose connection between where-provenance and the view update problem. (If I want to update a data element in the output, what elements in the input need to be changed.) Recently, [10] has proposed using the deterministic model described here for view maintenance in scientific databases.

2   A Deterministic Model

We describe the data model in [6] where the *location* of any piece of data can be uniquely described by a *path*. This model uses a variation of existing edge-labeled tree models for semistructured data [14,13]. It is more restrictive in that the out-edges of each node have distinct labels; it is less restrictive because these labels may themselves be pieces of semistructured data[1]. Figure 1 shows how certain common data structures can be expressed in this "deterministic" model of semistructured data. Here, any node in the deterministic tree is uniquely determined by a path of edge labels from root node to that node. These paths are analogous to *l*-values in programming language terminology. We will describe shortly how relations can be cast in this model by using the keys as edge labels. Any object-oriented or semistructured database with *persistent* object identifiers for all structures can also be expressed. There is also a variety of hierarchical data formats that implicitly conform to this model. Notably ACeDB [9], a lightweight DBMS originally developed as a database for genetic data conforms rather closely to this model and also supports certain operations such as "deep union" which are essential to the techniques developed in this paper.

2.1   Syntax and Operations

Values. We use the notation $x{:}y$ to denote a pair whose label is x and value is y. We can think of x as the edge label and y as the subtree under it. We use the notation $\{x_1{:}y_1,...,x_n{:}y_n\}$ to denote a set of such pairs. Since the edge-labels $x_1,...,x_n$ are distinct, this notation describes a *finite partial function* from values to values. A set of values $\{s_1,...,s_n\}$ can always be described in our model by mapping each element in the set to some standard constant (c in Figure 1). The last example shows how edge labels can be themselves pieces of semi-structured data. Value equality can be computed inductively.

---

[1] For the purposes of normal forms, these pieces of semistructured data are required to be "linear".

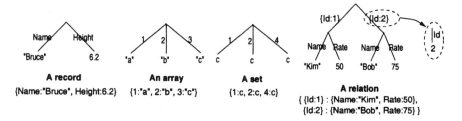

Fig. 1. Examples of data structures represented in our syntax.

Paths. We use the notation $x_1.x_2.....x_n$ for paths. In the last example of Figure 1, the path $\{\texttt{Id:1}\}$ identifies the value $\{\texttt{Name:"Kim"}, \texttt{Rate:50}\}$ and the path $\{\texttt{Id:1}\}.\texttt{Rate}$ identifies the value 50.

Abbreviation. We use $e_1.e_2.....e_{n-1}{:}e_n$ as a shorthand for $\{e_1{:}\{e_2{:} \{...\{e_{n-1}{:}e_n\}...\}\}\}$. We can think of $e_1.e_2.....e_{n-1}$ as the path leading to the value e_n. For example, $\{\texttt{Id:1}\}.\texttt{Name:Kim}$ is an abbreviation for $\{\{\texttt{Id:1}\}{:}\{\texttt{Name:Kim}\}\}$.

Traversal. We use $v(p)$ to denote the subtree identified by a path p in value v. If path p does not occur in v, then $v(p)$ is undefined. For example: $\{\texttt{a:1,b:2}\}(\texttt{c})$ is undefined while $\{\{\texttt{c:3}\}{:}\texttt{1,b:2}\}(\{\texttt{c:3}\})$ is 1.

Path representation. Observe that any value in our model can be described by specifying the set of all paths to the constants at the terminal nodes. We call this the *path representation* of v. For example, the path representation of $\{\texttt{a:}\{\texttt{1:c,3:d}\}\}$ is $\{(\texttt{a.1,c}),(\texttt{a.3,d})\}$.

Definition 1. (Substructure) w is a *substructure* of v, denoted as $w \sqsubseteq v$, if the path representation of w is a subset of the path representation of v.   □

Example. $\texttt{a:}\{\texttt{1:c,3:d}\} \sqsubseteq \texttt{a:}\{\texttt{1:c,2:b,3:d}\}$ but $\texttt{a:}\{\texttt{1:c,3:d}\} \not\sqsubseteq \texttt{b.a:}\{\texttt{1:c,3:d}\}$. It is easy to see that since our model is deterministic, if $w \sqsubseteq v$ then w occurs as a part of v in a unique way.

Definition 2. (Deep Union) The *deep union* of v_1 with v_2, written as $v_1 \sqcup v_2$ is the value whose path representation is the union of the path representations of v_1 and v_2. Note that the result may not be a partial function in which case the deep union is undefined.   □

Example. The deep union of $\{\texttt{a:1,b.c:2}\}$ and $\{\texttt{b.d:4,e:5}\}$ is $\{\texttt{a:1,b:}\{\texttt{c:2,} \texttt{d:4}\},\texttt{e:5}\}$ while the deep union of $\{\texttt{a:1,b.c:2}\}$ and $\{\texttt{b.c:3,e:5}\}$ is undefined.

2.2 An Encoding of Relations

We can encode relations as follows. Each relation name forms the label of an outgoing edge from the root node which is in turn mapped to the set of keys from that relation. Each key of a relation is then mapped to the corresponding tuple it identifies in the relation. If there is no key, the tuples are modeled as a

where $p_1 \in e_1$,	where $sp_1 \in D_1$,	where Composers.x.born:$u \in D$,
$\vdots$	$\vdots$	$u < 1700$
$p_n \in e_n$,	$sp_n \in D_n$	collect $\{year:u\}$:C
condition	condition	
collect e	collect se	
(a)	(b)	(c)

Fig. 2. (a) General form and (b) normal form of a query fragment. (c) An example.

set, that is, the entire tuple becomes an edge label. As an example, suppose we have two relations Composers and Works as shown below. The key for Composers is name and Works has a compound key (name, opus). The figure below also shows the encoding of the relations into our model. We see that keys of a tuple are placed on an edge in our model. If a tuple contains a compound key, we could model the entire compound key as a "linear" piece of semistructured data on the edge. That is, each key is placed one after another on the same edge. It does not matter which order we serialize the keys so long as this is done in a consistent manner.

Composers

name	born	period
"J.S. Bach"	1685	"baroque"
"G.F Handel"	1685	"baroque"
"W.A Mozart"	1756	"classical"

Works

name	opus	title
"J.S. Bach"	"BMV82"	"I have enough."
"J.S. Bach"	"BMV552"	NULL
"G.F Handel"	"HMV19"	"Art thou troubled?"

```
{ Composers:
    {{name:"J.S. Bach"}: {born:1685, period:"baroque"},
     {name:"G.F. Handel"}: {born:1685, period:"baroque"},
     {name:"W.A. Mozart"}: {born:1756, period:"classical"}},
  Works: {{{name:"J.S. Bach"}.opus:"BMV82"}:
              { title: "I have enough." },
          {{name:"J.S. Bach"}.opus:"BMV552"}:
              { title: "-" },
          {{name:"G.F Handel"}.opus:"HMV19"}:
              { title: "Art thou troubled?" }} }
```

2.3   XML

At first sight, XML does not conform to a deterministic model. Insofar as some formal model for XML has been developed in the Document Object Model (DOM) [15] it is that of a *node*-labeled graph in which child labels may be repeated. The fact that it is node labeled is a minor irritant. Uniqueness is more serious. However, in the absence of any system of keys (see [16]) we can still fall back on the property, specified by the DOM, that child nodes can be uniquely identified by their positions and attribute nodes by their names. We defer the details of the translation of XML and a query language such as XML-QL [8] into our deterministic model and query language to the full version of this paper.

3   A Query Language

Query languages for semistructured data [3] are based on a general syntactic form shown in Figure 2(a). The p_is are patterns whose syntax follows the syntax for data (as defined in the previous section) augmented with variables[2]. Expressions $e, e_1, ..., e_n$ are essentially the same as patterns but may contain "where ...

---

[2] In semistructured query languages, patterns can also include regular expressions on the edge labels. We will not deal with such patterns in this paper.

collect..." expressions (nested queries). *condition* is simply a boolean predicate on the variables of the query.

The interpretation of a "where ... collect..." expression is as follows: consider each assignment of the variables in the expression that makes each pattern p_i a substructure of the corresponding expression e_i. For each such assignment, evaluate the *condition*. If it is true, add the (instantiated) value of e to the output. Finally "union" together the output values. This interpretation is quite general, but to make it precise we must (a) define what we mean by "union" and (b) say what values a variable can bind to (a constant, an arbitrary value, or something in between). Languages, see [13,5] vary in their choice of the "union" operation. In our case, we use the deep union operation. Thus the output of the query in Figure 2(c) is {year:1685}:C even though this value is emitted twice. A consequence of this is that the result of a query maybe undefined.

We add the deep union operation to our language, and the general syntax can be summarized by the following grammar:

$e ::=$ **where** $p \in e, \dots, p \in e,$ *condition* **collect** $e \mid e \sqcup e \mid \{e : e\} \mid c \mid x$

where c ranges over constants, x over variables, p over patterns and *condition* over conditions. Note that $\{e_1 : e'_1, \dots, e_n : e'_n\}$ is in fact a shorthand for $\{e_1 : e'_1\} \sqcup \dots \sqcup \{e_n : e'_n\}$. We refer to this query language, for want of a better term, as DQL (Deterministic QL). The syntax of the query language is quite general, but its interpretation is limited by the model. In order to set up the machinery to analyze provenance, we will make some restrictions both on the syntax and interpretation of queries for the soundness of our rewrite rules. First, we impose some syntactic restrictions.

Definition 3. (Well-Formed Query) A query Q is said to be *well-formed* if (a) no pattern p_i is a single variable, (b) each expression e_i is either a (nested) query or an expression that does not involve a query, and (c) each comparison is between variables or between variables and constants only. □

Conditions (a) and (b) are required for the soundness of our rewrite rules. Condition (c) restricts our queries to the "conjunctive" fragment for which containment of queries can be easily determined. In addition to well-formedness, we say a query is *well-defined* if it is not undefined on any input. For the rest of the paper, we consider only queries that are both well-formed and well-defined. The next restriction we place is on the interpretation of a query. For this, we need the notion of a *singular* expression, which consists of a single path terminated by a constant or variable.

Definition 4. (Singular expression) A expression e is *singular* if $e \neq (e_1 \sqcup e_2)$ for any non-empty and distinct expressions e_1 and e_2. □

Our restriction on the interpretation is that variables may only bind to singular values. At first sight, this seems very restrictive and the interpretation of a query is unusual. Consider the query (a) in Figure 3. It binds singular values to y, and the output is {{name:"J.S. Bach"}.born:1685, {name:"G.F. Handel"}.born:1685}. This is probably not the expected output for someone

where Composers.$x : y \in$ D,
    born.$u \in y$,
    $u < 1700$
collect $x : y$
(a)

where Composers.$x : y \in$ D,
    born.$u \in y$,
    Composers.$x : z \in$ D,
    $u < 1700$
collect $x : z$
(b)

Fig. 3. More example DQL queries. C denotes some constant.

familiar with, say, XML-QL in which variables bind to complete subtrees. However there is an easy translation, illustrated in query (b) from the XML-QL interpretation[3] into DQL. Note that the deep union reconstructs the subtree.

Restrictive as it may seem, DQL can capture positive (SPJU) relational queries and positive nested relational algebra ([12]). It is less expressive than XML-QL in that (a) it cannot express path patterns involving a Kleene-star(*), (b) it works only on hierarchical structures, and (c) the forms of Skolem function and nested query forms in XML-QL that can be simulated are limited. We omit the details in this paper.

Definition 5. (Normal Form) A query Q is said to be in *normal form* if Q has the form $Q_1 \sqcup ... \sqcup Q_m$ where each Q_i is as shown in Figure 2(b). sp_i and se is a singular pattern and singular expression respectively. D_i is a database constant and *condition* is a boolean predicate on the variables of the query. $\square$

Our main result in this section is that every well-formed query has an equivalent normal form which can be determined from our rewrite system $\mathcal{R}$. We omit the details of $\mathcal{R}$ and state the *strong normalization* result which says that starting from any well-formed query, any sequence of application of rewrite rules leads to a normal form in a finite number of steps.

Theorem 1. (Strong Normalization) The rewrite system $\mathcal{R}$ is strongly normalizing.

4   Two Meanings of Provenance

Equipped with a data model and query language, we are now in a position to formulate two meanings of provenance and to compute the provenance of a component d in a view $V = Q(D)$ where Q is as query and D is the source data. We will formulate the provenance of d as a query Q' that is completely determined by Q, D and d.

where
  Composers.{name:x}.{born:u,period:v} $\in$ D,
  Works.{{name:x}.opus:w}:$y \in$ D
collect
  {name:x}.{born:u, {opus:w}:y}

```
{ {name:"J.S. Bach"}:
    {born:1685,
    {opus:"BMV82"}:{title:"I have enough."},
    {opus:"BMV552"}:{title:"-"} },
  {name:"G.F. Handel"}:
    {born:1685,
    {opus:"HMV19"}:{title:"Art thou troubled?"}
    } }
```

---

[3] We assume that the XML-QL interpretation contains a skolem function that groups by composer names.

The above query, say Q_1 expresses a join on components of the database described in Section 2.2. Consider the value referenced by {name:"G.F Handel"}. born. This value was generated by Q_1 as any instance of the "collect" expression in which the variable x was bound to "G.F Handel" and u to 1685. We now look at the patterns in the "where" clause to find what (simultaneous) matches of these patterns caused these bindings. In this case there is only one such match consisting of the patterns (after instantiating the variables):

```
Composers.{name:"G.F.Handel"}.{born:1685,period:"baroque"}
Works.{{name:"G.F. Handel"}.opus:"HMV19"}.title:"Art thou troubled?"
```

Moreover if we apply Q_1 to any database that contains these structures, we will obtain an output that contains {name:"G.F. Handel"}.born:1685. This is the rationale for calling these structures the why-provenance of the value referenced by {name:"G.F Handel"}.born. However, if we are interested in the where-provenance of {name:"G.F Handel"}.born, we only need to look at the pattern(s) that bind the variable u to determine that it came from the path Composers.{name:"G.F Handel"}.born.

Our example suggests that one natural approach to compute provenance is via syntactic analysis of the query and this is the approach that we take.

5   Why-Provenance

In the model-theoretic approach to datalog programs described in [4], these programs are viewed as a set of first-order sentences describing the desired answer. For example, if we have a datalog rule $R(u) : -R_1(u_1), ..., R_n(u_n)$, we could associate the logical sentence: $\forall x_1, ..., x_m \bigwedge_{i \in [1..n]} R_i(u_i) \to R(u)$ where $x_1, ..., x_m$ are variables occuring the in the rule. A DQL query $\{e \mid p_1 \in D, ..., p_n \in D, condition\}$ could be viewed as the following logical sentence: $\forall x_1, ..., x_m$ $(\bigwedge_{i \in [1..n]} p_i \in D$ and $condition) \to e$ is in the output. $x_1, ..., x_m$ are variables which occurs in the query. Therefore a value v is provable if there exists a valuation that will make the premise true and puts v in the output.

As discussed earlier, the structures in the why-provenance example correspond to a proof for {name:"G.F Handel"}.born:1685. We call the collection of values taken from D that proves an output, a *witness* for the output. More specifically, we say a value s is a *witness* for a value t with respect to a query Q and a database D, if $t \sqsubseteq Q(s)$ and $s \sqsubseteq D$. The value shown below is a witness for {name:"G.F Handel"}.born:1685.

```
{ Composers.{name:"G.F. Handel"}.{born:1685, period:"baroque"},
  Works.{{name:"G.F. Handel"}.opus:"HMV19"}.title:"Art thou troubled?" }
```

5.1   Witness Basis

We now refine the notion of witness as introduced above to be explicitly tied to the structure of a given query as well as an input database. Specifically, for a singular value t, we only consider witnesses that correspond to the deep union of values taken from D (at the leaves of a proof tree for t) with respect to a query Q. For Q_1 and output $\{\text{name}:\text{"G.F Handel"}\}.\text{born}:1685$, the witness above corresponds to values at the leaves of the proof tree taken from D. The following is also a witness for the same value but it is not the result of deep union of values at the end of any proof tree for that value.

```
{ Composers.{{name:"G.F. Handel"}.{born:1685, period:"baroque"},
            {name:"W.A Mozart"}.{born:1756, period:"classical"}},
  Works.{{name:"G.F. Handel"}.opus:"HMV19"}.title:"Art thou troubled?" }
```

We describe next our notion of a *witness basis* which captures the set of all witnesses of the former type for any value t in $Q(D)$. Our definition closely follows the syntax of the query.

Definition 6. (Witness Basis) Consider a normal form query Q. The *witness basis* for a singular value t with respect to Q and D, denoted as $W_{Q,D}(t)$, is:

(1) If Q is of the form $Q_1 \sqcup ... \sqcup Q_n$ then $W_{Q,D}(t) = W_{Q_1,D}(t) \cup ... \cup W_{Q_n,D}(t)$.

(2) If Q is of the form $\{e \mid p_0 \in e_0, ..., p_n \in e_n, condition\}$, let Ψ be the set of all valuations on the variables of Q such that "where" clause of Q holds under each valuation in Ψ. Then, $W_{Q,D}(t) = \{[\![p_0]\!]_\psi \sqcup ... \sqcup [\![p_n]\!]_\psi \mid \psi \in \Psi, t = [\![e]\!]_\psi\}$. Note that e_i $(0 \leq i \leq n)$ is a database constant since Q is in normal form.

(3) Otherwise, $W_{Q,D}(t) = \{\}$.

More generally, for any well-formed query Q, we can define the witness basis by extending (2) as follows. We partition the set of $p_i \in e_i$ in the "where" clause of Q into two parts: $S_1 = \{p_i \mid e_i \text{ is the database constant } D\}$ and $S_2 = \{(p_i, e_i) \mid p_i \text{ is a pattern matched against a query } e_i\}$. We use $p_0^1, ..., p_k^1$ to denote the members of S_1 and $(p_0^2, e_0^2), ..., (p_m^2, e_m^2)$ to denote the members of S_2. Let Ψ be the set of all valuations on the variables of Q such that for each valuation in Ψ, "where" clause of Q holds. Then $W_{Q,D}(t) = \{P_1 \sqcup P_2 \mid \psi \in \Psi, t \sqsubseteq [\![e]\!]_\psi, P_1 = [\![p_0^1]\!]_\psi \sqcup ... \sqcup [\![p_k^1]\!]_\psi, P_2 = w_1 \sqcup ... \sqcup w_m$ where $w_i \in W_{\psi(e_i^2),D}([\![p_i^2]\!]_\psi)\}$. For a compound value t, the witness basis is the product of individual witness basis of singular values making up t. That is, consider $t = t_1 \sqcup ... \sqcup t_m$ where each t_i is singular. Then $W_{Q,D}(t) = \{w_1 \sqcup ... \sqcup w_m \mid w_i \in W_{Q,D}(t_i)\}$. $\square$

The general definition above looks for patterns which are matched against the database constant D and patterns which match against queries. The former is collected together as part of the witness under P. If the generator is a nested query, we inductively look for the witness basis of these patterns under the valuation and later combine the results together by taking the product. Next, we show that the witness basis of a well-formed query is in fact the same as the witness basis of its normal form.

Lemma 1. If $Q \rightsquigarrow Q'$ via the rewrite system $\mathcal{R}$, then for any value t in the output of $Q(D)$, $W_{Q,D}(t) = W_{Q',D}(t)$.

Computing a Witness Basis. We next show a procedure for finding $W_{Q,D}(t)$ where t is a singular value and Q is a query in normal form. That is, $Q = Q_1 \sqcup ... \sqcup Q_n$ and each $Q_i = \{e_i \mid p_{i1} \in D, ..., p_{ik_i} \in D, condition_i\}$. To look for members of the witness basis of t, we need to search for valuations on variables in each Q_i that will produce t. For those valuations that produce t, the deep union of p_{i1} to p_{ik_i} under each valuation is returned as a result. However, instead of searching the witness basis directly, we produce a query Q'_i, which when evaluated, will generate the witness basis. The "where" clause of Q'_i is the same as Q_i and the "collect" clause contains an output expression which is the deep union of all patterns in the "where" clause of Q_i placed on an edge. This is to prevent inter-mixing with other members of the witness basis. The algorithm for generating Q'_i from Q_i is described below. Why(t, Q, D) is simply Why$(t, Q_1, D) \sqcup ... \sqcup$ Why(t, Q_n, D). ψ is a valuation from e_i to t such that $\psi(e_i) = t$. This technique is sound and complete in the sense that the set of witnesses in $W_{Q,D}(t)$ is the same as the set of witnesses returned by Why$(t, Q, D)(D)$.

Algorithm: Why(t, Q_i, D)

> Let Δ denote the "where" clause of Q_i.
> Let Δ' denote the deep union of patterns in Δ.
> **if** there is a valuation ψ from e_i to t **then**
>> Return the query "where $\psi(\Delta)$ collect $\psi(\Delta')$:C"
>> (For simplicity, we did not serialize the output expression on the edge.)
> **else**
>> No query is returned
> **end if**

Theorem 2. (Soundness and Completeness) Let Q be a query in normal form and t be any singular value in the output of $Q(D)$. Then $W_{Q,D}(t)$ = Why$(t, Q, D)(D)$.

A Comparison. We point out here that our notion of witness basis coincides with the derivation of a tuple in [7] for SPJU queries where the general case of theta-join is considered. The details are deferred to the full version.

5.2 Minimal Witness Basis

Observe that a witness for a value is invariant under all equivalent queries but the witness basis is not. We show next that a subset of the witness basis, called *minimal witness basis*, is in fact invariant under queries with only equalities.

Definition 7. (Minimal Witness, Minimal Witness Basis) A value s is a *minimal witness* for a value t with respect to Q if $\forall s' \sqsubset s$ $t \not\sqsubseteq Q(s')$. The *minimal witness basis* for a value t with respect to a query Q and database D, denoted as $M_{Q,D}(t)$, is a maximal subset of $W_{Q,D}(t)$ such that $\forall m \in M_{Q,D}(t)$ $\nexists w \in W_{Q,D}(t)$ such that $w \sqsubset m$. □

Example: According to the query Q_1, introduced earlier, the witness shown in Section 5 is a minimal witness for {name:"G.F. Handel"}.born:1685 while the witness shown in Section 5.1 is not.

Theorem 3. (Invariance of Minimal Witness Basis under Equivalent queries) If Q and Q' are two equivalent well-formed queries with only equality conditions and t is contained in $Q(D)$ and $Q'(D)$, then $M_{Q,D}(t) = M_{Q',D}(t)$.

The proof of this theorem is based on a homomorphism theorem which shows that for the class of well-formed and well-defined queries (with equality conditions), query containment is equivalent to the existence of a homomorphism between the queries. Based on the ideas in [11], we can also extend this theorem to certain subclasses of queries with inequalities. Thus the invariance property of minimal witness basis in fact holds across this larger class of queries.

5.3   Cascaded Witnesses (Query Composition)

Suppose we have some data sources – a mixture of materialized views (V) and actual databases (D) – and a query written against these sources. We may choose to find the witness basis for a value with respect to these sources (our witnesses will therefore consist of values from both V and D) and subsequently finding the witness basis of those components taken from the views so that eventually, witnesses in the witness basis consist of only values from D. We show next that the witness basis obtained in this manner is the same as first "composing out" the views in the query using the composition rule in our rewrite system $\mathcal{R}$ and obtaining the witness basis according to the rewritten query. In fact, this result is an important special case of Lemma 1 where views are nested queries not sharing any variables with the outer query block.

Theorem 4. (Unnesting of Witnesses) Let D be a set of databases, V be a query written against D and Q be a query written against D and V. Then for a value t in $Q(D, V)$, $W_{Q', D}(t) = \{w \sqcup w' \mid (w \sqcup v') \in W_{Q, \{D, V(D)\}}(t), v'$ is the value taken from view $V(D)$, $w' \in W_{V, D}(v')\}$ where Q' is the rewritten query via our rewrite system $\mathcal{R}$ in which view V has been "composed out".

6   Where-Provenance

So far we have explored the issue of what pieces of input data validate the existence of an output value, for a given query. We now focus on identifying what pieces of input data helped create various values that appear in the output. The where-provenance of a specific value in the output is closely connected to the witnesses for the output in that only some parts of any witness are used to construct a specific output value. For instance, in the example described in Section 4, the output value "1685" in {name:"G.F. Handel"}.born:1685 depends only on Composers.{name:"G.F. Handel"}.born:1685 in the input. We refer to the path Composers.{name:"G.F. Handel"}.born in the input as the where-provenance of this output value. This informal description already suggests an intuitive procedure for determining the where-provenance of any specific value in the output: determine which output variable was bound to this specific value, and then identify the pieces of input data that were bound to this output variable. However, this intuition is fragile and there are many difficulties involved in formalizing this intuition as illustrated by the sequence of examples below. Consider the following two equivalent queries that look for employees with a salary of $50K :

$$Q_1 = \text{where } \text{Emps.}\{\text{Id:}x\}.\text{salary:}\$50K \in D,$$
$$\text{collect } \{\text{Id:}x\}.\text{salary:}\$50K$$

$$Q_2 = \text{where } \text{Emps.}\{\text{Id:}x\}.\text{salary:}y \in D,$$
$$y = \$50K$$
$$\text{collect } \{\text{Id:}x\}.\text{salary:}y$$

Suppose we wish to determine the where-provenance of \$50K in an output tuple. In case of query Q_1, there is no variable in the collect clause which the value \$50K can be identified with. The where-provenance of this value in Q_1 is the query itself since the value is hard-wired into the query output. For Q_2, the output variable y can be associated with the value \$50K and can be used to identify what contributed to this value. By convention, we will consider the where-provenance of a specific value in the output to be defined only if it can be associated with one or more variables in the output expression of a query. Otherwise, we will ascribe the where-provenance of a value to the query itself. This example illustrates that the notion of where-provenance is hard to keep invariant over equivalent queries in general.

Our next example shows that when multiple pieces of data may simultaneously contribute to a specific value in the output, it may be difficult to identify all the pieces.

$$Q_3 = \text{where } \text{Emps.}\{\text{Id:}x\}.\text{salary:}y \in D,$$
$$\text{Emps.}\{\text{Id:}x\}.\text{bonus:}y \in D$$
$$\text{collect } \{\text{Id:}x\}.\text{new\_salary:}y$$

$$Q_4 = \text{where } \text{Emps.}\{\text{Id:}x\}.\text{salary:}y \in D,$$
$$\text{Emps.}\{\text{Id:}x\}.\text{salary:}z \in D,$$
$$\text{Emps.}\{\text{Id:}x\}.\text{bonus:}z \in D$$
$$\text{collect } \{\text{Id:}x\}.\text{new\_salary:}y$$

In case of Q_3, the value associated with any new_salary component in the output originated from both the salary and bonus components of the corresponding employee. This is easily identified by tracking the output variable y through the query. But in Q_4, which is equivalent to Q_3, on any input data where salary and bonus are atomic values, one needs to recognize that z is always forced to agree with y and hence where-provenance is determined by y and z together. This suggests that in general the syntactic structure of a query may not suffice for identifying the where-provenance. Even in cases where syntactic analysis alone may work, this issue becomes rather difficult to handle once we consider nested queries. Consider the following two equivalent queries:

$$Q_5 = \text{where } R.x.y : z \in D,$$
$$S.x.y : z \in D$$
$$\text{collect } x.y : z$$

$$Q_6 = \text{where } R.x.y : z \in D,$$
$$S.t.u \in D,$$
$$t : u \in \left(\begin{array}{l} \text{where } R.x.y : z \in D \\ \text{collect } x.y : z \end{array} \right),$$
$$\text{collect } \{x.y : z, t : u\}$$

When applied to an input database $\{\text{R.1.2:3}, \text{S.1.2:3}\}$, these queries produce as output $1.2:3$. The where-provenance of value 3 in the output is $\{\text{R.1:2}, \text{S.1:2}\}$ in case of query Q_5. In contrast, where-provenance of the same value with respect to Q_6 requires one to identify that u binds to $y : z$ via the nested query. Then, the where-provenance is given by $\{\text{R.1:2}, \text{S.1:2}\}$ in this case as well.

A Syntactic Approach. The examples above highlight that for general queries, where-provenance is not invariant over the space of equivalent queries, and that a purely syntactic characterization of where-provenance is unlikely to yield a complete description of the where-provenance. However, we use the syntactic approach and identify a restricted class of queries referred to as *traceable queries*, for which where-provenance is preserved under rewriting. Our approach is based on formalizing our initial intuition of using variables in the output expression of a query as a means of identifying the where-provenance of a value. Specifically, for each successful valuation of the query, we systematically explore the pieces of input data contributing to the identified output variable; and we refer to this as the *derivation basis* of the output value. To determine where-provenance of a value resulting from a traceable query, it suffices to work with the normal form of the query. Once a query is in normal form, a straightforward procedure can be used to compute the derivation basis of a given value.

Paths. To identify the where-provenance of a value in our tree of values, we need to extend our notion of paths. We augment our syntax for paths with "%". For example, to refer to the value {name:"J.S. Bach"} which is a value on the edge of Composers relation, we could use the path Composers.{name:"J.S. Bach"}%. To refer to the value "J.S. Bach", we could use the path Composers. {name:"J.S. Bach"}%name.

We show next the definition of derivation basis (where-provenance) for queries in normal form. Informally, the derivation basis for $l{:}v$ finds a variable x in the output expression that will generate v. This can be done by partially matching $l{:}v$ against the output expression e. All the paths to x in the patterns of Q are then determined. Then, for any valuation that satisfies the "where" clause, the valuation of the patterns in the "where" clause will form the witness, and the valuation of the paths that point to x will be the where-provenance of $l{:}v$ with respect to this witness. Altogether, they form the derivation basis of $l{:}v$. We refer to the procedure that computes the derivation basis of $l{:}v$ as Where($l{:}v,Q,D$). It is similar to Why(t, Q, D) in that we generate a query which when applied to D will produce the derivation basis. The "where" clause of the generated query is the "where" clause of Q and the "collect" clause of the generated query emits two things: the patterns and the paths pointing to x in the "where" clause of Q.

Definition 8. (Derivation Basis) Consider a normal form query Q. The *derivation basis* for $l{:}v$ where v is an atomic value, denoted as $\Gamma_{Q,D}(l : v)$ with respect to Q and D, is defined as below:

(1) If $Q = Q_1 \sqcup ... \sqcup Q_n$ then $\Gamma_{Q,D}(l : v) = \Gamma_{Q_1,D}(l : v) \cup ... \cup \Gamma_{Q_n,D}(l : v)$.

(2) If Q has the form $\{e \mid p_0 \in e_0, ..., p_n \in e_n, condition\}$, let Ψ be the set of valuations on the variables of Q such that the "where" clause of Q holds under each valuation and $\psi(e)$ contains $l{:}v$. For each $\psi \in \Psi$, let p_{x_ψ} denote the path in e that points to a variable x_ψ such that there exists p' and p'' so that $l = p'.p''$ and $\psi(p_{x_\psi}) = p'$ and $\psi(x_\psi)(p'') = v$. Then, $\Gamma_{Q,D}(l : v) = \{([\![p_0]\!]_\psi \sqcup ... \sqcup [\![p_n]\!]_\psi, S) \mid \psi \in \Psi, S = \{\psi(p_i').p'' \mid p_i' \text{ is the path that points to variable } x_\psi \text{ in pattern } p_i, 0 \le i \le n\}\}$.

(3) Otherwise, $\Gamma_{Q,D}(l : v) = \{\}$.

More generally, the derivation basis of $l{:}v$ where v is a compound value is defined to be the derivation basis of all possible (path,value) pairs $p'{:}v'$ such that

$p'{:}v'$ points to a value in v. The derivation basis for multiple (path,value) pairs is defined to be the product of the derivation basis of individual (path,value) pairs. That is, $\Gamma_{Q,D}(p_1{:}v_1, p_2{:}v_2) = \Gamma_{Q,D}(p_1{:}v_1) * \Gamma_{Q,D}(p_2{:}v_2) = \{(w_1 \sqcup w_2, P_1 \cup P_2) \mid (w_1, P_1) \in \Gamma_{Q,D}(p_1{:}v_1), (w_2, P_2) \in \Gamma_{Q,D}(p_2{:}v_2)\}$. □

We omit the definition for queries in the general form and remark that the main difference is that it looks for the derviation basis inductively for patterns matched against nested queries. We show next that in dealing with the derivation basis for the class of traceable queries, we can restrict our attention to the derivation basis corresponding to their normal forms.

Definition 9. (Traceable Queries) A well-defined query Q is *traceable* if (a) each pattern in the query matches either against some database constant or against a subquery, (b) every subquery in Q is a view which does not share any variables with the outer scope (c) only a singular pattern is allowed to match against a subquery and (d) this pattern and output expression of the subquery consist of a sequence of distinct variables (variables do not repeat) and have the same length. □

Example: The first query below is not traceable because the variable u is being used in the inner query (this violates condition (b)). The second query is not traceable because an expression $\{y{:}w\}$ is used in the pattern sequence (this violates condition (d) where each expression in the sequence can only be a variable).

where $x : u \in D$,
$\quad y : z \in \left(\begin{array}{l} \text{where } u : v \in D \\ \text{collect } u : v \end{array} \right)$,
collect $x : z$

where $x : y \in D$,
$\quad \{y : w\} : z \in \left(\begin{array}{l} \text{where } u : v \in D \\ \text{collect } u : v \end{array} \right)$,
collect $x : y$

Proposition 1. If Q is a traceable query and $Q \rightsquigarrow Q'$ via rewrite system $\mathcal{R}$, then Q' is a traceable query.

Proposition 2. For the class of traceable queries, if $Q \rightsquigarrow Q'$ via rewrite system $\mathcal{R}$, then for any $l{:}v$ in the output of $Q(D)$, $\Gamma_{Q,D}(l : v) = \Gamma_{Q',D}(l : v)$.

7 Conclusions

We have described a framework for both describing and understanding provenance of data in the context of SPJU queries and views. Data provenance is examined from two perspectives, namely (1) Why is a piece of data in the output?, and (2) Where did a piece of data come from?

We have taken a syntactic approach to understanding both notions of provenance, and we have described a system of rewrite rules in which why-provenance is preserved over the class of well-defined queries and where-provenance is preserved over the class of traceable queries.

One interesting direction for future work is to identify necessary and sufficient conditions for the class of well-defined queries. Another interesting direction is to study how additional constraints on the input instances, e.g., functional dependencies, can help us obtain a more complete description of the where-provenance of a piece of data.

Acknowledgements. We thank Victor Vianu, Susan Davidson, Val Tannen and the Penn Database Group students for many useful exchanges; and the paper reviewers for many useful comments.

References

1. *INFOBIOGEN. DBCAT, The Public Catalog of Databases.*
   http://www.infobiogen.fr/services/dbcat/, cited 5 June 2000.
2. A. Woodruff and M. Stonebraker. Supporting fine-grained data lineage in a database visualization environment. In *ICDE*, pages 91–102, 1997.
3. S. Abiteboul, P. Buneman, and D. Suciu. *Data on the Web. From Relations to Semistructured Data and XML.* Morgan Kaufman, 2000.
4. S. Abiteboul, R. Hull, and V. Vianu. *Foundations of Databases.* Addison Wesley Publishing Co, 1995.
5. S. Abiteboul, D. Quass, J. McHugh, J. Widom, and J. Wiener. The lorel query language for semistructured data. *Journal on Digital Libraries*, 1(1), 1996.
6. P. Buneman, A. Deutsch, and W. Tan. A Deterministic Model for Semistructured Data. In *Proc. of the Workshop On Query Processing for Semistructured Data and Non-standard Data Formats*, pages 14–19, 1999.
7. Y. Cui and J. Widom. Practical lineage tracing in data warehouses. In *ICDE*, pages 367–378, 2000.
8. A. Deutsch, M. Fernandez, D. Florescu, A. Levy, and D. Suciu. *XML-QL: A Query Language for XML*, 1998. http://www.w3.org/TR/NOTE-xml-ql.
9. R. Durbin and J. T. Mieg. *ACeDB – A C. elegans Database: Syntactic definitions for the ACeDB data base manager*, 1992.
   http://probe.nalusda.gov:8000/acedocs/syntax.html.
10. H. Liefke and S. Davidson. Efficient View Maintenance in XML Data Warehouses. Technical Report MS-CIS-99-27, University of Pennsylvania, 1999.
11. A. Klug. On conjuncitve queries containing inequalities. *Journal of the ACM*, 1(1):146–160, 1988.
12. L. Wong. Normal Forms and Conservative Properties for Query Languages over Collection Types. In *PODS*, Washington, D.C., May 1993.
13. P. Buneman and S. Davidson and G. Hillebrand and D. Suciu. A Query Language and Optimization Techniques for Unstructured Data. In *SIGMOD*, pages 505–516, 1996.
14. Y. Papakonstantinou, H. Garcia-Molina, and J. Widom. Object exchange across heterogeneous information sources. In *ICDE*, 1996.
15. World Wide Web Consortium (W3C). *Document Object Model (DOM) Level 1 Specification*, 2000. http://www.w3.org/TR/REC-DOM-Level-1.
16. World Wide Web Consortium (W3C). *XML Schema Part 0: Primer*, 2000.
   http://www.w3.org/TR/xmlschema-0/.
17. Y. Zhuge, H. Garcia-Molina, J. Hammer, and J. Widom. View maintenance in a warehousing environment. In *SIGMOD*, pages 316–327, 1995.

Subsumption for XML Types

Gabriel M. Kuper and Jérôme Siméon

Bell Laboratories, 600 Mountain Avenue, 07974, NJ, USA
{kuper,simeon}@research.bell-labs.com
http://www-db.research.bell-labs.com/user/{kuper,simeon}

Abstract. XML data is often used (validated, stored, queried, etc) with respect to different types. Understanding the relationship between these types can provide important information for manipulating this data. We propose a notion of subsumption for XML to capture such relationships. Subsumption relies on a syntactic mapping between types, and can be used for facilitating validation and query processing. We study the properties of subsumption, in particular the notion of the greatest lower bound of two schemas, and show how this can be used as a guide for selecting a storage structure. While less powerful than inclusion, subsumption generalizes several other mechanisms for reusing types, notably extension and refinement from XML Schema, and subtyping.

1 Introduction

XML [5] is a data format for Web applications. As opposed to e.g., relational databases, XML documents do not have to be created and used with respect to a fixed, existing schema. This is particularly useful in Web applications, for simplifying exchange of documents and for dealing with semistructured data. But the lack of typing has many drawbacks, inspiring many proposals [2,3,4,10, 12,23,24,33] of type systems for XML. The main challenge in this context is to design a typing scheme that retains the portability and flexibility of untyped XML. To achieve this goal, the above proposals depart from traditional typing frameworks in a number of ways. First, in order to deal with both structured and semistructured data, they support very powerful primitives, such as regular expressions [2,10,26,33,28] and predicate languages to describe atomic values [2, 6,10]. Secondly, documents remain independent from their type, which allows the same document to be typed in multiple ways according to various application needs. These features result in additional complexity: the fact that data is often used with respect to different types, means that it is difficult to recover the traditional advantages (such as safety and performance enhancements) that one expects from type systems. To get these advantages back, one need to understand how types of the same document relates to each other.

In this paper, we propose a notion of subsumption to capture the relationship between XML types. Intuitively, subsumption captures not just the fact than one type is contained in another, but also captures some of the structural relationships between the two schemas. We show that subsumption can be used to facilitate commonly used type-related operations on XML data, such as type assignment, or for query processing.

J. Van den Bussche and V. Vianu (Eds.): ICDT 2001, LNCS 1973, pp. 331–345, 2001.
© Springer-Verlag Berlin Heidelberg 2001

We compare subsumption with several other mechanisms aimed at reusing types. Subsumption is less powerful than inclusion, but it captures *refinement* and *extension*, recently introduced by XML Schema [33], subtyping, as in traditional type systems, as well as the instantiation mechanism of [10,32]. As a consequence, subsumption provides some formal foundations to these notions, and techniques to take advantage of them.

We study the lattice theoretic properties of subsumption. These provide techniques to rewrite inclusion into subsumption. Notably we show the existence of a *greatest lower bound*. Greatest lower bound captures the information from several schemas, while preserving the relationship with them, and can be used as the basis for storage design.

Practical scenario. To further motivate the need for a subsumption mechanism for XML, consider the following application scenario. In order to run an integrated shopping site for some useful product, such as mobile phone jammers, company "A" accesses catalogs from various sources. The first catalog, on the left below, is taken from company "SESP" [22], while the second, on the right, is extracted from miscellaneous pages.

```
<products>                              <products>
 <jammer>                                <jammer>
  <company>SESP</company>                 <name>Static HP Jammer</name>
  <name>VHP Jammer</name>                 <price><onrequest/></price>
  <price><onrequest/></price>             <case><type>metal</type>
  <case><type>Mobile Attache Case</type>    <size>180x180x80mm
  </case></jammers>                           </size></case></jammer>
                                         <jammer>
 <jammer>                                 <company>JamLogic</company>
  <company>SESP</company>                 <name>Personal Jammer</name>
  <name>Full Milspec. Portable            <price><onrequest/></price>
       High  Power (HP) Jammer</name>     <input>Digital/Analog</input>
  <price><onrequest/></price>             <warranty>2 years</warranty>
  <case><type>Rugged military            </jammer>
             type case</type></case>     <jammer>
  <booster><range>1km</range></booster>   <name>Cell-Phone Jammer</name>
  <supplement>39</supplement></jammer>    <price>749</price></jammer>
  . . .                                    . . .
```

Company "SESP" only sells high power jammers, and provides precise information about their products as the SESP schema, given on the left hand side below[1]. This schema indicates that the SESPcatalog (we write types in upper case and element names in lower case), is composed of an element with name products, which has 0 or more children of type HPJammer ('*' stands for the Kleene star). HPJammers have a company sub-element which is always "SESP", a name, etc., and may have a booster option with a supplement cost. On the right-hand side is the schema used by company "A". Because it accesses jammer information from many places, it supports a more general description where

---

[1] Note that we will write some of the examples using the concrete schema syntax developed for the YAT System [10]

Jammers might not have a company information, and may have any kind of Option, with or without a supplement.

```
SESPCatalog := products *HPJammer;        IntegratedCatalog := products
                                                               * Jammer;

HPJammer :=                               Jammer :=
  jammer [ company [ "SESP" ],              jammer [ ?company [ String ],
           name [ String ],                          name [ String ],
           price [ Int | onrequest ],               price [Int|onrequest],
           case [ type [ String ],                  *(Option,
                  ?size [ String ] ],                  ?supplement [ Int ]
           ?(booster [ range [ Int ] ],                              ) ] ];
           supplement [ Int ] ) ];        Option := Symbol *Any;
```

Because it knows precisely the type of its data, company SESP can support more efficient storage (using, for instance, techniques in [14,18,31]), with fast access to the name, price and case information. But the fact that company "A" assumes a different type for the same data results in a mismatch. Verifying that type SESPCatalog is included in type IntegratedCatalog allows company "A" to make sure the information provided by SESP will conform to the structure expected by the application. However, this will not help in performing further operations, such as: actually assigning types of the integrated schema to elements of the SESP document, or understanding that the name and price elements can be efficiently accessed using the storage used by company SESP. Doing so requires to understand that the name and price in the Jammer type *are related to* the name and the price elements in the HPJammer type. We shall see that subsumption allows one to understand this relationship and to take advantage of it.

Another important use of typing is to support better query processing. To find all jammers that have a two years warranty, one can write the following YATL [10,16,11] query:

```
define q($x) = make $n
               match $x with products/jammer/{ name/$n,
                                               warranty/$w }
               where contains($w,"2 years");
```

whose input type is:

```
q_type := products * jammer [ *(Name | Warranty | Other) ];
Name := name * Any1;
Warranty := warranty * Any2;
Other := !name!warranty * Any;
Any1 := true [ Any* ]; Any2 := true [ Any* ]
```

where ! stands for tag negation, i.e., any tag other than name and warranty.

Company "A" might wish to support queries on all Jammers, but more efficient access for this query, i.e. for products with a warranty. The relational approach [30] would be to use a specific access structure for the warranty field, but the integrated schema does not mention it. We will see that the greatest

lower bound of the query type and the integrated schema is a new schema (with
an explicit warranty field) that can be used for storage design, while the relationships with the original schemas are preserved through subsumption.

Organization of the paper. Section 2 introduces the type system we will
use in the rest of the paper (essentially that of [2]) and the notion of type
assignment. Section 3 defines subsumption, investigates its properties and its
use for validation. Section 4 compares it to other relations on types, such as
inclusion, refinement and extension in XML Schema, etc. Section 5 studies the
greatest lower bound, the corresponding lattice, and how this can be used to
bridge the gap between inclusion and subsumption. Section 6 discusses how one
can take advantage of subsumption for storage and query processing. Section 7
summarizes related works and indicates directions for future work.

2   Data Model and Type System

Data model. The data model, based on ordered labeled trees with references,
is similar to other previously proposed models [10,15,25,28]. $\mathcal{O}$ denotes a fixed
(infinite) set of *object ids* and $\mathcal{L}$ a fixed set of *labels*. References are modeled as
a special type of node, that is labeled with a distinguished symbol "&" in $\mathcal{L}$ and
has exactly one child. The root of the database is treated specially: A database
is a tree with a root "△", which has *no* label, and cannot be referenced by any
node. (The reason for the special treatment of the root is explained later.)

Definition 1. *A database is a structure* $D = \langle O_D, label_D, children_D \rangle$, *where*

1. $O_D \subset \mathcal{O}$;
2. $label_D$ *is a mapping from* O_D *to* $\mathcal{L}$;
3. $children_D$ *is a mapping from* $O_D \cup \{\triangle\}$ *to* $\cup_{i \geq 0} O_D^i$; *If* $label_D(o) = \&$, *then*
   $children(o) \in O_D^1$;
4. *The structure that we obtain by considering only children of non-reference
   nodes (nodes with a label other than "&") is a tree.*

Example 1. The upper part of Figure 1 is a (partial) representation for the
Jammers document from Section 1 and would correspond to the following struc-
ture. $D = \langle O_D, label_D, children_D \rangle$, where $O_D = \{o_1, o_2, \ldots\}$, $children(\triangle) = [\ldots, o_1, \ldots]$, and

$$label(o_1) = jammer \quad children(o_1) = [o_{11}; o_{12}; o_{13}; o_{14}]$$
$$label(o_{11}) = company \quad children(o_{11}) = [o_{111}]$$
$$label(o_{111}) = \text{"SESP"} \quad children(o_{111}) = [\ ]$$
$$\vdots \qquad\qquad \vdots$$

Type system. We adopt the type system of [2,25], where predicates are used
to describe labels and regular expressions are used to describe children. Note
though that we do not handle unordered trees, and that we model references
in a slightly different way. Also, we choose not to use XML Schema [33], which

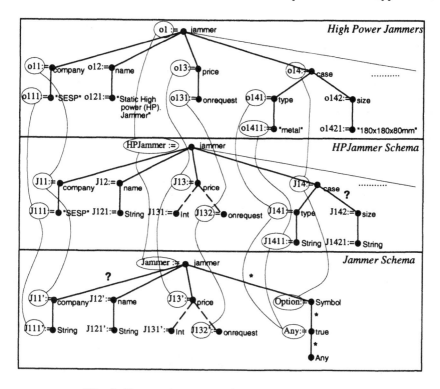

Fig. 1. Type assignment and subsumption mapping

is more a user syntax for types than a model, but we will explain later on how subsumption can be used in the context of XML Schema.

Let $\mathcal{T}$ be a fixed, infinite, set of *type names*, and $\mathcal{P}$ a fixed set of *label predicates*, which is closed under disjunction, conjunction, and complementation. We use τ, τ' etc., to denote elements of $\mathcal{T}$. Regular expressions over $\mathcal{T}$ are of the form ϵ, τ, $\&\tau$, (R_1, R_2), $(R_1 \mid R_2)$, or R_1^*, where R_1 and R_2 are regular expressions, and $\tau \in \mathcal{T}$. $L(R)$ denotes the language defined by the regular expression R, in which $\&\tau$ is treated as a single symbol.

Definition 2. *A type schema is a structure* $S = \langle T_S, predicate_S, regexp_S \rangle$, *in which*

1. T_S *is a finite subset of* $\mathcal{T}$;
2. $predicate_S$ *is a mapping from* T_S *to* $\mathcal{P}$ *with the property that for each* τ, *either* $predicate_S(\tau) = \{\&\}$, *or* $\& \notin predicate_S(\tau)$; *and*
3. $regexp_S$ *is a mapping from* $T_S \cup \{\triangle\}$ *to regular expressions over* T_S. *Whenever* $predicate_S(\tau) = \{\&\}$, $regexp_S(\tau)$ *must be of the form* $\tau_1 \mid \cdots \mid \tau_n$.

For convenience, we will sometimes describe schemas as $\tau \mapsto p; r$, where p and r are the predicate and regular expression corresponding to τ. We write $predicate(\tau) = \mathbf{true}$ to mean that it is satisfied by all tags *except* "&" – the restrictions on the interaction between reference and non-reference types guarantee that this will never cause any confusion.

Example 2. The middle part of Figure 1 is a (partial) representation of the schema for HP jammers and would correspond to the structure $\langle T_{cat}, p_{cat}, r_{cat}\rangle$, where T_{cat} is the set $\{\mathbf{catalog}, \mathbf{HPjammer}, \mathbf{J_{11}}, \mathbf{J_{12}}, \mathbf{J_{13}}, \mathbf{J_{14}}, \mathbf{J_{111}}, \ldots, \mathbf{J_{1421}}\}$, $regexp(\triangle)$ is **catalog**, and

$$predicate_{cat}(\mathbf{HPjammer}) = \{\text{jammer}\} \quad regexp_{cat}(\mathbf{HPjammer}) = \mathbf{J_{11}}, \mathbf{J_{12}}, \mathbf{J_{13}}, \mathbf{J_{14}}$$

$$\vdots \qquad\qquad\qquad\qquad\qquad \vdots$$

$$
\begin{aligned}
predicate_{cat}(\mathbf{J_{13}}) &= \{\text{price}\} & regexp_{cat}(\mathbf{J_{13}}) &= \mathbf{J_{131}}|\mathbf{J_{132}} \\
predicate_{cat}(\mathbf{J_{131}}) &= \{0, 1, \ldots\} & regexp_{cat}(\mathbf{J_{131}}) &= \epsilon \\
predicate_{cat}(\mathbf{J_{131}}) &= \{\text{onrequest}\} & regexp_{cat}(\mathbf{J_{132}}) &= \epsilon
\end{aligned}
$$

$$\vdots \qquad\qquad\qquad\qquad\qquad \vdots$$

Typing and Type Assignment

Definition 3. *Let D be a database and S a schema. We say D is of type S under the type assignment θ, and write $D :_\theta S$ iff θ is a function from $O_D \cup \{\triangle\}$ to $T_S \cup \{\triangle\}$ such that:*

1. *$\theta(\triangle) = \triangle$,*
2. *for each $o \in O_D$, $predicate_S(\theta(o)) \models label(o)$, and*
3. *for each $o \in O_D \cup \{\triangle\}$ with $children(o) = [o_1, \ldots, o_n]$, $\theta(o_1) \ldots \theta(o_n) \in L(regexp_S(\theta(o)))$.*

We say that D is of type S, and write $D : S$, iff $D :_\theta S$ for some θ. Models(S) is the set of databases of type S, i.e., $\{D \mid D : S\}$. It is immediate that $D :_\theta S$ and $D' \subseteq D$ (i.e., $O_{D'} \subseteq O_D$ and the corresponding labels and children are the same) imply $D' :_{\theta|O_{D'}} S$.

Example 3. Figure 1 illustrates the type assignment between the Jammer document and the HPJammer schema, corresponding to the following θ:

$$
\begin{aligned}
\theta(o_1) &= \mathbf{HPjammer} & \theta(o_{11}) &= \mathbf{J_{11}} \\
\theta(o_{13}) &= \mathbf{J_{13}} & \theta(o_{131}) &= \mathbf{J_{132}} \\
\theta(o_{14}) &= \mathbf{J_{14}} & \theta(o_{141}) &= \mathbf{J_{141}}
\end{aligned}
$$

$$\vdots \qquad\qquad\qquad\qquad\qquad \vdots$$

Type assignment is the most important information coming out of the typing process (also called *validation* in the XML world). Once computed, it allows the system to efficiently obtain the type of a given data whenever needed, e.g., in order to chose the storage or take query processing decisions at run time. Note that type assignment information is logically provided in the XML Query data model [15] by the Def_T reference[2].

However simple, our type system is powerful enough to capture most of the other proposals, including XML Schema. It can be used to represent existing

---

[2] http://www.w3.org/TR/query-datamodel/#def_t

type information from heterogeneous sources [10,32,2] or to describe mixes of structured and semistructured data. The two following remarks will also play an important role in the rest of the paper.

Remark 1. **Any** is the schema that such that D : **Any** holds for any database D:

$$\triangle \mapsto (\tau_{\text{anytype}} \mid \tau_{\text{anyref}})^*$$
$$\tau_{\text{anyref}} \mapsto \{\&\}; (\tau_{\text{anyref}} \mid \tau_{\text{anytype}})$$
$$\tau_{\text{anytype}} \mapsto \textbf{true}; (\tau_{\text{anytype}} \mid \tau_{\text{anyref}})^*$$

Remark 2. For each database D, one can define a schema S that types this database only, by taking T_S such that it contains exactly a type name τ for each object o in O_D, with $\theta(o) = \tau$, $predicate_S(\tau) = \{label_D(o)\}$ and $regexp_S(\tau) = children_D(o)$. Then, $D :_\theta S$ and $Models(S) = \{D\}$.

We will write $S_{[D]}$ the schema that types the database D only. We will call **None** the schema that types the empty database only. **None** has $T_{\text{None}} = \emptyset$ and $regexp_{\text{None}}(\triangle) = \epsilon$.

3   Subsumption

Intuitively, subsumption relies on a mapping between types (playing a role similar to type assignment for typing) and on inclusion between regular expressions over these types.

Definition 4. *Let S and S' be two schemas. We say that schema S subsumes S' under the subsumption mapping θ, and write $S \preceq_\theta S'$, iff θ is a function from $T_S \cup \{\triangle\}$ to $T_{S'} \cup \{\triangle\}$ such that:*

1. *$\theta(\tau) = \triangle$ iff $\tau = \triangle$.*
2. *For all $\tau \in T_S$, $predicate_S(\tau) \subseteq predicate_{S'}(\theta(\tau))$.*
3. *For all $\tau \in T_S \cup \{\triangle\}$, $\theta(L(regexp_S(\tau))) \subseteq L(regexp_{S'}(\theta(\tau)))$ (where θ is extended to words in the language in the natural way)*

We write $S \preceq S'$ if there exists a θ such that $S \preceq_\theta S$, and $S \approx S'$ for $(S \preceq S') \wedge (S' \preceq S)$: this is clearly an equivalence relation.

Example 4. Figure 1 illustrates the subsumption mapping between the **Jammer** and **HPJammer** types, corresponding to the following θ':

$$\theta'(\textbf{HPJammer}) = \textbf{Jammer} \qquad \theta'(\textbf{J}_{11}) = \textbf{J}'_{11}$$
$$\theta'(\textbf{J}_{111}) = \textbf{J}_{111} \qquad \theta'(\textbf{J}_{13}) = \textbf{J}'_{13}$$
$$\theta'(\textbf{J}_{14}) = \textbf{Option} \qquad \theta'(\textbf{J}_{141}) = \textbf{Any} \ldots$$

The following propositions cover the elementary properties of subsumption. The first states that type checking is a special case of subsumption, and is a direct consequence of Remark 2. The second and third propositions state the transitivity of subsumption, and more importantly of their underlying subsumption mapping, giving the means to propagate relationships between types.

Proposition 1. *Let S, S', S'' be three schemas, and D be a database.*

1. $D :_\theta S$ iff $S_{[D]} \preceq_\theta S$.
2. $S \preceq_{\theta_1} S'$ and $S' \preceq_{\theta_2} S''$ imply $S \preceq_{\theta_1 \circ \theta_2} S''$.
3. If $D :_{\theta_1} S$ and $S \preceq_{\theta_2} S'$, then $D :_{\theta_1 \circ \theta_2} S'$.

Using subsumption for validation. An important consequence of Prop. 1 is the ability to take advantage of subsumption for computing type assignments. Intuitively, if one has a type assignment for a given database, and a subsumption mapping from the original type to the new type, the new type assignment can be obtained by composing the mappings rather than by evaluating the type assignment from scratch.

This is especially useful as in most practical scenarios, including the one we sketched in Section 1, XML data is generated from a legacy source, along with its original schema (SESPCatalog). If instead of checking inclusion, company "A" computes subsumption between the two schemas, it obtains the new type-assignment at the same time. This approach has a number of advantages. First, the size of schema is orders of magnitude smaller than the data. Secondly, this can be done at compile time, without requiring to access the whole data.

Example 5. For instance, assume Company "A" runs a query to the SESP store that returns the jammer o_1. We know from θ in Example 2 that o_1 has type **HPJammer** and from θ' in Example 4, that **HPJammers** correspond to **Jammers** in the integrated schema. This gives us directly that the type of o_1 with respect to the integrated schema is **Jammer** (see also Figure 1).

4   Comparison with Inclusion, Extension, et al.

To get a better understanding of the scope of subsumption, we now compare it to other relations over types, notably, inclusion, XML schema's mechanisms of refinement and extension, subtyping, and the instantiation mechanism of [10].

Inclusion. Type inclusion is defined in terms of containment of models.

Definition 5. $S \subseteq S'$ iff $\mathrm{Models}(S) \subseteq \mathrm{Models}(S')$.

Of course, subsumption provides additional information compared to inclusion because of the subsumption mapping. A natural question is: can one always find a subsumption mapping between two types for which inclusion holds.

Proposition 2. *Let S and S' be two schemas. Then (1) $S \preceq S' \rightarrow S \subseteq S'$, but not conversely; and (2) $S \preceq S' \rightarrow S \subseteq S'$, and this implication is proper.*

Proof. (2) is trivial. (1) and (3) are direct consequences of Remark 2. To see why the implications are proper, consider the following type schemas:

$$
\begin{array}{rl}
S, S' & \tau_1 \mapsto \{a\}; \epsilon \\
 & \tau_2 \mapsto \{a\}; \epsilon \\
S & \triangle \mapsto \tau_1^*, \tau_2 \\
S' & \triangle \mapsto \tau_1, \tau_2^*
\end{array}
$$

Then both S and S' type precisely those databases for which $children(\triangle)$ are all leaves with tag "a", but neither $S \preceq S'$ or $S' \preceq S$.

As shown in [20,21], type inclusion can be used to type-check XML languages. Proposition 2 implies that some queries might type-check even though a subsumption mapping does not exist. In such a case one might not be able to take advantage of subsumption. Fortunately, we will see that there are many practical cases for which a subsumption mapping between types exists, including: when they are defined through XML Schema's refinement or extension mechanisms or when they are exported from a traditional type system with subtyping. Moreover, we will show (Proposition 1) that if $S'' \subseteq S$, then one can construct a schema S' equivalent to S for which $S'' \preceq S'$.

Extension and refinement in XML Schema. XML Schema: Part 1 [33] defines two subtyping-like mechanisms, called *extension* and *refinement*, aimed at reusing types. For obvious space limitations, we cannot explain all the complex features of XML Schema, so our presentation will rely on a simple modeling of these two mechanisms. In a nutshell, *extension* allows to add new fields at the end of a given type, while *refinement* provides syntactic means to restrict the domain of a given type.

Example 6. The following XML Schema declaration defines a Stated-Address by *refining* an Address to always have a unique state element and US-Address by extending Stated-Address with a new zip element.

```
<complexType name="Address">
  <element name="street" type="string"/>
  <element name="city"   type="string"/>
  <element name="state"  type="string" minOccurs="0" maxOccurs="1"/>
</complexType>

<complexType name="Stated-Address" base="Address"
                                   derivedBy="refinement">
  <element name="street" type="string"/>
  <element name="city"   type="string"/>
  <element name="state"  type="string" minOccurs="1" maxOccurs="1">
</complexType>

<complexType name="US-Address" base="Stated-Address"
                               derivedBy="extension">
  <element name="zip"    type="positiveInteger"/>
</complexType>
```

In our model, these three types would be defined as follows:

$$regexp(\textbf{Address}) = \textbf{Street}, \textbf{City}, \textbf{State}?, \tau_{\text{anytype}}*$$
$$regexp(\textbf{Stated-Address}) = \textbf{Street}, \textbf{City}, \textbf{State}, \tau_{\text{anytype}}*$$
$$regexp(\textbf{US-Address}) = \textbf{Street}, \textbf{City}, \textbf{State}, \textbf{Zip}, \tau_{\text{anytype}}*$$

The type τ_{anytype}, as defined in Remark 1, indicates the ability to have additional fields. Note that the subsumption relationship holds **US-Address** $\preceq$ **Stated-Address** $\preceq$ **Address**.

Proposition 3. *A type τ' derived by extension or refinement from a type τ is such that $\tau' \preceq \tau$.*

Proof Sketch: Refinement corresponds to adding a field at the end of a given type. This corresponds to regular expressions of the form: $regexp = \tau_1, \ldots, \tau_n,$ $\tau_{\text{anytype}}*$, and $regexp' = \tau_1, \ldots, \tau_n, \tau_{n+1}, \tau_{\text{anytype}}*$ for which subsumption holds with $\theta(\tau_{n+1}) = \tau_{\text{anytype}}$.

Extension can be obtained by restricting a datatype, which yields inclusion between predicates. minOccur and maxOccur restrictions corresponds to regular expressions of the form:

$$regexp = \underbrace{(\tau, \tau, \ldots, \tau)}_{n}, \underbrace{\tau?, \ldots, \tau?}_{m} \quad \text{and} \quad regexp' = \underbrace{(\tau, \tau, \ldots, \tau)}_{n'}, \underbrace{\tau?, \ldots, \tau?}_{m'}$$

Subsumption holds when $n \leq n'$ and $(n+m) \geq (n'+m')$. Union type restrictions correspond to regular expressions of the form $regexp = \tau_1 | \ldots | \tau_n | \ldots | \tau_{n+m}$, and $regexp' = \tau_1 | \ldots | \tau_n$ for which subsumption holds. The result follows by induction.

Subtyping. The literature proposes a large number of different mechanisms called or related to subtyping [8,27,29]. Basic subtyping usually relies on two mechanisms: additions of new attributes in tuples (e.g., { name: String; age: Int } <: { name: String }) and restrictions on atomic types (e.g., Int <: Float). The last mechanism is captured by predicate restrictions in our context, while the first is captured by adding Any* types when modeling tuples[3].

Instantiation. [10] proposes a notion of *instantiation* that corresponds to certain restrictions over types. This mechanism allows: restrictions on the label predicates, restrictions on the arity of collections (similar to the minOccur and maxOccur restrictions in XML schema), and restrictions on the unions. As for XML Schema, these restrictions yields only types for which subsumption holds.

5   Greatest Lower and Least Upper Bound

Let S and S' be two schemas. We consider equivalence classes of schemas with respect to subsumption $[S]_\approx$, ordered by $\preceq$, and show that this is a lattice. We first define the greatest lower bound, which intuitively is a schema describing the type information that is common to the given schemas.

We shall assume that whenever τ and τ' are in $\mathcal{T}$, so is the symbol $\tau \sqcap \tau'$. We need to define appropriately intersection of regular expressions: our regular expressions are over type names, but the intersection should be over the *semantics* of the types, not the names. For example, if the regular expressions are τ_1^* and (τ_2, τ_3), the intersection will be $((\tau_1 \sqcap \tau_2), (\tau_1 \sqcap \tau_3))$.

---

[3] Note however that our type system does not capture the unordered semantics of tuples.

Definition 6. *Let S and S' be two type schemas.*[4] *The* greatest lower bound $S \sqcap S'$ *and* least upper bound $S \sqcup S'$ *are the schemas with* $T_{S \sqcap S'} = \{\tau \sqcap \tau' \mid \tau \in T_S, \tau' \in T_{S'}\}$, $T_{S \sqcup S'} = T_S \cup T_{S'}$, *and*

$$S \sqcap S': \quad \begin{aligned} \triangle &\mapsto regexp_S(\triangle) \cap regexp_{S'}(\triangle) \\ \tau &\mapsto predicate_S(\tau); regexp_S(\tau) \cap regexp_{S'}(\tau') \end{aligned}$$

$$S \sqcup S': \quad \begin{aligned} \triangle &\mapsto regexp_{S'}(\triangle) \mid regexp_{S'}(\triangle) \\ \tau &\mapsto predicate_S(\tau); regexp_S(\tau) \qquad \tau \in T_S \\ \tau &\mapsto predicate_{S'}(\tau); regexp_{S'}(\tau) \qquad \tau \in T_{S'} \end{aligned}$$

Example 7. Consider the following two schemas (where τ_{anytype} is as in the definition of the schema **Any**).

$$S: \quad \begin{aligned} \triangle &\mapsto (\tau_1, \tau_{\text{anytype}}*) \\ \tau_1 &\mapsto \{a\}; \epsilon \end{aligned} \qquad S': \quad \begin{aligned} \triangle &\mapsto (\tau_{\text{anytype}}*, \tau_2) \\ \tau_2 &\mapsto \{b\}; \epsilon \end{aligned}$$

$$S \sqcap S': \quad \triangle \mapsto ((\tau_1 \sqcap \tau_{\text{anytype}}), (\tau_{\text{anytype}} \sqcap \tau_{\text{anytype}})*, (\tau_{\text{anytype}} \sqcap \tau_2))$$
$$\tau_1 \sqcap \tau_{\text{anytype}} \mapsto \{a\}; \epsilon$$
$$\tau_{\text{anytype}} \sqcap \tau_2 \mapsto \{b\}; \epsilon$$

where $\tau_{\text{anytype}} \sqcap \tau_{\text{anytype}}$ is the same as τ_{anytype} up to renaming.

The greatest lower bound of schemas requires intersection of regular expressions, that can lead to a blowup in the size of the schema but this is unlikely to happen in practice.

The greatest lower bound is the best description, with respect to subsumption, of all of the type information that we have about both schemas. In particular, if a database is typed by both S and S', it is also typed by $S \sqcap S'$. More generally:

Proposition 4. *1. $S \sqcap S' \preceq S$ and $S \sqcap S' \preceq S'$; $S \preceq S \sqcup S'$ and $S' \preceq S \sqcup S'$.*
2. If $S'' \preceq S$ and $S'' \preceq S'$, then $S'' \preceq S \sqcap S'$; similarly If $S \preceq S''$ and $S' \preceq S''$, then $S \sqcup S' \preceq S''$.
3. If $D : S$ and $D : S'$, then $D : S \sqcap S'$ and $D : S \sqcup S'$.

Theorem 1. $\mathcal{L} = \langle [S]_{\approx}, \sqcap_{\approx}, \sqcup_{\approx}, [\textbf{None}]_{\approx}, [\textbf{Any}]_{\approx} \rangle$ *is an incomplete distributive lattice without complement.*

The next theorem is essential as it gives a relationship between the syntactic definitions of $S \sqcap S'$ and $S \sqcup S'$ and the semantics of the respective schemas. The proof of this theorem relies on Remark 2, that connects typing, on which Models are defined, and subsumption.

Theorem 2. *For any schemas S and S', (1) Models$(S \sqcap S') =$ Models$(S) \cap$ Models(S') and (2) Models$(S \sqcup S') =$ Models$(S) \cup$ Models(S').*

---

[4] We assume for simplicity that T_S and $T_{S'}$ are disjoint. This can always be achieved by appropriate renaming.

The use of untagged roots was introduced in [2]. Our results give another, technical, reason why such special treatment of the root is needed. Specifically, if the database root were allowed to be tagged, then $\mathcal{L}$ would not be distributive. On the other hand, a data model based on forests rather than trees would not work either, as then $\text{Models}(S \sqcup S') = \text{Models}(S) \cup \text{Models}(S')$ would not hold.

Subsumption is weaker than inclusion, as there are schemas that are contained in other schemas without subsuming them. For this reason, the following Corollary is very important: it shows that whenever a schema S is contained in a schema S', S can be rewritten in an equivalent way such that S subsumes S'.

Corollary 1. *Let S and S' be two schemas such that* $\text{Models}(S) \subseteq \text{Models}(S')$. *Then there exists a schema S'' such that (1)* $\text{Models}(S'') = \text{Models}(S)$ *and (2)* $S'' \preceq S'$.

6 Practical Use of Subsumption

We now come back to our example from the introduction and illustrate how subsumption can be helpful for storage and query processing.

Standard relational techniques are used to design storage structures that take into account which queries are likely to be asked. If we take query q from the introduction, one might wish to find a schema S that would allow to store data in such a way this query is answered in an efficient way. However, if one only considers the integrated schema, one can only use the available information about Jammers. Existing techniques [14,18,31] would provide the following relational schema:

```
jammers(jid, company, name, price);
options(jid,att,treeid);
tree(treeid,...);
```

where the tree table is used to store any tree, playing a similar role to the overflow graph in [14].

The greatest lower bound can be used to derive a schema that includes the warranty attribute. After appropriate renaming of types, this is:

```
Warranty_Jammer :=
      jammer [ ?Company', Name', Price',
              *(  WarrantyOption' | (OtherOption', ?Supplement') ) ) ];
Company'          := company [ String ];
Name'             := name[ String ];
Price'            := price [ Int | onrequest ];
WarrantyOption'   := warranty * Any;
OtherOption'      := !warranty * Any;
Supplement'       := supplement [ Int ];
```

We can then use this information to store the data with a faster access to the warranty attribute, using the following relational schema:

```
jammers(jid, company, name, price);
jammers(jid, warranty);
options(jid,att,supplement,treeid);
tree(treeid,...);
```

We then need to evaluate query q on top of this storage. The key remark is that YAT_L [10,11] uses pattern matching with type expressions. This captures the navigation performed in other languages [1,13].

Following [9], the match clause of a YAT_L query is represented by a pattern-matching operation called *Bind*. *Bind* matches a regular expression with the data, and returns a binding between variables in the query and values in the document. In the case of query q, *Bind* p[$n,$w] where

```
p[$n,$w] := products * Jammer;
Jammer   := jammer [ *(Name | Warranty | Other) ];
Name     := name * ($n:Any1);
Warranty := warranty * ($w:Any2);
Other    := !name!warranty * Any;
Any1     := true [ Any* ]; Any2 := true [ Any* ]
```

Most XML processors evaluate similar operations by loading the document in memory and parsing it according to the given filter. This can be expensive and does not make use of the knowledge of how the document is stored (here with using the relational schema above).

Let θ be the subsumption mapping from the type of p[$n,$w] to the greatest lower bound:

$$\theta'(\text{Warranty\_Jammer}) = \text{Jammer} \qquad \theta'(\text{Company}') = \text{Other}$$
$$\theta'(\text{Name}') = \text{Name} \qquad \theta'(\text{Price}') = \text{Other}$$
$$\theta'(\text{WarrantyOption}') = \text{Warranty} \qquad \theta'(\text{OtherOption}') = \text{Other} \ldots$$

Through θ, we know that the values of $n
are the values of the elements of type Name' in the the stored schema, hence how to access them using the relational engine.

7   Related Work and Conclusion

Typing for XML is a heavily studied problem. Existing work covers the type systems themselves [2,10,12,33], type checking [20,26] and type inference [25,28]. XML types have been used for query formulation [19], query optimization [17,9], storage [14,31], and compile-time error detection [20]. A notion of subsumption for unordered semistructured data was proposed in [6] based on a graph bisimulation. Our work extends this approach to types that involve order and regular expressions. Typing in XDuce [20] relies on full type inclusion. [7] describes a notion of containment between XML DTDs, which are less expressive than our type system and is based on full inclusion with tag renaming.

There are many directions in which this work can be continued. First of all, while our work (and most other work in this area), uses a list model for data, for database applications a set semantics may be more appropriate, and therefore extending the results to sets (and bags) would be of interest. For applying the results to inheritance, as indicated above, one may want to be able to type an object in multiple ways – formally this may be captured by the greatest lower bound, but this does not provide the intuitive semantics desired here.

We have not discussed complexity in this paper. Typing a database is a special case of subsumption (where the database is itself the schema), and the complexity of typing is known [2] to be hard. Note, however, that complexity of checking subsumption is in the size of the schema rather than in the size the database. Furthermore, many of the problems that relate to typing become tractable in the case of *unambiguous* schemas: in our framework there are many possible definitions of ambiguity, such as the existence of a single typing, unambiguity up to reference nodes, unambiguous regular expressions, etc. Efficient evaluation of queries is one of the main motivations for this work. Many complex parameters must be taken into account in this context, such as the impact of storage structures, memory management issues, etc. To evaluate the real impact of subsumption, we consider an implementation of the techniques presented here in the context of the YAT System [10,9].

References

1. S. Abiteboul, D. Quass, J. McHugh, J. Widom, and J. L. Wiener. The Lorel query language for semistructured data. *International Journal on Digital Libraries*, 1(1):68–88, Apr. 1997.
2. C. Beeri and T. Milo. Schemas for integration and translation of structured and semi-structured data. In *Proceedings of International Conference on Database Theory (ICDT)*, Lecture Notes in Computer Science, Jerusalem, Israel, Jan. 1999.
3. R. Bourret, J. Cowan, I. Macherius, and S. St. Laurent. Document definition markup language (ddml) specification, version 1.0, Jan. 1999. W3C Note.
4. T. Bray, C. Frankston, and A. Malhotra. Document content description for XML. Submission to the World Wide Web Consortium, July 1998.
5. T. Bray, J. Paoli, and C. M. Sperberg-McQueen. Extensible markup language (XML) 1.0. W3C Recommendation, Feb. 1998. http://www.w3.org/TR/REC-xml/.
6. P. Buneman, S. B. Davidson, M. F. Fernandez, and D. Suciu. Adding structure to unstructured data. In *Proceedings of International Conference on Database Theory (ICDT)*, volume 1186 of *LNCS*, pages 336–350, Delphi, Greece, Jan. 1997.
7. D. Calvanese, G. D. Giacomo, and M. Lenzerini. Representing and reasoning on xml documents: A description logic approach. *Journal of Logic and Computation*, 9(3):205–318, 1999.
8. L. Cardelli. A semantics of multiple inheritance. *Information and Computation*, 76(2/3):138–164, 1988.
9. V. Christophides, S. Cluet, and J. Siméon. On wrapping query languages and efficient XML integration. In SIGMOD'2000, Dallas, Texas, May 2000.
10. S. Cluet, C. Delobel, J. Siméon, and K. Smaga. Your mediators need data conversion! In SIGMOD'1998, pages 177–188, Seattle, Washington, June 1998.
11. S. Cluet and J. Siméon. YAT$_L$: a functional and declarative language for XML. Draft manuscript, Mar. 2000.
12. A. Davidson, M. Fuchs, M. Hedin, M. Jain, J. Koistinen, C. Lloyd, M. Maloney, and K. Schwarzhof. Schema for object-oriented XML 2.0, July 1999. W3C Note.
13. A. Deutsch, M. F. Fernandez, D. Florescu, A. Y. Levy, and D. Suciu. A query language for XML. In *Proceedings of International World Wide Web Conference*, Toronto, May 1999.

14. A. Deutsch, M. F. Fernandez, and D. Suciu. Storing semistructured data with STORED. In SIGMOD'1999, pages 431–442, Philadelphia, Pennsylvania, June 1999.
15. M. F. Fernandez and J. Robie. XML Query data model. W3C Working Draft, May 2000. http://www.w3.org/TR/query-datamodel/.
16. M. F. Fernandez, J. Siméon, and P. Wadler (editors). XML query languages: Experiences and exemplars. draft manuscript, communication to the W3C, Sept. 1999.
17. M. F. Fernandez and D. Suciu. Optimizing regular path expressions using graph schemas. In ICDE'1998, Orlando, Florida, Feb. 1998.
18. M. N. Garofalakis, A. Gionis, R. Rastogi, S. Seshadri, and K. Shim. XTRACT: A system for extracting document type descriptors from XML documents. In SIGMOD'2000, pages 165–176, Dallas, Texas, May 2000.
19. R. Goldman and J. Widom. Data guides: Enabling query formulation and optimization in semistructured databases. In VLDB'1997, pages 436–445, Athens, Greece, Aug. 1997.
20. H. Hosoya and B. C. Pierce. XDuce: an XML processing language. In *International Workshop on the Web and Databases (WebDB'2000)*, Dallas, Texas, May 2000.
21. H. Hosoya, J. Vouillon, and B. C. Pierce. Regular expression types for XML. Submitted for publication, Mar. 2000.
22. http://sesp.co.uk/4.htm.
23. N. Klarlund, A. Moller, and M. I. Schwartzbach. DSD: A schema language for XML. In *Workshop on Formal Methods in Software Practice*, Portland, Oregon, Aug. 2000.
24. M. Makoto. Tutorial: How to relax. http://www.xml.gr.jp/relax/.
25. T. Milo and D. Suciu. Type inference for queries on semistructured data. In PODS'1999, pages 215–226, Philadephia, Pennsylvania, May 1999.
26. T. Milo, D. Suciu, and V. Vianu. Typechecking for XML transformers. In PODS'2000, Dallas, Texas, May 2000.
27. J. C. Mitchell. *Foundations for Programming Languages*. MIT Press, 1996.
28. Y. Papakonstantinou and V. Vianu. DTD inference for views of XML data. In PODS'2000, Dallas, Texas, May 2000.
29. F. Pottier. *Synthèse de types en présence de sous-typage: de la théorie à la pratique*. Thèse de doctorat, Université Paris VII, July 1998. http://pauillac.inria.fr/~fpottier/publis/these-fpottier.ps.gz.
30. R. Ramakrishnan and J. Gehrke. *Database Management Systems*. McGraw-Hill, 2000.
31. J. Shanmugasundaram, K. Tufte, C. Zhang, G. He, D. J. DeWitt, and J. F. Naughton. Relational databases for querying XML documents: Limitations and opportunities. In *Proceedings of International Conference on Very Large Databases (VLDB)*, Edinburgh, Scotland, Sept. 1999.
32. J. Siméon and S. Cluet. Using YAT to build a web server. In *International Workshop on the Web and Databases (WebDB'98)*, volume 1590 of *LNCS*, pages 118–135, Valencia, Spain, Mar. 1998.
33. H. S. Thompson, D. Beech, M. Maloney, and N. Mendelsohn. XML schema part 1: Structures. W3C Working Draft, Feb. 2000.

Towards Aggregated Answers for Semistructured Data

Holger Meuss[1], Klaus U. Schulz[1], and François Bry[2]

[1] CIS, University of Munich, Oettingenstr. 67, 80538 Munich, Germany
meuss@cis.uni-muenchen.de
[2] Institute for Computer Science, University of Munich, Oettingenstr. 67,
80538 Munich, Germany

1 Introduction

Semistructured data [5,34,23,31,1] are used to model data transferred on the Web for applications such as e-commerce [18], biomolecular biology [8], document management [2,21], linguistics [32], thesauri and ontologies [17]. They are formalized as trees or more generally as (multi-)graphs [23,1]. Query languages for semistructured data have been proposed [6,11,1,4,10] that, like SQL, can be seen as involving a number of variables [35], but, in contrast to SQL, give rise to arrange the variables in trees or graphs reflecting the structure of the semistructured data to be retrieved. Leaving aside the "construct" parts of queries, answers can be formalized as mappings represented as tuples, hence called *answer tuples,* that assign database nodes to query variables. These answer tuples underly the semistructured data delivered as answers.

A simple enumeration of answer tuples is problematic for several reasons. First, the number of answer tuples for a query may grow exponentially in the size of both, the query and the database. Second, even if the number of answer tuples is manageable, the frequent sharing of common data between distinct answer tuples is no more apparent in their enumeration.

In this article, it is first argued that enumerating answer tuples is often not appropriate and that *aggregated answers* are preferable. Then, a notion of aggregated answers called $\underline{C}$omplete $\underline{A}$nswer $\underline{A}$ggregate (CAA) generalizing [25,24] is introduced and algorithms for computing CAAs are given. We only consider CAAs for semistructured data: In this context, CAAs seem particularly attractive since they reflect the graph structure of the database and the query in a very natural way. It is shown that CAAs enjoy nice complexity properties: (1) While the number of answer tuples may be exponential in the size of the query, the size of the CAA is at most linear in the size of the query and quadratic in the size of the database; (2) the complexity of computing the CAA of a query depends on the query's structural complexity (i.e. whether it is a sequence, tree, graph, etc.) but is independent of the structural complexity of the database. For tree queries, efficient polynomial algorithms are given. Besides, CAAs seem to be particularly appropriate for *answer searching* and *answer browsing.*

This article is organized as follows. The need for aggregated answers and the basics of CAAs are illustrated with a motivating example in Section 2. Section 3

J. Van den Bussche and V. Vianu (Eds.): ICDT 2001, LNCS 1973, pp. 346–360, 2001.
© Springer-Verlag Berlin Heidelberg 2001

introduces a few preliminary notions. Section 4 gives the formal definition of CAAs. In Section 5, a hierarchy of query problems of increasing complexity is defined. In Section 6, we describe algorithms for computing the CAA and analyze their complexity, for each problem of the hierarchy. Query answering using CAAs is discussed in Section 8. Section 9 discusses related work. Section 10 is a conclusion. For space reasons, no proofs are given. They are given in the full version of this paper [26].

2   Motivating Example

Consider a database $\mathcal{D}$ (Figure 1) on research projects offering information on project managers, members and publications. Assume that the database is organized as a graph with labeled edges and nodes according to a model for semistructured data [9,19,1]. Projects x and their managers z such that the string "XML" occurs in a title element t (at any depth) of some articles y of projects x are retrieved by a query depicted in Figure 1. (The restructuring facilities of

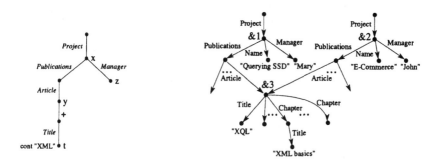

Fig. 1. An example query (left) and database (right)

full-fledge query languages for semistructured data [22,12,36] are not considered in this paper. Thus, only the "select" parts of queries are mentioned, possible "construct" parts are left implicit.)

Some of the articles retrieved by the query Q are common to several projects in the database $\mathcal{D}$ (Figure 1). Evaluated against the database $\mathcal{D}$, the query Q returns the answer tuples $\langle x \mapsto \&1, y \mapsto \&3, z \mapsto$ "Mary", $t \mapsto$ "XML basics"$\rangle$ and $\langle x \mapsto \&2, y \mapsto \&3, z \mapsto$ "John", $t \mapsto$ "XML basics"$\rangle$.

More generally, if the string "XML" occurs in k titles of article $\&3$, then Q admits $2k$ answer tuples all referring to $\&3$. Furthermore, if an article is shared by n projects, then Q has $n \cdot k$ answer tuples. In case of more complex queries and/or of database items with more complex interconnections, as often arise in Web and e-commerce servers, an enumeration of answer tuples à la Prolog or à la SQL results in a combinatorial explosion. If e.g. the functional dependency $Project \rightarrow$

Manager does not hold and if each of the two projects has m managers, then Q admits $2 \cdot k \cdot m$ answer tuples. In general, such a product giving the number of answers of a query like Q can have any number of factors, i.e. the number of answers is exponential.

Arguably, for many applications such an enumeration of answer tuples is not appropriate. Instead, a data structure stressing the common subelements shared between (parts of) answer tuples as well as their graph relationships would often be more convenient. Let us call *aggregated answer* such a hypothetical data structure. Aggregated answers can help to recognize "bottlenecks" in the "answer space". Furthermore, aggregated answers make advanced query answering forms possible, cf. Section 7.

In this paper, *Complete Answer Aggregates (CAAs)* are proposed as a formalization of such a notion of aggregated answer and CAAs are shown to be efficiently computable. A CAA reflects the graph structure of the query it is computed from. The CAA computed for Q over an example database (larger than $\mathcal{D}$) has a "slot", represented in the figure below by a rectangle, for each variable x, y, z, and t. A slot for variable v contains possible binding elements for v: E.g. the slot for x contains project identifiers and the slot for z contains manager identifiers. The edges in are *CAA links*. They represent (sequences of) database edges. Note that a presentation of a CAA such as in the following figure is not intended for end users.

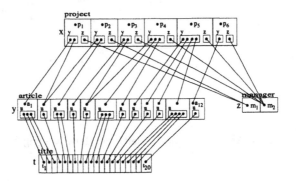

Admittedly, it is possible to generate in some cases simple kinds of aggregated answers with usual query languages like [4,10], but this requires nested queries that might be complex [1] (cf. Sec. 4.1). In contrast, with CAAs, no complex queries are needed and aggregated answers are obtained in all cases.

CAAs are nothing else than semistructured data items of a certain kind. Thus queries can be posed to CAAs. Provided that the implementation of the query language is "CAA aware", such a querying can be performed without requiring from the user or application issuing the query to be aware of the internal structure of the CAAs constructed during query evaluation. Thus, CAAs are a convenient basis for an iterative, or cascade style query-answering: The evaluation of a query yields a CAA which can be stored and in turn queried using the same query language. Such a cascade style query-answering is often sought for in e-commerce applications [18]. Cf. Section 7 for more details.

3   Preliminary Notions

Definition 1. *A database is a tuple $\mathcal{D} = (N, E, L_N, L_E, \Lambda_N, \Lambda_E)$ where*
- *N is a (finite) set of nodes,*
- *$E \subseteq N \times N$ is a set of directed edges,*
- *L_N is a (finite) set of node labels,*
- *L_E is a (finite) set of edge labels or features,*
- *$\Lambda_N : L_N \to 2^N$ is a (total) function assigning to each node label a set of nodes,*
- *$\Lambda_E : E \to L_E$ is a (total) function assigning labels to edges.*

$\mathcal{D}$ is a sequence (resp. tree, DAG, graph) database if the structure imposed by E upon N defines a (finite) set of sequences (resp. trees, DAGs, graphs).

For simplicity, we do not consider multigraphs with multiple edges between nodes. Note that sequence, tree, and DAG databases are acyclic and that nodes in sequence (resp. tree) databases have at most one parent and one child (resp. one parent). Node labels are aimed at modeling attributes and attribute values. Multiple node labeling is allowed, so as to model textual content: A label w of node n might express that a string w occurs in the textual content of n. In the sequel, regular expressions α over the alphabet L_E of edge labels will be considered.

Definition 2. *Let $\mathcal{D} = (N, E, L_N, L_E, \Lambda_N, \Lambda_E)$ be a database and α a regular expression over L_E. A node $d \in N$ is an α-ancestor of $e \in N$, if there exists a path from d to e such that the sequence of labels along the path belongs to the regular language $\mathcal{L}(\alpha)$ induced by α.*

Definition 3. *Let X be an enumerable set of variables and $\mathcal{D} = (N, E, L_N, L_E, \Lambda_N, \Lambda_E)$ a database. An atomic path constraint is an expression of the form*
- *$A(x)$ called a labeling constraint,*
- *$x \to_1 y$ called a child constraint,*
- *$x \to_f y$ called a f-child constraint,*
- *$x \to_+ y$ called a descendant constraint,*
- *$x \to_\alpha y$ called an α-descendant constraint,*

where $x, y \in X$, $A \in L_N$, $f \in L_E$, and α is a regular expression over L_E. Atomic path constraints of the latter four types are called edge constraints.

In the sequel, we only consider regular expressions α where the empty word ϵ does not belong to $\mathcal{L}(\alpha)$. Edge constraints of the form $x \to_1 y$, $x \to_f y$, and $x \to_+ y$ can be seen as special cases of α-descendant constraints. Without loss of generality, the (non-atomic) path constraints considered in this paper are conjunctions of atomic path constraints containing at most one atomic edge constraint $x \to_? y$ for each (ordered) pair (x, y) of query variables. Depending on their nature, edge constraints might impose sequence, tree, DAG, or graph structures on the variables.

Definition 4. *A sequence (resp. tree, DAG, graph) query is a conjunction of atomic path constraints the atomic edge constraints of which impose a sequence (resp. tree, DAG, graph) structure on its variables. If D is a database and Q a query with set of variables X_Q, then $(Q, X_Q, \mathcal{D})$ is an evaluation problem.*

Note that queries of either type can be represented as graphs.

Definition 5. *Let $\mathcal{D} = (N, E, L_N, L_E, \Lambda_N, \Lambda_E)$ be a database and Q a query. An* answer *to Q in $\mathcal{D}$ is a mapping μ that assigns a node in D to each variable in Q in such a way that*

- $\mu(x) \in \Lambda_N(A)$ *whenever Q contains the labeling constraint $A(x)$,*
- $(\mu(x), \mu(y)) \in E$ *whenever Q contains the child constraint $x \to_1 y$,*
- $(\mu(x), \mu(y)) \in E$ *and $\Lambda_E(\mu(x), \mu(y)) = f$ whenever Q contains the f-child constraint $x \to_f y$,*
- $\mu(x)$ *is an α-ancestor of $\mu(y)$ whenever Q contains the α-descendant constraint $x \to_\alpha y$.*

If $(Q, X_Q, \mathcal{D})$ is an evaluation problem and μ an answer to Q in $\mathcal{D}$, then μ is called a solution *of $(Q, X_Q, \mathcal{D})$.*

Note that according to Definition 5, cyclic, i.e. proper graph queries have no answers in acyclic, i.e. sequence, tree, or DAG databases.

4   Complete Answer Aggregates

Let $\mathcal{D} = (N, E, L_N, L_E, \Lambda_N, \Lambda_E)$ be a database and Q a query with set of variables X_Q.

Definition 6. *An* answer aggregate *for the evaluation problem $(Q, X_Q, \mathcal{D})$ is a pair (Dom, Π) such that*

- $\text{Dom} : X_Q \to 2^N$ *assigns to each variable of Q a set of nodes of $\mathcal{D}$ such that each $d \in \text{Dom}(x)$ has the label A if $A(x)$ is a labeling constraint of Q,*
- Π *maps each edge constraint $x \to_1 y$ (resp. $x \to_f y$, $x \to_+ y$, $x \to_\alpha y$) of Q to a set $\Pi(x, y) \subseteq \text{Dom}(x) \times \text{Dom}(y)$ such that for all $(d, e) \in \Pi(x, y)$ e is a child (resp. f-child, descendant, α-descendant) of d. A node $d \in \text{Dom}(x)$ is called a* target candidate *for x. A pair $(d, e) \in \Pi(x, y)$ is called a* link *between d and e.*

Definition 7. *An* instantiation *of an answer aggregate (Dom, Π) is a mapping μ that maps each $x \in X_Q$ to a node $\mu(x) \in \text{Dom}(x)$ such that $(\mu(x), \mu(y)) \in \Pi(x, y)$ whenever Q contains an edge constraint $x \to_1 y$, $x \to_f y$, $x \to_+ y$, or $x \to_\alpha y$. Each node of the form $\mu(x)$, as well as every link of the form $(\mu(x), \mu(y))$ (for $x, y \in X_Q$) is said to* contribute *to instantiation μ.*

Note that each instantiation of an answer aggregate for $(Q, X_Q, \mathcal{D})$ defines an answer to Q in $\mathcal{D}$.

Definition 8. *(Dom, Π) is a* complete answer aggregate (CAA) *for $(Q, X_Q, \mathcal{D})$ if every answer to Q in $\mathcal{D}$ is an instantiation of (Dom, Π) and if every target candidate and every link of (Dom, Π) contributes to at least one instantiation.*

Example 1. Assume that $Q = x_1 \to_+ x_2 \wedge x_2 \to_+ x_3 \wedge \cdots \wedge x_{q-1} \to_+ x_q$ and assume that D consists of $n > q$ nodes $d_1, \ldots, d_n$ sequentially ordered (i.e. $(d_i, d_{i+1}) \in E$ for all $1 \leq i \leq n-1$). Q has $\binom{n}{q}$ answers in D. For $q = 4$ and $n = 8$ the CAA representing the 70 answers (each mapping the four query variables to database nodes) is depicted below. For one possible instantiation, contributing nodes and links are highlighted.

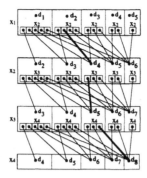

Lemma 1. *There exists a unique CAA for each evaluation problem.*

Size of CAAs. Let $(Q, X_Q, \mathcal{D})$ be an evaluation problem. In the following, q will denote the number of variables plus labeling constraints of Q, n the number of nodes of $\mathcal{D}$, and a the maximal number of ancestors of a database node plus the number of links between these nodes. Note that, if $\mathcal{D}$ is a sequence or a tree database, then a is bounded by $O(h)$ where h is the height of $\mathcal{D}$.

As a measure for the size of a CAA (Dom, Π) for $(Q, X_Q, \mathcal{D})$ it makes sense to retain the total number of target candidates and links in (Dom, Π), i.e. $\sum_{x \in X_Q} |Dom(x)| + \sum_{x,y \in X_Q} |\Pi(x, y)|$ (where $\Pi(x, y) := \emptyset$ if x and y are not related by an edge constraint in Q). Although the number of answers to a query Q may be exponential, the size of a CAA is at most linear in the size of the query and quadratic in the size of the database:

Theorem 1. *The size of the CAA for an evaluation problem $(Q, X_Q, \mathcal{D})$ is $O(q \cdot n \cdot a)$.*

The full version [26] of this paper describes situations, where a better bound $O(q \cdot n)$ can be obtained.

CAAs as Semistructured data: According to Definition 6, the links of the CAA for an evaluation problem (Q, X_Q, D) are not labeled. If $x \rightarrow_f y$ is an f-child constraint in Q, then the label f can obviously be attached to each link in $\Pi(x, y)$. If $x \rightarrow_1 y$ is a child constraint in Q, then each link of $\Pi(x, y)$ clearly represents a labeled edge of $\mathcal{D}$, i.e. can be labeled like this database edge. Thus, if all edge constraints of the query are child- or f-child constraints, the CAA trivially extends to a semistructured data item. If the query Q contains descendant constraints of the form $x \rightarrow_+ y$ or $x \rightarrow_\alpha y$ and if $\mathcal{D}$ is a sequence or tree database, then for each $(d, e) \in \Pi(x, y)$ there exists in D a unique path π from d to e. The corresponding sequence of labels can be attached to the link (d, e) of the CAA yielding a semistructured data item in this case, too. If $\mathcal{D}$ is a proper DAG graph database, a link $(d, e) \in \Pi(x, y)$ in general stands for a regular expression. Although this is less immediate than in the previous cases of sequence and tree databases, this expression can serve as a label of a CAA link. For space reasons, details are left out.

CAAs for extended query formalisms: Many query languages for XML data and semistructured data [11,6,23] allow for arbitrary value comparisons (joins), i.e. database leaves are assumed to carry values, and queries may contain value comparisons. A CAA does not suffice to completely represent exactly the answers to a query with value comparisons. Nonetheless, the CAA for the join-free part of the query can be built up representing a coarsening of the set of answers. Note that such a generalization of a query might speed up its evaluation and be appropriate for some applications such as e-commerce [18]. Extensions to CAA as defined here can be thought of for a faithful representation of the answers of a query with value comparisons.

5   A Query Hierarchy

We would like to clarify how the structural properties of both query and database affect the complexity of computing the CAA. To this end we introduce the following notions:

Definition 9. *Let $\mathcal{EP} = (Q, X_Q, \mathcal{D})$ be an evaluation problem. $\mathcal{EP}$ is of type S-S (Sequence-Sequence) if Q is a sequence query and D a sequence database. Evaluation problem of types S-T, S-D, S-G, T-S, T-T, T-D, T-G, D-S, D-T, D-D, D-G, and G-G are similarly defined: The first letter (S: sequence, T: tree, D: DAG, and G: graph) denotes the type of the query, the second, that of the database.*

The thirteen classes of evaluation problems of Definition 9 form a hierarchy of increasing structural complexity. This hierarchy does not include the types G-S, G-T, G-D, because they would correspond to evaluation problems with cyclic (i.e. type G) queries: According to Definition 5, evaluation problems with cyclic queries have no solutions in acyclic (i.e. type S, T, and D) databases. Note that all the evaluation problems of the types specified in Definition 9 are non-trivial in the sense that they might have solutions.

Definition 10. *A query is called* simple *if all its edge constraints are child, f-child, or descendant constraints. An evaluation problem $(Q, X_Q, \mathcal{D})$ is* simple *if Q is simple.*

According to Definitions 4 and 3, a query is simple if it does not involve regular expressions. For simple queries, the algorithms described in the next section have optimal complexity.

6   Computation of CAAs

In this section an algorithm for computing the CAA of a simple sequence query is first given. Then, its adaptation to simple tree queries is outlined. For space reasons, further adaptations, e.g. to tree queries involving regular path expressions, are not explained in this paper. A polynomial algorithm for this case is given in the full version [26].

Simple Sequence Queries

The algorithm depicted below takes a simple sequence query Q and a database $\mathcal{D}$ as arguments and computes the CAA (Dom_Q, Π_Q) for the evaluation problem induced by Q and $\mathcal{D}$. Starting from an empty domain (line 3) and an empty set of edges (line 4) the algorithm adds target candidates to the domains (slots) of the query variables (line 15) and adds appropriate links to the set of edges (lines 30, 37). A pair (x, d) is said to be "added" to express that target candidate d is added to the domain (slot) of x. Possibly, pairs (x, d) are added that are "illegal" in the sense that $d \notin Dom_Q(x)$.

```
 1 procedure Aggregate comp_agg(Q,db)
 2 begin
 3   Dom:=empty DomainSet;
 4   Π:=empty EdgeSet;
 5   q_l:=leaf of Q;
 6   for all nodes d in db do
 7     map(Dom,Π,q_l,d);
 8   Agg:=Aggregate(Dom,Π);
 9   clean(Agg);
10   return Agg;
11 end;
12
13 procedure boolean map(Dom,Π,x,dx)
14 begin
15   add dx to Dom(x);
16   if dx satisfies the labeling
17     constraints of x then
18   begin
19     if x=root then return true
20     else
21     begin
22       y:=parent(x);
23       Anc:=appr_ancestors(dx,x,y);
24       map_found:=false;
25       for all dy_i ∈ Anc do
26         if dy_i ∉ Dom(y) then
27           if map(Dom,Π,y,dy_i) then
28           begin
29             map_found:=true;
30             add (y,x,dy_i,dx) to Π;
31           end
32         else
33         begin
34           if not is_red(Dom,y,dy_i) then
35           begin
36             map_found:=true;
37             add (y,x,dy_i,dx) to Π;
38           end;
39         end;
40       if map_found=false then
41         color_red(Dom,x,dx);
42       return map_found;
43     end;
44   else /*labeling constraints not satisfied*/
45   begin
46     color_red(Dom,x,dx);
47     return false;
48   end;
49 end;
```

Illegal pairs are detected and marked "red" (lines 41, 46). Only "legal" links, i.e., links in Π_Q, are introduced. As a last step, for each red pair (x, d) node d is deleted from the slot of x. After this slot "cleaning" (line 9), the CAA (Dom_Q, Π_Q) is obtained.

Let $x_1, \ldots, x_p$ be the ordered sequence of query variables such that $x_i \to_? x_{i+1}$ $(1 \leq i < p)$ occurs in the simple sequence query. The algorithm starts with the (unique) query leaf x_p (line 5). The outermost loop (line 6) calls for each database node d_p the recursive function map. This function returns a boolean value indicating whether the pair (x_p, d_p) is legal. First, the pair is added (line 15). Assume the pair (x_i, d_i) has been added. If $i = 1$, then the pair is legal (line 19). Otherwise (x_i, d_i) is legal if and only if there exists a legal pair (x_{i-1}, d_{i-1}) such that (d_{i-1}, d_i) satisfies the edge constraint $x_{i-1} \to_? x_i$ in Q. Hence, for each "appropriate" ancestor d_{i-1}, which depends on the kind of the edge constraint, it is checked whether (x_{i-1}, d_{i-1}) is a legal pair (lines 27, 34). Two cases are distinguished:

1. If (x_{i-1}, d_{i-1}) has not been previously added, then the legality of (x_{i-1}, d_{i-1}) is checked by a recursive call of the function map (line 27).

2. Otherwise (x_{i-1}, d_{i-1}) is illegal if it is marked red (line 34).

In both cases, if (x_{i-1}, d_{i-1}) is legal then a link between (x_{i-1}, d_{i-1}) and (x_i, d_i) is added (lines 30, 37). After inspection of all appropriate ancestors of d_i, the pair (x_i, d_i) is marked red if no legal pair (x_{i-1}, d_{i-1}) is found (line 40). Similarly (x_{i-1}, d_{i-1}) is marked red if d_i does not satisfy all labeling constraints of x_i (line 46).

Complexity: Clearly, for each pair (x, d), map is called at most once. Hence, the total number of calls to this function is bounded by the maximal number of pairs $q \cdot n$. Under the assumption that each database node has links pointing to parent nodes, computing the set of appropriate ancestors of a target candidate x_i takes time $O(a)$. Whether a node x_i satisfies a given labeling constraint $A(x_i)$ can be checked in constant time. Since each labeling constraint refers to a unique query variable, the total time needed for all tests related to labeling constraints is $O(q \cdot n)$. Cleaning takes time $O(q \cdot n)$. Therefore, the overall complexity is $O(q \cdot n \cdot a)$.

Simple Tree Queries

In the case of simple tree queries we introduce the notion of an *adapter point* as the bottom-most common query node of two query paths. The query paths are processed consecutively. For each query path, the above algorithm is modified as follows: When reaching an adapter point x_{i-1} that has already been visited during processing of another path, no new target candidate for slot x_{i-1} is introduced. Furthermore, only the already collected non-red target candidates (x_{i-1}, d_{i-1}) are used for links between target candidates in x_{i-1} and x_i. If, after a query path has been fully processed, a target candidate (x_{i-1}, d_{i-1}) for an adapter point x_{i-1} has no links to a target candidate in x_i, then it is marked red.

With simple tree queries, cleaning is more complicated. Call *downwards isolated* target candidates (x_{i-1}, d_{i-1}) such that for some child x_i of x_{i-1} there are no links from (x_{i-1}, d_{i-1}) to a target candidate within the slot x_i. After entering all target candidates, downwards isolated target candidates are detected. Since they are illegal, they are marked red. Removal of red nodes may result in new downwards isolated target candidates. The removal of red target candidates is based upon a variant of (the second part of) the well-known AC-4 arc-consistency algorithm [29].

Complexity: Since the recursive calls do not fill slots of adapter points twice, in this case as well no target candidates are processed twice in the first part of the algorithm. This gives a time complexity of $O(q \cdot n \cdot a)$ for this part. For cleaning an adaption of arguments from [29] yields time complexity $O(q \cdot n \cdot a)$. Space complexity is still $O(q \cdot n \cdot a)$.

Adding Regular Path Expressions

A simple modification suffices to adapt the algorithms for sequence and tree queries described above to queries involving regular path expressions. At line 23, if the query contains an α-descendant constraint $y \to_\alpha x$, then the set of appropriate ancestors of the current node dx is now the set of all α-ancestors of the database node dx.

The computation of the sets of α-ancestors needs some extra time. Using standard techniques from automata and graph theory, it is shown in the full version [26] that the resulting time complexity is $O(q^2 \cdot n \cdot a)$.

Simple DAG and Graph Queries

Four evaluation problems of the hierarchy turn out to be NP-complete with respect to combined complexity.

Define the *weight* of a node (resp. variable) of a database (resp. query) as 1 plus the number of labels attached to the node (resp. variable). Define the *size* of a database (resp. query) as the sum of the weights of its nodes (resp. variables) and its the number of edges. Define the *size* of an evaluation problem $(Q, X_Q, \mathcal{D})$ as the sum of the size of Q and the size of $\mathcal{D}$. It is shown in the full version [26] that so-called 1-in-3 problems over positive literals [13] can be encoded as D-T evaluation problems, using a polynomial translation. The following theorem is a simple consequence.

Theorem 2. *Whether a simple D-T (resp. D-D, D-G, G-G) evaluation problem $(Q, X_Q, \mathcal{D})$ has a solution is NP-complete with respect to the size of $(Q, X_Q, \mathcal{D})$.*

Table 1. Complexity for computing the CAA resp. (*) for deciding solvability

		Database			
		S	T	D	G
Queries	S	$O(q \cdot n \cdot a)$	$O(q \cdot n \cdot a)$	$O(q \cdot n \cdot a)$	$O(q \cdot n \cdot a)$
without	T	$O(q \cdot n \cdot a)$	$O(q \cdot n \cdot a)$	$O(q \cdot n \cdot a)$	$O(q \cdot n \cdot a)$
reg. path	D	$O(q \cdot e \cdot n^3 \cdot a)$	(*) NP-compl.	(*) NP-compl.	(*) NP-compl.
expressions	G	-	-	-	(*) NP-compl.
Queries with	S	$O(q^2 \cdot n \cdot a)$	$O(q^2 \cdot n \cdot a)$	$O(q^2 \cdot n \cdot a)$	$O(q^2 \cdot n \cdot a)$
reg. path expr.	T	$O(q^2 \cdot n \cdot a)$	$O(q^2 \cdot n \cdot a)$	$O(q^2 \cdot n \cdot a)$	$O(q^2 \cdot n \cdot a)$

Table 1 summarizes the complexity results for the computation of CAAs (resp. for deciding solvability, marked with *) given in this section. The case D-S in the upper table is established in the full version [26]. The parameter e denotes the number of edges in the query.

Due to the results on the size of CAAs (cf. Section 4), the bounds given at lines S and T of the upper table are optimal.

In practice the worst case time complexity for computing a CAA can be exponential with D-T, D-D, D-G and G-G evaluation problems. This could be faced by a polynomial-time computation of an "upper approximation" to the CAA, i.e. an answer aggregate yielding not only all answers, but also possibly containing target candidates or links not contributing to any answer. Such an upper approximation to a CAA can be obtained by first selecting a spanning tree T of the considered query, then compute the CAA for the subquery induced by this spanning tree. Links representing possible interpretations of the query edges that have been omitted from Q might then be added. Arc consistency techniques [29] can be used to erase nodes and edges that do not contribute to any instantiation.

7   Advanced Query Answering Using CAAs

Once the CAA for an evaluation problem has been computed, it can be exploited for advanced query answering techniques we call *answer searching* and for *answer browsing*. These notions are explained referring to the example of Section 2: A query Q to a research project database $\mathcal{D}$ retrieves projects x and the managers z of these projects such that the string "XML" occurs in a title element u (at any depth) of some article y of a project x.

Answer Searching: In essence, the CAA of a query is a data structure making explicit the interdependencies between the answers to a query. Comparing queries and investigating the interrelationships between the various answers to a query is needed in many applications. CAAs can be used for scanning, comparing, filtering, ordering in the style of search engines as well as for analyzing in any other manner the answers to a query. Particularly promising are search primitives for detecting commonalities and differences between answers, computation of aggregate values like averages, maxima and minima. Note that the nodes of database items stored in a CAA potentially give access to the subelements rooted at these nodes, thus giving rise to a semantically rich "answer searching".

The set of answers for the above-mentioned query Q can be searched for:
• managers leading the highest number of project,
• for managers leading at least 2 projects,
• for projects with at least 10 XML articles.
To answer such queries, aggregate values have to be computed from the CAA of query Q. Note that such semantically related aggregate values are often computed in the same query. Many database applications like molecular biology sequence analysis and e-commerce require to perform such advanced comparisons from large answer sets computed from some "base query" [18].

In many cases, the querying of the CAA of a base query can be carried out automatically. In some cases however, such an automatic "search" is not sufficient or not possible, an interactive "browsing of the answer space" is desirable.

Answer Browsing: A visualization of a CAA for a query can be a convenient basis for browsing the answers to that query. One can easily identify nodes of the CAA of query Q, like project 5, that deserve special attention by looking at the number of departing article links of CAA 1 in Figure 2. More elaborate visualization facilities would make it possible to directly browse between e.g. projects, articles, titles by following the links of the CAA.

If the CAA has a large number of nodes, then the user might get "lost in answer space". In such cases, it might be beneficial to restrict the visualization to a *view of the CAA*. In case of query Q, one might wish to restrict, say, the CAA to information associated with projects with at least three XML related articles. Also, *slot hiding* can provide with a better overview. Note that slot hiding corresponds to the projection operator of relational databases. If slot hiding is applied, then CAA links are inherited. Applying slot hiding to the running example yields CAA 2 depicted in Figure 2.

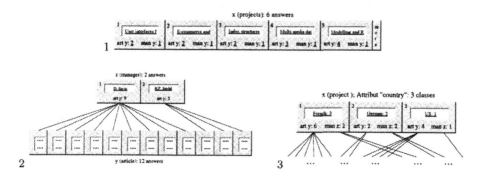

Fig. 2. Three presentation forms of CAAs

A further visualization technique based upon CAAs is *clustered aggregation*. Assuming that nodes have further attributes, CAA nodes that have identical attribute values can be merged. In case of query Q, if projects have a "country" attribute, if projects p_1, p_3, p_4 are French, projects p_2 and p_6 are German, and if p_5 is a US-project, then applying clustered aggregation might yield CAA 3 of Figure 2. This presentation might be used to show which countries have projects of interest and how many.

General picture: cascade style query-answering: The possibilities for automated search as well as interactive browsing of answer sets the CAAs offer suggests that, for many applications, query answering can be processed in two or more successive phases, the first of which resulting in the construction and storing of the CAA, the following phases consisting in an inspection of this CAA or in the construction of further, more specialized CAAs. CAA inspection can consist both in an automated search or in an interactive browsing. In addition, to help analyzing and/or browsing answers, such a query answering based upon CAAs can help to react rapidly to user query requests.

Cascade style query-answering query answering is possible with any query language, indeed. The contribution of CAAs lies in an intermediate data structure supporting this form of query answering which can be efficiently computed. Note that for many novel applications such as e-commerce such a cascade style query-answering is needed [18].

8   Related Work

Tree Databases: For tree queries and tree databases, a simplified form of CAA based on the Tree Matching formalism [20] has already been introduced in [25, 24]. The present paper significantly extends over this early work.

Query formalisms for semi-structured data: Several query models for XML and semistructured data have been designed and/or implemented and used [23, 3,33,15,30,31,4,10], cf. [4,10] for surveys. These query models are more ambitious than the model presented in this paper, however, in contrast to this paper they are not devoted to *aggregating answers*. Thus, the contribution of this paper is widely orthogonal and complementary.

Conjunctive queries: The queries considered in this paper are a special case of the conjunctive queries over relational databases as investigated in, e.g., [7,16]. However, it must be stressed that the distinction between tree queries and DAG or graph queries does *not* correspond to the conventional distinction between acyclic and cyclic conjunctive queries in database theory.

The distinction of database theory between acyclic and cyclic conjunctive queries refers to the hypergraph of the query, which is an undirected graph. In contrast, the query atoms considered in this paper are unary (labeling constraints) or binary (edge constraints). A binary atom $r(x, y)$ imposes a fixed orientation $x \to y$ on $\{x, y\}$ which reflects the direction of edges in the database. The conjunctions considered in this paper are such that the set of their binary atoms induces a sequence, tree, DAG, or graph structure on the query. Hence, the NP-hardness result for DAG-queries given in Section 6 is not in conflict with general results on polynomial tractability of acyclic conjunctive queries.

Dynamic programming and constraint reasoning: The algorithms described in Section 6 are closely related to methods of dynamic programming and to the arc-consistency techniques for constraint networks, cf. the full version [26] for details.

Index structures: Index structures as discussed in [23,2,14,28,27] can be used to improve the practical efficiency of the computation of CAAs. Details can be found in the full version [26].

9   Conclusion

The paper motivated and introduced "complete answer aggregates (CAAs)" as a model for aggregating the answers to a sequence, tree, DAG, or graph query in a semistructured database. Algorithms for the computation of CAAs for queries of various structural kinds have been presented. A hierarchy of evaluation problems the CAAs of which can be computed in polynomial time (with respect to combined complexity) has been given. Cases have been characterized where computation of CAAs (emptiness problem) is NP-complete.

The query model presented in this paper has been implemented for the special case of tree queries and of tree databases. The implementation is being tested with large collections of complex structured documents. The prototype currently available does not handle regular path expressions, but can cope with left-to-right order constraints between the children of a query node, as needed in document management. The necessary adaptation of the notion of a CAA as well as the mathematical and algorithmic background is given in [25,24]. For this expanded signature, the time complexity of the algorithm for computing the CAA is $O(q \cdot n \cdot a \cdot log(n))$. The additional logarithmic factor comes from the fact that order information is not being taken into account and handled during query evaluation. An "answer browser" based on CAAs is currently being developed.

References

1. S. Abiteboul, P. Buneman, and D. Suciu. *Data on the Web: From Relations to Semistructured Data and XML.* Morgan Kaufmann Publishers, 2000.
2. R. Baeza-Yates and G. Navarro. Integrating contents and structure in text retrieval. *SIGMOD Record,* 25(1):67–79, 1996.
3. The BBQ Page. http://www.npaci.edu/DICE/MIX/BBQ/, May 2000.
4. A. Bonifati and S. Ceri. A comparative analysis of five XML query languages. *SIGMOD Record,* March 2000.
5. P. Buneman. Semistructured data. In *Proc. ACM PODS'97,* 1997.
6. S. Ceri, S. Comai, E. Damiani, P. Fraternali, S. Paraboschi, and L. Tanca. XML-GL: a graphical language for querying and restructuring XML documents. *Computer Networks,* 31(11–16):1171–1187, May 1999.
7. A. K. Chandra and P. M. Merlin. Optimal implementation of conjunctive queries in relational data bases. In *Proc. 9th Annual ACM Symp. on Theory of Computing,* 1977.
8. XML/CML - Chemical Markup Language. http://www.nottingham.ac.uk/pazpmr/README, 1999.
9. M. Consens and A. Mendelzon. Graphlog: a visual formalism of real life recursion. In *Proc. ACM PODS'90,* 1990.
10. A. Deutsch, M. Fernandez, D. Florescu, A. Levy, D. Maier, and D. Suciu. Querying XML data. *IEEE Data Bulletin,* 22(3):10–18, 1999.
11. A. Deutsch, M. Fernandez, D. Florescu, A. Levy, and D. Suciu. XML-QL: A query language for XML. Submission to the WWW Consortium: http://www.w3.org/TR/NOTE-xml-ql/, August 1998.
12. M. Fernandez, J. Siméon, and P. Wadler. XML query languages: Experiences and exemplars. Draft, http://www-db.research.bell-labs.com/user/simeon/xquery.ps, 1999.
13. M. R. Garey and D. S. Johnson. *Computers and Intractibility: A Guide to the Theory of NP-Completeness.* W. H. Freeman and Company, New York, 1979.
14. R. Goldman and J. Widom. Dataguides: Enabling query formulation and optimization in semistructured databases. In *Proc. VLDB'97,* 1997.

15. R. Goldman and J. Widom. Interactive query and search in semistructured databases. In *WebDB'98, Proc. Int. Workshop on the Web and Databases*, 1998.
16. G. Gottlob, N. Leone, and F. Scarcello. The complexity of acyclic conjunctive queries. In *Proc. 39th Annual Symp. on Foundations of Computer Science*, 1998.
17. N. Guarino, editor. *Int. Conf. on Formal Ontology in Information Systems*. IOS Press, 1998.
18. A. Gupta. Some database issues in e-commerce. Invited talk at the Int. Conf. on Extending Database Theory, http://www.edbt2000.uni-konstanz.de/invited/talks.html, 2000.
19. M. Gyssens, J. Paredaens, J. V. den Bussche, and D. V. Gucht. A graph-oriented object database model. *IEEE Transactions on Knowledge and Data Engineering*, 6(4):572–586, Aug. 1994.
20. P. Kilpeläinen. *Tree Matching Problems with Applications to Structured Text Databases*. PhD thesis, Dept. of Computer Science, University of Helsinki, 1992.
21. A. Loeffen. Text databases: A survey of text models and systems. *SIGMOD Record*, 23(1):97–106, Mar. 1994.
22. D. Maier. Database desiderata for an xml query language. In *QL'98 - The Query Languages Workshop*, 1998.
23. J. McHugh, S. Abiteboul, R. Goldman, D. Quass, and J. Widom. Lore: A database management system for semistructured data. *SIGMOD Record*, 26(3), 1997.
24. H. Meuss. *Logical Tree Matching with Complete Answer Aggregates for Retrieving Structured Documents*. PhD thesis, Dept. of Computer Science, University of Munich, 2000.
25. H. Meuss and K. U. Schulz. Complete answer aggregates for structured document retrieval. Technical Report 98-112, CIS, University of Munich, 1998. Submitted.
26. H. Meuss, K. U. Schulz, and F. Bry. Towards aggregated answers for semistructured data. Technical report, Institute for Computer Science, University of Munich, 2000. http://www.cis.uni-muenchen.de/~meuss/agg_answers_full.ps.gz.
27. H. Meuss and C. Strohmaier. Improving index structures for structured document retrieval. In *IRSG'99, 21st Annual Colloquium on IR Research*, 1999.
28. T. Milo and D. Suciu. Index structures for path expressions. In *ICDT'99, Proc. 6th Int. Conf. on DB Theory*, 1999.
29. R. Mohr and T. C. Henderson. Arc and path consistency revisited. *Artificial Intelligence*, 28:225–233, 1986.
30. F. Neven and T. Schwentick. Query automata. In *PODS'99*, 1999.
31. F. Neven and T. Schwentick. Expressive and efficient pattern languages for tree-structured data. In *Proc. ACM PODS'00*, 2000.
32. J. Oesterle and P. Maier-Meyer. The gnop (german noun phrase) treebank. In *First International Conference on Language Resources and Evaluation*, pages 699 – 703, 1998.
33. The Strudel Page. http://www.research.att.com/sw/tools/strudel/, May 2000.
34. D. Suciu. An overview of semistructured data. *SIGACT News*, 29(4), 1998.
35. J. D. Ullman. *Database and Knowledge-Base Systems, Volumes I and II*. Computer Science Press, 1989.
36. World Wide Web Consortium: XML Query Requirements. W3C Working Draft, http://www.w3.org/TR/2000/WD-xmlquery-req, August 2000. Eds. D. Chamberlin and P. Frankhauser and M. Marchiori and J. Robie.

Orthogonal Range Queries in OLAP [*]

Chung Keung Poon[1]

Dept. of Computer Science, City U. of Hong Kong, China
ckpoon@cs.cityu.edu.hk

Abstract. We study the problem of pre-computing auxillary information to support on-line range queries for the sum and max functions on a datacube. For a d-dimensional datacube with size n in each dimension, we propose a data structure for range max queries with $O((4L)^d)$ query time and $O((12L^2 n^{1/L} \gamma(n))^d)$ update time where $L \in \{1, ..., \log n\}$ is a user-controlled parameter and $\gamma(n)$ is a slow-growing function. (For example, $\gamma(n) \leq \log^* n$ and $\gamma(2^{4110}) = 3$.) The data structure uses $O((6n\gamma(n))^d)$ storage and can be initialized in time linear to its size. There are three major techniques employed in designing the data structure, namely, a technique for trading query and update times, a technique for trading query time and storage and a technique for extending 1-dimensional data structures to d-dimensional ones. Our techniques are also applicable to range queries over any semi-group and group operation, such as min, sum and count.

1 Introduction

Recently, research in On-Line Analytical Processing (OLAP) [14] has attracted a lot of attention. A popular data model for OLAP applications is the data cube [19] or the multi-dimensional databases [15,1]. In this model, an aggregate database with d functional attributes and one measure attribute is viewed as a d-dimensional array. Each dimension corresponds to a functional attribute and the value of an array entry corresponds to the measure attribute. One of the main research focuses is concerned with the orthogonal range query problems, i.e., the pre-computation of auxillary information (data structures) to support on-line queries of various functions such as SUM, COUNT, AVERAGE, MAX and MIN over values lying within an orthogonal region, see [22,21,23,18,7]. These queries provide useful information for companies to analyze the aggregate databases built from their data warehouses.

A generic orthogonal range query problem can be stated as follows. Given an aggregate database $\mathcal{F}$ with N records, each consisting of a key field corresponding to a point in a d-dimensional space and a value field, preprocess $\mathcal{F}$ such that subsequent queries $f(R_1, R_2, \ldots, R_d)$ can be answered efficiently. Here f is a function definable over a variable number of values, such as MAX, MIN, SUM, COUNT, ENUMERATE, etc; and the query $f(R_1, R_2, \ldots, R_d)$ asks for the value

[*] This research was fully supported by a grant from the Research Grants Council of the Hong Kong SAR, China [Project No. 9040314 (RGC Ref. No. CityU 1159/97E)].

J. Van den Bussche and V. Vianu (Eds.): ICDT 2001, LNCS 1973, pp. 361–374, 2001.
© Springer-Verlag Berlin Heidelberg 2001

when applying f on all the values lying within the orthogonal region $R_1 \times R_2 \times \cdots \times R_d$ where R_i specifies an interval in the i-th dimension, for $1 \leq i \leq d$. For example, the query $\text{MAX}(R_1, R_2, \ldots, R_d)$ asks for the maximum among all values lying within the orthogonal region $R_1 \times R_2 \times \cdots \times R_d$. The query $\text{ENUMERATE}(R_1, R_2, \ldots, R_d)$ asks for all the values present in the range.

Note that the query regions are unknown before the preprocessing and the data structure should be capable of handling all possible query regions. One solution for the problem is to store nothing except the original database. Then query may take $O(N)$ time in the worst case. We call this the *lazy* approach. Another solution, which we call the *workaholic* approach, is to pre-compute the answers for all possible query regions. Then query takes constant time but there are $O(N^2)$ pre-computed answers to be stored. As N is typically very large in OLAP applications, both solutions are unsatisfactory. Therefore, the crux of the problem is to design a data structure with close to constant query time and nearly linear storage simultaneously. Added to the difficulty of the problem is the fact that the database $\mathcal{F}$ may change over time. Therefore, another performance measure for the data structure is its update time.

1.1   Previous Results in Computational Geometry

There is a rich body of research on orthogonal range queries when the data points are sparsed. Under this data distribution, merely storing the points in a space-efficient manner while allowing users to quickly locate the points within an orthogonal region (so that they can subsequently be enumerated at constant time per point) is highly non-trivial. Therefore, the range enumeration problem is of central importance and has been extensively studied, see [3,16,24,6,5,4,8,9]. As it turns out, many of the ideas used in these data structures can be adapted for other range queries.

For range sum and count problems, a classical data structure is the *ECDF tree* of Bentley [4] obtained by applying his *multi-dimensional divide-and-conquer* technique. It requires $O(N \log^{d-1} N)$ storage and has $O(\log^d N)$ query time. Using the idea of *downpointers*, Willard [27] improved the query time by a factor of $\log N$. Chazelle [9] further improved the storage by a factor of (roughly) $\log N$. For example, for any $d \geq 2$, and any small constant $\epsilon > 0$, he exhibited data structures with $O(N \log^{d-2} N)$ storage and $O(\log^{d-1} N)$ query time for range count queries, and $O(N \log^{d-2+\epsilon} N)$ storage and $O(\log^{d-1} N)$ query time for range max queries. He also observed that 1-dimensional range max queries can be answered in constant time and $O(N)$ space by combining the Cartesian tree of Vuillemin [26] and the nearest common ancestor algorithm of Harel and Tarjan [20].

To handle updates as well, the best known data structures typically require $O(\log^d N)$ update time, see Willard [27], Willard and Lueker [28]. Also, allowing for updates often incurs a slowdown in the query time. For example, Willard and Lueker [28] devised a transformation that adds range restriction capabilities to dynamic data structures by increasing query time by a factor of $O(\log N)$, provided the aggregate function f satisfies certain decomposability conditions.

If fast update time is imperative in an application, then the structure by Ravi Kanth and Ambuj Singh [25], which has $O(\log N)$ update time and $O(N^\epsilon)$ query time, may be an alternative.

Various lower bounds suggest that these results are close to optimal, see [10, 11]. In particular, it was proved in [11] that $\Omega((\log N/\log(2S/N))^{d-1})$ is a lower bound on the query time for range sum and max queries when the data structure uses $O(S)$ storage and is oblivious to the values of the data points. (In fact, the result applies to any semigroup operation possessing the so-called *faithfulness* property, which is enjoyed by most semigroups). For the dynamic range sum and count problems, Fredman [17] proved that $\Omega(N(\log N)^d)$ time is necessary for performing a sequence of N operations containing insertions, deletions and queries.

1.2   New Perspective in OLAP Environment

Ho ET. AL. [22] pointed out that the non-linear storage requirement may pose a problem when applying the above data structures in an OLAP application. In particular, the $O(\log^{d-1} N)$ factor can be devastating in an OLAP application which has, say, $d = 10$ dimensions and $N = 10^6$ records. Given the lower bounds mentioned before, it seems difficult, if not impossible, to build data structures to support efficient OLAP queries. On the other hand, it is also observed that data points often form clusters in many applications, see [22] and [13] for example. Suppose the data set is sufficiently dense or clusters of dense data points can be found readily [30], it is reasonable to consider orthogonal range queries in the following situation which we call the *dense settings*. The data points are stored in a multidimensional array of size n in each dimension and there are $N = n^d$ data points in the array. (In contrast, N is much less than n^d in the *sparse settings* discussed in the previous subsection.) The index of the array is assumed to be integral. (If the original dimension is non-integral, we can work with the rank space of that dimension.)

Under the dense settings, Ho ET. AL. [22] proposed the *prefix sum* data structure that achieves $O(2^d)$ query time for range sum queries while using only $O(N)$ extra storage. The update cost is, however, $O(N)$ in the worst case. Geffner ET. AL. [18] designed an extension of the data structure, called the *relative prefix sum*, which requires only $O(\sqrt{N})$ update cost. Chan and Ioannidis [7] further studied the tradeoff between the query and update costs. They proposed the *hierarchical rectangle cube* and the *hierarchical band cube*, both of which are experimentally shown to outperform the relative prefix sum structure. Fredman [17] gave data structures that support prefix sum queries and updates in $O(\log^d N)$ time using $O(N \log^d N)$ storage.

For range maximum queries, [22] studied a quad-tree-like structure which takes $O(N)$ storage. In the worst case, it answers queries in $O(\log N)$ time in the 1-dimensional case and $\Omega(N^{1-1/d})$ time for d-dimensional case. Ho ET. AL. [21] then investigated various techniques to improve the average query time. Chazelle and Rosenberg [12] designed a much more efficient data structure which has $O(\alpha^d(s,n))$ query time when $O(s^d)$ storage is allowed where $\alpha(s,n)$, the functional inverse of Ackermann's function, is an extremely slow-growing function.

1.3   Our Contributions

In this paper, we design several data structures for range queries by exploiting the properties in the dense settings. Our data structures are array-based rather than linked-list based. Both the query and update algorithms involve index calculations, array accesses and applications of the queried operator (e.g., MAX, SUM). Number of operator applications is bounded above by the number of array accesses. Time for index calculation is negligible compared with array accesses when d is large in our construction. Moreover, if arrays are stored in secondary storage, cost of array accesses dominates that of CPU computations. Therefore, our formula only accounts for the number of array accesses.

First, we propose a data structure for 1-dimensional prefix max queries (a special case of range queries). For a 1-dimensional array of size n, the data structure has $O(L)$ query time, $O(Ln^{1/L})$ update time and requires $O(n)$ storage, where $L \in \{1, \ldots, \log n\}$ is a user-controlled parameter. When $L = 1$, the query time is the fastest but update is slow. As L increases, query time increases while update time decreases. When $L = \log n$, both query and update requires $O(\log n)$ time. Our technique is applicable to any semi-group or group operation. In particular, we have a data structure for 1-dimensional prefix sum queries having the same performance. By an observation in [2,22], the structure also answers 1-dimensional range sum queries in $O(L)$ time.

Second, we propose a data structure for 1-dimensional range max queries which has $O(L)$ query time, $O(L^2 n^{1/L} \gamma(n))$ update time and $O(n\gamma(n))$ storage where $\gamma(n)$ is a slow-growing function, e.g., $\gamma(n) \leq \log^* n$. Putting $L = 1$, our structure requires at most 4 array look-ups. This is the fastest query time among all known data structures with such a small assymptotic storage complexity. The previously best result requires 7 look-ups by [12]. As we will see next, the constant is important when we extend the data structure for higher dimensional queries. Our construction borrows a lot from the recursive technique of [12]. However, we have a better base case construction and this brought about a constant factor improvement in the query time for the same assymptotic storage complexity.

Third, we define a class of data structures called oblivious storage schemes and propose a technique to extend such a data structure for 1-dimensional range queries to multi-dimensional range queries. Our technique generalizes the one used in [12] by taking care of updates as well. Applying it to our 1-dimensional range max structures (which is an oblivious storage scheme), we obtain a d-dimensional range max structure which has $O((4L)^d)$ query time, $O((12L^2 n^{1/L} \gamma(n))^d)$ update time and $O((6n\gamma(n))^d)$ storage, where $L \in \{1, \ldots, \log n\}$. Similarly, we obtain a d-dimensional range sum structure which has $O((2L)^d)$ query time, $O((2Ln^{1/L})^d)$ update time and $O((2n)^d)$ storage. This generalizes the results of [22,18,17].

The rest of the paper is organized as follows. Section 2 and 3 contain data structures for 1-dimensional prefix and range max queries respectively. In Section 4, we discuss the concept of oblivious storage scheme and its application to generalizing 1-dimensional structures to higher dimensions. Finally, Section 5 contains some open problems.

2   One-Dimensional Prefix Max Queries

A prefix max query is a query of the form, $MAX(0, i)$, i.e., the lower end-point of the range is fixed at index 0. Our construction, to be described shortly, is applicable to any commutative semigroup or group operator, including min, sum, count, etc. In particular, it results in a data structure for 1-dimensional prefix sum queries having the same performance. As observed in [2,22], $SUM(i, j) = SUM(0, j)$ - $SUM(0, i - 1)$. Therefore, this structure can also answer 1-dimensional range sum queries in twice amount of time.

Without loss of generality, we assume the size of array A is $n = b^L$ for some integers $b > 1$ and $L \geq 1$. To explain the data structure, consider an $(L + 1)$-level complete b-ary tree. We assign the n entries of A to the $b^L = n$ leaves of this tree. Next, we assign to each internal node the maximum value among the leaves of its subtree. Then to each node (leaf or internal), we compute and store a 'prefix-max' value which is equal to the maximum of the 'assigned' values of its left siblings and itself. To facilitate the discussion, we label the tree with array indices as follows. First, we number the levels from 0 at the leaves up to L at the root. The leaves are then labelled from 0 to $n - 1$ starting from the left. Internal nodes at level 1 are labelled from 0 to $(n/b) - 1$, and in general nodes at level w are labelled from 0 to $(n/b^w) - 1$. See Figure 1 for an illustration when $b = 3$, $L = 3$.

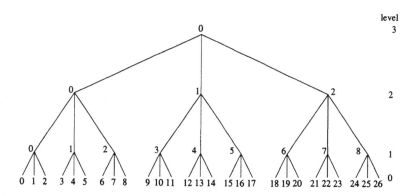

Fig. 1. A tree structure for $b = 3$, $L = 3$

Initialization and Storage: For every integer $w = 1$ to L, we define A_w as an array with n/b^w entries, indexed from 0 to $n/b^w - 1$, so that

$$A_w[i] = \max\{A[ib^w + j] \mid 0 \leq j < b^w\}$$
$$= \max\{A_{w-1}[ib + j] \mid 0 \leq j < b\}.$$

Referring to Figure 1, $A_w[i]$ contains the 'assigned' value at node i in level w. We do not really store these L arrays. Instead, we store the prefix max of these arrays and the base array A. (For uniformity, we let $A_0 = A$.) More precisely, for every integer $w = 0$ to $L - 1$, we compute and store the array $P_w[0..n/b^w - 1]$ so that

$$P_w[i] = \max\{A_w[j] \mid b\lfloor i/b \rfloor \leq j \leq i\}.$$

Obviously, computing all the P_w's requires $O(n)$ time and storing them requires

$$\sum_{w=0}^{L-1} n/b^w \leq n\frac{1}{1 - 1/b} \leq 2n$$

storage for $b \geq 2$.

Query: To answer the query $\mathrm{MAX}(0, n - 1)$, simply return $P_{L-1}[b - 1]$. For a query, $\mathrm{MAX}(0, i)$, where $i \leq n - 2$, we convert $i + 1$ (the length of the interval $[0..i]$) to a base-b number. The w-th digit will tell us which entry in P_w is needed. Specifically, let the base-b representation of $i + 1$ be $I_{L-1}I_{L-2}\cdots I_0$ where I_w is the w-th digit. (Since $i + 1 \leq n - 1 = b^L - 1$, there are at most L non-zero digits.) Then we calculate

$$I'_{L-1} = I_{L-1} - 1$$
$$I'_{L-2} = b(I'_{L-1} + 1) + I_{L-2} - 1$$
$$\vdots$$
$$I'_1 = b(I'_2 + 1) + I_1 - 1$$
$$I'_0 = b(I'_1 + 1) + I_0 - 1$$

and $\mathrm{MAX}(0, i) = \max\{P_w[I'_w] \mid 0 \leq w < L, I_w \neq 0\}$. Therefore, query takes at most L array look-ups (and $O(L)$ time for index calculation).

Update: When an update is made in the base array A, at most b entries in each of the prefix max arrays need to be changed. In particular, if $A[i]$ is updated, then for each $w = 0$ to L, $A_w[i_w]$, where $i_w = \lfloor i/b^w \rfloor$, may also be changed. Therefore, $P_w[i_w..\lfloor i_w/b \rfloor b + b - 1]$ (or at most b entries in P_w) has to be changed and no other changes are needed.

Now, we show how to update each P_w in $O(n^{1/L})$ time. Suppose we have updated $P_{w'}$'s for all $w' < w$, and $P_w[j']$ for all $j' < j$. To update $P_w[j]$, consider node j in level w of the tree. We first initialize it to the maximum of its subtree, i.e., set $P_w[j] = P_{w-1}[bj + b - 1]$. (If $w = 0$, then set $P_w[j] = A[j]$ instead.) Next, if the node does not have a left sibling, i.e., $j \bmod b = 0$, then we are done with $P_w[j]$. Otherwise, set $P_w[j]$ to the maximum between $P_w[j - 1]$ and $P_w[j]$. The total update cost is at most $2Ln^{1/L}$ array reads/writes (and $O(Ln^{1/L})$ time for index computation).

3   One Dimensional Range Max Queries

We first present a simple data structure called the *Bi-directional Prefix Max Structure (BPM)* which is the key to our data structures. Putting suitable parameters to our BPM structure, we obtain a data structure which answers range max queries in 2 array lookups but requires a logarithmic blow-up in storage. We then reduce the blow-up factor by using a recursion technique in [12]. Throughout this section, we often refer to sub-intervals with boundaries located at certain positions. For convenience, we call an interval $[i, j]$ an a-*interval* if i is a multiple of a and $i + a = j + 1$. We define $i_{(a)} = \lfloor i/a \rfloor a$, i.e., the largest multiple of a less than or equal to i.

3.1   The Bi-directional Prefix Max Structure

We define the (l, h)-*bi-directional prefix max structure* for an array $A[0..n-1]$, denoted $BPM(A, l, h)$, as a collection of $2h$ arrays, $PR_0, PR_1, \ldots, PR_{h-1}$, and $PL_0, PL_1, \ldots, PL_{h-1}$, each of length n. For $0 \leq w < h$, the content of array PL_w and PR_w is as follows:

$$PL_w[i] = \max\{A[j] \mid i_{(2^w l)} \leq j \leq i\}$$
$$PR_w[i] = \max\{A[j] \mid i \leq j \leq i_{(2^w l)} + 2^w l - 1\}$$

This requires $2nh$ storage cells and can be initialized in $O(nh)$ time. Given a query $\text{MAX}(i, j)$ where $\lfloor i/(2^w l) \rfloor + 1 = \lfloor j/(2^w l) \rfloor$ for some integer $w \in \{0, \ldots, h-1\}$, the range $[i, j]$ spans across two adjacent $2^w l$-intervals. Therefore, $\text{MAX}(i, j) = \max\{PR_w[i], PL_w[j]\}$. We will describe the calculation of w later when we have specific values for the parameters l and h.

For an update to $A[i]$, we need to modify at most $2l$ elements in PL_0 and PR_0, namely, $PL_0[i..i_{(l)} + l - 1]$ and $PR_0[i_{(l)}..i]$. Similarly, we need to change at most $4l$ elements in PL_1 and PR_1, ..., and $2^h l$ elements in PL_{h-1} and PR_{h-1}. Therefore, updating $BPM(A, l, h)$ requires at most $O(2^h l)$ array accesses. We can reduce the update time by the technique in Section 2. We pick the same L for the prefix max structure of each $2^w l$-interval for each w. Update time for a PR_w or PL_w is then reduced to $2L(2^w l)^{1/L}$ array accesses. Summing up from $w = 0$ to $h-1$, updating requires $8L^2(2^h l)^{1/L}$ array accesses. However, $4nh$ storage cells are required and each query takes $2L$ array look-ups.

Now we turn to the parameters l and h. If l is too large, some queries may lie within an l-interval. If h is too small, some queries may span across many $2^{h-1}l$-intervals. Both types of queries cannot be answered efficiently by $BPM(A, l, h)$. To eliminate these queries, we can put $l = 2$ and $h = \log n - 1$. Given a query $\text{MAX}(i, j)$, let w be the leftmost bit position at which the binary representations of i and j differ. (So $0 \leq w \leq \log n - 1$ if $i \neq j$.) Then $\lfloor i/2^w \rfloor + 1 = \lfloor j/2^w \rfloor$ and $\text{MAX}(i, j) = \max\{PR_w[i], PL_w[j]\}$. If $i = j$, then $\text{MAX}(i, j)$ is simply asking for $A[i]$ which is $PL_0[i]$ if i is even and $PR_0[i]$ if i is odd. For the index calculation, w can be determined by taking the exclusive-or of the binary representations of i and j; and then computing the position of the leftmost '1' by a look-up table.

In summary, a $BPM(A, 2, \log n - 1)$ structure answers range max queries with 2 array lookups, uses $2n(\log n - 1)$ storage cells and can be initialized in $O(n \log n)$ time. With the tradeoff technique in Section 2, it requires $2L$ array look-ups for a query, $8L^2 n^{1/L}$ array accesses for an update, $4n(\log n - 1)$ storage and $O(n \log n)$ for initialization.

3.2 A Tradeoff between Query Time with Storage

We can reduce the storage by having an ensemble of BPM structures with suitably chosen parameters. For the time being, we ignore the handling of updates. The idea, mainly due to [12], is to recursively construct a data structure for an array of size n which has query time t and storage kn. We denote by $R(t, k)$ the maximum n for which such a data structure is realizable by our construction.

We first consider the base case which consists of several subcases. When only 1 array look-up is allowed, we use the workaholic approach mentioned in Section 1. Since we need to store $n(n + 1)/2$ answers, we have $R(1, k) = 2k - 1$. When at most 2 look-ups are allowed, we use $BPM(A, 2, \log n - 1)$. Therefore, $R(2, k) = \lfloor 2^{k/2+1} \rfloor$. At the other extreme where $k = 1$ (i.e., no extra storage other than A itself), we use the lazy approach and therefore $R(t, 1) = t$. For simplicity, we choose $R(t, 2) = R(t, 3) = t$ when $t \geq 3$.

For the recursive case where $t \geq 3$ and $k \geq 4$, we apply the recursion technique taken from [12]. Let $a = R(t, k - 3)$. We classify the queries into two types, those lying within an a-interval (type 0) and those spanning across at least two a-intervals (type 1). We handle type 0 queries by recursively constructing $R(t, k)/a$ data structures, one for each a-interval, with query time t and storage $(k - 3)a$ each. In total, they consume $(k - 3)a \times R(t, k)/a = (k - 3)R(t, k)$ storage. For type 1 queries, we separate the query range into (at most) three parts, the left and right parts containing incomplete a-intervals and the middle part containing zero or more complete a-intervals. We compute the maximums of the left and right parts in 2 steps by $BPM(A, a, 1)$ which has $2R(t, k)$ storage. We compute the maximum of the middle part by a data structure for another array A' containing the maximum of each a-interval of A. Note that A' has size $R(t, k)/a$, and we are allowed $t - 2$ look-ups and $a \cdot R(t, k)/a$ storage for this data structure. Therefore, we choose $R(t, k)/a = R(t - 2, a)$ and hence

$$R(t, k) = R(t, k - 3) \cdot R(t - 2, R(t, k - 3))$$

Our formula is slightly different from that in [12], which is $R(t, k) = R(t, k - 6) \cdot R(t - 2, 2R(t, k - 6))$ with an appropriate change of variables. Compared with theirs, we obtain better query time for the same assymptotic growth rate of storage. For instance, when $t = 4$, we obtain a data structure with $O(n \log^* n)$ storage while the construction in [12] requires $t = 5$ in order to have $O(n \log n)$ storage, and $t = 7$ to have $O(n \log^* n)$ storage. Below, we give two tables comparing our results.

	k		
t	1	4	7	10
2	2	8	22	64
4	4	32	2^{22}	$2^{2097175}$

(a) our value of $R(t, k)$

	k		
t	2	8	14	20
5	4	16	64	256
7	4	64	2^{50}	$2^{2^{7.5 \times 10^{14}}}$

(b) Value of $R(t, k)$ in [12]

Fig. 2. Comparision between our result and [12]'s

3.3   Details for the $t = 4$ Case

We now describe the details for index calculation, trading query and update costs, and the handling when $n < R(t, k)$ for the chosen t and k. Assuming a blow-up factor of $O(\log^* n)$ in storage is tolerable in practice, we will concentrate on the case where $t = 4$.

From previous tables and formulas, the blow-up factor, k, of storage increases in steps of 3 in our construction (and 6 in [12]). However, observe that $BPM(A, 2, 1)$ can handle queries spanning across at most four 2-intervals in 4 lookups. Similarly, $BPM(A, 4, 1)$ and A together can handle queries spanning across at most four 4-intervals in 4 lookups. Thus we set $R(4, 2) = 8$ and $R(4, 3) = 16$. Applying the previous recursive construction, we obtain a smoothier increases in the storage blow-up factor:

					k					
t	1	2	3	4	5	6	7	8	9	10
4	4	8	16	32	256	8192	2^{22}	2^{137}	2^{4110}	$2^{2097175}$

Unrolling the recursions, our structure is composed of groups of BPM structures. Suppose the size of array A is n such that $R(t, k - 1) < n \leq R(t, k)$ for some k. Assume k is a multiple of 3. Then the number of groups is determined as follows. Define a function $g(r) = R(4, k)$ where $r = k/3$. Then

$$g(1) = 16$$
$$g(r) = 2^{g(r-1)/2+1} \times g(r - 1) \qquad \text{for } r > 1.$$

(If $k \equiv 2 \bmod 3$, we set $r = (k + 1)/3$ and $g(1) = 8$. If $k \equiv 1 \bmod 3$, we set $r = (k + 2)/3$ and $g(1) = 4$. We omit these similar cases here.) Note that $g(r)$ is a power of 2 for all r. With this change of variables, $g(r)$ is the maximum n for which our recursive construction takes only r recursion levels. Define $\gamma(n)$ as the smallest integer, r, such that $g(r) \geq n$. It can be shown that $\gamma(n) \leq \log^* n$ where $\log^* n = \min\{p \mid \log^{(p)} n \leq 2\}$ and $\log^{(p)} n$ is defined as: $\log^{(0)} n = n$, $\log^{(p)} n = \log(\log^{(p-1)} n)$ for $p > 0$. Our structure will have $\gamma(n)$ groups of BPM structures. For $1 \leq w < \gamma(n)$, we define the arrays $A_w[0..n/g(w) - 1]$ as

$$A_w[i] = \max\{A[j] \mid i \cdot g(w) \leq j < (i + 1) \cdot g(w)\}.$$

Group 0, consisting of A and $BPM(A, 4, 1)$, handles queries within a $g(1)$-interval. Group 1 consists of $BPM(A_1, 2, g(1)/2)$ and $BPM(A, g(1), 1)$ for queries within a $g(2)$-interval (which consists of $2 \cdot 2^{g(1)/2}$ $g(1)$-intervals). In general, for $1 \leq w \leq \gamma(n) - 2$, group w consists of $BPM(A_w, 2, g(w)/2)$ and $BPM(A, g(w), 1)$ which can handle queries within a $g(w + 1)$-interval. For $w = \gamma(n) - 1$, $2^{g(w)/2}$ can be much larger than n and padding A with $2^{g(w)/2} - n$ dummy elements would be a mistake. Thus we choose $BPM(A_w, 2, \log(\lceil \frac{n}{g(w)} \rceil) - 1)$ (instead of $BPM(A_w, 2, g(w)/2)$) and $BPM(A, g(w), 1)$ for group $w = \gamma(n) - 1$. (Note: $g(\gamma(n) - 1) < n$ by definition).

Initialization and Storage: Group 0 BPM structures take $3n$ storage cells. For $0 < w < \gamma(n)$, group w BPM structures take $2(\frac{n}{g(w)} \cdot \frac{g(w)}{2}) + 2n = 3n$ cells. Hence the total space required is $3\gamma(n)n$. Initialization is also easy, using $O(n\gamma(n))$ time.

Query: To answer a query $MAX(i,j)$, we find the smallest integer w such that $\lfloor i/g(w+1)\rfloor = \lfloor j/g(w+1)\rfloor$. Then i, j fall into the same $g(w+1)$-interval but in different $g(w)$-intervals. Therefore, $MAX(i,j) = \max\{MAX(i,i'-1),$ $MAX(i',j'-1), MAX(j',j)\}$ where $i' = \lceil i/g(w)\rceil g(w)$ and $j' = \lfloor j/g(w)\rfloor g(w)$. For the first and last sub-ranges, we look up $BPM(A,g(w),1)$. That is,

$$MAX(i,i'-1) = PR_0[i]$$
$$MAX(j',j) = PL_0[j]$$

where PR_0 and PR_0 are arrays in $BPM(A,g(w),1)$. For the middle sub-range, we search for the range $[i'',j'']$ in $BPM(A_w,2,g(w)/2)$ where $i'' = \lfloor i'/g(w)\rfloor$ and $j'' = \lfloor (j'-1)/g(w)\rfloor$. That is,

$$MAX(i',j'-1) = \max\{PL_{p-\log g(w)}[i''], PR_{p-\log g(w)}[j'']\}$$

where p is the leftmost bit at which the binary representations of i and j differs. Therefore, it takes at most 4 array look-ups. For the index calculation, we determine p as described in Subsection 3.1. For w, we check the range of p. If $p < 4$, then $w = 0$. If $4 \le p < 13$, then $w = 1$. If $13 \le p < 4110$, then $w = 2$, etc. This can be done in constant time by using a look-up table of size $O(\log n)$.

Update: To process an update, each BPM structure needs to be changed. Updating $BPM(A,g(w),1)$ takes $O(g(w))$ time for each $1 \le w \le \gamma(n)-1$. Updating $BPM(A_w,2,g(w)/2)$ takes $O(2^{g(w)/2})$ time for each $1 \le w \le \gamma(n)-2$. For $w = \gamma(n)-1$, updating $BPM(A_w,2,\log(n/g(w))-1)$ takes $O(n/g(w))$ time. Observe that $2^{g(w-1)/2} \le g(w)$ and that $g(\gamma(n)-1) < n$. Therefore, the total worst case update time is

$$O(\sum_{w=1}^{\gamma(n)-1} g(w)) + O(\sum_{w=1}^{\gamma(n)-2} 2^{g(w)/2}) + O(\frac{n}{g(\gamma(n)-1)}) = O(n).$$

Using the technique in Section 2, updating $BPM(A,g(w),1)$ takes $4Ln^{1/L}$ accesses for each $1 \le w \le \gamma(n)-1$. Updating $BPM(A_w,2,g(w)/2)$ for $1 \le w \le \gamma(n)-2$ and $BPM(A_w,2,\log(\lceil\frac{n}{g(\gamma(n)-1)}\rceil)-1)$ takes $8L^2n^{1/L}$ accesses each. Hence it takes $12L^2n^{1/L}\gamma(n)$ accesses in total. Query now takes $4L$ look-ups and storage becomes $6n\gamma(n)$.

4   Extension to Higher Dimensions

In this section, we define a class of data structures called oblivious storage scheme and describe a technique to extend such data structures for 1-dimensional range queries to higher dimensions.

4.1   Oblivious Storage Scheme

Informally, an oblivious storage scheme is a data structure in which the set of storage cells to be examined or changed is determined by the query region or update position rather than on the values in the array. Similar concepts were introduced in [17,29,11]. Here we describe a definition suitable for our purpose. Let A be an array over a commutative semigroup G. An *oblivious storage scheme* for A is a triple, $(B, \mathcal{Q}, \mathcal{U})$, where

1. B is an array of storage cells containing elements in G,
2. $\mathcal{Q}$ is a set of programs, one for each query region, and
3. $\mathcal{U}$ is a set of programs, one for each update position.

The storage cost of the scheme is the size, m, of B. For each query region, R, the corresponding program in $\mathcal{Q}$ is a sequence of integers, $(\mu_0, \ldots, \mu_{m-1})$, such that

$$\sum_{r \in R} A[r] = \mu_0 B[0] + \cdots + \mu_{m-1} B[m-1]$$

where '+' is the addition operation in G. When answering a query, extra temporary storage may be needed to evaluate the expression. However, we do not charge it towards the storage since they are temporary. When evaluating the expression, those terms with μ's equal to 0 need not be added. Thus, the number of non-zero μ's is taken as the query cost. In general, we require all the μ's to be non-negative. However, if G is a group, then we also allow negative μ's.

For each update position, r, the corresponding program in $\mathcal{U}$ consists of a sequence of instructions in one of the following forms: (i) $B[j] =$ new value for $A[r]$, (ii) $B[j] = \lambda_0 B[0] + \cdots \lambda_{m-1} B[m-1]$ where the λ's are integers if G is a group, and non-negative integers if G is a semi-group. The total number of non-zero λ's in all the instructions is taken as the update cost.

Our prefix and range max structures, the prefix sum structure of [22] and the relative prefix sum structure of [18] are all oblivious storage schemes. On the other hand, the combination of Cartesian tree [26] and the nearest common ancestor algorithm [20] for 1-dimensional range max is not.

4.2   Combining Oblivious Storage Schemes

Let S and S_{d-1} be oblivious storage schemes for a 1-dimensional array of size n and a $(d-1)$-dimensional array of size n^{d-1} respectively. We can combine them into an oblivious storage scheme, S_d, for a d-dimensional array A of size n^d as follows. Suppose S requires m storage cells and S_{d-1} requires m_{d-1} storage cells. Then we will make use of two arrays of storage cells, $C[0..m-1, 0..n^{d-1}-1]$ and $B[0..m-1, 0..m_{d-1}-1]$. For each position r in dimension 2 to d, we follow S and construct a storage scheme for the subarray $A[0..n-1, r]$ using $C[0..m-1, r]$ as the storage cells. Next, for each position i in dimension 1, we follow S_{d-1} and construct a storage scheme for the subarray $C[i, 0..n^{d-1}-1]$ using $B[i, 0..m_{d-1}-1]$ as the storage cells. The total storage of the new scheme is $m(n^{d-1} + m_{d-1})$.

Note that if the storage cells of S_{d-1} and S includes a copy of the original array, then the array C need not be stored in S_d. Then the storage becomes mm_{d-1}.

Let the query program for region $R_2 \times \cdots \times R_d$ in S_{d-1} be $(\mu_0, \ldots, \mu_{m_{d-1}-1})$ and that for R_1 in S be $(\eta_0, \ldots, \eta_{m-1})$. Then the query program for $R_1 \times \cdots \times R_d$ in S can be derived as follows:

$$\sum_{i,r} A[i,r] = \sum_r (\eta_0 C[0,r] + \cdots + \eta_{m-1} C[m-1,r])$$

$$= \eta_0 (\mu_0 B[0,0] + \cdots + \mu_{m_{d-1}-1} B[0, m_{d-1}-1])$$
$$+ \cdots + \eta_{m-1}(\mu_0 B[m_{d-1},0] + \cdots + \mu_{m_{d-1}-1} B[m_{d-1}-1, m-1])$$
$$= \sum_{i,j} \eta_i \mu_j B[i,j]$$

If there are p and q non-zero η's and μ's respectively, there will be pq non-zero $(\eta\mu)$'s. Hence the query cost of S is the product of that of S_{d-1} and S.

Similarly, the update program for (i,r) in S can be derived as follows. Let U and U_{d-1} be the update programs for i in S and for r in S_{d-1} respectively. Furthermore, let the set of indices of storage cells that appeared on the left hand side of U be $\{j_1, \ldots, j_l\}$. These are the storage cells of S that are updated by U. Then the update program for (i,r) executes the program U on $C[0..m-1, r]$, followed by the program U_{d-1} on $B[j_1, 0..m_{d-1}-1]$, $\cdots$, $B[j_l, 0..m_{d-1}-1]$. (That is U_{d-1} is executed l times.) Thus, if the two programs have cost t and t_{d-1} respectively, then the new program have cost $t + t_{d-1}t = t(1 + t_{d-1})$.

Applying this composition technique repeatedly to a 1-dimensional structure with query time t_q, update time t_u and storage m which does not contain the base array A, we obtain a d-dimensional structur with query time t_q^d, update time at most $2t_u^d$ and storage dm^d. If the structure contains A, the storage is only m^d. Applying to our 1-dimensional range max structure, we obtain a d-dimensional range max structure with $O((4L)^d)$ query time, $O((12L^2 n^{1/L}\gamma(n))^d)$ update time and $O((6n\gamma(n))^d)$ storage. Applying to our 1-dimensional range sum structure, we obtain a d-dimensional range sum structure which has $O((2L)^d)$ query time, $O((2Ln^{1/L})^d)$ update time and $O((2n)^d)$ storage.

5   Conclusion

We have designed efficient data structures for range sum and max queries. The range sum structure generalizes that of [22,18,17]. Our range max structure has constant query time and almost linear space It handles updates more efficiently than [12] which is basically a static structure. It would be nice to have a truly linear space and constant time range max structure, or a proof that linear space is impossible.

References

1. R. Agrawal, A. Gupta, and S. Sarawagi. Modeling multidimensional databases. In *13th International Conference on Data Engineering*. IEEE, 1997.

2. J. L. Bentley and M. I. Shamos. A problem in multivariate statistics: algorithms, data structure and applications. In *15th Allerton Conference on Communications, Control and Computing*, pages 193–201, 1977.

3. J.L. Bentley. Multidimensional binary search trees used for associative searching. *Communications of the ACM*, 18(9):509–517, 1975.

4. J.L. Bentley. Multidimensional divide-and-conquer. *Communications of the ACM*, 23(4):214–228, April 1980.

5. J.L. Bentley and H.A. Maurer. Efficient worst-case data structures for range searching. *Acta Informatica*, 13:155–168, 1980.

6. A. Bolour. Optimal retrival algorithms for small region queries. *SIAM Journal on Computing*, 10(4):721–741, November 1981.

7. C.Y. Chan and Yannis E. Ioannidis. Hierarchical prefix cubes for range-sum queries. In *Proceedings of ACM International Conference on Very Large Data Bases*, pages 675–686, 1999.

8. Bernard Chazelle. Filtering search: A new approach to query-answering. *SIAM Journal on Computing*, 15(3):703–724, August 1986.

9. Bernard Chazelle. A functional approach to data structures and its use in multidimensional searching. *SIAM Journal on Computing*, 17(3):427–462, June 1988.

10. Bernard Chazelle. Lower bounds for orthogonal range searching: I. the reporting case. *Journal of the ACM*, 37(2):200–212, April 1990.

11. Bernard Chazelle. Lower bounds for orthogonal range searching: II. the arithmetic model. *Journal of the ACM*, 37(3):439–463, July 1990.

12. Bernard Chazelle and Burton Rosenberg. Computing partial sums in multidimensional arrays. In *5th Annual Symposium on Computational Geometry*, pages 131–139, 1989.

13. D.W. Cheung, B. Zhou, B. Kao, K. Hu, and S.D. Lee. DROLAP - a dense-region based approach to on-line analytical processing. In *10th International Conference on Database and Expert Systems Applications (DEXA'99)*, 1999.

14. E.F. Codd. Providing OLAP (on-line analytical processing) to user-analysts: an IT mandate. Technical report, E.F. Codd and Associates, 1993.

15. The OLAP Council. MD-API the OLAP application program interface version 0.5 specification. Technical report, September 1996.

16. R.A. Finkel and J.L. Bentley. Quad trees: A data structure for retrievel on composite keys. *Acta Informatica*, 4:1–9, 1974.

17. Michael Fredman. A lower bound on the complexity of orthogonal range queries. *Journal of the ACM*, 28(4):696–705, 1981.

18. S. Geffner, D. Agrawal, A. El Abbadi, and T. Smith. Relative prefix sums: An efficient approach for querying dynamic olap data cubes. In *15th International Conference on Data Engineering*, pages 328–335. IEEE, 1999.

19. Jim Gray, Adam Bosworth, Andrew Layman, and Hamid Pirahesh. Data cube: A relational aggregation operator generalizing group-by, cross-tab, and sub-totals. In *12th International Conference on Data Engineering*, pages 152–159. IEEE, 1996.

20. Dov Harel and Robert Endre Tarjan. Fast algorithms for finding nearest common ancestors. *SIAM Journal on Computing*, 13(2):338–355, May 1984.

21. Ching-Tien Ho, Rakesh Agrawal, Nimrod Meggido, and Jyh-Jong Tsay. Techniques for speeding up rang-max queries. Technical report, IEEE Research Report, April 1997.

22. Ching-Tien Ho, Rakesh Agrawal, Nimrod Megiddo, and Ramakrishnan Srikant. Range queries in olap data cubes. In *ACM SIGMOD Conference on the Management of Data*, pages 73–88, 1997.

23. Ching-Tien Ho, Jehoshua Bruck, and Rakesh Agrawal. Partial-sum queries in olap data cubes using covering codes. *IEEE Transactions on Computers*, 47(12):1326–1340, 1998.
24. D.T. Lee and C.K. Wong. Worst-case analysis for region and partial region searches in multidimensional binary search trees and balanced quad trees. *Acta Informatica*, 9:23–29, 1977.
25. K.V. Ravi Kanth and Ambuj K. Singh. Efficient dynamic range searching using data replication. Technical Report TRCS97-12, University of California at Santa barbara, 1997.
26. Jean Vuillemin. A unifying look at data structures. *Communications of the ACM*, 23(4):229–239, 1980.
27. D.E. Willard. New data structures for orthogonal queries. *SIAM Journal on Computing*, 14(1):232–253, February 1985.
28. D.E. Willard and G.S. Lueker. Adding range restriction capability to dynamic data structures. *Journal of the ACM*, 32(3):597–617, July 1985.
29. Andrew Yao. On the complexity of maintaining partial sums. *SIAM Journal on Computing*, 14(2):277–288, May 1985.
30. Bo Zhou, David W. Cheung, and Ben Kao. A fast algorithm for density-based clustering in large database. In *Methodologies for Knowledge Discovery and Data Mining (PAKDD'99)*, pages 338–349, 1999.

Reasoning about Summarizability in Heterogeneous Multidimensional Schemas

Carlos A. Hurtado[1] and Alberto O. Mendelzon[2]

[1] University of Toronto (chl@db.toronto.edu)
[2] University of Toronto (mendel@db.toronto.edu)

Abstract. In OLAP applications, data are modeled as points in a multidimensional space. Dimensions themselves have structure, described by a schema and an instance; the schema is basically a directed acyclic graph of granularity levels, and the instance consists of a set of elements for each level and mappings between these elements, usually called *rollup functions*. Current dimension models restrict dimensions in various ways; for example, rollup functions are restricted to be total. We relax these restrictions, yielding what we call *heterogeneous schemas*, which describe more naturally and cleanly many practical situations. In the context of heterogeneous schemas, the notion of *summarizability* becomes more complex. An aggregate view defined at some granularity level is *summarizable* from a set of precomputed views defined at other levels if the rollup functions can be used to compute the first view from the set of views. In order to study summarizability in heterogeneous schemas, we introduce a class of constraints on dimension instances that enrich the semantics of dimension hierarchies, and we show how to use the constraints to characterize and test for summarizability.

1 Introduction

The multidimensional model is becoming increasingly important as a logical layer for visualizing and querying data in OLAP scenarios. A key aspect of multidimensional data is the separation of *factual* and *dimensional* data. While dimensions represent descriptive and relatively static data, facts depict event-based data, represented as points in spaces defined by dimensions.

A number of multidimensional models for OLAP [CT97][HMV99a][LAW98] [JLS99] have recently incorporated dimensions as first-class entities in query and update languages. In the logical layer, a dimension is composed of a schema and an instance. The dimension schema includes a directed acyclic graph (DAG) of levels, called *hierarchy schema*, where levels may have attributes associated with them. Levels can be viewed as foreign keys of tables containing values for the attributes.

On the other hand, a dimension instance consists of a set of members for each level, called *member sets*; and a hierarchy relation that models the ancestor/descendant relation between the members. For instance, we may have *Toronto* as a member of a level *City* in a dimension representing locations. In

J. Van den Bussche and V. Vianu (Eds.): ICDT 2001, LNCS 1973, pp. 375–389, 2001.

most of the models [CT97] [HMV99a] [HMV99b], the hierarchy relation is represented by a set of functions between member sets, called *rollup functions*. Usually, we say that a level l_1 *rolls up* to another level l_2 when there exists an edge from l_1 to l_2 in the hierarchy, meaning that there is a rollup function from l_1 to l_2.

1.1 Heterogeneous Dimensions

Suppose we have a dimension representing stores in Canada and the USA. While the stores in Canada roll up to cities and to provinces, the stores in the USA roll up to cities and to states. Figures 1 (B), and (C) show two possible dimension hierarchies for the location dimension (we abstract away the attributes); a possible instance is depicted in Figure 1(D). Notice that in the schemas (B) and (C) the rollup functions are total. An alternative schema for representing this dimension is depicted in Figure (A). However, here we have that the rollup functions between *City* and *State*, and between *City* and *Province* are partial, because some cities do not have states while others do not have provinces.

At this point, we need to introduce some terminology that will be central in this paper, and which we formalize in the next section. A dimension schema is *homogeneous* if for every pair of levels l_1 and l_2 such that l_1 rolls up to l_2 we have that in every dimension instance conveyed in the schema, the rollup function is a total function from the member set of l_1 to the member set of l_2. A dimension schema is *strictly homogeneous* if it is homogeneous and it has only one level that is at the bottom of the hierarchy schema; a dimension schema is *heterogeneous* if it is not homogeneous.

Coming back to our example, the schema (A) is heterogeneous becuse in the instance of Figure 1 (D), the rollup function between *City* and *State* is a partial function from $\{NewYork, Toronto\}$ to $\{NYstate\}$. On the other hand, the schema (B) is homogeneous, and the schema (C) is is strictly homogeneous. The choice between schemas (A), (B), or (C) depends on factors like the attributes that the levels share, and how we would like to group members into levels in the dimension. The schemas that allow heterogeneity could be better in many situations. As an example, if we restrict the schemas (B) and (C) to be homogeneous, the insertion of the stores in Washington D.C. would require a new sub-hierarchy *StoreWashington-CityWashington* below the level *Country*, where *CityWashington* contains, in any instance, only one member (because *Washington* is the only city in *USA* that does not have a *State*.) Modeling heterogeneity allows the fusion of levels that represent the same granularity of aggregation, reducing the complexity of the schema and, therefore, of query formulation. The benefit of having a more flexible model at the logical layer can also be propagated to the storage layer. For instance, heterogeneity allows the fusion of levels that share attributes, while keeping separate levels with different attributes.

We end this section by noting that current dimension models [CT97] [HMV99a] [HMV99b] [JLS99] do not allow heterogeneity.

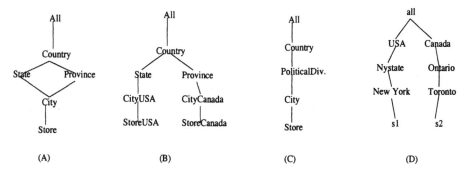

Fig. 1. (A) (B) (C) Three alternative dimension hierarchies for the location dimension. (D) An instance of the location dimension.

1.2 Summarizability

Data cubes [GBLHP96] comprise the computation of a set of aggregate views, called cube views, which represent facts aggregated at different granularities (set of levels taken from a set of dimensions). Different fundamental functionalities for OLAP, like *aggregate navigation*, *cube computation*, and *cube maintenance* [CD97], among others, require the derivation, using pre-defined aggregate queries, of cube views from other pre-computed cube views, transparently to the user. In order to do this, the system must determine which derivations are correct; in other words, whether a cube view can be derived from other cube views through predefined aggregate queries.

The notion of summarizability [RS90] refers to the conditions under which we can correctly derive any cube view defined at a level l_2 from a cube view defined at a level l_1 by aggregating using the rollup functions between l_1 and l_2 of a particular dimension. In order to allow summarizability the data cube must be *distributive*, i.e., its aggregate functions must be distributive [GBLHP96]. A *distributive aggregate function af* can be computed on a set by partitioning the set into disjoint subsets, aggregating each separately, and then computing the aggregation of these partial results with another aggregate function[1] that we denote by af^c.

The central problem we address in this paper is: how we can infer summarizability in distributive data cubes from the dimension schema, without having to analyze the dimension instance? In particular, it has been shown [HRU96] that, in strictly homogeneous dimensions, correct summarizations correspond to the edges of the dimension hierarchy, as depicted in the following example. We give the formalization using the relational algebra with bag semantics, extended with the *generalized projection operator* to express aggregation [AGS+96]. The generalized projection operator, Π_A, is an extension of the duplicate-eliminating

---

[1] Among the SQL aggregate functions, $COUNT$, SUM, MIN, and MAX are distributive. We have that $COUNT^c = SUM$; for SUM, MIN, and MAX we have $af^c = af$.

projection, where A can include both regular and aggregate attributes. For simplicity, all the aggregates of cube views are assumed to be on a single attribute.

Example 1. Consider the dimension with schema depicted in Figure 1 (B). From the schema we can infer the correctness of the summary operation that computes the total sales per province from the total sales per cities in Canada: $\Pi_{Province,Sum(Sales)}(Sales\_CityCan \bowtie \Gamma_{CityCan}^{Province})$, where $\Gamma_{CityCan}^{Province}$ represents the rollup function from the cities of Canada to the provinces.

In this paper we extend the notion of summarizability, previously introduced for dimensions over strictly homogeneous schemas, in order to consider derivations from *sets of levels* to levels in dimensions over dimension schemas that are not strictly hierarchical. The following example shows the extra complexity of inferring summarizability in heterogeneous dimension schemas.

Example 2. Consider the hierarchy schema of the location dimension of Figure 1 (A). Consider the cube views *Sale_Province*, and *Sale_State* representing the total sales per province and state, respectively, and defined as follows:

$$Sale\_Province = \Pi_{Province,Sum(Sales)}(Sales\_Store \bowtie \Gamma_{Store}^{Province})$$
$$Sale\_State \quad = \quad \Pi_{State,Sum(Sales)}(Sales\_Store \bowtie \Gamma_{Store}^{State})$$

Consider the following aggregation that derives the total sales per Country from *Sale_Province*, and *Sale_State*:

$$\Pi_{Country,Sum(Sales)} (\Pi_{Country,Sum(Sales)}(Sales\_Province \bowtie \Gamma_{Province}^{Country})) \uplus$$
$$(\Pi_{Country,Sum(Sales)}(Sales\_State \bowtie \Gamma_{State}^{Country}))$$

where $\Gamma_{l_1}^{l_2}$ represents the rollup function from l_1 to l_2; and $\uplus$ represents the *additive union* which adds the multiplicity of the tuples. Intuitively, we could say that this derivation is correct, because there are no stores that roll up to a state and to province at the same time. However, we cannot infer the correctness of this derivation from the schema (A), because it does not capture precisely the possible set of instances we are modeling; in particular, it does not explicitly disallow a store that rolls up to both a state and a province.

The question that arises at this point is: what additional constraints we have to add in order to keep the ability to reason about summarizability in heterogeneous schemas.

1.3   Contributions and Outline

In this paper we introduce a dimensional model that accounts for heterogeneity. We define the notion of summarizability for heterogeneous dimensions, which smoothly extends the notion of summarizability for homogeneous dimensions. We identify four classes of dimension schemas, that go from strictly homogeneous to a class of schemas we call *hierarchical schemas*, that allow heterogeneity but keep a notion of ordering between the granularities defined by levels.

We introduce a class of constraints, *split constraints*, that enrich the semantics of dimension hierarchies. Finally, we solve the problem of deciding summarizability in hierarchical dimensions constrained with split constraints. The solution is obtained from a sound and complete axiomatization of a subclass of split constraints.

The remainder of the paper is organized as follows. Section 2 introduces the model for dimensions, along with the formalization of the notion of summarizability. Section 3 introduces the new constraints we propose. The inference problem for summarizability is studied in Section 4. In Section 5 and Section 6 we show related work, conclude and outline some of the prospects for future work.

2   Heterogeneous Dimensions

In this section, we describe our framework for modeling dimensions. A dimension schema will consist of a hierarchy schema and a set of constraints.

2.1   Hierarchy Schema

We define a hierarchy schema in the same fashion as in [JLS99] and [HMV99a], but allowing heterogeneity, multiple hierarchical paths, and multiple bottom levels. Multiple hierarchical paths are frequently required as argued in [HMV99a], [CT97] . Allowing multiple bottom levels makes it possible to have more natural schemas in several situations as shown in [JLS99].

Consider a set of members $\mathbf{E}$, a set of levels $\mathbf{L}$, and set of attributes $\mathbf{A}$.

Definition 1 (Hierarchy Schema). *A hierarchy schema is a tuple $G = (L, \nearrow, \mathcal{A}, \sigma)$, where $L \subseteq \mathbf{L}$ is a set of levels with a distinguished level All; $\nearrow$ is a binary relation on L such that $(L, \nearrow)$ conforms a rooted DAG with All as root (we denote by $\nearrow^*$ the transitive closure of $\nearrow$); $\mathcal{A} \subseteq \mathbf{A}$ is a set of attributes; and $\sigma : L \to 2^{\mathcal{A}}$ assigns to each level a set of attributes.*

We refer to the set of bottom levels of a hierarchy schema, $\{l \in L \mid \neg \exists l' \in L : l' \nearrow l\}$, as L_{Bottom}. Given two levels $l_a, l_b \in L$, we denote by Υ_{l_a, l_b} the set of paths between l_a and l_b in G.

2.2   Dimension Instance and Schema

An instance of a dimension is obtained by specifying a set of members for each level, along with the descendant/ancestor relation $<$ between them.

Definition 2 (Dimension Instance). *A dimension instance is a tuple $(G, \mathcal{E}, <, \mathcal{T})$, where G is a hierarchy schema; $\mathcal{E}$ is a set of sets of members in $\mathbf{E}$, one set $\mathcal{E}_l$ for each level $l \in L$, where we denote by $\mathcal{E}_d$ the union of the member sets of a dimension d; $<$ is a relation between members conforming a rooted DAG with root all, where we denote by $\ll$ the transitive closure of $<$; and finally, $\mathcal{T}$ is a set of relations that contains one relation $\mathcal{T}_l$, with attributes $\sigma(l) \cup \{l\}$, for every* *level $l \in L$. The following conditions hold: (1) the member set of a level l, $\mathcal{E}_l$, is the active domain of l in $\mathcal{T}_l$, and l is a key of $\mathcal{T}_l$; (2) for every pair of members e_a, e_b such that $e_a \in \mathcal{E}_{l_a}$, $e_b \in \mathcal{E}_{l_b}$ and $e_a < e_b$, we have $l_a \nearrow l_b$, and there are no members $e_1, \ldots, e_n \in \mathcal{E}_d$ such that $e_a < e_1 < \ldots e_n < e_b$; (3) for every member $e \in \mathcal{E}_d$ such that $e \neq \texttt{all}$ we have $e << \texttt{all}$.*

The first condition says that the relation for level l contains exactly one tuple for each element in $\mathcal{E}_l$. The second condition essentially says that the edges in the dimension hierarchy represent links between levels, that must exist whenever we have a *direct* descendant/ancestor relation between some pair of members in the levels. And finally, the last condition states that all the members reach the top member $\texttt{all}$. Note that the member sets are not necessarily disjoint.

Given a dimension d, a *leaf member* is a member $e \in \mathcal{E}_d$ with no descendant members. An important feature of the model is that it may have leaf members in non-bottom levels. This allows updating the dimension, as shown in [HMV99b] (for instance, we might want to add a city but do not yet have stores that belong to it.) However, in order to simplify the presentation, we make two assumptions: (a) all the leaf members belong to the bottom levels; and (b) the member sets of the bottom levels are pairwise disjoint. We define a *base level*, denoted by l_{base}, containing the union of the member sets of the bottom levels. The results in this paper can be extended to dimensions where (a) and (b) does not hold by a more detailed treatement of base members, which basically consists in defining them as id's of the leaves.

Definition 3 (Rollup Operators). *Given a dimension instance h, we define the direct rollup operator, that takes a dimension and two of its levels l_1, l_2 and gives a relation with attributes l_1 and l_2 defined as follows: $d\Gamma_{l_1}^{l_2} = \{(x_1, x_2) \mid x_1 \in \mathcal{E}_{l_1} \wedge x_2 \in \mathcal{E}_{l_2} \wedge x_1 < x_2\}$. We have the rollup operator with the same signature of $d\Gamma$ which gives a relation with attributes l_a and l_2 defined as follows: $\Gamma_{l_1}^{l_2} = \{(x_1, x_2) \mid x_1 \in \mathcal{E}_{l_1} \wedge x_2 \in \mathcal{E}_{l_2} \wedge x_1 << x_2\}$. The base rollup operator takes a level l a defines the relation, with attributes l_{base} and l, that groups the base elements to it, and is defined as follows: $\Gamma_{l_{base}}^{l} = \{(x, y) \mid x \in \mathcal{E}_{l_{base}} \wedge y \in \mathcal{E}_l \wedge x << y\}$.*

The following are some basic properties of the rollup operators: given a dimension instance d we have: (a) if $\neg(l_a \nearrow l_b)$ then $d\Gamma_{l_a}^{l_b} = \emptyset$; (b) if $\neg(l_a \nearrow^* l_b)$ then $\Gamma_{l_a}^{l_b} = \emptyset$; (c) if $\Upsilon_{l_a, l_b} = \{l_a l_b\}$ then $\Gamma_{l_a}^{l_b} = d\Gamma_{l_a}^{l_b}$.

Definition 4 (Partitioned Instances). *A dimension instance is partitioned when all its rollup relations are single valued (partial functions). The partitioning property appears as an inherent constraint in the the dimension models of [CT97], [HMV99a], [LAW98], and [JLS99]. It requires that each member in the base level reach, through $\Gamma_{l_{base}}^{l}$, not more that one member in each level l. In this sense, each levels represent partitioned classifications of the base members. In the sequel we assume that all dimension instances are partitioned.*

We are ready to define dimension schema as a hierarchy schema plus a set of constraints in some constraint language $\mathcal{CL}$. In Section 3 we introduce a specific $\mathcal{CL}$, the language of split constraints.

Definition 5 (Dimension Schema). *A CL-dimension schema is a tuple $ds = (G, \Sigma)$ where G is a hierarchy schema; and $\Sigma \subseteq CL$.*

The constraint language must have a notion of satisfaction, denoted by $\models_{CL}$. A dimension instance d is over a dimension schema ds if $G_d = G_{ds}$, $d \models_{CL} \Sigma$. Given a dimension schema ds we denote by $\mathcal{I}(ds)$ the set of dimension instances that are over ds.

2.3 Classes of Dimension Schemas

The following definition formalizes the classes of dimension schemas we mentioned in Section 1.

Definition 6 (Homogeneous and Heterogeneous Dimension Schemas).
A dimension schema ds is homogeneous *if every dimension d over ds satisfies: for every pair of levels l_1, l_2 such that $l_1 \nearrow l_2$ we have that $\Gamma_{l_1}^{l_2} : \mathcal{E}_{l_1} \to \mathcal{E}_{l_2}$ is a total function. A dimension schema is* strictly homogeneous *if it is homogeneous, and has a single bottom level. A dimension schema is* heterogeneous *if it is not homogeneous.*

In a homogeneous dimension instance, the ordering of the levels provided by the graph is exactly the same as the ordering of the grains represented by the levels. In other words, as we move up the hierarchy schema we reach levels that represent coarser partitions of the base members. Furthermore, the rollup functions capture precisely the containment relation between the partitions of levels connected in the graph. These two properties can no longer be true in heterogeneous dimension instances.

In order to formalize this intuition, let us define the notion of overlap, as introduced for classification schemas in statistical databases [Mal93]. The overlap between two levels l_1 and l_2 is a relation $\Theta_{l_1}^{l_2}$ with signature $\mathcal{E}_{l_1} \times \mathcal{E}_{l_2}$ that has an edge between the members e_1 and e_2 iff the intersection of the sets of base members that reach them is non-empty. The overlap between two levels can be defined with the following relational-algebra expression: $\Theta_{l_1}^{l_2} = \pi_{l_1,l_2}(\Gamma_{l_{base}}^{l_1} \bowtie \Gamma_{l_{base}}^{l_2})$. We say that $l_1 \preceq l_2$ in a dimension instance d if $\Theta_{l_1}^{l_2} = \Gamma_{l_1}^{l_2}$, That is, $l_1 \preceq l_2$ means: (a) the grain of l_1 is finer than the grain of l_2 because the overlap is a function (possibly partial); and (b) the rollup function $\Gamma_{l_1}^{l_2}$ captures precisely the containment relation between the grains of l_1 and l_2.

Example 3. The dimension instance of Figure 2 satisfies $City \preceq State$, i.e., there is no City c and State s such that they overlap and c does not roll up to s. Another way to think of the fact that $City \preceq State$ is as follows: if there is a store that rolls up to a city c and to a state s, then c rolls up to s.

It is important to note, that in general $\preceq$ is not transitive, i.e., if a dimension instance h satisfies $l_1 \preceq l_2$, and $l_2 \preceq l_3$ it does not necessarily satisfy $l_1 \preceq l_3$.

Example 4. Consider the dimension instance depicted in Figure 2. Although we have *City* $\preceq$ *SaleDistrict*, and *SaleDistrict* $\preceq$ *SaleRegion*, we do not have *City* $\preceq$ *SaleRegion*, because two stores which roll up to *NewYork*, such as s_1 and s_2, roll up to two different sale regions, r_1 and r_2.

Definition 7 (Hierarchical Dimension Schemas). *A dimension schema ds is* hierarchical *if for every pair of levels* $l_1, l_2 \in L_{ds}$ *such that* $l_1 \nearrow l_2$ *we have that every dimension instance* $d \in \mathcal{I}(ds)$ *satisfies* $l_1 \preceq l_2$. *A dimension schema ds is* strictly hierarchical *if for every pair of levels* $l_1, l_2 \in L_{ds}$ *such that* $l_1 \nearrow^* l_2$ *we have that every dimension instance* $d \in \mathcal{I}(ds)$ *satisfies* $l_1 \preceq l_2$.

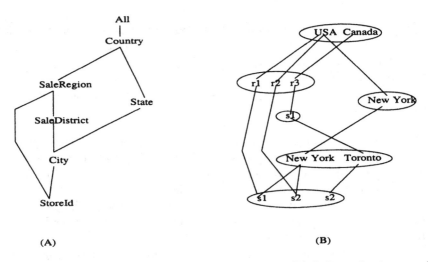

Fig. 2. (A) A hierarchy schema of a Location dimension; (B) A dimension instance for (A).

The relationship among the classes of schemas is given by the following chain of inclusions: Strictly Homogeneous $\subset$ Homogeneous $\subset$ Strictly Hierarchical $\subset$ Hierarchical .

2.4   Summarizability

In this section we extend the notion of summarizability to heterogeneous dimensions. A level represents a granularity of aggregation. In this sense, a level l can be associated with a one-dimensional cube view with no select conditions, that has the following form: $\Pi_{l,m=af(m)}(\Gamma^l_{l_{base}} d \bowtie F)$, where d is a dimension; F is a relation, called a *fact table*, with a special attribute m called the *measure*, and with l_{base} included in its attributes; af is an aggregate function; and l is a level. This cube view will be abbreviated as $cv(d, F, l, af(m))$.

Sumarizability of levels in a dimension is related to the correct derivation of one dimensional cube views from other one dimensional cube views using rollup relations for grouping. Such derivations involve queries of the form: $\Pi_{l,af^c(m)}(\biguplus_{i \in 1...n}(\pi_{l,m}\Gamma_{l_i}^l d \bowtie F_i))$. Intuitively, we are aggregating a set of fact tables $F_1, \ldots, F_n$, using the rollup mappings $\Gamma_{l_1}^l, \ldots, \Gamma_{l_n}^l$.

Definition 8 (Summarizability). *Given a dimension instance d, a set of levels $L = \{l_1, \ldots, l_n\}$, and a level l, l is* summarizable *from L in d if for every fact table F, and distributive aggregate function af, we have: $cv(d, F, l, af(m)) = \Pi_{l,af^c(m)}(\biguplus_{i \in 1...n}(\pi_{l,m}(\Gamma_{l_i}^l \bowtie cv(d, F, l_i, af(m)))))$ Given a dimension schema ds, a set of levels $L = \{l_1, \ldots, l_n\}$, and a level l, l is* summarizable *from L in ds if l is summarizable from L in every instance d in $\mathcal{I}(ds)$.*

Example 5. In the dimension instance of Figure 2, we have that *Country* is summarizable from $\{SaleDistrict, State\}$, but it is not summarizable from $\{SaleRegion, State\}$.

The following lemma gives an alternative definition of summarizability.

Lemma 1 (Summarizability). *A level l is summarizable from a set of levels $L = \{l_1, \ldots, l_n\}$ in a dimension instance d iff $\Gamma_{l_{base}}^l = \biguplus_{i \in 1...n} \pi_{l_{base},l}(\Gamma_{l_{base}}^{l_i} \bowtie \Gamma_{l_i}^l)$*

Recall that we are assuming that the dimension is partitioned. From Lemma 1 we have that a level l is summarizable from a single level l_1 in a dimension d iff $\Gamma_{l_{base}}^l = \Gamma_{l_{base}}^{l_1} \bowtie \Gamma_{l_1}^l$.

3 Split Constraints

In this section we propose a class of constraint we call *split constraints*. The intuition behind them is that usually there are dependencies between the rollup functions that start from a common level. For example, we could say that the cities that roll up to states do not roll up to any province in the location dimension of Example 1.

To start, a *split expression* $\alpha(x)$ *for level l* is a propositional formula (with the usual connectives $\neg, \wedge, \vee, \supset, \Leftrightarrow$, and $\oplus$ for exclusive disjunction) over atoms of the form $\exists x_i : \Gamma_l^{l_i}(x, x_i)$, or $\exists x_i : d\Gamma_l^{l_i}(x, x_i)$. Note that all the atoms represent rollup from a common level l, and the only free variable is x. We use $\bot$ and $\top$ to denote the false and the true proposition respectively.

Definition 9 (Split Constraints). *A split constraint for level l is an expression $\forall x \in \mathcal{E}_l : \alpha(x)$, where $\alpha(x)$ is a split expression for level l. A dimension instance d satisfies a split constraint s, denoted $d \models s$, if s is true when each fact $\Gamma_l^{l_i}(x, x_i)$ and $d\Gamma_l^{l_i}(x, x_i)$ is interpreted respectively by the direct and indirect rollup relations of d. A* base split constraint *is a split constraint whose atoms all rollup from l_{base}.*

Example 6. The split constraint: $\exists x_1 : \Gamma_l^{l_1}(x, x_1) \supset \exists x_2 : \Gamma_l^{l_2}(x, x_2)$ says that if a member e in l rolls up to a member e_1 in l_1, then e rolls up to a member in l_2.

Note that, if we associate the variables of the atoms with the level that they bind to, abstracting away the arguments and the existential quantifiers in the atoms, we can write split constraints in an abbreviated form. For example, the split constraint in the last example can be written as $\Gamma_l^{l_1} \vee \Gamma_l^{l_2}$.

Example 7. We can impose the following set of split constraints over the skeleton of Figure 2 (A). $\Sigma_S = \{(a)\ \Gamma_{StoreId}^{City}, (b)\ \Gamma_{City}^{SaleDistrict} \oplus \Gamma_{City}^{State}, (c)\ \Gamma_{SaleDistrict}^{SaleRegion}, (d)\ \Gamma_{SaleRegion}^{Country}, (e)\ \Gamma_{State}^{Country}\}$.

The following example depicts the use of direct rollup atoms in a split constraint.

Example 8. The split constraint: $d\Gamma_{City}^{State} \supset \neg\Gamma_{City}^{County}$ says that if a city rolls up *directly* to a state it does not roll up to any county.

We can characterize, using base split constraints, structural anomalies that can be present in a schema. A level could be *empty*, i.e., l could be constrained to not have any members in any instances of the schema; formally, this is captured by $\neg\Gamma_{l_{base}}^l$. Even if we have a pair of levels l_1, l_2 such that $l_1 \nearrow l_2$, the rollup function between them could be empty in all the instances of the schema; in this case we have $\neg\Gamma_{l_{base}}^{l_1} \vee \neg\Gamma_{l_{base}}^{l_2}$. Finally, we can have a dimension schema that is unsatisfiable; this can be characterized as $\neg\Gamma_{l_{base}}^l$ for every $l \in l_{base}$. As an example, if we imposed Γ_{City}^{State} to the schema of Example 7 *SaleDistrict* would be an empty level.

4   Inferring Summarizability

In this section we give an algorithm for testing summarizability in the dimension instances defined by a given hierarchical dimension schema, where the constraint language consists of split constraints. Therefore, unless otherwise stated, we assume that the dimension schemas mentioned are hierarchical and $\mathcal{CL}$ is the class of split constraints.

4.1   Conditions for Summarizability

In this section, we show that the problem reduces to testing inference of base split constraints. Given a dimension schema ds, and two of its levels, l_1, l_n, we define the following split expression:

$$\Delta_{l_1, l_n} \equiv_{def} \begin{cases} \bigvee_{l_1 \ldots l_n \in \Upsilon_{l_1, l_n}} (\Gamma_{l_{base}}^{l_1} \wedge \ldots \wedge \Gamma_{l_{base}}^{l_n}) & \text{if } l_1 \nearrow^* l_n \\ \bot & \text{otherwise.} \end{cases}$$

Note that if $l_1 \nearrow l_n$ then $\Delta_{l_1}^{l_n}$ is equivalent to $\Gamma_{l_{base}}^{l_1} \wedge \Gamma_{l_{base}}^{l_n}$, and if there is no path from l_1 to l_n it is equivalent to $\bot$. The intuition behind the above expression is that if we have Δ_{l_1, l_n}, then every base member e_b reaches an element e_n in

l_n passing through some element e_1 in l_1. For instance, if we state $\Delta_{l_1,l} \oplus \Delta_{l_2,l}$, then every base element reaches an element in l passing trough l_1, or through l_2, but not through l_1 and l_2. Note that the above statements do not always hold for non hierarchical dimension schemas.

Now, we give a lemma that characterizes summarizability in terms of a base split constraint.

Lemma 2. *A level l is summarizable from a set of levels $L = \{l_1, \ldots, l_n\}$ in a hierarchical dimension d iff $d \models \Gamma^l_{l_{base}} \supset (\Delta_{l_1,l} \oplus \cdots \oplus \Delta_{l_n,l})$.*

The intuition behind Lemma 2 is that in order for l to be summarized from L, we need that every base member e_b that reaches a member e in l, reaches e passing trough one and only one of the levels in L.

Example 9. Consider the Location dimension depicted in Figure 2. Assume that it is hierarchical, and the base level is denoted by *Store*. We have that *Country* is summarizable from $\{SaleDistrict, State\}$ iff $Location \models \Gamma^{Country}_{StoreId} \supset$ $((\Gamma^{SaleDistrict}_{StoreId} \wedge \Gamma^{SaleRegion}_{StoreId} \wedge \Gamma^{Country}_{StoreId}) \oplus (\Gamma^{State}_{StoreId} \wedge \Gamma^{Country}_{StoreId}))$. Note that the above split expression can be simplified to: $\Gamma^{Country}_{StoreId} \supset ((\Gamma^{SaleDistrict}_{StoreId} \wedge \Gamma^{SaleRegion}_{StoreId}) \oplus \Gamma^{State}_{StoreId})$.

4.2   Derivation of Base Split Constraints

In the previous section, we found necessary and sufficient conditions for summarizability in terms of base split constraints. In this section, we give a sound and complete set of inference rules for implication of base split constraints. The notion of implication is stated as follows: given a dimension schema ds and split constraint α, we say that $ds \models \alpha$ if for every dimension instance $d \in \mathcal{I}(ds)$ we have $d \models \alpha$. We denote by Σ^+_B the set of base split constraints $\{\beta \mid ds \models \beta\}$.

The first two derivation rules we introduce reflects the assumptions (a) and (b) in Section 2.2, respectively.

Rule 1 *For every level $l \in L \setminus L_{Bottom}$ we have $\Gamma^l_{l_{base}} \supset \bigvee_{\{l_i \mid l_i \nearrow l\}} \Gamma^{l_i}_{l_{base}}$.*

Rule 2 *We have $\bigoplus_{l_i \in L_{Bottom}} \Gamma^{l_i}_{l_{base}}$.*

Rule 1 states that there are no leaves in the internal levels, and Rule 2 says that every base member reaches one and only one member in a bottom level. The next rule reflects the condition (3) of Definition 2.

Rule 3 *for every level $l \in L$ such that $l \neq All$, we have Γ^{All}_l.*

Next, we show how to transform split constraints into equivalent base split constraints. We will do this by expressing atoms in terms of base rollup atoms. We need the following definition: given a dimension schema ds and two of its levels l_a and l_b we have:

$$d\Delta_{l_a,l_b} \equiv_{def}$$

$$\begin{cases} \Gamma^{l_a}_{l_{base}} \wedge \Gamma^{l_b}_{l_{base}} \wedge \neg(\bigvee_{l_a l_1 \ldots l_n l_b \in \Upsilon_{l_a,l_b}} \Gamma^{l_1}_{l_{base}} \wedge \ldots \wedge \Gamma^{l_n}_{l_{base}}) & \text{If } \{l_a l_b\} \subset \Upsilon_{l_a,l_b} \\ \Gamma^{l_a}_{l_{base}} \wedge \Gamma^{l_b}_{l_{base}} & \text{if } \Upsilon_{l_a,l_b} = \{l_a l_b\} \\ \bot & \text{otherwise} \end{cases}$$

For instance, the base split constraint $d\Delta_{l_a,l_b}$ states that every base element reaches an element e_b in l_b, passing trough an element e_a in l_a that reaches directly e_b.

Now, we give a characterization of the relationship between split and base split constraints.

Lemma 3. *Given a dimension schema ds, and a split constraint α, then for every hierarchical dimension d over ds we have $d \models \alpha$ iff $d \models \Gamma^l_{l_{inf}} \supset \alpha'$, where α' is obtained from α by replacing every indirect rollup atom $\Gamma^{l_i}_l$ with Δ_{l,l_i}, and replacing every direct rollup atom $d\Gamma^{l_i}_l$ with $d\Delta_{l,l_i}$.*

The following rule that transforms split constraints to base split constraints comes from Lemma 3.

Rule 4 *Given a split constraint α, then we have $\Gamma^l_{l_{inf}} \supset \alpha'$, where α' is obtained from α by replacing every indirect rollup atom $\Gamma^{l_i}_l$ with Δ_{l,l_i}, and replacing every direct rollup atom $d\Gamma^{l_i}_l$ with $d\Delta_{l,l_i}$.*

The last rule we give shows that base split constraints can be derived from other base split constraints using propositional logic derivation. Let $\models_{prop}$ be the propositional implication of two base split constraint when considering rollup atoms as propositional variables.

Rule 5 *If we have the split constraints $\alpha_1, \ldots, \alpha_n$, and $\alpha_1, \ldots, \alpha_n \models_{prop} \beta$, then we have β.*

Finally, we show that the given axiomatization is sound and complete for deriving Σ_B^+.

Theorem 1 (Soundness and Completeness of Base Split Inference). *Rules 1, 2, 3, 4, and 5 are sound and complete for Σ_B^+.*

Example 10. Consider the base split constraint that we have to test in Example 9 in order to decide whether $Country$ is summarizable from $\{SaleDistrict, State\}$:

(*) $\Gamma^{Country}_{StoreId} \supset ((\Gamma^{saleDistrict}_{StoreId} \wedge \Gamma^{SaleRegion}_{StoreId}) \oplus \Gamma^{State}_{StoreId})$. Now, we give a derivation for (*).

(1) $\Gamma^{City}_{StoreId} \supset \Gamma^{SaleDistrict}_{StoreId} \oplus \Gamma^{State}_{StoreId}$	Rule 4 from split constraint (b)
(2) $\Gamma^{SaleDistrict}_{StoreId} \oplus \Gamma^{State}_{StoreId}$	Rule 5 from (1) and split constraint (a)
(3) $\Gamma^{SaleDistrict}_{StoreId} \Leftrightarrow (\Gamma^{SaleDistrict}_{StoreId} \wedge \Gamma^{SaleRegion}_{StoreId})$	Rule 5 from split constraint (c)
(4) $(\Gamma^{SaleDistrict}_{StoreId} \wedge \Gamma^{SaleRegion}_{StoreId}) \oplus \Gamma^{State}_{StoreId}$	Rule 5 from (2) and (3)
(5) $\Gamma^{Country}_{StoreId}$	sequence of applications of Rules 1 and 5
(*)	Rule (5) from (4) and (5)

4.3   Complexity

The following theorem gives a lower bound for the problem of inferring summarizability from a given dimension schema.

Theorem 2. *Given a dimension schema ds, a level l and a set of levels L, whether l is summarizable from L in every dimension $d \in \mathcal{I}(ds)$ is coNP-hard.*

Proof. (Sketch) Transformation from VALIDITY.

An upper bound of $O(n^2 2^n)$, where n is the number of levels of the hierarchy schema, can be obtained by the algorithm in Figure 3. The upper bound is basically caused by the steps (2) and (3) of the algorithm, which are in $O(n^2 2^n)$.

Input: A heterogeneous dimension schema ds, a level $l \in L_{ds}$, and a set $L \subseteq L_{ds}$
Output: Whether l is summarizable from L in all the instances of ds
(1) Apply Rules 1 and 2, and 3, having Σ_I
(2) Apply Rule 4 to every split constraint in Σ_I and Σ, giving Σ_{BS}.
(3) For every level $l_i \in L$ compute $\Delta_{l_i,l}$
(4) If $\Sigma_{BS} \models_{prop} \Gamma^l_{l_{inf}} \supset (\Delta_{l_1,l} \oplus \ldots \oplus \Delta_{l_n,l})$ then return true; else return false
Input: A homogeneous dimension schema ds, a level $l \in L_{ds}$, and a set $L \subseteq L_{ds}$
Output: Whether l is summarizable from L all the instances of ds
(1) Let $L' = L \cap \{l' \mid l' \nearrow^* l\}$
(2) If every bottom level that reaches l reaches exactly one level in L' then return true; else return false.

Fig. 3. Algorithms for testing summarizability: (Above) in a hierarchical dimension schema with split constraints, (Below) in a Homogeneous Dimension Schema without empty levels.

It is easy to show that testing summarizability in strictly homogeneous schemas is in polytime; we only have to check whether there is exactly one level in L that reaches l in the dimension hierarchy. The following lemma shows that testing summarizability in homogeneous schemas without empty levels is also in polytime.

Lemma 4. *Testing summarizability in an homogeneous schema without empty levels is in polytime.*

Proof. (Sketch) A polytime algorithm is given in Figure 3.

5   Related Work

Cabibbo and Torlone [CT97] introduced one of the first formal models for OLAP dimensions; it allows representing only strictly homogeneous dimensions. Further models [LAW98], [HMV99a] have the same restriction. Jagadish et al. [JLS99] introduce in their model the ability to represent non-strict homogeneous schemas, referring to them as *unbalanced*. Although they motivate the need for modeling heterogeneity, their model does not go beyond homogeneity. The model of Lehner et al. [LAW98] considered a case of heterogeneity arising between levels and attributes, that has a trivial treatement using null values.

The notion of summarizability was introduced by Rafanelli and Shoshani [RS90] as a property of statistical objects. Lenz and Shoshani [LS97] give conditions for summarizability of a level from a single level. Using a different, rather informal framework, they basically state that if (a) $l_1 \nearrow^* l_2$, (b) the rollup relations are functions, and (c) they are total between member sets, then l_1 is summarizable from l_2 in a dimension d. They refer to condition (b) as the rollup relations being *disjoint*, and condition (c) as being *complete*. Assuming that the dimension is partitioned (or disjoint in their terminology), the above conditions are basically equivalent to the special case of Lemma 1 when summarizability is from a single level.

Split constraints have the flavor of the *disjunctive existential constraints* (dec's) introduced by Goldstein [Gol81], which basically specify where null values may occur in a relation. Let us denote by $\mathcal{T}_d$ the relational table that represents the dimension instance d realized as a single table in the star schema. Intuitively, $\mathcal{T}_d$ is the relation that has as attributes the levels $L \cup \{l_{base}\}$, and is defined by the outer-join of the base rollup relations. It easy to show that the partitioned property of a dimension d is equivalent to having l_{base} as a key for $\mathcal{T}_d$. Basically, a dec says that whenever a tuple is non-null for an attribute, it must be non-null for all the attributes in at least one set of attributes in a given list. Only a subset of bottom split constraints can be represented using dec's over $\mathcal{T}_d$; split constraints are more general because they allow any propositional condition on non-null attributes.

6   Conclusion

The restriction of homogeneity in current dimension models leads to unnatural dimension schemas in many real situations. The relaxation of this condition, however, weakens the ability to reason about summarizability in the schema. We identify a class of constraints that overcome this problem and enrich the semantics of dimension schemas. We solve the the problem of inferring summarizability in a class of heterogeneous schemas. The problem is still open for non partitioned, and heterogeneous schemas in general. The exploration of further classes of constraints and their relation with summarizability is also a challenging problem to pursue.

It is interesting to note that homogeneous dimension schemas convey data in exactly the same way as hierarchical data models. Furthermore, the notion of heterogeneity and the results of this paper extend to hierarchical data modeling in general.

Summarizability is a particular case of the problem of using materialized views to compute aggregate views [SSJL96]. Little has been said about the interplay between constraints and aggregate view rewriting in the context of OLAP dimensions and hierarchies. Our work establishes the foundations for further research in this area.

Acknowledgements. This research was supported by the National Science and Engineering Research Council and the Institute for Robotics and Intelligent Systems of Canada.

References

[AGS+96]   R. Agrawal, A. Gupta, S. Sarawagi, P. Deshpande, S. Agarwal, J. Naughton, and R. Ramakrishnan. On the computation of multidimensional aggregates. In *Proceedings of the 22nd VLDB Conference*, Bombay, India, 1996.

[CD97]   S. Chaudhuri and U. Dayal. An overview of data warehousing and OLAP technology. In *ACM SIGMOD Record 26(1)*, March 1997.

[CT97]   L. Cabibbo and R. Torlone. Querying multidimensional databases. In *Proceedings of the 6th DBPL Workshop*, East Park, Colorado, USA, 1997.

[GBLHP96]   J. Gray, A. Bosworth, A. Layman, and H. H. Pirahesh. Data cube : A relational operator generalizing group-by, cross-tab and sub-totals. In *Proceedings of the 12th IEEE-ICDE Conference*, New Orleans, Los Angeles, USA, 1996.

[Gol81]   B. A. Goldstein. Constraints on null values in relational databases. In *Proceedings of the 7th VLDB Conference*, Cannes, France, 1981.

[HMV99a]   C. Hurtado, A. Mendelzon, and A. Vaisman. Maintaining data cubes under dimension updates. In *Proceedings of the 15th IEEE-ICDE Conference.*, Sydney, Australia, 1999.

[HMV99b]   C. Hurtado, A. Mendelzon, and A. Vaisman. Updating OLAP dimensions. In *Proceedings of the 2nd IEEE-DOLAP Workshop*, Kansas City, Missouri, USA, 1999.

[HRU96]   V. Harinarayan, A. Rajaraman, and J. Ullman. Implementing data cubes efficiently. In *Proceedings of the 1996 ACM-SIGMOD Conference*, Montreal, Canada, 1996.

[JLS99]   H. V. Jagadish, L. V. S. Lakshmanan, and D. Srivastava. What can hierarchies do for data warehouses? In *Proc. of the 25th VLDB Conference*, Edinburgh, Scotland, UK, 1999.

[LAW98]   W. Lehner, H. Albrecht, and H. Wedekind. Multidimensional normal forms. In *Proceedings of the 10th SSDBM Conference*, Capri, Italy., 1998.

[LS97]   H. J. Lenz and A. Shoshani. Summarizability in OLAP and statistical databases. In *Proceedings of the 9th SSDBM Conference*, Olympia, Washington, USA, 1997.

[Mal93]   Francesco Malvestuto. A universal-scheme approach to statistical databases containing homogeneous summary tables. In *ACM Transactions on Database Systems, Vol. 18, No. 4.*, December 1993.

[RS90]   M. Rafanelli and A. Shoshani. Storm: A statistical object representation model. In *Proceedings of the 5th SSDBM Conference*, Charlotte, N.C., USA, 1990.

[SSJL96]   D. Srivastava, D. Shaul, H. V. Jagadish, and A. Levy. Answering queries with aggregation using views. In *Proceedings of the 22nd VLDB Conference*, Bombay, India, 1996.

Estimating Range Queries Using Aggregate Data with Integrity Constraints: A Probabilistic Approach

Francesco Buccafurri[1], Filippo Furfaro[2], and Domenico Saccà[3]

[1] DIMET, University of Reggio Calabria, 89100 Reggio Calabria, Italy,
bucca@ing.unirc.it
[2] DEIS, University of Calabria, 87030 Rende, Italy, furfaro@si.deis.unical.it
[3] ISI-CNR & DEIS, 87030 Rende, Italy, sacca@unical.it

Abstract. In fast OLAP applications it is often advantageous to provide approximate answers to range queries in order to achieve very high performances. A possible solution is to inquire summary data rather than the original ones and to perform suitable interpolations. Approximate answers become mandatory in situations where only aggregate data are available. This paper studies the problem of estimating range queries (namely, sum and count) over aggregate data using a probabilistic approach for computing expected value and variance of the answers. The novelty of this approach is the exploitation of possible integrity constraints about the presence of elements in the range that are known to be null or non-null. Closed formulas for all results are provided, and some interesting applications for query estimations on histograms are discussed.

1 Introduction

Traditional query processing deals with computing exact answers by possibly minimizing response time and maximizing throughput. However, a recent querying paradigm, on-line analytical processing (OLAP) [11,13,5], often involves complex range queries over very large datacubes (i.e., multidimensional relations with dimension and measure attributes) so that the exact answer may require a huge amount of time and resources. As OLAP queries mainly deals with operations of aggregation (e.g., count and sum) of the measure values on dimension ranges, an interesting approach to improve performances is to store some aggregata data and to inquiry them rather than the original data thus obtaining approximate answers — this approach is very useful when the user wants to have fast answers without being forced to wait a long time to get a precision which often is not necessary.

The possibility of returning approximate answers for range queries has been first explicitly addressed in [12] but, in that case, the approximation is temporary since results are output on the fly while the tuples are being scanned and, at the end, after all original tuples are consulted, the user will eventually get the correct answer.

J. Van den Bussche and V. Vianu (Eds.): ICDT 2001, LNCS 1973, pp. 390–404, 2001.
© Springer-Verlag Berlin Heidelberg 2001

The issue of computing approximate range query answers by never accessing original tuples but only consulting aggregate data has very recently started receiving a deal of attention. Typical approaches consist in re-using statistical techniques which have been applied for many lusters inside query optimizers for selectivity estimation [17]. We recall that three major classes of statistical techniques are used for selectivity estimation: *sampling, histograms* and *parametric modeling* — see [2] for a detailed survey. Interesting applications of sampling and histogram techniques already exist, see for instance [8,9] and [10], respectively. The usage of sampling techniques are also used for approximate join-queries answering [1]. A recent technique for selectivity estimation, wavelet-based histograms, has been already applied to approximate answering of range queries [18].

In this paper we propose a probabilistic approach to compute approximate answers to range queries (in particular, count and sum queries) by consulting a compressed representation of the datacube, that is a partition of the datacube into blocks of possibly different sizes storing a number of aggregate data (number of non-null tuples and sum of their measure values) for each block. Our approximated results will come with a detailed analysis of the possible error so that, if the user is not satisfied with the obtained precision, s/he may eventually decide to submit the query on the actual datacube. In this case, it is not necessary to run the query over all tuples but only on those portions of the range that do not fit the blocks.

Our approach is not concerned with the problem of finding the most effective compressed representation of a datacube to increase accuracy in query estimation — instead this is the main goal of the sampling and histogram techniques mentioned above. We are involved with the "apparently" simpler problem of performing interpolation of aggregate data once the compressed representation for the datacube has been decided. This means that our approach can be also used to interpolate data from summarized ones for which detail tuples are not available. This case has been first studied in [6] and interesting results have been obtained by enforcing the optimization of some criterion like the smoothness of the distribution of values. Our approach does not make any assumption on data distribution and perform estimations extending the probabilistic framework introduced in [3].

The novelty of our approach is that we exploit additional information on a datacube that is often available under the form of integrity constraints. In particular, we assume the existence of constraints stating that a minimum number of null or non-null tuples are present in given ranges. Such a situation often arises in practice. For instance, given a datacube whose dimensions are the time (in terms of days) and the products while the measure is the amount of daily product sales, realistic integrity constraints are that the sales are null during the week-end while at least 4 times a week the sales are not null.

In the paper we analyze two types of integrity constraints:

- *number of elements that are known to be null:* we are given a function $LB_{=0}$ returning, for any range R, a lower bound to the number of null tuples occurring in D — so $|R| - LB_{=0}(R)$ is an upper bound on the number of non-nulls occurring in the range;

- *number of elements that are known to be non-null:* we are given a function $LB_{>0}$ returning, for any range R, a lower bound for the number of non-null tuples occurring in R.

The two functions $LB_{=0}$ and $LB_{>0}$ are assumed to be monotone, to require a little amount of additional storage space and to be computable very efficiently — actually in time constant w.r.t. the size of the compressed datacube. Possible future research directions could explore other types of integrity constraints: then the problem of interpolating data from compressed representation could eventually enter the field of knowledge discovery and data mining. This explain why we have above stressed that the problem is only apparently simple.

Our problem is therefore the following: given a range R inside a datacube block B for which we know the count t (the number of non-null tuples) and the sum s of their measure values, we want to compute the estimation (mean and variance) of the count t_R and the sum s_R for the range R, knowing that $(|R| - LB_{=0}(R)) \le t_R \le LB_{>0}(R)$ and $(|\bar{R}| - LB_{=0}(\bar{R})) \le t_{\bar{R}} \le LB_{>0}(\bar{R})$, where $\bar{R}$ is the range in B complementary to R.

The results we provide are formulas for mean and variance of both count and sum queries; besides the formulas are closed so that they can be computed very efficiently. For instance, suppose that the block B has size 120, the number of non-nulls in it is 80 and their sum is 12000 and that the range R consists of the first 30 tuples in the block. Without integrity constraints we have that the expected value for s_R is obviously $(30/120) \times 12000 = 3000$ — note that the knowledge about the number of non-nulls does not contribute to the estimation. Suppose now that we know that at least 4 of the first 20 tuples in the block are null but at least 2 of them are not null; moreover, at least half of the last 20 tuples are not null. Thus, $LB_{=0}(R) = 4$, $LB_{>0}(R) = 2$, $LB_{=0}(\bar{R}) = 0$ and $LB_{>0}(\bar{R}) = 10$. By applying our formulas we now obtain that the expected value for s_R is 4100.

Estimating mean values is not enough in most situations: we also need to compute the possible error in the estimation. For instance, given a block of size 100 and sum 10000 and given a range R coinciding with half of the block, the expected value for the sum in R is independent from the number of non-nulls in B. But it is obvious that the error in the case this number is 2 is much higher than for the case with, say, 90 non-nulls; so we need to consult the variance of the estimation before concluding that it is meaningful. Our results include closed formulas also for the variance of both count and sum queries. Indeed the proofs of such formulas are rather long and complex so we have included only one proof in the appendix. Besides, for reason of space, all the other proofs are either left out or only sketched.

The paper is organized as follows. In Section 2 we introduce the compressed representation of a datacube and the integrity constraints about the number of null or non-null tuples in the datacubes ranges. In Section 3 we fix the probabilistic framework for estimating *count* and *sum* range queries on a datacube M by means of random queries variables over the population of all datacubes which both have the same aggregate data as M and satisfies the integrity constraints. For the sake of the presentation, in Section 4 we perform range query estimation for the simple case that only integrity constraints about the null tuples are available (i.e., only the function $LB_{=0}$ is given); the general case is treated in the subsequent section. Finally, in Section 6 we give some interesting applications of our formulas for the estimation of frequency distribution inside a bucket of a histogram [14,15,16]. The most common approach is the *continuous value assumption* [17]: the sum of frequencies in a range of a bucket is estimated by linear interpolation. We shall show that this computation does not yield a correct estimation for the case of bucket whose extremes (or at least one of them) is known to be not null. This situation, that arises for many of the most popular histogram representations, can be formalized in terms of our integrity constraints, thus obtaining more accurate estimations as well as the evaluation of their errors.

2   Compressed Datacubes and Integrity Constraints

Let $\mathbf{i} = <i_1,\ldots,i_r>$ and $\mathbf{j} = <j_1,\ldots,j_r>$ be two r-tuples of cardinals, with $r > 0$. We extend common operators for cardinals to tuples in the obvious way: $\mathbf{i} \leq \mathbf{j}$ means that $i_1 \leq j_1,\ldots i_r \leq j_r$; $\mathbf{i}+\mathbf{j}$ denotes the tuple $<i_1+j_1,\ldots,i_r+j_r>$ and so on. Given $p \geq 0$, $\mathbf{p}^r$ (or simply $\mathbf{p}$, if r is understood) denotes the r-tuple of all p. Finally, $[\mathbf{i}..\mathbf{j}] = [i_1..j_1,\ldots,i_r..j_r]$ denotes the range of all tuples from $\mathbf{i}$ to $\mathbf{j}$, that is $\{\mathbf{q}|\ \mathbf{i} \leq \mathbf{q} \leq \mathbf{j}\}$.

A *multidimensional relation* R is a relation whose scheme consists of $r > 0$ *dimensions* (also called *functional attributes*) and $s > 0$ *measure attributes*. The dimensions are a key for the relation so that no two tuples have the same dimension value. For the sake of presentation but without loss of generality, we assume that

- $s = 1$ and the domain of the unique measure attribute is the set of cardinals, and
- $r \geq 1$ and the domain of each dimension q, $1 \leq q \leq r$, is the range $[1..n_q]$, where $n_q > 2$, i.e., the projection of R on the dimensions is a subset of $[1..\mathbf{n}]$, where $\mathbf{n} = <n_1,\ldots,n_r>$.

Given any range $[\mathbf{i}..\mathbf{j}]$, $1 \leq \mathbf{i} \leq \mathbf{j} \leq \mathbf{n}$, we consider the following *range queries* on R:

- *count query:* $count^{[\mathbf{i}..\mathbf{j}]}(R)$ denotes the number of tuples of R whose dimension values are in $[\mathbf{i}..\mathbf{j}]$, and
- *sum query:* $sum^{[\mathbf{i}..\mathbf{j}]}(R)$ denotes the sum of all measure values for those tuples of R whose dimension values are in $[\mathbf{i}..\mathbf{j}]$.

Since the dimension attributes are a key, the relation R can be naturally viewed as a $[1..\mathbf{n}]$ matrix (i.e., a *datacube*) M of elements with values in $\mathcal{N}$ such that for each $\mathbf{i} \in [1..\mathbf{n}]$, $M[\mathbf{i}] = v$ if the tuple $<\mathbf{i},v>$ is in R or otherwise $M[\mathbf{i}] = 0$ — then $\mathbf{i}$ is a *null element* if either $<\mathbf{i},0>$ is in R or no tuple with dimension value $\mathbf{i}$ is present in R. The above range queries can be now re-formulated in terms of array operations as follows:

- $count^{[i..j]}(R) = count(M[i..j]) = |\{q| \ q \in [i..j] \text{ and } M[q] > 0\}|$;
- $sum^{[i..j]}(R) = sum(M[i..j]) = \sum_{q \in [i..j]} M[q]$.

We next introduce a *compressed representation* of the relation R by dividing the datacube M into a number of blocks and by storing a number of aggregate data for each of them. To this end, given $\mathbf{m} = <m_1, \ldots, m_r>$ in $[1..n]$, a *m-compression factor* for M is a tuple $F = <f_1, \ldots, f_r>$, such that for each q, $1 \leq q \leq r$, f_q is a $[0..m_q]$ array for which $0 = f_q[0] < f_q[1] < \cdots < f_q[m_q] = n_q$. For each $\mathbf{k} = <k_1, \ldots, k_r>$ in $[1..m]$, let $F^+(\mathbf{k})$ and $F^-(\mathbf{k})$ denote the tuples $<f_1[k_1], \ldots, f_r[k_r]>$ and $<f_1[k_1 - 1] + 1, \ldots, f_r[k_r - 1] + 1>$, respectively . Therefore, F divides the range $[1..n]$ into $m_1 \times \cdots \times m_r$ blocks $B_{\mathbf{k}}$, one for each tuple $\mathbf{k} = <k_1, \ldots, k_r>$ in $[1..m]$; the *block* $B_{\mathbf{k}}$ has range $[F^-(\mathbf{k})..F^+(\mathbf{k})]$ and size $(f_1[k_1] - f_1[k_1 - 1]) \times \cdots \times (f_r[k_r] - f_r[k_r - 1])$ if $\mathbf{k} > 1$ or $f_1[k_1] \times \cdots \times f_r[k_r]$ otherwise.

For instance, consider the $[1..10, 1..6]$ matrix M in Figure 1(a), which is divided into 6 blocks as indicated by the double lines. We have that $\mathbf{m} = <3, 2>$, $f_1[0] = 0$, $f_1[1] = 3$, $f_1[2] = 7$, $f_1[3] = 10$, and $f_2[0] = 0$, $f_2[1] = 4$, $f_2[2] = 6$. The block $B_{<1,1>}$ has size 3×2 and range $[1..3, 1..4]$; the block $B_{<1,2>}$ has size 3×2 and range $[1..3, 5..6]$, and so on.

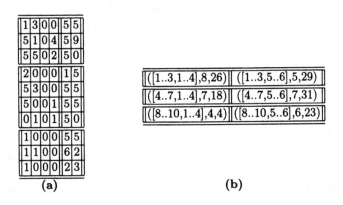

(a)   (b)

Fig. 1. A two-dimensional datacube and its compressed representation

A *compressed representation* of the datacube M consists of selecting a m-compression factor F and storing the following aggregate data on the F-compressed blocks of M:

- the $[1..m]$ matrices $M_{count,F}$ and $M_{sum,F}$ such that for each $\mathbf{k} \in [1..m]$,

$$M_{cs,F}[\mathbf{k}] = cs(M[F^-(\mathbf{k})..F^+(\mathbf{k})])$$

where cs stands for *count* or *sum*;

The compressed representation of the datacube M in Figure 1(a) is represented in Figure 1(b) by a matrix of triples, one for each block; the values of each triple indicates respectively the range, the number of non-null elements and the sum of the elements in the corresponding block. For instance, the block $B_{<1,1>}$ has range $[1..3, 1..4]$ and 8 non-null elements with sum 26; the block $B_{<1,2>}$ has range $[1..3, 5..6]$ and 5 non-null elements with sum 29, and so on.

We assume that the we are given a compressed representation of a datacube M as well as additional information on M under the form of integrity constraints on the content of M. The representation of such constraints needs a little amount of additional storage space; besides, the requirements defined by the constraints are expressed in terms of aggregate data which are computed by suitable function in constant time — thus the functions are not dependent on the actual contents of M. As discussed in the Introduction, data distributions often match this property in real contexts. For instance, consider the case of a temporal dimension with granularity *day* and a measure attribute storing the amount of sales for every day. In this case, given any temporal range, it is easily recognizable a number of *certain* null values, corresponding to the holidays occurring in that range. In such cases, the constraints provide additional information that can be efficiently computed with no overhead in terms of storage space on the compressed representation of M.

Let $2^{[1..n]}$ be the family of all subsets of indices in $[1..n]$. We analyze two types of integrity constraints:

- *number of elements that are known to be null:* we are given a function $LB_{=0} : 2^{[1..n]} \to \mathcal{N}$ returning, for any D in $2^{[1..n]}$, a lower bound to the number of null elements occurring in D; the datacube M satisfies $LB_{=0}$ if for each D in $2^{[1..n]}$, $\sum_{i \in D} count(M[i]) \leq |D| - LB_{=0}(D)$, where $|D|$ is the number of elements of M in D;
- *number of elements that are known to be non-null:* we are given a function $LB_{>0} : 2^{[1..n]} \to \mathcal{N}$ returning, for any D in $2^{[1..n]}$, a lower bound for the number of non-null elements occurring in D; the datacube M satisfies $LB_{>0}$ if for each D in $2^{[1..n]}$, $\sum_{i \in D} count(M[i]) \geq LB_{>0}(D)$.

The two functions $LB_{=0}$ and $LB_{>0}$ are monotone: for each D', D'' in $2^{[1..n]}$, if $D' \subset D''$ then both $LB_{=0}(D') \leq LB_{=0}(D'')$ and $LB_{>0}(D') \leq LB_{>0}(D'')$.

Suppose that $LB_{=0}([4..6, 1..3]) = 3$ and $LB_{>0}([4..6, 1..3]) = 1$ in our running example. Then we infer that the number of non-null elements in the range $[4..6, 1..3]$ is between 1 and $(6 - 4 + 1) \times (3 - 1 + 1) - 3 = 6$. Note that the compressed representation of M in Figure 1(b) only says that the block $[4..7, 1..4]$ has 7 non-nulls; so, from this information, we only derive that the bounds on the number of non-null elements in $[4..6, 1..3]$ are 0 and 7.

3   The Probabilistic Framework for Range Query Estimation

We next introduce a probabilistic framework for estimating the answers of range queries (*sum* and *count*) by consulting aggregate data rather than the actual datacube. To this aim, we consider the queries as random variables and we give their estimation in terms of mean and variance. More precisely, a range query Q on a given datacube M is estimated by a random query variable $\tilde{Q}$, defined by applying Q on a datacube $\tilde{M}$ extracted from the population of all datacubes, whose compressed representations is 'compatible' with the one of M. Thus, the estimation of the range query Q is only based on the knowledge of the compressed representation of M. A crucial point in such estimation is the definition of population 'compatible' with the compressed representation of the given datacube M.

We start from the population of the datacubes having the same aggregate data that we assume available for M: $M_{cs,F}^{-1}$ is the set of all the $[1..n]$ matrix M' of elements in $\mathcal{N}$ for which both $M'_{count,F} = M_{count,F}$ and $M'_{sum,F} = M_{sum,F}$. We next restrict the population $M_{cs,F}^{-1}$ by considering only those datacubes which satisfy a given set of integrity constraints on the number of non-null elements.

Let us now define the random variables for the estimation of the count and the sum query.

Let the query $count(M[i..j])$ and $sum(M[i..j])$ be given and let $LB_{=0}$ and $LB_{>0}$ be two integrity constraints that are satisfied by M. We shall estimate the two queries with the two random query variables $count(\tilde{M}[i..j])$ and $sum(\tilde{M}[i..j])$, respectively, in the following two cases:

1. for $\tilde{M}$ extracted from the population $\sigma_{LB_{=0}}(M_{cs,F}^{-1}) = \{M'|\ M' \in M_{cs,F}^{-1}$ and M' satisfies $LB_{=0}\}$; thus we estimate the number and the sum of the non-null elements in $M[i..j]$ by considering the population of all datacubes having both the same sum and the same number of non-nulls in each block as M and satisfying the lower bound constraint enforced by the function $LB_{=0}$ on the number of null elements occurring in each range;

2. for $\tilde{M}$ extracted from the population $\sigma_{LB_{=0},LB_{>0}}(M_{cs,F}^{-1}) = \{M'|\ M' \in M_{cs,F}^{-1}$ and M' satisfies $LB_{=0}$ and $LB_{>0}\}$; thus we estimate the number and the sum of the non-null elements in $M[i..j]$ by restricting the population of the previous case to those datacubes which also satisfy the lower bound constraint enforced by the function $LB_{>0}$ on the number of non-null elements occurring in each range.

We observe that Case 1 can be derived from the more general Case 2 but, for the sake of presentation, we first present the simpler case and then we move to the general case.

Once the datacube population for a random variable $query(\tilde{M}[i..j])$ (where $query$ stands for $count$ or sum) is fixed, we have to determine its probability distribution and then its mean and variance — recall that both mean and variance are defined by the operator E. Concerning the mean, due to the linearity of E we have:

$$E(query(\tilde{M}[i..j])) = \sum_{B_q \in TB_F(i..j)} M_{query,F}[q] + \sum_{B_k \in PB_F(i..j)} E(query(\tilde{M}[i_k..j_k]))$$

where

1. $TB_F(i..j)$ returns the set of blocks B_q that are totally contained in the range $[i..j]$, i.e., both $i \leq F^-(q)$ and $F^+(q) \leq j$,
2. $PB_F(i..j)$ returns the set of blocks B_k that are partially inside the range, i.e., $B_k \notin TB_F(i..j)$ and either $i \leq F^-(k) \leq j$ or $i \leq F^+(k) \leq j$, and
3. for each $B_k \in PB_F(i..j)$, i_k and j_k are the boundaries of the portion of the block B_k which overlaps the range $[i..j]$, i.e., $[i_k..j_k] = [i..j] \cap [F^-(k)..F^+(k)]$.

For example, for the datacube in Figure 1(a), given $i = <4,3>$ and $j = <8,6>$, the block $B_{<2,2>}$ is totally contained in the range, the blocks $B_{<2,1>}$, $B_{<3,1>}$, $B_{<3,2>}$ are partially contained in the range (with boundaries $[4..7, 3..4]$, $[8..8, 3..4]$ and $[8..8, 5..6]$, respectively), and the blocks $B_{<1,1>}$, $B_{<1,2>}$ are outside the range.

Concerning the variance, we assume statistical independence between the measure values of different blocks so that its value is determined by summing the variances of all partially overlapped blocks, thus introducing no covariance.

$$\sigma^2(query(\tilde{M}[i..j])) = \sum_{B_k \in PB_F(i..j)} \sigma^2(query(\tilde{M}[i_k..j_k])).$$

It turns out that we only need to study the estimation of a query ranging on one partial block as all other cases can be easily re-composed from this basic case. Therefore, from now on we assume that the query range $[i..j]$ is strictly inside one single block, say the block B_k, i.e., $F^-(k) \leq i \leq j \leq F^+(k)$. We use the following notations and assumptions:

1. b, $b > 1$, is the size of B_k, thus b is the number of elements in B_k;
2. $b_{i..j}$, $1 \leq b_{i..j} < b$, is the size of $[i..j]$, that is the number of elements in the range;
3. $t = M_{count,F}[k]$, $1 \leq t \leq b$, is the number of non-null elements in B_k;
4. $s = M_{sum,F}[k]$, $s \geq max(1,t)$, is the sum of the elements in B_k;
5. $t^U_{i..j} = b_{i..j} - LB_{=0}([i..j])$ and $t^L_{i..j} = LB_{>0}([i..j])$ are respectively an upper bound and a lower bound on the number of non-null elements in the range $[i..j]$;
6. $t^U_{i\tilde{.}j} = b_{i\tilde{.}j} - LB_{=0}([i\tilde{.}j])$ and $t^L_{i\tilde{.}j} = LB_{>0}([i\tilde{.}j])$ are respectively an upper bound and a lower bound on the number of non-null elements in the block B_k outside the range $[i..j]$;
7. $t^U = t^U_{i..j} + t^U_{i\tilde{.}j} = b - LB_{=0}([i..j]) - LB_{=0}([i\tilde{.}j])$ and $t^L = t^L_{i..j} + t^L_{i\tilde{.}j} = LB_{>0}([i..j]) + LB_{>0}([i\tilde{.}j])$, where $[i\tilde{.}j]$ denotes the set of elements that are in B_k but not in the range $[i..j]$; t^U and t^L are an upper bound and a lower bound on the number of non-null elements in B_k.

Observe that the functions $LB_{=0}$ and $LB_{>0}$ are computed for the ranges $[i..j]$ and $[i\tilde{.}j]$ but not for the whole block B_k. Indeed, t^L and t^U do not in general coincide with $LB_{>0}([F^-(k)..F^+(k)])$ and $b - LB_{=0}([F^-(k)..F^+(k)])$, respectively, as the latter ones may be stricter bounds. For instance, suppose that the block stores the bimonthly sales of a store and we want to estimate the sales in the first month. The integrity constraints say that the store closes 4 days every month and an additional day every two months. So $t^U = 60 - 4 = 56$ and not 55. Thus the additional day is not taken into account but this does not affect at all the accuracy of the estimation: indeed we have available the actual number of opened days for the block of two months.

4   Case 1: Range Query Estimation Using Upper Bounds on the Number of Non-null Elements

In this section we only consider upper bounds on the number of non-null elements in the ranges $[i..j]$ and $[\tilde{i}..j]$ which are derived by the function $LB_{=0}$. We define the random variables $count(\tilde{M}[i..j])$ and $sum(\tilde{M}[i..j])$ by extracting $\tilde{M}$ from the population $\sigma_{LB_{=0}}(M_{cs,F}^{-1})$ of all datacubes having both the same sum and the same number of non-nulls in each block as M and satisfying the upper bound constraints on the number of elements in each range. We assume that both $t_{i..j}^L$ and t^L are equal to zero, i.e., both $LB_{>0}([i..j]) = 0$ and $LB_{>0}([\tilde{i}..j]) = 0$.

Theorem 1. *Let $C_1([i..j]) = count(\tilde{M}[i..j])$ and $S_1([i..j]) = sum(\tilde{M}[i..j])$ be two integer random variables ranging from 0 to t and from 0 to s, respectively, defined by taking $\tilde{M}$ in the datacube population $\sigma_{LB_{=0}}(M_{cs,F}^{-1})$. If $t_{i..j}^L = t^L = 0$ then for each $t_{i..j}$ and $s_{i..j}$, $0 \le t_{i..j} \le t_{i..j}^U$ and $0 \le s_{i..j} \le s$, the joint probability distribution $P(C_1([i..j]) = t_{i..j}, S_1([i..j]) = s_{i..j})$ is equal to:*

$$P(C_1([i..j]) = t_{i..j}, S_1([i..j]) = s_{i..j}) = \frac{Q(t_{i..j}^U, t_{i..j}, s_{i..j}) \cdot Q(t_{\tilde{i}..j}^U, t_{\tilde{i}..j}, s_{\tilde{i}..j})}{Q(t^U, t, s)}$$

where $t_{\tilde{i}..j} = t - t_{i..j}$, $s_{\tilde{i}..j} = s - s_{i..j}$, and

$$Q(\bar{t}_u, \bar{t}, \bar{s}) = \begin{cases} 0 & \text{if } (\bar{t} = 0 \wedge \bar{s} > 0) \vee (\bar{t} > 0 \wedge \bar{s} < \bar{t}) \vee \bar{t} > \bar{t}_u \\ 1 & \text{if } \bar{t} = 0 \wedge \bar{s} = 0 \\ \binom{\bar{t}_u}{\bar{t}} \cdot \binom{\bar{s}-1}{\bar{s}-\bar{t}} & \text{otherwise.} \end{cases}$$

Proof. (Sketch) The probability distribution does not change if we reduce the size of the range and of the block by removing certain null elements. Therefore, the size of the block B_k is assumed to be t^U and, then, the size of the query query becomes $t_{i..j}^U$. We can now see the block as a vector, say V, of t^U elements with values in $[1..s]$ such that their total sum is s and the number of non null elements is t. We divide V into two subvectors V' and V'' such that V' consists of the first $t_{i..j}^U$ elements and V'' of the last $t_{\tilde{i}..j}^U = t^U - t_{i..j}^U$ ones. The probability of the event $(C_1([i..j]) = t_{i..j} \wedge S_1([i..j]) = s_{i..j})$ is then equal to the probability that V' contains $t_{i..j}$ non-null elements whose sum is $s_{i..j}$. Let denote by $\bar{P}$ this probability. Observe that the event implies that V'' contains $t - t_{i..j}$ non null-elements whose sum is $s - s_{i..j}$. It is then easy to see that $\bar{P}$ is equal to

$$\frac{Q(t_{i..j}^U, t_{i..j}, s_{i..j}) \cdot Q(t^U - t_{i..j}^U, t - t_{i..j}, s - s_{i..j})}{Q(t^U, t, s)}$$

where $Q(\bar{t}_u, \bar{t}, \bar{s})$ is the number of possible configurations for a vector of size $\bar{t}_u$ containing exactly $\bar{t}$ non-null elements with total sum $\bar{s}$.

$Q(\bar{t}_u, \bar{t}, \bar{s})$ can be determined by considering all possible ways of distributing the sum $\bar{s}$ into $\bar{t}$ non-fixed positions by assigning to each of such elements a value from 1 to s. If we fix the positions of the $\bar{t}$ non-null elements,we obtain that the number of such configurations is:

$$m(\bar{t}, \bar{s}) = \binom{\bar{t} + (\bar{s} - \bar{t}) - 1}{\bar{s} - \bar{t}} = \binom{\bar{s} - 1}{\bar{s} - \bar{t}}.$$

As the positions for the $\bar{t}$ non-null elements are not fixed, we have to multiply $m(\bar{t}, \bar{s})$ by the number of all possible dispositions of $\bar{t}$ non-nulls over xd positions, that is

$$n(\bar{t}_u, \bar{t}) = \binom{\bar{t}_u}{\bar{t}}.$$

Hence, $Q(\bar{t}_u, \bar{t}, \bar{s}) = n(\bar{t}_u, \bar{t}) \cdot m(\bar{t}, \bar{s})$. □

Mean and variance of the random variable $C_1([i..j])$ are presented in the next proposition.

Proposition 1. *Let $C_1([i..j])$ be the random variables defined in Theorem 1. Then, mean and variance are, respectively:*

$$E(C_1([i..j])) = \frac{t_{i..j}^U}{t^U} \cdot t$$

$$\sigma^2(C_1([i..j])) = t \cdot (t^U - t) \cdot t_{i,j}^U \cdot \frac{t_{i..j}^U}{(t^U)^2 \cdot (t^U - 1)}$$

Proof. (Sketch) Consider the vector V, V' and V'' defined in the proof of Theorem 1. The event $(C_1([i..j]) = t_{i..j})$ is equivalent to the event that V' contains exactly $t_{i..j}$ non-null elements. Observe that the probabilty that an element is not null is equal to t/t^U. Hence $(C_1([i..j]) = t_{i..j})$ is in turn equivalent to the event of extracting $t_{i..j}$ non-nulls from V in $t_{i..j}^U$ trials. This probability is described by the well-known hypergeometric distribution [7]. □

Now we determine mean and variance of the random variable $S_1([i..j])$.

Theorem 2. *Consider the random variable $S_1([i..j])$ defined in Theorem 1. Then, mean and variance of $S_1([i..j])$ are, respectively:*

$$E(S_1([i..j])) = \frac{t_{i..j}^U}{t^U} \cdot s$$

$$\sigma^2(S_1([i..j])) = \frac{s \cdot t_{i,j}^U \cdot t_{i..j}^U}{t^{U2} \cdot (t^U - 1) \cdot (t + 1)} \cdot [t^U \cdot (2 \cdot s - t + 1) - s \cdot (t + 1)].$$

Proof. (Sketch) Consider the vector V, V' and V'' defined in the proof of Theorem 1. The event $(S_1([i..j]) = s_{i..j})$ is equivalent to the following event: the sum of all elements in V' is $s_{i..j}$. From $s = \sum_{1 \leq i < t^U} V[i]$, we derive $s = \sum_{1 \leq i < t^U} E(V[i])$ by linearity of the operator E. Further, the mean of random variable $V[i]$ is equal to the mean of the random variable $V[j]$, for any i, j, $1 \leq i, j \leq t^U$. Indeed, for symmetry, the probability that an element of V assumes a given value is independent on the position of this element inside the vector. Let denote by m this mean. From the above formula for s it then follows that $m \cdot t^U = s$, thus $t = s/t^U$. Consider now the vector V'. Let S' be the random variable representing the sum of all elements of V'. Then $E(S') = t^U_{i..j} \cdot m$. Hence, $E(S') = t^U_{i..j} \cdot s/t^U$.

The variance can be obtained using its definition. To this end, we first need to determine the probability distribution of $S_1([i..j])$ from the joint probability distribution obtained in Theorem 1. The detailed proof is rather elaborated and, for the sake of presentation, is included in the appendix. □

Note that the mean of the random variable $S_1([i..j])$ representing the sum query does not depend on the number t of non-null elements in the block B_k. On the other hand, the knowledge about certain null elements derived by the function $LB_{=0}$ does influence the value of the sum. Indeed, the mean depends both on the size of the query range w.r.t. the size of the block and on the number of the nulls that are already known to be in the range and in the complementary part of the block.

5   Case 2: Range Query Estimation Using Both Lower Bounds and Upper Bounds on the Number of Non-null Elements

We are now ready to perform the estimation of range queries in the general case where the datacube population is the set $\sigma_{LB_{=0}, LB_{>0}}(M^{-1}_{cs,F})$ of all datacubes having the same aggregate data (count and sum) as M and satisfying both constraints: the lower bound on the number of null elements occurring in each range and the lower bound on the number of non-null elements.

Theorem 3. *Let $C_2([i..j]) = count(\tilde{M}[i..j])$ and $S_2([i..j]) = sum(\tilde{M}[i..j])$ be two integer random variable ranging from 0 to t and from 0 to s, respectively, defined by taking $\tilde{M}$ in the datacube population $\sigma_{LB_{=0}, LB_{>0}}(M^{-1}_{cs,F})$. Then, for each $t_{i..j}$ and $s_{i..j}$, $t^L_{i..j} \leq t_{i..j} \leq t^U_{i..j}$ and $0 \leq s_{i..j} \leq s$, the joint probability distribution $P(C_2([i..j]) = t_{i..j}, S_2([i..j]) = s_{i..j})$ is equal to:*

$$P(C_2([i..j]) = t_{i..j}, S_2([i..j]) = s_{i..j}) = \frac{N(t^U_{i..j}, t_{i..j}, s_{i..j}, t^L_{i..j}) \cdot N(t^U_{\tilde{i..j}}, t_{\tilde{i..j}}, s_{\tilde{i..j}}, t^L_{\tilde{i..j}})}{N(t^U, t, s, t^L)}$$

where $t_{\widetilde{i..j}} = t - t_{i..j}$, $s_{\widetilde{i..j}} = s - s_{i..j}$, and

$$N(\bar{t}_u, \bar{t}, \bar{s}, \bar{t}_l) = \begin{cases} 0 & \text{if } \bar{t} > \bar{t}_u \vee \bar{t} > \bar{s} \vee (\bar{t} = 0 \wedge \bar{s} > 0) \\ 1 & \text{if } \bar{t} = 0 \wedge \bar{s} = 0 \\ \left(\dfrac{\bar{t}_u - \bar{t}_l}{\bar{t} - \bar{t}_l}\right) \cdot \left(\dfrac{\bar{s} - 1}{\bar{s} - \bar{t}}\right) & \text{otherwise} \end{cases}$$

Proposition 2. *Consider the random variable* $C_2([i..j])$ *of Theorem 3. Then, mean and variance are:*

$$E(C_2([i..j])) = t_{i..j}^L + \frac{t_{i..j}^U - t_{i..j}^L}{t^U - t^L} \cdot (t - t^L)$$

$$\sigma^2(C_2([i..j])) = \frac{t_{i..j}^U - t_{i..j}^L}{t^U - t^L} \cdot (t - t^L) \cdot \frac{[(t^U - t^L) - (t_{i..j}^U - t_{i..j}^L)] \cdot (t^U - t)}{(t^U - t^L) \cdot (t^U - t^L - 1)}$$

Theorem 4. *Consider the random variable* $S_2([i..j])$ *of Theorem 3. Then, mean and variance are:*

$$E(S_2([i..j])) = t_{i..j}^L \cdot \frac{s}{t} + (t_{i..j}^U - t_{i..j}^L) \cdot \frac{s}{t} \cdot \frac{t - t^L}{t^U - t^L}.$$

$$\sigma^2(S_2([i..j])) = \alpha \cdot (t_{i..j}^U - t_{i..j}^L) \cdot \frac{t - t^L}{t^U - t^L} \cdot \left[1 + (t_{i..j}^U - t_{i..j}^L - 1) \cdot \frac{t - t^L - 1}{t^U - t^L - 1}\right] +$$
$$(\beta + 2 \cdot \alpha \cdot t_{i..j}^L) \cdot (t_{i..j}^U - t_{i..j}^L) \cdot \frac{t - t^L}{t^U - t^L} + (\alpha \cdot t_{i..j}^{L\,2} + \beta \cdot t_{i..j}^L) - \gamma^2$$

where:

$$\alpha = \frac{s \cdot (s+1)}{t \cdot (t+1)}, \beta = \frac{s \cdot (s-t)}{t \cdot (t+1)} \text{ and } \gamma = t_{i..j}^L \cdot \frac{s}{t} + (t_{i..j}^U - t_{i..j}^L) \cdot \frac{s}{t} \cdot \frac{t - t^L}{t^U - t^L}.$$

Note that, unlike the case 1, the mean $S_2([i..j])$ of the random variable representing the sum query depends on the number t of non null elements occurring in the block B_k. Indeed, in this case, the information encoded in the function $LB_{>0}$ actually invalidates the symmetry condition about the aggregate information used for the estimation, on which the independence of the mean from t is based. This happens since $LB_{>0}$ returns a number of certain non-null elements, thus giving a positive contribution both to the count and the sum query. Thus, such positions cannot be eliminated in order to re-formulate the query into a new query applied on a block with indistinguishable positions as it happens for the Case 1.

Also in this case, the mean is not in general a linear function respect to the size of the query, since it depends both on $t_{i..j}^U$ (and then on $LB_{=0}([i..j])$) and on $t_{i..j}^L$ (and then on $LB_{>0}([i..j])$). Thus, once again, the estimation depends on the actual distribution of the values inside the block and not only on the aggregate information concerning count and sum of the block.

6 Estimation of Range Queries on Histograms

Histograms are mono-dimensional compressed datacube that are used to summarize the frequency distribution of an attribute of a database relation for the estimation of query result sizes [14,15,16]. The estimation is made using aggregate data such as the number t of non-null values in each block (bucket in the histogram terminology) B_k, the total frequency sum s in B_k and the boundaries of B_k. A crucial point for providing good estimations is the way the frequency distributions for original values are partitioned into buckets. Here we assume that the buckets have been already arranged using any of the known techniques and we therefore focus on the problem of estimating the frequency distribution inside a bucket.

The most common approach is based on the *continuous value assumption* [17]: the sum of frequencies in a range of a bucket is estimated by linear interpolation. It thus corresponds to equally distributing the overall sum of frequencies of the bucket to all attribute values occurring in it. This result can be derived from Theorem 2 by assuming that there are no integrity constraints on the number of null and non-null elements.

Corollary 1. *Let B_k be a block of a histogram and let $S_3([i..j]) = sum(\tilde{M}[i..j])$ be an integer random variable ranging from 0 to s, defined by taking $\tilde{M}$ in the datacube population $M_{cs,F}^{-1}$. Then mean and variance of $S_3([i..j])$ are, respectively:*

$$E(S_3([i..j])) = \frac{b_{i..j}}{b} \cdot s$$

$$\sigma^2(S_3([i..j])) = \frac{s \cdot b_{i..j} \cdot (b - b_{i..j})}{b^2 \cdot (b-1) \cdot (t+1)} \cdot [b \cdot (2 \cdot s - t + 1) - s \cdot (t+1)].$$

Thus our approach gives a model to explain the linear interpolation and, besides, allows to evaluate the error of the estimation, thus exploiting the knowledge about the number t of non-nulls in a block — instead t is not mentioned in the computation of the mean.

We now recall that the classical definition of histogram requires that both lowest and highest elements (or at least one of them) of any block are not null (i.e., they are attribute values occurring in the relation). A block for which the extreme elements are not null are called *2-biased*; if only the lowest (or the highest) element is not null then the block is called *1-biased*.

So far linear interpolation is also used for biased blocks thus producing a wrong estimation — it is the case to say a "biased" estimation. We next show the correct formulas that are derived from Theorem 4.

Corollary 2. *Let B_k be a block of a histogram and let $S_4([i..j]) = sum(\tilde{M}[i..j])$ be an integer random variable ranging from 0 to s, defined by taking $\tilde{M}$ in the datacube population $\sigma_{LB_{>0}}(M_{cs,F}^{-1})$. Then*

1. *if the block B_k is 1-biased and* i *is the lowest element of the block then mean and variance of $S_4([i..j])$ are, respectively:*

$$E(S_4([i..j])) = \frac{s}{t} + (b_{i..j} - 1) \cdot \frac{s}{t} \cdot \frac{t-1}{b-1},$$

$$\sigma^2(S_4([i..j])) = \alpha \cdot (b_{i..j} - 1) \cdot \tfrac{t-1}{b-1} \cdot \left[1 + (b_{i..j} - 2) \cdot \tfrac{t-2}{b-2}\right] + (\beta + 2 \cdot \alpha) \cdot (b_{i..j} - 1) \cdot \tfrac{t-1}{b-1} + (\alpha + \beta) - E(S_4([i..j]))^2$$

2. *if the block B_k is 1-biased and* i *is not the lowest element of the block then mean and variance of $S_4([i..j])$ are, respectively:*

$$E(S_4([i..j])) = b_{i..j} \cdot \frac{s}{t} \cdot \frac{t-1}{b-1},$$

$$\sigma^2(S_4([i..j])) = \alpha b_{i..j} \cdot \frac{t-1}{b-1} \cdot \left[1 + (b_{i..j} - 1) \cdot \frac{t-2}{b-2}\right] + \beta \cdot b_{i..j} \cdot \frac{t-1}{b-1} - E(S_4([i..j]))^2$$

3. *if the block B_k is 2-biased and either* i *or* j *is an extreme element of the block then mean and variance of $S_4([i..j])$ are, respectively:*

$$E(S_4([i..j])) = \frac{s}{t} + (b_{i..j} - 1) \cdot \frac{s}{t} \cdot \frac{t-2}{b-2},$$

$$\sigma^2(S_4([i..j])) = \alpha \cdot (b_{i..j} - 1) \cdot \tfrac{t-2}{b-2} \cdot \left[1 + (b_{i..j} - 2) \cdot \tfrac{t-3}{b-3}\right] + (\beta + 2 \cdot \alpha) \cdot (b_{i..j} - 1) \cdot \tfrac{t-2}{b-2} + (\alpha + \beta) - E(S_4([i..j]))^2$$

4. *if the block B_k is 2-biased and neither* i *nor* j *is an extreme element of the block then mean and variance of $S_4([i..j])$ are, respectively:*

$$E(S_4([i..j])) = b_{i..j} \cdot \frac{s}{t} \cdot \frac{t-2}{b-2},$$

$$\sigma^2(S_4([i..j])) = \alpha b_{i..j} \cdot \frac{t-2}{b-2} \cdot \left[1 + (b_{i..j} - 1) \cdot \frac{t-3}{b-3}\right] + \beta \cdot b_{i..j} \cdot \frac{t-2}{b-2} - E(S_4([i..j]))^2$$

where:

$$\alpha = \frac{s \cdot (s+1)}{t \cdot (t+1)} \text{ and } \beta = \frac{s \cdot (s-t)}{t \cdot (t+1)}.$$

The above formulas have been used in [4] to replace the continuous value assumption inside one of the most efficient methods for histogram representation (the maxdiff method [16]) and have produced some meaningful improvements in the performance of the method.

In [16,15], another method for estimating frequency sum inside a block is proposed, based on the *uniform spread assumption*: the t non-null attribute values in each bucket are assumed to be located at equal distance from each other and the overall frequency sum is therefore equally distributed among them. This method does not give a correct estimation unless we assume that nun-nulls are scattered on the block in some particular, unrealistic way. Our approach gives instead an unbiased estimation.

References

1. S. Acharya, P.B. Gibbons, Poosala, S. Ramaswamy. Join Synopses for Approximate Query Answering, In *Proc. of SIGMOD International Conference On Management Of Data* June 1999.

2. Barbara, D., DuMouchel, W., Faloutsos, C., Haas, P.J., Hellerstein, J.M., Ionnidis, Y., Jagadish, H.V., Johnson, T., Ng, R., Poosala, V., Ross, K.A., Sevcik, K.C., The New Jersey data reduction report, *Bulletin of the Technical Committee on Data Engineering 20*, 4, 3-45, 1997.

3. Buccafurri, F., Rosaci, D., Sacca', D., Compressed datacubes for fast OLAP applications, *DaWaK 1999*, Florence, 65-77.

4. Buccafurri, F., Pontieri, L., Rosaci, D., Sacca', D., Improving Range Query Estimation on Histograms, unpublished manuscript, 2000.

5. Chaudhuri, S., Dayal, U., An Overview of Data Warehousing and OLAP Technology, *ACM SIGMOD Record 26(1)*, March 1997.

6. C. Faloutsos, H. V. Jagadish, N. D. Sidiripoulos. Recovering Information from Summary Data. In *Proceedings of the 1997 VLDB Very Large Data Bases Conference*, Athens, 1997

7. W. Feller, *An introduction to probability theory and its applications.* John Wiley & Sons, 1968.

8. P. B. Gibbons and Y. Matias. New sampling-based summary statistics for improving approximate query answers. In *Proceedings of the 1998 ACM SIGMOD International Conference on Management of Data*, Seattle, Washington, June 1998

9. P.B.Gibbons, Y.Matias, V.Poosala. AQUA Project White Paper, At *http://www.bell-labs.com/user/pbgibbons/papers*, 1997.

10. P.B.Gibbons, Y.Matias, V.Poosala. Fast incremental maintenance of approximate histograms, *Proc. of the 23rd VLDB Conf.*, 466-475, August 1997.

11. Gray, J., Bosworth, A., Layman, A., Pirahesh, H., Data Cube: A Relational Aggregation Operator Generalizing Group-By, Cross-Tab, and Sub-Total, *Proc. of the ICDE 1996*, pp. 152-159

12. J. M. Hellerstein, P. J. Haas, H. J. Wang. Online Aggregation. In *Proceedings of 1997 ACM SIGMOD International Conference on Management of Data*, pages 171-182, 1997

13. Harinarayan, V., Rajaraman, A., Ullman, J. D., Implementing Data Cubes Efficiently, *Proc. of the ACM SIGMOD 1996*, pp. 205-216

14. Y. Ioannidis, V. Poosala. Balancing histogram optimality and practicality for query result size estimation. In *Proceedings of the 1995 ACM SIGMOD International Conference on Management of Data*, pages 233-244, 1995

15. V. Poosala. *Histogram-based Estimation Techniques in Database Systems.* PhD dissertation, University of Wisconsin-Madison, 1997

16. V. Poosala, Y. E. Ioannidis, P. J. Haas, E. J. Shekita. Improved histograms for selectivity estimation of range predicates. In *Proceedings of the 1996 ACM SIGMOD International Conference on Management of Data*, pages 294-305, 1996

17. P. G. Selinger, M. M. Astrahan, D. D. Chamberlin, R. A. Lorie, and T. T. Price. Access path selection in a relational database management system. In *Proc. of ACM SIGMOD Internatinal Conference*, pages 23-24, 1979

18. J. S. Vitter, M. Wang, B. Iyer. Data Cube Approximation and Histograms via Wavelets. In *Proceedings of the 1998 CIKM International Conference on Information and Knowledge Management*, Washington, 1998

Constraint-Based Clustering in Large Databases

Anthony K. H. Tung[1], Jiawei Han[1], Laks V.S. Lakshmanan[2], and
Raymond T. Ng[3]

[1] Simon Fraser University, {khtung, han}@cs.sfu.ca
[2] IIT – Bombay & Concordia U, laks@cs.concordia.ca
[3] University of British Columbia, rng@cs.ubc.ca

Abstract. Constrained clustering—finding clusters that satisfy user-specified constraints—is highly desirable in many applications. In this paper, we introduce the constrained clustering problem and show that traditional clustering algorithms (e.g., k-means) cannot handle it. A scalable constraint-clustering algorithm is developed in this study which starts by finding an initial solution that satisfies user-specified constraints and then refines the solution by performing confined object movements under constraints. Our algorithm consists of two phases: *pivot movement* and *deadlock resolution*. For both phases, we show that finding the optimal solution is NP-hard. We then propose several heuristics and show how our algorithm can scale up for large data sets using the heuristic of *micro-cluster sharing*. By experiments, we show the effectiveness and efficiency of the heuristics.

1 Introduction

Cluster analysis has been an active area of research in computational statistics and data mining with many algorithms developed. However, few algorithms incorporate user-specific constraints in cluster analysis. Many studies show that constraint-based mining is highly desirable since it often leads to effective and fruitful data mining by capturing application semantics [NLHP98, KPR98,LNHP99]. This is also the case in cluster analysis.

Formally, the unconstrained clustering problem can be defined as follows.
Unconstrained Clustering (UC): Given a data set D with n objects, a distance function $df : D \times D \longrightarrow \Re$, and a positive integer k, find a k-*clustering*, i.e., a partition of D into k disjoint clusters $(Cl_1, \ldots, Cl_k)$ such that $DISP = (\sum_{i=1}^{k} disp(Cl_i, rep_i))$ is minimized.

The "dispersion" of cluster Cl_i, $disp(Cl_i, rep_i)$, measures the total distance between each object in Cl_i and the *representative* rep_i of Cl_i, i.e., $disp(Cl_i, rep_i)$ is defined as $\sum_{p \in Cl_i} df(p, rep_i)$. The representative of a cluster Cl_i is chosen such that $disp(Cl_i, rep_i)$ is minimized. Finding such a representative for each cluster is generally not difficult. For example, the k-means algorithm uses the centroid of the cluster as its representative, which can be calculated in linear time.

The constrained clustering problem can be defined as follows.
Constrained Clustering (CC): Given a data set D with n objects, a distance function $df : D \times D \longrightarrow \Re$, a positive integer k, and *a set of constraints $\mathcal{C}$*, find a k-*clustering*

J. Van den Bussche and V. Vianu (Eds.): ICDT 2001, LNCS 1973, pp. 405–419, 2001.
© Springer-Verlag Berlin Heidelberg 2001

$(Cl_1, \ldots, Cl_k)$ such that $DISP = (\sum_{i=1}^{k} disp(Cl_i, rep_i))$ is minimized, and *each cluster Cl_i satisfies the constraints C, denoted as $Cl_i \models C$.*

A fundamental difference between the UC and CC problems is that the unconstrained clustering algorithms are designed to find clusterings satisfying the *nearest rep(resentative) property* (NRP), defined below, whereas for the CC problem, the NRP may conflict with constraint satisfaction.

The Nearest Rep(resentative) Property (NRP): Let $(Cl_1, \ldots, Cl_k)$ be the k-clustering computed by the algorithm, and let rep_i denote the representative of cluster Cl_i, $1 \le i \le k$. Then a data object $p \in D$ is placed in a cluster Cl_j iff rep_j is the closest to p among all the representatives, i.e., $(\forall p \in D)(\forall 1 \le j \le k)$ $[p \in Cl_j \Leftrightarrow (\forall i \ne j)$ $df(p, rep_j) \le df(p, rep_i)]$.

In this paper, we study the CC problem. A taxonomy of constraints useful in applications is presented in Section 2. In Section 3, we review works related to the CC problem, and in Section 4, we analyze the major challenges of CC. In Section 5, we develop an algorithm for CC under an existential constraint. In Section 6, we study how to scale up our algorithm by *micro-cluster sharing*. The experiments evaluating the effectiveness of the proposed heuristics are reported in Section 7. Section 8 discusses the handling of other SQL aggregate constraints, and Section 9 concludes the paper.

2   A Taxonomy of Constraints for Clustering

Depending on the nature of the constraints and applications, the CC problem can be classified into the following categories.

1. Constraint on individual objects: This constraint confines the set of objects to be clustered, e.g., cluster only luxury mansions of value over one million dollars. It can be easily handled by preprocessing (e.g., performing selection using an SQL query), after which the problem reduces to an instance of the UC problem.
2. Obstacle objects as constraints: A city may have rivers, bridges, highways, lakes, mountains, etc. Such obstacles and their effects can be captured by redefining the distance functions $df()$ among objects. Once that is done, the problem again reduces to an instance of the UC problem.
3. Clustering parameters as "constraints": Some "constraints" may serve as the parameters in a clustering algorithm, e.g., the number of clusters, k. Such parameters, though specifiable by users, are not considered as constraints in our study.
4. Constraints imposed on each individual cluster: This is the theme of our study. Within this class, we focus on constraints formulated with SQL aggregates.

Let each object O_i in the database D be associated with a set of m attributes $\{A_1, \ldots, A_m\}$. The value of an attribute A_j of an object O_i is denoted as $O_i[A_j]$.

Definition 1 (SQL Aggregate Constraints). Consider the aggregate functions $agg \in \{max(), min(), avg(), sum()\}$. Let θ be a comparator function, i.e.,

$\theta \in \{<, \leq, \neq, =, \geq, >\}$, and c represent a numeric constant. Given a cluster Cl, an SQL aggregate constraint on Cl is a constraint in one of the following forms: (i) $agg(\{O_i[A_j] \mid O_i \in Cl\}) \; \theta \; c$; or (ii) $count(Cl) \; \theta \; c$. □

In this paper, we mainly focus on one type of constraints, called **existential constraints**:

Definition 2 (Existential Constraints). Let $W \subset D$ be any subset of objects. We call them **pivot** objects. Let c be a positive integer. An **existential constraint** on a cluster Cl is a constraint of the form: $count(\{O_i | O_i \in Cl, O_i \in W\}) \geq c$. □

Pivot objects are typically specified via constraints or other predicates. For example, in a market segmentation problem, pivot objects might be *frequent customers*. See Section 8 for a discussion on the generality of existential constraints.

3   Related Work

Cluster analysis has been an active area in computational statistics and data mining. Clustering methods can be categorized into partitioning methods [KR90, NH94], hierarchical methods [KR90,ZRL96], density-based methods [EKSX96], grid-based methods [WYM97,AGGR98], and model-based methods [HaKa00]. However, none of the existing methods incorporates user-specified constraints.

A problem somewhat similar to the CC problem is the facility location problem [STA97], mostly studied in operational research and theoretical computer science. It tries to locate k facilities to serve n customers such that the traveling distance from the customers to their facility is minimized. However, the only type of constraints they studied are constraints on the capacity of the facility, i.e., each facility can only serve a limited number of customers. If we assume that customers cannot be "split" between two facilities (as we do for CC), the resultant solution will require an increase both in the number of facilities and in the capacity of these facilities. However, if the customers can be "split", only the number of facilities needs to be increased. Such an increase in number of facilities and capacity is inappropriate for the CC problem as we treat user's constraints as hard constraints.

Since CC is a kind of constrained optimization problem, mathematical programming naturally comes to mind. Our concern, however, is its scalability with respect to a large database. To cluster n customers into k clusters, a mathematical programming approach will involve at least $k \times n$ variables. As n can be as large as a few millions, it is very expensive to perform mathematical programming. As can be seen later, our solution for handling a very large dataset involves a novel concept called *micro-cluster sharing*. This may correspond to dynamic combining and splitting of equations in a mathematical program, which has not been considered in mathematical programming but could be an interesting future direction for performing mathematical programming in large databases.

4   The Nearest Representative Property (NRP)

We first consider the theoretical implication of adding constraints to clustering, by examining the popular k-means algorithm although the discussion generalizes to other algorithms, such as the k-medoids algorithm.

Given a set of constraints $\mathcal{C}$, a "solution" space for the CC problem is defined as,

$$ClSp(\mathcal{C}, k, D) = \{(Cl_1, \ldots, Cl_k) \mid \forall 1 \leq i, j \leq k : \emptyset \subset Cl_j \subset D \ \& \ Cl_j \models \mathcal{C} \ \& $$
$$\cup \, Cl_j = D \ \& \ Cl_i \cap Cl_j = \emptyset, \text{ for } i \neq j\}$$

We refer to $ClSp(\mathcal{C}, k, D)$ as the (constrained) clustering space. Clusterings found by the k-means algorithm satisfy the NRP. Accordingly, the *constrained mean solution space* is defined as:

$$MeanSp(\mathcal{C}, k, D) = \{(Cl_1, \ldots, Cl_k) \mid (Cl_1, \ldots, Cl_k) \in ClSp(\mathcal{C}, k, D)$$
$$\& \ \forall 1 \leq j \leq k, \forall q \in D : (q \in Cl_j \ \Leftrightarrow \ (\forall i \neq j : df(q, p_j) \leq df(q, p_i)))\}$$

where p_j is the centroid of cluster Cl_j. It should be clear by definition that the mean space $MeanSp()$ is a strict subset of the clustering space $ClSp()$. To understand the role played by the NRP, let us revisit the situation when the set of constraints $\mathcal{C}$ is empty. The k-means algorithm does the smart thing by operating in the smaller $MeanSp()$ space than in the $ClSp()$ space. More importantly, the following theorem says that there is no loss of quality. Unless stated otherwise, proofs of the results in this paper can be found in [TNLH00] but are omitted here for lack of space.

Theorem 1. A clustering $\mathcal{UCL}$ is an optimal solution to the UC problem in the space $ClSp(\emptyset, k, D)$ iff it is an optimal solution to the UC problem in the mean space $MeanSp(\emptyset, k, D)$.   □

Like virtually all existing clustering algorithms, the k-means algorithm does not attempt to find the global optimum. This is because the decision problem corresponding to k-clustering is NP-complete even for $k = 2$ [GJ79]. Thus, the k-means algorithm focuses on finding local optima. Theorem 1 can be generalized from the global optimum to a local optimum.

The point here is that $MeanSp(\emptyset, k, D)$ contains the "cream" of $ClSp$ $(\emptyset, k, D)$, in that the global and local optima in $ClSp(\emptyset, k, D)$ are also contained in the smaller $MeanSp(\emptyset, k, D)$. This nice situation, however, does not generalize to the CC problem. For example, suppose there are only four customers with three located close to each other at one end of a highway, and the fourth at the other end. If the CC problem is to find two clusters with (at least) two customers in each, it is easy to see that it is impossible to satisfy the constraint and the NRP simultaneously.

To resolve this conflict, we adopt the policy that the user-defined constraints take precedence over the NRP. Specifically, the algorithm to be presented next regards the set $\mathcal{C}$ to be hard constraints that must be satisfied. The NRP, on the other hand, is treated as a "soft" constraint in the sense that it is satisfied as much as possible by the minimization of ($\sum_{i=1}^{k} disp(Cl_i, rep_i)$). But there is no guarantee that every object is in the cluster corresponding to its nearest center.

5   Clustering without the Nearest Representative Property

In this section, we will develop an algorithm to perform CC under an existential constraint. An important difference of our method from the UC algorithms is that our algorithm tries to find a good solution by performing cluster refinement in the constraint space, $ClSp(C, k, D)$, which we represent using a *clustering locality graph*, $\mathcal{G} = (\mathcal{V}, \mathcal{E})$, described as follows:

- The set $\mathcal{V}$ of nodes is the set of all k-clusterings. More precisely, it is the unconstrained clustering space $ClSp(\emptyset, k, D)$. Nodes which satisfy existential constraint (EC) are called *valid nodes*, and those that do not are called *invalid nodes*.
- There is an edge e between two nodes $C\mathcal{L}_1, C\mathcal{L}_2$ in the graph iff they are different by only one pivot object, i.e., $C\mathcal{L}_1$ of the form $(Cl_1, \ldots, Cl_i, \ldots, Cl_j, \ldots, Cl_k)$, whereas $C\mathcal{L}_2$ of the form $(Cl_1, \ldots, Cl_i - \{p\}, \ldots, Cl_j \cup \{p\}, \ldots, Cl_k)$ for some pivot object $p \in Cl_i$ & $j \neq i$. If a node $C\mathcal{L}_2$ is connected to $C\mathcal{L}_1$ by an edge, then $C\mathcal{L}_2$ is called a *neighbor* of $C\mathcal{L}_1$ and vice versa.

With such a graph, a naive algorithm to solve the CC problem given k and EC is to first pick a valid node in the locality graph and move to a valid neighboring node which gives the highest decrease in $DISP$. Intuitively, such a node movement is a cluster refinement process similar to the k-means algorithm which tries to refine the clustering by moving objects to the nearest center to reduce $DISP$. The cluster refinement process terminates when no node of lower $DISP$ is found. The algorithm will then output $C\mathcal{L}$ as the solution. However, this is a generate-and-test algorithm which is inefficient since the number of neighbors of a node is potentially large. To improve its efficiency, the number of nodes to be examined needs to be restricted.

5.1   Cluster Refinement under Constraints

To derive a more efficient algorithm for CC, we first define a set of *unstable pivots* given a valid node $C\mathcal{L} = (Cl_1, \ldots Cl_k)$.

Definition 3. (Unstable Pivots) A set of unstable pivots, S, with respect to $C\mathcal{L}$ is a collection of all pivots in D such that each $s \in S$ belongs to some Cl_i in $C\mathcal{L}$ but s is nearer to a representative of some Cl_j, $j \neq i$. $\square$

Using S, we form a subgraph of $\mathcal{G}$, viz., $SG = (SV, SE)$, where the set of nodes SV is defined as follows: (1) (base case) the initial node $C\mathcal{L}$, representing the chosen valid clustering is in SV; (2) (inductive case) for any node $C\mathcal{L}$ in SV, if (i) there is an object s in Cl_i whose nearest cluster representative is in Cl_j, and (ii) $C\mathcal{L}$ is of the form $(Cl_1, \ldots, Cl_i, \ldots, Cl_k)$, then the node $C\mathcal{L}'$ of the form $(Cl_1, \ldots, Cl_i - \{s\}, \ldots, Cl_j \cup \{s\}, \ldots, Cl_k)$ is also in SV; and (3) there is no other node in SV. Intuitively, once S is defined, the subgraph SG includes all the nodes that are reachable from $C\mathcal{L}$ via the movements of some $s \in S$ to their nearest cluster. Let us denote the $DISP$ of any node v with respect to a set of representatives REP as $DISP_{REP}(v)$.

Theorem 2. $DISP_{REP'}(CL') \leq DISP_{REP}(CL)$ *for any nodes* CL, CL' *in* SG *as above, REP and REP' being the set of representatives for CL and CL' respectively.*

Proof: Let $REP = (rep_1, ..., rep_k)$ and $REP' = (rep'_1, ..., rep'_k)$. The dispersion of CL' calculated with respect to REP will be $DISP_{REP}(CL') = (\sum_{i=1}^{k} disp(Cl'_i, rep_i))$.

We first observe that

$$DISP_{REP}(CL') \leq DISP_{REP}(CL)$$

This is because the set of representatives is the same on both sides of the inequality and since CL' can be obtained by moving some $s \in S$ to their nearest representative in REP, the reduction in dispersion will result in the above observation. On the other hand, since REP' is a set of representatives for CL', by definition they will minimize the dispersion for $Cl'_1, ..., Cl'_k$, we thus have the following inequality,

$$DISP_{REP'}(CL') \leq DISP_{REP}(CL')$$

By combining these two inequalities together, we have

$$DISP_{REP'}(CL') \leq DISP_{REP}(CL') \leq DISP_{REP}(CL) \quad \square$$

By Theorem 2, we conclude that our clusters can in fact be refined just by searching SG. There are two advantages to doing this. First, our efficiency improves because the number of nodes to be searched is reduced, and the movement always leads to progressive refinement in clustering quality. This in itself does *not* guarantee the chosen neighbor is valid. Second, instead of considering only neighbors, SG allows us to consider nodes that are many steps away.

Given SG, we adopt the steepest descent approach and plan a path along the valid nodes of SG which leads to a new valid node CL' with minimized dispersion in SG. We call this problem the *Best Path (BP) Problem*. To plan the path, only unstable pivots in a surplus cluster (cluster which have more objects than required by EC) can be moved. We call such an object, a *movable* object. To gain more insight into the BP problem and to derive an algorithm for solving it, we introduce a concept called *pivot movement graph* which can be used to represent the state of clustering in each node of SG.

Definition 4. *(Pivot Movement Graph)* A *pivot movement graph* is a directed graph in which each cluster is represented by a node. An edge from Cl_i to Cl_j indicates that there is at least one unstable pivot object in Cl_i that has Cl_j as its nearest center. These objects are represented as labels on the edge. The reduction in $DISP$ when an unstable object is moved to its nearest center is shown next to each of these objects. $\square$

Figure 1 shows an example of a pivot movement graph which is under the constraint "$\forall i, count(Cl_i) \geq 50$". As such, the surplus clusters at this instance are Cl_1, Cl_3 and Cl_5. Figure 2 shows the actual situation depicted by the pivot movement graph in Figure 1. For clarity, only the unstable pivots and the cluster representatives (marked by a "×") are shown. Given a pivot movement graph, a *Pivot Movement (PM)* problem is the problem of computing a schedule of movements for the unstable objects in the graph such that the total reduction in $DISP$ is maximized.

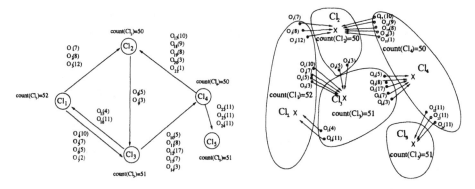

Fig. 1. A Pivot Movement Graph   **Fig. 2.** The Actual Situation.

Theorem 3. *The BP problem is equivalent to the PM problem.*

Proof: Given an optimized solution for BP, we follow the path given in the solution and move the pivots in the corresponding pivot movement graph. This will give a maximized reduction in dispersion. Similarly, if an optimized schedule is given for PM, we can follow the schedule and move along a path where each node in the path corresponds to a state of the pivot movement graph when the schedule is followed. This will bring us to a node with minimized dispersion in SG. □

Given their equivalence, it suffices to focus on the PM problem.

Definition 5. (The PM Decision Problem) Given a pivot movement graph and an existential constraint EC, the PM decision problem is to determine whether there is a schedule of movements of objects around the clusters such that EC is satisfied at all times and the total dispersion being reduced is $\geq B$ where B is a numeric constant. □

Two observations hint at the difficulty of this problem. (1) The movement of an unstable pivot object could possibly trigger a series of movements of other unstable pivot objects. For example, by moving O_3 from Cl_1 to Cl_2, Cl_2 now has 51 pivot objects, and thus we could move O_8 from Cl_2 to Cl_3. We refer to such a series of triggerings as a **movement path**. (2) Given a surplus cluster with more than one outgoing edge, the choice of the outgoing edge that minimizes $DISP$ in the resultant movement path is not obvious. Indeed we can show:

Theorem 4. The PM decision problem is NP-complete.
Proof: See [TNLH00]. □

Furthermore, by using a result given in [KMR97], we can show that it is not possible to compute in polynomial time a constant factor approximation for the PM problem. Thus, an alternative is to use heuristics which could work well in practice and efficient enough for handling a large dataset. The purpose of the heuristic is to iteratively pick an edge in the pivot movement graph and move an unstable object on the edge to its nearest representative thus forming a schedule of movements for the unstable pivots.

We experiment with two heuristics. The first is a **random heuristic** in which a random edge is selected from those edges that originate from a surplus cluster; whereas the second is a **look-ahead** l heuristic which looks ahead at all possible movement paths originating from a surplus cluster, of length up to l, and selects the best among them. The selected movement path is then activated, resulting in a movement of up to l objects depending on the length of the path. Since there are at most $k(k-1)$ edges, there are at most $O(k(k-1)^{l+1})$ movement paths. While there exist optimization strategies that can avoid examining all the qualifying movement paths of length l, the worst case complexity of this heuristic remains $O(k(k-1)^{l+1})$. Thus, the value of l is designed to be a small integer.

Using these heuristics, our corresponding movement in $\mathcal{SG}$ will eventually reach a node $\mathcal{CL}''$ where future movement is no more possible. We then repeat the process and form a new subgraph $\mathcal{SG}$ for processing.

5.2   Handling Tight Existential Constraints

While the cluster refinement algorithm discussed earlier works well under most constraints, problem arises when the constraint EC is tight, i.e., when it is nearly impossible to be satisfied. For example, given $k = 5$, $|D| = 100$ and $EC = \{count(Cl_i) \geq 20\}, 1 \leq i \leq 5$, our algorithm may get into a *deadlock cycle*. A sequence of clusters $\langle Cl_1, \ldots, Cl_k, Cl_1 \rangle$ is said to be in a *deadlock cycle* of length k if (a) all the clusters are non-surplus; and (b) there is an edge in the pivot movement graph from Cl_i to $Cl_{i+1}, 1 \leq i \leq k-1$ and one from Cl_k to Cl_1, respectively.

In terms of the graph, $\mathcal{SG}$, a tight EC means that $\mathcal{SG}$ contains a large number of invalid nodes and refining the clusters by movement through only valid nodes is not possible. In view of this, a deadlock resolution phase is added before computing a new subgraph $\mathcal{SG}$. The objective of the deadlock resolution phase is to provide a mechanism to jump over a set of invalid nodes by resolving deadlock in the pivot movement graph. Similar to the PM problem, we can prove (in a way similar to that for Theorem 4) that resolving deadlock optimally is NP hard.

Similarly, we can show that there is also no constant factor approximation algorithm for the deadlock resolution problem which runs in polynomial time. Thus, we resort to the following heuristic based on a randomized strategy. It conducts a depth-first search on the pivot movement graph to find any deadlock cycle. Suppose the deadlock cycle detected is $\langle Cl_1, \ldots, Cl_k, Cl_1 \rangle$. Let n_i denote the number of unstable pivot objects appearing as labels on the edge from Cl_i to Cl_{i+1}. Then let n_{max} denote the minimum n_i value among the edges in the cycle, i.e., $n_{max} = min_{1 \leq i \leq k}\{n_i\}$. This marks the *maximum* number of unstable objects that can be moved across the *entire* cycle without violating EC. Once the n_{max} value has been determined, the heuristic would move the unstable pivot objects with the top-n_{max} highest reduction in $DISP$ across each edge of the cycle causing the cycle to be broken.

5.3 Local Optimality and Termination

Having introduced our algorithm, we will now look at its formal properties by analyzing the two main phases of the algorithm: *pivot movement* and *deadlock resolution*. Our algorithm essentially iterates through these two phases and computes a new subgraph SG at the end of each iteration.

Local Optimality Result. Having modeled our cluster refinement algorithm as a graph search, we would like to establish that at the end of each iteration, the clustering obtained corresponds to a local minimum in the subgraph SG. However, since all dispersion of nodes in SG is actually computed with respect to the cluster representatives of CL, when there is a pivot movement, say object p moved from Cl_i to Cl_j, both the representatives of Cl_i and that of Cl_j change, and the set of unstable pivots S can also change, which means that SG itself must be recomputed. This process is time-consuming, especially for our look-ahead heuristic which must recompute SG every step it looks ahead. Because of this, we choose to freeze the representatives of each cluster and avoid the recomputation of SG. As such, the cost of each node CL in the subgraph SG is not the true dispersion but rather the "approximated" dispersion, denoted as $\widehat{disp}(CL)$, relative to the fixed representatives. Now we can establish the following result. Intuitively, at the end of the pivot movement phase, no surplus cluster in the pivot movement graph has an outgoing edge. Thus, it is not possible to find a valid neighbor of the current one that has a lower dispersion.

Lemma 1. The clustering obtained at the end of the pivot movement phase is a local minimum in the subgraph SG, where cost is based on approximated dispersion $\widehat{disp}(CL)$. $\square$

Interestingly, a deadlock cycle of length k corresponds to a path $\langle CL_1, \ldots, CL_{k+1}\rangle$ in SG, such that the first node/clustering CL_1 and the last node CL_{k+1} are valid, but *all the other nodes are not*. This is a very interesting phenomenon because resolving a deadlock cycle amounts to jumping from one valid node to another via a sequence of invalid nodes in SG. In particular, if deadlock cycles are resolved after the pivot movement phase as in our algorithm, then we jump from a valid local minimum to another (which is not a neighbor) with a strictly lower value of dispersion.

Lemma 2. The clustering obtained at the end of the deadlock resolution phase is a local minimum in the subgraph SG, where cost is based on approximated dispersion $\widehat{disp}(CL)$. $\square$

Termination of the Algorithm. Since each move in the graph SG corresponds to a reduction in the number of unstable pivot objects, and the number of unstable pivot objects is finite, both the object movement phase and deadlock resolution phase will terminate. Moreover, since we move to a node of lower $DISP$ for every iteration, and G is a finite clustering space, it is impossible to have the $DISP$ value decreasing forever. Thus, the algorithm terminates.

6   Scaling the Algorithm by Micro-Cluster Sharing

For clustering large, disk-resident databases, many studies have adopted a *micro-clustering* methodology (e.g., [ZRL96,WYM97,BFR98,KHK99]), which "compresses" data objects into *micro-clusters* in a pre-clustering phase so that the subsequent clustering activities can be accomplished at the micro-cluster level. To ensure that not much quality is lost, a maximum radius on a micro-cluster is imposed.

By micro-clustering, in our cluster refinement, instead of moving one unstable object across the edges of a pivot movement graph at a time, we have to move one micro-cluster. However, since each micro-cluster can contain more than one pivot object, it may not be possible to move a micro-cluster away from a surplus cluster without invalidating the constraint. Similar complication arises when resolving deadlock since there is no guarantee that for each edge in a cycle, the total number of pivot objects in the micro-clusters to be moved add up to exactly n_{max}.

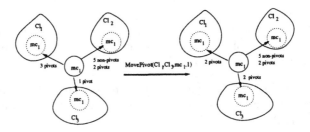

Fig. 3. An Example of Micro-cluster Sharing

To resolve these problems, we introduce a novel concept called *micro-cluster sharing*. Given a micro-cluster with n non-pivot objects and m pivot objects, the n non-pivot objects will always be allocated to the nearest cluster, while the m pivot objects can be shared among multiple clusters. For example, consider Figure 3 in which micro-cluster mc_1 is formed from 5 non-pivot objects and 6 pivot objects. It is shared by three clusters, Cl_1, Cl_2 and Cl_3. Since Cl_2 is the nearest to mc_1, it owns all 5 of mc_1's non-pivot objects and also 2 pivot objects from mc_1. Cl_1, on the other hand, contains 3 pivot objects from mc_1, while Cl_3 has 1 pivot object from mc_1.

To record the sharing or "splitting" of mc_1 into multiple clusters, we use the notation $Cl_i.mc_1$ to represent the part of mc_1 that is in Cl_i. During the pivot movement and deadlock resolution phases, if p objects of $Cl_i.mc_1$ are to be moved to Cl_j, the algorithm calls a function MovePivot(Cl_i, Cl_j, mc_1, p) which updates the numbers in $Cl_i.mc_1$ and $Cl_j.mc_1$ accordingly. In Figure 3, MovePivot(Cl_1, Cl_3, mc_1, 1) moves one pivot object from $Cl_1.mc_1$ to $Cl_3.mc_1$.

Given the MovePivot() function, the problem of being unable to shift micro-clusters around the clusters is effectively solved since the micro-clusters can now be dynamically split and combined to cater to the condition for swapping. Since the number of objects in a micro-cluster is small enough for all of them to fit in main memory, the above heuristic requires a minimum amount of I/O.

The remaining issue that we need to address is at the end of clustering, how to determine the *actual objects* in a micro-cluster mc that are to be assigned to $Cl_1, \ldots, Cl_q$, where these are all the clusters for which $Cl_i.mc$ is positive. We adopt the following greedy heuristic: For all the non-pivot objects in mc, they are all assigned to the nearest center/cluster. This is to reduce $DISP$ as much as possible. Consider the set of distances defined as: $\{df(O, Cl_i) \mid O$ is a pivot object in mc, and $1 \leq i \leq q\}$. Sort this set of distances in ascending order. Based on this order, the pivot objects are assigned to the cluster as near as possible, while satisfying the numbers recorded in $Cl_1.mc, \ldots, Cl_q.mc$.

7 Performance Analysis

We report our performance study, which evaluates the efficiency and effectiveness of the proposed heuristics. All the experiments were performed on a 450Mhz Intel Celeron, with 64MB of main memory, and an IBM 7200 rpm disk-drive.

Two datasets were used in our experiments. The first, DS1, is a dataset of a courier company for planning collection centers based on the locations of their frequent customers (see [TNLH00]). The second, DS2, is synthetic, generated following the synthetic datasets used in [ZRL96]. For lack of space, we report our experiments on DS2 only.

For the constraints, we made all data objects to be pivot objects in order to give most vigorous tests to our algorithms. Micro-clustering in our experiments was done using the CF-tree in the BIRCH algorithm [ZRL96] which only needs to scan through the database once. Note that BIRCH is used here as a pre-processing step and it's data structure is not utilized in any part of our algorithm.

To separate the different heuristics used in our algorithms, we denote an algorithm as **RandLS** if it uses the *random heuristic* in pivot movement and **LAHLS-1** if *look-ahead-l heuristic*. For the micro-cluster sharing version of the two algorithms, the term "Micro" is added, i.e., **MicroRandLS** and **MicroLAHLS-1**.

Our synthetic dataset was generated using a modification of the synthetic dataset from [ZRL96], with skewed density distribution for testing the scalability of our algorithms and how constraints affect the clustering of a dataset. Essentially, there was a $M \times M$ grid in which cluster centers were placed. The distance between neighboring centers in the same row or column was set to 1. For a cluster centered at the coordinate $(row, column)$, $((row - 1) \times M + column) \times 50$ points were generated following a 2-d normal distribution with center at $(row, column)$ and variance 0.5^2. By design, the density of the synthetic data was skewed, being least dense at the top-left corner of the grid and most dense at the bottom-right. The value of M was varied from 4 to 8, generating datasets with various sizes and numbers of clusters. Figure 5 shows the parameters used for each dataset.

As shown in Figure 6(a), the order of effectiveness of the various algorithms generally remains unchanged with *LAHLS* giving the best quality of clustering. The running times of both *MicroRandLS* and *MicroLAHLS-4* remain relatively low as both $|D|$ and k increase. For a dataset with 104000 tuples, the running times of *MicroRandLS* and *MicroLAHLS-4* were around 1100 and 1500 seconds respectively.

To see the effect that an existential constraint has on the clustering, we look at the output of *MicroLAHLS-4* in Figure 4 which shows a synthetic dataset with $M = 8$. The clustering was done with the existential constraint of "$count(Cl_i) \geq 812$" imposed. Since the actual clusters that were generated near the top-left corner generally contained less than 812 points, there was a shift of cluster centers from the top-left corner towards the dense region at the bottom-right corner.

To summarize, our experimental results show that the our algorithm is effective for constrained clustering. Among the heuristics, micro-cluster sharing clearly delivers good efficiency and scalability. The gain in efficiency far offsets the small loss in quality. Finally, the look-ahead heuristic with small l (e.g., 4) appears to be the best candidate for pivot movement.

M	k	$|D|$	c	No. of Micro-clusters
4	16	6800	212	1410
5	25	16250	325	2523
6	36	33300	462	4050
7	49	61250	625	7079
8	64	104000	812	8253

Fig. 4. 64 Clusters with $\geq$ 812 Objects Each.

Fig. 5. Parameters for Synthetic Dataset.

8   Discussion: Handling Other SQL Aggregate Constraints

We have presented a cluster refinement algorithm which handles a *single existential constraint*. In this section, we first examine how the algorithm can be extended to handle constraints containing single SQL aggregate, where the constrains are classified into five classes (see Table 1) based on their behavior with respect to constrained clustering: *existential, existential-like, universal, averaging,* and *summation*.

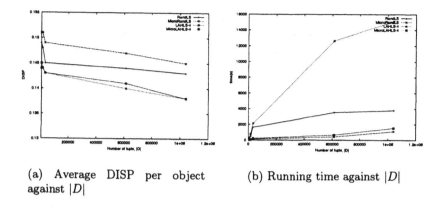

(a) Average DISP per object against $|D|$

(b) Running time against $|D|$

Fig. 6. Performance of Various Algorithms as $|D|$ Varies.

Table 1. A Classification of SQL Constraints

	$<$ or $\leq$	$\neq$	$=$	$>$ or $\geq$
min	existential	existential-like	existential-like	universal
max	universal	existential-like	existential-like	existential
count	existential-like	existential-like	existential	existential
avg	averaging	averaging	averaging	averaging
sum	summation	summation	summation	summation

1. Universal constraints: These are constraints in which a specific condition must be satisfied by *every* object in a cluster. For example, $min(\{O_i[A_j]|O_i \in Cl_i\}) \geq c$ requires that every object's A_j-value be $\geq c$. This can be reduced to the UC problem as discussed for constraints on individual objects in Section 2.

2. Existential-like constraints: These constraints are similar in nature to existential constraints, and our algorithm can handle them with simple modification. For example, $count(Cl_i) \leq c$ is an existential-like constraint. Instead of moving surplus objects around, the objective here is to move "holes" around to achieve the maximum reduction in $DISP$. If a cluster Cl_i contains m objects, $m < c$, it has $c - m$ holes, meaning that $c - m$ objects can still be moved into it. When an object is moved from Cl_j into Cl_i, a hole is moved from Cl_i into Cl_j. Correspondingly, a *hole movement graph* can be generated which could be used to guide movement in the locality graph.

3. Averaging and Summation constraints. For these kinds of constraints, even computing an initial solution is an NP-hard problem similar to a bin-packing or knapsack problem [GJ79]. Handling general averaging and summation constraints in clustering is an interesting problem for future work.

Finally, we consider the situation when there are multiple conjunctive existential constraints. The local search algorithm can easily be modified to handle existential constraints when the sets of pivot objects for these constraints do not overlap. The algorithm can then set up a different pivot movement graph for each constraint, and move the pivot objects in different graphs independently. However, for situations where the sets of pivot objects do overlap, again we can show even computing an initial solution is NP-hard. Handling multiple general existential constraints is another interesting problem for future work.

9   Conclusions

In this paper, we introduced and studied the constrained clustering problem, a problem which arises naturally in practice, but barely addressed before. A (constrained) cluster refinment algorithm is developed, which includes two phases of movement in a clustering locality graph: *pivot movement* and *deadlock resolution*. Our experimental results show that both phases are valuable. To scale up the algorithm for large databases, we proposed a micro-cluster sharing strategy whose effectiveness is also verified by our experiments. Our algorithm can also be extended to handle some other kinds of constraints, however, handling general averaging and summation constraints, as well as handling general multiple existential constraints, are interesting topics for future research. Thanks to a reviewer of this paper, we have come to know of a recent study by Bradley et al. [BBD00] on a version of constrained clustering problem similar to ours. Unlike us, their main motivation is using cardinality constraints for better quality clustering. Scalability and applicability to other types of constraints are not addressed. Despite these differences, a quantitative comparison between the two approaches would be an interesting future work.

References

[AGGR98] R. Agrawal, J. Gehrke, D. Gunopulos, and P. Raghavan. Automatic subspace clustering of high dimensional data for data mining applications. In *SIGMOD'98*.

[BBD00] P. Bradley, K. P. Bennet, and A. Demiriz. Constrained k-means clustering. In *MSR-TR-2000-65*, Microsoft Research, May 2000.

[BFR98] P. Bradley, U. Fayyad, and C. Reina. Scaling clustering algorithms to large databases. In *KDD'98*.

[EKSX96] M. Ester, H.-P. Kriegel, J. Sander, and X. Xu. A density-based algorithm for discovering clusters in large spatial databases. In *KDD'96*.

[GJ79] M. Garey and D. Johnson. *Computers and Intractability: a Guide to The Theory of NP-Completeness*. Freeman and Company, New York, 1979.

[HaKa00] J. Han and M. Kamber *Data Mining: Concepts and Techniques*. Morgan Kaufmann, 2000.

[KHK99] G. Karypis, E.-H. Han, and V. Kumar. CHAMELEON: A hierarchical clustering algorithm using dynamic modeling. *COMPUTER*, 32:68–75, 1999.

[KMR97] D. Karger, R. Motwani, and G. D. S. Ramkumar. On approximating the longest path in a graph. *Algorithmica*, 18:99–110, 1997.

[KPR98]   J. M. Kleinberg, C. Papadimitriou, and P. Raghavan. A microeconomic view of data mining. *Data Mining and Knowledge Discovery*, 2:311–324, 1998.

[KR90]   L. Kaufman and P. J. Rousseeuw. *Finding Groups in Data: an Introduction to Cluster Analysis*. John Wiley & Sons, 1990.

[LNHP99] L. V. S. Lakshmanan, R. Ng, J. Han, and A. Pang. Optimization of constrained frequent set queries with 2-variable constraints. In *SIGMOD'99*.

[NH94]   R. Ng and J. Han. Efficient and effective clustering method for spatial data mining. In *VLDB'94*.

[NLHP98] R. Ng, L. V. S. Lakshmanan, J. Han, and A. Pang. Exploratory mining and pruning optimizations of constrained associations rules. In *SIGMOD'98*.

[STA97]   D. B. Shmoys, E. Tardos, and K. Aardal. Approximation algorithms for facility location problems. In *STOC'97*.

[TNLH00] A. K. H. Tung, R. Ng, L. Lakshmanan, and J. Han. Constraint-based clustering in large databases. www.cs.sfu.ca/pub/cs/techreports/2000/CMPT2000-05.pdf.

[WYM97]   W. Wang, J. Yang, and R. Muntz. STING: A statistical information grid approach to spatial data mining. In *VLDB'97*.

[ZRL96]   T. Zhang, R. Ramakrishnan, and M. Livny. BIRCH: an efficient data clustering method for very large databases. In *SIGMOD'96*.

On the Surprising Behavior of Distance Metrics in High Dimensional Space

Charu C. Aggarwal[1], Alexander Hinneburg[2], and Daniel A. Keim[2]

[1] IBM T. J. Watson Research Center
Yorktown Heights, NY 10598, USA.
charu@watson.ibm.com
[2] Institute of Computer Science, University of Halle
Kurt-Mothes-Str.1, 06120 Halle (Saale), Germany
{ hinneburg, keim }@informatik.uni-halle.de

Abstract. In recent years, the effect of the curse of high dimensionality has been studied in great detail on several problems such as clustering, nearest neighbor search, and indexing. In high dimensional space the data becomes sparse, and traditional indexing and algorithmic techniques fail from a efficiency and/or effectiveness perspective. Recent research results show that in high dimensional space, the concept of proximity, distance or nearest neighbor may not even be qualitatively meaningful. In this paper, we view the dimensionality curse from the point of view of the distance metrics which are used to measure the similarity between objects. We specifically examine the behavior of the commonly used L_k norm and show that the problem of meaningfulness in high dimensionality is sensitive to the value of k. For example, this means that the Manhattan distance metric (L_1 norm) is consistently more preferable than the Euclidean distance metric (L_2 norm) for high dimensional data mining applications. Using the intuition derived from our analysis, we introduce and examine a natural extension of the L_k norm to fractional distance metrics. We show that the fractional distance metric provides more meaningful results both from the theoretical and empirical perspective. The results show that fractional distance metrics can significantly improve the effectiveness of standard clustering algorithms such as the k-means algorithm.

1   Introduction

In recent years, high dimensional search and retrieval have become very well studied problems because of the increased importance of data mining applications [1], [2], [3], [4], [5], [8], [10], [11]. Typically, most real applications which require the use of such techniques comprise very high dimensional data. For such applications, the curse of high dimensionality tends to be a major obstacle in the development of data mining techniques in several ways. For example, the performance of similarity indexing structures in high dimensions degrades rapidly, so that each query requires the access of almost all the data [1].

J. Van den Bussche and V. Vianu (Eds.): ICDT 2001, LNCS 1973, pp. 420–434, 2001.

It has been argued in [6], that under certain reasonable assumptions on the data distribution, the ratio of the distances of the nearest and farthest neighbors to a given target in high dimensional space is almost 1 for a wide variety of data distributions and distance functions. In such a case, the nearest neighbor problem becomes ill defined, since the contrast between the distances to different data points does not exist. In such cases, even the concept of proximity may not be meaningful from a qualitative perspective: a problem which is even more fundamental than the performance degradation of high dimensional algorithms.

In most high dimensional applications the choice of the distance metric is not obvious; and the notion for the calculation of similarity is very heuristical. Given the non-contrasting nature of the distribution of distances to a given query point, different measures may provide very different orders of proximity of points to a given query point. There is very little literature on providing guidance for choosing the correct distance measure which results in the most meaningful notion of proximity between two records. Many high dimensional indexing structures and algorithms use the euclidean distance metric as a natural extension of its traditional use in two- or three-dimensional spatial applications. In this paper, we discuss the general behavior of the commonly used L_k norm $(x, y \in \mathcal{R}^d, k \in \mathcal{Z},\ L_k(x, y) = \sum_{i=1}^{d}(\|x^i - y^i\|^k)^{1/k})$ in high dimensional space. The L_k norm distance function is also susceptible to the dimensionality curse for many classes of data distributions [6]. Our recent results [9] seem to suggest that the L_k-norm may be more relevant for $k = 1$ or 2 than values of $k \geq 3$. In this paper, we provide some surprising theoretical and experimental results in analyzing the dependency of the L_k norm on the value of k. More specifically, we show that the relative contrasts of the distances to a query point depend heavily on the L_k metric used. This provides considerable evidence that the meaningfulness of the L_k norm worsens faster with increasing dimensionality for higher values of k. Thus, for a given problem with a fixed (high) value of the dimensionality d, it may be preferable to use lower values of k. This means that the L_1 distance metric (Manhattan Distance metric) is the most preferable for high dimensional applications, followed by the Euclidean Metric (L_2), then the L_3 metric, and so on. Encouraged by this trend, we examine the behavior of *fractional* distance metrics, in which k is allowed to be a fraction smaller than 1. We show that this metric is even more effective at preserving the meaningfulness of proximity measures. We back up our theoretical results with empirical tests on real and synthetic data showing that the results provided by fractional distance metrics are indeed practically useful. Thus, the results of this paper have strong implications for the choice of distance metrics for high dimensional data mining problems. We specifically show the improvements which can be obtained by applying fractional distance metrics to the standard k-means algorithm.

This paper is organized as follows. In the next section, we provide a theoretical analysis of the behavior of the L_k norm in very high dimensionality. In section 3, we discuss fractional distance metrics and provide a theoretical analysis of their behavior. In section 4, we provide the empirical results, and section 5 provides summary and conclusions.

2   Behavior of the L_k-Norm in High Dimensionality

In order to present our convergence results, we first establish some notations and definitions in Table 1.

Table 1. Notations and Basic Definitions

Notation	Definition
d	Dimensionality of the data space
N	Number of data points
$\mathcal{F}$	1-dimensional data distribution in $(0,1)$
X_d	Data point from $\mathcal{F}^d$ with each coordinate drawn from $\mathcal{F}$
$dist_d^k(x,y)$	Distance between $(x^1, \ldots x^d)$ and $(y^1, \ldots y^d)$ using L_k metric $= \sum_{i=1}^{d} [(x_1^i - x_2^i)^k]^{1/k}$
$\| \cdot \|_k$	Distance of a vector to the origin $(0, \ldots, 0)$ using the function $dist_d^k(\cdot, \cdot)$
$Dmax_d^k = \max\{\|X_d\|_k\}$	Farthest distance of the N points to the origin using the distance metric L_k
$Dmin_d^k = \min\{\|X_d\|_k\}$	Nearest distance of the N points to the origin using the distance metric L_k
$E[X]$, $var[X]$	Expected value and variance of a random variable X
$Y_d \rightarrow_p c$	A vector sequence $Y_1, \ldots, Y_d$ converges in probability to a constant vector c if: $\forall \epsilon > 0\ lim_{d \to \infty} P[dist_d(Y_d, c) \le \epsilon] = 1$

Theorem 1. Beyer et. al. (Adapted for L_k metric)
If $lim_{d \to \infty}\ var\left(\frac{\|X_d\|_k}{E[\|X_d\|_k]}\right) = 0$, then $\frac{Dmax_d^k - Dmin_d^k}{Dmin_d^k} \rightarrow_p 0$.

Proof. See [6] for proof of a more general version of this result.

The result of the theorem [6] shows that the difference between the maximum and minimum distances to a given query point [1] does not increase as fast as the nearest distance to any point in high dimensional space. This makes a proximity query meaningless and unstable because there is poor discrimination between the nearest and furthest neighbor. Henceforth, we will refer to the ratio $\frac{Dmax_d^k - Dmin_d^k}{Dmin_d^k}$ as *the relative contrast.*

The results in [6] use the value of $\frac{Dmax_d^k - Dmin_d^k}{Dmin_d^k}$ as an interesting criterion for meaningfulness. In order to provide more insight, in the following we analyze the behavior for different distance metrics in high-dimensional space. We first assume a uniform distribution of data points and show our results for $N = 2$ points. Then, we generalize the results to an arbitrary number of points and arbitrary distributions.

---

[1] In this paper, we consistently use the origin as the query point. This choice does not affect the generality of our results, though it simplifies our algebra considerably.

Lemma 1. *Let $\mathcal{F}$ be uniform distribution of $N = 2$ points. For an L_k metric,*
$$lim_{d\to\infty} E\left[\frac{Dmax_d^k - Dmin_d^k}{d^{1/k-1/2}}\right] = C \cdot \left(\frac{1}{(k+1)^{1/k}}\right)\sqrt{\left(\frac{1}{2 \cdot k+1}\right)}, \text{ where } C \text{ is some con-}$$
stant.

Proof. Let A_d and B_d be the two points in a d dimensional data distribution such that each coordinate is independently drawn from a 1-dimensional data distribution $\mathcal{F}$ with finite mean and standard deviation. Specifically $A_d = (P_1 \ldots P_d)$ and $B_d = (Q_1 \ldots Q_d)$ with P_i and Q_i being drawn from $\mathcal{F}$. Let $PA_d = \{\sum_{i=1}^{d}(P_i)^k\}^{1/k}$ be the distance of A_d to the origin using the L_k metric and $PB_d = \{\sum_{i=1}^{d}(Q_i)^k\}^{1/k}$ the distance of B_d. The difference of distances is $PA_d - PB_d = \{\sum_{i=1}^{d}(P_i)^k\}^{1/k} - \{\sum_{i=1}^{d}(Q_i)^k\}^{1/k}$.

It can be shown [2] that the random variable $(P_i)^k$ has mean $\frac{1}{k+1}$ and standard deviation $\left(\frac{k}{k+1}\right)\sqrt{\left(\frac{1}{2\cdot k+1}\right)}$. This means that $\frac{(PA_d)^k}{d} \to_p \frac{1}{(k+1)}$, $\frac{(PB_d)^k}{d} \to_p \frac{1}{(k+1)}$ and therefore

$$\frac{PA_d}{d^{1/k}} \to_p \left(\frac{1}{k+1}\right)^{1/k}, \quad \frac{PB_d}{d^{1/k}} \to_p \left(\frac{1}{k+1}\right)^{1/k} \tag{1}$$

We intend to show that $\frac{|PA_d-PB_d|}{d^{1/k-1/2}} \to_p \left(\frac{1}{(k+1)^{1/k}}\right)\sqrt{\left(\frac{2}{2\cdot k+1}\right)}$. We can express $|PA_d - PB_d|$ in the following numerator/denominator form which we will use in order to examine the convergence behavior of the numerator and denominator individually.
$$|PA_d - PB_d| = \frac{|(PA_d)^k - (PB_d)^k|}{\sum_{r=0}^{k-1}(PA_d)^{k-r-1}(PB_d)^r} \tag{2}$$

Dividing both sides by $d^{1/k-1/2}$ and regrouping the right-hand-side we get:
$$\frac{|PA_d - PB_d|}{d^{1/k-1/2}} = \frac{|((PA_d)^k - (PB_d)^k)|/\sqrt{d}}{\sum_{r=0}^{k-1}\left(\frac{PA_d}{d^{1/k}}\right)^{k-r-1}\left(\frac{PB_d}{d^{1/k}}\right)^r} \tag{3}$$

Consequently, using Slutsky's theorem [3] and the results of Equation 1 we obtain
$$\sum_{r=0}^{k-1}\left(\frac{PA_d}{d^{1/k}}\right)^{k-r-1} \cdot \left(\frac{PB_d}{d^{1/k}}\right)^r \to_p k \cdot \left(\frac{1}{k+1}\right)^{(k-1)/k} \tag{4}$$

Having characterized the convergence behavior of the denominator of the right hand side of Equation 3, let us now examine the behavior of the numerator:
$|(PA_d)^k - (PB_d)^k|/\sqrt{d} = |\sum_{i=1}^{d}((P_i)^k - (Q_i)^k)|/\sqrt{d} = |\sum_{i=1}^{d}R_i|/\sqrt{d}$. Here R_i is the new random variable defined by $((P_i)^k - (Q_i)^k) \; \forall i \in \{1, \ldots d\}$. This random variable has zero mean and standard deviation which is $\sqrt{2} \cdot \sigma$ where

---

[2] This is because $E[P_i^k] = 1/(k+1)$ and $E[P_i^{2k}] = 1/(2 \cdot k + 1)$.

[3] **Slutsky's Theorem:** Let $Y_1 \ldots Y_d \ldots$ be a sequence of random vectors and $h(\cdot)$ be a continuous function. If $Y_d \to_p c$ then $h(Y_d) \to_p h(c)$.

σ is the standard deviation of $(P_i)^k$. The sum of different values of R_i over d dimensions will converge to a normal distribution with mean 0 and standard deviation $\sqrt{2} \cdot \sigma \cdot \sqrt{d}$ because of the central limit theorem. Consequently, the mean average deviation of this distribution will be $C \cdot \sigma$ for some constant C. Therefore, we have:

$$\lim_{d \to \infty} E\left[\frac{|(PA_d)^k - (PB_d)^k|}{\sqrt{d}}\right] = C \cdot \frac{k}{k+1}\sqrt{\frac{1}{2 \cdot k + 1}} \qquad (5)$$

Since the denominator of Equation 3 shows probabilistic convergence, we can combine the results of Equations 4 and 5 to obtain

$$\lim_{d \to \infty} E\left[\frac{|PA_d - PB_d|}{d^{1/k - 1/2}}\right] = C \cdot \frac{1}{(k+1)^{1/k}}\sqrt{\frac{1}{2 \cdot k + 1}} \qquad (6)$$

We can easily generalize the result for a database of N uniformly distributed points. The following Corollary provides the result.

Corollary 1. *Let $\mathcal{F}$ be the uniform distribution of $N = n$ points. Then,*
$$\left(\frac{C}{(k+1)^{1/k}}\right)\sqrt{\left(\frac{1}{2 \cdot k + 1}\right)} \le \lim_{d \to \infty} E\left[\frac{Dmax_d^k - Dmin_d^k}{d^{1/k - 1/2}}\right] \le \left(\frac{C \cdot (n-1)}{(k+1)^{1/k}}\right)\sqrt{\left(\frac{1}{2 \cdot k + 1}\right)}.$$

Proof. This is because if L is the expected difference between the maximum and minimum of two randomly drawn points, then the same value for n points drawn from the same distribution must be in the range $(L, (n-1) \cdot L)$.

The results can be modified for arbitrary distributions of N points in a database by introducing the constant factor C_k. In that case, the general dependency of $Dmax - Dmin$ on $d^{\frac{1}{k} - \frac{1}{2}}$ remains unchanged. A detailed proof is provided in the Appendix; a short outline of the reasoning behind the result is available in [9].

Lemma 2. *[9] Let $\mathcal{F}$ be an arbitrary distribution of $N = 2$ points. Then,*
$$\lim_{d \to \infty} E\left[\frac{Dmax_d^k - Dmin_d^k}{d^{1/k - 1/2}}\right] = C_k, \text{ where } C_k \text{ is some constant dependent on } k.$$

Corollary 2. *Let $\mathcal{F}$ be the arbitrary distribution of $N = n$ points. Then,*
$$C_k \le \lim_{d \to \infty} E\left[\frac{Dmax_d^k - Dmin_d^k}{d^{1/k - 1/2}}\right] \le (n-1) \cdot C_k.$$

Thus, this result shows that in high dimensional space $Dmax_d^k - Dmin_d^k$ increases at the rate of $d^{1/k - 1/2}$, independent of the data distribution. This means that for the manhattan distance metric, the value of this expression diverges to ∞; for the Euclidean distance metric, the expression is bounded by constants whereas for all other distance metrics, it converges to 0 (see Figure 1). Furthermore, the convergence is faster when the value of k of the L_k metric increases. This provides the insight that higher norm parameters provide poorer contrast between the furthest and nearest neighbor. Even more insight may be obtained by examining the exact behavior of the relative contrast as opposed to the absolute distance between the furthest and nearest point.

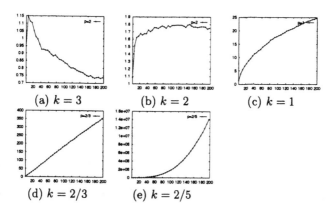

(a) $k = 3$ (b) $k = 2$ (c) $k = 1$

(d) $k = 2/3$ (e) $k = 2/5$

Fig. 1. $|Dmax - Dmin|$ depending on d for different metrics (uniform data)

Table 2. Effect of dimensionality on relative (L_1 and L_2) behavior of relative contrast

Dimensionality	$P[U_d < T_d]$		Dimensionality	$P[U_d < T_d]$
1	Both metrics are the same		10	95.6%
2	85.0%		15	96.1%
3	88.7%		20	97.1%
4	91.3%		100	98.2%

Theorem 2. *Let $\mathcal{F}$ be the uniform distribution of $N = 2$ points. Then,*

$$\lim_{d \to \infty} E\left[\left(\frac{Dmax_d^k - Dmin_d^k}{Dmin_d^k}\right) \cdot \sqrt{d}\right] = C \cdot \sqrt{\frac{1}{2 \cdot k + 1}}.$$

Proof. Let A_d, B_d, $P_1 \dots P_d$, $Q_1 \dots Q_d$, PA_d, PB_d be defined as in the proof of Lemma 1. We have shown in the proof of the previous result that $\frac{PA_d}{d^{1/k}} \to \left(\frac{1}{k+1}\right)^{1/k}$. Using Slutsky's theorem we can derive that:

$$\min\{\frac{PA_d}{d^{1/k}}, \frac{PB_d}{d^{1/k}}\} \to \left(\frac{1}{k+1}\right)^{1/k} \tag{7}$$

We have also shown in the previous result that:

$$\lim_{d \to \infty} E\left[\frac{|PA_d - PB_d|}{d^{1/k-1/2}}\right] = C \cdot \left(\frac{1}{(k+1)^{1/k}}\right) \sqrt{\left(\frac{1}{2 \cdot k + 1}\right)} \tag{8}$$

We can combine the results in Equation 7 and 8 to obtain:

$$\lim_{d \to \infty} E\left[\sqrt{d} \cdot \frac{|PA_d - PB_d|}{\min\{PA_d, PB_d\}}\right] = C \cdot \sqrt{1/(2 \cdot k + 1)} \tag{9}$$

Note that the above results confirm of the results in [6] because it shows that the relative contrast degrades as $1/\sqrt{d}$ for the different distance norms. Note

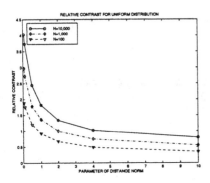

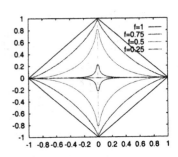

Fig. 2. Relative contrast variation with norm parameter for the uniform distribution

Fig. 3. Unit spheres for different fractional metrics (2D)

that for values of d in the reasonable range of data mining applications, the norm dependent factor of $\sqrt{1/(2 \cdot k + 1)}$ may play a valuable role in affecting the relative contrast. For such cases, even the relative rate of degradation of the different distance metrics for a given data set in the same value of the dimensionality may be important. In the Figure 2 we have illustrated the relative contrast created by an artificially generated data set drawn from a uniform distribution in $d = 20$ dimensions. Clearly, the relative contrast decreases with increasing value of k and also follows the same trend as $\sqrt{1/(2 \cdot k + 1)}$.

Another interesting aspect which can be explored to improve nearest neighbor and clustering algorithms in high-dimensional space is the effect of k on the relative contrast. Even though the expected relative contrast always decreases with increasing dimensionality, this may not necessarily be true for a given data set and different k. To show this, we performed the following experiment on the Manhattan (L_1) and Euclidean (L_2) distance metric: Let $U_d = \left(\frac{Dmax_d^2 - Dmin_d^2}{Dmin_d^2} \right)$ and $T_d = \left(\frac{Dmax_d^1 - Dmin_d^1}{Dmin_d^1} \right)$. We performed some empirical tests to calculate the value of $P[U_d < T_d]$ for the case of the Manhattan (L_1) and Euclidean (L_2) distance metrics for $N = 10$ points drawn from a uniform distribution. In each trial, U_d and T_d were calculated from the same set of $N = 10$ points, and $P[U_d < T_d]$ was calculated by finding the fraction of times U_d was less than T_d in 1000 trials. The results of the experiment are given in Table 2. It is clear that with increasing dimensionality d, the value of $P[U_d < T_d]$ continues to increase. *Thus, for higher dimensionality, the relative contrast provided by a norm with smaller parameter k is more likely to dominate another with a larger parameter.* For dimensionalities of 20 or higher it is clear that the manhattan distance metric provides a significantly higher relative contrast than the Euclidean distance metric with very high probability. Thus, among the distance metrics with integral norms, the manhattan distance metric is the method of choice for providing the best contrast between the different points. This result of our analysis can be directly used in a number of different applications.

3   Fractional Distance Metrics

The result of the previous section that the Manhattan metric ($k = 1$) provides the best discrimination in high-dimensional data spaces is the motivation for looking into distance metrics with $k < 1$. We call these metrics fractional distance metrics. A **fractional distance metric** $dist_d^f$ (L_f norm) for $f \in (0, 1)$ is defined as:

$$dist_d^f(x, y) = \sum_{i=1}^{d} \left[(x^i - y^i)^f \right]^{1/f}.$$

To give a intuition of the behavior of the fractional distance metric we plotted in Figure 3 the unit spheres for different fractional metrics in $\mathcal{R}^2$.

We will prove most of our results in this section assuming that f is of the form $1/l$, where l is some integer. The reason that we show the results for this special case is that we are able to use nice algebraic tricks for the proofs. The natural conjecture from the smooth continuous variation of $dist_d^f$ with f is that the results are also true for arbitrary values of f. [4]. Our results provide considerable insights into the behavior of the fractional distance metric and its relationship with the L_k-norm for integral values of k.

Lemma 3. *Let $\mathcal{F}$ be the uniform distribution of $N = 2$ points and $f = 1/l$ for some integer l. Then,*

$$\lim_{d \to \infty} E\left[\frac{Dmax_d^f - Dmin_d^f}{d^{1/f - 1/2}} \right] = C \cdot \left(\frac{1}{(f+1)^{1/f}} \right) \sqrt{\left(\frac{1}{2 \cdot f + 1} \right)}.$$

Proof. Let $A_d, B_d, P_1 \ldots P_d, Q_1 \ldots Q_d, PA_d, PB_d$ be defined using the L_f metric as they were defined in Lemma 1 for the L_k metric. Let further $QA_d = (PA_d)^f = (PA_d)^{1/l} = \sum_{i=1}^{d}(P_i)^f$ and $QB_d = (PB_d)^f = (PB_d)^{1/l} = \sum_{i=1}^{d}(Q_i)^f$. Analogous to Lemma 1, $\frac{QA_d}{d} \to_p \frac{1}{f+1}$, $\frac{QB_d}{d} \to_p \frac{1}{f+1}$.

We intend to show that $E\left[\frac{|PA_d - PB_d|}{d^{1/f - 1/2}} \right] = C \cdot \left(\frac{1}{(f+1)^{1/f}} \right) \sqrt{\left(\frac{1}{2 \cdot f + 1} \right)}$. The difference of distances is $|PA_d - PB_d| = \{ \sum_{i=1}^{d}(P_i)^f \}^{1/f} - \{ \sum_{i=1}^{d}(Q_i)^f \}^{1/f} = \{ \sum_{i=1}^{d}(P_i)^f \}^l - \{ \sum_{i=1}^{d}(Q_i)^f \}^l$. Note that the above expression is of the form $|a^l - b^l| = |a - b| \cdot (\sum_{r=0}^{l-1} a^r \cdot b^{l-r-1})$. Therefore, $|PA_d - PB_d|$ can be written as $\{ \sum_{j=1}^{d} |(P_i)^f - (Q_i)^f| \} \cdot \{ \sum_{r=0}^{l-1}(QA_d)^r \cdot (QB_d)^{l-r-1} \}$. By dividing both sides by $d^{1/f - 1/2}$ and regrouping the right hand side we get:

$$\frac{|PA_d - PB_d|}{d^{1/f - 1/2}} \to_p \{ \frac{\sum_{i=1}^{d} |(P_i)^f - (Q_i)^f|}{\sqrt{d}} \} \cdot \{ \sum_{r=0}^{l-1} \left(\frac{QA_d}{d} \right)^r \cdot \left(\frac{QB_d}{d} \right)^{l-r-1} \} \quad (10)$$

By using the results in Equation 10, we can derive that:

$$\frac{|PA_d - PB_d|}{d^{1/f - 1/2}} \to_p \{ \frac{\sum_{i=1}^{d} |(P_i)^f - (Q_i)^f|}{\sqrt{d}} \} \cdot \{ l \cdot \frac{1}{(1+f)^{l-1}} \} \quad (11)$$

---

[4] Empirical simulations of the relative contrast show this is indeed the case.

This random variable $(P_i)^f - (Q_i)^f$ has zero mean and standard deviation which is $\sqrt{2} \cdot \sigma$ where σ is the standard deviation of $(P_i)^f$. The sum of different values of $(P_i)^f - (Q_i)^f$ over d dimensions will converge to normal distribution with mean 0 and standard deviation $2 \cdot \sigma \cdot \sqrt{d}$ because of the central limit theorem. Consequently, the expected mean average deviation of this normal distribution is $C \cdot \sigma \cdot \sqrt{d}$ for some constant C. Therefore, we have:

$$\lim_{d \to \infty} E \left[\frac{|(PA_d)^f - (PB_d)^f|}{\sqrt{d}} \right] = C \cdot \sigma = C \cdot \left(\frac{f}{f+1} \right) \sqrt{\left(\frac{1}{2 \cdot f + 1} \right)}. \quad (12)$$

Combining the results of Equations 12 and 11, we get:

$$\lim_{d \to \infty} E \left[\frac{|PA_d - PB_d|}{d^{1/f - 1/2}} \right] = \left(\frac{C}{(f+1)^{1/f}} \right) \sqrt{\left(\frac{1}{2 \cdot f + 1} \right)} \quad (13)$$

An direct consequence of the above result is the following generalization to $N = n$ points.

Corollary 3. *When $\mathcal{F}$ is the uniform distribution of $N = n$ points and $f = 1/l$ for some integer l. Then, for some constant C we have:*

$$\left(\frac{C}{(f+1)^{1/f}} \right) \sqrt{\left(\frac{1}{2 \cdot f + 1} \right)} \leq \lim_{d \to \infty} E \left[\frac{Dmax_d^f - Dmin_d^f}{d^{1/f - 1/2}} \right] \leq \left(\frac{C \cdot (n-1)}{(f+1)^{1/f}} \right) \sqrt{\left(\frac{1}{2 \cdot f + 1} \right)}.$$

Proof. Similar to corollary 1.

The above result shows that the absolute difference between the maximum and minimum for the fractional distance metric increases at the rate of $d^{1/f - 1/2}$. Thus, the smaller the fraction, the greater the rate of absolute divergence between the maximum and minimum value. Now, we will examine the relative contrast of the fractional distance metric.

Theorem 3. *Let $\mathcal{F}$ be the uniform distribution of $N = 2$ points and $f = 1/l$ for some integer l. Then,*

$$\lim_{d \to \infty} \left(\frac{Dmax_d^f - Dmin_d^f}{Dmin_d^f} \right) \sqrt{d} = C \cdot \sqrt{\frac{1}{2 \cdot f + 1}} \text{ for some constant } C.$$

Proof. Analogous to the proof of Theorem 2.

The following is the direct generalization to $N = n$ points.

Corollary 4. *Let $\mathcal{F}$ be the uniform distribution of $N = n$ points, and $f = 1/l$ for some integer l. Then, for some constant C*

$$C \cdot \sqrt{\frac{1}{2 \cdot f + 1}} \leq \lim_{d \to \infty} E \left[\frac{Dmax_d^f - Dmin_d^f}{Dmin_d^f} \right] \leq C \cdot (n-1) \cdot \sqrt{\frac{1}{2 \cdot f + 1}}.$$

Proof. Analogous to the proof of Corollary 1.

This result is true for the case of arbitrary values f (not just $f = 1/l$) and N, but the use of these specific values of f helps considerably in simplification of the proof of the result. The empirical simulation in Figure 2, shows the behavior for arbitrary values of f and N. The curve for each value of N is different but all curves fit the general trend of reduced contrast with increased value of f. Note that the value of the relative contrast for both, the case of integral distance metric L_k and fractional distance metric L_f is the same in the boundary case when $f = k = 1$.

The above results show that fractional distance metrics provide better contrast than integral distance metrics both in terms of the absolute distributions of points to a given query point and relative distances. This is a surprising result in light of the fact that the Euclidean distance metric is traditionally used in a large variety of indexing structures and data mining applications. The widespread use of the Euclidean distance metric stems from the natural extension of applicability to spatial database systems (many multidimensional indexing structures were initially proposed in the context of spatial systems). However, from the perspective of high dimensional data mining applications, this natural interpretability in 2 or 3-dimensional spatial systems is completely irrelevant. Whether the theoretical behavior of the relative contrast also translates into practically useful implications for high dimensional data mining applications is an issue which we will examine in greater detail in the next section.

4   Empirical Results

In this section, we show that our surprising findings can be directly applied to improve existing mining techniques for high-dimensional data. For the experiments, we use synthetic and real data. The synthetic data consists of a number of clusters (data inside the clusters follow a normal distribution and the cluster centers are uniformly distributed). The advantage of the synthetic data sets is that the clusters are clearly separated and any clustering algorithm should be able to identify them correctly. For our experiments we used one of the most widely used standard clustering algorithms - the *k-means algorithm*. The data set used in the experiments consists of 6 clusters with 10000 data points each and no noise. The dimensionality was chosen to be 20. The results of our experiments show that the fractional distance metrics provides a much higher classification rate which is about 99% for the fractional distance metric with $f = 0.3$ versus 89% for the Euclidean metric (see figure 4). The detailed results including the confusion matrices obtained are provided in the appendix.

For the experiments with real data sets, we use some of the classification problems from the UCI machine learning repository [5]. All of these problems are classification problems which have a large number of feature variables, and a special variable which is designated as the class label. We used the following simple experiment: For each of the cases that we tested on, we *stripped off* the

---

[5] $http://www.cs.uci.edu/~mlearn$

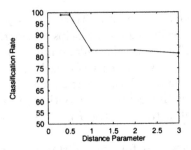

Fig. 4. Effectiveness of k-Means

class variable from the data set and considered the feature variables only. The query points were picked from the original database, and the closest l neighbors were found to each target point using different distance metrics. The technique was tested using the following two measures:

1. Class Variable Accuracy: This was the primary measure that we used in order to test the quality of the different distance metrics. Since the class variable is known to depend in some way on the feature variables, the proximity of objects belonging to the same class in feature space is evidence of the meaningfulness of a given distance metric. The specific measure that we used was the total number of the l nearest neighbors that belonged to the same class as the target object over all the different target objects. Needless to say, we do not intend to propose this rudimentary unsupervised technique as an alternative to classification models, but use the classification performance only as an evidence of the meaningfulness (or lack of meaningfulness) of a given distance metric. The class labels may not necessarily always correspond to locality in feature space; therefore the meaningfulness results presented are evidential in nature. However, a consistent effect on the class variable accuracy with increasing norm parameter does tend to be a powerful way of demonstrating qualitative trends.

2. Noise Stability: How does the quality of the distance metric vary with more or less noisy data? We used *noise masking* in order to evaluate this aspect. In noise masking, each entry in the database was replaced by a random entry with masking probability p_c. The random entry was chosen from a uniform distribution centered at the mean of that attribute. Thus, when p_c is 1, the data is completely noisy. We studied how each of the two problems were affected by noise masking.

In Table 3, we have illustrated some examples of the variation in performance for different distance metrics. Except for a few exceptions, the major trend in this table is that the accuracy performance decreases with increasing value of the norm parameter. We have show the table in the range $L_{0.1}$ to L_{10} because it was easiest to calculate the distance values without exceeding the numerical ranges in the computer representation. We have also illustrated the accuracy performance when the L_∞ metric is used. One interesting observation is that the accuracy with the L_∞ distance metric is often worse than the accuracy value by picking a record from the database at random and reporting the corresponding target

Table 3. Number of correct class label matches between nearest neighbor and target

Data Set	$L_{0.1}$	$L_{0.5}$	L_1	L_2	L_4	L_{10}	L_∞	Random
Machine	522	474	449	402	364	353	341	153
Musk	998	893	683	405	301	272	163	140
Breast Cancer (wdbc)	5299	5268	5196	5052	4661	4172	4032	3021
Segmentation	1423	1471	1377	1210	1103	1031	300	323
Ionosphere	2954	3002	2839	2430	2062	1836	1769	1884

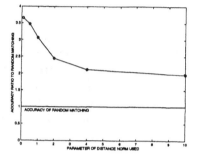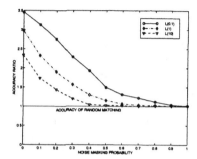

Fig. 5. Accuracy depending on the norm parameter

Fig. 6. Accuracy depending on noise masking

value. This trend is observed because of the fact that the L_∞ metric only looks at the dimension at which the target and neighbor are furthest apart. In high dimensional space, this is likely to be a very poor representation of the nearest neighbor. A similar argument is true for L_k distance metrics (for high values of k) which provide undue importance to the distant (sparse/noisy) dimensions. It is precisely this aspect which is reflected in our theoretical analysis of the relative contrast, which results in distance metrics with high norm parameters to be poorly discriminating between the furthest and nearest neighbor.

In Figure 5, we have shown the variation in the accuracy of the class variable matching with k, when the L_k norm is used. The accuracy on the Y-axis is reported as the ratio of the accuracy to that of a completely random matching scheme. The graph is averaged over all the data sets of Table 3. It is easy to see that there is a clear trend of the accuracy worsening with increasing values of the parameter k.

We also studied the robustness of the scheme to the use of noise masking. For this purpose, we have illustrated the performance of three distance metrics in Figure 6: $L_{0.1}$, L_1, and L_{10} for various values of the masking probability on the machine data set. On the X-axis, we have denoted the value of the masking probability, whereas on the Y-axis we have the accuracy ratio to that of a completely random matching scheme. Note that when the masking probability is 1, then any scheme would degrade to a random method. However, it is interesting to see from Figure 6 that the L_{10} distance metric degrades much faster to the random performance (at a masking probability of 0.4), whereas the L_1 degrades to random at 0.6. The $L_{0.1}$ distance metric is most robust to the presence of noise in the data set and degrades to random performance at the slowest rate. These results are closely connected to our theoretical analysis which shows the rapid lack of discrimination between the nearest and furthest distances for high values of the norm-parameter because of undue weighting being given to the noisy dimensions which contribute the most to the distance.

5   Conclusions and Summary

In this paper, we showed some surprising results of the qualitative behavior of the different distance metrics for measuring proximity in high dimensionality. We demonstrated our results in both a theoretical and empirical setting. In the past, not much attention has been paid to the choice of distance metrics used in high dimensional applications. The results of this paper are likely to have a powerful impact on the particular choice of distance metric which is used from problems such as clustering, categorization, and similarity search; all of which depend upon some notion of proximity.

References

1. Weber R., Schek H.-J., Blott S.: A Quantitative Analysis and Performance Study for Similarity-Search Methods in High-Dimensional Spaces. *VLDB Conference Proceedings*, 1998.
2. Bennett K. P., Fayyad U., Geiger D.: Density-Based Indexing for Approximate Nearest Neighbor Queries. *ACM SIGKDD Conference Proceedings*, 1999.
3. Berchtold S., Böhm C., Kriegel H.-P.: The Pyramid Technique: Towards Breaking the Curse of Dimensionality. *ACM SIGMOD Conference Proceedings*, June 1998.
4. Berchtold S., Böhm C., Keim D., Kriegel H.-P.: A Cost Model for Nearest Neighbor Search in High Dimensional Space. *ACM PODS Conference Proceedings*, 1997.
5. Berchtold S., Ertl B., Keim D., Kriegel H.-P. Seidl T.: Fast Nearest Neighbor Search in High Dimensional Spaces. *ICDE Conference Proceedings*, 1998.
6. Beyer K., Goldstein J., Ramakrishnan R., Shaft U.: When is Nearest Neighbors Meaningful? *ICDT Conference Proceedings*, 1999.
7. Shaft U., Goldstein J., Beyer K.: Nearest Neighbor Query Performance for Unstable Distributions. Technical Report TR 1388, Department of Computer Science, University of Wisconsin at Madison.
8. Guttman, A.: R-Trees: A Dynamic Index Structure for Spatial Searching. *ACM SIGMOD Conference Proceedings*, 1984.
9. Hinneburg A., Aggarwal C., Keim D.: What is the nearest neighbor in high dimensional spaces? *VLDB Conference Proceedings*, 2000.
10. Katayama N., Satoh S.: The SR-Tree: An Index Structure for High Dimensional Nearest Neighbor Queries. *ACM SIGMOD Conference Proceedings*, 1997.
11. Lin K.-I., Jagadish H. V., Faloutsos C.: The TV-tree: An Index Structure for High Dimensional Data. *VLDB Journal*, Volume 3, Number 4, pages 517–542, 1992.

Appendix

Here we provide a detailed proof of Lemma 2, which proves our modified convergence results for arbitrary distributions of points. This Lemma shows that the asymptotical rate of convergence of the absolute difference of distances between the nearest and furthest points is dependent on the distance norm used. To recap, we restate Lemma 2.

Lemma 2: *Let $\mathcal{F}$ be an arbitrary distribution of $N = 2$ points. Then,* $\lim_{d\to\infty} E\left[\frac{Dmax_d^k - Dmin_d^k}{d^{1/k-1/2}}\right] = C_k$, *where C_k is some constant dependent on k.*

Proof. Let A_d and B_d be the two points in a d dimensional data distribution such that each coordinate is independently drawn from the data distribution $\mathcal{F}$. Specifically $A_d = (P_1 \ldots P_d)$ and $B_d = (Q_1 \ldots Q_d)$ with P_i and Q_i being drawn from $\mathcal{F}$. Let $PA_d = \{\sum_{i=1}^{d}(P_i)^k\}^{1/k}$ be the distance of A_d to the origin using the L_k metric and $PB_d = \{\sum_{i=1}^{d}(Q_i)^k\}^{1/k}$ the distance of B_d.

We assume that the kth power of a random variable drawn from the distribution $\mathcal{F}$ has mean $\mu_{\mathcal{F},k}$ and standard deviation $\sigma_{\mathcal{F},k}$. This means that: $\frac{PA_d^k}{d} \to_p \mu_{\mathcal{F},k}$, $\frac{PB_d^k}{d} \to_p \mu_{\mathcal{F},k}$ and therefore:

$$PA_d/d^{1/k} \to_p (\mu_{\mathcal{F},k})^{1/k}, \quad PB_d/d^{1/k} \to_p (\mu_{\mathcal{F},k})^{1/k}. \tag{14}$$

We intend to show that $\frac{|PA_d - PB_d|}{d^{1/k-1/2}} \to_p C_k$ for some constant C_k depending on k. We express $|PA_d - PB_d|$ in the following numerator/denominator form which we will use in order to examine the convergence behavior of the numerator and denominator individually.

$$|PA_d - PB_d| = \frac{|(PA_d)^k - (PB_d)^k|}{\sum_{r=0}^{k-1}(PA_d)^{k-r-1}(PB_d)^r} \tag{15}$$

Dividing both sides by $d^{1/k-1/2}$ and regrouping on right-hand-side we get

$$\frac{|PA_d - PB_d|}{d^{1/k-1/2}} = \frac{|(PA_d)^k - (PB_d)^k|/\sqrt{d}}{\sum_{r=0}^{k-1}\left(\frac{PA_d}{d^{1/k}}\right)^{k-r-1}\left(\frac{PB_d}{d^{1/k}}\right)^r} \tag{16}$$

Consequently, using Slutsky's theorem and the results of Equation 14 we have:

$$\sum_{r=0}^{k-1}\left(PA_d/d^{1/k}\right)^{k-r-1} \cdot \left(PB_d/d^{1/k}\right)^r \to_p k \cdot (\mu_{\mathcal{F},k})^{(k-1)/k} \tag{17}$$

Having characterized the convergence behavior of the denominator of the right-hand-side of Equation 16, let us now examine the behavior of the numerator: $|(PA_d)^k - (PB_d)^k|/\sqrt{d} = |\sum_{i=1}^{d}((P_i)^k - (Q_i)^k)|/\sqrt{d} = |\sum_{i=1}^{d} R_i|/\sqrt{d}$. Here R_i is the new random variable defined by $((P_i)^k - (Q_i)^k) \; \forall i \in \{1, \ldots d\}$. This random variable has zero mean and standard deviation which is $\sqrt{2} \cdot \sigma_{\mathcal{F},k}$ where $\sigma_{\mathcal{F},k}$ is the standard deviation of $(P_i)^k$. Then, the sum of different values of R_i over d dimensions will converge to a normal distribution with mean 0 and standard deviation $\sqrt{2} \cdot \sigma_{\mathcal{F},k} \cdot \sqrt{d}$ because of the central limit theorem. Consequently, the mean average deviation of this distribution will be $C \cdot \sigma_{\mathcal{F},k}$ for some constant C. Therefore, we have:

$$\lim_{d \to \infty} E\left[\frac{|(PA_d)^k - (PB_d)^k|}{\sqrt{d}} \right] = C \cdot \sigma_{\mathcal{F},k} \tag{18}$$

Since the denominator of Equation 16 shows probabilistic convergence, we can combine the results of Equations 17 and 18 to obtain:

$$\lim_{d \to \infty} E\left[\frac{|PA_d - PB_d|}{d^{1/k-1/2}} \right] = C \cdot \frac{\sigma_{\mathcal{F},k}}{k \cdot \mu_{\mathcal{F},k}^{(k-1)/k}} \tag{19}$$

The result follows.

Confusion Matrices. We have illustrated the confusion matrices for two different values of p below. As illustrated, the confusion matrix for using the value $p = 0.3$ is significantly better than the one obtained using $p = 2$.

Table 4. Confusion Matrix- p=2, (rows for prototype, colums for cluster)

1208	82	9711	4	10	14
0	2	0	0	6328	4
1	9872	104	32	11	0
8750	8	74	9954	1	18
39	0	10	8	8	9948
2	36	101	2	3642	16

Table 5. Confusion Matrix- p=0.3, (rows for prototype, colums for cluster)

51	115	9773	10	37	15
0	17	24	0	9935	14
15	10	9	9962	0	4
1	9858	66	5	19	1
8	0	9	3	9	9956
9925	0	119	20	0	10

On Optimizing Nearest Neighbor
Queries in High-Dimensional Data Spaces

Stefan Berchtold[1], Christian Böhm[2], Daniel Keim[3], Florian Krebs[2], Hans-Peter Kriegel[2]

[1] stb gmbh, Ulrichsplatz 6, 86150 Augsburg, Germany
{Stefan.Berchtold}@stb-gmbh.de
[2] University of Munich, Oettingenstr. 67, 80538 Munich, Germany
{boehm,kriegel}@informatik.uni-muenchen.de
[3] University of Halle-Wittenberg, Kurt-Mothes Str. 1, 06099 Halle (Saale), Germany
keim@informatik.uni-halle.de

Abstract. Nearest-neighbor queries in high-dimensional space are of high importance in various applications, especially in content-based indexing of multimedia data. For an optimization of the query processing, accurate models for estimating the query processing costs are needed. In this paper, we propose a new cost model for nearest neighbor queries in high-dimensional space, which we apply to enhance the performance of high-dimensional index structures. The model is based on new insights into effects occurring in high-dimensional space and provides a closed formula for the processing costs of nearest neighbor queries depending on the dimensionality, the block size and the database size. From the wide range of possible applications of our model, we select two interesting samples: First, we use the model to prove the known linear complexity of the nearest neighbor search problem in high-dimensional space, and second, we provide a technique for optimizing the block size. For data of medium dimensionality, the optimized block size allows significant speed-ups of the query processing time when compared to traditional block sizes and to the linear scan.

1. Introduction

Nearest neighbor queries are important for various applications such as content-based indexing in multimedia systems [10], similarity search in CAD systems [7, 17], docking of molecules in molecular biology [21], and string matching in text retrieval [1]. Most applications use some kind of feature vector for an efficient access to the complex original data. Examples of feature vectors are color histograms [20], shape descriptors [15, 18], Fourier vectors [23], and text descriptors [14]. According to [3], nearest neighbor search on high-dimensional feature vectors may be defined as follows:

Given a data set DS of points in a d-dimensional space $[0, 1]^d$, find the data point NN from DS which is closer to the given query point Q than any other point in the DS. More formally:

$$NN(Q) = \{\bar{e} \in DS | \forall e \in DS: \|\bar{e} - Q\| \le \|e - Q\|\}.$$

A problem of index-based nearest neighbor search is that it is difficult to estimate the time which is needed for executing the nearest neighbor query. The estimation of the time, however, is crucial for optimizing important parameters of the index structures such as the block size. An adequate cost model should work for data sets with an arbitrary number of dimensions and an arbitrary size of the database, and should be applicable to different data distributions and index structures. Most important, however, it should provide accurate estimates of the expected query execution time in order to allow an optimization of the parameters of the index structure.

In a previous paper [3], we proposed a cost model which is very accurate for estimating the cost of nearest-neighbor queries in high-dimensional space. This cost model is based on ta-

J. Van den Bussche and V. Vianu (Eds.): ICDT 2001, LNCS 1973, pp. 435–449, 2001.

bles which are generated using the Montecarlo integration method. Although expensive numerical integration occurs only in the compile time of the cost estimator, not in the execution time (when actually determining the cost of query execution), expensive numerical steps are completely avoided in the cost model proposed in this paper. Based on recent progress in understanding the effects of indexing high-dimensional spaces [4], we develop a new cost model for an index-based processing of nearest neighbor queries in high-dimensional space. The model is completely analytical allowing a direct application to query optimization problems. The basic idea of the model is to estimate the number of data pages intersecting the nearest neighbor sphere by first determining the expected radius of the sphere. Assuming a certain location of the query point and a partition of the data space into hyperrectangles, the number of intersected pages can be represented by a staircase function. The staircase function results from the fact that the data pages can be collected into groups such that all pages in a group have the same "skewness" to the query point. Each page in the group is intersected simultaneously and, therefore, the cost model results in a staircase function.

The model has a wide range of interesting theoretical and practical applications. The model may, for example, be used to confirm the known theoretical result [24] that the time complexity of nearest neighbor search in a very high dimensional space is linear. Since the model provides a closed formula for the time complexity (depending on the parameters: dimensionality, database size, and block size), the model can also be used to determine the practically relevant break-even dimensionality between index-based search and linear scan (for a given database size). For dimensionalities below the break-even point, the index-based search performs better, for dimensionalities above the break-even point, the linear scan performs better. Since the linear scan of the database can also be considered as an index structure with an infinite block size, the query optimization problem can also be modeled as a continuous block size optimization problem. Since our model can be evaluated analytically and since the block size is one of the parameters of the model, the cost model can be applied to determine the block size for which the minimum estimated costs occur. The result of our theoretical analysis is surprising and shows that even for medium-dimensional spaces, a large block size (such as 16kB for 16 dimensions) clearly outperforms traditional block sizes (2 kByte or 4 KByte) and the linear scan. An index structure built with the optimal block size always shows a significantly better performance, resulting in traditional block sizes in lower dimensional spaces and to a linear scan in very high dimensions. Also, the query processing cost will never exceed the cost for a linear scan, as index structures typically do in very high dimensions due to a large number of random seek operations. A practical evaluation and comparison to real measurements confirms our theoretical results and shows speed-ups of up to 528% over the index-based search and up to 500% over the linear scan. Note that a cost model such as the one proposed in [3] can hardly be used for a parameter optimization because of the numerical component of the model.

2. Related Work

The research in the field of nearest neighbor search in high-dimensional space may be divided into three areas: index structures, nearest neighbor algorithms on top of index structures, and cost models.

The first index structure focusing on high-dimensional spaces was the TV-tree proposed by Lin, Jagadish, and Faloutsos [16]. The basic idea of the TV-tree is to divide attributes into attributes which are important for the search process and others which can be ignored because these attributes have a small chance to contribute to query processing. The major drawback of the TV-tree is that information about the behavior of single attributes, e.g. their selectivity, is required. Another R-tree-like high-dimensional index structure is the SS-tree [25] which uses spheres instead of bounding boxes in the directory. Although the SS-tree clearly outperforms the R*-tree, spheres tend to overlap in high-dimensional spaces and therefore, the performance also degenerates. In [13], an improvement of the SS-tree has been proposed, where the concepts of the R-tree and SS-tree are integrated into a new index structure, the SR-tree. The directory of the SR-tree consists of spheres (SS-tree) and hyperrectangles (R-tree) such that the area corresponding to a directory entry is the intersection between the sphere and the hyperrectangle. Another approach has been proposed in [6]. The X-tree is an index structure adapting the algorithms of R*-trees to high-dimensional data using two techniques: First, the X-tree introduces an overlap-free split algorithm which is based on the split history of the tree. Second, if the overlap-free split algorithm would lead to an unbalanced directory, the X-tree omits the split and the corresponding directory node becomes a so-called supernode. Supernodes are directory nodes which are enlarged by a multiple of the block size. Another approach related to nearest neighbor query processing in high-dimensional space is the parallel method described in [4]. The basic idea of the declustering technique is to assign the buckets corresponding to different quadrants of the data space to different disks, thereby allowing an optimal speed-up for the parallel processing of nearest neighbor queries.

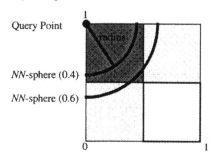

Figure 1: Two-dimensional Example for the Data Pages Affected by the Nearest Neighbor Search for an Increasing NN-distance

Besides the index structures, the algorithms used to perform the nearest neighbor search are obviously important. The algorithm of Rousopoulos et. al. [19] operates on R-trees. It traverses the tree in a top-down fashion, always visiting the closest bounding box first. Since in case of bounding boxes there always exists a maximal distance to the closest point in the box, the algorithm can prune some of the branches early in the search process. The algorithm, however, can be shown to be suboptimal since, in general, it visits more nodes than necessary, i.e., more nodes than intersected by the nearest neighbor sphere. An algorithm which avoids this problem is the algorithm by Hjaltason and Samet [12]. This algorithm traverses the space partitions ordered by the so-called MINDIST which is the distance of the closest point in the box to the query point. Since the algorithm does not work in a strict top-down fashion, the algorithm has to keep a list of visited nodes in main memory. The algorithm can be shown to be time-optimal [3]; however, in high-dimensional spaces, the size of the list, and therefore the required main memory, may become prohibitively large.

The third related area are cost models for index-based nearest neighbor queries. One of the early models is the model by Friedman, Bentley, and Finkel [11]. The assumptions of the model, however, are unrealistic for the high-dimensional case, since N is assumed to converge to infinity and boundary effects are not considered. The model by Cleary [9] extends the Friedman, Bentley, and Finkel model by allowing non-rectangular-bounded pages, but still does not account for boundary effects. Sproull [22] uses the existing models for optimizing the nearest neighbor search in high dimensions and shows that the number of data points must be exponential in the number of dimensions for the models to provide accurate estimates. A cost model for metric spaces has recently been proposed in [8]. The model, however, has been designed for a specific index-structure (the M-tree) and only applies to metric spaces. In [3], a cost model has been proposed which is very accurate even in high-dimensions as the model takes boundary effects into account. The model is based on the concept of the Minkowsky-sum which is the volume created by enlarging the bounding box by the query sphere. Using the Minkowsky-sum, the modeling of the nearest neighbor search is transformed into an equivalent problem of modeling point queries. Unfortunately, when boundary effects are considered, the Minkowsky-sum can only be determined numerically by Montecarlo integration. Thus, none of the models can be used to optimize the parameters of high-dimensional indexing techniques in a query processor.

3.   A Model for the Performance of Nearest Neighbor Queries in High-Dimensional Space

As a first step of our model, we determine the expected distance of the query point to the actual nearest neighbor in the database. For simplification, in the first approximation we assume uniformly distributed data[1] in a normalized data space $[0,1]^d$ having a volume of 1. The nearest neighbor distance may then be approximated by the volume of the sphere which on the average contains one data point. Thus,

$$Vol_{Sp}^d(NN\text{-}dist) = \frac{1}{N} \quad \Leftrightarrow \quad \frac{\sqrt{\pi}^d}{\Gamma(d/2 + 1)} \cdot NN\text{-}dist^d = \frac{1}{N}$$

where $\Gamma(n)$ is the gamma function $(\Gamma(x + 1) = x \cdot \Gamma(x), \ \Gamma(1) = 1$ and $\Gamma(1/2) = \sqrt{\pi})$, which may be approximated by $\Gamma(n) \approx (n/e)^n \cdot \sqrt{2 \cdot \pi \cdot n}$. From the above equation, the expected nearest neighbor distance may be determined as

$$NN\text{-}dist(N, d) = \sqrt[d]{\frac{\Gamma(d/2 + 1)}{N \cdot \sqrt{\pi}^d}} = \frac{1}{\sqrt{\pi}} \cdot \sqrt[d]{\frac{\Gamma(d/2 + 1)}{N}}$$

In general, the number of data points is not growing exponentially, which means that not all dimensions are used as split axes. Without loss of generality, we assume that the first d' dimensions have been used as split dimensions. Thus, d' may be determined as

$$d' = \left\lceil \log_2 \left(\frac{N}{C_{eff}} \right) \right\rceil .$$

For simplification, we further assume that each of the d' split dimensions has been split in the middle.

To determine the number of pages which are intersected by the nearest neighbor sphere, we now have to determine the number of pages depending on $NN\text{-}dist(N,d)$. In our first approximation, we only consider the simple case that the query point is located in a corner of the data space[2]. In figure 1, we show a two-dimensional example for the data pages which are affected by the nearest neighbor search for an increasing $NN\text{-}dist(N, d)$. Since the data space is assumed to be normalized to $[0,1]^d$ and since the data pages are split at most once, we have to consider more than one data page if $NN\text{-}dist(N, d) \geq 0.5$. In this case, two additional data pages have to be accessed in our two-dimensional example (cf. figure 1). If $NN\text{-}dist(N, d)$ increases to more than $0.5 \cdot \sqrt{2}$, we have to consider even more data pages, namely all four

---

1. In section 5, we provide an extension of the model for non-uniform data distributions.
2. In high-dimensional space, this assumption is not unrealistic since most of the data points are close to the surface of the data space (for details see [5]).

pages in our example. In the general case, we have to consider more data pages each time the NN-dist(N,d) exceeds the value $0.5 \cdot \sqrt{i}$. We therefore obtain

$$NN\text{-}dist(N, d) = 0.5 \cdot \sqrt{i} \qquad \text{(for } i = 1 \ldots d\text{')}$$

$$\Leftrightarrow \quad i = \left(\frac{NN\text{-}dist(N, d)}{0.5}\right)^2 \qquad \text{(for } i = 1 \ldots d\text{')}$$

$$\Leftrightarrow \quad i = \left(\frac{\dfrac{1}{\sqrt{\pi}} \cdot \sqrt[d]{\dfrac{\Gamma(d/2 + 1)}{N}}}{0.5}\right)^2 \qquad \text{(for } i = 1 \ldots d\text{')}$$

$$\Rightarrow \quad i \approx \frac{2 \cdot (d + 2)}{e \cdot \pi} \cdot \sqrt[d]{\frac{\pi \cdot (d + 2)^3}{4 \cdot e^2 \cdot N^2}} \qquad \text{(for } i = 1 \ldots d\text{')}$$

The number of data pages which have to be considered in each step are the data pages that differ in i of the d' split dimensions, which may be determined as $\binom{d'}{i}$.

d	dimension
N	number of data points
$\lvert db \rvert$	size of the database
#b	number of data pages in the database
$\lvert b \rvert$	page size
u	storage utilization
d'	number of split dimensions
C_{eff}	average number of data points per index page
T_{IO}	I/O time (disc access time independent from the size of the accessed data block)
T_{Tr}	transfer and processing time (linearly depends on the size of the accessed data block)
NN-dist($\lvert db \rvert$, d)	nearest neighbor distance depending on $\lvert db \rvert$ and d
P(N,d)	number of data pages depending on N and d
P($\lvert db \rvert$, d)	number of data pages depending on $\lvert db \rvert$ and d
X(#b)	percentage by which the linear scan is faster

Table 1: Important Symbols

Integrating the formulas provides the number of data pages which have to accessed in performing a nearest neighbor query on a database with N data points in a d-dimensional space:

$$P(N, d) \; = \; \sum_{k = 0}^{\frac{2 \cdot (d + 2)}{e \cdot \pi} \cdot \sqrt[d]{\frac{\pi \cdot (d + 2)^3}{4 \cdot e^2 \cdot N^2}}} \binom{d'}{k} .$$

In the following, we determine the development of $P(N, d)$ for a constant size database ($|db| = const$). In this case, the number of data pages is also constant

$$\#b \; = \; \frac{|db|}{|b| \cdot u}$$

and the number of data points linearly depends on the database size $|db|$ and the dimensionality d

$$N \; = \; \frac{|db|}{d} .$$

The nearest neighbor distance NN-dist now depends on the dimensionality (d) and the size of the database ($|db|$)

$$NN\text{-}dist(|db|, d) \; = \; \frac{1}{\sqrt{\pi}} \cdot \sqrt[d]{\frac{d \cdot \Gamma(d/2 + 1)}{|db|}}$$

and since $C_{eff} = |b| \cdot u / d$, the number of split dimensions d' becomes

$$d' \; = \; \left\lceil \log_2 \left(\frac{N}{C_{eff}} \right) \right\rceil = \left\lceil \log_2 \left(\frac{|db|}{|b| \cdot u} \right) \right\rceil .$$

The number of data pages which have to be accessed in performing a nearest neighbor query in d-dimensional space can now be determined as

$$P(|db|, d) \; = \; \sum_{k = 0}^{\frac{2 \cdot (d + 2)}{e \cdot \pi} \cdot \sqrt[d]{\frac{\pi \cdot d^2 \cdot (d + 2)^3}{4 \cdot e^2 \cdot |db|^2}}} \left(\begin{array}{c} \left\lceil \log_2 \left(\frac{|db|}{|b| \cdot u} \right) \right\rceil \\ k \end{array} \right)$$

In figure 2, we show the development of $P(|db|, d)$ depending on the dimensionality d. $P(|db|, d)$ is a staircase function which increases to the maximum number of data pages ($\#b$). The staircase property results from the discontinuous increase of $P(|db|, d)$ each time

$$NN\text{-}dist(N, d) \geq 0.5 \cdot \sqrt{i} \quad (for \; i = 1...d') ,$$

which is a consequence of using the corners of the data space as query points. Since for practical purposes this assumption is not sufficient, in section 5 we extend the model to consider other query points as well.

4. Evaluation

After introducing our analytical cost model, we are now able to compare the time needed to perform an index-based nearest neighbor search with the sequential scan of the database. Let us first consider the factor by which a sequential read is faster than a random block-wise access. Given a fixed size database ($|db|$) consisting of $\#b = |db| / (|b| \cdot u)$ blocks, the time needed to read the database sequentially is $T_{IO} + \#b \cdot T_{Tr}$. Reading the same database in a

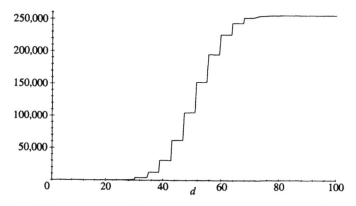

Figure 2: Number of Page Accesses as Determined by our Cost Model

block-wise fashion requires $\#b \cdot (T_{IO} + T_{Tr})$. From that we get the factor X, by which the sequential read is faster, as

$$X(\#b) \cdot \#b \cdot (T_{IO} + T_{Tr}) = T_{IO} + \#b \cdot T_{Tr} \quad \Rightarrow \quad X(\#b) = \frac{\#b \cdot (T_{IO} + T_{Tr})}{T_{IO} + \#b \cdot T_{Tr}}$$

In figure 3a, we show the development of $X(\#b)$ depending on the size of the database for realistic system parameters which we measured in our experiments ($T_{IO} = 10$ ms, $T_{Tr} = 1.5$ ms). Note that for very large databases, $X(\#b)$ converges against a system constant

$$\lim_{\#b \to \infty} X(\#b) = \frac{T_{IO} + T_{Tr}}{T_{Tr}} .$$

It is also interesting to consider the inverse of $X(\#b)$, which is the percentage of blocks that could be read randomly instead of sequentially reading the whole database. The function $1/(X(\#b))$ is plotted in figure 3b for a constant database size.

Let us now compare the time needed to perform an index-based nearest neighbor search with the time needed to sequentially search the database. The time needed to read the database

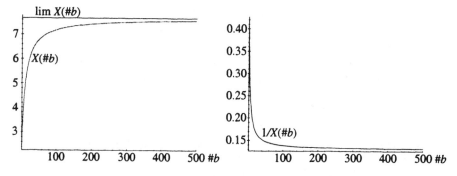

a. Factor by which seq. scan is faster

b. Percentage of pages which can be read randomly instead of seq. scan

Figure 3: Development of $X(\#b)$ and $1/X(\#b)$

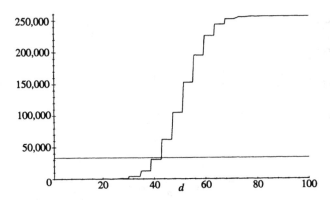

Figure 4: Comparison of Index-based Search and the Sequential Scan Depending on the Dimensionality d for a Fixed-Size Database

sequentially is $T_{IO} + \#b \cdot (T_{Tr} + T_{CPU})$, and the time needed to randomly access the necessary pages in an index-based search is

$$T_{IndexSearch}(|db|, d) = (T_{IO} + T_{Tr}) \cdot \sum_{k=0}^{\frac{2 \cdot (d+2)}{e \cdot \pi} \cdot \sqrt[d]{\frac{\pi \cdot d^2 \cdot (d+2)^3}{4 \cdot e^2 \cdot |db|^2}}} \left(\left\lceil \log_2 \left(\frac{|db|}{|b| \cdot u} \right) \right\rceil \atop k \right)$$

In figure 4, the time resulting from the two formulas is shown for a fixed database size of 256,000 blocks. Note that in the example for $d = 44$, the linear scan becomes faster than the index-based search. In figure 5, we show the time development depending on both, the dimensionality and the database size. It is clear that for all realistic parameter settings, there exists a dimensionality d for which the linear scan becomes faster than the index-based search.

This fact is summarized in the following lemma:

Lemma: *(Complexity of Index-based Nearest Neighbor Search)*
For realistic system parameters (i.e., $T_{IO} > 0$, $|db| > |b|$, and $u > 0$), there always exists a dimension d , for which the sequential scan is faster than an index-based search. More formally,

$$\forall |db| \; \exists \tilde{d}: \; T_{IndexSearch}(|db|, \tilde{d}) \; > \; T_{LinScan}(|db|) .$$

Idea of the Proof:
From our previous observations, it is clear that $T_{IndexSearch}(|db|, \tilde{d})$ increases faster than $T_{LinScan}(|db|)$ and finally all data blocks of the database are read. This is the case for

$$\frac{2 \cdot (\tilde{d} + 2)}{e \cdot \pi} \cdot \sqrt[d]{\frac{\pi \cdot \tilde{d}^2 \cdot (\tilde{d} + 2)^3}{4 \cdot e^2 \cdot |db|^2}} = \log_2 \left(\frac{|db|}{|b| \cdot u} \right) ,$$

in which case the index-based search randomly accesses all blocks of the database. A sequential read of the whole database is faster than the block-wise access by a factor of

$$X(\#b) \; = \; \frac{|db| \cdot (T_{IO} + T_{Tr})}{|b| \cdot u \cdot T_{IO} + |db| \cdot T_{Tr}}$$

and therefore, the correctness of the lemma is shown. q.e.d.

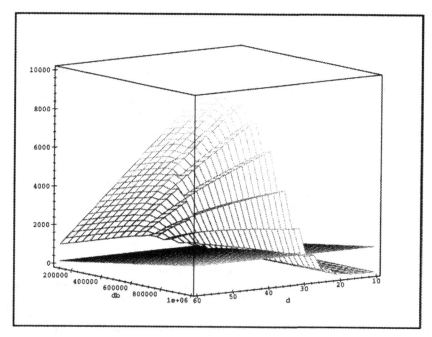

Figure 5: Comparison of Index-based Search and the Sequential Scan Depending on the Database Size |db| and the Dimensionality d

Note that this result confirms the pessimistic result by Weber et al. [24] that nearest neighbor search in high-dimensional space has a linear time complexity. In figure 6, we compare the performance estimations of our numerical model [3] and the new analytical model (proposed in this paper) to the performance of the R*-tree [2] on a uniformly distributed data set with a fixed number of data pages (256) and varying dimensionality (d = 2 ... 50). As one can see, the analytical cost model provides an accurate prediction of the R*-tree's performance over a wide range of dimensions. Even for low and medium dimensions, the prediction of our model is pretty close to the measured performance.

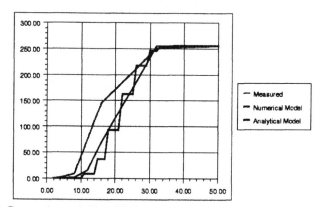

Figure 6: Comparison of Cost Models and Measured R*-Tree Performance Depending on the Dimension

5. Optimized Processing of Nearest Neighbor Queries in High-Dimensional Space

The objective of this section is to show, how the results obtained above can be used for an optimization of the query processing. We have shown in section 4 that data spaces exist, where it is more efficient to avoid an index-based search. Instead, the sequential scan yields a better performance. In contrast, for low-dimensional data spaces, multidimensional index structures yield a complexity which is logarithmic in the number of data objects. In this section, we show that it is optimal for data spaces with moderate dimensionality to use a logical block size which is a multiple of the physical block size provided by the operating system. Therefore, we have to consider three different cases of query processing: (1) Index-based query processing with traditional block size (4 KByte) in low-dimensional data spaces, (2) Sequential Scan processing in high-dimensional data spaces and (3) Index-based query processing with enlarged block-size in medium-dimensional data spaces. As the sequential scan can be considered as an index with infinite block size, the third case subsumes case (2). Case (1) is trivially subsumed by case (3). Therefore, the problem is reduced to a single optimization task of minimizing the access costs by varying the logical block size.

In order to obtain an accurate estimation of the minimum-cost blocksize, especially in the presence of non-uniform data distributions, we have to slightly extend our model. Hence, we express the expected location of the query point more accurately than assuming the query point to be in a corner of the data space. If we assume that the location of the query point is uniformly distributed, we are able to determine the expected distance *Edist* of the query point to the closest corner of the data space. However, the formula for *Edist* is rather complex and therefore not applicable for practical purposes. Instead, we use the following empirically derived approximation of the formula which is very accurate up to dimension 100:

$$Edist = \frac{d^{0.53}}{4}$$

Figure 7 compares the exact and the approximated distances demonstrating the good accuracy of the approximation.

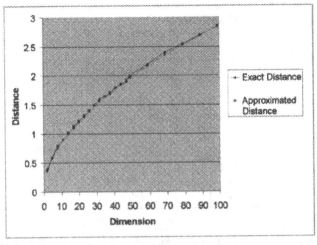

Figure 7: Approximated distance of the query point to the closest corner of data space

If we assume that the query point is located on the diagonal of the data space, we can adapt our model using the approximate value of *Edist*. In this case, we have to consider more data pages each time *NN-dist*(N, d) exceeds the value $\left(0.5 - \frac{d^{0.53}}{4\sqrt{d}} \right) \cdot \sqrt{i}$ rather than exceeding $0.5 \cdot \sqrt{i}$ in the original model. Thus, our extended cost function turns out as:

$$\frac{d+2}{e \cdot \pi \cdot \left(0.5 - \frac{d^{0.53}}{4\sqrt{d}} \right)^2} \cdot \sqrt[d]{\frac{\pi \cdot (d+2)^3 \cdot d^2}{4 \cdot |db|^2 \cdot e^2}}$$

$$\sum_{k=0} \qquad \left(\left\lceil \log_2\left(\frac{|db|}{|b| \cdot u} \right) \right\rceil \atop k \right).$$

Figure 8 depicts the graph of the extended cost model with varying dimension and varying block size. As the model is discrete over the dimensions, there are some staircases. On the other hand, the model is continuous over the blocksize and therefore, amenable to an optimi-

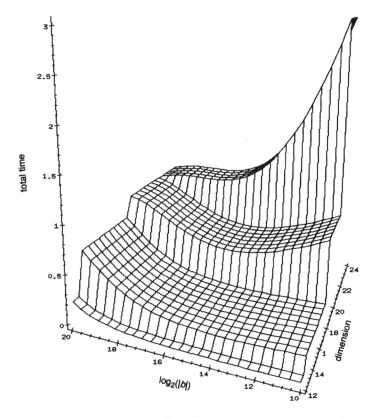

**Figure 8: Graph of the Extended Cost Function: The staircase in the front is associat-
ed to dimensions for which a minimum block size yields least cost. The staircase in the back shows dimensions for which sequential scan causes less
costs than index search whereas the staircase in the middle shows minimum
cost for an optimal block size in a medium size range.**

zation by differentiation. In Figure 8, all three cases can be seen: For low dimensions (staircase in the front), the cost function is monotonously increasing with increasing block size. Therefore, the lowest possible blocksize should be taken. In the high-dimensional case (staircase in the back), the cost function is monotonously decreasing with increasing block size. Therefore, the optimal blocksize is infinite, or in other words, we are supposed to use sequential scan instead of indexing.

The most interesting phenomenon is the staircase in the middle. Here the cost function is monotonously falling to a minimum and then monotonously increasing. The cost function has obviously a single minimum and no further local extrema, which facilitates the search for the optimum. In order to find the block size for which the minimum cost occur, we simply derive the cost function with respect to the block size. The derivative of the cost function $T_{\text{IndexSearch}}(|db|, d, |b|)$ can be determined, as follows:

$$\frac{\partial T_{\text{IndexSearch}}(|db|, d, |b|)}{\partial |b|} =$$

$$= \frac{\partial}{\partial |b|}(T_{IO} + |b| \cdot T_{Tr}) \cdot \frac{d+2}{e \cdot \pi \cdot \left(0.5 - \frac{d^{0.53}}{4\sqrt{d}}\right)^2} \cdot \sqrt[d]{\frac{\pi \cdot (d+2)^3 \cdot d^2}{4 \cdot |db|^2 \cdot e^2}} \sum_{k=0} \left(\left\lceil \log_2\left(\frac{|db|}{|b| \cdot u}\right)\right\rceil \atop k\right)$$

$$= \frac{d+2}{e \cdot \pi \cdot \left(0.5 - \frac{d^{0.53}}{4\sqrt{d}}\right)^2} \cdot \sqrt[d]{\frac{\pi \cdot (d+2)^3 \cdot d^2}{4 \cdot |db|^2 \cdot e^2}} \sum_{k=0} \frac{\partial}{\partial |b|}\left((T_{IO} + |b| \cdot T_{Tr})\left(\left\lceil \log_2\left(\frac{|db|}{|b| \cdot u}\right)\right\rceil \atop k\right)\right)$$

$$= \frac{d+2}{e \cdot \pi \cdot \left(0.5 - \frac{d^{0.53}}{4\sqrt{d}}\right)^2} \cdot \sqrt[d]{\frac{\pi \cdot (d+2)^3 \cdot d^2}{4 \cdot |db|^2 \cdot e^2}} \sum_{k=0} \left(\log_2\left(\frac{|db|}{|b| \cdot u}\right) \atop k\right) \cdot (T_{Tr} + (T_{IO} + |b| \cdot T_{Tr}) \cdot \%)$$

with $\% = \dfrac{\Psi\left(\log_2\left(\frac{|db|}{|b| \cdot u}\right) - k + 1\right) - \Psi\left(\log_2\left(\frac{|db|}{|b| \cdot u}\right) + 1\right)}{|b| \cdot \ln(2)}$, where Ψ is the well-known

digamma function, the derivative of the natural logarithm of the Γ-function:

$$\Psi(x) = \frac{\partial}{\partial x} \ln(\Gamma(x)).$$

The derivative of $T_{\text{IndexSearch}}$ is continuous over $|b|$. Three cases can be distinguished: (1) The derivative is positive over all block sizes. In this case, the minimum block size is optimal. (2) The derivative is negative. Then, an infinite blocksize is optimal and the search is processed by sequentially scanning the only data page. (3) The derivative of the cost function has a zero value. In this case, the equation

$$\frac{\partial T_{\text{IndexSearch}}(|db|, d, |b|)}{\partial |b|} = 0$$

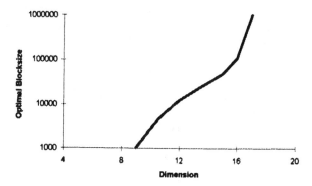

Figure 9: Optimal Block Size for Varying Dimensions

has to be solved, determining the optimal blocksize $|b| = |b|_{opt}$. Finding the optimal blocksize can be done by a simple binary search. As the cost function is smooth, this will lead to an optimal blocksize after a small (logarithmic) number of steps.

The development of the optimal block size over varying dimensions and varying database sizes is depicted in Figure 9. The position of the optimum is, as expected, heavily affected by the dimension of the data space. At dimensions below 9, it is optimal to use the minimal block size of the system, in this case 1KByte. In contrast, when searching in a 17-dimensional data space (or higher), the optimal block size is infinite. Therefore, the sequential scan yields the best performance in this case. The position of the optimum also depends on the database size. Figure 10 shows the optimal block size with varying the database size. Although the variation is not very strong, the optimal block size is decreasing with increasing the database size. We therefore suggest a dynamical adaption of the block size if the database size is unknown a priori.

Finally, we are going to evaluate the accuracy of our cost model. For this purpose, we created indexes on real data containing 4, 8, and 16-dimensional Fourier vectors (derived from CAD data, normalized to the unit hypercube). The size of the databases was 2.5 and 1.0 MBytes. Figure 11 shows the results of these experiments (total elapsed time in seconds), revealing the three different cases of query processing mentioned in the beginning of this section. The

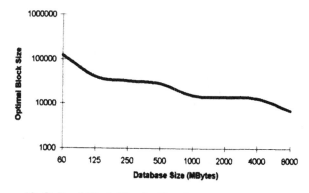

Figure 10: Optimal Block Size for Varying Sizes of the Database

left side shows the results of the 4-dimensional data space, where normal index based query processing with small block sizes is optimal. To the right, we have the high-dimensional case, where the infinite block size (sequential scan) is optimal. The interesting case (8-dimensional data space) is presented in the middle. Here, the performance forms an optimum at a block size of 32KBytes, which is very unusual in database applications. The query processing software using this logical block size (16 contiguous pages of the operating system) yields substantial performance improvements over the normal index (258%) as well as over the sequential scan (205%). The maximal speedup reached in this series of experiments was 528% over normal index processing and 500% over the infinite block size (sequential scan).

6. Conclusions

In this paper, we propose a new analytical cost model for nearest neighbor queries in high-dimensional spaces. The model is based on recent insights into the effects occurring in high-dimensional spaces and can be applied to optimize the processing of nearest neighbor queries. One important application is the determination of an optimal block size depending on the dimensionality of the data and the database size. Since the linear scan can be seen as a special configuration of an index structure with an infinite block size, an index structure using the optimal block size will perform in very high dimensions as good as a linear scan of the database. For a medium dimensionality, the optimal block size leads to significant performance improvements over the index-based search and the linear scan. An experimental evaluation shows that an index structure using the optimal block size outperforms an index structure using the normal block size of 4 KBytes by up to 528%.

References

[1]   Altschul S. F., Gish W., Miller W., Myers E. W., Lipman D. J.: 'A Basic Local Alignment Search Tool', Journal of Molecular Biology, Vol. 215, No. 3, 1990, pp. 403-410.

[2]   Beckmann N., Kriegel H.-P., Schneider R., Seeger B.: 'The R*-tree: An Efficient and Robust Access Method for Points and Rectangles', Proc. ACM SIGMOD Int. Conf. on Management of Data, Atlantic City, NJ, 1990, pp. 322-331.

[3]   Berchtold S., Böhm C., Keim D., Kriegel H.-P.: 'A Cost Model For Nearest Neighbor Search in High-Dimensional Data Space', Proc. ACM PODS Int. Conf. on

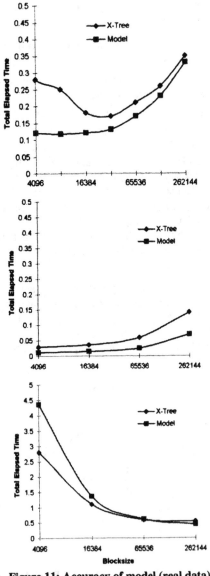

Figure 11: Accuracy of model (real data)

Principles of Databases, Tucson, Arizona, 1997.

[4] Berchtold S., Böhm C., Braunmüller B., Keim D., Kriegel H.-P.: *'Fast Parallel Similarity Search in Multimedia Databases'*, Proc. ACM SIGMOD Int. Conf. on Management of Data, Tucson, Arizona, 1997.

[5] Berchtold S., Keim D. A.: *'High-dimensional Index Structures: Database Support for Next Decades's Applications'*, Tutorial, Proc. ACM SIGMOD Int. Conf. on Management of Data, 1998, p. 501.

[6] Berchtold S., Keim D., Kriegel H.-P.: *'The X-tree: An Index Structure for High-Dimensional Data'*, 22nd Conf. on Very Large Databases, 1996, Bombay, India.

[7] Berchtold S., Keim D., Kriegel H.-P.: *'Fast Searching for Partial Similarity in Polygon Databases'*, VLDB Journal, Dec. 1997.

[8] Ciacia P., Patella M., Zezula P.: *'A Cost Model for Similarity Queries in Metric Spaces'*, Proc. ACM PODS Int. Conf. on Principals of Databases, Seattle, WA, 1998, pp. 59-68.

[9] Cleary J. G.: *'Analysis of an Algorithm for Finding Nearest Neighbors in Euclidean Space'*, ACM Transactions on Mathematical Software, Vol. 5, No. 2, June 1979, pp.183-192.

[10] Faloutsos C., Barber R., Flickner M., Hafner J., et al.: *'Efficient and Effective Querying by Image Content'*, Journal of Intelligent Information Systems, 1994, Vol. 3, pp. 231-262.

[11] Friedman J. H., Bentley J. L., Finkel R. A.: *'An Algorithm for Finding Best Matches in Logarithmic Expected Time'*, ACM Transactions on Mathematical Software, Vol. 3, No. 3, September 1977, pp. 209-226.

[12] Hjaltason G. R., Samet H.: *'Ranking in Spatial Databases'*, Proc. 4th Int. Symp. on Large Spatial Databases, Portland, ME, 1995, pp. 83-95.

[13] Katayama N., Satoh S.: *'The SR-Tree: An Index Structure for High-Dimensional Nearest Neighbor Queries'*, Proc. ACM SIGMOD Int. Conf. on Management of Data, 1997.

[14] Kukich K.: *'Techniques for Automatically Correcting Words in Text'*, ACM Computing Surveys, Vol. 24, No. 4, 1992, pp. 377-440.

[15] Jagadish H. V.: *'A Retrieval Technique for Similar Shapes'*, Proc. ACM SIGMOD Int. Conf. on Management of Data, 1991, pp. 208-217.

[16] Lin K., Jagadish H. V., Faloutsos C.: *'The TV-tree: An Index Structure for High-Dimensional Data'*, VLDB Journal, Vol. 3, 1995, pp. 517-542.

[17] Mehrotra R., Gary J. E.: *'Feature-Based Retrieval of Similar Shapes'*, Proc. 9th Int. Conf. on Data Engineering, Vienna, Austria, 1993, pp. 108-115.

[18] Mehrotra R., Gary J. E.: *'Feature-Index-Based Similar Shape Retrieval'*, Proc. of the 3rd Working Conf. on Visual Database Systems, March 1995.

[19] Roussopoulos N., Kelley S., Vincent F.: *'Nearest Neighbor Queries'*, Proc. ACM SIGMOD Int. Conf. on Management of Data, 1995, pp. 71-79.

[20] Shawney H., Hafner J.: *'Efficient Color Histogram Indexing'*, Proc. Int. Conf. on Image Processing, 1994, pp. 66-70.

[21] Shoichet B. K., Bodian D. L., Kuntz I. D.: *'Molecular Docking Using Shape Descriptors'*, Journal of Computational Chemistry, Vol. 13, No. 3, 1992, pp. 380-397.

[22] Sproull R.F.: *'Refinements to Nearest Neighbor Searching in k-Dimensional Trees'*, Algorithmica 1991, pp. 579-589.

[23] Wallace T., Wintz P.: *'An Efficient Three-Dimensional Aircraft Recognition Algorithm Using Normalized Fourier Descriptors'*, Computer Graphics and Image Processing, Vol. 13, pp. 99-126, 1980.

[24] Weber R., Schek H.-J., Blott S.: *'A Quantitative Analysis and Performance Study for Similarity-Search Methods in High-Dimensional Spaces'*, Proc. Int. Conf. on Very Large Databases, New York, 1998.

[25] White, D., Jain R.: *'Similarity Indexing with the SS-Tree'*, Proc. 12th Int. Conf. on Data Engineering, New Orleans, LA, 1996, pp. 516-523.

Author Index

Lecture Notes in Computer Science

For information about Vols. 1–1899
please contact your bookseller or Springer-Verlag

Vol. 1766: M. Jazayeri, R.G.K. Loos, D.R. Musser (Eds.), Generic Programming. Proceedings, 1998. X, 269 pages. 2000.

Vol. 1791: D. Fensel, Problem-Solving Methods. XII, 153 pages. 2000. (Subseries LNAI).

Vol. 1799: K. Czarnecki, U.W. Eisenecker, Generative and Component-Based Software Engineering. Proceedings, 1999. VIII, 225 pages. 2000.

Vol. 1812: J. Wyatt, J. Demiris (Eds.), Advances in Robot Learning. Proceedings, 1999. VII, 165 pages. 2000. (Subseries LNAI).

Vol. 1932: Z.W. Raś, S. Ohsuga (Eds.), Foundations of Intelligent Systems. Proceedings, 2000. XII, 646 pages. (Subseries LNAI).

Vol. 1933: R.W. Brause, E. Hanisch (Eds.), Medical Data Analysis. Proceedings, 2000. XI, 316 pages. 2000.

Vol. 1934: J.S. White (Ed.), Envisioning Machine Translation in the Information Future. Proceedings, 2000. XV, 254 pages. 2000. (Subseries LNAI).

Vol. 1935: S.L. Delp, A.M. DiGioia, B. Jaramaz (Eds.), Medical Image Computing and Computer-Assisted Intervention – MICCAI 2000. Proceedings, 2000. XXV, 1250 pages. 2000.

Vol. 1937: R. Dieng, O. Corby (Eds.), Knowledge Engineering and Knowledge Management. Proceedings, 2000. XIII, 457 pages. 2000. (Subseries LNAI).

Vol. 1938: S. Rao, K.I. Sletta (Eds.), Next Generation Networks. Proceedings, 2000. XI, 392 pages. 2000.

Vol. 1939: A. Evans, S. Kent, B. Selic (Eds.), «UML» – The Unified Modeling Language. Proceedings, 2000. XIV, 572 pages. 2000.

Vol. 1940: M. Valero, K. Joe, M. Kitsuregawa, H. Tanaka (Eds.), High Performance Computing. Proceedings, 2000. XV, 595 pages. 2000.

Vol. 1941: A.K. Chhabra, D. Dori (Eds.), Graphics Recognition. Proceedings, 1999. XI, 346 pages. 2000.

Vol. 1942: H. Yasuda (Ed.), Active Networks. Proceedings, 2000. XI, 424 pages. 2000.

Vol. 1943: F. Koornneef, M. van der Meulen (Eds.), Computer Safety, Reliability and Security. Proceedings, 2000. X, 432 pages. 2000.

Vol. 1945: W. Grieskamp, T. Santen, B. Stoddart (Eds.), Integrated Formal Methods. Proceedings, 2000. X, 441 pages. 2000.

Vol. 1948: T. Tan, Y. Shi, W. Gao (Eds.), Advances in Multimodal Interfaces – ICMI 2000. Proceedings, 2000. XVI, 678 pages. 2000.

Vol. 1949: R. Connor, A. Mendelzon (Eds.), Research Issues in Structured and Semistructured Database Programming. Proceedings, 1999. XII, 325 pages. 2000.

Vol. 1951: F. van der Linden (Ed.), Software Architectures for Product Families. Proceedings, 2000. VIII, 255 pages. 2000.

Vol. 1952: M.C. Monard, J. Simão Sichman (Eds.), Advances in Artificial Intelligence. Proceedings, 2000. XV, 498 pages. 2000. (Subseries LNAI).

Vol. 1953: G. Borgefors, I. Nyström, G. Sanniti di Baja (Eds.), Discrete Geometry for Computer Imagery. Proceedings, 2000. XI, 544 pages. 2000.

Vol. 1954: W.A. Hunt, Jr., S.D. Johnson (Eds.), Formal Methods in Computer-Aided Design. Proceedings, 2000. XI, 539 pages. 2000.

Vol. 1955: M. Parigot, A. Voronkov (Eds.), Logic for Programming and Automated Reasoning. Proceedings, 2000. XIII, 487 pages. 2000. (Subseries LNAI).

Vol. 1960: A. Ambler, S.B. Calo, G. Kar (Eds.), Services Management in Intelligent Networks. Proceedings, 2000. X, 259 pages. 2000.

Vol. 1961: J. He, M. Sato (Eds.), Advances in Computing Science – ASIAN 2000. Proceedings, 2000. X, 299 pages. 2000.

Vol. 1963: V. Hlaváč, K.G. Jeffery, J. Wiedermann (Eds.), SOFSEM 2000: Theory and Practice of Informatics. Proceedings, 2000. XI, 460 pages. 2000.

Vol. 1965: Ç. K. Koç, C. Paar (Eds.), Cryptographic Hardware and Embedded Systems – CHES 2000. Proceedings, 2000. XI, 355 pages. 2000.

Vol. 1966: S. Bhalla (Ed.), Databases in Networked Information Systems. Proceedings, 2000. VIII, 247 pages. 2000.

Vol. 1967: S. Arikawa, S. Morishita (Eds.), Discovery Science. Proceedings, 2000. XII, 332 pages. 2000. (Subseries LNAI).

Vol. 1968: H. Arimura, S. Jain, A. Sharma (Eds.), Algorithmic Learning Theory. Proceedings, 2000. XI, 335 pages. 2000. (Subseries LNAI).

Vol. 1969: D.T. Lee, S.-H. Teng (Eds.), Algorithms and Computation. Proceedings, 2000. XIV, 578 pages. 2000.

Vol. 1970: M. Valero, V.K. Prasanna, S. Vajapeyam (Eds.), High Performance Computing – HiPC 2000. Proceedings, 2000. XVIII, 568 pages. 2000.

Vol. 1971: R. Buyya, M. Baker (Eds.), Grid Computing – GRID 2000. Proceedings, 2000. XIV, 229 pages. 2000.

Vol. 1972: A. Omicini, R. Tolksdorf, F. Zambonelli (Eds.), Engineering Societies in the Agents World. Proceedings, 2000. IX, 143 pages. 2000. (Subseries LNAI).

Vol. 1973: J. Van den Bussche, V. Vianu (Eds.), Database Theory – ICDT 2001. Proceedings, 2001. X, 451 pages. 2001.

Vol. 1974: S. Kapoor, S. Prasad (Eds.), FST TCS 2000: Foundations of Software Technology and Theoretical Computer Science. Proceedings, 2000. XIII, 532 pages. 2000.

Vol. 1975: J. Pieprzyk, E. Okamoto, J. Seberry (Eds.), Information Security. Proceedings, 2000. X, 323 pages. 2000.

Vol. 1976: T. Okamoto (Ed.), Advances in Cryptology – ASIACRYPT 2000. Proceedings, 2000. XII, 630 pages. 2000.

Vol. 1977: B. Roy, E. Okamoto (Eds.), Progress in Cryptology – INDOCRYPT 2000. Proceedings, 2000. X, 295 pages. 2000.

Vol. 1983: K.S. Leung, L.-W. Chan, H. Meng (Eds.), Intelligent Data Engineering and Automated Learning – IDEAL 2000. Proceedings, 2000. XVI, 573 pages. 2000.

Vol. 1987: K.-L. Tan, M.J. Franklin, J. C.-S. Lui (Eds.), Mobile Data Management. Proceedings, 2001. XIII, 289 pages. 2001.